# City-Region 2020

# City-Region 2020

Integrated planning for a
sustainable environment

## Joe Ravetz

with the
Sustainable City-Region Working Group
chaired by

### Peter Roberts

Town & Country Planning Association

Earthscan Publications Ltd, London

First published in the UK in 2000 by
Earthscan Publications Ltd

A catalogue record for this book is available from the British Library

ISBN      1 85383 606 0 paperback
          1 85383 607 9 hardback

Illustrations and design by the author
Printed and bound by Bell & Bain Ltd, Glasgow
Cover design by John Burke from a photograph by Jan Chlebic

For a full list of publications please contact:

Earthscan Publications Ltd
120 Pentonville Road
London, N1 9JN, UK
Tel:  +44 (0)171 278 0433
Fax: +44 (0)171 278 1142
Email: earthinfo@earthscan.co.uk
http://www.earthscan.co.uk

Earthscan is an editorially independent subsidiary of Kogan Page Ltd and
publishes in association with WWF-UK and the International Institute for
Environment and Development

The *Sustainable City-Region Programme* has been supported by:
Centre for Employment Research at Manchester Metropolitan University;
European Regional Development Fund; the 10 local authorities of Greater Manchester;
Pieda DTZ plc; Eversheds;  Economic and Social Research Council.

This book is printed on elemental chlorine free paper

# CONTENTS

## PART II: KEY SECTORS

## PART III:  PUTTING IT TOGETHER

# ACKNOWLEDGEMENTS

The Sustainable City-Region Working Group would like to acknowledge the generous support which has made this publication possible from:

**Centre for Employment Research at Manchester Metropolitan University**

**Manchester University**

**European Regional Development Fund**

**the ten local authorities of Greater Manchester**

**Economic and Social Research Council**

**Pieda DTZ plc**

**Eversheds**

**a private Trust**

*Members of the Sustainable City-Region Working Group, drawn from the TCPA and the local authorities and universities in Greater Manchester, have each contributed immense amounts of time and expertise. The working group was chaired by:*

Professor Peter Roberts, University of Dundee

*The full working group included:*

Prof Andrew Blowers, Open University; Prof Michael Breheny, University of Reading; (the late) Michael Brown, Landscape Architect; Glyn Carter, London Borough of Barnet; Dr Mike Clark, University of Central Lancashire; Nic Clifford, Manchester City Council; Mike Gordon, Mike Gordon Consultancy; Jon Fox, Peterborough City Council; Herbie Girardet, Footprint Films Ltd; Prof David Hall, Oxford Brookes University; Dr Peter Hopkinson, University of Bradford; Dr Ros Howell, Manchester Metropolitan University; Brian Parker, Transport Consultant; Ralph Rookwood, former Chair of TCPA; Lee Shostak, EDAW; Adrian Webb, Planning Consultant; Paul Winter, Eversheds; Dr Stephen Young, Manchester University.

*The Group would like to acknowledge the support of many individuals in local authorities, development agencies, utilities, industries and civic organizations, who have contributed freely their enthusiasm and expertise. In particular the Group would like to thank:*

Aidan Roe, Andrew Ross, Bernd Kasemir, Bob Christie, Callum Thomas, Chris Church, Cindy Warwick, Dave Carter, Dave Gibbs, Dave Raper, David Rudlin, David Tarlo, Denise Servante, Eddie Scott, Graeme Bell, Graham Haughton, Helmut Lusser, Ian Christie, John Atkins, Jim Longhurst, Jim Watt, John Handley, Keith Howcroft, Les Coop, Lindsay Smales, Michael Carley, Mike Shields, Nick Falk, Pam Warhurst, Phil Barton, Richard Leese, Ron Cockayne, Sara Parkin, Silvio Funtowicz, Simon Shackley, Steven Kirkby, Stuart Murray, Ted Kitchen, Terry Thomas, Walter Menzies

# FOREWORD

**Rt Hon Michael Meacher MP**

*Minister of State for the Environment and
Member of Parliament for Oldham West*

Sustainable development implies a commitment to quality in every sense of the word. It is also about quality of analysis, of our situation and needs, as well as those of future generations. This detailed analysis of a long-established metropolitan area illustrates the extraordinary challenge of knowing and understanding major cities, and of anticipating and guiding their future evolution.

In developing a coherent national sustainable development strategy we need more systematic and in-depth analysis of urban environments. This is a useful contribution to the debate on how to take forward sustainable development in the UK. I congratulate the Town & Country Planning Association for grappling assiduously with the dynamics of an urban region as large and complex as Greater Manchester, and producing this stimulating study.

*Michael Meacher*

# PREFACE

## Peter Roberts

*Professor of European Strategic Planning, University of Dundee, and Chair of the Sustainable City-Region Working Group*

This book builds on the research which was undertaken during the early 1990s by the Town & Country Planning Association's Sustainable Development Group. A report of this work was published in 1993 as *Planning for a Sustainable Environment*. This set out an agenda for change, based around the concept of 'social city-regions' in which a balanced portfolio of policies could be applied, to help avoid environmental damage, social distress and economic decline.

The next step for the TCPA was to demonstrate in practice the ideas and models that had been advanced. From a number of potential case studies, the Greater Manchester metropolitan region was eventually selected as a test-bed. A research partnership and working group was established between the TCPA, Manchester Metropolitan University and the ten local authorities of Greater Manchester, with funding from these partners together with the European Regional Development Fund.

The research gathered a huge body of evidence, and developed a powerful organizing framework. It has now produced a report at the leading edge of international thinking on sustainable urban development, particularly for the older industrial city-regions. Conurbations such as Greater Manchester are home to a substantial part of the European population, and the successful management of change in such regions is a test of the ingenuity and determination of politicians, planners, the private sector and communities alike.

Our great cities are pools of opportunity and potential. However, they have often been deflected from achieving a quality lifestyle for everyone, due to the unthinking and irresponsible rush for growth that has characterized much of the past two hundred years. At long last the 'muck and brass' philosophy of the past is shifting to a more responsible and balanced approach to the planning and management of change. This report brings together much of this new thinking and practice and, in addition, it provides a practical model to help coordinate and integrate both strategy and action.

It is appropriate that this book will be published in 1999. This year marks the centenary of the establishment of the TCPA, and *City-Region 2020* is a worthy successor to Ebenezer Howard's *Tomorrow: a Peaceful Path to Real Reform*. The book is a tribute to the dedication and diligence of Joe Ravetz and his colleagues who have undertaken this research, and the TCPA owes them a considerable debt of thanks.

In addition, on behalf of the TCPA, can I express my thanks to everyone who has participated in the 'Sustainable City-Region' research programme. As part of our continuing programme of work we will monitor and review the response to this book, and we welcome your comments and reactions to the ideas and messages contained in the following pages.

# ABOUT THIS BOOK

## Author's note

*I would like to pay tribute to the memory of Michael Brown, Landscape Designer, who died in 1996. His inspired contributions to this project among many others will be missed by all who worked with him.*

*I would like to pay special thanks to Peter Roberts, without whose enthusiasm and foresight this project would not have happened. I would like to thank the staff at Earthscan, and the researchers at the Centre for Urban & Regional Ecology, for their boundless patience.*

*Finally, the long journey in forming these ideas, and from ideas to publication, would not have been possible without Amanda, Jerry and Alison.*

*Scope:* For such a wide ranging investigation we have focused only on the key themes. Each sector or topic is in outline form, summarizing arguments which are often complex and controversial, and there will be inevitable gaps in the coverage of many technical subjects.

*Sources:* Information is taken from local sources wherever possible, but many topics are only covered at a regional or national level, and many 'best guesses' have been made for local data. All charts and graphs refer to Greater Manchester (GM) unless otherwise specified. Targets refer to 2020, and trends and changes for the period 1995–2020 unless otherwise specified. Boundaries are taken as the local authority boundaries of the 10 GM Districts unless otherwise specified. All data for GM is drawn from official sources unless otherwise specified.

*Further information:* This publication has been drawn from a more detailed *'Technical Report'* which covers in some depth each of the key sectors. An *'Overview'* and *'Methods and Tools'* working papers are also available. The Sustainable City-Region research programme continues with related projects including appraisal methods, integrated economic evaluation, resource flow audits, scenario workshops and a web-based 'Sustainability Atlas'. Details are on the Sustainable City-Region website at **www.art.man.ac.uk/planning/cure.**

*Attribution:* The views expressed are those of the author as advised by the Sustainable City-Region Working Group, and do not necessarily reflect the views of the TCPA or the sponsoring organizations. While every effort has been made to ensure accuracy, the author and the Working Group cannot accept responsibility for any errors or omissions.

# PART I

*The story begins with the question – what does sustainable development mean, if anything, in cities and regions? 'The State of the City-Region' shows the dynamic and problematic reality of the case-study, the conurbation of Greater Manchester. 'Trends and Prospects' follows the moving picture, and points to alternative paths or scenarios for the future. 'City-Region 2020' shows one of these paths in outline, as a vision and guide for the journey to follow.*

# INTRODUCTION

*Sustainable, a. (f.prec.+-ABLE. Cf. SUSTENABLE)*
*capable of being upheld or defended: maintainable*

## What if ...?

Sustainability is the watchword for the new millennium, and a guiding theme for all human activity. It is also a never-ending quest for 'having our cake and eating it' – not only economic growth with social justice, but environmental protection into the bargain.

For the 'developed' nations of the North, the race for affluence stretches their environmental limits, even while their social fabric is fragmented by unemployment and exclusion. For 'developing' nations the need for basic shelter and services is overwhelming, but 'development' too often destroys the natural resource base. For the world in total, problems such as climate change and species loss are raising the stakes to the brink of catastrophe – and as five billion people reach out for western levels of affluence, current trends cannot continue.

What has this global agenda got to do with cities, regions, or planning? This is a multi-layered question, which we explore through a detailed case study.

In most industrial countries most people live in or near cities, and the workings of such cities are implicated in most environmental damage. But urban activity now reaches right across 'city-region' territories, from city centres to remote countryside. And while each city-region is the result of a unique history, for the future there are many forking paths, from utopias to nightmares. Planning, in its widest sense – strategic management of environmental, economic and social change – has the challenge of steering large and complex city-regions towards more benign futures.

To begin this, we need some kind of vision or goal to work towards. That is why we start with the question:

### 'what if ...?'

What if a city-region was to become truly 'sustainable' within our lifetimes? What changes could we see on the ground? Would economics, politics or technology provide the answers? Would there be jobs for the unemployed, and where would the money come from? What if plans and policies could be fully integrated between all sectors? These are the kind of questions which guide this inquiry into 'integrated planning for long term sustainable development'.

A hundred years ago Ebenezer Howard took up a similar challenge, in the waste and deprivation of both town and country. The result was not only a physical model for garden cities, but an economic model for local industry and social welfare.[1] More recently the TCPA set out envi-

---

1 Howard 1898: Hall & Ward 1998

ronmental goals for all areas of urban development.[2]

Here we follow through that agenda. We ask
how such ideas might fit together on the ground
– not so much in a one-off new settlement, as in
the much larger 'reality test' of restructuring and
re-engineering existing cities and regions.

And the reality test here is challenging indeed – the dynamic and problematic conurbation of Greater Manchester (GM).[3] GM is a world
icon for style and sport, and a thriving centre for
finance, media, education and culture. It is also
a city where a million people live amidst poverty,
obsolete industry and crumbling buildings – the
'human landfills' of a post-industrial wasteland.[4]
GM contributes 1/700th of the global climate
change effect, air pollution is high, life expectancies are short, suicide and depression are rife.
Just as the industrial revolution began here, so
might the post-industrial sustainability revolution – but it will not be a simple or easy transition.

## Complexity & contradiction

Such a challenge depends on a high level of
'joined-up thinking' – but this is a perennial
quest, with many contradictions and few simple
solutions. So we have taken a sceptical view of
many claims, both from the 'business as usual'
and the 'sustainability' camps. In practical terms
we tread a very thin line between 'cynical
greenwash' and 'misplaced idealism'. Both are
plentiful.

At the start we find that most real-time problems cross the boundaries of subjects and sectors, and that most available information doesn't
seem to fit the problem. We find that many
sustainability goals are in conflict – for instance,
bottom-up decision-making versus strategic
planning. We find huge gaps between principles and practice – the core concept of
sustainability is about long term thinking, but
most of us struggle with uncertainty day by day.
We find that any practical question is surrounded
by trade-offs such as efficiency vs equality, with

few clear answers in sight *(Box 1.1)*. It is no
wonder that busy practitioners take the 'S' label
and stick it on whatever they were doing anyway.

## Putting it together

Faced with this, we have aimed to see the wood
for the trees. We have used best available information, and we have invented methods and tools
where none existed. The result is a demonstration of what is possible in the integrated planning and restructuring of a major conurbation. It
is a source-book for long term policy and strategy. It is also a demonstration of methods and
tools for similar projects elsewhere.

These methods have been developed
around the basic sustainability themes – balance
and integration – to be explored below.

Our starting point is the physical city-region,
its form and fabric, its resource inputs and outputs, and its pressures and impacts on local and
global environments. But to tackle such physical problems we have to look 'upstream' at their
roots and causes in sectors such as housing or
transport, and look at how far these sectors meet
human needs or demands. We also have to look
'downstream' of the problem, at the environmental impacts caused, and the final outcomes for
individuals or societies. Overall, we can look at
the balance of 'needs' and 'outcomes', upstream
and downstream, and put the question of how
far it is 'sustainable' in the shorter and longer
term – whether we get the totality of what we
need, as individuals, city-regions or nations. This
balance of needs and outcomes is at the core of
the methods below.

---

**Box 1.1    COMPLEXITY & CONTRADICTION**

A fine example is the question of 'where will the
people go?' *(Chapter 5)*. Households in the UK are
becoming smaller as people live longer and more
independently, and huge numbers of new dwellings
will be needed. Should we allow everybody to trade
up, and build all over the countryside? Should we
protect rural land, and keep the poor in high density
urban areas? Is there a win-win solution that keeps
everybody happy, and if so, why has it not yet worked?

Adapted from  Breheny & Hall 1997

---

2 Blowers 1993
3 GM is used for Greater Manchester throughout: not to be
confused here with genetic modification, or General Motors
4 Davis 1998

Another theme is integration – or in more topical terms 'joined-up thinking'. The solutions to many problems in transport, for instance, are often in other sectors such as housing or industry, and vice versa. But in practice each sector tends to draw a line around its own concerns – so a 'sustainable' transport strategy has to extend mainstream transport thinking towards wider issues, from climate to communities. On the principle that the whole is greater than the sum of the parts, we look at a hundred industries in a dozen sectors, to see the linkages and the bigger picture – less detail, but more synergy.

A third theme is that of space and time. Just as people live and work in places, rather than sectors, there is a clear logic for putting together problems and opportunities by territory – the neighbourhood, city, bio-region or whichever is the most appropriate for the task. This project looks beyond many others at the implications 'on the ground' of sustainable development.[5] It also looks at the time dimension of restructuring and re-engineering, as a process over a medium and long horizon.

The case-study approach here also brings special opportunities – a kind of mental laboratory where a city can be taken to pieces and put back together again. Looking at one city-region in depth can help to show the linkages between many problems and solutions. GM is of course a unique mix, but not unlike many post-industrial cities. The core themes, if not the fine detail, will be relevant to most cities and regions in the developed world and elsewhere. If we substituted Birmingham, Barcelona or Berlin for GM, how much would be different or common between them?

## Applications

Such a quest, in the long tradition of envisioning the ideal city, is a fascinating journey in its own right. But meanwhile there are urgent and controversial policy debates in the UK, Europe and elsewhere:

- Housing, transport, waste management and many other sectors show rising pressures and conflicts between economic growth, social needs and environmental protection.
- New regional governance in the UK aims to bring together economic, social and environmental strategy, but the institutions, resources or methods are not always up to the job.
- Urban regeneration appears more intractable than ever, as many former approaches have failed, while again the needs outstrip the resources.
- Public services are perennially short of funds, even while the fabric of society is torn by unemployment and exclusion.
- Local and regional economies are caught in the race for global competitiveness, where the pace of change, and the risks of dependency and polarization seem greater than ever.

For these and similar issues there are few simple solutions – each is a tangle of economic, social and environmental problems with many conflicting viewpoints. For such issues, the principle of sustainability is not just a cosy marketing label, or a clever academic game, or a mediaeval theology. Sustainability has to be an over-arching guiding theme, a combination of vision and practice, to be interpreted at every step of the way.

## Caveats

In practice, one person's vision is another's blind spot, especially where it concerns the broad and fuzzy theme of sustainability. Decision-makers often assume that sustainability can be 'achieved', as if cities were like machines whose problems can be fixed with a tune-up or a new part. Our analysis suggests quite the opposite – a view of cities which lurch restlessly between crisis and opportunity, where today's solutions become tomorrow's problems.

Another misconception is that sustainability is a scientific quantity to be measured on a scale. Again we suggest the opposite – that there is rarely a single 'true path' of sustainability, more often a tangle of interactions, the results of which may be more or less efficient, equitable and risk-avoiding, depending on who measures them.

5 Roberts 1995: Cohen 1993

There is also a view that a city-region can somehow be an island of sustainability, as if insulated from the world around it. Cities may be autonomous in some ways, but they are driven by the global system in most other ways. If the sustainable development of a city is like turning round a supertanker, the crew cannot ignore the storm-force gale of the global economy around them, or the disputes over who is captain.

The upshot is that everything said here about GM is conditional – a local transport strategy, for instance, will not get very far without linking actions at national and global scale. At the same time higher level actions need to take account of how they fit together at the local or regional level. This interplay of scales and functions is another recurring theme.

Finally we have to keep asking 'who or what' we are trying to sustain.[6] If we can demolish an obsolete house to make way for one which is more beautiful and efficient, could we do the same with an obsolete city? Are we setting out to sustain the city, its people, the global environment, or all of these? The question of 'who or what' is at the heart of this project and its approach to linking different kinds of knowledge. That is why, at the end of the day, we avoid simple conclusions and ten-point lists, in favour of in-depth debate. If this book enriches such debate it will have achieved its aims.

# BACKGROUND

World leaders met in 1992 at the UN Conference on Environment and Development – the Rio Summit – and then again at New York in 1997.[7] There was a common agenda, in that environmental damage caused by economic development was endangering the well-being, and possibly the survival, of present and future generations. Major global environmental problems, such as disruption to the climate, had finally produced a commitment to address their causes. The result was a large set of declarations – 'Agenda 21' – aimed at improving the environmental sustainability of economic development.[8] Agenda 21 was based on the commonly accepted definition of sustainable development, from the 'Brundtland Report':[9]

*'to provide for the needs of the present generation without compromising the abilities of future generations to meet their needs'*

One way to interpret this definition is through the concept of a 'balance' of needs – between local and global, present and future, and material and environmental *(Fig 1.1)*.[10]

Behind the environmental rhetoric, the real business of Agenda 21 was overtly political – the link between economic development, international trade, environmental impacts, and the gap between rich and poor. Since 1960, income inequality between the richest and poorest 20% of the world's population has increased from 30:1 to 75:1, and the 200 richest individuals now possess as much wealth as half the world's population *(Fig 1.2)*.[11] In this sense the environmental agreements – the Conventions on Biological Diversity, Climate Change, Desertification, Forestry, and the Commission on Sustainable Development – were diversions from the core agenda, while being major achievements in their own right.

Rio gave a huge impetus to discussion at every level, but results, unsurprisingly, have fallen short of promises.[12] The full Agenda 21 programme was costed at $128 billion, one tenth of the global arms budget, but only a small fraction of this has been found. Some environmen-

6 Mitlin & Satterthwaite 1996
7 This section was kindly drafted by Ralph Rookwood
8 Centre for Our Common Future 1993
9 World Commission on Environment & Development 1987

10 the vital distinctions between 'need', 'demand' and 'greed' are so problematic that we coined the term 'gneed'
11 United Nations Development Programme 1998
12 Dodds & Biggs 1997

Fig 1.1  ### *SUSTAINABILITY BALANCE*    Fig 1.2   ### *RICH vs POOR*

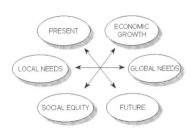

Balance of opposing goals and values.
Source: based on WCED 1987.

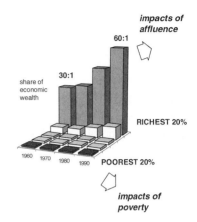

Income disparity of top & bottom 20% of world population.
Source: UNDP 1996

tal problems have been contained, such as ozone depletion, while others continue almost unabated, such as forest destruction.

While the gap between rich and poor grows, the GATT world trading system excludes social and environmental policies which might hinder international trade. The current instability in the world economy is a sign that there are no simple solutions or safe fall-back positions – the global roller coaster is effectively out of control.

## The urban agenda

One of the most alarming global trends is runaway urbanization in developing countries – three-quarters of the world's 30 largest conurbations are in the South and East, each of them larger than many nations, and containing the most extreme environmental problems.[13] Meanwhile, in countries such as the UK, 80% of people are already in urban areas, and there is an opposite trend of 'counter-urbanization' or outward migration – threatening the viability of both urban and rural areas, and dependent on high-impact lifestyles and technologies.[14] Urbanization and counter-urbanization can be seen as two sides of the same coin, reflecting different stages in a general urban development path, where cities are both the 'engines' and the 'dustbins' of economic growth *(Fig 1.3)*.

There is a clear linkage between urbanization and Agenda 21, and this is the focus of global meetings such as 'Habitat II'.[15] Such meetings tend to be once removed from mainstream decisionmaking, but are essential for building networks and spreading 'best practices', some of which are used as examples here.[16] In Europe, the urban agenda was set out in the Green Paper on the Urban Environment.[17] It was then developed through the Aalborg Charter, the Lisbon Declaration, the EU Climate Alliance, the EU Sustainable Cities Project,[18] the Euronet database, and many others.[19]

In the UK the 'sustainable city' is now a guiding theme, and there is some consensus on a model of more compact, mixed use urban form.[20] But the principle is often slippery in practice – not least with the evidence that current policies would at best save a tiny proportion of urban climate emissions.[21] And in practice, long term environmental risks are secondary to present-day needs for jobs and houses: local government is still under-funded and disempowered: and for most hard decisions – such as where to build the houses – there is much conflicting advice. While policy-makers grasp for simple fixes

13 Girardet 1994
14 Herington 1990

15 Binde 1996
16 UNCHS 1996
17 CEC 1990
18 EU Expert Group 1996
19 http://www.euronet.uwe.ac.uk
20 DETR 1998: 'Sustainable Urban Development'
21 Breheny 1995

and print glossy leaflets, there is widespread confusion over the complex and many-layered challenge of the 'sustainable city'.

## Global linkages

Southern cities appear to be increasing their environmental impacts faster than those in the North, where relatively stable populations and more advanced technology have contained most local environmental problems.  But cities in the North are the consumers and financiers of material and products from the South – the '20% with the 80%' – the affluent minority who consume the majority of global resources.[22]  So while city-regions such as GM grapple with their own social and environmental problems, they also have a wider responsibility to the cities of the South. As well as reducing their expropriation and colonization of Southern resources, they can provide examples, incentives and transfers to Southern cities of low-impact technology, market infrastructure, consumer aspirations and political institutions – the essential components of a sustainable development path.

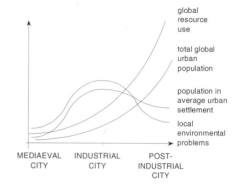

Fig 1.3   **URBANIZATION & ENVIRONMENT**

global resource use

total global urban population

population in average urban settlement

local environmental problems

MEDIAEVAL      INDUSTRIAL          POST-
CITY                CITY            INDUSTRIAL
                                      CITY

General trends in urban development / environmental impact, with 'environmental Kuznets curves':
Source: adapted from Kuznets 1963, Ekins 1997, World Bank 1992

At the same time there is much that Northern cities can learn from their Southern counterparts, where activities such as recycling, self-build and social trading are often much more advanced.  We aim to show that sustainable development in a northern city-region depends on global linkages and transfers both ways.

# URBAN ENVIRONMENTAL SUSTAINABILITY

In the rest of this chapter we look at ways to unravel some of the tangled questions raised above. We look at how the principles of sustainable development apply to cities and regions, and outline the methods and tools developed during the research.

To simplify the task we start with three linked definitions:[23]

1) 'Urban environmental sustainability' – the balance of urban systems with their long term environmental resource base. As each of these has many definitions and constantly

changes, 'sustainability' is a direction not a fixed goal.

**+**

2) 'Urban development':  the evolution and restructuring of urban systems in their global context – also a direction, not a goal.

**=**

3) 'Sustainable urban development': actions which steer the evolutionary process of 'urban development' towards the moving balance of 'environmental sustainability'.

22 Galbraith 1977
23 in this section the term 'urban' is taken generally to mean a city, regional or city-region system:

Fig 1.4 **ENVIRONMENT ~ ECONOMY ~ SOCIETY**

Fig 1.5  **LADDER of LOCAL SUSTAINABILITY**

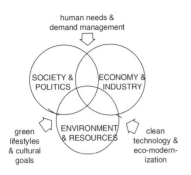

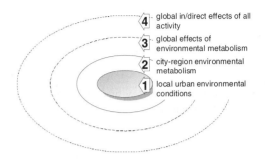

Overlapping agendas and discourses in sustainable development

Layers of analysis and responsibility for urban systems and global impacts.

Another approach is to look at the role of cities as providers of economic, social and environmental functions – as shown by the well-known three-ball sign *(Fig 1.4)*:

- environment: to reduce environmental impact and resource use to 'sustainable' levels, and enhance environmental quality and safety.
- economy: to enhance long term resilience, competitiveness, employment, and equitable distribution of resources.
- society: to enhance health, education, security, equity, cohesion, diversity and 'quality of life'.

Each of these is instrumental to the others – environmental protection is essential for all human life, economic development is needed for environmental protection, and social progress is needed for a stable economy. Actions that hit the bullseye or the overlap between three circles, are the 'win-win' strategies that attract support from all directions. In reality there are many 'win-lose' strategies – solving one problem while creating several others.

Such goals might be applied directly to a self-contained island – but cities and regions are by nature specialized and intensive hubs of activity, taking resources and producing goods and services for elsewhere. So we need to look at the city-region with several kinds of linkages to the outside world, as with a 'ladder' of local sustainability *(Fig 1.5)*.[24] Most cities are seeking to improve their local environments, such as air quality or derelict land. Some cities are starting to look at the urban-hinterland or 'bio-region' system of energy, water and nutrients.[25] A third level concerns the global impacts of the urban system, such as energy and climate change. A wider and deeper view looks at the direct and indirect effects, global and local, of all activity – physical, economic, social and political. If a company headquarters is sited in GM, for instance, how much responsibility does the city bear for that company's subsidiaries on the other side of the world? Such a question may have more to do with ethics than science.

## Environment & resources

The middle steps of this ladder focus on the environmental 'metabolism' of a city-region – a system of activity which maintains itself with continuous flows of inputs and outputs – as does a living organism *(Fig 1.6)*. For a conurbation such as GM, the total flow, including water, is about 2000 million tonnes per year, or about 0.2% of the world total, and the overall efficiency or ratio of primary to 'useful' materials can be estimated at less than 5% *(Chapter 8)*.[26]

24 Stren, White & Whitney 1994
25 Sale 1988

Fig 1.6     **URBAN ENVIRONMENTAL METABOLISM**

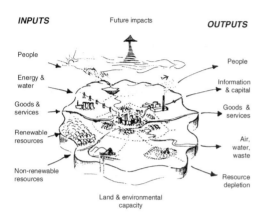

General outline of material inputs and outputs.
Source: based on Douglas 1983: Girardet 1994.

Fig 1.7     **ENVIRONMENTAL TARGETS**

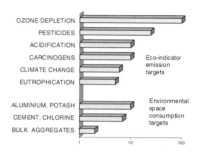

'Environmental space': aggregated long term targets for reductions in environmental impacts and material throughput.
Source: based on Sachs 1998, Carley & Spapens 1998, Pre Consultants 1995, Wackernagel & Rees 1995, McLaren et al 1997

The concept of 'eco-cycles' in environmental metabolism looks at how flows of substances such as water and carbon continuously circulate through the biosphere. Cities tend to disrupt such natural and self-organizing cycles with a 'linear' metabolism – natural resources are sucked in, and pollution and wastes are pushed out. A city or region which contains its own eco-cycles would tend to be less vulnerable and damaging, or more 'sustainable' – such a cycle might be food which is locally grown, digested and its nutrients returned to the soil. Even where the cycle is on the global scale it can still be 'sustainable', if its side-effects or risks are acceptable. GM for instance could operate a 'carbon cycle', offsetting its emissions by planting forests elsewhere which also supply its timber needs *(Chapter 9)*.

An urban metabolism can be analysed in terms of its environmental 'stocks' such as the urban fabric and renewable resources, and 'flows' such as direct resource inputs and waste outputs. Some types of stock are obvious and measurable, such as the area of urban greenspace – but others are more intangible, such as the human welfare provided by the same greenspace.

Such stocks and flows are organized in 'patterns' – structural arrangements of land-uses or activities in space and time. Within the same area of greenspace, for instance, different layouts or management systems might change its social amenity function. Any city-region accounting system should include estimates for both tangible and intangible stocks, flows and patterns.[27]

Each eco-cycle's stocks and flows take place within certain limits, or 'capacities' – the ability of environments and eco-systems to absorb pollution and disruption without damage or adverse effects. But environments and eco-systems are continually changing, and the definition of uncertain or irreversible effects needs both human and technical judgement. Even for simple questions, causes and effects can be complex – the link between a smoky chimney and ill-health may be obvious but difficult to prove. To tackle this there are new methods for capacity assessment at local and global scales, and these are the basis for the environmental targets used throughout this project *(Fig 1.7)*:

- Critical Capacity: level of pollution which causes significant or irreversible damage to human or ecological health.[28]

---

26 World Resources Institute 1997

27 EU Expert Group 1996
28 Critical Loads Advisory Group 1993
29 Rees & Wackernagel 1995

Fig 1.8 **LOCAL & GLOBAL**

Very approximate orders of spatial scales.

Fig 1.9 **NOW. SOON and LATER**

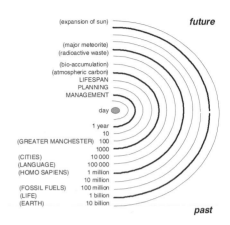

Very approximate orders of temporal scales.

- Ecological Footprint: the notional land area needed to supply primary energy, materials and products.[29]
- Environmental Space: estimates the global equal distribution of resources and assimilation capacity.[30]
- Ecological Rucksack: a ratio of total material consumption to useful outputs of goods or services.[31]
- Eco-indicators: global targets for environmental pressures to minimize human and ecological risk.[32]
- Natural Step: long term goals for zero emissions, zero minerals use and zero toxic chemical accumulation.[33]
- Urban Capacity: acceptable pressures and thresholds in the physical, environmental, social and economic functions of cities.[34]

The most far-reaching environmental capacity problem is perhaps global climate change, of which the largest human cause is fossil fuel use, and we give this a special priority in Chapter 9.

## Space & time

The themes of metabolism, eco-cycles and capacity above are each relative to units in space and time, and there may be different thresholds for global, national, or local levels. The majority of the impacts of an urban system are indirect and non-local – while cleaner technology may improve local air quality, heavy industries may move overseas to produce materials which are then imported back. So a total impact and capacity assessment has to look at supply chains at local, regional, national and global scales.

In this project, for practical reasons, we draw a line at the political boundary of GM, while keeping in view other units such as the bio-region where relevant (*Chapter 14*). Putting together all possible spatial scales, it turns out that a city-region is halfway between an individual and the world (*Fig 1.8*). At each of these scales there are activity patterns and a functional territory where a metabolism and capacities can be identified.

This also raises the question – what is a city-region? The concept was put forward with the term 'conurbation', as a territorial system of city–hinterland relationships.[35] A city-region

30 Carley & Spapens 1997
31 Sachs 1997
32 Pre Consultants 1995
33 Hawken 1996
34 Entec 1998: Jacobs 1998

35 Geddes 1915

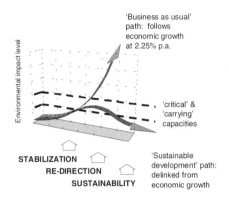

Fig 1.10   **PHASES of SUSTAINABLE DEVELOPMENT**

'Business as usual' path: follows economic growth at 2.25% p.a.

Environmental impact level

'critical' & 'carrying' capacities

STABILIZATION
RE-DIRECTION
SUSTAINABILITY

'Sustainable development' path: delinked from economic growth

General outline of key phases in the 'de-linking' of economic growth from sustainable levels of environmental impact.

might be defined by its politics, industry, commuting, river basins or others, and there are perennial efforts to re-arrange the political map around the optimum pattern *(Chapter 14).*[36]

At higher spatial levels, location is crucial – the position of GM as gateway to a peripheral region is crucial to its prospects. At lower spatial levels, within the city-region each area type contains a profile of problems and opportunities, and the phenomenon of 'uneven development' is the focus for urban regeneration *(Chapter 12).*[37] The spatial implications of environmental strategy in each area type are outlined at the end of each 'key sector' chapter in Part II.

The time dimension also shows nesting layers, from past to present and future – putting in modest perspective the one-generation horizon of this project *(Fig 1.9).* Longer term risks, such as atmospheric carbon or radio-active waste, can be seen in relation to the lifespan of a human, a city-region, or the earth itself.

Steering the course of urban development towards environmental sustainability implies a major restructuring and re-engineering of urban form and fabric. This of course takes time. Long term trends show rising economic growth linked to rising environmental impact, and sooner or later such impacts cross environmental capacity limits. So the 'de-linking' of economic growth from environmental damage is essential to allow one to rise while the other reduces. Such a de-linking process is different in each sector or industry, but there are several key stages *(Fig 1.10):*

- 'Stabilization' of environmental impacts and pressures – slowing the rate of growth in material damage in the shorter term.
- 'Redirection' of trends in impacts and pressures, towards significant reduction in the medium term.
- 'Sustainability' in levels of impacts and pressures, taking all activity to within long term capacity limits.

With a medium and longer time horizon we can also look at alternative 'scenarios' – composite explorations of possible future conditions, trends and transitions *(Chapter 3).* In each chapter we review four possible scenarios, with a focus on a 'business as usual' (BAU) projection, and a 'sustainable development' (SD) scenario, this last being explored in depth. Such scenarios include both discussion and technical calculation, as shown in the boxes and charts of Parts II and III. For practical reasons again we focus on the year 2020 and the decade 2020–30 as a horizon. This allows actual 1995 base data to be projected to 2020 – or estimated for 2000 and projected to 2025. Such a generation timescale is short enough to be grounded in current trends, and long enough to see major restructuring of the urban system.

36 Senior 1967
37 Breheny & Rookwood 1993

# URBAN DEVELOPMENT

Urban environmental sustainability is not a fixed blueprint on a blank sheet – cities are continually evolving and interacting with the world around them. And of course this world itself is in an overwhelming state of flux. Alongside the endless race of economic growth, there are several key transitions:

- 'Globalization': integration of investment, production, trade and consumption.[38]
- 'Connexivity': global networks through information and communications technology (ICT), media, international travel.[39]
- 'Post-fordism': dissolution of former more stable economic, social and political structures.[40]
- 'Exclusion': new patterns of polarization, unemployment and dependency for large sections of the population.

Behind such trends lie the 'long waves' of economic development, a combination of technology, communications and economic changes *(Fig 1.11)*.[41] And in parallel is another transition of human activity itself – from 'primary' resource-based sectors, to 'secondary' manufacturing, to 'tertiary' services, to 'quaternary' knowledge-based and cultural activity. For several centuries secondary activity was the basis of the industrial city, of which GM was arguably the world's first. Local and imported materials were processed via labour, land and capital, producing goods for export along water or railway corridors. Economic specialization and 'advantage' could be defined in terms of the city-region's location and resources as a 'material processor' *(Fig 1.12)*.[42]

That model is now in transition to a more post-industrial 'city of flows'.[43] The city-region now functions more as a node in a global 'hypergrid' – networks of motorways and airports for movement of people and goods, and networks of satellites and wires for movement of information and capital. Many patterns of urban activity and urban form are turning inside out, as the growth nodes of production and consumption migrate to the urban fringe or 'edge city' – retail, leisure and business parks with easy links

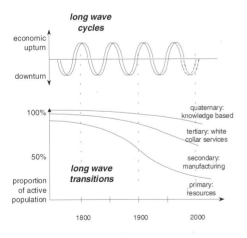

Fig 1.11    **CYCLES & TRANSITIONS**

Overview of structural cycles and transitions in economy, technology and society.
Source: adapted from Schumpeter 1939, Handy 1992.

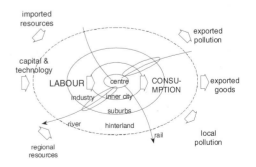

Fig 1.12    **CITY as MATERIAL PROCESSOR**

General system flows in a typical industrial city-region: based on geography of Greater Manchester.

---

38 Townroe 1996: Dicken 1998
39 Mulgan 1997:
40 Amin 1994
41 Schumpeter 1939: Brotchie Hall & Newton 1987
42 Solow 1970
43 Castells 1998
44 Garreau 1994

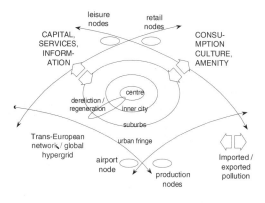

Fig 1.13          **CITY as INFORMATION PROCESSOR**

Flows of capital, information and cultures in a post-industrial globalized city-region; based on geography of Greater Manchester.

to the hypergrid *(Fig 1.13)*.[44] The city itself, and its people's 'reason for being there', centres on services and consumption, and its cultural 'cachet' competes in a global hierarchy.

There are many paradoxes in such a transition – GM contains 19th and 21st century cultures and economies side by side. And while production and consumption globalize, there is a counter trend of 'localization' – a new kind of 'place advantage' in culture and amenity.[45] In physical terms, edge cities are 'counter-urbanized', while historic centres are 're-urbanized' and industrial areas 'regenerated'. In social terms, 'uneven development' creates clusters of unemployment and exclusion. In environmental terms, the bulk of a city-region's resources and impacts come and go through the global hypergrid which is increasingly privatized and deregulated, and where environmental management is an even greater challenge than before.

# URBAN SUSTAINABLE DEVELOPMENT

The concept of 'urban sustainable development' brings together 'environmental sustainability' with 'urban development' – a rich mixture indeed. One starting point looks again at the triangle of economy-environment-society, and the resource management concepts of stocks, flows, patterns and limits. Then there is one more crucial factor – 'dynamics' – meaning the evolutionary potential of human activity and ingenuity to turn problems into opportunities.

## Economy & environment

Economic activity has traditionally been the exploiter of natural resources – so how can there be a 'sustainable economy'? A very simple balance is shown in the equation $I = P \times A \times T$, which shows environmental impact as a function of population, affluence and technology *(Fig 1.14)*.[46] Doubling average levels of affluence, while halving environmental impact, requires a 'factor of four' increase in material efficiency.[47] If the world population also doubles in the meantime, a factor of eight or ten increase is needed – a full-scale 'de-materialization'.[48]

In reality the economic stocks and flows represented by 'affluence' are not only in money, but in social and environmental resources, 'capital' or 'welfare'. Some of these resources can be traded on the market, some of them can be measured but not traded, and others can be valued only as functions or intangible qualities.[49] If such resources are to be protected they have to be 'internalized' within economic markets and social systems. Different kinds of stocks and flows can be seen in a mapping of production, consumption and 'welfare' *(Fig 1.15)*.[50] This

45 Dicken 1998
46 Meadows, Meadows & Randers 1992

47 von Weizsacker & Lovins 1997
48 World Business Council for Sustainable Development 1994
49 CAG & Land-Use Consultants 1997
50 Ekins 1994

**Fig 1.14**    **AFFLUENCE & EFFLUENCE**

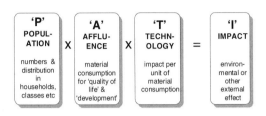

Basic ratios linking population, affluence, technology, environment.
Source: Meadows et al 1992: Olson 1993

**Fig 1.15**    **CAPITAL STOCKS & FLOWS**

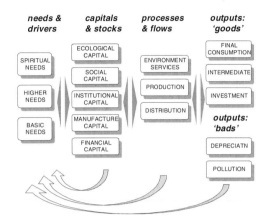

General framework for linking different forms of capital and consumption.
Source: simplified and re-arranged from Ekins & Max-Neef 1994.

highlights the flows between different kinds of capital, and the challenge of environmental economics – how to define market values for non-market resources *(Chapter 13)*.[51]

Beyond the static balance sheet picture of stocks and limits are the 'dynamics' of economic and business activity.[52] Such dynamics might include innovation, skills, competitiveness and indeed optimism – the factors which turn environmental problems into economic opportunities. Fostering such dynamics is the general aim of 'ecological modernization', reducing ecological impacts while expanding the economy, by transforming production and consumption.[53] Its overall goal of a 'sustainable economy' has many layers *(Chapter 10)*:

- Environmentally sustainable economy: activity and trading systems which co-exist with local and global capacities and limits.
- Socially sustainable economy: provision and equitable distribution of income, goods, services, security and employment.
- Financially sustainable economy: a viable balance of investment, savings, consumption, added value, autonomy and competitiveness.

## Society & environment

Following through the logic of the 'affluence' equation above, we can explore the human 'needs' which lie behind it. A needs equation cannot sensibly be put into numbers, but would include:

*human needs x cultural factors x fulfilment factor = affluence levels*

This shows very simply that social systems with cultural norms which encourage non-material needs are more likely to be environmentally sustainable.[54] For instance, the GM climate emission targets could be met tomorrow if thermal clothing was worn at all times – but current lifestyle factors make this highly unlikely *(Chapter 11)*. A balance sheet approach looks at stocks of human 'welfare' from the service provided by environmental resources. Some of these can be measured through economic markets, but other welfare factors are more qualitative – a sense of 'place', for instance, is crucial for neighbourhood vitality, but it cannot necessarily be measured or traded.[55]

As for the dynamics which turn problems into opportunities, there are actions at every level

51 Bowers 1996
52 Ravetz 1999d
53 Hajer 1995

54 Max-Neef 1994
55 Ravetz 1997

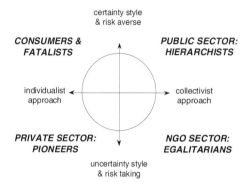

**Fig 1.16**        **CULTURAL TYPES**

certainty style
& risk averse

**CONSUMERS &**                    **PUBLIC SECTOR:**
**FATALISTS**                       **HIERARCHISTS**

individualist ←                    → collectivist
approach                            approach

**PRIVATE SECTOR:**                **NGO SECTOR:**
**PIONEERS**                        **EGALITARIANS**

uncertainty style
& risk taking

General outline of human types in cultural theory. ('NGO' = 'non governmental organization').
Source: adapted from Douglas & Wildavsky 1986; Thomson 1994.

and sector of society. 'Social capacity' enables the cohesion and integrity of individuals, families, groups and networks: 'political capacity' enables empowerment of individuals and communities: and 'cultural capacity' enables diversity, identity, and the values which support sustainability

In practice such values, often taken as self-evident, contain many contradictions:

- 'Futurity': responsibility to f uture generations is fundamental: but most individuals operate with very short time horizons.[56]
- 'Equity': equity in the present generation is difficult to define, let alone achieve: even the concept of 'sustainability' can be seen as a trick to further the exploitation of the poor South by the rich North.[57]
- 'Risk': the 'precautionary approach' seeks responsible action in the face of environmental risk: in practice there are many other kinds of risk to be balanced.[58]
- 'Ecology': a 'deep green' approach sees nature as sacrosanct, while a 'pale green' approach gives priority to human needs: there may not be an objective truth behind one or the other.[59]

In this project we have focused on a middle way approach – 'mid-green' and 'mid-equity', which aims to bridge the gap between principles and practice. While these differences cannot always be reconciled, awareness of alternative views can help to mediate conflict and build consensus. One approach is 'cultural theory', a typology of the styles of individuals and institutions, showing different combinations of risk aversion and collective mentality *(Fig 1.16)*.[60] Meanwhile investigation of alternative views has to find out what people really think – street-level research in Lancashire has shown huge alienation and distrust between different sections of society.[61]

## Economy & society

For the third side of the triangle, we have to admit now – we have no masterplan to solve all human problems. But sustainability themes do provide a fresh approach to perennial debates.[62]

In almost all public services there is a dire shortage of resources, while elsewhere many people lack useful or fulfilling activity. The obvious step is to link one with the other through the 'third sector' *(Chapter 10)*. But to bypass the money system needs not only new policies, but new channels for social interaction. In practical terms cooperation is crucial for the success of public transport, housing, urban ecology and others – where people share gardens with friends, for instance, they may increase amenity while using less space.[63]

Such cooperation and mutual aid in turn depends on rebuilding social cohesion and shared norms and values. But in practice there is an explosion of diversity – in organizations, networks, activities and cultures, as now manifest in the boundless jungle of the internet.[64] Such diversity is potentially unstable, and many future scenarios envisage civic breakdown, cyber-drugs and corporate gangsterism.[65] Such diversity is also a potential strength, encouraging deeper levels of human capacity, and again turning problems into opportunities.

56 Rabl 1996
57 Redclift 1994
58 O'Riordan 1995
59 Pearce 1993

60 Thompson 1990
61 MacNaghten & Urry 1997
62 Jacobs 1996
63 Ravetz 1998
64 Mulgan 1997
65 Gibson 1984

All this is a backdrop to the visible and practical agenda for sustainable urban development – re-claiming land, re-structuring economies, re-engineering the infrastructure, re-imaging urban identity, and re-defining new roles for cities and their people in a globalized era. Sustainable urban development is a many-headed theme, with politicians, designers, economists, activists, engineers and managers each bringing their own angle and their own language. Coordinating such diversity is a huge but essential challenge if cities and regions are to steer towards a more sustainable development path.

# METHODS & TOOLS

Here we take a step back and look for common threads and ways to link different forms of knowledge. The result is a set of methods and tools which were developed during the research, and which should be useful to similar projects.

## Systems thinking

In reality an urban economy or urban environment is not a simple or predictable unit at any scale – it is more like a 'complex system', where many parts constantly interact and organize themselves into ever-more intricate patterns.[66]

Almost every natural habitat – such as a woodland – contains endless layers of complexity, at every scale down to the microscopic. Any definition of 'sustainability' depends on the frame of reference – even sudden change or catastrophe, such as a forest fire, may be part of a longer term cycle.[67] As there are few fixed boundaries around any 'system', its definition depends on the nature of the question – if we are looking at a woodland, the watershed might be one kind of boundary, but the species types might be another. Likewise in a city-region, almost any component – a house, a housebuilder, or a housing industry – can each be seen as a 'system'. Each system responds to changing pressures, problems and opportunities, to sustain its existence and its functions.

A systems perspective on sustainability looks at the qualities of viability, integrity and longevity – sustainability, in other words – of any system, as manifest in a set of system functions *(Fig 1.17)*.[68] A system has to survive by utilizing its available resources and throughput of energy and materials.[69] It has to deal with diverse conditions, respond to short term changes, and adapt to long term changes. Most importantly it has to co-exist with other systems, both larger and smaller, by containing its exter-

Fig 1.17     *SYSTEMS PERSPECTIVE*

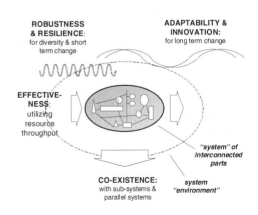

General functions of systems & their 'sustainability'.
Source: adapted from McLoughlin 1969: Bossel 1996: Clayton & Radcliffe 1996

---

66 Funtowicz, O'Connor & Ravetz 1994
67 Hollings 1986

68 Bossel 1996: Clayton & Radcliffe 1996
69 Odum 1983

nal impacts which could affect its resource base. To fulfil these functions there are key qualities which reflect the system's capacity for survival, resilience and integrity:

- cybernetic feedback and communication – ability to respond to pressure or change.[70]
- self-organization – capacity to innovate and generate diversity.[71]
- emergence – capacity to evolve to higher levels of self-organization.

With a systems perspective, seemingly unpredictable behaviour can be traced via 'attractors' – relatively stable or recurring patterns of organization and activity.[72] Self-organizing patterns can be seen in every aspect of the natural world – sustainable agriculture also depends on synergy with such patterns.[73] Human-made patterns can be seen in the spatial arrangement of cities – with the same stocks of houses and streets, different spatial patterns might aid or reduce human amenity.[74] Looking at cities as complex systems opens the door to understanding how cities can evolve, organize and regenerate themselves.[75]

## Integrated assessment

The systems view is also very useful in seeing how different kinds of stocks and flows work together, both environmental, economic and social. But the sustainability theme seems to demand more than this. A housebuilding firm, for instance, might be successful and profitable, but do its products respect the global climate? Does the housing industry as a whole improve local services? Wherever we look, the sustainability theme combines the economic, environmental and social. It also extends beyond the conventional boundaries of each industry or sector – in our finite world almost everything is connected to almost everything else.[76]

The systems view above hinges on the concept of metabolism – the flows of energy, materi-

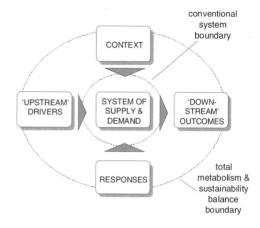

Fig 1.18          **TOTAL METABOLISM**

General concept of integrated assessment of a 'total metabolism': a causal chain which translates upstream 'drivers' to downstream 'outcomes'. Source: Ravetz 2000

als and activity patterns, for example in the house above.[77] For the sustainability question, we have to ask what lies 'upstream' of the house – the social needs fulfilled, or economic demand met, which are not necessarily the same thing. Then we have to ask what lies 'downstream' of the house – its final outcomes or impacts. In this way we can see the house and its functions, not just as a physical metabolism, but a total or 'informational' metabolism, with social, economic and environmental dimensions *(Fig 1.18)*.

One way to picture this total metabolism is by a kind of mental mapping of cause and effect, or 'upstream' and 'downstream'.[78] It seems that for the kind of sustainability issues relevant at the city-region scale, environmental problems are typically caused by economic activity, and economic activity is typically caused by social needs and demands. Putting these together, the result is a very approximate chain of cause and effect from upstream to downstream, and this shows directly the balance of sustainability between 'what we need' and 'what we get'. For example, the total metabolism of the transport sector

70 Ashby 1956
71 Kay & Schneider 1994
72 Gleick 1993
73 Mollison 1988
74 Alexander 1986
75 Portugali 1997
76 Mulgan 1997

77 O'Regan & Moles 1996
78 Ravetz 2000

Fig 1.19   **INTEGRATED ASSESSMENT**

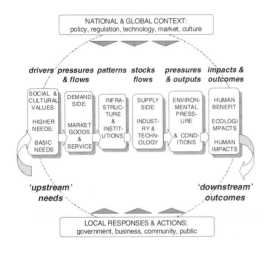

Integrated assessment framework for mapping of 'total metabolism' and 'sustainability balance'.
Source:  adapted from EEA 1995, OECD 1993.

- The context of assumptions on national or global policy, regulation, markets and technology can be shown above.
- Local actions which may alter various links in the system, aiming to improve its performance or sustainability, can be shown below.

Such an 'integrated assessment' mapping only puts on one piece of  paper what every good manager knows instinctively.  Its structure is an extension of the common OECD 'pressure-state-response' and the EEA 'driving forces' frameworks.[79]  It is not an objective description as such, more a tool for investigation.  It provides a total systems mapping, with 'hard' supply–demand equations in the centre, and more 'soft' or intangible social and cultural values surrounding them.  It can be used as a guide to 'hard' systems modelling or 'soft' systems analysis of social and political 'discourse'.  It is also a linking framework for identifying strategies, agencies, indicators, targets, and appraisals as below.

As with any mapping or mental model, there are endless possible levels of detail: the very general level shown here is akin to a route map showing only the very largest features. Even this shows how sectors such as housing or transport, can meet multiple needs with single actions, or single needs with multiple actions, and each generating multiple outcomes. It also shows how simple actions often backfire – for instance why building new roads can increase congestion.

This combination of 'integrated assessment' mapping with the 'total metabolism' systems approach is a powerful double tool for exploring the sustainability theme.  The systems mappings at the beginning of each chapter in Parts II and III show in outline the main features of each sector, as a route-map for more detailed discussion.

shows such a balance – we need access and opportunity, but we end up with congestion and climate change, unless there are changes at each step between.  A total metabolism mapping should include cultural, social, economic, political, spatial, technological, environmental and ethical dimensions, arranged in a rough order from upstream to downstream *(Fig 1.19)*:

- The left hand column shows cultural and lifestyle factors – needs and desires for mobility, identity and so on.
- These pressures translate to economic markets and mode activity levels – 'demand' for trips in cars or buses.
- Market demands interact with the urban infrastructure both physical and human – such as the road network or the police force.
- 'Supply-side' technology provides services together with external impacts – emissions and congestion.
- These externalities cause pressures and impacts on environmental resources – climate change or acid rain.
- Human outcomes can be both positive and negative, with the final balance weighted by social priorities or ethical values.

## Integrated Sustainable Cities Assessment Method

Following the logic through, we applied the 'integrated assessment' and 'total metabolism' mapping approach to this research.  One result is this book.  Another result is a prototype package of methods and tools, the 'Integrated

79 EEA 1995 & OECD 1993
80 Ravetz 2000

Sustainable Cities Assessment Method'
(ISCAM).[80] This is a platform which links a
number of applications, which surface in various
parts of this book:

- 'systems mapping' or integrated assessment
  of the total metabolism, as above.
- 'accounting', to compare scenarios, and to
  identify chains of indicators and targets.
- 'strategies' for sets of actions coordinated
  between different parts of the metabolism.
- 'agencies' which can achieve such actions
  in the context of barriers and constraints.
- 'appraisal' of the sustainability of systems,
  projects or programmes.

The accounting component is also available in
the form of a prototype software tool.[81]

The ISCAM starts by scoping the problem
in question, whether large or small, understanding the nature of the metabolism, and drawing
up a systems mapping as above.

'Accounting' then puts flesh on the bones
of the mapping, starting with the indicators which
are relevant and measurable. But as any one
indicator is a small piece of the jigsaw, we need
to link 'families' of indicators in extended chains
of cause and effect.[82] For example, an indicator
of 'high public transport use' might show an eco-
city, or simply a poor city, depending on other
factors such as utilization or emissions – we need
the wider picture to see each part in context. The
ISCAM systems mapping provides a useful
structure for these chains. An indicator chain
from the transport sector, for instance, shows
linkages all the way from culture to climate
change:

- cultural: desire for access and mobility;
- social: work and lifestyle patterns;
- economic: travel demand by mode;
- infrastructure: network performance;
- technology: fuel efficiency by mode;
- environmental: emissions by mode;
- ecological: acidification and climate impacts;
- outcomes: economic, environmental, social.

Fig 1.20   **INTEGRATED SUSTAINABLE
CITIES ASSESSMENT METHOD**

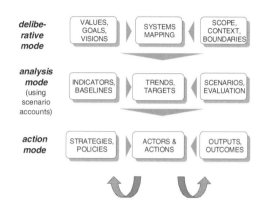

General scope of ISCAM method & accounting tool: many feedback
cycles and loops are possible between each stage.
Source: adapted from Checkland 1990, Friend & Hickling 1987

To be meaningful, each indicator needs a target
– but targets likewise can mean little in isolation.
We need linked sets of targets, each of which
reflect a balance of scientific goals, social values, economic resources and political constraints.
The ISCAM software selects the features of the
city-region system which can be easily measured and linked, and puts them on a set of
spreadsheets, with minimum data requirements
and nothing hidden – 'what you see is what you
get'. A standard format for each sector shows
the total metabolism factors above – drivers,
pressures, stocks, patterns, flows and impacts –
arranged as a set of alternative scenarios:

- current values, and historic where available;
- business-as-usual (BAU) trends;
- sustainable development (SD) targets.

The factors which are most sensitive and critical
to the total system are represented by 'core indicators'. For each of these the distance between
BAU 'trends' and SD 'targets' is shown as a
'trend–target' index. The core indicators and
their indices can be explored and linked to
indepth political and economic debates. Such debates are an integral part of the process of forming scenarios, and scenarios which look beyond

81 Details on www.art.man.ac.uk/planning/cure
82 Levett 1996

Fig 1.21   **SUSTAINABILITY APPRAISAL**

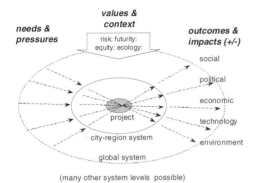

(many other system levels possible)

General linkages between individual projects and programmes,
and their context of city-region and global systems.

the frame of conventional thinking are essential for any kind of long range strategy.[83]

'Strategies' or coordinated sets of actions, can then be formed on the basis of the system mapping and the scenario accounts, as a balance of problems, constraints and opportunities. The ISCAM system mapping shows how strategies overlap – for instance that housing, transport and employment strategies have to coordinate to avoid failure and gain added value.

'Agencies' to carry out the actions can be identified on the basis of the strategies. The ISCAM systems mapping shows how political and institutional factors are generally part of the problem, and that new kinds of institutions may be needed. So each sector in the city-region has a 'strategy', and each 'strategy' has an 'agency'. Depending on the situation, this could be either a formal body with funding, such as a city-region 'energy agency', or an informal network, or collaborative partnership *(Chapter 14)*.

In summary, the ISCAM approach which links these various tools is also the methodology for the 2020 research process *(Fig 1.19)*:

- firstly it explores the scope and nature of the problem, using the system mapping;
- accounting tools help to define indicators and targets, and explore alternative scenarios;

- a third stage explores the implications of the selected scenarios for actions and agencies.

# Sustainability appraisal

The crunch comes with hard decisions – should a derelict urban site be used for housing or allotments? The ISCAM is a useful guide to the sustainability appraisal of such questions.[84] The 'trend–target' index for each indicator is also the beginning of an appraisal – the difference between 'where we are heading', and 'where we want to be'. The systems mapping shows how projects are driven by 'upstream' needs, fulfilling a purpose, and resulting in 'downstream' outcomes. Nesting layers of environmental strategy in time and space are a basis for weighing up benefits and impacts *(Fig 1.20)*.

In practice most 'real' decisions are surrounded by uncertainty and conflict, and 'sustainability' itself is a direction and shifting balance. So a 'sustainability appraisal' of any project or programme is not so much a fixed answer, as a process of investigation, which should be multi-sectoral, multi-cultural and so on *(Chapter 15)*.[85] The question – 'is this house or housing industry sustainable?' – can be seen in its context – 'it depends on what or whom we want to sustain'.

After all this complexity, how can the ISCAM capture the basics of the city-region with some simple 'headline' indicators?  The logic above might suggest three key ratios – economy/environment, environment/society, and society/economy – an approach which national and other indicators projects could do well to follow.[86]  For practical purposes we can take proxies for such ratios, estimated pro rata per person:

- economy/environment: GDP/$CO_2$ emissions;
- environment/society:  $CO_2$/housing floorspace;
- society/economy: housing floorspace/GDP.

Such a circle of indicators show an outline sustainability balance of 'needs' to 'outcomes'. This is useful in comparison and trend analysis, as in the examples to follow *(Chapter 2)*.

---

83 Schwartz 1996

84 Ravetz 2000
85 Carley & Christie 1993
86 DETR 1999: 'Sustainability Counts'

# ABOUT THE PROJECT

This report is the outcome of an inquiry into 'integrated planning for long term integrated sustainable development in a northern conurbation'. It builds on the work of the TCPA Sustainable Development Group, published as *Planning for a Sustainable Environment*.[87] This was based on a holistic view of city-regions, where each component had a role to play, and it showed how different policy menus could apply in city centres, inner areas, suburbs and so on.

The next step was to test these ideas with a case-study of an actual city-region, where more in-depth analysis could show the conflicts and synergies between sectors. To carry this out, a partnership was formed between the TCPA and the Centre for Employment Research at Manchester Metropolitan University. Funding came from the European Regional Development Fund in conjunction with the Global Forum 94 event, the 10 districts of GM, and corporate sponsors as listed.

The aims of the project were to look further, wider and deeper than other current studies, and to investigate how principles could apply to practice, in a typical case-study city-region:

- strategic time horizon for urban restructuring;
- spatial perspective on each type of territory;
- environmental, social, economic linkages;
- goals, targets and strategies for key sectors;
- action recommendations for national and local government, business, community and the public;
- demonstration and guidance for sustainability strategies and appraisals, Local Agenda 21 and similar programmes.

## Report structure

The report aims at a logical structure, although in practice each theme is linked to almost every other:

- Part I *(Chapters 1–4)* looks at principles and methods: GM in the past and present: future trends and prospects: and a scenario for 2020.
- Part II *(Chapters 5–10)* looks in more detail at each of the key environmental sectors.
- Part III *(Chapters 11–15)* looks at how to put the many strategies and actions together – in public services, regeneration, investment funding, and politics and governance.

Each chapter in Parts I and II follows a common pattern. First we look at the trends, prospects and possible scenarios, and use the 'integrated assessment' system mapping to explore the total metabolism and possible goals and targets. Then we look in more detail at each industry and sub-sector. Finally we look at how to make it happen, in terms of 'who' does what, 'where' on the ground, and a comparison with other city-regions. The thorny question of costs and benefits is the subject of current research, and is discussed here only in outline *(Chapter 13)*.[88]

In each chapter there are summary boxes of goals and strategies, showing the relevant roles and responsibilities with a shorthand:

- GOV: national government, agencies, EU;
- LA: local authorities, agencies and related partnerships;
- BUS: business, industry, professions, finance;
- COM: community groups, NGOs, networks;
- PUB: public, consumers, individuals.

In each category there is a code to show very roughly 'who does what':

87 Blowers 1993                              88 Ravetz 2000c

– direct or major responsibility shown by ●

– indirect or minor responsibility shown by ○

## Project methods

The research approach aimed at a holistic and longer-term perspective on the city-region system, and to help achieve this, developed the ISCAM methods and tools above.

The research process started with a 'forecasting' approach of trend analysis, drawing on government and industry data where possible. It then combined this with a 'backcasting' approach, using scenario techniques to envision possible futures and then work back towards policies and strategies.[89] While the methodology is more holistic and wide-ranging than that of many projects, the ISCAM scenario accounting tool provides a sound mathematical grounding. The available space allows only for summaries and extracts from the scenario accounts, but the full set with details of the software is available on the Sustainable City-Region website.[90]

With a general shortage of data, linkages, methods and tools, the research aims to draw together whatever evidence is relevant to a focus on the 'real-world' prospects for various possible scenarios for sustainable development.

In practice the process of assembling and linking such a case is anything but straightforward – there are many feedback cycles, lateral moves, and apparent dead ends. The result aims at a fine line between idealism and practicality; between detailed policy recommendations and general research findings; and between scientific evidence and political reality. Hopefully, similar attempts in the future – integrated planning for long term sustainable development – can usefully build on this prototype.

89 Dreborg 1996

90 www.art.man.ac.uk/planning/cure

# THE STATE
# of the
# CITY-REGION

*From this foul drain the greatest stream of human industry flows out to fertilize the whole world. From this filthy sewer pure gold flows. Here humanity attains its most complete development and its most brutish.*
De Tocqueville, Manchester, 1834

Manchester a century ago was the classic 'shock city' – with the world's first global trading economy, railway station, trade union congress, retail cooperative, programmable computer and many other landmarks. A journey from east to west crosses many layers of this history like rings on a tree – from the birth of the textile industry in the Pennine valleys, to the sunrise business parks surrounding the 'world's best' airport.

The city is still dynamic and problematic. It has the world's best known football club, and the UK's liveliest youth scene. It has the largest higher education campus, and the largest concentration of digital creative industries in Europe. It also has the worst pollution, mortality and depression rates in the UK. About a million people live amidst poverty, unemployment and dereliction.

Greater Manchester (GM) is a sprawling conurbation surrounding the City of Manchester, partly an extension and partly a different level of urbanization *(Box 2.1)*. Two and a half million people – half the population of Scotland – are housed in a ring of satellites around a large ur-

ban core, where many former settlements have merged. To the east and north are low hills surrounding a mixed urban fringe, and to the west and south is a patchwork of small towns and large suburbs. GM sits at a national crossroads, halfway between Scotland and the south, and the motorway network is used by the new estates and business parks as a gigantic high street. GM is also the gateway to a 'peripheral' European region, a big brother to its struggling neighbour of Merseyside, a playground for wealthy commuters, and a stop-off for Lake District globetrotters.

As a guide to where future pressures are coming from, some vital statistics for the city-region are shown below in order of their annual growth rate under 'business as usual' projections *(Box 2.2)*.

## The changing city

Manchester sprang to the world's attention in June 1996, when the largest ever mainland IRA bomb devastated a whole quarter of the city centre.[1] Within days a partnership Task Force was

---

1 While this event was devastating, the air raids of Christmas 1940 caused 363 deaths and 1300 fires, and destroyed 30000 houses and 10 acres of the city centre.
2 Averley 1997

Fig 2.1

## GREATER MANCHESTER

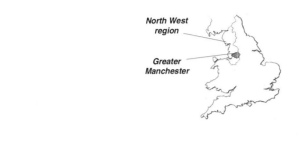

North West
region

Greater
Manchester

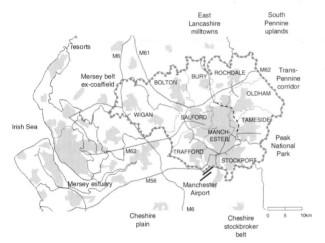

East
Lancashire
milltowns

South
Pennine
uplands

resorts

M6 M61

Mersey belt
ex-coalfield

BOLTON

BURY ROCHDALE

M62 Trans-
Pennine
corridor

OLDHAM

WIGAN SALFORD

TAMESIDE

Irish Sea

MANCH-
ESTER

Peak
National
Park

M62 TRAFFORD

STOCKPORT

M56

M6

Manchester
Airport

Mersey estuary

Cheshire
plain

Cheshire
stockbroker
belt

0   5   10km

Box 2.1

## THE CITY-REGION

Greater Manchester (GM) is a conurbation of over 2.5 million people in the industrial heart of the north west region of the UK. It grew rapidly as the world centre of the textile industry, and now has a diverse economy of about £25bn GDP, with strengths in chemicals, electronics and general manufacturing. Outside of London it has the largest finance, law, media, research and higher education clusters in the UK. It also contains some of the worst unemployment, deprivation and housing.

Greater Manchester (GM) is the name of the former Metropolitan County which contained 10 districts; following its abolition in 1986 these are now 'unitary' or autonomous local authorities. The Districts include the Cities of Manchester and Salford, which suffer the worst conditions, along with the metropolitan districts of Rochdale and Oldham. The outer districts of Bury, Stockport and Trafford are areas of growth and affluence, and Bolton, Tameside and Wigan are somewhere between. This of course is a generalization of a very complex pattern of wealth and poverty.

GM has long been a multi-ethnic centre for many groups including Norse, Flemish, German, Jewish, Irish, Scottish, Asians and Chinese. Manchester itself has been a European city since AD79, when Roman troops started a 331-year military occupation at the fort of 'Mancunium'.

formed, a design competition was organized, and the selected masterplan is now being built in one of Europe's largest building sites.[2] New pedestrian routes link the station with the river and cathedral, and the much-reviled Arndale shopping mall is being re-connected with the surrounding streets. When complete, the rebuilding will have created a new gateway around a new generation of culture, leisure and retail – while some asked the question as to why a bomb was needed to improve the city centre.[3]

To the south in Hulme, the last of the notorious deck-access blocks was demolished, to be replaced by a more traditional low-rise pattern, as part of a re-invention of urban design around

the 'sustainable community' concept.[4] One project in particular, 'Homes for Change', is a shining example of human scale, mixed use and low-impact development.[5] To the east, a huge area of industrial dereliction is now seeing new life, with the national cycling stadium and the 2002 Commonwealth Games site providing a major boost to image and investment. Meanwhile to the north, the difficulties of projects such as the Miles Platting Development Trust show that there is no quick fix for compound physical, social and economic decline.[6] Surrounding the regional centre is still a swathe of older neighbourhoods and newer estates on the brink of a downward spiral of dependency, unemploy-

3 Shostak 1997
4 Hulme City Challenge 1994

5 Rudlin & Falk 1999
6 Robson 1994

Box 2.2

## *GM ~ VITAL STATISTICS*

| | |
|---|---|
| 'world's best' airport with 35000 trips per day | 8% |
| GDP of £25 billion per year | 2.5% |
| about 1 million cars: 6 million trips per day | 2% |
| nearly 100 000 other buildings | 2% |
| derelict land on 6% of urban area | 1.8% |
| about 1 million dwellings | 1% |
| 700 000 bus trips per day, 70000 local rail | 1% |
| energy use;  90 billion kWhr per year | 1% |
| $CO_2$ emissions:  32 million tonnes per year | 0.7% |
| waste arising 11 million tonnes per year | 0.7% |
| over 2.5 million people | 0.2% |
| urban area 55000 hectares: 43% of total | 0.1% |
| 8000 km roads: 152 km motorways: 350 km railways | |
| land area 128600 hectares or 500 square miles | |

Showing annual growth rates from current trends and 'business as usual'
projections. Sources: GMR 1995, AGMA 1995, Manchester City 1996

ment and crime. Further afield to the west are flagship regeneration areas such as Salford Quays and Trafford Park, where the former docks of the Ship Canal have been transformed into sunrise business parks.

On the periphery, one of the UK's largest out-of-town malls threatens to take 20% of trade from some surrounding centres, and possibly cause gridlock across the conurbation.[7] Even this is but the tip of an iceberg – travel demand and congestion both grow in parallel with new thinking on integrated transport. The M60 orbital motorway will shortly be complete, opening up further swathes to development, and decimating one of Oldham's most precious urban parks. The worst pinch point is on the east–west M62 corridor, where a scheme for a parallel motorway has been shelved for the moment, but where traffic is well over the design capacity,

and almost total gridlock is frequent. Although public transport strategies are now 'in', users and managers alike struggle with the deregulated and fragmented bus and rail industries. And while the town halls print glossy cycling strategies, many cyclists are not impressed and stage mass demonstrations in the city centre.

Manchester Airport is arguably the gateway to the entire north of England, with a capacity of 30 million passengers per year when its controversial second runway is complete. While newer aircraft reduce the noise 'footprint', surface transport flows are massive and rising rapidly, and the projected effects of aircraft emissions could undermine any sensible climate emissions strategy for the city-region *(Chapter 6)*. The axis of the airport, universities, Trafford Park and regional centre forms an international 'technopole' of sunrise industries and global investment flows, with a massive influence across the region.

Beyond are the suburbs – mile upon mile of estates where at first sight there is little change. But under the surface, many households now contain multiple careers, many children now have computers instead of street games, and many local services struggle to survive.

The surrounding urban fringe is a fragmented landscape of marginal farming, waste tips, motorways, power lines, reclaimed river valleys, garden centres and 'horsiculture' or riding stables. The Red Rose Community Forest project aims to convert much fringe land to mixed woodlands, but progress so far is slow. Beyond, the barren emptiness of the South Pennine uplands conceals many structural shifts, from farming to leisure industries, and from native communities to commuters and teleworkers.

7 Deakin 1996

# THE STORY SO FAR

Manchester and its satellites were the world's first global industrial city, and a model for free-market capitalism. In parallel they have also been pioneers in social investment and strategic planning. In many ways the 2020 project stands in this tradition, with similar goals – environment, economy, society – and we aim to draw from past lessons to inform future prospects.

Manchester City Council came into being in 1853 with an agenda of reform, at a time when riots, cholera and starvation were commonplace.[1] The city was then a classic model of industrial development – activity in the centre was shifting to commerce and finance, creating extravagant merchant palaces, and pushing industry and housing outwards. The first networks for water, gas and drainage were built in the heyday of Victorian municipal engineering, while the Co-operative movement was established in a tiny shopfront in Rochdale. In 1891 the first social housing was built, and later a demonstration garden suburb.[2]

By 1901 the population had doubled to nearly its present size, even while average life expectancy was 29 years.[3] While the tide was turning for the textile industry, the pressure of growth was huge: the first city-region body was founded in 1920, with an ambitious agenda for investment and modernization. In 1926 Manchester City began the country's first municipal satellite township at Wythenshawe, but its plans for an integrated and self-contained community were never realized – the estate became an overspill and sink of deprivation adjacent to the wealthy Cheshire suburbs.[4] Elsewhere, while new boulevards and parks were laid out on a grand scale, the oncoming wave of industrial restructuring brought large-scale unemployment, and the air was thick with dispute and radical ferment.[5]

## Reconstruction & redevelopment

The war damage gave impetus to a reconstruction programme, set out in three large-scale plans in 1945–47, covering the city and an extended hinterland or city-region.[6] These plans aimed to sweep away older industries and create a modern road network – even Manchester Town Hall was to be replaced in concrete, with a grand avenue leading down to the river. Up to half the inner city population was to be moved in a massive dispersal across the region.[7] Manchester and Salford lost 20% of their populations, but due to inertia and infighting, most migrants ended up in the suburbs of the outer districts.[8] Many areas of over 25 dwellings to the acre were razed to the ground, and it is ironic that the 'compact city' approach is now reinventing this level of density, albeit for very different reasons.

The Development Plan of 1961 was even more radical, proposing comprehensive redevelopment, mass rehousing, industrial zoning, highways and car parks.[9] The ill-fated Hulme Crescents were put up at a time when a new council flat was highly prized by tenants, but elsewhere, redevelopment had drastic effects on many families and communities.[10] In areas such as Rochdale, a lower-impact 'community development' approach was shown to be cheaper and more beneficial to communities under stress.[11]

## City-region strategy

The clearance of a quarter of a million slums, and modernization of the transport network, demanded increasing levels of cooperation across the city-region. But the planned dispersal of population coincided with the unplanned migration and decimation of industry – and with hindsight, the result was the devastating hollowing-out of the city which still exists today.

---

1 Engels 1845
2 Manchester City Council 1996
3 Ashton 1934
4 Hardy 1991
5 Greenwood 1938

6 City of Manchester 1945
7 Lancashire County Council 1951
8 Rodgers 1986
9 Nicholas & McWilliam 1962
10 Ministry of Housing & Local Government 1970
11 Community Projects Foundation 1986

The GM County Council was set up in 1974 but lasted only 12 years – during its short and not always popular life, the County coordinated public transport and road building, green belts and river valley programmes, the GMEX exhibition centre and the Castlefield urban heritage park. The County's Structure Plan of 1979 posed three alternatives – free market, interventionist, and a middle way, which in the event was the consensus.[12]   But the tide was turning for strategic planning, and the incoming government promoted a market-led approach with centrally-funded Development Corporations in Central Manchester and Trafford Park. Meanwhile the hard-pressed outer districts encouraged community-based initiatives for declining estates such as Hulme and Langley.[13]

Such lessons have generally been learned the hard way, and the bold redevelopments of former generations have shifted towards a more subtle partnership approach.  As GM emerges from the ashes of the world's first industrial revolution, it is a very topical test bed for the 'post-industrial revolution' of sustainable development.

# WEALTH & HEALTH

The GM economy is again dynamic and problematic – with a long and thorny transition from its former manufacturing and trading base, to a new mix of high- tech and service industries. The city's industrial structure has been diversifying ever since the waning of the textile industry at the beginning of the century, and now has with strengths in chemicals, pharmaceuticals and electronics, and weaknesses in vulnerable industries such as defence.[14]   The universities and international airport are major catalysts for R&D and inward investment, and Manchester is now the largest finance, law, professional and media centre in the UK outside London.[15]   Leisure is one of the fastest growing sectors, and for instance Manchester United is now the world's most valuable football club and brand-name.

Behind this upbeat profile is a story of industrial shake-out on a massive scale.[16]   As a result, most economic indicators are still 10% below national averages, with manufacturing investment at 20% below, and self employment at 30% below *(Fig 2.2)*.   Some projections show growth rates in local GDP above the national average – however, few sectors are likely to generate new employment, and many will show further reductions, with a short term projection of –1% loss of employment per year.[17]   The overall unemployment level is just above the national average, but many areas suffer long term unemployment of 20–40%. While economic development and regeneration schemes strive to upgrade training, there is likely to be further polarization between those with and without the crucial assets of transferable skills.

## The people

The population of GM has dropped by nearly half a million people over the last 40 years – one in five persons – with waves of migration across and beyond the region.  Some inner areas have been almost totally cleared for roads and industry, while some towns on the urban fringe have doubled in size.  At the same time, the average household size has dropped from 3.3 to 2.5 persons per household, and further reductions are the main cause of growing numbers of households, projected at over 200,000 in GM in the next 20 years *(Chapter 5)*.[18]

The population at large is caught between inner decline and outer growth, and large areas hover somewhere in the middle.   Again, many social indicators for GM are 10% worse than the national average, and those for dependency, health, education and crime all tell a similar story *(Fig 2.3)*. But these averages hide local clusters

12 Greater Manchester County, 1977 & 1979
13 Manchester City Council 1986
14 GMR 1996

15 known as FIRE = finance, insurance, real estate
16 Lloyd 1980
17 NW Economic Research Consortium 1994
18 DOE 1995 'Projections of Households'

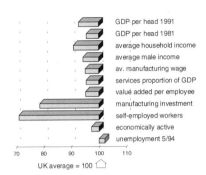

Fig 2.1 **ECONOMIC INDICATORS**

GDP per head 1991
GDP per head 1981
average household income
average male income
av. manufacturing wage
services proportion of GDP
value added per employee
manufacturing investment
self-employed workers
economically active
unemployment 5/94

UK average = 100

Data for Greater Manchester relative to UK average.
Source: CSO 1998.

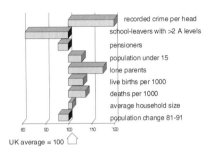

Fig 2.2 **SOCIAL INDICATORS**

recorded crime per head
school-leavers with >2 A levels
pensioners
population under 15
lone parents
live births per 1000
deaths per 1000
average household size
population change 81-91

UK average = 100

Data for Greater Manchester in percentage relative to UK.
Source CSO 1994.

– area mapping shows how social problems are compounded in some inner areas, with ill-health, crime, unemployment and pollution all overlapping *(Chapter 11)*.

At the same time there is a dense network of neighbourhood activity, community organizations, ethnic cultures and mutual self-help. GM has a long history of radical politics, including the Luddite movement (1828), cooperative movement (1844), trade unionism (1868), women's suffrage (1860s), and hosting the Pan-African Congress (1946). This tradition continues to pioneer social innovations.

## Running the city

The GM County administration was disbanded in 1986, leaving all local government functions to 10 unitary authorities or 'Districts'. Joint functions such as public transport support and emergency services continue with the Association of Greater Manchester Authorities (AGMA). Services such as energy and water, invented by local authorities a century ago, are now privatized on a regional basis and increasingly owned and traded on the global market.

Each district has a political and economic agenda somewhere between 'management of growth', and 'regeneration by the bootstraps'.[19] While there are coordinating actions for city-region issues such as EU funding, industrial sites and airports, on the ground there is continuing conflict over parking, retail development and inward investment.[20] This is partly a result of huge variations in the problems and pressures on each district – the most extreme case being Manchester City, containing the most extreme concentrations of poverty and wealth side by side.

Meanwhile the city-region as a political unit and functional territory has in some ways been overtaken by the new regional agenda of the UK. The North West (NW) is one of the most active and cohesive regions in the UK, and a powerful set of public-private partnerships has launched a new generation of bodies including a regional Development Agency, a local authority Assembly, and various collaborative agencies. The city-region or metropolitan agenda, whether 'sustainable' or otherwise, will need be fitted to this new order, even while many details are yet to emerge *(Chapter 14)*.[21]

19 Kitchen 1997
20 DOE 1989 'Strategic Guidance': Williams 1998
21 Jackson & Roberts 1999

# ENVIRONMENT & RESOURCES

The urban environment of GM is in many ways a total mess – the legacy of several centuries of industry, with degradation of air, water and land, vacancy, dereliction, unfit and obsolete housing.[22]   Many critical capacities are exceeded, and the urban metabolism and 'footprint' causes 0.1– 0.2% of global material flows and impacts *(Chapter 8).* On another level the environment is a kind of opportunity – as shown by the two thirds of wildlife sites in GM on derelict or vacant land.

The question now is where we are heading. The chart below shows key 25-year trends projected forward to 2020, assuming 'business as usual' with existing policies: of the selected indicators, only water quality and sulphur emissions show positive trends *(Fig 2.4).*

This highly urbanized city-region already recycles most of its land – 80% of development in GM is on 'brown' sites – but the other 20% still causes the loss of 80 hectares of open land per year *(Chapter 5).* Within the urban area, 6% is derelict and about 8% is vacant, while in the urban fringe there is as much vacant land again, much agriculture is marginal, and the surrounding uplands are eroded and unproductive. Woodlands cover only 2% of the area, and ancient woodlands less than 1%.   There are over 400 sites of biological interest (SBIs) and 17 sites of special scientific interest (SSSIs), and most of these are on urban or derelict land, forming a very unique set of habitats.

Air quality has improved in recent decades, but the regional centre is still titled pollution 'capital' of the UK. Transport is the main source of air pollution, and even the improvements from cleaner vehicles may be overtaken by future growth in traffic. Most of GM is subject to acid loading beyond its critical capacity, with damage to soils, eco-systems and buildings.

Local rivers, especially the lower Mersey, are notoriously polluted, and even with the largest watershed partnership in Europe, many are still effectively lifeless. There is toxic contamination on perhaps 10% of urban land, with 'areas of search' including heavy industry, minerals, utilities and the 620 'closed' waste disposal sites. Nearly all the waste stream of 12 million tonnes per year is transported to landfills in neighbouring counties. Municipal recycling in GM takes only 3% of the total, waste minimization schemes are in the very early stages, and there is no clear strategy for future waste management.

## Metabolism & footprint

The state of the local environment is one symptom of the external impact or 'footprint' of the urban metabolism. Sizing the footprint starts with physical inputs and outputs *(Box 2.3),* and extends to an overall 'material flow analysis' *(Chapter 8).*[23]   We find that human consumption of energy and water is a fraction of the natural input from sun and rain, but water forms 90% of the total material input to the urban system. Of the remainder, the largest inputs are in construction materials and fossil fuels. Minerals generally accumulate in the system, while fossil fuels are converted to carbon, both locally and elsewhere via power generation.

The 'ecological footprint' is the notional land area needed to produce all material inputs and assimilate all pollution outputs.[24]  For an average industrial economy this is estimated as at least 5 hectares per person:  on that basis the GM footprint would be about 100 times its own area, or half the size of the UK. In practice, the supply chains for GM involve every branch of industry from all corners of the world, and a full assessment of this would be impossibly complex. So a simpler approach might assume that GM's supply chains and material flows are indirectly responsible for global impacts per year, pro-rata to the city's share of international trade flows:[25]

22 Wood, Lee et al 1974

23 Sachs 1997
24 Rees & Wackernagel 1995
25 Estimated pro rata from World Resources Institute 1996:
UNCHS 1996:  UNDP
1998

Fig 2.3　**ENVIRONMENTAL TRENDS**

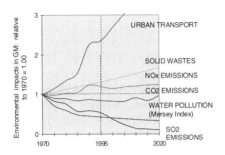

Actual trends & 'business as usual' projections for emissions and
conditions in GM, relative to 1970. Various sources.

Box 2.3　**INPUTS & OUTPUTS**

Data for GM at 1995 base with 'business as usual' projections to
2020. All figures in 1000 tonnes per year unless otherwise stated.

| MATERIAL | MAIN SOURCES | FLOW | B.A.U. TRENDS |
|---|---|---|---|
| **OUTPUTS** | | | |
| CO2: | households | 6000 | 10% |
| | industry | 7600 | 15% |
| | transport inc.air | 7500 | 80% |
| CH$_4$ | landfill /agriculture | 200 | 25% |
| SO$_x$ | electricity | 200 | −80% |
| NO$_x$ | electricity | 34 | −10% |
| | transport | 68 | −40% |
| CO | transport | 300 | −30% |
| waste | sewage | 64 | |
| | municipal | 1200 | 25% |
| | industry / comm. | 8000 | |
| | inert | 3100 | |
| **INPUTS** | | | |
| water | total consumption | 360 million t/yr | 10% |
| | precipitation | 1250 million t/yr | 5-10% |
| energy | direct solar input | 1 million GWh/yr | |
| | energy demand | 90000 GWh/yr | 8-25% |
| fuels | electricity | 8000 GWh/yr | 65% |
| | gas | 3.8 million m3 | 50% |
| | oil & aviation fuel | 3.1 million t/yr | 55% |
| | coal | 4.4 million t/yr | -50% |
| constructn | cement | 700 | 100% |
| | sand & aggregates | 10000 | 100% |
| | bricks & blocks | 450 | 100% |
| | timber | 75 | 100% |
| industry & | metals (total) | 400 | 25% |
| commerce | plastic | 750 | 100% |
| | paper | 750 | 60% |
| food / drink | vegetables & fruit | 400 | |
| | meat, grain, dairy | 520 | |

Estimated various sources incl. ONS 1997, Biffa 1997

- deforestation: 15,000 hectares of rainforest lost (more than the GM community forest will plant over 40 years);
- desertification: 3 million tonnes biomass lost;
- marine pollution: 60,000 tonnes of oil spilled;
- species extinction: between 100–1000 lost;
- displaced persons: 80,000 people (would fill the 50,000 empty homes in GM every year).

How can we set meaningful targets in the face of such huge impacts? 'Environmental space' is one approach – the principle that access to global resources should be divided equally – and material resources and pollution capacity can then be calculated on a global or national basis.[26] The method depends on many assumptions, but most results show that most environmental impacts and resource supply chains for GM need to be reduced by a factor of four in the medium term, and ten or more in the longer term. This challenging goal can be taken as the basis for interim environmental targets.[27]

Another approach is through capacity assessments. 'Carrying capacities' are the sustainable yields of renewable resources, and 'critical capacities' are those where exceedence is irreversible, where stocks cannot be rebuilt once the limit is crossed. Both have a scientific grounding but can be difficult to apply. The Pen-

nine uplands are acidified beyond their critical loading, but actual damage to vegetation and eco-systems is not always easy to measure.[28] The most obvious breaches of social 'urban capacity' are the effects of traffic on pedestrians, and this is one of the themes of the 2020 transport strategy *(Chapter 6)*. A broader question is the 'urban capacity' of the city-region for growth – not a simple issue, as the line between acceptable development and unacceptable 'cramming' is defined as much by culture and lifestyle, as by physical space.[29] The many different capacity limits which might apply in each sector are explored in Part II.

26 McLaren 1997: Carley & Spapens 1997
27 Weizsacker & Lovins 1997

28 Critical Loads Advsory Group 1993
29 Ravetz 1998

# SUSTAINABILITY ASSESSMENT

This lightning tour of conditions, trends and impacts leads up to the million dollar question –

*'is the city-region sustainable?'*

Of course there are many ways to answer this question, as it all depends on who or what is being 'sustained'.

The first and best approach is to ask the people – many of whom are now debating and defining indicators of 'sustainability' under the aegis of Local Agenda 21 *(Chapter 11)*. Most of these public indicators are more concerned with social and economic problems than with technical environmental issues. The UK 'local indicators' programme ran a pilot project in Oldham, where 24 indicators were selected as a snapshot of local sustainable development *(Box 2.4)*.[30]  The former NW Regional Association also carried out a 'sustainability audit', with a single indicator for each of 11 themes.[31] Both these show that much data is missing, incomplete or incompatible, but the results are a useful first approximation for issues of public concern. However there may be a risk that such indicators represent self-selecting groups in LA21 – focus group research on a wider cross section in Lancashire found widespread alienation and distrust of authority and 'policy' in all its forms.[32]

Such indicators are useful for snapshots or slices of life in the city, but even if all the data were available, it is often difficult to say what which indicators should be selected, and what each one should aim for. Without targets – the 'sustainability' factor – indicators have little practical application. But such a sustainability factor is often slippery to define, and so the whole exercise is easily devalued.

One approach would be to add up the 'stocks' or resources of the city-region – land, buildings and so on – in a kind of balance sheet. However, there are problems with adding different kinds of resources, with selecting those that are important, and dealing with cross-boundary effects. Another approach is with a global assessment such as ecological footprint, but this also has to take averages and assumptions at the global scale.

The approach here is to take the city-region not as a static entity, but a dynamic system; to identify a linked set of key measurable indicators; and to look at the gap between 'where we are heading' and 'where we want to be' for each of these indicators. Using the ISCAM software *(Chapter 1)*, these indicators are linked together into a consistent set of scenarios; for a 'business as usual' (BAU) projection, and a 'sustainable development' (SD) scenario for the total urban-environment system.

Using this approach to the question above, the aggregate 'trend–target' index of sustainability for GM scores an overall  –

---

**Fig 2.4**

## *LOCAL SUSTAINABILITY INDICATORS*

Sample data from Oldham MBC

| | |
|---|---|
| Companies with recycling schemes | |
| Recycling rate for domestic waste: | 2.8% |
| Good air quality days at a variety of sites: | |
| Percentage of river mileage in each class | |
| Non-domestic ponds with frogs & newts | |
| Population within 400m of basic services | <50% |
| Homes with energy rating of 5 or above | |
| School children with free school dinners | 27% |
| Population in receipt of income support | 18% |
| Population with mental health problems | |
| Live births underweight <2.5kg | 7% |
| Passenger miles on public transport | –2% p.a. |
| Population who feel safe to go out at night | |
| Street cleanliness index | |
| Children with >5 A-C passes at GCSE | +5% p.a. |
| Adult literacy levels | |
| Voluntary sector on council committees | 22 |
| Electorate voting in local elections | <30% |
| People using library / gallery / museum | +8% p.a. |
| Buildings with disabled access | |
| Population within 400m public open space | |
| Quality of life: (public attitude survey) | |

(no data shows research in progress)
Source Oldham MBC 1995

---

30 LGMB & Touche Ross 1995:  Oldham MBC 1996
31 NW Regional Association 1996
32 McaNaghten et al 1995

Fig 2.4 **TREND-TARGET EVALUATION**

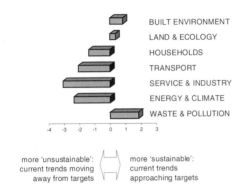

BUILT ENVIRONMENT
LAND & ECOLOGY
HOUSEHOLDS
TRANSPORT
SERVICE & INDUSTRY
ENERGY & CLIMATE
WASTE & POLLUTION

-4   -3   -2   -1   0   1   2   3

more 'unsustainable':       more 'sustainable':
current trends moving       current trends
away from targets           approaching targets

Indices of 'trend to target' evaluation aggregated by sector for GM, as at 1995:
data drawn from many government sources for ISCAM scenario accounts.
Source: Ravetz 2000a.

## ' –20% '

What does this mean?   Roughly, that for the average of all the selected 'core indicators', linked in consistent scenarios based on government projections and best available evidence, conditions in GM are moving *away* from each target, at 20% of the rate needed to meet such targets within 25 years.  In other words, things in total are getting worse before they get better.

The averages of the trend—target scores for each sector are drawn from the complete listing of core indicators in the Appendix *(Fig 2.5)*.  The built environment and pollution sectors show modest progress towards their environmental targets.  Domestic, transport and energy sectors each show minus scores, reflecting the challenge in 'de-linking' economic growth from environmental impact. The services and industry sector scores highlight the fact that most economic targets are moving away from the UK average at present.

Most of these trend—target scores are based on actual physical conditions and impacts, and do not include any 'responses' in policies or programmes – policies for energy efficiency, for example, would show their effects only in future years. And of course many issues are not measurable at all – social cohesion, enterprise culture, the 'feel-good factor' and others are perhaps the most important of any qualities, and the most difficult to define.  For these, there is no substitute for public debate and an open policy process.

# OTHER CITY-REGIONS

If the 2020 project is a demonstration of long term sustainable development for one city-region –the question is, how far is this useful to other cities or regions, in the UK or abroad?

Generally, the principles are common, while the details will be unique to each.

In the highly urbanized UK, the conurbations of the West Midlands, South Wales, Merseyside, West Yorkshire, South Yorkshire, Teesside, Tyneside and Strathclyde, are the most comparable to GM in population, economic structure, urban environment and general dynamics.  There are also other regional or county-wide clusters, such as Avon or the East Midlands, with a more diffuse structure and boundary.  In Europe each country contains one or more provincial city-regions of similar size, such as Lyons, Barcelona, Milan or the Ruhr. Many capitals such as Stockholm, Athens or Lisbon are also similar, although the political role of a capital is clearly different.

This project focuses at the city-region level, as this represents the key factors of financial, professional and educational resources, as well as a large urban population – overall, an effective functional territory *(Chapter 14)*. Many European city-regions have greater political autonomy, while in the UK they tend to have less. Those specialized in single industries such as ship-building or steel, tend to have greater restructuring and adjustment problems than others which are more diverse. Those on the periphery, either physically, economically or politically, tend to continue their dependency relative to those in the centre. The 'intangibles' of politics, culture, education, confidence and image appear to be increasingly crucial factors in a city-region's development prospects in a global hierarchy of urban hubs. Meanwhile it is the very tangible problems of dereliction, air quality and poor housing which provide the impetus for environmental action.

With this complex set of activities and relationships each city-region type has a different profile of problems or opportunities, and legacies or prospects:

- *physical structure*: housing conditions, space and fitness standards, public amenity, urban infrastructure
- *environmental conditions*: basic air, water, ground, landscape and townscape provision and quality
- *environmental metabolism:* input & output of energy, water and materials: economic and social efficiency, distribution of environmental services
- *spatial structure*: land-uses and trends: accessibility and density: protected and green land: vacant and derelict land: housing-jobs-services linkages
- *transport & communications:* access and location, urban infrastructure, ICT networks, diffusion and applications, media and cultural communications
- *industry & technology:* basic facilities and processes for primary, manufacturing, trade and commerce, communications and distribution, innovation & entrepreneurism
- *economic structure:* industrialization path, competitive advantage, added value, re-investment, labour skills, occupational structure, industrial vulnerability
- *social structure*: migration and household structure: education, health, crime, average incomes, inequalities, exclusion and disadvantagement: lifestyle, 'quality of life'

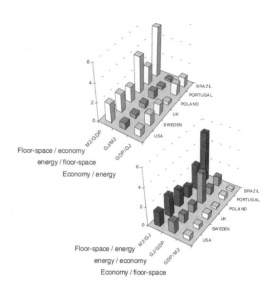

Fig 2.6  **ECONOMY / ECOLOGY / SOCIETY**

International comparison of indicators of compound ratios between economy, environment and social welfare.
M² = average housing space per capita in urban areas
GJ = average annual consumption of commercial energy per capita
GDP = average economic activity per capita

Source: based on World Resources Institute 1997: UNCHS 1996: UNDP 1998: European Environment Agency 1996

- *political structure*: autonomy and governance, institutional organizations & networks, civic society and public decision-making
- *cultural structure*: norms and values, kinship & community networks, cohesion & cooperation.

Each of these dimensions is a complex story with its own internal logic and multiple outcomes. So how can the sustainability factor be put in simple terms? As most things are linked to most other things, it makes sense to identify the most critical and sensitive of the linkages. This can be done in highly aggregated measures, in a triangle of ratios between economy, environment and society *(Chapter 1)*:

- economy–environment: £GDP / energy use in GJ per person per year
- environment–society: energy in GJ / housing floor space per person;

- society–economy: housing floorspace / £GDP of economic activity.

Climate emissions could be a more meaningful indicator than energy use, however international comparison of carbon is difficult as each country has its own given mix of energy sources. In the event, information on even these basic indicators is not easy to find, and anything for a city or regional unit makes many assumptions about boundaries, averages and so on. But even a very rough comparison of simple national data provides food for thought *(Fig 2.6)*.[33]

The results show that the UK is abour middle of the range in environmental-economic efficiency, and perhaps more advanced in social-environmental efficiency than expected.

This is of course very rough and ready, and it could be taken much further in the analysis of efficiency, efficacy and effectiveness.[34] What is more important, and much more difficult to sum up, are the complex internal and external relationships, the development trajectory, and the more intangible political, social and cultural problems and opportunities in each city-region.

Would a 2020-type project in each of these city-regions lead to similar results? It is fair to say that the results would depend on the context, and that the point of this kind of exercise is to encourage debate and forward thinking, rather than detailed policies. Each city-region will decide for itself where its priorities lie, with the problems and opportunities at hand.

33 data from EEA 1996: Eurostat 1997: UNDP 1998: World Resources Institute 1996          34 Bergstrom & Nilsson 1996

# 3

# TRENDS & PROSPECTS

*'Prediction is never easy, especially*
*where it concerns the future'*
Paul Dirac

Experience often shows that today's solutions, can easily rebound into tomorrow's problems. One possible outcome for our city-region – an eco-fable which is hopefully fictititious – shows how environmental improvement might disrupt society, or vice versa. It shows how cities are complex and contradictory, even with the best of intentions *(Box 3.1)*. It also points beyond a view of cities and regions as static islands with clear boundaries, towards a view which is dynamic, evolving, complex, multi-layered and inter-dependent.

So in this chapter we look at the moving picture. Our starting points are the key trends and dynamics of change at local and global level. These point towards many possible perspectives or scenarios for an uncertain future, and ways of managing such uncertainty. A key question for the city-region is the implication of alternative scenarios for its overall shape, size, and the dynamic of urbanization. Finally we look at ways to turn vision into action – the general process of capacity building and business planning

## Economy & society

Whatever happens in the city-region is increasingly driven by the hectic pace of the global economy. Two trillion dollars of volatile capital circle the world every day, and as the digital nervous system of the internet spreads like wildfire, the inter-connectedness of organizations and people can only increase.[1] The dominant theme is 'globalization' – the integration of economic activity on a world scale. Another theme is that of 'post-Fordism', where former economic and political structures evolve towards a more diverse pattern.[2] The result is a set of global dynamics which are fundamental to any version of sustainable urban development *(Chapter 10)*:[3]

---

**Box 3.1**

### THE BEST OF INTENTIONS

Imagine that the very best in eco-management makes our city-region clean and green. But the result is that property prices shoot up, local businesses are forced out, there are labour shortages and homeless migrants. Eco-lifestyles are enforced by LA21 vigilantes who hunt down cars, tobacco and other relics of the industrial age. As the local economy collapses into turmoil, a multi-national media company buys out the leases, and turns the city into a highly profitable eco-theme park using immigrant labour. Their plans are backed up by a 'sustainability appraisal' with projections of increased social welfare and eco-efficiency.

---

1 Mulgan 1997
2 Amin 1997:
3 Handy 1996

- Integration – the dominant trend of liberalized free trade, with frameworks such as the Single European Market, GATT and others.[4]
- De-regulation – blurring the boundaries between state and market, reducing market barriers, tariffs and business controls.
- Flexible specialization – large corporate industries shift towards down-sizing, sub-contracting and out-sourcing.
- Restructuring – rapid change and obsolescence of industrial infrastructure, technology, skills and occupations.
- New urban hierarchy – an emerging framework of global hubs and peripheries, or control and dependency, between cities and nations.[5]

A city-region such as GM is in a particular position in this hierarchy. With an industrial base which is partly obsolete, and partly booming with hi-tech and tertiary activities, it is a major hub to a peripheral region, and at the same time saddled with social and economic decline and dependency. Whether the two worlds will converge or diverge is an open question. A globalized 'sunrise' high-tech reconomy could be serviced by upwardly mobile finance and media professionals, while surrounding them could be many redundant communities on a downward spiral of dependency and decline. New patterns of activity in the third sector may or may not be able to bridge between one world and another *(Chapter 10)*. For businesses and employees in both worlds, there is likely to be accelerating competition, together with structural changes in the nature of work and management.[6]

In parallel are some equally fundamental social dynamics at both local and global scales:

- Demographic trends – changing age structure, gender balances, family structures, disposable time and income, and household organization.
- Cultural trends – differentiation and a shift from former patterns towards individual or community self-identity, empowerment and alternative states of consciousness, both psychic, digital, chemical and bio-engineered.
- Psychological trends – increasing aspirations for identity, community, affluence and fulfilment, alongside the symptoms of stress, depression and alienation.
- Social trends – polarization and segmentation of communities into those with or without work, opportunities, networks and norms: in spite of government efforts, further diffusion of the 'moral economy'.

Overall, such trends might lead to an ageing population with rising disposable time and money, chasing diminishing job opportunities and expanding lifestyle activities. Parents and children in particular may struggle with the diffusion of career structures, family structures, and the increasing alienation of the public realm. The overall result could be another kind of fragmentation which cuts across the division of work-rich and work-poor – in this case the the opportunities of diversity and empowerment, in contrast to those of alienation and stress *(Chapter 11)*.

Similar trends can be seen with post-Fordist local government and 'governance', as the former model of centralized service provision is replaced by one of 'enabling' in partnership with other organizations *(Chapter 14)*.

From where we stand now, such trends may seem set to continue, although the future is full of surprises. But what is interesting is that both the goal-posts and the nature of the 'ball-game' changes – work, family and city structures have all changed in nature as well as in size. Many visions of the future are quite pessimistic, even without 'side-swipes' such as famine or climate change – suggesting large-scale conflict not so much between governments, as between cultures and corporate interests.[7] The same corporate interests may be forced towards transparency and expanded stakeholding, to survive in a super-fluid knowledge-based economy.[8] The implication for cities centres on their role not only as producers and consumers, but as arenas for conflict between the local and global, and between social norms and the dynamics of change.[9]

4 Institute of Development Policy & Management 1999
5 Hall & Hay 1986
6 Elkington 1997: Rifkin 1995

7 Castells 1997
8 Elkington 1997
9 Gibson 1984

# Information revolution

One of the most potent forces on the future city-region is almost invisible on the surface. Information and communications technology (ICT) is rapidly changing the nature and location of production and consumption – it is also changing the nature of societies and communities, in a new era of global 'connexity'.[10] ICT offers a new and powerful nervous system for any human activity or organization, locally and globally.[11] ICT is also instrumental to several technological revolutions – not only the digital, but the quantum and biotechnology revolutions, each of which has the potential to transform not only communications but life itself.[12]

Manchester University produced the world's first stored memory computer in 1948. Fifty years on, high-band networks have linked major clusters of education and health, the city has pioneered one of the first public access 'hosts', there is a chain of 'electronic village halls' for community access, and economic development is coordinated by the European 'inter-regional information society initiative' (IRIS-I).[13] In practice most public sector schemes are rapidly overtaken by the ICT-led transformation of business, and the current annual doubling of internet traffic and trading.[14]

But this shows only the tip of an iceberg. Globalized business communication, together with internet shopping, healthcare, education, and of course culture and entertainment, all add up to a transformation of cities and urban activity at least as far-reaching as in the industrial revolution.[15] While computer speeds and capacities double every 1–2 years on average, the effect of a projected 10,000-fold increase by 2020 is almost beyond the imagination *(Fig 3.1)*. It would also be approaching the physical limits of current silicon technology, and to continue past there, molecular, quantum or biological computing would be needed, as yet still at the concept stage. But while the hardware leaps ahead, the constraints are often at the software and

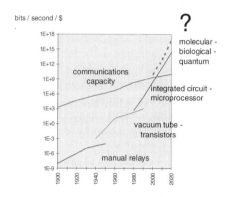

Fig 3.1 **INFORMATION & COMMUNICATIONS**

Trends in ICT: computing power in bits/second/$1 cost:
standard communications bandwidth in bits / second.
Source: adapted from Graham & Marvin 1996: Ayres 1998.

'useware' end, where applications, skills and end-uses are still thin on the ground.[16]

The implications for the physical city alone are huge – daily commuting could be much reduced, but replaced by a more resource-intensive demand for inter-city and international travel.[17] Tele-work lifestyles could spread across the region, if not Europe or the world, far beyond any planning controls. Energy demand in 'smart' houses could be greatly reduced, while new applications hardly yet dreamed of draw in further demand.[18] Artificial climates for outdoor spaces, for instance, may help to increase the vitality of urban spaces, at the cost of huge energy flows.

While digital debate and decisionmaking could well bring new dimensions to urban governance, this is not a simple solution to the problems of representation. In the wider picture, ICT is instrumental to a post-modern perspective on cities and urban life as a 'space of flows'.[19] The ICT networks themselves are one layer in such space, and the nodes and hubs are another. A third layer is the pattern of dominance and exploitation as managed by the new elite, and cities again may be the prime arenas for such conflicts.[20]

10 Mulgan 1997: Solesbury 1999
11 Gates 1999
12 Kaku 1999
13 Manchester Telematics Partnership 1995
14 The Economist 28/06/99
15 Graham & Marvin 1996

16 Sardar & Ravetz 1996
17 Gillespie 1992: Mitchell 1999
18 Miles 1994: Bartlett School 1999
19 Castells 1997
20 Harvey 1989

## Environment & resources

The physical city-region itself shows a changing pattern of risks and opportunities. Many common environmental pollutants, such as acidifying emissions, are being replaced with the more insidious hazards of modern production and consumption – genotoxics, carcinogens or food chain viruses. As heavy industry migrates overseas, the clean-up of the urban environment shows gradual improvement, while rising affluence generates consumption of imported goods and thus exported pollution.

On the ground, local territorial conflicts are mounting over 'positional goods' such as amenity, location and proximity. Sectors such as housing, transport and waste management are each embroiled in controversies over environmental risk and justice, and these also mark and define new social groupings and sub-cultures.[21] New ways of managing such conflicts will be needed, whether or not they are labelled as 'sustainability', while the post-industrial environmental agenda hinges on rising affluence and aspirations for identity-creating goods and lifestyles of all kinds. It will also be marked by the polarization of communities, and housing, transport or waste management may come to revolve around such polarization.

# FUTURE SCENARIOS

If the trends above are more or less clear, is the future so determined? Not at all. Many such trends are extremely fuzzy, contradictory, and highly sensitive to intervention and unexpected events. To deal with the uncertainty of future possibilities, we need 'scenarios' – asking the question 'what if' certain trends are followed with certain actions in certain conditions. Scenarios are not predictions or forecasts, but tools which can help to adapt and respond to change as it emerges.[22]

One kind of scenario is based on forecasting, which projects forward from current trends as far as they can be sensibly taken. Another kind is based on 'backcasting' – a more creative envisioning of future possible conditions, which then informs back to to policies or actions which may enable such possibilities.[23] The scenario accounts in the chapters to follow contrast one type with the other – in other words the trend projections of 'business as usual' (BAU) with the goal-seeking 'sustainable development' (SD) scenarios.

## National & world scenarios

The concept of sustainability emerged with the 'limits to growth' arguments of the 1970s, and many computer-baseed global scenarios were pioneered by multi-national companies.[24] The World Business Council for Sustainable Development explored in 1997 a range of scenarios with three clear 'givens' or likely assumptions for the middle of the next century – a world population in the region of 10 billion, a further wave of technological innovation, and ICT as the primary driver for organizing and networking economic and social activity:[25]

- A 'first raise our growth' (FROG) scenario continues current trends of economic development and corporate dominance, with many social and environmental impacts.
- A 'Geopolity' scenario is based on governance in the public interest, at the cost of some economic opportunities.
- A 'Jazz' scenario sees communications as the catalyst for new global and local networks and partnerships, vastly more transparent

21 Beck 1994
22 Schwartz 1996
23 Robinson 1990

24 Meadows, Meadows & Randers 1973
25 World Business Council 1997

and accountable than today, which together can deliver a more sustainable outcome.

At the UK level, with a progressive centre government in place for some years to come, there are again several directions that national policy might follow over the next decade or two:

- Economic agenda: priority for GDP growth, competitiveness, material consumption, technology innovation.
- Social agenda: welfare redistribution, strong public services, cultural diversity, and community cohesion.
- Environmental agenda: non-material quality of life, conservation of resources, ecological values – possibly the least likely direction as at present.

Such contrasting approaches have been explored through national scenario projects and computer models.[26] For the UK and other EU economies, the overall result is generally more favourable under environmental policies. This assumes that any environmental taxes are 'fiscally neutral', in other words that funds are used to reduce employment taxes, stimulating the economy while improving the environment *(Chapter 13).*[27] However, modelling such effects is often problematic and restricted by its own assumptions on economic and political dynamics.[28] For a more rounded menu of possibilities, the simple scenario directions above can be extended to many possible combinations of growth and change *(Fig 3.2)*:[29]

- lifestyles – social change or social inertia;
- economic growth – high or low;
- politics – interventionist or free-market;
- institutions – globalization or regionalization;
- technology innovation – rapid or slow;
- environmental protection – strong or weak;
- cultural perspectives – entrepreneurial, organizational or ecological.

While such a menu of possibilities for national and world futures forms the backdrop to the 2020

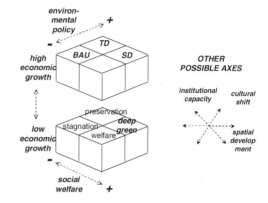

**Fig 3.2          SCENARIO COMBINATIONS**

Conceptual matrix for alternative scenarios: possibilities shown for main axes of environment policy, economic growth, social welfare priorities. Alternative axes are also possible. Key:-
BAU = business as usual
TD = technology development
SD = sustainable development

project, we clearly cannot explore every possible combination. Instead we have worked with a 'bottom-up' backcasting approach, envisioning a set of desirable or 'SD' scenarios for the city-region, based on the integrated assessment mapping approach to the sustainability of inter-connected systems *(Chapter 1).* National and world scenarios are then envisioned, and assumed in outline only, as a plausible set of conditions which would support and facilitate the city-region SD scenario. To highlight the SD path, some simple alternatives are also charted for comparison, and their trends and targets are particularly visible for physical sectors such as energy or transport. A typical range of possibilities includes *(Fig 3.3)*:

- ***business as usual scenario (BAU):*** continuation of current social and economic trends;
- ***technology development scenario ('pale green'):*** accelerated innovation and economic growth;
- ***sustainable development scenario (SD):*** a win-win combination of gradual shifts in environmental, social and economic spheres;
- ***deep ecology scenario ('deep green'):*** rapid shift towards bio-centric values and lifestyles.

26 Tindale & Holtman 1996
27 Employment Studies Institute 1994
28 Ekins 1996
29 IPCC 1996

Fig 3.3   ***ALTERNATIVE SCENARIOS***

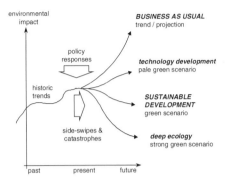

General pattern for alternative scenarios in environmental impact and resource use.

Out of these possibilities the SD or 'mid-green' scenario is explored in depth, and then compared to the others in a scenario review at the start of each chapter in Parts II and III. It is then compared in numbers to the baseline or BAU scenario, using the ISCAM core accounts and 'trend-target' indices. Many elements of the SD scenario at the city-region level, such as power generation or international travel, directly assume a similar outlook for the national context – otherwise progress in the city-region would be practically impossible. Each national scenario in turn depends on a European and world scenario, where again the 2020 project assumes a balance of optimism and realism.[30]

## Business as usual scenario

The BAU scenario for GM draws from government and industry trends and projections, and its general direction is outlined above. Sectors such as transport and energy show rapid increases in consumption, and slower increases in exported pollution and waste. Local pollution and dereliction are contained and replaced by more invisible and invidious effects such as carcinogens and genotoxics. The urban environment continues to polarize between private wealth and public squalor. In the local economy, the trend towards 'jobless growth' continues, while

ICT increases the stratification and polarization between rich and poor. For many communities, stress and alienation increase, and the conditions of the excluded 'underclass' spread over large parts of the city.

As well as projecting current trends, the BAU scenario envisions many things as staying still – possibly management, aspirations, culture and kinship – and this kind of continuity and stability is a significant factor.

## Technological scenario

The 'technology development' scenario envisions more rapid innovation and take-up, within current market conditions and social priorities. Transport, for instance, might be shifted to clean engines and smart systems – improving air quality, but leaving the problems of congestion, unequal access, and the global impacts of the car and oil industries. Business could revolve around a vastly extended ICT system both local and global, so that every input of production or output of consumption is distributed and networked in real time. For every environmental problem there are prospects for technological solutions – but experience shows that such solutions bring their own risks. This is shown by the rise and fall of the genetic food industry, or the nuclear industry which believed that energy would be 'too cheap to meter'.[31] In recent decades, rising efficiency in buildings, transport and industry has been outweighed by further growth in demand, showing that technology on its own is generally not a complete solution to environmental problems, or for that matter most others.[32]

## Deep ecology scenario

Many see the solution to current problems in a rapid shift in social lifestyles, cultural values and institutional norms – not always realizing that such rapid shifts bring their own kind of risk. While the choice of lifestyle can double or halve environmental impacts, these are often due to deep-seated cultural and psychological patterns.[33] But the potential for change should not be under-estimated – roads protestors have done

30 Krause et al 1995

31 Patterson 1986
32 Camagni Capello & Nijkamp 1998
33 Noorman & Uiterkamp 1998

perhaps as much as anything to shift public thinking, and their arrival at the Manchester airport runway development was a national event, covered by the media with a mixture of disgust and admiration.[34]

A deep green city-region would see people who were happy in their neighbourhood, working organic allotments, recycling and sharing resources, and working together for the renewal of a caring society. 'Deep ecology' is about a rediscovery of non-material quality of life and spiritual values – a powerful if indirect influence on the majority as well as the converts. While the environmental lobby is founded on the values of deep ecology, many of its strands are implicated with territorial and class boundaries – where the rhetoric to consume less often comes from those who have more than others. Nevertheless a deep ecology scenario is an essential reference point for comparison with other more probable outcomes.

## Sustainable city-region

The SD scenario attempts to bridge the gap between deep green ideals, technological potential, the negative barriers of inertia and materialism, and the positive assets of stability and continuity. It also incorporates moderate rates of change in politics, institutions, economics and industry. This very fine line is explored in detail in the rest of this book. It is also based on some fundamental themes which emerge from the integrated systems approach.

One is that of 'enlightened self-interest' – lateral thinking and networking to channel the dynamic of individualist and materialist desire towards collective benefit *(Chapter 11)*. Another is the theme of coordination for added value – where there is more to be gained by integration, whether in transport, housing or public services. A third theme is the evolutionary perspective – with continuous flux and change in all aspects of the city-region, the potential is not so much to create change as to steer the changes in motion.

# THE SHAPE OF THE CITY-REGION

Each of these possible scenarios, at local, national and global level, has implications for the overall shape and nature of the city-region – the question of where the people live, work and play. This is central to the built environment agenda of Chapter 5, but also to each other sector – urbanization being the physical manifestation of trade, employment, regeneration, communications and others. For GM, as for most post-industrial city-regions, there are several parallel trends, as shown by  migration data *(Fig 3.4)*:[35]

- Thinning out: the reducing size of the average household means that the population of most existing areas is gradually dispersing, as demand rises for space, privacy, amenity and identity.

- Urbanization:  the traditional spread of urban areas at their peripheries.
- Counter-urbanization: the wider diffusion of urban populations across rural areas.
- Re-urbanization: the return of populations with choice to city centres, inner cities and regeneration areas.
- Centralization: inter-urban and regional migration towards the south-east, shire counties and coastal areas.
- Uneven development: the spatial polarization of growth and decline, opportunity and deprivation, security and risk.

These trends combined then show up in the controversial government projections for land and housing, and the thorny business of finding

34 Wall 1999
35 Champion 1996

Fig 3.4

### URBANIZATION

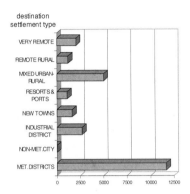

destination
settlement type

Annual net migration from UK 'principal metropolitan cities'

Migration from 'principal metropolitan cities' in the UK: from 1991 Census.
Source: data from Champion et al 1997

sites for development is then based on estimates and assumptions which are slender and volatile. But what happens on the ground is due to many factors beyond calculation – educational reforms, for instance, may have crucial effects on urban quality of life with large impacts on migration patterns.[36] Consumer studies show an overwhelming desire for 'sustainable communities', implying high levels of security, amenity and accessibility, and locations with a good combination then generate a market price with its threshold of exclusion.[37] The trends of economic and social fragmentation are likely to accelerate the polarization of urban and rural areas, as the wealthy and more mobile secure their private versions of the 'sustainable community'.[38]

But even this is based on a traditional view of what cities are about, which is now challenged by the 'technology development' scenario. Following current trends suggests that, within a generation, housing and education may be distributed and networked just as retail and employment are becoming now – that the desired norm will be to access a range of living-working positions at different distances around the world. Even now, GM has a strong global identity, as shown by the worldwide membership of Man-

chester United, which is itself a thoroughly multinational team. Such alternative virtual city-region identities – a 'space of flows and potentials', rather than a 'place of home and work' – are likely to multiply, as economic and social activity is globally networked.

Meanwhile the 'deep ecology' scenario offers a now familiar menu – that people should live and work locally, consume less space and share resources with the neighbours. The effect on the city-region would be to consolidate its existing shape and structure, with major environmental improvements and cohesion of communities. In the context of a networked society this may be even more idealistic than it is now, but also increasingly relevant – for many problems of social polarization and resource depletion there appear to be few alternatives. This is the model of the 'compact city' of the EU and the Urban Villages forum;[39] the distributed new garden city;[40] and the Urban Task Force with its programme for an urban renaissance.[41] While such a scenario is supported at the highest levels, it seems to defy many current trends – business specialization, consumer choice and rising affluence among many others.

## Spatial development scenario

Each of these scenarios playing out in parallel point towards the key question – what would the SD scenario imply for the shape and size of the city-region? This of course has to be seen with historical perspective on the changing functions of cities and regions, caught in the uncertain shift from industrial to post-industrial city-region *(Fig 3.5)*.

Urban form is a key factor in the environmental and social sustainability of a city-region, and yet linkages between urban form and environmental impact are complex and uncertain.[42] For the wider picture we have to look beyond the trends of urbanization, and weigh up the complex and multiple needs, demands, supplies and external impacts of alternative paths. For instance, both urbanization and counter-urbanization are often seen as evils to be contained, for

36 Ravetz 1998
37 Rapoport 1986: MacNaghten & Urry 1997
38 Newby 1996

39 CEC 1990
40 Hall & Ward 1998
41 Urban Task Force 1999
42 Breheny 1991

which the 'compact city' approach promotes an alternative model.[43] This may have benefits in social terms, if people want to live in dense vibrant neighbourhoods. In environmental terms, there are few clear relationships between critical 'life-support' limits and the mix of urban and rural land-use – the issue being more 'how people live' as much as 'where they live'.[44] Given the unusual size and density of GM, which in many respects was assembled too rapidly for an industrial order which is now obsolete, there would be a case for allowing its population to disperse at will. But in this event the effects on both surrounding communities and the remaining population would be drastic, as the deprived and dependent could be squeezed out of the countryside to cluster in a declining city.

Such counter-urbanization would be at the regional or national scale, and so a full assessment would be beyond the remit of this project. Within our boundaries, the overall balance of direct and indirect costs and benefits seems to favour an equal inward and outward migration, or overall population stability. If, and only if, such stability is the result of choice for urban quality of life, rather than coercion and exclusion from the alternatives, then other benefits might follow:

- maintains cohesion and viability of local communities and economies within the city;
- promotes efficient urban form and reduces demands for land, transport, energy and other resources;
- reduces environmental pressures and impacts on surrounding areas.

To promote such shifts as desirable choices rather than unwanted barriers, for both individuals and organizations, depends on working with the underlying dynamics, both physical, social and economic:

- redirecting aspirations towards quality of location rather than quantity of space;
- restructuring of urban form for greater efficiency, accessibility and amenity value;

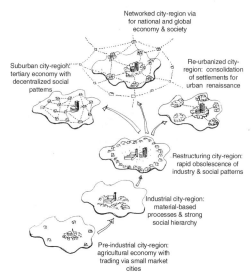

Fig 3.5   **DYNAMICS OF URBANIZATION**

Networked city-region via for national and global economy & society

Suburban city-region: tertiary economy with decentralized social patterns

Re-urbanized city-region: consolidation of settlements for urban renaissance

Restructuring city-region: rapid obsolescence of industry & social patterns

Industrial city-region: material-based processes & strong social hierarchy

Pre-industrial city-region: agricultural economy with trading via small market cities

General trajectories of urban & regional development: showing 3 alternative versions of post-industrial city-region.

- management of accessibility and mobility, by internalizing the external costs of transport.

Such a redirection needs active intervention from policy, going far beyond the conventional containment of the green belt, to an active coordination of all the features that make up urban viability and quality of life.

## Area development scenario

Such an overall stabilization scenario then involves the dynamics of change in each component of the city-region, as part of a balanced portfolio. Re-urbanization can enable new urbanist lifestyles via regeneration of the inner urban fabric and economy. Counter-urbanization can enable new rural lifestyles via eco-restoration and diversification of the landscape. In between, sustainable 'sub-urbanization' is a key to improving quality of life for a large majority.[45] Each of these area development strategies should be based on the combined dynamics or underlying forces in each settlement type (Fig 3.6):

43 CEC 1990
44 Breheny & Hall 1997: Ravetz 1998                45 Gwilliam et al 1999

Fig 3.6          **SPATIAL DYNAMICS**

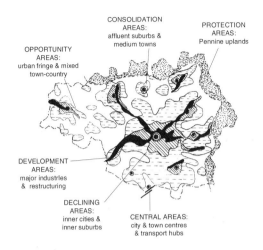

General development dynamics for each of the main settlement types:
Sources: derived from UDP's of Salford & Oldham MBC: based on
Breheny & Rookwood 1993

- Opportunity areas: areas of rapid change
  and restructuring with a legacy of negative
  assets such as contamination and dereliction; investment capitalizes on potential assets of location and large scale sites.
- Regeneration areas: a legacy of social, economic and environmental problems; invest-

ment needs to be generated indigenously
as far as possible, through social and economic development and environmental improvement.

- Consolidation areas: general stability of infrastructure and socio-economic resources,
  as in the affluent suburbs. More indirect
  environmental impacts have to be tackled
  through gradual and strategic development
  of urban form and fabric.
- Protection areas: positive environmental
  assets under pressure, where change and
  development are directly constrained by
  critical capital and critical capacities.

In each of these the environmental assets or
'stocks' vary from negative to positive quality,
the pressures or 'flows' vary from internal to external, and the impacts from direct to indirect.
Somewhere in the middle are large areas of suburban housing, where apparent stability conceals
large indirect environmental impacts. Some of the
GM Unitary Development Plans (UDPs) are also
based on such area types.[46]

Overall, the spatial dimension of the SD scenario contains a balanced diversity between each
of its components. The challenge for policies is
to coordinate this within a holistic city-region
framework.[47]

# MANAGING CHANGE

Steering from the 'business as usual' towards
the 'sustainable development' scenario is no
mean feat – the fundamental dynamics of human
desire, market forces, political governance, as well
as a massive urban form and fabric, all have to be
redirected from their current trajectories. To do
this needs the traditional qualities of vision, leadership, commitment, expertise and patience, for
which there is little substitute. It also needs the
practicalities of resources or 'capacity' for action, and 'strategy' or intelligence to guide such
action, as below.

## Powers & resources

Many organizations compete for the mandate to
represent the interests of the public or consumers. But while the natural responsibility and stewardship for the city starts and ends with local
authorities, they are hemmed in by legal and financial constraints. Businesses in turn are
hemmed in by their bottom line and shareholder
values. In turn, national government is hemmed
in by business, the media, the electorate and
world markets. At each level of the tree there are
certain rights, responsibilities, restrictions, and

46 See especially the UDP's of Oldham, Salford & Trafford
47 Breheny & Rookwood 1993

Fig 3.6          **LOCAL AUTONOMY**

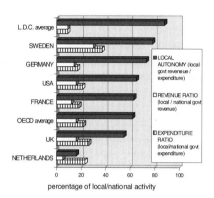

International comparison of local/national autonomy, revenue
& expenditure ratios.
Source: based on Satterthwaite 1996

Fig 3.7          **BUSINESS PLANNING**

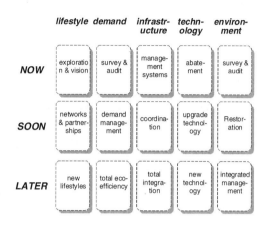

General strategic programme or business plan for sustainable development.

limited room for manoeuvre. The question for the city-region here is how much room – or what are the resources for local action?

Such resources can be seen as the 'capacity' for positive change in each of the dimensions above – cultural, social, economic, political, technological, infrastructure and so on.

Cultural resources are perhaps the starting point – with commitment and a vision factor, many things become possible. In urban development, for instance, local authorities can move ahead of the game, using planning agreements to fulfil environmental goals.[48] This might be seen as risking loss of trade – alternatively as the means towards environmental leadership,

increased quality of life and the investment which flows from it. A local authority can act as a catalyst in bringing together businesses, the civic community and the public – raising awareness, creating visions, building consensus and action networks to achieve results that no individual party can *(Box 3.2)*.

Local economic resources and autonomy can be seen in the balance between local and national governments. An international comparison shows the local/national 'expenditure ratio', the local/national 'revenue ratio', and the degree of 'autonomy', or the balance of local revenue and expenditure [49] *(Fig 3.7)*. Local government autonomy in the UK is on the low end of the scale, with revenues covering only 55% of expenditure, and strict controls on investment or business activity.[50] The result is that forward investment in environmental infrastructure is very difficult – the public sector cannot raise the capital, and the private sector cannot wait for the return. This suggest that new forms of partnerships and consortiums could bridge this gap as part of a market transformation *(Chapter 13)*.

Political or institutional resources concern structures and decision-making processes, both

Box 3.2

**LOCAL VISION**

The Hamilton-Wentworth Sustainable Community Vision 2020 initiative is an ongoing collaborative process in which the regional government works with thousands of citizens, to turn a jointly developed community vision into reality. Since 1993 a strategy has been formed with recommendations for 400 specific actions. The result so far is major improvements to the local environment, with profound changes in the structure of local government.

Source UNCHS 1996

48 Section 106 of the UK Town & Country Planning Act 1990 enables negotiated agreements between developer and local planning authority

49 Satterthwaite 1996
50 This is a very simple picture of the complex system of local government assessments and allowances

formal and informal, in the public, private and third sectors *(Chapter 14)*. There is copious advice on institutional 'capacity-building' from the UK local authority associations;[51] UN Centre for Human Settlements;[52] and the European Expert Group on Sustainable Cities *(Box 3.3)*.[53] In practice, institutional capacity seems very low in many organizations, submerged with inertia and infighting, empire-building, budget tightening, and the pitfalls of 'management by objectives'. This highlights the role of catalysts such as Local Agenda 21 or other visioning exercises, in kick-starting new networks and cultures in corporate bodies.

## Strategic planning

For each sector of the city-region, a general strategic business planning approach is a tool which links short term actions with longer term goals. Above is a 'generic' or typical business plan which can be applied to almost any sector or programme *(Fig 3.8)*. Based on the 'integrated assessment' framework from Chapter 1, this shows actions on the 'demand' and the 'supply' side, which may take place now, soon and later.

In general, the actions needed now or in the next few years include those which cost little, need no changes in current legislation and lifestyle patterns, and for which appropriate and viable technologies exist. This would include information gathering, performance monitoring, staff training and organization capacity-building, with practical applications such as:

- land-use: temporary uses for vacant and derelict land;
- buildings: energy investment partnerships;
- transport: traffic calming, integrated public travel information;
- ecology: community-based urban tree planting and greening;
- waste: household goods exchange centre.

Actions which can be carried out 'soon', perhaps in the next 5 or 10 years, are those with low cost or viable investment returns, and needing only minor changes to legislation and market structure. Practical applications in GM would include:

- energy: first phase of an energy agency consortium for comprehensive city-wide upgrading;
- transport: new vehicle technologies in public fleets, combined with integrated planning;
- waste: comprehensive household sorting and recycling at source.

Looking to 2020 and beyond, actions for 'later' include those which depend on new legislation, market structures, technology development or large scale investment. For GM these would include all the key recommendations set out in Parts II and III.

## Horizontal actions

The actions for 'soon' and 'later' may depend on future conditions which cannot be predicted – but they also depend on a continuous process of assembling resources, information, expertise, partnerships and commitment. And rather than starting from a clean slate, each of the actions

---

Box 3.3

### EUROPEAN SUSTAINABLE CITY PRINCIPLES

- **ECO-SYSTEMS:** an ecological and holistic approach to the management of urban areas and the implementation of sustainable solutions
- **INTEGRATION:** improved integration of the economic, social and environmental dimensions of sustainability across policy sectors and government levels
- **CAPACITY:** appropriate institutional and organizational capacity for managing urban areas for sustainability
- **COHERENCE:** policy and action coherence so the development of sustainability at the local level is not undermined by governments & EU
- **EXCHANGE:** measures to avoid wasteful duplication of work and to enhance the productive exchange of experience
- **EFFECTIVENESS:** both the enhanced application of existing policies, programmes and mechanisms, and, where necessary, the development of new ones.

Source EU Expert Group 1996

---

51 LGMB 1992
52 UNCHS 1996
53 EU Expert Group 1996

has to build on what is already in progress, often in a state of rapid change. To encourage and enable such positive change, there are several kinds of 'horizontal' actions which local government can lead in partnership with others:

- *City-wide SOE*: (state of the environment) reporting and auditing, covering every aspect of the urban environment and metabolism, together with its trends and projections.[54] Social audits work on similar principles, using more in-depth investigation of public perceptions and problems.

- *Standardized EMAS*: (environmental management & audit systems) for all public policies & programmes.[55] In itself EMAS does not guarantee improvement, but it sharpens the tools for defining and monitoring progress towards such improvement.

- *Supply chain policies*: comprehensive environmental and ethical policies for all public purchasing, distribution and contracting *(Chapter 10)*.[56]

- *Vision and consensus building*: following the 'first steps' with the 'next steps' for the LA21 movement, towards a wider & deeper programme involving stakeholders at every level of society *(Chapter 14)*.[57]

## Future prospects

In practice there is confusion on the multi-layered concept of sustainable development, and this is not helping progress. The environmental agenda is often seen as an add-on to existing practices, and the general climate is against long term investment. The 'precautionary principle' can work both ways – uncertain risks in the future are balanced against the risks of disrupting existing practices and vested interests in the present. The social agenda hinges on the themes of equity and participation – fine in theory, but in practice society contains complex structures which by nature are inequitable and exclusive. The economic agenda is beginning to take on environmental management, but this is often a side-show in the global race for competitiveness.

Each of these dynamics can be countered with the themes outlined here, and explored in more detail in the following chapters – capacity, strategic planning, horizontal actions. Central to the argument of this project is that a city-region is an effective unit of organization which can enhance each of these qualities.

Around the UK, the areas which have made most progress on sustainability policy – Sutton, Bath, Cheshire, Leicester and so on – are generally those with greener environments and higher living standards *(Box 3.4)*. This might suggest that GM has to 'get rich' before it can 'go green' – the 'first raise our growth' scenario as above. On the other hand, where the vision factor can be raised along with cultural, economic and political resources, then it is possible to do both.

---

**Box 3.4**  ***ENVIRONMENT CITIES***

In 1990 four cities in the UK were designated as models for urban environmental management and sustainability. Leicester was selected as the first on the grounds of its track record and commitment. A partnership structure was set up to carry out survey, research and monitoring of indicators, with a series of key projects such as recycling, pollution awareness, cycle routes, and green corridors. The agency ENVIRON now employs over 30 people based at a demonstration eco-house

Source: BT Environment Cities 1994

---

54 Barton & Bruder 1996
55 LGMB 1995
56 Simpson 1994

57 Carley & Christie 1993

# CITY-REGION 2020

*'Cities and thrones and powers stand in time's eye*
*almost as long as flowers, which do daily die,*
*but as new buds put forth to glad new men,*
*out of the spent and unconsidered earth, new cities rise again'*
Rudyard Kipling 1906

What might a sustainable city-region look like in 25 years? Clearly, the sprawling mass of GM is not the easiest or prettiest place to start.

From the trends, dynamics and scenarios in previous chapters, we can put together outlines, sketches and visions. We can then apply them to each kind of territory, from city centres to remote rural areas. On the ground such areas overlap in a complex pattern – any one location might be an inner city, regeneration and peripheral area at the same time. So these sketches are a menu broadly based on the problems and opportunities of GM, to be fitted to each location according to the agenda in hand.

The key to the whole picture is the synergy factor – the potential for people to live and work together, improve the physical surroundings, gain more happiness with less damage, and simply look after each other. It is also the synergy between industries and sectors – a sustainable transport strategy, for instance, is little use without parallel strategies for the economy, housing, regeneration and so on. Each part links to the others, and the whole is greater than the sum of the parts.

This is why we need to look at each physical component of the city-region, as below. Then we need to look at each environmental key sector – transport, energy and so on, as in Part II. Finally we need to look at the social and economic processes which put them together, as in Part III.

In reality there are countless plans and policies for improving every aspect of the city-region. Many of these have taken on board the language and principles of the sustainability agenda. The challenge is to sort out the rhetoric from the reality, and the one-off bright ideas from those which are part of a larger concept. So for each area type we aim to highlight the added value and key features of a sustainability agenda which is fully integrated into long term strategy and short term action. Such features include the perennial menu:

- integrated long term environmental management;
- coordinated problem-solving public services and social strategy;
- partnership long term investment for market transformation;
- lateral opportunities in cultural diversity and the social economy.

Is this a utopian vision? There is a long tradition of idealistic thinking on cities and societies, and of course reality always falls short. But utopian vision does not have to be achieved to have a place and a purpose. The 2020 project aims to point towards the ideal without losing touch with reality.

We cannot assume, for instance, that planners will take into account all possible needs and demands, both short and long term, for every decision. We cannot assume, at least in our lifetime, that people will become much more altruistic and nature-loving, that businesses will sacrifice profit for principles, or that those with power and money will hand them over to those without. Certainly we cannot assume that people will end their love affairs with their cars, or live in less space rather than more, without very strong incentives to do so.

What we can show is the potential for combining enlightened self-interest with social benefit – the added value and synergy factor, as above. In many ways this is part of the current quest for the 'third way', the 'stakeholder society', and similar guiding themes looking for practical applications.[1] With a modernizing government of the progressive centre, the UK has perhaps the best chance in a generation of realizing some of these ideals. But speaking realistically, solving today's problems is more likely to lead towards tomorrow's problems than a mythical utopia. It is fascinating to speculate what kind of problems would be found in a 'sustainable city-region' of the future.

The 'vision statements' to follow, in large text and concept sketches, are very similar to the aspirations of Local Agenda 21, City Pride and many other vision-building initiatives. Manchester, like most other cities, is in many ways a city of dreams – the rebuilding of its bomb damage, like the rebuilding of Hulme, and the development of the 'world's best' airport, has become a focus for collective visions of the city. In *City-Region 2020* we look at an area about a thousand times larger, over a generation timescale, but the aim is similar – to match vision to reality.

# CITY CENTRES

City centres are the nodes and hubs of the global system, with a role as much to do with signals and symbols as physical presence. Manchester city centre is the heart of GM and its gateway to the world. It is physically small compared to its surroundings, with 0.3% of the land area and 5% of the travel – but as the hub of the conurbation it houses 10% of all employment and 30% of all office space. After decades of decline and dereliction, the rebuilding of the 1996 bomb damage provided the impetus,with lashings of loose money from the Millennium and Lottery funds, and a general fashion for urban lifestyles. With a massive upturn in retail, leisure and cultural development, Manchester is now booming, with one of the largest building sites, indoor arenas, youth scenes and creative quarters in the UK.

Even so, much of the centre is still degraded with traffic congestion and vacant buildings, and the whole area is something of an island marooned in the midst of major roads, industrial parks, decline and dereliction. The centres of surrounding towns show a similar mix. The challenge is to balance the physical improvements urgently needed, with the needs of a competitive global marketplace, and with local needs for social equity and accessibility – at present many parts of the centre are contested territories between different classes and sub-cultures.[2]

One crucial issue for the physical centre is transport. In spite of much evidence for the benefits of traffic calming, the business community has still to be convinced.[3] But the balance of roads, parking and public transport is one of the keys to quality and competitiveness, and total

1 Giddens 1998

2 Taylor, Evans & Fraser 1996
3 PIEDA 1995

Fig 4.1

## CITY & TOWN CENTRES

Outline of integrated city centre and town centre strategies

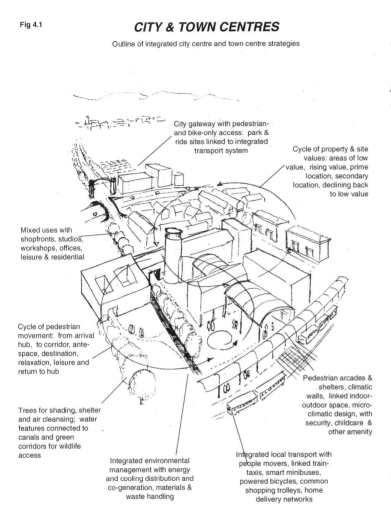

City gateway with pedestrian- and bike-only access: park & ride sites linked to integrated transport system

Cycle of property & site values: areas of low value, rising value, prime location, secondary location, declining back to low value

Mixed uses with shopfronts, studios, workshops, offices, leisure & residential

Cycle of pedestrian movement: from arrival hub, to corridor, ante-space, destination, relaxation, leisure and return to hub

Trees for shading, shelter and air cleansing; water features connected to canals and green corridors for wildlife access

Integrated environmental management with energy and cooling distribution and co-generation, materials & waste handling

Integrated local transport with people movers, linked train-taxis, smart minibuses, powered bicycles, common shopping trolleys, home delivery networks

Pedestrian arcades & shelters, climatic walls, linked indoor-outdoor space, micro-climatic design, with security, childcare & other amenity

*The sustainable city centre of 2020 is vibrant and dynamic, yet friendly and human scale. Streets and public spaces are sheltered and flourishing with green-ery and wildlife, and there are facilities and entertainments for diverse lifestyles. Get-ting around is easy and safe, with fully inte-grated public transport, and tree-lined avenues with trams, 'people movers' and electric city-bugs. Buildings new and old are de-signed with flexibility and efficiency, forming sheltered courtyards, squares and gardens. Each quarter houses a different mixture of uses, so that shopping, lei-sure, commerce and housing each gain in vitality and added value. As a global gateway, the city centre provides for the world's best while welcoming all classes and cultures.*

blanket pedestrianization could easily backfire. This suggests phasing local actions in parallel with national policies, so that over a period the centre can begin to manage car traffic alongside other modes. The result will be a fully accessible environment, with several layers or degrees of pedestrianized space linked to green corridors, complemented by 'people movers' and 'travelators', trams and responsive minibuses, linked train-taxis, home delivery services, and pos-sibly electric city-bugs *(Chapter 6)*.

The transport question is in many ways a barometer of wider issues. A successful centre, whether for city or town, depends on the quality of experience of its users and visitors – so the routes which people may take need to be seen as part of a whole cycle, as in the diagram above. Such transient cycles are also linked to those of much longer timescales, such as the property cycle. This sees a physical and financial move-ment of values and locations from low to rising, prime, secondary, to declining – each with a unique role in the life of the city.[4] The application of such themes would see streets and squares with mixed uses in a human-scale environment, using historic assets in a diverse family of urban quarters. Many former warehouses and some modern offices will be turned to housing, while others will suit flexible workspace for cultural industries. To compete with out-of-town shopping, the centre needs an integrated retail strategy to an equal or better standard – including coordinated information, security, conveniences and home deliveries.[4]

The centre also needs clearly defined gateways to mark symbolic boundaries, encourage access for pedestrians and cyclists, and link with development corridors along main public transport routes. Environmental best practice is important both in itself and for the signals it sends elsewhere – all buildings should be upgraded or built to the highest energy efficiency, and supplied from a central CHP network which could recycle waste heat. Large commercial buildings and complexes should provide public atriums, with a diversity of micro-climates and sheltered spaces. These should also link with wildlife habi-

tats and the green corridor network along canals, rivers and other water features.

Many of these themes are already in the UDPs and initiatives such as City Pride, the 'Millennium' development and others – so what is the 'sustainability' added value?

- environmental best practice and integrated systems within overall city-region strategy;
- coordination of investment in property, construction, transport, public services and others;
- social strategy to ensure facilities and accessibility for all classes and cultures.

The surrounding district and town centres face similar problems and opportunities on a smaller scale, although many are struggling hard against out-of-town competition. Each centre likewise needs its own integrated town centre management within an overall city-region strategy. Again the competition from the out-of-town business and retail sites is in many ways an opportunity to re-define and re-engineer the nature and function of town centres.

# DEVELOPMENT AREAS

A wide band across the middle of GM contains areas of 'development opportunity' – for which an alternative title might be 'obsolescence and dereliction'. The scale of change and poisonous legacy from industrial restructuring is huge, in areas such as the Ship Canal corridor and East Manchester. Obvious problems include negative image, contamination and dereliction, high development costs, obsolete infrastructure, declining local services, and unskilled labour. The regeneration industry is huge and active in GM, with many flagship projects to be seen. On pure acreage of large-scale derelict land, it may just now be winning, provided that there is not another industrial shake-out around the corner. But there is also an insidious downward spiral that seems to affect a broad swathe around the re-

gional centre, where current levels of effort may not be enough to reverse the fatal combination of physical dereliction, economic obsolescence and social exclusion.

Of the many meanings of 'sustainable regeneration' explored in Chapter 12, one concerns the role of development areas in re-engineering the whole city-region for greater sustainability. The need for large scale change is an opportunity for innovative solutions in more sustainable urban form. This needs a strategic approach which can capitalize on locational potential in order to take on the negative costs of land and infrastructure. It also needs a coordinated approach between businesses, utilities, financiers and others, which adjusts current market structures for added value and longer term benefit.

---

[4] URBED & Hillier Parker 1995

Fig 4.2

## DEVELOPMENT OPPORTUNITY AREAS

Outline of integrated industrial restructuring and regeneration area strategy

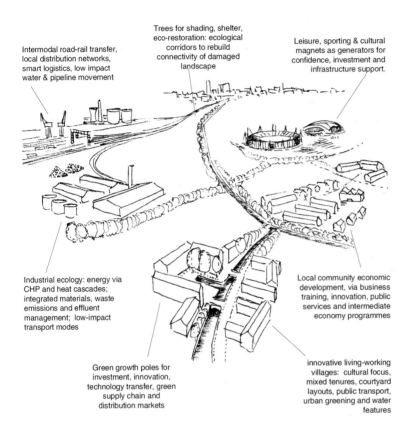

Intermodal road-rail transfer, local distribution networks, smart logistics, low impact water & pipeline movement

Trees for shading, shelter, eco-restoration: ecological corridors to rebuild connectivity of damaged landscape

Leisure, sporting & cultural magnets as generators for confidence, investment and infrastructure support.

Industrial ecology: energy via CHP and heat cascades; integrated materials, waste emissions and effluent management; low-impact transport modes

Local community economic development, via business training, innovation, public services and intermediate economy programmes

Green growth poles for investment, innovation, technology transfer, green supply chain and distribution markets

innovative living-working villages: cultural focus, mixed tenures, courtyard layouts, public transport, urban greening and water features

*Regeneration areas are dynamic zones of opportunity which attract the best and most creative development, as vital parts of the future city-region. For business there are multi-mode freight interchanges, and industrial ecology networks for integration of energy and waste flows. For local communities there is work, training and leisure in a diverse range of environmentally-friendly enterprises. New urban communities are building residential-commercial villages around dynamic watersides and townscapes, with ecological transport and leisure facilities.*

The application of this on a pilot area is explored in the 'green zone' concept *(Chapter 12)*.

Current programmes appear to be doing all they can to succeed against the odds, and promote similar goals, so what is the added value of the 'sustainability' agenda? Again the agenda here focuses on integrated long term strategy:

- integrated environmental management and best practice within city-region framework;
- innovative industrial, commercial and residential clusters or villages;
- longer term approach within a 25 year framework;

- coordination of economic development with local labour markets and public services.

Development opportunity areas can then become the generators for the restructuring of the city-region around. As in Emscher Park in the Ruhr, success may come through working with the remains of the industrial landscape rather than sweeping them away completely. There are no certain solutions to the re-invention of the nature and function of the city in these areas. There is rather a wide open opportunity for exploring new and creative urban environments for working and living.

# INNER CITY AREAS

Many inner city areas in GM are a fragmented patchwork of older housing and newer public estates, mixed with industry and vacant or derelict land, and cut through by major roads. A large swathe around north and east Manchester, with surrounding parts of Salford, Oldham, Trafford and Tameside, is on the brink of a spiral of decline, with compounded physical, economic and social problems.

Meanwhile the inner cities are also home to a huge diversity of lifestyles and communities,

and these are the starting point for any strategy. Public services should engage with the voluntary or 'third sector', to unlock the hidden resources of people with high levels of unemployment and dependency. Community regeneration and local enterprise can generate jobs and improve the environment and housing stock, in locally-based partnership schemes.[5]

Much of the housing stock is aged, and in some areas large-scale renewal may be needed in the next few decades. This is an opportunity

*Inner cities are now vibrant and diverse neighbourhoods, providing housing and jobs for existing and new residents. Urban village centres with many services are in easy walking distance of most homes, along green and traffic-free streets, where children can play safely while walking to school. All housing is built or upgraded to 'best practice' in energy efficiency, health and security. Travel by any mode is easy and pleasant from the local neighbourhood hub.*

*Each local centre contains a wide range of jobs and businesses; and a neighbourhood office coordinates many self-help enterprises, social trading activity and integrated public services.*

Fig 4.3

## INNER CITY AREAS

Outline of integrated inner city and transition area strategy

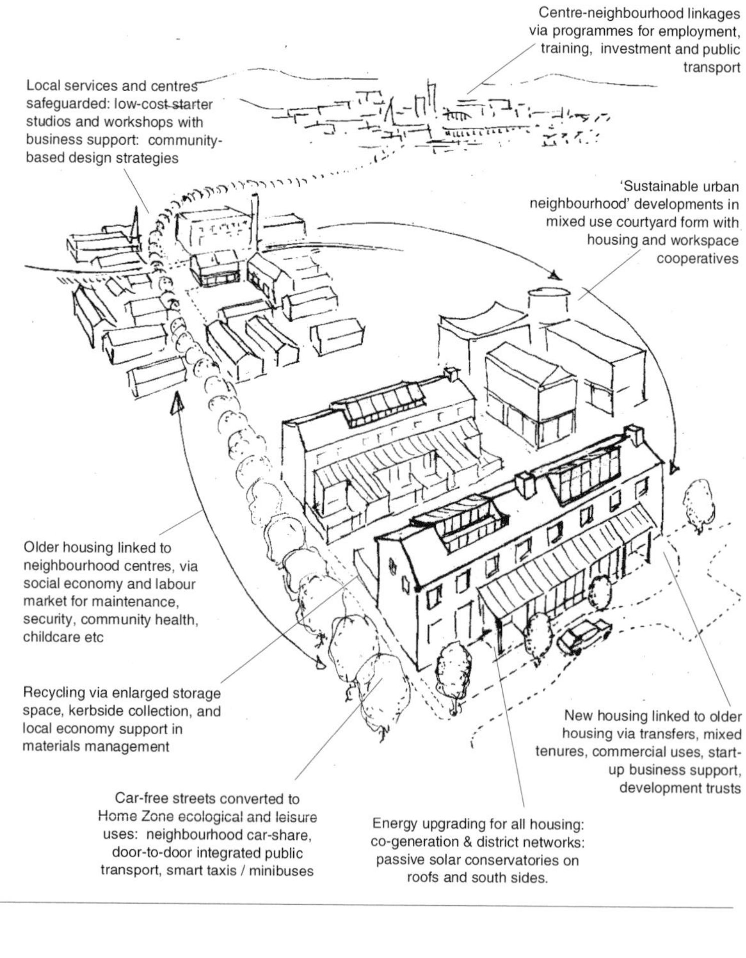

Centre-neighbourhood linkages via programmes for employment, training, investment and public transport

Local services and centres safeguarded: low-cost starter studios and workshops with business support: community-based design strategies

'Sustainable urban neighbourhood' developments in mixed use courtyard form with housing and workspace cooperatives

Older housing linked to neighbourhood centres, via social economy and labour market for maintenance, security, community health, childcare etc

Recycling via enlarged storage space, kerbside collection, and local economy support in materials management

New housing linked to older housing via transfers, mixed tenures, commercial uses, start-up business support, development trusts

Car-free streets converted to Home Zone ecological and leisure uses: neighbourhood car-share, door-to-door integrated public transport, smart taxis / minibuses

Energy upgrading for all housing: co-generation & district networks: passive solar conservatories on roofs and south sides.

for restructuring, clustering and consolidation of neighbourhood units, towards a more sustainable pattern of houses, services, transport and green space *(chapter 5)*. Rebuilding fragmented neighbourhoods is a long term process, but there are many immediate actions – traffic calming, green space and housing improvements each generate jobs with visible results.

Many of these goals are included in current regeneration policies and programmes; so what is the added value of the 'sustainability' agenda?

- long term strategy for neighbourhood structure and consolidation;
- integrated environmental management and best practice within city-region strategy;
- investment partnershipswhich link local authorities and public agencies, businesses and local communities;
- intermediate labour market to link employment training and businesses support with public services.

# SUBURBAN AREAS

The suburbs are the largest and apparently most stable component of the city-region. Such respectability can conceal huge diversity of social and economic change. Their problems and impacts are often less visible, the result of affluence in the owner-occupied suburbs, and the result of poverty in the social housing estates. Problems for both include lack of local services and jobs, high car dependency, high energy demand, backlog of housing maintenance, polarization of communities, and general alienation particularly for the youth and elderly.

In some ways the suburbs are a very 'sustainable' urban form, if success is defined as flexibility, adaptability and self-organization – and this quality is often missed by the 'compact city' lobby.[6] But this devolved owner-occupier pattern relies on high levels of affluence and generates other social problems. A strategy for 'suburban sustainability' looks at both the local problems and opportunities, their wider environmental impacts, and the role of the suburbs in the overall framework for the city-region.

Current development policies for suburban areas are fairly few and general – they are not often seen as a 'problem' and hence attract

little attention. The added 'sustainability' dimension includes:

- extension of city-region regeneration to suburban areas for restructuring land-use and building stock;
- long term consolidation of neighbourhood units, by clustering housing and mixed uses with local hubs;
- integrated environmental management and best practice for transport, waste, energy, ecology;
- investment partnerships for upgrading of energy and environment standards in all housing.

The flexibility and loose structure of suburban forms of settlement is often criticized by urban form advocates who see wasted space. From another angle such flexibility is an invaluable resource for the emerging shape of the global economy and a liberalized society – networked, responsive, fast-changing, client- and culture-focused. Any strategies for suburban areas should aim to maximize such a resource, while managing and containing their more negative aspects.

5 Ward 1991
6 Gwilliam et al 1999

*The suburbs can now start to improve their own quality of life and reduce the load they place on the world around them. Local centres become more viable by clustering new housing and employment around public transport hubs, while local jobs and useful activity are generated for the young and old. Public transport networks become more flexible and responsive to deal with dispersed travel over larger areas. Housing is upgraded to best practice in energy and environmental standards, through partnership investment funding. Residential streets are planted and linked to green corridors circling the city, and gardens are havens for wildlife and organic cultivation.*

Fig 4.4

## SUBURBAN & EX-URBAN AREAS

Outline of integrated suburban area strategy

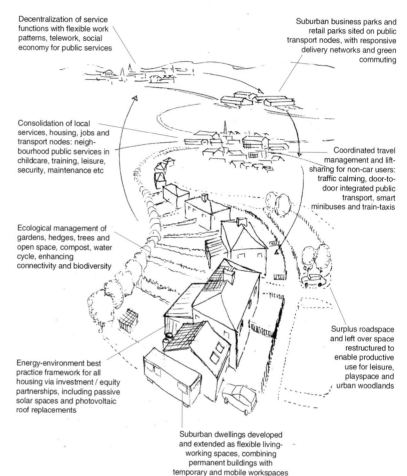

Decentralization of service functions with flexible work patterns, telework, social economy for public services

Suburban business parks and retail parks sited on public transport nodes, with responsive delivery networks and green commuting

Consolidation of local services, housing, jobs and transport nodes: neighbourhood public services in childcare, training, leisure, security, maintenance etc

Coordinated travel management and lift-sharing for non-car users: traffic calming, door-to-door integrated public transport, smart minibuses and train-taxis

Ecological management of gardens, hedges, trees and open space, compost, water cycle, enhancing connectivity and biodiversity

Surplus roadspace and left over space restructured to enable productive use for leisure, playspace and urban woodlands

Energy-environment best practice framework for all housing via investment / equity partnerships, including passive solar spaces and photovoltaic roof replacements

Suburban dwellings developed and extended as flexible living-working spaces, combining permanent buildings with temporary and mobile workspaces

# URBAN FRINGE & COUNTRYSIDE

Surrounding the urban core is a rambling area of urban fringe – a mixed landscape of old towns and villages, commuter settlements, former industrial sites and out-of-town business parks, marginal farms, vacant land, sewage farms, motorways and power lines. Within this are areas of growth and development pressure, and those with decline and dereliction, and many between with an uncertain future. Tackling the problems and opportunities of this patchwork is as complex as in the city – the general aim is not so much to turn the tide of counter-urbanization, but to manage the process in a more sustainable

way. The strategies for rural development, farming, conservation, woodlands and leisure uses, are the diverse pieces of this complex jigsaw *(chapter 7)*.

At present, urban fringe and rural areas are battlegrounds between the 'conservationists' and the 'developers' – in practice both have a role to play. The effective containment of development pressure is a key to the prospects of the conurbation as a whole. At the same time lifestyle and technological shifts mean that the urban fringe is a massive resource for both living and working. In such a fertile situation, new ap-

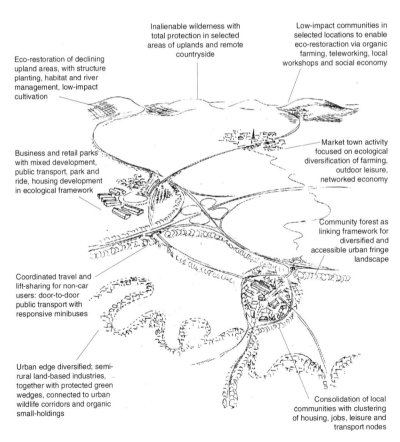

**Fig 4.5**

## *URBAN FRINGE & COUNTRYSIDE*

Outline of integrated urban fringe and countryside strategy

Inalienable wilderness with total protection in selected areas of uplands and remote countryside

Low-impact communities in selected locations to enable eco-restoration via organic farming, teleworking, local workshops and social economy

Eco-restoration of declining upland areas, with structure planting, habitat and river management, low-impact cultivation

Business and retail parks with mixed development, public transport, park and ride, housing development in ecological framework

Market town activity focused on ecological diversification of farming, outdoor leisure, networked economy

Community forest as linking framework for diversified and accessible urban fringe landscape

Coordinated travel and lift-sharing for non-car users: door-to-door public transport with responsive minibuses

Urban edge diversified; semi-rural land-based industries, together with protected green wedges, connected to urban wildlife corridors and organic small-holdings

Consolidation of local communities with clustering of housing, jobs, leisure and transport nodes

*Urban fringe and rural areas are ecological havens for people living closer to the land while being part of the city. A rethink of the green belt promotes landscape diversity, sustainable land management, mixed organic farming and community woodlands. New technologies spread city-based employment towards local communities, with access by demand-responsive public transport. For the surrounding uplands, countryside policies set out 'inalienable' wilderness, alongside areas where eco-restoration can start to regenerate the fertility and diversity of the landscape.*

proaches to low-impact development could allow greater engagement between people and the land. Many countryside and landscape programmes are now aiming in this direction, so what is the 'sustainability' added value?

- extending city-wide regeneration to the urban fringe for buildings, transport, economy and public services;
- integrated environmental management within city-region framework;
- containing road traffic with more integrated, flexible and reponsive public transport networks;
- integrated land management for agriculture, forestry, ecology and leisure;
- new forms of tenure, equity and stake-owning in land and businesses, to enable positive uses and long term investment.

Beyond the fringe on its northern and eastern edges are some fairly remote uplands. Here the native population is being replaced by incoming commuters, the soil and eco-systems are struggling with acid rain, and the landscape structure is falling into disrepair. In such areas the 'unspoilt wilderness' value is high, although the landscape is degraded in many ways, and any change or development is strongly resisted. A holistic approach would set out a series of policy layers; 'inalienable wilderness' would be protected from any development. Other areas will be under 'eco-restoration', with remedial landscape management and regeneration of woodlands and hedgerows; while others are 'homesteading' areas, encouraging local organic cultivation and diversification of rural economies, with both land-based and IT-based industries.

# ECONOMY & SOCIETY

To round off this composite sketch of a vision factor, we flag up some key features be hind the visible surface of the city-region – its economy and employment; and its lifestyle and communities. Again at this stage these are deliberate wish-lists, with all the hard questions still to face, but they represent a composite menu of possibilities to then be worked out in detail.

For a city-region green economy of 2020, there are several overlapping trends and dynamics in progress *(chapter 10)*:

- ecological modernization of business & industry;
- greening of consumption, purchasing and investment;
- social trading and third sector activity for economic resilience and public services;
- market transformation to incorporate ecological and social economy in all sectors.

*The 21st century economy at last begins to work for people, rather than the other way round. Most jobs are high-skill, high-added value, and flexible according to needs and circumstances. Most businesses are low-impact, socially responsible, equitably owned, and competitive in world markets. Information technology is the key to coordinating skills, services, locations, materials and clients, both for global and local enterprises. All financial institutions operate with clear social and environmental objectives, particularly for local investment, and all large organizations purchase and contract through green and ethical supply-chains. While the globalizing economy cannot provide secure full employment for all, there are many other layers to the local economy, from self-help enterprise to social trading networks, and as many people choose part-time flexible lifestyles, neighbourhood activity thrives.*

Each of these combines in a composite scenario which reflects the best of what is possible and desirable.

The economy, of course, is instrumental to society as a whole. To talk about a sustainable society, as far as such a thing can be defined, is the closest approach yet to a fully utopian vision *(Chapter 11)*. In a City-Region 2020 vision for lifestyles, communities, public services and social strategy in general, we can sketch in outline only a few key themes:

- cohesion, self-help, third sector social economy;
- cultural diversity and individual empowerment;
- integration and coordination of all public services;
- an open, flexible civic society which heals its divisions and nurtures its people.

Each of these fits together in a composite vision of how lifestyles and public services could change positively in all aspects. Superimposed on these aspirations would be the trends and dynamics discussed in Chapter 3, of demographic, cultural and social change. This suggests that the now-conventional menu of 'local communities' should not be the only theme on the agenda, and that we should not ignore the opportunities and pressures brought by globalization and liberalization – the internet, the media, businesses and employment, interest groups, cultural and religious networks and so on. The challenge is not to return to some Arcadian myth but to invent viable futures for new problems and opportunities.

*Many 21st century lifestyles change for the better as people find more localized and flexible patterns of work and leisure. Neighbourhood networks work in parallel to global networks, sharing resources and a sense of belonging and support. Both absolute and relative poverty rapidly reduce, as social networks provide continuous family support for prevention, and cultivate self-help for adaptation, with basic needs met at marginal cost by city-region consortiums.*

*Healthy lifestyles are widespread, supported by environmental best practice at work and home, and community-based paramedics help to deliver integrated self-help positive and preventative health. Crime rates and fear of crime fall rapidly with preventative measures, widespread social networks, and a multicultural approach to young people's needs and opportunities. Education becomes more integrated and responsive, schools are pro-active eco-centres providing self-development through practical skills, and all pupils and their families have personal advocates for self-directed project-based learning. Community action and the voluntary sector expand through new social trading networks for social and environmental services. Most decision-making is open and interactive, with digital tools at the neighbourhood level.*

*Local Agenda 21 continues at the leading edge – the creation of new visions and social networks, bringing together public, private and community sectors.*

# PART II

# Key sectors

Here we look at each of the key sectors and industries which link human activity with the environment. In many ways the city-region is like a human body – in which case, the 'Built Environment' represents its flesh and bones, and 'Transport' is its circulation and nervous system. 'Ecology' is about its genetic inheritance, 'Pollution' focuses on its metabolism of inputs and outputs, and 'Energy' represents its fundamental physics. Finally 'Economy and work' looks at the many layers of production, trade and consumption, in the city-region and the world around it.

# THE BUILT ENVIRONMENT

*'When we build, let us think that we build for ever'*
John Ruskin

Cities are the hubs for the organization, if not the exploitation, of their hinterlands. The bricks and mortar, and streets and spaces, are the physical matrix which contain this dynamic. But the transition of cities is now in full swing, from industrial 'material processors' to post-industrial 'information processors'. In future the structure and nature of cities may change in ways that are hard to imagine.

Meanwhile the bricks and mortar remain, in GM as a chaotic jumble of housing and industry, places and spaces, new and old. While buildings fall vacant and crumble, the fuel they consume spreads emissions and impacts around the world. While local people struggle for territory and security, rising affluence continues to spread concrete across the countryside.

This chapter looks at how to steer the built environment – the urban form and fabric – towards greater sustainability. But the built environment is not a simple thing. With many environmental, economic and social angles to explore, we sketch here only the key features:

- urban form, land-use and social resources – themes which centre on spatial patterns.
- urban functions in housing and property – focusing on supply–demand interactions.

- urban fabric and its demands for energy and materials – themes concerning the physical metabolism.

## Trends & tensions

Industrial restructuring has left widespread dereliction and contamination on up to 10% of the GM urban area, a quarter of all housing is over 100 years old, and 40% is unfit or in poor condition. The people have departed from many inner areas, leaving large gaps in the urban fabric, while the pressure for development mounts at the periphery and beyond. The city-region's building stock produces climate change emissions of a tenth of 1% of the world total, and this could increase by a quarter in the next 25 years. For this and many similar problems, improvements to efficiency are overtaken by rising demand for space, mobility, comfort and identity.

A built environment in transition is both cause and effect of economic problems, with widespread mismatch of locations and values in property and housing. The result is the boom in sunrise business and leisure parks adjacent to areas of dereliction and dependency. The built environment is also cause and effect of social problems, as a manifestation of cultural change and class conflict – decaying buildings and fragmented neighbourhoods impact on health, social cohesion, and the viability of the city.

## Future prospects

For the future, such trends could lead in several alternative directions or 'scenarios':

- *BAU scenario*: increasing space per person and per employee; increasing levels of servicing, energy and resource use. Many neighbourhoods are abandoned as areas of growth and decline polarize, while green belts become a preserve of the rich.
- *technology scenario*: 'smart' houses and workplaces are common, but savings in energy and resource use are outweighed by increased space and comfort. Universal tele-work, leisure and education polarizes communities and disperses lifestyles over a wide radius.
- *SD scenario:* moderate lifestyle shift, public service coordination and gradual clustering of neighbourhoods help to stabilize population in the cities. New institutions and investment channels help to achieve major energy and resource efficiency in buildings.
- *deep green scenario:* lifestyle shift increases viability of dense urban communities and shared tenures in mixed uses, and reduces demand for property. Zero energy buildings are common and green belts become eco-belts for food and wildlife.

## Development metabolism

To explore the 'sustainability' scenario in more depth, we have to consider again what is to be sustained – is it the physical city, its people, or the global environment?[1] *(Chapter 1)*. Such a question involves the many roles, functions, linkages and impacts of the built environment as a total system.

At the very simplest, tangible resources such as land and buildings can be counted as 'stocks', and gains or losses counted as 'flows' on a

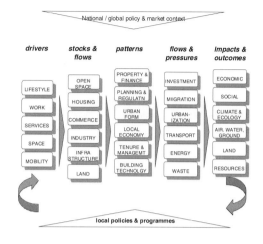

Fig 5.1     **BUILT ENVIRONMENT**

Built environment 'total metabolism' system mapping

balance sheet. Long term trends can be seen in context – for instance in GM, there is about 80 years' supply of non-protected rural land at current rates of consumption. But the built environment is much more than numbers – it has many roles, in supporting livelihoods, institutions and communities and cultures. Primary human 'needs' and demands are met through a complex and self-organizing system, resulting in many kinds of outputs and 'outcomes'.[2] The outline of the total system can be seen with a 'total metabolism' system mapping for urban development and construction *(Fig 5.1)*.

Such a mapping shows some of the many linkages between lifestyles on the demand-side, patterns of urban form and infrastructure, technology on the supply-side, and the impacts and outcomes, from social exclusion to climate change. The 'sustainability', or otherwise, of the system appears as a dynamic balance between pressures on each side, rather than a fixed solution. This shows, for instance, how the need and demand for housing space needs to be balanced with the environmental and human impacts of space provision – to redress any imbalance, shifting lifestyles and expectations on the demand side may be as important as

[2] Mitlin & Satterthwaite 1996                              [2] Portugali 1996

Fig 5.2   *PATTERNS in URBAN FORM: (1)*

private territory
local amenity
garden environment
car access
public transport
urban environment
local jobs & services
communal space

— *suburban model - space extensive*

⋯ *'urbanist' model - space intensive*

Balances and trade-offs in location profile of human settlements at any scale:
Source: adapted from Alexander 1985: Mollison 1991.

provision on the supply side. It shows that quality of space may be as important as quantity, which is very topical for the prospects for re-urbanization. It also shows the theme of integration – that single objectives are entangled with many others, and that success is likely to come through a holistic approach to the total system.

The spatial dimensions of such a balance revolve on the location decisions and trade-offs of individuals or organizations *(Fig 5.2)*. This shows the need for privacy and territory in tension with the need for public spaces and services – and in a market economy, the better the balance, the higher the price. Different generic patterns, such as suburban or 'new urbanism' models, can shift the balance one way or the other, both in physical form and in perceptions or aspirations. This approach underlies a series of 'patterns in urban form' as in the following sections – generic spatial arrangements which underpin and facilitate the many roles of the built environment.[3]

Such patterns recall the many 'ideal city' visions over the years, which are even now being re-invented in the UK as elsewhere. But now there are new ingredients in the mix – post-industrial affluence, global environmental change, cultural diversity and so on – placing new demands on the traditional goals of city planning. One theme is that of diversity – that any single model or pattern, whether for compact cities or out-of-town suburbs, is unlikely to be a universal solution, and that a balanced portfolio is a more robust approach.[4] Another theme is that of 'process not product' – in the context of overwhelming change, more effective and sustainable built environments will come from a 'process' which is continuous and collaborative, rather than the 'product' of a fixed blueprint *(Chapter 12)*.[5]

## Towards a sustainable built environment

Within this picture of change and complexity, we can begin to map out practical goals for a 'sustainable built environment', at various scales from the household to the city-region.

For urban form, there is a goal for efficient and equitable location and land-use patterns, including for indirect effects on transport and energy. At the neighbourhood level, the maintenance and revitalization of local services and jobs can be aided by spatial patterns of 'clustering' and consolidation. For housing and property, the tensions between supply and demand can be eased by managing demand and coordinating supply. Cultural heritage, both official and informal, is clearly 'critical capital' to be conserved and enhanced, as is urban ecology. The longer term trend in energy demand from buildings needs to be 'dematerialized' or reduced by a factor of between four and ten, with healthy and adaptable buildings as standard. Such a re-engineering of the urban fabric can be summed up with a target of reducing carbon emissions by 35% from the building stock.

While such goals are admirable, in practice we find huge gaps between problems and solutions – 'sustainable urban form', for instance, in practice means the spatial form of an urban system which may be more or less sustainable in its own terms.[6] Even where such goals can be defined, moving towards them is a long term

3 Alexander 1986: Mollison 1988

4 TCPA 1998
5 Healey 1997
6 Breheny 1991

process – the turnover of buildings and land is 1–2% per year, and there is massive inertia built into the system. There is also endemic conflict and competition in the way the city is structured, and no strategy, whether sustainable or otherwise, is likely to achieve social harmony and cooperation overnight. So for each action we have to consider who gains and loses, both from the end result, and the process of moving towards it. Finally, we should be wary of newly fashionable advice – the European historic cores which inspire 'new urbanism' are generally surrounded by suburbs and business parks, showing that both are part of a larger whole.[7]

Translating such goals into practical targets, and linking them together is the theme of the rest of this chapter. Before that, the last question is how to identify indicators and targets to help monitor change and progress. Again, many of the most important features of the built environment cannot easily be pinned down – it is easy to measure numbers of houses or parks, but harder to assess whether they provide security and well-being. Some of the more tangible factors can be seen in the 'core indicators' table below, and this shows 'business as usual' (BAU) projections alongside 'sustainable development' (SD) targets *(Box 5.1)*. This is then combined with a more general outline of goals and strategies which follows *(Box 5.2)*. At the end of the chapter we review the agenda for 'making it happen' – with an outline of actions from each of public and private actors, on the ground in each area type, and a comparison of GM in the context of other European city-regions.

---

**Box 5.1**

### BUILT ENVIRONMENT ~ INDICATORS & TARGETS

| | | 1995 | BAU 2020 | SD 2020 | trend/ target index |
|---|---|---|---|---|---|
| **URBAN DEVELOPMENT** | | | | | |
| total urban land | Km² | 550 | 578 | 564 | 5 |
| new hsg gross pop.density | pp/ha | 88 | 88 | 120 | 7 |
| industrial land/GDP | M²/£K | 4.2 | 3.5 | 3.3 | 8 |
| total derelict land | Km2 | 32 | 30 | 11 | 1 |
| hh within 400m of local centres | % | 18% | 14% | 30% | -4 |
| retail space % out of town | % | 19% | 42% | 15% | -10 |
| % households exposed >1000 vpd | % | 20% | 40% | 5% | -10 |
| **HOUSEHOLDS** | | | | | |
| energy intensity new stock | GJ/m²/y | 1.25 | 1.00 | 0.75 | 5 |
| total final energy demand | PJ/y | 96.1 | 115.8 | 88.6 | -10 |
| % energy via direct renewables | % | 0.01% | 2.0% | 12.0% | 2 |
| % energy via CHP heat | % | 0.4% | 5.0% | 15.0% | 3 |
| domestic $CO_2$ emissions incl power | MtCO2/y | 8.2 | 7.5 | 4.8 | 2 |
| unfit hsg in need of replacement | 1000's | 129 | 193 | 78 | -10 |
| % hh in energy poverty | % | 28% | 35% | 0% | -3 |
| % homeless / hsg stress/ neg.equity | % | 20% | 25% | 0% | -3 |
| % new hsg with BREEAM or similar | % | 3% | 9% | 100% | 1 |

BAU = business as usual projection
SD = sustainable development scenario

---

**Box 5.2**

### BUILT ENVIRONMENT ~ GOALS & STRATEGIES

| | G O V | L A P | B U S | C O M | P U B |
|---|---|---|---|---|---|
| **LAND & URBAN FORM:** | ● | ● | ● | ● | |
| Growth of urbanization stabilized, critical capital to be safeguarded: use vacant & derelict land for urban restructuring | | | | | |
| **SOCIAL CITY:** | ○ | ● | ○ | ● | ○ |
| Neighbourhood vitality via clustering of housing & services: enhance cultural heritage, local forums & community actions for liveable city | | | | | |
| **HOUSING:** | ○ | ● | ● | ○ | ● |
| Projected household demand met mainly within urban area: at least 1/2 of new hsg to be high density near to local centres. | | | | | |
| **PROPERTY & SERVICES:** | ○ | ● | ● | ○ | ● |
| Consolidate local services, contain outward spread of retail & public services, use accessibility planning for employment. | | | | | |
| **BUILDING ENERGY:** | ○ | ● | ● | | ○ |
| Energy in housing reduced by 40%: other buildings by 25%: all existing building to 1995 standards, new hsg to NHER 10 | | | | | |
| **ENVIRONMENT & RESOURCES:** | ○ | ● | ○ | | ○ |
| All buildings 'good' standard on BRE assessment: environmental health audits | | | | | |

GOV ~ government: LA ~ local authorities & partnerships: BUS ~ business: COM ~ community & 3rd sector: PUB ~ public

---

# URBAN FORM & LAND-USE

The changing balance of people, land, and urban form is under continuous pressure from development – not just the development of buildings, but the dynamics of demand for space, amenity, competitiveness and so on. Both housing and commercial floorspace increase at 1–2% per year, and site area rather faster, with a doubling time in the region of 30–50 years.[8] The outcome is generally an outward spread which then contributes to urban decline, waste of land, and increased car-dependency. On the other hand any restrictions in land supply could lead to housing shortages, loss of open space, and migration of wealthier households. So a 'sustainable' urban form for any city is a complex balance of many needs and goals, at larger and smaller scales.

With a clear core and satellite structure, GM is a classic industrial conurbation – some of the mill towns and suburbs around the periphery are still distinct units, while others have merged into a large mass around the regional centre. The density of the urban area is 45 persons/ha (gross), with average net housing densities of 25 dwellings/ha – in fact near the current good practice standards.[9] Open land is urbanized or developed at nearly 1km$^2$ per year, although 80% of all development in GM is already on 'brown' urban sites. However, development of 'white' land not in the Green Belt is over 1% of the total per year, with less than 80 years' supply to go.

After decades of thinning out and de-population, both planned and spontaneous, there is a strong policy goal to provide for the current population and its projected increase of 2% per decade.[10] However GM already has the highest urban density in the UK outside of London – and while 'brown' and derelict land is plentiful, high amenity sites and open spaces are more scarce. The current UK target for 60% of development to be on 'brown' or re-used sites, is not so relevant in GM, which achieves 80% and has a different range of problems.[11] The 'sustainable' solution is of course to re-use wasted assets in the urban area while protecting critical assets on the fringe – the 'brownfield agenda'. But such a solution would need a re-think of current patterns of housing and economic development – on the demand side, the aspirations and expectations of consumers, and on the supply side, the constraints of financiers, developers, contractors and agents. There are many possible actions, from taxation to planning controls, with various pros, cons and side-effects.

## Density, transport & energy

Much argument on urban form focuses on the linkage of urban size and density to transport and energy demand *(Fig 5.3)*.[12] The evidence is sketchy, there are many intervening factors,[13] and the effect of planning policy would have very marginal effects on travel demand.[14] Other things being equal the optimum pattern appears to be in free-standing medium-sized settlements of about 80– 100 pph (persons per hectare) net,

Fig 5.3  **DENSITY & TRANSPORT**

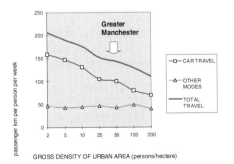

Estimated transport demand by average urban density: based on travel data & settlement analysis in UK cities & regions.
Source: ECOTEC 1993, Owens & Cope 1995.

8 Fothergill et al, 1987
9 'gross' density refers to the whole population divided by area: 'net' density refers to individual sites, excluding the rest of the city

10 DoE 1995 & DETR 1999 'Household projections'
11 DETR 1998 'Planning for communities of the future'
12 Owens & Cope 1992
13 Stead, Titheridge & Williams 1999
14 Breheny 1995

or 40–50 pph gross density. In fact this is already the average population density of GM:[15] the travel intensity, or distance per person per week, of GM as a whole is 10% less than London, 50% more than Merseyside, and 15% less than the UK average for small cities. The satellite pattern and mixture of uses found in GM are also similar to the recommended 'dispersed nucleated' structure.[16] This is not to say that conditions are ideal in GM, more that the impact of future development patterns should be tested against current baselines.

Such density-energy linkages can be extended to include energy use in buildings, the potential for combined heat and power (CHP), and urban food cultivation. The evidence here is very approximate, but there seems to be a threshold at about 25 pph, beyond which increasing densities brings diminishing returns.

## Green belts

The foundation of modern planning, the green belt, is under mounting pressure in GM as elsewhere, as the national household projections suggest that over 200,000 new dwellings may be required by 2020.[17] The local green belt boundary follows the urban edge closely, and is maintained in most of the current UDPs. In reality the green belt in GM is anything but green – three quarters is within 1km of urban areas, and a useful corridor for motorways, power lines and other infrastructure.[18]

As most of the green belt was drawn around the urban boundaries in 1974, it is not necessarily the optimum shape for the longer term – and at present motorways, employment sites and the airport are taking significant chunks for development. Together with related designations such as 'areas of landscape value' and 'river valleys', the green belt boundaries may need a rethink for new problems and opportunities:

- degraded / derelict land where development would promote enhancement and after-use;
- rural areas where diversification needs leisure or ecological development;

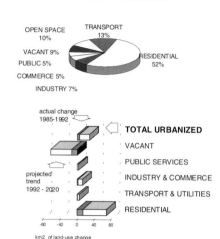

Fig 5.4 **LAND-USES & TRENDS**

Land use types and land-use trends 1985-1992 and projected to 2020.
Source: GMR 1995

- smaller settlements where development would enhance viability of local services;
- green wedges in the urban area which would benefit from green belt extensions,

There is also a need for long-term stability of green belt boundaries and policies, as any uncertainty tends to inflate 'hope' values and undermine investment. On balance there is a strong case for maintaining the total stock of green belt areas, with any essential development compensated by green belt extensions and positive restoration elsewhere. As for the green belt land itself, large areas are degraded and under-used, and their future prospects should be steered towards the theme of an 'eco-belt' *(Chapter 7)*.

## Land uses & quality

The urban area in GM takes up 43% of the total, and within this, housing accounts for over half, transport at 13% and open space at 10%.[19] On current trends 30 km[2] of rural land would be developed by 2020, and the entire stock of urban and fringe vacant land would be used up. The projected growth of land for services, employ-

15 ECOTEC 1993
16 Breheny Gent & Lock 1995
17 DETR 1999 'Household projections'
18 Elson et al 1991

19 All land-use data from GMR 1996

Fig 5.5 **PATTERNS in URBAN FORM: (2)**

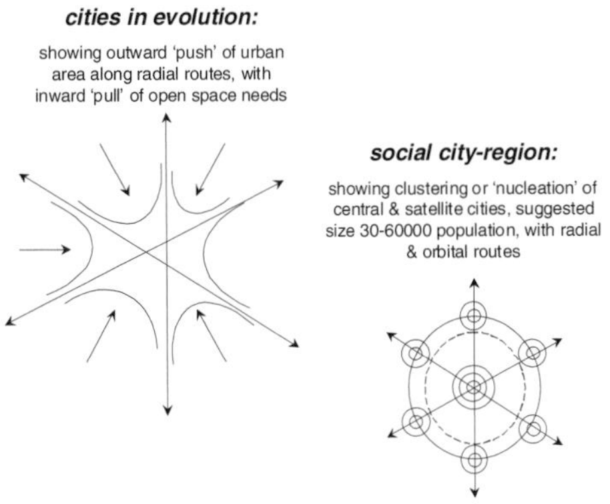

**cities in evolution:**
showing outward 'push' of urban
area along radial routes, with
inward 'pull' of open space needs

**social city-region:**
showing clustering or 'nucleation' of
central & satellite cities, suggested
size 30-60000 population, with radial
& orbital routes

General requirements & patterns for conurbation forms:
Source: based on Geddes 1915: Howard 1898.

ment and transport would itself take nearly half the current vacant land *(Fig 5.4)*.

How can the size and shape of the urban area be maintained, while providing for growth and development? Multiple and diverse land-use is one approach.[20] Transport-related land has huge potential for conversion to public and residential space through traffic calming. Housing land may intermingle with employment areas via networking and teleworking, and spare land on industrial and institutional estates can become wildlife and cultivation areas. In each case land policies and practices should aim to use available space more efficiently, equitably, and with increased added value.

The other key resource is vacant and derelict land, currently at 10% and 7% of the urban area, without counting left-over corners and strips attached to other uses.[21] Vacancy and dereliction are by-products of industrial restructuring, and some vacant land is inevitable while land-uses change. Even if all vacant land was developed for housing, at current densities it would provide for less than half of the projected dwellings needed, and in practice much of it is quite unsuitable for housing. But vacant land is

an essential resource in the long term restructuring of urban form:

- consolidation of neighbourhood units;
- development clustering for housing growth;
- new networks of green corridors and necklaces.

The 3200 hectares of derelict land has been roughly constant for two decades, as reclamation has been balanced by new dereliction. Much is concentrated in areas such as East Manchester, where the negative image, cost and risk of reclamation are barriers to development. If a 25-year programme was to reduce dereliction to a third of current levels, assuming that new dereliction continues at its current rate, reclamation activity would need to double *(Chapter 8)*. Meanwhile each derelict or vacant site could play a potential role in long term neighbourhood strategy as below, and where long term uses are uncertain, short term activity should be generated through local partnerships.[22]

## Urban form strategy

In the wider view, the question of urban form is much more than simple density and brown-green choices – it is about the spatial structure of human activities. This is not a new theme – a century ago, the garden city concept of the forerunner to the TCPA aimed at planned clusters of communities, as a response to overcrowded cities and countryside deprivation *(Fig 5.5)*.[23] The agenda, at least in the developed world, is now not so much about new settlements, as about restructuring existing cities for social and ecological goals – the theme of clustering and differentiation for viability and cohesion is equally valid, although the means to achieve it is vastly different.

Current development policy focuses on the study of 'urban capacity' or ability of urban areas to intensify, and the NW region for one has generated new methods to do this.[24] But capacity is both a technical and social issue – the vi-

20 Nijkamp 1991
21 National Land-Use Database 1999

22 Handley 1996
23 Howard 1898: Geddes 1915
24 Clarke 1997

ability of land for development depends on the social acceptance of densities, mixed uses and other factors.[25]   Many European cities show that higher densities are viable when combined with the right mix of lifestyles, cultures, tenures and public services. While sieve maps and the numbers game are a necessary step, urban capacity also involves creative visions of the future city.[26]

To achieve such broad shifts in the direction of urban development, all possible options need to be explored, in legislation, markets and regulation, of which these are a selection:

- greenfield levy combined with brownfield subsidy.[27]

- powers for public land assembly and voluntary consortiums
- resolving liability conflicts for contaminated land and reclamation.[28]
- reform of the business rating system to favour local enterprises
- extending planning controls to density and tenure

In practice, such moves on the supply side are likely to be marginal and gradual, and there may be more to be gained by more structural changes. New forms of tenure, mixed use design, and consortium finance would boost the demand side for brownfield sites, as below.

# THE SOCIAL CITY-REGION

In contrast to the macro-scale of urban form above, the human and neighbourhood agenda looks at the meso- and micro-scale. Many neighbourhoods in cities such as GM have merged into sprawl fragmented by roads, and many outer areas are dormitories with few jobs or services. The principles of human-scale neighbourhoods are nothing new, but it seems we have to re-interpret them for the post-industrial city.[29]   The first issue is the linkage between homes, jobs and services. Viable units in education, retail and other services require a 10–20000 population range, and a viable walking distance for most people is about 4–1000m, depending on the quality of the environment *(Fig 5.6)*.[30]

Both these can be achieved by clustering of higher density housing and mixed employment around local centres, in mainly pedestrianized units of up to 1km radius.[31]   Clusters of neighbourhood units can be arranged around public transport loops and district centres with special-

ized services, with an interlocking 'eco-structure' or matrix of green spaces. Highways should be in a tree pattern with restricted through routes – walking or cycling locally, and public transport between neighbourhoods should be the first choice *(Fig 5.7)*.

Fig 5.6    ***DENSITY & ACCESSIBILITY***

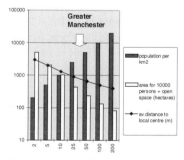

GROSS DENSITY OF URBAN AREA (persons/hectare)

Average relationship of population, area & distance to local centres serving 10000 people, including for open space standard at 3.3. hectares per 1000.

25 ENTEC 1998
26 Ravetz 1998: Sherlock 1990
27 Urban Task Force 1999
28 Winter 1998
29 Jacobs 1964
30 Hass-Klau 1992:
31 Rudlin & Falk 1999

Fig 5.7    *PATTERNS in URBAN FORM: (3)*

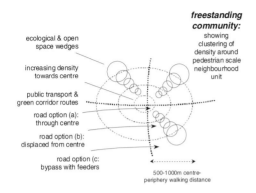

General patterns for single neighbourhood units, freestanding and within urban grid.
Source: based on Alexander 1986, Calthorpe 1994, Rudlin & Falk 1999

Fig 5.8    *PATTERNS in URBAN FORM: (4)*

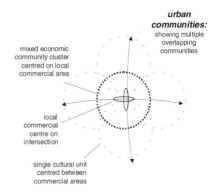

General patterns for overlapping cultural & economic neighbourhood units within urban grid.
Source: based on Alexander 1986: Calthorpe 1994: Tjallingi 1995

In practice the neighbourhood unit, 'pedestrian pocket', or 'transit-oriented development' is only a starting point for a complex conurbation such as GM. In contrast to much current advice, urban vitality and richness are not necessarily increased by a single choice for local services, even if they were desirable for residents.[32] For the crucial question of road access, the alternatives range from a route through the centre to an external bypass, each with problems and opportunities. For social communities, perhaps the most complex of any urban patterns, there are alternative types of pattern for the overlapping of community units. An economic unit could be centred on existing road-based commercial centres, whose catchments might cover several cultural units. Any one cultural unit might access several local centres and be contained within the cells of the road network *(Fig 5.8)*.[33] Both economic and cultural units in practice overlap with tenure and land-use units, and this richer kind of mixture contrasts with the now conventional advice for 'mixed uses'.[34]

## Urban grain & texture

If these multi-layered patterns for neighbourhood units are translated to a continuous urban area,

as in GM, there are some interesting possibilities for urban 'micro-form' *(Fig 5.9)*. Public transport routes and green corridors may be parallel but removed from the main road network, as in the upper diagram; or alternate to the road network, shown below, as in some new towns.[35] Each has implications for accessibility, commercial services, the overlapping of communities, and the 'richness' of the city.[36] Of course such generic patterns have to be translated to a reality which is complex and messy, but the theme of multiple nodes is a useful approach for inner and outer areas.[37]

Average distances in GM from dwellings to local centres are about 750m, or twice the modern standard for acceptable walking distance. A policy of doubling average housing densities within 4–500m of local centres could accommodate up to half of all new development within this radius by 2020, depending on land availability, and the population contained would increase to an average of 5000, or half the catchment.[38] Such a scenario is closely linked to traffic reductions which enable pedestrianization on alternate routes, and residential traffic calming will increase pedestrian travel and the effective catchment.[39] If a similar restructuring was to continue up to

32 Calthorpe 1993
33 Rapaport 1986
34 Jenks, Burton & Williams 1996

35 Percy 1996
36 Greenhalgh & Worpole 1998
37 Newman, Kenworthy & Vintila 1992
38 Ravetz & SCRWG1996: est.from map surveys & statistical calculation
39 Hass-Klau 1992

2050, three quarters of the population in principle could be within easy walking distance of local centres.

## The liveable city

In Manchester itself there has been a rediscovery of the neighbourhood principle – the 'City Development Guide' draws on the experience of redevelopment in Hulme, and sets out urban design principles and guidelines for 'sustainable neighbourhoods' *(Box 5.3)*.[40]

While this has been adopted by Manchester, and serves as a model to other districts, the Guide is perhaps limited by its visual-based and site-based remit.[41] While the one-off flagship sites are only a starting point, a far greater challenge is in the vast expanses of mixed commercial areas and anonymous suburbs, where the task will take decades. In the shorter term there are many ways to improve urban liveability – with details such as junctions, crossings, entrances and pedestrian routes all urgently needed. The 'home zone' pedestrian street concept is now official policy, but there are few funds to carry it out – again, innovative thinking on finance and institutional arrangements is needed.

And for this the role of local communities is paramount – each neighbourhood should have a local forum or similar body to map out development strategies, promote liveable streets, and anticipate problems and opportunities *(Chapter 14)*. Housing estates can be managed more effectively and at lower cost through estate management boards.[42] Town centres can be

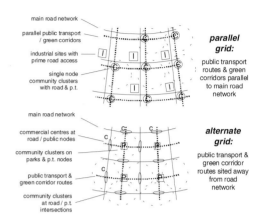

Fig 5.9 **PATTERNS in URBAN FORM: (5)**

main road network

parallel public transport / green corridors

industrial sites with prime road access

single node community clusters with road & p.t.

**parallel grid:**

public transport routes & green corridors parallel to main road network

main road network

commercial centres at road / public nodes

community clusters on parks & p.t. nodes

public transport & green corridor routes

community clusters at road / p.t. intersections

**alternate grid:**

public transport & green corridor routes sited away from road network

General patterns for combinations of neighbourhood units within urban grid: to be adapted to local circumstances. Based on Alexander 1986: Calthorpe 1994: Tjallingi 1995

transformed by local businesses in collaboration.[43] Area regeneration can be kick-started by local development trusts, with appreciation on property values returned to the community.[44] In an age of globally networked virtual communities, the 'product' of neighbourhood-based action is only half the story – the 'process' of bringing people and organizations together itself builds community capacity and cohesion *(Chapter 11)*.[45]

## Cultural heritage

The cultural heritage and 'time-depth' of buildings and townscapes, as with natural heritage, is 'critical capital' and equally irreplaceable.[46] In resource management terms, some wastage of assets is inevitable, and the total stock will always need to be replenished with new additions.[47] In practice this means that historic resources can be living and working parts of the city, and adapted in the spirit in which they were built, while new designs should aim to achieve the quality and value worthy of future conservation.

To equal the richness of cities such as Oxford or Bath, GM would need a ten-fold increase

---

40 Manchester City Development Guide 1995
41 Symes & Pauwels 1999
42 Power 1994

43 Urbed & Hiller Parker 1995
44 Monaghan 1997
45 Abbott 1995
46 Land Use Consultants 1995

Fig 5.10 **CULTURAL HERITAGE**

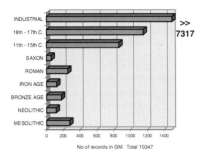

Recorded sites and monuments by date of earliest records.
Source GMAU 1995

in its historic density. Such a step change could be achieved over the next century, if for instance an average of one in fifteen new buildings were of a quality and distinctiveness suitable for the future heritage stock.[48] This applies not only to flagship buildings, but everyday townscapes of industry and housing – common elements such as corners and crossroads should each contribute identity and creative design.

There are over 2500 listed buildings in GM, and while parts of the centre are comparable to other historic cities, the 'listing density' is low at 1 per 20 hectares of urban area (*Fig 5.10*). Historic buildings in GM are concentrated in small 19th century leftovers, the older commercial centres, and ethnic or religious communities: one unique type is the 'Manchester' warehouse, a legacy of the city's mercantile wealth in the 19th century.[49] Another is the 'Lancashire' multi-storey textile mill, but of the former 2400 mills across the city, only a quarter have survived. Local conservation areas are still being designated, and the 200 such areas in GM now include many examples of 19th century housing, which up to 20

years ago were being declared for clearance as unfit. The challenge is to marry conservation and adaptation in a practical sense: an energy-climate strategy, for instance, will need to be creative in the upgrading of listed buildings.

## Social city strategy

In a sprawling conurbation such as GM, the prospects seem daunting – neighbourhood restructuring may take decades, local needs are outweighed by financial pressures, and people and businesses tend to spread out rather than 'bunch up'.[50] But the benefits of strong, diverse and liveable neighbourhood units can be seen in areas of high amenity and high value (*Box 5.4*). While planning practice tends to focus on site-by-site allocations, a creative and community-based neighbourhood strategy, coupled with integrated strategy for finance, fiscal policy, transport and so on, would turn problems into opportunities and gain from numerous benefits:

- provision for growth in household numbers;
- accessibility and viability of local services;
- low-impact transport and car dependency;
- increased security and liveability;
- green corridors linking local centres;
- reduced development pressure on green belt and countryside areas.

---

Box 5.4 **URBAN NEIGHBOURHOODS**

The city of Freiburg has pedestrianized 90% of residential areas and planted 1/4 million trees on former streets, many of which are locally managed. The highway network has been reorganized into a 'tree' to avoid rat-running. All public transport is on a common ticket system, with 60 trams per hour on main routes.

Source: EU Expert Group 1996

---

47 Lichfield 1987
48 Ravetz 1996
49 Wilkinson 1986

50 Hooper 1994

# HOUSING & HOUSEHOLDS

The first question for any city is how it shelters its people. While GM is a major conurbation in one of the richest nations in the world, up to 40% of its housing is unfit or needing repair, factors which compound with unemployment and ill-health. At the same time, 'levelling up' and provision of new housing to current standards on the scale needed would have large impacts on land-use and environmental resources. There is also more to the housing problem than numbers of units – while there are 15,000 families in GM registered as homeless, half of them in Manchester, over 50000 dwellings lie vacant.[51]

For the future there is a very big question – 'where should the people go?'[52] The average size of household in GM is projected to reduce from 2.45 to 2.14 people per household, and the number of households may rise by 140–210 000 over the next 25 years *(Fig 5.11)*. Including for replacement of unfit housing, a quarter of all dwellings in GM could be new by 2020 – much of the older stock will also be near the end of its life and needing large scale renewal, putting further pressure on housing land. Most of the new households will be for single persons or smaller units, whereas most of the supply in GM is in larger family dwellings. Meanwhile the industry suggests that smaller households are more likely to be upwardly mobile with flexible family arrangements, and demand for space is also likely to increase with new patterns of teleworking and local social economies.[53] The projections themselves can be questioned as to whether they are self-fulfilling prophecies or packages of assumptions, and there are many more arguments on tenure, social housing investment, affordability, equity, and the benefit system.[54]

As land is perhaps the most finite resource of all, its distribution is a key question. In a nutshell, the more private space we take, the less public space is left: by building multi-storey we

can increase the internal space but decrease the external space per person. But the desire for space and territory is one of the deepest roots in human psychology:[55]

- life-cycle aspirations for space and territory – people growing up in a two-room terrace will tend to aspire to something bigger.
- desire for identity through sub-cultures, by sharing spaces with like-minded people, with polarisation of the remainder.
- desire to 'have one's cake and eat it', in locations with access to green fields, jobs and services – the result is seen on the fringe and other locations with the highest prices.

Current distribution of private and public space in GM is shown for typical 19th and 20th century neighbourhood types *(Fig 5.12)*. The 21st century target shows average net housing densities of up to 100 pph (20 dwellings/acre), about the optimum for access to local services, renewable energy and CHP networks. However, this densification of the 21st century housing type but conflicts not only with basic psychology as

Fig 5.11  **HOUSEHOLD PROJECTIONS**

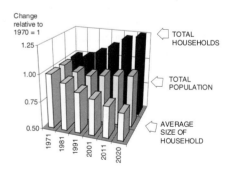

Trends & projections in households & population for GM to 2016, with extrapolation to 2020.
Source GMR 1994: DETR 1998 & DOE 1995

---

51 Power & Mumford1999: local data from AGMA 1994, Manchester City 1995
52 Breheny & Hall 1996
53 Housebuilders Federation 1996:
54 Bramley & Watkins1995

55 Ravetz 1998

Fig 5.12   **SPACE:  QUANTITY & QUALITY**

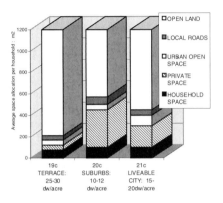

Average space requirements for urban form types:  based on sample map surveys of GM, with projected figures for 21st century development: open land component in proportion to actual urban/ rural land ratio.
Source Ravetz 1996a

Fig 5.13   **PATTERNS in URBAN FORM: (6)**

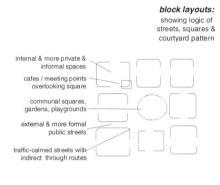

General patterns for street & block layout.
Source:  based on Jacobs 1966, Alexander 1986, Calthorpe 1994

above, but the general conservatism of the property industry.[56]  So the challenge is to turn a problem into an opportunity, for quality of location rather than quantity of space per person, by clustering around positive attractions. One possible scenario for housing to 2020 shows how the projected demand could be met almost entirely within the urban area by a combination of clustering and conversion *(Box 5.5).*[57]

## Housing forms & layouts

The increase in single person households coincides with the need to increase housing densities – but such housing needs to be adaptable to home-working, teleworking, extended families and sub-division, as in the '21st century homes' concept.[58]  Meanwhile the effects of rising disposable incomes are likely to increase the demand for space, both internal and external.  Such demand can be met by design patterns which increase space efficiency and added value, while maintaining privacy, external space and 'defensible' space.  Plan forms such as courtyards, and sectional forms such as maisonettes and step forms, can be seen in further 'patterns' of urban form, which aim at mixed uses,

mixed households and mixed tenures within a clear hierarchy of external and internal space *(Fig 5.13).*[59]

In London and most European cities, land prices and cultural differences make higher density living both necessary and viable. While GM is for the most part a low-rise city, a combination of development strategy and value-added land prices would encourage a similar urbanist culture.  In waterfront regeneration for instance, younger mobile households are attracted to housing with cachet, attitude and nightlife. Households with families are attracted to high standards of security, childcare and local schooling.  The 'housing' challenge is in fact more of an 'urbanism' challenge.[60]

It is also clear that lifestyle shifts are crucial for people to gain the added value from proximity – where people agree to share collective space such as gardens, and facilities such as childcare, everybody is better off.  But this needs a re-think of current housing tenure, investment and benefit systems, where the former model of nuclear family owner-occupation is in many ways outdated in an age of mobile and flexible careers and households. There is a case for flexible and portable finance packages which allow mobility between locations and tenures. The most positive

56 Rydin 1995
57 Rudlin & Friends of the Earth 1998
58 URBED & Newbury-King 1995

59 Barton, Davis & Guise 1995
60 Ravetz 1999c

alternative tenure is the self-build cooperative, which encourages compatible people to work together and share facilities *(Box 5.6)*. For the mainstream, the 'housing plus' concept in social housing, aiming to coordinate facilities and services for added value, needs to be extended to all tenures.[61]

## Rehabilitation & renewal

Some of the UK's worst housing conditions are in GM – with 6% of dwellings 'unfit', 16% in poor condition, and 17% in need of major repair. Physical conditions are compounded by area decline, social poverty, and low prices which undermine investment. For public and social landlords, the resources available are shrinking, private landlords have few incentives, and owner occupiers with insecure jobs and static values also have diminishing ability to invest.[62]

The life-cycle of the housing stock is also a long term question – over half the local stock is pre-war, much of it far below modern standards, and many public sector estates are still in dire need of major rehabilitation. The improvement grants of the 1970–80s were often a 'quick fix'

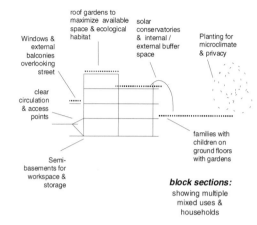

Fig 5.14 **PATTERNS in URBAN FORM: (7)**

roof gardens to maximize available space & ecological habitat

solar conservatories & internal / external buffer space

Planting for microclimate & privacy

Windows & external balconies overlooking street

clear circulation & access points

families with children on ground floors with gardens

Semi-basements for workspace & storage

**block sections:**
showing multiple mixed uses & households

General patterns for street & block section in urban context.
Source:  based on Jacobs 1966, Alexander 1986, Calthorpe 1994

modernization, often to the benefit of owners and speculators, while much of the basic fabric still deteriorates, so by 2020 many dwellings may again be approaching the end of their material lives. For public housing, incentives are needed for tenants' improvements, while for private housing, packages of expertise and finance should be available. This should be backed up with a system of 5-yearly inspections or 'MOTs', for the condition, health and energy efficiency of every dwelling.[63] In Manchester the 'Care & Repair' scheme operates a package of basic security and insulation, coupled with mortgage finance and job training for local people.[64] Other areas are trying to form various partnerships and consortium with lenders and builders, but the situation is fragmented and needs a national framework.

## Sustainable housing strategy

Overall by 2020, a quarter of all dwellings in the city-region will be newly developed, so it is crucial that 'best practice' in layout and design can help to restructure the urban form and fabric for new kinds of household. Another third of dwellings which are unfit should have comprehen-

| Box 5e | | | |
|---|---|---|---|
| **HOUSING DEVELOPMENT SCENARIO** | | | |
| | LAND AREA (ha) | AVERAGE DENSITY | UNITS |
| Local centres infill | 200 | 100 dw/ha | 20000 |
| Local mixed development | 200 | 75 dw/ha | 15000 |
| 30% of urban vacant land | 1000 | 50 dw/ha | 50000 |
| 60% of peripheral vacant land | 1500 | 30 dw/ha | 45000 |
| 50% vacant space over shops/offices | | | 10000 |
| 50% vacant indust-rial conversions | | | 5000 |
| Larger house subdivisions | | | 10000 |
| Rural ecological housing | 500 | 30 dw/ha | 15000 |
| TOTAL | 3500 ha | | 175000 |
| (mid range estimate requirement to 2020) | (7% of urban area) | | |

Approximate estimates for new housing supply to 2020: vacant land areas include for projected new vacancies to 2020.
Sources: based on GMR 1995, AGMA 1995, DOE 1993

61 Scottish Homes 1994
62 Groves et al 1999
63 Joseph Rowntree Foundation 1999 #
64 Cahill & National Housing Federation1999

sive rehabilitation with long term finance packages, while a further quarter of dwellings nearing the end of their material lives will need renewal or major life-cycle improvements. Upgrading the entire housing stock of GM over 25 years would involve a consortium programme covering 30,000 houses per year. This would also traffic-calm and green all residential areas, increasing amenity and usable space around dwellings, and involving local communities in integrated programmes of social investment, intermediate labour and business support. The key to building communities, rather than just housing, is in the added value of community involvement, mixed uses and social facilities such as childcare, security, maintenance and quality standards in local schools. Such integrated packages are now a policy goal for social housing providers, as in the 'housing plus' theme, and

increasingly for private housebuilders, but the average practice has a long way to catch up. A city-region 2020 housing strategy has a role to play in this, not so much by direct provision, as by coordinating and raising standards across all parts of the industry.

---

**Box 5.6**    *SUSTAINABLE MIXED USE*

The 'Homes for Change' development in the Hulme area of Manchester provides 88 flats with workspace in a high density, high quality courtyard on half a hectare of reclaimed land. With a dual housing and work cooperative structure, the development has combined design participation, self-build, state of the art energy efficiency, local business development and a cultural events space.

Source: Rudlin & Falk 1999

---

# SERVICES & INDUSTRY

Commercial and industrial property is a very different industry from housing, but many of its critical questions are similar – rising demand for space and amenity, polarization into growth and decline, and the growing resource demands of the building stock. Here we look at the supply-side for physical sites and premises; further on, Chapter 10 looks at the demand-side from business and services.

The former city-scape of GM, as famously depicted in the paintings of L.S.Lowry, was marked with multi-storey 'Lancashire' textile mills. Most of these have been closed and replaced by more specialized and space-intensive industries, and a vast range of secondary and consumer services. Single storey 'B1' and distribution sheds on peripheral estates dominate the development scene, and the total industrial land

allocated or under construction is nearly half of the existing area, showing a rapid rate of expansion and turnover of land-use.[65] Regional planning guidance (RPG) up to now has promoted motorway corridors for larger manufacturing and distribution, increasing road freight and commuting, with some conflict from other advice on regeneration and transport reduction.[66] Each district competes for economic growth with a place on the ladder of modernization, centred on the 'technopole' axis between the airport and regional centre.

Commercial and industrial floorspace per job tends to increase on average by 1.5–2% per year – such a trend continued to 2020 would show a growth of 40–65%, amounting to more than the entire current stock of vacant land.[67] Much sustainability thinking advocates 'mixed uses', but in a city such as GM many uses are already mixed, with many negative results. In the longer term demand for high quality sites could come up against the limits of land supply – and as with housing, either outward migration or internal restriction would reduce the viability of the city-region. Similar strategies for accessibility also apply – the ABC system is one which matches locations with the type of transport demand and supply *(Chapter 6)*.[68]

While there is no shortage of brownfield industrial sites, larger investors tend to look elsewhere in search of size, amenity and access.[69] GM has a portfolio of 29 'strategic sites' for leading-edge industries – half are on former urban land and half on greenfield, two thirds have good amenity, but only a few have public transport connections.[70] There is also conflict between employment and open space in the urban area – in Trafford, for instance, one site will take 40 hectares of green belt open land, strategically placed for the airport, the universities and the motorways. Where such losses are unavoidable, such development should aim at maximum benefits to the local environments and economies, through development agreements, employer's transport and local labour schemes.

## Consumer services

Commercial retailing and high street services, and public services such as education and health, are each in a state of flux – restructuring, specializing, centralizing and networking. Internet trading is set to explode over the next decade, and could transform high streets as we know them. But the role of services is not only economic but social, as the keys to the public realm, access for the disadvantaged, and urban viability. The huge growth of retail parks in the last 20 years is parallel to the decline of local centres, and some in GM have vacancy rates of over 20%.[71] In the 'pipeline' of retail planning applications, the space proposed is more than half of the space already open, and half of this is out-of-town.[72] Clearly the retail parks have set standards for

security and convenience, to which town centres must aspire.

The most extreme case is the newly-opened Trafford Centre shopping mall, opposed bitterly by nearly all local authorities and environ-mentalists, but sited on what is arguably an urban brownfield site.[73] This is a gilded baroque cathedral promising a heaven of credit-card consumption – to criticize it on the basis of 'shopping' catchments is perhaps missing the point, that such a spectacle is more about consumer identities and fantasies.[74] The eco-efficiency of such a development can and should be greatly improved, but the forces of retail restructuring, global media and ICT are such that it adapts to consumer fashion or dies.

As large retailers offer more and more similar products and services, competitiveness is likely to be in niche branding, and it is interesting that the 'high street' is now being re-invented, under one roof with one checkout and one security system. With basic purchases and services via internet, ICT-based local customer service may increase the viability of traditional high street outlets, particularly where combined with 'added value' of security, automated checkouts, childcare and social facilities. So the city-region services strategy has the challenge of working with large and small retailers, to promote viability of local centres through integrated management of town centres, transport, public facilities and others.[75] There are many angles to this, and what applies to retailers also applies to public services such as health and education. The planning agenda should make mixed uses for retail developments mandatory, the fiscal agenda should encourage small traders via reform of the business rating system, and the commercial agenda should seek competitiveness by combining ICT with customer value.

## Property strategy

For environmental efficiency, the first priority is for the existing building stock. Over 10% or 30 million ft$^2$ of commercial buildings in GM are va-

68 Amundsen 1995
69 INWARD 1995
70 AGMA 1994
71 Roger Tym & Partners 1986
72 AGMA 1994

73 Deakin 1994
74 Henley Centre 1999
75 URBED & Hillier Parker 1995

cant, and converting half this space to housing could provide 15,000 homes.[76] Meanwhile half of all shops and offices, and a quarter of factories and warehouses in GM are over 100 years old – often occupied by more vulnerable industries, with less efficient premises, but in close proximity to the workforce.[77] Industrial regeneration areas need to be coordinated with energy and transport programmes, while new buildings need to be 'industry best' to contribute to the 2020 energy-climate strategy. Larger industrial estates and business clusters also have potential for 'industrial ecology' energy and materials management networks *(Chapter 10)*.

These environmental and social goals, and the many business opportunities above, each combine in a 2020 property strategy:

- Transport management through location policies, commuting schemes, lorry routing and local distribution networks.
- High-tech industry clustered in specialized technopoles: bulk industries sited on rail and water transport connections.
- Office developments located for public transport access and mixed public facilities.
- Retailing and other services maintained in local centres, via land allocations, land assembly, integrated town centre management and business rating reform.
- Local health, education and public services networked via ICT, sited for pedestrian access, and combined with other facilities.

# ENERGY & ENVIRONMENT

The most direct impact of the 1.1 million buildings of GM is through their energy demand of 50000 million kwh per year, accounting for over half the city-region's climate change emissions, or about 15 million tonnes of $CO_2$ per year. In recent decades the 'floorspace efficiency' of the building stock has increased by 7-10% per decade, but not as rapidly as space per person, comfort standards and the numbers of modern appliances. Such trends will continue, with energy use in buildings projected to rise by about 10% per decade, unless positive action is taken.[78] The effect of climate change over several decades may reduce heating demand by 20%, but this could be outweighed by the use of air conditioning for summer cooling.[79] *(Chapter 9)*.

While energy efficient technology is proven, there are many financial and institutional obstacles. Falling energy prices undermine efficiency investment – payback periods for business are 1–2 years, and those for householders are shorter, and much viable

investment is stopped by inertia, uncertainty and split responsibilities between landlords and tenants. Meanwhile over a third of all households suffer energy poverty, with costs to public health and building maintenance in GM of £200 million per year.[80]

There are several approaches to urban energy strategy – improving efficiency on the demand side, and providing renewable sources and CHP on the supply side *(Chapter 9)*. Unfortunately there are conflicts – higher efficiency on the demand side often means lower viability on the supply side. Success may depend on diversity, where each area would develop an integrated energy strategy based on current conditions and future prospects, coordinating demand and supply.[81] But in practice, energy is rarely the first priority for businesses or households, so effective energy strategies have to achieve results via parallel programmes such as health, regeneration and economic development.

76 estimate based on Lowe & Petherick 1989
77 DoE 1996 (Housing & construction statistics)
78 DTI 1995 (Eenergy paper 65)
79 DETR 1998 (climate change programme)

80 Boardman 1992
81 Guy & Marvin 1996

**Box 5.7**

## DOMESTIC ENERGY SCENARIO

Summary of sustainable development scenario for domestic energy and climate emissions in GM to 2020.

| | unit | 1995 Total | BAU 2020 Total | SD 2020 Total | SD shares | Change 95/SD |
|---|---|---|---|---|---|---|
| **DWELLINGS** | | | | | | |
| HH av.size | p/unit | 2.50 | 2.13 | 2.13 | | -15% |
| HH number | Million | 1.03 | 1.27 | 1.27 | | 24% |
| Current stock | Million | 1.03 | 0.99 | 0.93 | 0.73 | -10% |
| New dwellings | Million | 0.00 | 0.28 | 0.35 | 0.27 | # |
| Exg.floorspace | $m^2$/unit & $10^0.m^2$ | 77.19 | 74.49 | 69.5 | 75.00 | -10% |
| New floorspace | $m^2$/unit & $10^0.m^2$ | 0.00 | 27.82 | 25.9 | 75.00 | # |
| TOTAL FLOORSPACE | $10^0.m^2$ | 77.19 | 102.31 | 95.4 | | 24% |
| **DEMAND** | | | | | | |
| Exg.stock intensity | $GJ/m^2/y$ | 1.25 | 1.18 | 1.00 | | -20% |
| New stock intensity | $GJ/m^2/y$ | # | 1.00 | 0.75 | | -40% |
| Exg.demand | PJ/y | 96.1 | 88.1 | 69.2 | | -28% |
| New demand | PJ/y | # | 27.7 | 19.3 | | # |
| TOTAL DEMAND | PJ/y | 96.1 | 115.8 | 88.6 | | -8% |
| **FINAL USES** | | | | | | |
| Space heat | PJ/y | 50.9 | 57.9 | 35.4 | 40% | -30% |
| Water & cooking | | 23.1 | 23.2 | 17.7 | 20% | -23% |
| Lighting | | 4.8 | 5.8 | 4.4 | 5% | -8% |
| Refridge | | 7.7 | 17.4 | 8.9 | 10% | 15% |
| Other power | | 9.6 | 11.6 | 22.1 | 25% | 130% |
| TOTAL | PJ/y | 96.1 | 115.8 | 88.6 | 100% | -8% |
| **FINAL ENERGY** | | | | | | |
| Electric | PJ/y | 16.2 | 23.2 | 17.7 | 20% | 9% |
| Gas | | 63.4 | 76.5 | 44.3 | 50% | -30% |
| Oil | | 1.8 | 2.3 | 1.8 | 2% | -2% |
| Coal | | 14.4 | 5.8 | 0.9 | 1% | -94% |
| direct renewable | | 0.0 | 2.3 | 10.6 | 12% | # |
| Heat | | 0.4 | 5.8 | 13.3 | 15% | # |
| TOTAL | PJ/y | 96.1 | 115.8 | 88.6 | 100% | -8% |
| **$CO_2$** | | | | | | |
| total $CO_2$ incl power | $MtCO^2/y$ | 8.22 | 7.51 | 4.8 | | -41% |

Source: ISCAM scenario accounts for GM: sources as in text.
'BAU' = business as usual projection: 'SD' = sustainable development scenario
'SHARES' shows percentage proportions of SD total: 'RATE' shows annual growth rate for SD total: 'CHANGE' shows percentage growth from 1995 – SD 2020 scenario.

**Fig 5.15**     **ENERGY in HOUSING**

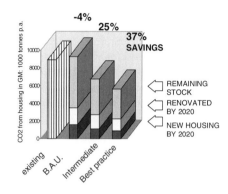

Scenarios for energy & carbon emissions from total housing stock in GM to 2020. Source: EEO 1993, GMR 1995

## Energy in housing

A fifth of housing in GM by 2020 may be new, with potential for 'best practice' at NHER 10 rating, reducing energy demand to about 25% of current levels, for about 1-2% extra on overall costs.[82] When life-cycle maintenance and management savings are factored in, low-energy construction can save over 15% of total costs.[83] For the great bulk of existing and older houses, the investment payback may be 5-15 years, depending on how far efficiency upgrading is combined with renovation and rehabilitation.

In the 2020 energy-climate scenario below, the domestic target is for 'final energy' reductions of 10% from current levels. New dwellings would be built at NHER 10 rating, renovated houses to NHER 9, and the whole of the remaining stock upgraded to at least 1995 building regulations standards or NHER 7. This would result in $CO_2$ emissions reductions of 40% from current levels, assuming improvements in the 'energy intensity' per unit of floorspace of 20% for existing and 60% for new housing *(Fig 5.11)*. With higher standards of insulation and heat recovery, there would be a greater proportion of electricity used for refrigeration, cooling, and home working. Most coal and oil would be replaced by a 20% contribution from local CHP, with a further 5% from on-site solar renewables *(Box 5.7)*.

In practice, there are diminishing returns in increasing insulation, and to approach 'zero-energy' standards involves complete re-engineering for heat recovery and integrated element design, needing special expertise and equipment. Meanwhile the largest consumption growth comes from appliances such as freezers and dishwashers, with a large latent demand in GM from lower-income households. This suggests that incentives for purchasing and maintenance of low-energy technology is crucial. Another simple

82 NHER (National Home Energy Rating) is one of several efficiency rating schemes
83 Ecologica 1995: Whitelegg Smith & Williams 1998

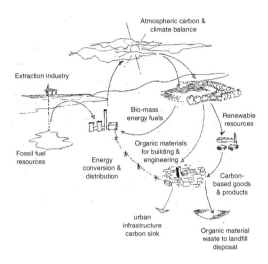

Fig 5.16 **URBAN CARBON CYCLE**

Outline of urban carbon cycle including atmospheric & anthropogenic sinks & sources. An integrated energy-carbon strategy aims to balance the stocks, flows, capacities and impacts at each point in the cycle.

target would be to replace every lightbulb in the city with low energy fittings, saving up to 8% of total $CO_2$ emissions.

## Life-cycles & eco-cycles

Building fabric is the largest cause of environmental impact, not only from energy use, but from huge volumes of bulk materials, and a vast range of toxic substances. The average new house contains about 30 tonnes of 10,000 different types of components, many of them shipped from around the world.[84] The bulk material shifted to extract and process these materials is upwards of 100 tonnes per house, and every year GM builds about 6–7000 houses and about 1 million $m^2$ of commercial floorspace.[85]

While large scale urban renewal is hailed as 'sustainable development', the benefits have to be balanced with the impacts of construction. As yet there is no simple way of calculating this balance. Methods such as 'BREEAM' contain an outline-type checklist, but even with this only

about 1% of construction in GM is assessed as yet.[86] Standards should be set and negotiated by local authorities using any available means, so that by 2020 all new and renovated buildings meet the principle of 'best practical environmental option', translated as the BREEAM 'good' standard *(Box 5.8)*. An example has been set by the West Midlands Housing Association, the first to let a building contract, not only on price, but on energy and environment rating.[87]

Buildings 'embody' large amounts of stored energy in materials, typically about 5– 10 years' worth of energy-in-use, two thirds of which is in cement, bricks, blocks and plaster.[88] Building standards should include for assessment of embodied energy, which can be reduced by 75–80% with alternative materials such as timber framing and cladding.[89] Zero-energy buildings should include for tree planting to absorb the carbon emitted by their embodied energy – for an average house this would be about 20 broadleaf trees. The total construction industry in GM embodies emissions of 1 million tonnes of carbon per year, which could be taken up by about 1 million hectares of mixed forest, on 8 times the city area.[90] If this was managed as part of a city-region carbon eco-cycle, it would produce several times the existing demand for timber, paper and board, which would then substitute for other materials in a 'carbon-neutral' construction industry *(Fig 5.16)*. In practice such a forest would be overseas in an 'international offset', and if it were to take up the overall total emis-

Box 5.8 **GREEN DESIGN**

Stockport MBC has created a 'Green Development Guide' with practical advice for best practice in new development. Applicants for planning and building permission are strongly advised to follow the Guide, and to submit building designs to a BREEAM assessment, and the effects are being monitored with thermal imaging.

**Source: Stockport MBC 1996.**

84 Vale & Vale 1991
85 Sachs 1997

86 'Building Research Establishment Environmental Assessment Method': BRE 1998
87 Architects Journal 23/01/98 p15
88 Vale 1995
89 Buchanan & Honey 1992
90 Brown & Adger 1994
91 Grubb, Brack & Vrolijk 1998

sions from GM, its area would have be the size of the UK.[91]

About 20% of the total impact of an average building is at the construction stage, about 80% in use and maintenance over 50 years, and about 2% at the demolition and disposal stage. Meanwhile the rate of change in housing and business increases, and many commercial and public buildings are obsolete in 20 years. Designing buildings for flexibility and adaptability to new uses is crucial to reducing life-cycle impacts.[91]

## Materials & environments

Bulk materials in GM alone demand over 10 million tonnes of aggregates, of which 20% is produced locally.[92] Demolition aggregates are largely recycled but mostly as low-grade bulk fill material, and there is a strong case for 'higher level' recycling of up to 75% of bulk material.[93] Such impacts can be greatly reduced by careful specification of bulk materials which are recycled or from local sources.

Total life-cycles for common materials and constructions are now being assessed for their contribution to climate change, acidification, toxics, eutrophication and other impacts (*Fig 5.17*). An 'ecological' specification can produce about one tenth the life-cycle environmental impact of a standard design and construction, with a 60% reduction in energy use, and a 15% capital and maintenance saving over 60 years.[94]

Building environments are often seriously deficient. Common problems such as air quality, heating and lighting controls, trace gases from materials or furnishings, and electromagnetic fields, are clearly linked to employee stress and sickness.[95] Future building standards should tackle these problems with regular health monitoring of all buildings, either at point of transfer or at five-year intervals, and backed up with public health information.[96] Energy upgrading can also create health problems, with sealed environments increasing the risks of condensation and stale air, and these will increase with the onset of climate change. While a high-impact high-tech ap-

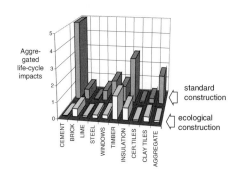

Fig 5.17    **ECOLOGICAL BUILDING**

Weighted environmental life-cycle impacts compared by standard & ecological multi-storey domestic construction.
Source: Ecologica 1995

proach would use air handling and conditioning, a more sustainable low-impact approach would use passive ventilation, 'breathing wall' construction, natural cooling and planting.[97]

## Energy–environment strategy

The key to energy-environment strategies, as above, is to link them to social and economic goals. Energy efficiency is a prime area for job creation and local business development – investment in housing in GM would be over £80 million per year, mostly recouped by consumer savings within five years. The housing energy programme could generate directly 8000 jobs, and including commercial property would increase this to 12–15000 jobs, mostly manual, locally based and suited to training and business development.

Such a programme could be led by a city-region Energy Agency, a partnership or consortium of developers, financiers, landlords, utilities, equipment suppliers and consumers. Its key role would be to set up financial mechanisms and packages to complete the circle from forward investment to consumer savings (*Chapter 9*).

91 Brand 1994
92 GM Geological Unit 1989
93 Howard Humphreys & Partners 1994
94 Whitelegg, Smith & Williams 1999
95 Curwell, March & Venables 1990
96 Institute of Environmental Health 1996

97 Holdsworth 1994
98 March Consulting 1995

Manchester City recently carried out a set of policy studies on an Energy Agency, but at the time deregulation and continued falls in energy prices undermined the prospects of forward investment.[98]   But with the liberalized market structure now in place, and tremendous oppportunities in the utilities market, there is a strong case for a city-region consortium to take on the challenge of integrated energy planning which combines demand, supply, infrastructure and social investment.[99]

# MAKING IT HAPPEN

The built environment strategy for the city-region is an umbrella, which aims to coordinate a wide range of overlapping industry strategies:

- development strategy, for urban form, land-use and strategic developments;
- neighbourhood strategy, for consolidation and viability of local units;
- housing strategy, for coordination of finance, tenures, design and rehabilitation;
- property strategy, for sites and premises, economic regeneration and local services;
- energy efficiency strategy, with an agency which can bring together lenders, developers, utilities, consumers and regeneration agencies;
- environmental health strategy for healthy buildings and low-impact construction.

This is a broad spread of activity with many linkages and overlaps, and each industry will need to establish its own role and profile.  The key is in joined-up thinking and action at the city-region scale, maximizing opportunity and added value wherever possible.   The city-region Energy Agency, for instance, would be  a consortium of financiers, developers, landlords, designers, suppliers, utilities and consumers, and once established it could extend its role to other areas.

The 'horizontal' actions of systems for auditing, monitoring, targeting, management, investment purchasing and others are perhaps the starting point for the city-region framework. Accounting for trends and targets in urban development is not simple, but is essential to a meaningful strategy process.  A sample of the ISCAM accounts with linked indicators and targets, is shown below for the SD scenario *(Box 5.9)*.

The prime movers for the city-region strategy are local authorities.  In principle these already subscribe to many of the goals and targets raised here, but in practice there is often a lack of powers and resources to achieve them. Local actions can start on integrated land-use and transport planning, with strategic programmes for regeneration of the building stock. The energy efficiency strategy can be a catalyst for economic and social regeneration, initially in areas of energy poverty, and then extending from there. GM presents good opportunities for partnerships, due to its size, technological expertise and economic dynamism – local authorities should take the lead in city-wide consortiums for energy, building construction, reclamation and others.

Such moves often start from unresolved policy tensions where the scale of the problem

---

**Box 5.10**   *ECO-FEEDBACK*

An eco-feedback scheme was set up in Middlesbrough to enable consumers to see directly the costs of their energy use. This was combined with free house surveys, information on efficiency and eco-labelling for appliances.  Energy use was reduced by 15% during the 6 months trial period.

Source BT Environment City 1994

---

Box 5.9

## BUILT ENVIRONMENT SCENARIO

Summary of sustainable development scenario for urbanization and land-use in GM to 2020.

| | unit | 1995 Total | BAU 2020 Total | SD 2020 Total | SD shares / rates | Cha- nge 95/SD |
|---|---|---|---|---|---|---|
| **URBANIZATION** | | | | | | |
| TOTAL AREA of GM | Km² | 1280 | 1280 | 1280 | | |
| TOTAL URBAN LAND | | 550 | 578 | 564 | 44% | 2% |
| direct urbanization / rate p.a. | Km²/y | | 28 | 14 | 0.1%pa | |
| indirect urbanization / rate p.a. | Km²/y | | 55 | 28 | 0.2% pa | |
| TOTAL direct/indirect urban | | 550 | 633 | 591 | 46% | 8% |
| TOTAL indirect/direct rural | | 730 | 648 | 689 | | -6% |
| **LAND INTENSITY** | | | | | | |
| Services area / services GDP | m²/£ | 3.35 | 2.2 | 2.17 | | -35% |
| Industrial area / industry GDP | m²/£ | 4.25 | 3.5 | 3.34 | | -21% |
| Transport land / pass.travel | m²/km·y | 3.82 | 2.7 | 2.75 | | -28% |
| **HOUSING** | | | | | | |
| Household av.size | p/hh | 2.50 | 2.13 | 2.13 | | -15% |
| Household number | Million | 1.03 | 1.27 | 1.27 | | 24% |
| Dwelling stock / replace.rate | Million | 1.03 | 0.98 | 0.93 | 73% | -10% |
| no & pop.in new dwellings | Million | 0 | 0.29 | 0.35 | 27% | |
| Exg residential area & density | Km² | 308 | 293 | 277 | 71p/ha | -10% |
| New residential area & density | | | 71 | 61 | 120p/ha | |
| TOTAL HOUSING LAND | | 308 | 363.5 | 338 | | 10% |
| **URBAN LAND** | | | | | | |
| Housing | Km² | 308 | 363.6 | 338 | 60% | 10% |
| Services | | 44 | 51.7 | 50 | 9% | 14% |
| Industry | | 28 | 32.7 | 33 | 6% | 20% |
| Transport & infra. | | 72 | 75.7 | 61 | 11% | -15% |
| Open space | | 55 | 43.0 | 70 | 12% | 27% |
| Vacant | | 44 | 12.0 | 12 | 2% | -73% |
| TOTAL URBAN LAND | | 550 | 578.7 | 564 | | 3% |
| **DERELICT LAND** | | | | | | |
| New dereliction area & rate | Km² | 25 | 25.0 | 19.2 | 2.4%pa | -23% |
| Reclaimed area & rate | | 27 | 27.0 | 40.0 | 5.0%pa | 48% |
| TOTAL DERELICT LAND | | 32 | 30.0 | 11.2 | | -65% |
| **RURAL LAND** | | | | | | |
| Agriculture | Km² | 430 | 407.0 | 407.0 | 56% | -5% |
| Woodland & forestry | | 23 | 48.0 | 90.0 | 12% | 291% |
| Leisure & recreation | | 72 | 81.0 | 90.0 | 12% | 25% |
| Wildlife habitat (designated) | | 15 | 30.0 | 39.0 | 5% | 160% |
| Mineral/landfill | | 7 | 1.0 | 3.0 | 0% | -57% |
| Other & vacant | | 186 | 142.0 | 94.0 | 13% | -49% |
| TOTAL RURAL LAND | | 733 | 709.0 | 723.0 | 0% | -1% |

Source: ISCAM scenario accounts for GM, with sources as in text.
'BAU' = business as usual projection: 'SD' = sustainable development scenario
'SHARES' shows percentage proportions of SD total: 'RATE' shows annual growth rate for SD total: 'CHANGE' shows percentage growth from 1995 – SD 2020 scenario.

exceeds the means to deal with it – as seen in housing, transport, regeneration and many others. The greatest challenge in such cases is at the institutional level, where new kinds of networks and institutional partnerships are needed for joined-up action.

## Government

All this of course depends on a national framework for markets, regulation, local resources, and coordination with sectors such as transport and energy. The UK government is raising many of the right questions, but it will take more to shift the inertia of the property markets, construction industries, and consumers themselves.[100] The lack of progress on the Home Energy Conservation Act, for instance, shows not a failing of individual local authorities, but the need for 'joined-up' institutions to bridge the gaps between suppliers and consumers.[101]

Key government actions for the 2020 built environment strategy include: resolving of liability for contaminated land, a system for return of betterment, and reversing hidden subsidies from greenfield to brownfield sites. For housing, a market and finance package is needed to support energy efficiency, flexible housing tenures, higher density mixed uses, and energy- environment best practice. For commercial property, the business rating system should encourage urban redevelopment, local services and efficiency investment.

Such moves should then filter through the fiscal system – VAT on energy conservation, for instance, is several times that on consumption, and this anomaly should be reversed immediately.[102] The regulated market framework between energy providers, investors and consumers should encourage efficiency investment. Finally to put all this into motion requires powers and resources for local authorities, including borrowing and lending, to enable them to lead consortiums and partnerships.

## Business, developers, property

Business and industry have a key role through investment and location decisions, and by setting standards for construction and energy efficiency, both inhouse and through purchasing and contracting chains. Most businesses can save a tenth of their energy simply by good management, and double that by profitable investment. While larger businesses are often better equipped with environmental expertise, SMEs need packages for expertise and investment. In many cases the investment chain comes back to the banks and institutions, and national action is needed to encourage responsible choices by local financiers and businesses.

100 DETR 1998 (Sustainable Construction)
101 Local Government Chronicle
102 Association for the Conservation of Energy 1996

Fig 5.18

## BUILT ENVIRONMENT STRATEGY

Outline of integrated city-region 2020 development strategy

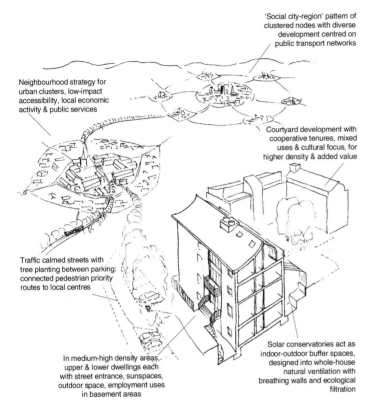

'Social city-region' pattern of clustered nodes with diverse development centred on public transport networks

Neighbourhood strategy for urban clusters, low-impact accessibility, local economic activity & public services

Courtyard development with cooperative tenures, mixed uses & cultural focus, for higher density & added value

Traffic calmed streets with tree planting between parking: connected pedestrian priority routes to local centres

In medium-high density areas, upper & lower dwellings each with street entrance, sunspaces, outdoor space, employment uses in basement areas

Solar conservatories act as indoor-outdoor buffer spaces, designed into whole-house natural ventilation with breathing walls and ecological filtration

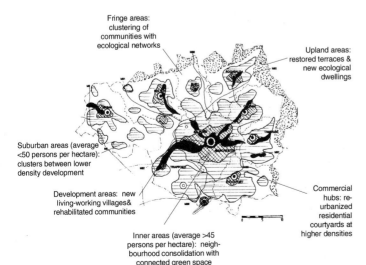

Fringe areas: clustering of communities with ecological networks

Upland areas: restored terraces & new ecological dwellings

Suburban areas (average <50 persons per hectare): clusters between lower density development

Development areas: new living-working villages & rehabilitated communities

Commercial hubs: re-urbanized residential courtyards at higher densities

Inner areas (average >45 persons per hectare): neighbourhood consolidation with connected green space

Coordination of many overlapping activities demands new techniques for the many professions involved, and a realization of mutual benefit through collaboration. Property agents will see rising values by extending their scope to the joined-up urban agenda. Planners and designers need to consider energy, ecology, community development and others. Developers and builders can add value by addressing the 'upstream' context of urban issues, and the 'downstream' use and re-use of buildings.

## Consumers & public

Lifestyle and cultural shifts can easily alter the apparently iron rule of the market, in housing, services and resources – people will tend to save energy when they have the motivation and tools to save it, and cooperate in the use of urban space, given the opportunity and the means to do so. Effective awareness-raising involves much more than typical advertising campaigns, or even LA21 programmes – employers, retailers, health, education and many others need to work in partnership to enable consumers and communities to make responsible lifestyle choices *(Box 5.10)*.

## Putting it together

The spatial 'dynamics' of urban development are the framework for fitting together all these strategies, policies and programmes on the ground *(Chapter 3)*. For each of the main settlement types the dynamics of development and policy menus in each area include: *(Fig 5.18)*:

- *city centres*: consolidation, innovation, human scale liveable public realm, transport and accessibility management, adaptable building stock
- *development & industrial areas*: reclamation, large scale urban villages, safeguard existing industry, accessibility planning for development, new leisure and cultural uses, ecological networks
- *inner city areas:* consolidation of neighbourhood structure, clustering of housing and services around public transport, traffic calming and pedestrian routes, new ecological networks, upgrading all housing and infrastructure
- *suburban areas:* neighbourhood restructuring, clustering of housing and services, traffic calming and planting, housing life-cycle maintenance
- *urban fringe areas:* upgrading older housing, zero-energy new housing, clustering of housing and services, diversification in low-impact land-uses

## GM in context

GM is fairly typical of older northern post-industrial cities, with an average population dispersal of 0.5% per year. In contrast, in southern and eastern Europe, many cities have doubled in size in two decades, and some developing cities have growth rates of 5%, putting enormous pressure on infrastructure, local economies and the management of urban growth:

- urban densities in most EU cities are higher, and in the east and south several times higher, than in the looser urban form of GM;
- residential density, or living space per person, varies from twice the UK averages in affluent Norway and Switzerland, to half in eastern and southern countries;
- average household sizes are smaller than GM only in affluent cities, and generally larger in rural areas, and sizes of double the UK averages are common in the developing world;

- housing conditions and services vary enormously between urban and rural areas – while safe water and sanitation are now taken for granted in the urbanized UK, there are many developing cities with less than half the population on mains services;
- energy efficiency can be assessed with the ratio of domestic energy consumption to average floorspace. Some northern countries have double UK efficiency levels, despite harsher climates; eastern countries have larger consumption with smaller areas, while southern countries use more power in cooling.

The upshot is that GM is not untypical of northern EU post-industrial cities, but its growth dynamics, and spatial structure contrast with those of eastern and southern cities. Sustainable development strategies for the built environment will be unique to each city, but the general principles apply throughout – spatial consolidation, integrated supply-demand provision, integrated efficiency investment, and partnership structures for political and economic integration.

---

**Box 5.11**

### *SUMMARY ~ BUILT ENVIRONMENT*

The 2020 development strategy aims to restructure and consolidate the physical and spatial form of the city-region and its building stock, to encourage local economies, cohesive communities, and diverse lifestyles:

- neighbourhood strategy which clusters and revitalizes local centres, jobs and services
- housing development to provide over 20% new dwellings in all sizes and tenures
- property development to promote local centres, mixed uses, travel management
- vacant and derelict land re-used as short or long term resource in urban restructuring
- every new building to be built and operated to energy-environment best practice standard, to reduce $CO_2$ emissions by 40%
- every existing building to be upgraded to best practice via city-wide regeneration
- all buildings to be monitored regularly and environmental health hazards greatly reduced

# TRAVEL & TRANSPORT

*'The car is the carapace, the shell and the armour of modern suburban man'*
Marshall McLuhan

Mobility is the basis for modern lifestyles, and transport is the 'maker or breaker' of cities. But the transport system is also breaking local and global limits, and future trends are set to bring the system itself to a halt. While access and opportunity are basic rights in modern society, the long-standing link between economic growth and transport growth has somehow to be 'decoupled'.

Most people now agree on this – but would prefer to see others' travel restricted before their own. The 'predict and provide' philosophy is over in the UK, at least in principle, and there is a new generation of local transport plans and partnerships seeking an 'integrated' transport system. But will this be enough to contain the inexorable demand and desire for mobility?

We cannot provide all the answers here to a problem which is bound to run and run. The ideals of an integrated and sustainable transport system are now quoted everywhere, but the practice seems ever further out of reach. So we take here a lateral view of the total metabolism of the transport system – far beyond the question of getting from 'a to b', and more about the connectivity and complexity of places, people, organizations and networks. To tackle this needs a step change beyond current thinking.

First we look at transport demand and supply in the light of wider environmental issues, and the social aspects of urban accessibility. Then for car traffic, diversification of access and coordination with travel management is likely to be more effective and acceptable than restriction. For public transport, integration between modes and networks is the key. Freight, logistics and business travel have to be linked to economic development strategies. For air travel, the massive growth in traffic has to be networked across the region and contained within a global climate strategy.

## Problems & prospects

A typical morning on the orbital motorway around GM is a kind of technological Armageddon – articulated lorries nose to tail, vehicle flows of 10,000 per hour, with frequent gridlocks dominated by mobile phone chatter. Not far away are large areas of the city with surprisingly few cars or buses. With an average weekly travel of 200 km per person in 18 trips, 83% is by car, 13% by public transport and 2% by bicycle.[1]  Buses and

---

1 All local statistics from GM Transport Unit 1996, GMPTA 1994, AGMA 1997 (walking not included in local travel data)

trains have reduced their total mileage by a third since deregulation, but the 'Metrolink' light rapid transit (LRT) now carries 35,000 passengers a day. Peak hour speeds have reduced by a third in a decade, and severe congestion has spread from radial to inner and outer orbital routes.

The impacts of transport are a familiar litany – the fastest growing source of climate emissions, and the largest cause of urban air pollution, with the oil and auto industries causing half of global ecological damage.[2] The 'external' environmental costs of transport amount to several times the direct costs, and congestion in GM could cost £1bn per year *(Chapter 13)*.[3] Social impacts concern especially the 60% of people who are not car owners, even while 83% of all miles travelled are by car. Half of urban residents are seriously affected by noise; 1 in 160 people are killed, and 1 in 15,000 are injured on the roads in GM every year.

If current trends continued, total urban traffic could increase by 40% over the next 25 years, with many bottlenecks coming to a complete halt.[4] One million cars in GM already take a parking area equivalent to all vacant land, as more female, younger, older and poorer people continue to acquire them. Information and communications technologies (ICT) are crucial to future travel patterns – their effect might reduce routine urban journeys more suited to public transport, while increasing irregular and longer-distance journeys, which are more suited to cars and air travel.[5] On the supply side, ICT has huge potential to improve the capacity and safety of roads, and the flexibility and performance of public transport.

## Future prospects

Alternative future scenarios for travel and transport show clearly the tension between social, economic and environmental goals:[6]

- **BAU scenario:**  increasing congestion and use of cars as all round work / leisure centres whether mobile or stationary: deregulation

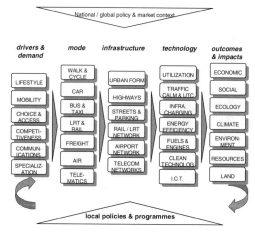

**Fig 6.1    TRANSPORT METABOLISM**

Total metabolism system mapping for travel and transport.

and decline of public transport, and further expansion of air travel on offshore airports;
- **technology scenario:** ICT helps traffic management and journey planning, clean vehicles help energy efficiency and emissions reductions, but travel volumes and distances continue to increase;
- **SD scenario:** current traffic growth is contained and diverted to low-impact modes, with a combination of lifestyle shift, travel coordination, technological development and re-organization of urban form;
- **deep green scenario:** major travel reductions as people rediscover local lifestyles and work patterns, combined with zero-emissions fuels in recyclable vehicles.

## Transport metabolism

'Sustainability' for the transport system involves a balance of its many roles and linkages. Physical, economic and social factors can be seen in an 'integrated assessment' mapping of the total system, showing the many linkages between human needs, culture and lifestyle, travel demand, infrastructure, transport mode and technology, impacts and outcomes *(Fig 6.1)*. Improving the balance of needs and outcomes,

2 Freund & Martin 1994
3 est. from Confederation of British Industry 1994
4 DETR 1999 (National Road Traffic Forecasts)
5 Graham & Marvin 1996
6 Institute of Transport Studies 1998: Engineering Council 1997

or problems and opportunities, involves actions at each stage.

For the GM economy, for instance, there are several million people within an hour's travel time by road, and half of the UK's industry within two hours, with ever-widening choice and specialization available to businesses and consumers. Economic competitiveness appears to hinge on such specialization, and the growth trend in transport closely reflects the 2–2.5% rate of long term economic growth.[6] An economic view also looks at the uncosted 'externalities' of transport impacts, and seek to internalize these for the optimum total costs and benefits *(Chapter 13)*.

The social role of transport focuses on the need for choice and accessibility, and common syndromes such as inaccessibility and inequity. Much recent car traffic growth has been taken by female, younger, older and poorer people who previously travelled little, but there is still high latent demand for car ownership as the key to choice and opportunity. For most households car ownership is a major threshold – once the investment is made, every mile travelled then becomes cheaper, locking in the household to the technology.

On the physical level, transport systems have shaped the interaction of people and places long before mass car travel – the first wave of suburbs were enabled by railways and trams in most industrial cities. The property and development industries rely implicitly on transport growth for competitiveness and the added value of location. Technical innovation tends to increase speed and accessible distance, travel demand tends to expand to certain time thresholds, and the viability of land-uses follows accordingly.[7] This suggests that demand will tend to exceed supply, until a balance is reached by shifts or constraints on either side:

- increases in supply – environmental damage;
- physical congestion – economically inefficient;
- direct regulation – politically unpopular;
- direct charges – socially regressive.

The question of transport mode hinges on the 'great divide' between private and public. Environmental arguments often ignore the social and cultural roles of cars – as symbols of status, identity and erotic power, and as providers of mobile living rooms, offices and store-rooms.[8] These multiple roles enable and encourage new patterns – not only in journeys, but networked lifestyles, involving cross-country, flexible, unscheduled, continuous mobility. Such patterns have enabled new land-uses and activities, with the result that public transport would now be unsuited and inefficient for the majority of journeys even if it was available. The result is that 'taming the car' is not only about transport, but the restructuring of society and economy.

## Towards sustainable transport

A 'sustainable' transport strategy aims to balance the many economic, environmental and social roles and linkages above – not so much in a fixed blueprint, but a continuous adaptation to problems and opportunities.

The first and now conventional theme is integration – enabling all parts of the system to work together efficiently and equitably. The total system should reduce travel demands where possible, provide for essential car needs, and shift the bulk of travel towards lower impact modes. Achieving this hinges on the second theme – diversification – of ownerships, access to infrastructure, modes and technologies, journey types and travel patterns. And in practice the multiple goals of 'sustainable' transport are totally dependent on parallel strategies in planning, housing, public services and so on – the third theme of 'coordination' of transport with economy and society.

The UK national strategy is a bold statement of principle, if not (yet) of action.[9] This strategy also stresses integration, but has some way to go in the themes of diversification and coordination, to break the stalemate of the familiar policy menu.[10] Following through the logic of these theme generates some topical goals and targets, as in passenger transport:

6 Standing Committee on Assessment of Trunk Roads 1999
7 Webster, Bly & Paulley 1988
8 Freund & Martin 1993
9 DETR 1998 (A New Deal for Transport)
10 Owens 1998

- private transport: widen car access to reduce ownership incentives; contain traffic within local capacity; diversify and widen access to road space.
- public transport: fully integrated, responsive and flexible networks for door-to-door travel, with diverse modes, improved facilities, and easier transfer to and from private transport.
- integrated travel management: universal business and site travel plans, car pools, load and trip sharing, responsive minibuses, green commuter schemes, multi-modal park and ride.

For freight, integrated networks and coordinated routing should reduce impacts. For air and international travel, airports should develop their roles as integrated multi-modal hubs. The whole transport sector should be an integral part of the 2020 energy-climate strategy *(Chapter 9)*. These goals and strategies are outlined in Box 6.2 which also shows the main actors and agencies which might be responsible.

Core indicators for conditions, trends and targets of a 2020 transport strategy are shown below; these focus only on the tangible, leaving aside more complex social or environmental issues. Each indicator is shown with a 'trend-target' index for the gap between current trends and selected targets, drawn from the transport-environment SD scenario in the next section *(Box 6.1)*. Following on are the goals and strategies which aim at a practical balance between social, economic and environmental agendas *(Box 6.2)*. Again, the aim is a rounded view of the problems and opportunities for the key 'factors, sectors and actors', not only in transport, but the physical connectivity of economy and society.

---

**Box 6.1**

### TRAVEL & TRANSPORT ~ TRENDS & TARGETS

| | | 1995 | BAU 2020 | SD 2020 | Trend target index |
|---|---|---|---|---|---|
| | | | | | % |
| pass.travel.economic.int | km/y/£GDP | 2460 | 2214 | 1722 | 30 |
| freight-economy intensity | t.km/y/£ | 0.42 | 0.46 | 0.28 | -30 |
| cycle/walk>1km | Mkm/y | 695 | 1133 | 2204 | 30 |
| total surface pass.travel | Mkm/y | 18739 | 28334 | 22037 | 30 |
| total air pass.travel | Mkm/y | 10549 | 31648 | 21099 | 50 |
| total freight traffic | Mt.km/y | 8210 | 15172 | 9241 | 10 |
| total final energy demand | PJ/y | 82.7 | 154.3 | 67.9 | -100 |
| total $CO_2$ | $MtCO_2$/y | 7.1 | 13.0 | 5.9 | -100 |
| av.pers.trav.car/noncar | ratio | 3.0 | 5.0 | 2.0 | -100 |
| % children asthma | % | 15% | 30% | 3% | -100 |
| total transport fatalities | no | 146 | 91 | 15 | 40 |

Summary 'core indicators' with trends & targets from ISCAM scenario accounts for GM 1995-2020.
BAU = business as usual projection from trend
SD = sustainable development scenario

---

**Box 6.2**

### TRAVEL & TRANSPORT ~ GOALS & STRATEGIES

| | G O V | L A P | B U S | C O M | P U B |
|---|---|---|---|---|---|
| **ENVIRONMENT:** Growth in total passenger & freight travel stabilized at 20% over 1995 levels: $CO_2$ reduce by 20%: air emissions reduce by 50-90%: promote clean vehicle fleets; protect local env capacities | ● | ○ | ○ | | |
| **ACCESSIBILITY:** site location by accessibility profile: city-wide pedestrian routes, traffic calming & cycle networks | ○ | ● | ○ | ○ | ○ |
| **HIGHWAYS & TRAFFIC:** shift 25% of urban car travel to other modes: UTC & parking for demand management: expand car access via trip sharing, public / employer car pools & demand responsive networks | ● | ● | ● | ○ | ○ |
| **PUBLIC TRANSPORT:** Triple public trans. to 30% of urban travel, with integrated networks & services for responsive & flexible door-to-door service | ● | ● | ○ | ○ | ○ |
| **FREIGHT TRANSPORT:** freight & commercial traffic growth stabilized at 20% above 1995 levels: 20% inter-urban freight transferred to rail / water: city-wide light distribution systems. | ● | ○ | ● | | |
| **AIR TRAVEL:** growth stabilized at 250-300% current levels via demand management & fuel duty: future airport as integrated regional hub. | ● | ● | ○ | | |

GOV ~ government & EU: LA ~ local authorities & partnerships:
BUS ~ business & finance: COM ~ community & 3rd sector: PUB ~ public

# TRANSPORT & ENVIRONMENT

The impact of travel all depends on how it is done – the energy consumption of different modes per passenger mile varies by a factor of 20, from that of a large petrol cars to a fully laden bus. However if the 'performance' factors of space, speed, and flexibility are taken into account, the efficiency and cost-effectiveness of cars are relatively high *(Fig 6.2)*.[11] So the problem is not only one of travel 'from a to b' – it is the standards to which we have become accustomed.[12] Raising occupancy rates is one key to energy efficiency, for both cars and public transport, and multi-occupant schemes are on trial around the UK. However, the net gains may be marginal, and if public transport networks are extended closer to homes and jobs, occupancies and efficiencies could be lowered.

There is also huge scope for increased efficiency in cars – a 40% improvement is quite viable with current technology, and 'hypercars' are now operating at over 300 mpg.[13] A European 'voluntary agreement' sets out targets for a 30% improvement in new vehicles by 2010, but this conflicts with strong lobbying from the oil industry. Since the oil crisis of the 1970s, fuel/power ratios in the average vehicle have doubled, but such gains are outweighed by increased performance, power and travel demand.

## Clean technology

Transport is the main source of urban air pollution, and as well as gross emissions there are now hazards such as catalytic converters, tyre dust and petrol vapours *(Chapter 8)*. The EU 'Auto-Oil' project aims to improve engines and fuels over the next decade to cut emissions per mile by 20–50%. While these targets are a great advance, local and regional traffic and travel management is needed in parallel, if the UK 'air quality management strategies' are to succeed.[14]

Many alternative technologies are on trial without a clear winner as yet – some EU cities are experimenting with electric vehicles or 'city-bugs', but until the power itself comes mainly from renewable sources, city-bugs have only local benefits. Gas engines are cleaner and produce 20% less carbon, and some UK cities have started to convert their fleets to gas, although small releases of methane could be a problem. Renewable fuels such as ethanol and rapeseed oil each produce emissions and odours, and the most promising technology could be a complete hybrid of petrol, electric and hydrogen fuel-cells. The projected effects of different technologies and policies can be seen on climate emissions *(Fig 6.3)*.[15]

The main efficiency incentive in the UK at present is the 'escalator' of 6% increase in fuel duty per year, and there is a case for doubling this with a graduated purchase tax linked to eco-labelling.[16] Although the auto industry is fully multi-national, clean technology can be encouraged at the city-region level via natural gas for commercial fleets, and electric city-bugs for personal travel *(Box 6.3)*. To achieve this

**Fig 6.2** *PERFORMANCE EFFICIENCY:*

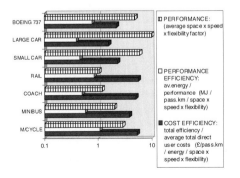

Aggregated indices on aggregated scale for performance factors including energy, space, speed, flexibility, direct cost.
Source: Ravetz 1996b: Freund & Martin 1994

11 Ravetz & SCR Group 1996c
12 Whitelegg 1993
13 von Weizsacker & Lovins 1997

14 Quality of Urban Air Review Group 1993: ENDS Vol 256/22
15 Hughes 1994
16 RCEP 1994

**Fig 6.3**

## ROADS POLICY OPTIONS

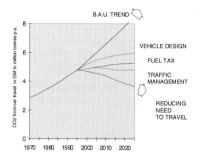

Effects estimated for national & local policy measures on total CO2 emissions from car travel in GM, shown cumulatively.
Source: Hughes 1994

**Fig 6.4**

## INTEGRATED TRANSPORT SCENARIO

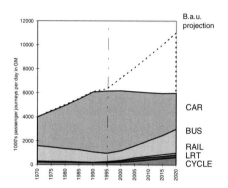

Historic trends & projected targets for GM urban area to 2020:
Source: based on ISCAM scenario accounts with data from GMPTE 1994

**Box 6.3**

### TRANSPORT-ENVIRONMENT SCENARIO ACCOUNT

| | unit | 1995 Total | BAU 2020 Total | SD 2020 Total | SD shares / rates | Change 95/SD |
|---|---|---|---|---|---|---|
| **INTENSITY** | | | | | | |
| pass.travel intensity | km/y/£GDP | 2460 | 2214 | 1722 | | -30% |
| freight economic intensity | Mt.km/y/£GD | 0.42 | 0.46 | 0.28 | | -33% |
| **PRIVATE** | | | | | | |
| car/mcl | $10^6$ km/y | 15695 | 21817 | 6611 | 30% | -58% |
| electric/other | | 0 | 1983 | 5509 | 25% | # |
| cycle/walk>1km | | 695 | 1133 | 2204 | 10% | 217% |
| bus/taxi | | 1312 | 1700 | 2204 | 10% | 68% |
| gas/other bus | | 0 | 283 | 2644 | 12% | # |
| LRT | | 111 | 567 | 1102 | 5% | 896% |
| train local/national | | 926 | 850 | 1763 | 8% | 90% |
| TOTAL SURFACE | $10^6$ km/y | 18739 | 28334 | 22037 | 100% | 18% |
| total pass.trans.energy | PJ/y | 41.4 | 61.3 | 23.9 | | -42% |
| | | | | | | |
| **AIR** | | | | | | |
| total pass.air travel | $10^6$ km/y | 10549 | 31648 | 21099 | | 100% |
| total final energy | PJ/y | 22.2 | 53.8 | 26.4 | | 19% |
| Surface travel generated | $10^6$ km/y | 520 | 1560 | 1040 | | 200% |
| | | | | | | |
| **FREIGHT** | | | | | | |
| Air | Mt.km | 160 | 910 | 370 | 4% | 131% |
| diesel lorry | | 6250 | 7586 | 1848 | 20% | -70% |
| gas/other lorry | | 0 | 3793 | 3696 | 40% | # |
| Rail | | 1400 | 1972 | 2772 | 30% | 98% |
| water/pipeline | | 400 | 759 | 554 | 6% | 39% |
| TOTAL FREIGHT | Mt.km | 8210 | 15172 | 9241 | 100% | 13% |
| total final energy | GJ | 19.2 | 39.2 | 17.6 | | -8% |
| | | | | | | |
| **FINAL ENERGY** | | | | | | |
| Electric/other | PJ/y | 1.2 | 5.5 | 11.2 | 17% | 818% |
| Gas | | 0.0 | 7.8 | 8.8 | 13% | # |
| Oil | | 81.5 | 141.1 | 47.9 | 70% | -41% |
| TOTAL DEMAND | PJ/y | 82.7 | 154.3 | 67.9 | 100% | -18% |
| | | | | | | |
| **CARBON** | | | | | | |
| total $CO_2$ from transport incl power | MtCO₂ | 7.1 | 13.0 | 5.9 | | -16% |

Summary of sustainable development scenario for 2020 transport-environment strategy in GM.
'BAU' = business as usual projection: 'SD' = sustainable development scenario
'SHARES' shows percentage proportions of SD total: 'RATE' shows annual growth rate for SD total: 'CHANGE' shows growth from 1995 – SD 2020 scenario.

would need a full policy menu – infrastructure for fuelling and servicing, petrol-free zones, graduated parking charges, mileage allowances, employer subsidies and tax breaks, purchasing and contracting schemes, and subsidized clean car clubs.[17]

## Environment–transport scenario

Putting together plausible assumptions on technology, markets, politics and lifestyles, and comparing with current trends, we can sketch the outline of an integrated transport-environment scenario for GM *(Fig 6.4 and Box 6.3)*. This leaves some room for growth from current travel levels, in the light of current trends, rising disposable income, and levelling up across the population. The passenger scenario anticipates 30% reductions in the 'travel economic intensity' indicator (passenger km/person/£GDP) – so while GDP increases by 2.25% per year, total travel increases at less than half that rate.

The scenario envisages a stabilization of the growth in car traffic – reduced in the inner urban area, with small growth on the periph-ery – and half of this shifted to gas or electric vehicles. Buses see their total mileage tri-

---

17 Bain & Pettitt: Environmental Transport Association 1994

pled, and half the fleet converted to natural gas. LRT travel is increased tenfold, covering all radial corridors in the city-region, while local rail is tripled up to network capacity. While there is an 18% growth in total passenger mileage, its energy and emissions show a 30% reduction from 1995 levels.

For air travel the scenario follows the current airport expansion programme, and then stabilizes by 2020 at 2.5 times current levels, or a throughput of 40 million per year. Assuming a 40% efficiency and utilization improvement, the result would be energy and emissions growth of 25%. For freight, the key indicator of 'freight economic intensity' (tonne-km/£GDP) is assumed to reduce by 30%, rather than stay level in the BAU scenario, leaving room for freight travel growth of 13%. Most of this shifts to gas-powered or other clean vehicles, with a doubling of rail freight and 40% increase in water and pipeline movement. The overall result of the strategy would be a 14% reduction in energy demand from 1995 to 2020, and a 20% reduction in $CO_2$ emissions, which is in line with the 2020 energy-climate strategy.

Such an outline summary shows the broad trends in quantities of journeys, energy and so on – but what it cannot show is the diversification of travel types, purposes, access to opportunities and other features as below.

---

**Box 6.4  CLEAN VEHICLE PROJECT**

The European-funded 'Zero Emission Vehicles for Urban Society' project operates a consortium for volume buying of gas, electric, ethanol and rape-seed powered vehicles, together with fuelling systems and maintenance support. Local authorities with large vehicle fleets are the first buyers for an initial target of 1000 vehicles, and will develop a public infrastructure from there.

Source: Lusser 1996

---

# ACCESSIBILITY

While transport engineering tends to focus on 'mobility', the real issue is arguably that of 'accessibility' – an urban form and activity-pattern which enables access to homes, jobs and services with the greatest social equity, the least travel and lowest impact modes.

For this, the first question is why and how do people travel? The statistics tell us that leisure and business trips are longer than average, others are shorter: leisure and 'personal' journeys account for over half of all mileage travelled, and are the fastest growing journey types *(Fig 6.5-6.6)*. Businesses and services are increasingly specialized, and family and social networks extended – for a city-region such as GM there is a business and social catchment of several million within one hour's drive time.

Some facilities, if not all, can be de-centralized and brought closer to their users, the goal of the current mantra – 'planning to reduce the need to travel'. Analysis shows that over several decades such a policy might reduce local travel demand by perhaps 15%, assuming a rapid growth in walking and cycling.[18] It also assumes a de-centralization of businesses and public services, against the trend of specialization and rationalization. It also involves clustering of development around transport nodes and local centres, in a long term urban form strategy *(Chapter 5).*[19]

To steer land-uses and activities towards a transit-oriented pattern, physical development needs to be related to its 'accessibility profile'. In principle this is simply good planning practice, but in a large urban area many sites are in a free-for-all which assumes that the whole area is equally suitable for high traffic volumes. One method is to map accessibility in terms of

18 ECOTEC 1993
19 Calthorpe 1993

Fig 6.5          **TRAVEL PURPOSES**                Fig 6.6          **TRAVEL TYPES & MODES**

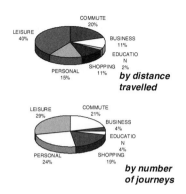

*by distance travelled*

*by number of journeys*

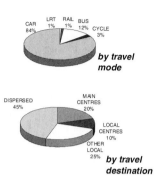

*by travel mode*

*by travel destination*

By no. of journeys in GM & interpolated for NW region: walking not included.
Source: GMPTE 1995 & AGMA 1996.

Data for GM & interpolated from NW region: walking not included.
Source: GMPTE 1995 , AGMA 1996 & CSO 1995

proximity to different networks.[20] Another approach is the Dutch 'ABC' system which aims to match land-uses with transport provision, so that large trip generators are located close to nodes of high public transport availability.[21] But in the sprawling mix of GM there are very few nodes which meet the 'A' standards, and major public transport nodes tend also to be surrounded by major roads. This suggests that public transport strategy should work more closely with long term accessibility planning, a task made more complex by deregulation.

## Walking & cycling

At a thousand times the fuel–distance ratio of an average car, cycling is the ultimate in transport eco-efficiency – the government wants to expand cycling to 12% of journeys, and cycle

networks feature strongly in local transport plans.[22] But the reality is a long way behind – cycle lanes are blocked, junctions are hazardous, drivers are aggressive, and the English winter puts off all but the hardy. For cycling strategy we have to look to European cities, where cycle lanes are totally integrated in the streetscape, with 'micro-mopeds' for the less fit, and many neighbourhoods are extended 'home zones'.[23] A wheel and spoke network is planned for the river valleys and green corridors of GM, and this needs filling in with a finer grain to link all local centres with dedicated cycle lanes and junctions. Half the roads in the city-region could be re-engineered for full cycling capability over 20 years at about 20km per district per year, at a modest rate of investment.

Walking depends on the quality and safety of the environment – 'acceptable' distances vary from 200m in typical urban conditions, to 1000m on green and traffic-calmed routes.[24] On some corridors in GM, up to 35% of all trips are by walking or cycling, but the quality and safety of such travel are low – even now, road junctions are being 'improved', with large radii, higher speeds, and complex barriers, to the detriment of pedestrians.

Pedestrian-friendly design is proven and simply needs wider application *(Box 6.5).* For residential areas, traffic calming should be stand-

Box 6.5      **ACCESSIBLE CITIES**

- Hammersmith has pioneered 'accessibility mapping' for proximity to public transport
- Groningen in the Netherlands makes over half of its work trips by bicycle
- The centres of most German cities and towns are pedestrianized
- Oldham has led the way in GM for traffic calming of residential areas

20 DETR 1998 (Sustainable Urban Development)
21 DoE 1996 #

22 Dept of Transport 1996 (National cycling strategy)
23 Hass-Klau 1996
24 Knoflacher 1995

ard, with the benefits in property values alone recouping the investment, and all local centres should link to their catchments with dedicated routes. Every junction and crossing point on every road should be re-engineered for a clear and direct pedestrian path with clear priorities, in a balance with the needs of vehicles. For commercial areas, pedestrian layers should combine timed access with physical space and parking, for the optimum balance of amenity, commercial benefit and security.

# ROADS & TRAFFIC

The car offers a Faustian bargain – apparently endless mobility, at the price of one city – and as the majority transport mode, the future of the city depends on it. The UK 'New Deal' for integrated transport begs many questions, and has hardly attempted to shift the inertia of 'car culture' – where the response of almost every section of society to transport problems is to increase its use of cars.[25] Bypassing such a stalemate needs integrated thinking on the total system – including travel demand, the highway network, parking, and car ownership. And as transport 'problems' are in many ways the result of social 'opportunities' – access and choice for the female, old, young or poor – any strategy has to start from that point.

Motorway traffic has increased in GM by 70% over the last decade, and some links carry over 150,000 vehicles per day (vpd), or twice their design capacity *(Fig 6.7)*.[26] Urban peak speeds reduce by 3% per year while the rush hour lengthens, and the urban air is often 'poor'. Congestion patterns show peaks and troughs, and the worst has shifted from radial to orbital routes.

'Local environmental capacity' is a guiding principle for traffic management within appropriate limits, particularly for the worst effects of pollution and disturbance in local centres and residential areas on major roads. Applying local capacity limits to traffic levels would aim to reduce flows on many roads from over 20,000 to under 10,000 vpd. Speeds should be within the 20–30 mph range for optimum levels of emissions, use of road space, safety and congestion, as the general standard for all traffic in proximity to pedestrians.

## Network management

Applying such capacity limits relies on shifting much car traffic to other modes, targeting particular journey types for school, work, shopping and deliveries. Demand management for schools, for instance, is a big issue with parents, and will conflict with the goal of educational 'choice', but there is a clear need to re-invent the school bus, lift-sharing and safe routes to schools. Similar packages could work for workplaces, shopping, and local deliveries.

For the network itself, demand for roadspace is always likely to exceed capacity – and rather than unplanned congestion being the limiting factor, demand management by incentive and coordination may be a better option. Electronic Urban Traffic Control (UTC) systems are in place in cities such as GM, and could be extended to cover the wider network. Traffic management would spread peak flows and pressure points, and give real-time information on congestion and parking space. It would extend the differentiation of roadspace, with dedicated lanes and priorities for buses, low-impact or multi-occupant vehicles. It would also differentiate destinations, by routing main highways close but not through local centres, with loops for short stays and drop-offs. Local highways should be designed to inhibit rat-runs and less essential journeys, and traffic- calmed home zones would be standard in all residential areas.

On the economic side, electronic road pricing is seen as the best means of providing signals and feedback to road users. Such pricing could be by length of journey, by certain areas, or at certain times, or with certain congestion, and each

25 DETR 1998 (A new deal for transport)
26 GM Transportation Unit 1996

of these raises technical and political questions. The experiments in progress in the UK are mostly in freestanding cities, and different problems would apply in a larger diffused city-region such as GM. For the inner urban area, obvious places for cordon boundaries would be the orbital ring road and inner relief road when complete – but each of these would encourage businesses to relocate outside the boundary. The optimum solution could be a graduated distribution of charges for areas and links, which includes both peripheral and urban travel, as part of a total economic package covering ownership, licensing, fuels, access, and parking, with ICT as the medium of exchange.

Bypasses, junction and link improvements aim to relieve congestion, but generally increase capacity and speeds – displacing congestion rather than solving it. The completion of the relief route around the GM regional centre, for instance, may reduce through traffic by pedestrianization, but the overall effect is estimated at 20% extra vehicle movements. Such improvements should aim to minimize local congestion and pollution, while not increasing total network capacity – needing new cost-benefit assessment methods, and designing for optimum rather than maximum speeds.[27]

## Parking

Ironically, parking as the place of zero mobility is right at the centre of transport strategy – the essential link between people, highways, places, activities and property values. Parking policy is a perennial problem, but also an opportunity for strategic management. It also raises all the issues of social inequity, inefficiency, displacement and even white collar crime – for instance park-and-ride schemes may reduce urban congestion at the price of increased peripheral traffic.[28]

Parking is an obvious focus for economic measures, and the new national tax on workplace parking is a step in this direction, although the exclusion of retail parking can only encourage the outward migration of shopping and shoppers. City and town centre parking should be in edge-of-centre locations, with connections to

Fig 6.7                    **HIGHWAY TRENDS**

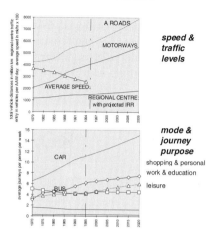

B.A.U. trends & projections as from DoT 'middle' scenario with GM data (upper) & UK data (lower):
Source GMTU 1994.

pedestrian routes and 'people movers', and linked to various pedestrian layers as above. Parking charges are also an opportunity for incentives on clean, small and multi-occupancy vehicles. Residential parking should be restricted in areas of high accessibility, and designed to fit within pedestrianized streets – the UK's first 'car-free' housing development is now being built in Edinburgh. At the conurbation level, a ring of park-and-ride sites with rail and LRT connections is proposed, and these should be more viable and effective as multi-modal development nodes.

## Widening car access

The divide between car and non-car owners is one of the greatest cleavages in modern society. For most travellers the demands of equality, status and convenience result in car purchase – and once that threshold is crossed, every mile travelled becomes cheaper, with a lock-in effect for ownership, and a lock-out effect for public transport. A lateral approach might seek to by-pass this effect by widening access to car use, in a flexible and journey-specific package.

The many roles of cars range from local to national, from work to leisure, and not least, for status and identity.[29] Different provisions should be made for each of these roles – larger cars used

27 SACTRA 1996
28 Goodwin 1994                         29 Freund & Martin 1994

Fig 6.8    **TRANSPORT ATTITUDES**        Fig 6.9    **INTEGRATED URBAN POLICIES**

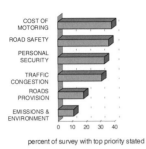

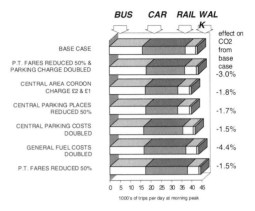

Top six transport concerns of British drivers: from AA / NOP survey 1996:
Source: AA Magazine 1997.

Estimated effect of alternative policies on morning peak flows into
regional centre: also showing effect on $CO_2$ emissions in relation to
base case.
Source: GMTU 1996.

irregularly should be available on a pool basis, with smaller or city-cars available on a network. One good incentive for car clubs is to provide access to more exotic models. Regular travel to work could be provided by coordinated minibus schemes, while business travel should be contained by a progressive taxation system, and substituted by video-conferencing where possible. Car sharing networks are now common in Europe, some of them supported by major manufacturers, and many are run on a neighbourhood non-profit basis*(Box 6.6)*.[30] Surveys of public attitudes to driving show that a direct environmental approach is likely to be less effective than direct incentives in cost and time, and car sharing schemes have to demonstrate such benefits *(Fig 6.8)*.[31]

## Integrated highway strategy

What makes transport policy particularly fascinating is that solving one problem invariably creates others – for instance, improved public transport could encourage outward migration, making it harder for city dwellers to access suburban employment markets.[32] So for real progress a high degree of policy integration is essential. Various options were tested in Manchester for public transport charges, parking spaces, and area charges around a 'cordon' *(Fig 6.9)*.[33] The optimum menu included reducing public trans-

port fares by 50%, and doubling parking charges, and the results included a 10% shift of car to bus traffic, and a 3% reduction in energy consumption – useful, but fairly marginal against the scale of the problem. The results of other modelling exercises are similar, each showing that the only policies which make serious inroads on congestion and emissions are those which are politically unthinkable.

Beyond current policy options, it is clear that the issues of car ownership, technology, infrastructure and parking have to be tackled as a total system. It is also clear that the great car-owning public, and those still aspiring, will not

---

Box 6.6

### EU CAR MANAGEMENT

- Most residential streets in the Netherlands are fully pedestrianized as 'woonerfs' with planting and playspace
- The 'Stattauto' car pool scheme in Berlin has 40 cars for 400 members who now find travel cheaper and easier.
- Earthworks and landscaping to shield residents from major traffic noise and pollution are standard
- Buses in London and Brighton, and council vehicles in Leeds, are running on natural gas
- The French town of La Rochelle has a fleet of electric cars for hire

---

30 Bain & Pettitt: Environment Transport Association 1994
31 AA Magazine 1997: Environmental Research & Information Centre 1997
32 Webster, Bly & Paulley 1989
33 Transport Research Laboratory 1995

easily be persuaded to make sacrifices. Any policy moves should be gradual and tapered, to enable adaptation by businesses and households who depend on the network, and avoid displacement of activity to elsewhere. Such a total system approach should cover both supply and demand sides for car use and the network:

- demand management via road or cordon pricing, priority lanes, preferential parking, organizational travel plans, demand-responsive services, load and trip sharing;

- vehicle modes shifted towards eco-efficient electric or gas 'city-cars', encouraged by priority parking and roadspace allocation;
- network management via differentiation and transfer of roadspace to low-impact modes, with UTC and other telematics systems;
- parking allocation and charging, with priority for shared or low-impact vehicles;
- widen access to car-based travel through demand-responsive minibuses, car and trip sharing, car pools and networks.

# PUBLIC TRANSPORT

Public transport is generally seen as the solution to urban mobility – but any major shift of car traffic to public transport would totally overload the network, and the travel patterns now enables by the car would be in any case less viable and efficient by public transport. Current trends in work and lifestyle suggest that the traditional 'Fordist' model of public transport as a mass transit provider from suburbs to workplaces, is in many ways outmoded. For public transport to compete with private, it will need to develop a more flexible, responsive and lifestyle-oriented service, with seamless, flexible, secure, door-to-door travel, by day or night, with personal baggage, minimum waiting, and 'smart' ticketing. The key theme is again that of integration, between modes, operators and destinations. Another is the theme of diversification of different modes and patterns of access, and a third is the theme of coordination with demand-side users. UK national policy is aiming in this direction, and the GM Passenger Transport Authority (PTA) is as advanced as any in the UK. But much more is needed for public transport to take a lead in a fully integrated system.

## Bus network

Buses are by far the largest public service, providing 700,000 journeys per day in GM, or 12%

of the total. If a quarter of urban car traffic was shifted to buses, bus capacity would need to triple, and this could overwhelm many streets and interchanges. On the ground the bus system is difficult to use and manage – the tangled GM network map is described as 'jelly', almost impossible to use as a route-finder, and the PTA now has to deal with over 50 private operators. And while the deregulation of 1986 resulted in fragmentation and decline, a return to public monopoly is not on the cards.[34]

Current policy rhetoric favours public transport, but is likely to fall short of its aims, in order not to challenge the status quo of car ownership.[35] Beyond current constraints, a more strategic 'quality' programme would start with a clear hierarchy of express, trunk, district, local and neighbourhood routes. Current schemes such as 'Busway Transit' should be extended to common fares, ticketing and information, between operators and other transport modes. Interchanges should be desirable hubs of activity, with shopping, security, on-line information, telephones, childcare, and business facilities. Every urban bus stop should be a local activity node, with cafes, stalls, taxis and other mixed uses which all add up to vitality and security, as in most European cities. Road space on major routes should be re-organized to allow for several lev-

---

34 GM PTE 1995
35 DETR 1998 (From workhorse to thoroughbred)

Fig 6.10 **PUBLIC TRANSPORT SCENARIO**

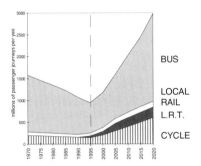

Historic trends & projected targets to 2020:
Source: based on ISCAM scenario accounts with data from GMPTE 1994

els of bus or LRT service, and segregated from major through traffic where possible *(Box 6.7)*. Finally, scheduled bus services should be one half of a larger network which provides a wide range of demand-responsive minibus and taxi services, to complete the 'one-stop' seamless and secure door-to-door service.

## Local rail & LRT

The local rail network provides about 70,000 journeys per day in GM or over 1% of total travel. After long term decline, local rail has seen a revival, although many off-peak services still run almost empty. Some improvements are in the pipeline, but investment was disrupted by the franchising process, and some inner city stations are still being run down and closed. In an era of flexibility the best prospects for such a fixed network may be in development partnerships, linking new services with related development on multi-modal interchanges, together with more flexible train-taxi-minibus links. The rail network itself is limited by central pinch-points, and the long-discussed link between the two mainline city-centre stations may one day be viable, when all external benefits are included. Together with signal improvements, this could help to raise traffic up to the effective network capacity, at several times current levels.

In contrast to 'heavy' rail, the GM MetroLink – a tram system on new street track and existing rail routes – has become the symbol of the modernizing city. In reality its current 35,000 trips per day amount to half of 1% of total travel, connecting relatively affluent suburbs. Further extensions to the airport and other satellite destinations are in the pipeline, and the fully developed network could take 2–3% of all journeys, or nearly half of all trips to the regional centre. However there is competition with freight for the limited number of track slots, and laying new track is very costly. The eco-efficiency of LRT depends on the national power system – at present, the environmental benefits of LRT are strictly local.

Future developments in the fixed-route network may be with cheaper dual road-rail systems, on radial and possibly orbital routes. Success also depends on how LRT is integrated with other modes, as the route viability threshold of about 20,000 trips per day requires concentrated corridors of movement. Such concentrations could be enhanced with multi-mode interchanges, park-and-ride and LRT-taxi extensions as below.

## Multi-modal strategy

Public transport operators and regulators still tend to work on a supply-side agenda of services and interchanges. Clearly, bus and rail should be clean and frequent, but this on its own is not necessarily enough. Public transport will need to reinvent its role and image in the context of a networked, deregulated, consumer-oriented, post-Fordist world. The agenda of integration and diversification involves new kinds of modes, such as the linked 'train-taxis' in the Netherlands,

---

**Box 6.7** **INTEGRATED TRANSIT**

In Curitiba, a regional capital of Brazil, major routes contain several bus lanes with express, district and local services, plus a separate bicycle lane. Car traffic is separately routed one block away from local centres, enabling pavement cafes, stalls and other services to be at the centre of public space. Lower-income people can exchange recycled goods and materials for free public transport passes.

Source: Gilbert et al 1996: Rabinovitch 1996

or the flexible taxi-minibuses in the Middle East. It also bridges the public–private divide, as with park-and-ride sites and demand-responsive mini-buses. It also concerns the institutional frame-work, where the current fragmentation between providers, regulators and users needs to be bridged, not so much with a large organization but with a responsive network.

For instance the GM transport sector is worth £2 billion per year, with masses of data on vehicle and passenger flows, but very little is known about the demand side – the detail of why and where people are travelling. ICT may be the catalyst which enables real-time data on travel demand to be collated instantaneously and fed to an integrated network of providers on the supply side.

Public funding is strictly limited in the UK, as elsewhere, and private finance will be the main source of investment. New forms of partnership are needed to achieve the concept of a fully inte-grated and responsive transit system. The new generation of 'local transport plans' aims at this goal, as does the national encouragement for quality partnerships, but there is a long way to go in linking private operators to an integrated system. In the meantime, the PTA in a city-re-gion such as GM has to make slow progress by coordination, voluntary agreement and very modest incentives.

Overall, there are compelling reasons for a doubling or tripling of public transport travel over 25 years, with an expanded diversity of modes *(Fig 6.10)*. But while the technology exists now, the markets and institutions are highly frag-mented, as are the land-use and travel-activity patterns of the city-region. The reinvention of public transport is one of the prime challenges for the future city-region.

.

# BUSINESS & FREIGHT

For business travel and freight, there is a chal-lenge – economic growth appears to depend on transport growth, but it is now clear that unlim-ited transport growth is not an option. Hence business-led demand management is not only desirable but essential, for the long term future of almost any business *(Chapter 10)*.

One of the assets of GM is its strategic loca-tion for business logistics, and regional plan-ning still promotes development on the motorway corridors.[36] The trends of specialization and 'just in time' delivery depend on continuing growth in road freight, which is projected to dou-ble at about 2025.[37] Such trends are demand-led, and demand management would alter commer-cial logistics accordingly – the problem is that freight is a national and international factor of industry, and restrictions could very easily dis-place activity elsewhere. So the challenge is to show that demand management is not good not only for the environment, but also for business.

National fuel duty and licence increases have inevitably raised strong opposition from busi-nesses, and positive incentives will be needed to compensate further moves. The government's 'sustainable distribution' theme is moving in the right direction, but needs backing up with local and regional activity. The city-region has the advantage of critical mass for forward invest-ment: a strategic combined-mode freight system could in principle halve the number of long dis-tance HGV movements.[38] Strategic route man-agement should operate through area licensing schemes, linked to trans-shipment depots for local distribution. Local networks should pro-mote cleaner and quieter vehicles for the bulk of e-business and consumer deliveries.[39] The 2020 transport strategy shows the combined effect – where freight growth is slowed to 0.5% per year, with a shift of diesel lorry traffic to cleaner vehi-cles, and a shift of longer distance freight from road to rail, water or pipeline.

36 Dept of Environment 1996 (RPG 13)
37 DETR 1999 (National Road Traffic Forecasts)
38 DETR 1998 (Sustainable Distribution)
39 Whitelegg 1995: McKinnon 1991

## Railfreight & water

The rail network in GM is used mainly for 'train-load' type bulk loads – the Euroterminal at Trafford Park has a capacity of 4 million tonnes per year, or two-thirds that of the Channel Tunnel. Since privatization, railfreight has increased rapidly to a total of 3 million 'tonnes lifted' in GM, in comparison to 65 million from road freight. Many rail routes are still adjacent to areas of heavy industry, but the longer term growth prospects for freight capacity are uncertain, not least due to pressure for track slots from passenger services and future LRT networks. If all existing sidings and line routes were safeguarded, an integrated multi-mode combination of 'piggy-back' technologies with local distribution networks could feasibly achieve a tripling of railfreight traffic, up to a total of 20% of all freight tonne-miles.[40]

The Manchester Ship Canal was a major engineering feat a century ago, and still carries about 6.5 million tonnes or 10% of total freight in GM, downstream of the city. Other deep sea ports on the Transpennine corridor on either side of GM have a capacity of 100 million tonnes. With the continuing globalization of manufacturing, and the growing constraints on the land-based Trans-European Networks, water has a promising future as the most efficient mode for long-distance bulk loads.

## Business & commuting

Business travel is perhaps the hardest journey type to influence – delays are expensive, trips are urgent, and privacy and image are crucial. The role of the car as a mobile office seems indispensable for the majority of business trips, which account for 12% of all miles travelled. Up to now company taxation and allowances encouraged car dependency: the modest incentives in the UK national budget for low-impact cars and lower mileages began to reverse this, and need following up. Larger employers and business parks should set up car pools for business trips, and operate travel management plans as standard.

For commuting journeys, at 20% of the total, the usual advice is to plan for mixed employment and housing. In practice many areas of GM are already mixed – but in a labour market of 2.5 million people, with growing numbers of dual-career households, lengthy home–work distances appear inevitable, and the highest car usage is on the periphery, where jobs tend to be more specialized and public transport less effective. In the sectors and occupations more suitable for localized labour markets, major employers should be pressed to coordinate access from public transport nodes, or demand responsive minibus systems, with incentives for clean vehicles and car-sharing.

# AIR TRAVEL

Manchester Airport has put the city on the international map – recently voted the 'world's best airport', it now moves over 16 million passengers and 100,000 tonnes of freight per year. The expansion programme now in progress will provide for 30 million passenger movements by 2005, or half the current capacity of Heathrow. 50,000 jobs are now related to the airport, one of the most successful of any publicly-owned enterprise in the UK.[41]

National and world projections are for a 5–6% growth rate – a fearsome doubling of air traffic every 15 years.[42] But urban airports such as Manchester are constrained by site area, access and noise limits, not to mention global climate impacts, and future expansion at Manchester will be difficult beyond the projected 40–45 million movements by 2015. Such inevitable conflict between supply and demand points towards several possible scenarios:

40 RCEP 1994
41 Manchester City holds 55% and the other GM Districts hold 5% each. Manchester Airport's share of total UK traffic is similar to the NW region's share of UK population, but half of its international passengers are from other regions.

42 Civil Aviation Authority 1994

a) high-growth BAU demand-led scenario, with traffic doubling between 2005 and 2020 and then beyond, possibly with an offshore airport in the Irish Sea;
b) a lower-growth demand-led scenario, which would expand the existing site to the full, and network operations with other regional airports;
c) an environment-led scenario, which would stabilize demand beyond 2005 and develop the airport as an integrated regional transport hub.

The economic and social benefits of expanding air travel are huge, and have to be balanced with the environmental costs – but this is not simple, as any local or regional constraints could lead to traffic diverting elsewhere.[43] For both demand in general, and the supply via Manchester airport, there are many questions raised:

- how far air travel should be 'demand-led', or constrained by taxes or regulation;
- whether global impacts are the responsibility of the airport, the national infrastructure, the carriers, the passengers, or the travel industry;
- which local environmental impacts can be balanced against which economic benefits;
- how the airport could develop as an integrated multi-modal transport hub, and the operator as a diversified service provider.

Such questions are naturally surrounded by scientific uncertainty and public controversy – so here we can only sketch some options for air travel and the airport, playing a positive part in an integrated transport–environment strategy.

## Environmental issues

There are growing concerns on the global impact of air travel, the fastest growing transport mode. There are also great uncertainties, as the effects of vapour trails and $NO_x$ emissions could magnify those of $CO_2$ emissions by several times;[44] a working estimate used here assumes

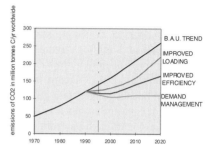

Fig 6.11  **AIR TRAVEL & CLIMATE CHANGE**

World projections for alternative aviation policy scenarios.
Source: CAA 1992, RCEP 1994.

that total impacts are double the $CO_2$ component.[45] Most aviation emissions do not appear in the national accounts, and the allocation for international flights is not resolved. At present the $CO_2$ emissions estimated for flights from Manchester are between 2–5 million tonnes per year, and including for other emissions brings the total to 5–10 million tonnes $CO_2$ equivalent, or a third of the total from GM.[46] The 'carbon-per-job' ratio is about 150 tonnes C/job, or 12 times the UK average.

On the ground, by far the largest source of emissions is from the road traffic flows of over 50000 vpd – the projection for 2005 is 124000 vpd, or enough to fill a motorway, and the airport will be the largest single destination outside of the regional centre. The airport is committed to providing public transport for 25% of all trips, with a combination of rail, LRT and buses, but this will hardly affect the huge growth in road traffic.

The controversial second runway development is now in progress, with the loss of 10 acres

43 Logan 1992
44 Schuman 1995: Association of European Research Establishments in Aeronautics 1996: Wennberg et al 1998

45 RCEP 1994
46 In the absence of detailed studies there are several ways to estimate $CO_2$ emissions from flights to/from Manchester, assuming equal apprtionment between origin & destination:
(a) pro rata from global passenger numbers and global $CO_2$ emissions: 4.8 mtCO$_2$/yr
(b) pro rata from fuel supplied at Heathrow and used by British Airways: 2.3mtCO$_2$/yr
(c) pro rata from global passenger numbers, average journey leg and specific energy coefficient: 2.0 mtCO$_2$/yr
(d) pro rata from global passenger-km, UK and Manchester proportion: 2.8 mtCO$_2$/yr
estimates based on RCEP 1994, IPCC 1998, British Airways 1994 & Whitelegg 1992: details in Ravetz & SCR Group 1996c

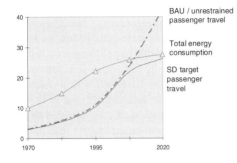

**Fig 6.12**   ***AIR TRAVEL SCENARIO:***

BAU / unrestrained passenger travel

Total energy consumption

SD target passenger travel

Scenario for air travel in NW region, via Manchester or other destinations. Passenger travel in billion km/yr. total energy demand in PJ/yr. Assumes demand management and/or constraint with 35% efficiency improvement, 25% utilization improvement from 1995-2020.
Source: ISCAM scenario accounts with data from CAA 1992, RCEP 1994

of ancient woodland, 4km of hedges and a section of the wildlife-rich Bollin Valley – to be compensated with comprehensive restoration and management. The population affected by noise will stay level over the next decade, as new 'Chapter 3' aircraft become widespread, and there is continuous environmental monitoring with the most advanced system in Europe. The airport is very aware that it relies on community relations, which it fosters through active sponsorship and public affairs.

## Sustainable air travel?

Questions on regional, national or global air travel management are totally linked. Expansion of the UK regional airports will relieve congestion around London, and allow more efficient single-leg flights from northern England to overseas.[47] It is also likely that business and consumer demand will increase, whether or not the local airport expands – but as with roads, new infrastructure tends to increase both capacity and demand.[48] Hence 'sustainable air travel' is not so much a local or regional matter, as a national, EU and global issue. In any case the networking of the infrastructure is now underway –

with its new financial freedom, Manchester is now acquiring Humberside airport, which would also compete with a proposed private airport in South Yorkshire.

The economic benefits of the airport are huge – as the global gateway to the region, it could support indirectly over 5% of the population.[49] But while the North West contains the largest regional airport in the UK, it is still one of the poorest regions, and over half the passenger movements are holiday charters, of which the bulk are outward bound. This raises questions on the employment projections, the economic benefits of overseas tourism, and indeed the pattern of economic growth which excludes the costs of its external impacts.[50] The airport's role as an economic generator is also crucial to development and property values across the region – already many nearby sites are under pressure for business premises and airport parking, and the challenge is to turn such pressures into opportunities for business and employment.

For global impacts, possible effects of policy and technology can be seen on $CO_2$ projections *(Fig 6.11)*. While there are few substitutes for aviation fuel, advanced technology might reduce emissions by a third, and demand management through fuel taxation could provide the incentive for better utilization. Fuel costs account for 15% of total costs, so its price would have to multiply several times for a significant effect on demand. There is also scope for substitution by high speed rail for journeys to London and western Europe, although this itself has major environmental impacts.[51]

If 'sustainable air travel' means anything, it has to link air travel growth with climate strategy. The emissions estimates above, pro rata for GM, show that global warming emissions are growing at 300-600 ktCO$_2$ equivalent per year – about the total rate of reduction required by the 2020 energy–climate strategy.[52] As the current growth rate in air travel emissions overtakes the target reduction rate for all other emissions, there is clear conflict between environmental and eco-

47 Cave 1992
48 RCEP 1994
49 Manchester Airport 1993

50 NW Green Party 1996
51 Whitelegg 1993
52 calculation based on the estimates and assumptions as above, with a very large margin of uncertainty:
current CO$_2$ apportionment for NW air travel – 2-5mtCO$_2$/yr:
current CO$_2$ equivalent incl related effects – 4-10mtCO$_2$/yr

nomic goals. One approach would be to take the transport sector as a whole, and redistribute emissions and targets between different modes. So an integrated transport strategy might aim to slow air travel growth after 2005, so that its total in 2020 is perhaps 2.5 times current levels *(Fig 6.12)*. Assuming that 40% gains in efficiency and utilization factors can be found, the effect would be a modest 20% rise in energy and emissions over the period, to be offset by reductions in other modes.

In reality, even modest levels of demand management will be controversial with users and operators – air miles being the ultimate prize in a mobile consumer society. A creative approach should aim to do what the runway Public Inquiry could not, to look at wider prospects on both demand and supply sides, and in particular the potential for diversified networks.

This scenario might see the airport as the hub of multiple transport and communications modes, including high-speed and light rail, demand-responsive buses and minibuses, and advanced VR-conferencing. Road access and parking would be contained within local limits, while airport facilities would be networked across the region and the UK. The pressures of rising demand would be contained with a combination of taxation, mode substitution, and ICT. Travel-intensive industries would be linked with airport operations for minimum impact and maximum added value through diversification into other service industries. The airport, and air travel in general, would be an integral part of a city-region level 2020 transport–environment strategy, bringing economic and environmental pressures and opportunities into balance.

# MAKING IT HAPPEN

The city-region is one of the most effective levels for the integration and coordination of transport strategy. But at present there is fragmentation, short-termism, modest tokens from government, and widespread paralysis from local government. A multi-sectoral integrated city-region transport strategy would use the combined weight of a consortium for bargaining power, expertise and added value:

- strong incentives for clean technology
- diversification of ownership and access
- integration of diverse networks
- coordination of supply and infrastructure with journey demand and cultural mobility
- use of ICT as the catalyst for integration, diversification and coordination

The forthcoming 'local transport plans' (LTPs) will be seen, in GM as elsewhere, as a test case for integration at the city-region level. The LTPs should recognize at the start the scale of the barriers and inertia to change, and the need for

new networks and partnerships to overcome the problems of fragmentation. In the shorter term, ICT systems may be able to deliver the most results for the minimum costs, for both demand and supply sides. In parallel, a city-wide home zones programme should begin on the reclaiming of the streets from the tyranny of the car, setting the signal for future directions *(Box 6.8)*.

## Government actions

The UK government has now at least the intention of an integrated strategy – but arguably this is trying to fit a former 'business as usual' approach with a former 'public transport is good for you' approach.[53] The 2020 strategy here aims at a more future-oriented, post-Fordist and responsive form of integration.

To achieve its stated aims, the government needs to extend the agenda of the transport White Paper in several directions. Economic signals such as licence fees, fuel tax, tax allowances and infrastructure charges should be extended

---

53 Hillman 1999

**Fig 6.13**    ***TRAVEL & TRANSPORT STRATEGY***

Outline of integrated city-region 2020 transport strategy

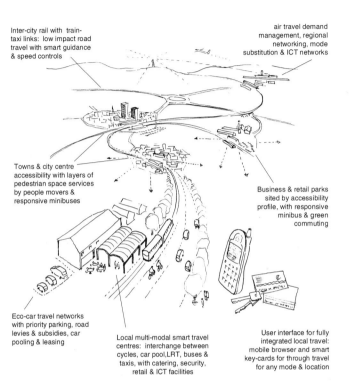

Inter-city rail with train-taxi links: low impact road travel with smart guidance & speed controls

air travel demand management, regional networking, mode substitution & ICT networks

Towns & city centre accessibility with layers of pedestrian space services by people movers & responsive minibuses

Business & retail parks sited by accessibility profile, with responsive minibus & green commuting

Eco-car travel networks with priority parking, road levies & subsidies, car pooling & leasing

Local multi-modal smart travel centres: interchange between cycles, car pool,LRT, buses & taxis, with catering, security, retail & ICT facilities

User interface for fully integrated local travel: mobile browser and smart key-cards for through travel for any mode & location

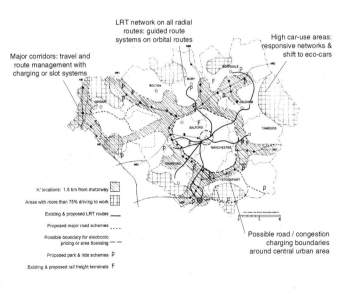

LRT network on all radial routes: guided route systems on orbital routes

High car-use areas: responsive networks & shift to eco-cars

Major corridors: travel and route management with charging or slot systems

'A' locations: 1.5 km from motorway

Areas with more than 75% driving to work

Existing & proposed LRT routes

Proposed major road schemes

Proposed boundary for electronic pricing or area licensing

Proposed park & ride schemes  p

Existing & proposed rail freight terminals  F

Possible road / congestion charging boundaries around central urban area

and made to 'bite' on a gradual and incremental basis. Direct subsidies on a major scale are needed to accelerate the development of urban infrastructure such as LRT, local car-sharing schemes, and ICT smart systems. Vehicle technology should be advanced by common standards and labels for manufacturers and consumers, with incentives at every stage for eco-efficiency. Greater powers and resources are needed for PTAs to coordinate private operators and strategic planning for highways and public transport. Local authorities themselves need financial resources, to take a lead in joining transport infrastructure with urban development.

## Business & public

The results lie in the hands of businesses and individuals – with journeys, modes, technologies, and ownership increasingly due to cultural and social choices as much as economic necessity. Every firm should have a transport management plan coordinated with freight, public networks and private schemes, in consultation with the LTP partnership. Similar travel plans should be integral to every project proposal.

Public awareness campaigns and other social marketing are likely to have only marginal effect, unless tied to the things that really matter to consumers. If vehicle eco-labelling schemes were linked to real incentives such as priority parking, shifts in behaviour would follow. The greatest challenge is to foster the networks and culture of cooperation and mutual aid, to break the lock-in effects of car ownership, and enable car- and lift-sharing, school runs, car-free housing and many others.

## Putting it together

The results of such strategies and actions over 25 years are then played out in the different settlement types across the city-region *(Fig 6.14)*:

- In city and town centres, public and pedestrian travel will dominate, with radial routes segregated for cars, city-cars, cycles, buses and LRT. Pedestrian areas will be layered for a balance of access and commerce, major centres will be served with 'people movers', while parking moves to the periphery.
- In development areas, highway improvements may serve business and urban village developments, with strategic locations for railfreight and public transport links.
- For inner urban areas, traffic calming and intensive public transport should accompany a diversification of car access through car-sharing pools and networks, promoting car-free housing, school runs, shopping and others.
- In suburban areas, cars and city-cars will be integrated with flexible and responsive public transport, local traffic management, and provision for retail, school and employers' transport.
- Urban fringe sites and developments should have transport management plans with employers' and home delivery schemes, and responsive public transport with park-and-ride for city access and local demand management.
- Rural areas should integrate transport management with local capacity limits, car-sharing and multi-mode access to responsive public networks.

## Context

As a densely mixed industrial and post-industrial city-region, GM is about midway between the extremes of affluence and poverty, and between decentralization and centralization.

GM is at the high end of the European average for urban personal transport energy con-sumption (16GJ/person/year). This is about twice that of Asian cities, about half that of Commonwealth cities, and a quarter that of some USA cities.[54] Transport trends are in line with the western EU average of 3% annual growth in car travel, 1.8 in bus, and 6.8% in air travel from 1970–1990. In contrast, for eastern Europe and many other developing nations, car travel growth is 10%, whereas air travel is the same as in the UK.[55]

For public safety, many EU cities have much lower injury rates than the 6200 per million in GM, whereas its death rates of 60 per million are about average. Car ownership in GM is about four times the world average – half that of the USA, slightly lower than France or Germany, but up to 100 times that of some developing nations where even buses and bicycles are luxuries.[56]

Overall, GM is quite similar to other larger EU city-regions in its urban form, industrial struc-ture, and consumer expectations. Where it dif-fers is in the institutional context, which for transport is often far in advance in the EU. There are also marked differences between GM and dif-ferent settlement types in the UK, where for in-stance historic cities are able to draw clear lines around concentric zones. However, the acceler-ating networking of businesses and lifestyles, may submerge local differences in a tide of glo-bally networked mobility.

---

**Box 6.8**

### *SUMMARY ~ TRAVEL & TRANSPORT*

The 2020 transport strategy aims to balance mo-bility, efficiency and equity in the transport me-tabolism. There are three key themes: integration of modes: diversification of technologies: and co-ordination with other sectors:

- demand management via accessibility plan-ning, integrated travel management, and re-engineering for walking and cycling
- promote clean vehicles, smart systems, and clubs for car access without ownership
- stabilize traffic growth, with large shift to other modes and low-impact vehicles
- fully integrated and responsive ICT-based pub-lic transport to rival car performance
- freight and distribution coordinated with multi-mode interchanges and local networks
- air travel growth within environmental limits, with the airport as an integrated transport hub

---

54 Newman & Kenworthy 1989
55 European Environment Agency 1996
56 UNCHS 1996

# LAND & ECOLOGY

*'In seed time learn, in harvest teach, in winter enjoy'*
William Blake

All human life is contained within its biological matrix – an endlessly subtle and complex web of activity, from micro-organisms to continental habitats. There are many guesses at the number of species in the world, but it is clear that they are being lost at a fearsome rate. On many grounds – ecological, medicinal, aesthetic or ethical – there is an urgent need to halt such catastrophic destruction.[1]

And while rural landscapes in the UK continue to be urbanized and industrialized, cities themselves have the potential for an endless diversity of new habitats. The derelict and lefto-ver sites and corners of a post-industrial city are quickly reclaimed by other species. But even these communities can be threatened by the in-tensification of living and working in the sup-posedly 'sustainable' cities of the future. So how can cities be revitalized while providing for other species? And how can the surrounding hinterland, now largely disconnected, be a posi-tive part of the urban biological metabolism?

While the sustainability principles of eco-logical diversity and abundance seem clear, their application to land and ecology is as complex and multi-layered as anywhere else. So our aim here is not to produce a fixed blueprint, more an integrated approach to the process of manag-ing land-based activities and resources.

First we look at the area-based patterns of the city, its fringe and its hinterland. Then we look at the roles and functions of wildlife and habitat, food and agriculture, and natural re-sources in forestry and minerals. Finally we look at how to 'make it happen', where and by whom.

## Trends & tensions

The densely populated county of GM was once famous for its fertile pastures and water mead-ows – 150 years later, over half its area remains as open land, but often degraded and lacking vegetation or positive use. Most of this open land is 'urban fringe' within sight and sound of built-up areas, with the remainder in the denuded uplands of the Pennines. Agricultural land cov-ers about two thirds, leisure uses cover a tenth, and woodlands about a fiftieth of the total. Agriculture itself is changing, with family farms giving way to larger agri-business units and part-time small-holding, while employment on the land dwindles.

Half of all vacant land in GM is on the ur-ban periphery, and much of this is low amenity and degraded by motorways and powerlines.

1 DoE 1994 (Biodiversity)

On current trends, over 20 km² or 3% of the total open land could be developed for housing and other uses by 2020 – while a third of the urban fringe could also be planted with community woodland within 40 years. Most open land in GM is above the critical load for acidity, ground-level ozone standards are regularly exceeded, and rivers are burdened with both rural and urban wastes.[2] What was an agricultural hinterland is rapidly becoming an urban front garden and back yard, used and abused.

## Future prospects

For the complex and many-layered system of land and ecology, envisioning future possibilities is more suited to scenario-based or 'what-if' approaches than any computer model:

- **BAU scenario:** current trends of intensification continue in agricultural areas, gentrification continues in fringe areas, and packaged tourism continues in wilderness areas. Habitats and landscape features compete for space with roads and leisure uses.
- **technology scenario:** ICT-based management systems re-organize farming and landscape management, with zoning to segregate managed leisure areas, teleworking communities, and bio-engineered production
- **SD scenario:** new patterns of ownership encourage mixed uses, community woodlands and low impact communities. Land reform increases public access and small-holding, with urban greening and eco-restoration of agricultural and upland areas.
- **deep green scenario:** rapid return to small-scale organic, permaculture and mixed forest farming. Many city-dwellers grow food in or near their living space, and the green belt is transformed to an eco-belt of low-impact villages and land trusts.

## Ecological metabolism

The land and ecology of the city-region contains many overlapping roles, functions, linkages and pressures, and we need to untangle

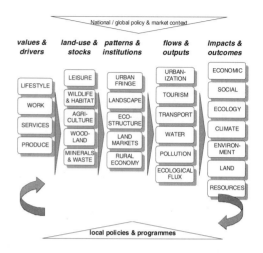

Fig 7.1   **LAND & ECOLOGY METABOLISM**

Total metabolism of land & ecology seen with an integrated assessment system mapping.

the way these work in physical, economic and social dimensions. As above, we can look at the total human-environment system with a mapping of the metabolism of cause and effect*(Fig 7.1)*. This of course is hugely simplified starting point, deserving much detailed exploration. While the physical interactions of soil, water and species are complex and uncertain, for physical–human interactions there is no single description.[3] The mapping shows how human needs and values are generally the drivers for physical activity and change, and such economic and cultural forces shape the distribution of land-uses across the city-region. Such uses form different kinds of 'patterns' in landscapes, food chains or ecological communities, and each then results in flows of physical and human resources. The outcomes of such flows are many and diverse, from economic and social impacts, to environmental damage and resource depletion across the area.

But what is this area? The former industrial city drew natural resources from its geographical hinterland or 'bio-region', but the post-industrial city now draws resources from around the world.[4] The dynamic of the physical hinterland is displaced – a container and sink for ur-

2 Critical Loads Advisory Group 1993

3 O'Callaghan 1995
4 Sale 1989

banization and new kinds of urban activity. Green Belts, for instance, are in many ways more important for the urbanization they prevent, than for what they are themselves. And the seemingly green hinterland is in many ways more intensely urban than many parts of the city itself – a container of wealth-consumption and wealth- creation, with sunrise industry aided by ICT and transport.[5]   At the same time, many rural communities are polarized, as land-based employment dwindles and incomers dominate local housing and services.[6]

The traditional division of town and country came from a time when the majority had little leisure or disposable income.[7]  But the needs of newly-affluent people for landscape and leisure now conflict with other people and other uses, both urban and rural. Countryside access also manifests power and class struggle within rural areas and between city and country – the first mass trespass demonstration for the public 'right to roam' was organized from Manchester in 1932, and the 'countryside lobby' now shows a potent if disorganized groundswell.[8]  While most urban areas are built on intricate patterns of property differentials, urban fringes can show highly variable changes in value and content. Conflict and competition are likely to increase along with affluence, active leisure, and cultural differentiation – one person's leisure park or self-build village is another's blot on the landscape.

Such human dynamics show many layers of function and dependency, at many scales. Each area has multiple roles and linkages in itself, in its surroundings, in its city or region, and globally. A similar picture applies to physical systems – water and groundwater cycles, soil and geomorphology, environmental stress and critical capacity, landscape structure and pattern, and ecological succession. This last factor highlights another common theme – that of continuous flux and change in the movement of eco-cycles, eco-systems and human activity.

Such a complex picture shows why straightforward definitions of sustainability are rare for land and ecology. Sectors such as agriculture

demonstrate the inter-dependence of local and global, and of human and natural processes.[9] Resource scientists seek out the bio-geophysical fundamentals but struggle with human agency.[10]  Ecologists look at the resilience of eco-systems, but recognize that communities of species never stay still.[11] Resource economists try to add up natural capital as 'critical' or 'substitutable', but in practice such definitions can be dubious.[12]  An alternative approach looks at the functional roles of natural assets such as landscapes, but has to deal with functions which are many and varied.[13]

## Towards sustainable land & ecology

Faced with such complexity, there is clearly no single or final definition of sustainability for land and ecology.  Looking at the many layers of landscape in the city-region we have to proceed gradually, asking at each step how alternative directions in land and ecology influence or impact on the economic, social and environmental processes at hand.

What stands out are some key strategic choices, ethical as much as scientific. One is the balance of town and country – urban needs for amenity versus rural needs for economic activity.  A second choice is in how far rural areas should be de-populated to serve the needs of urban containment, or re-populated through a process of counter-urbanization.  A third strategic choice concerns the balance of humans and other species – ecological priorities versus productivity in agriculture and other primary industries.

Such choices are not necessarily either–or, but they do show that not all objectives can be met in all cases. But for each strategic choice there is the potential to turn problems into opportunities. New kinds of multiple land-uses, for instance, may enlarge the choices available – while developers create leisure parks and other uses 'appropriate to rural settings', ecological small-holdings are also now in mainstream think-

5 Breheny 1996
6 Newby 1996
7 Williams 1972
8 MacFarlane 1998
9 O'Riordan & Cobb 1996

10 Munasinghe 1994
11 Holling 1986
12 MacDonald Hanley & Moffat 1999
13 CAG & Land Use Consultants 1997

ing, suggesting that the two could possibly be combined.[14]

The urban development theme might see sustainability for the urban fringe and hinterland as meeting the needs of the city for containment, amenity, access to leisure and wildlife areas, with an appropriate level of production. An ecological theme would see the potential for post-industrial fringes and hinterlands to evolve a diverse and resilient landscape, increasing their contribution to regional and global bio-diversity and bio-mass, with many social and economic benefits. A resource management theme would focus on urban supply chains in food, timber, minerals and organic wastes, with the goals of reducing pollution and increasing efficiency, both locally and globally. A rural development perspective focuses on opportunities for rural communities and local economies under pressure from urbanization.

Many of these goals appear in current policies, but the perennial fragmentation and conflict of different actors and agencies in the urban fringe are barriers to progress. The aim of the 2020 land-ecology strategy is to combine such diverse goals, for greater synergy and added value.

In the light of such multiple goals, finding indicators and setting targets for each sector is a challenge. For tangible features such as urban open space there are national standards – but for urban wildlife, rising numbers can easily reflect better surveys rather than better conditions, and there is often little data available. Some guidance is gained from looking at the environmental scenario accounts for the city-region. Below is a selection of 'core indicators' which highlight overall trends, possible targets, and the distance between them *(Box 7.1)*. Such targets then apply back to the goals and strategies in each sector *(Box 7.2)* – again, not so much a blueprint but a pointer to further discussion.

---

**Box 7.1**

### LAND & ECOLOGY ~ TRENDS & TARGETS

| | | 1995 | BAU 2020 | SD 2020 | Trend-target index |
|---|---|---|---|---|---|
| | | | | | % |
| urban open/green space | km2 | 55 | 43 | 70 | -80 |
| total rural land | km2 | 733 | 709 | 723 | 40 |
| total woodland area | km2 | 23 | 48 | 90 | 40 |
| other designated habitat | km2 | 15 | 30 | 39 | 60 |
| % food supply organic grown | % | 0.5% | 2.5% | 20.0% | 10 |
| % soil with >7% organic matter | % | 10% | 5% | 20% | -50 |

Summary 'core indicators' with trends & targets from ISCAM scenario accounts for GM 1995-2020.
BAU = business as usual projection from trend
SD = sustainable development scenario

---

**Box 7.2**

### LAND & ECOLOGY ~ GOALS & STRATEGIES

| | GOV | LAP | BUS | COM | PUB |
|---|---|---|---|---|---|
| **CITY GREENING:** Neighbourhood eco-structure: double tree cover: full green corridor network: eco-water management: urban farms/eco-schools | ○ | ● | ○ | ○ | ○ |
| **URBAN FRINGE:** Containment & regeneration of urban areas: maintain / increase green belt & diversify to eco-belt: double provision for leisure | ○ | ● | ○ | | |
| **WILDLIFE & HABITAT:** double bio-mass & species numbers: promote urban habitats; hedgerows, woodlands, wetlands, uplands; community forest woodland cover from 2% to 25-30% | ○ | ● | ○ | ● | ○ |
| **FOOD & AGRICULTURE:** urban & fringe organic cultivation for up to 10% of food supply: set up markets, distribution, agriculture extensification | ● | ○ | ● | ● | ● |
| **FORESTRY & MINERALS:** Woodland management for local timber production. Provide for aggregates & sandstones to meet demand managed UK minerals strategy | ○ | ● | ● | | |

GOV ~ government & EU: LA ~ local authorities & partnerships:
BUS ~ business & finance: COM ~ community & 3rd sector: PUB ~ public

---

# GREENING THE CITY

Every city-region has a unique pattern and structure as a starting point for ecological restructuring – GM for instance has a distinctive natural bowl and river valley geography. Amidst the sprawl of roads, industry and housing, ecological habitats and communities are often lacking, while elsewhere huge grassed spaces have little definition or purpose. Ecological restructuring works at each level – conurbation, districts, neighbourhoods, streets, blocks and dwellings – to form new patterns of urban 'eco-morphology'.[15] Many urban areas now contain more biodiversity than the industrialized countryside which surrounds them, and yet many people still aspire to a house with a view of trees and fields – if the city is to retain its people it must offer such opportunities.

A thriving urban ecology hinges on diversity – in habitats, communities, micro-climates, nutrients, soils, water and energy flows. Urban streets and squares, allotments, country parks and remote wilderness each have a place and a role to play. The edges of each area are the most diverse and active, for both ecological resilience and human interest – so the connectivity and inter-penetration of each habitat type with others is crucial.

At the city-region scale, green wedges and fingers of river valleys, railways and canal corridors tend to be degraded by roads and other infrastructure. So the interface between urban and natural landscapes needs several layers of strategic planning. Green corridors along roads and other routes should link the 'stepping stones' of a countryside and urban parks in a range of sizes. Different degrees of urbanized cultivation would link new and ancient woodlands, intensive and extensive habitats and leisure uses *(Fig 7.2)*.

At the local level, the 2020 neighbourhood strategy encourages a finer-grain eco-structure, taking up opportunities from the housing and transport strategies *(Chapters 5 and 6)*. Traffic calming of residential areas enables planting of streets and public spaces on a large scale, and re-connects each local centre to its catchment with a detailed network of green routes. These link with green fingers and wedges, surrounding each neighbourhood with stepping stones of open land for allotments and community woodland.

There is a strategic network of green corridors already mapped out for GM, and this should extend to second or third tiers, easily accessible from all dwellings, with a total length of perhaps 2000km or a quarter of all roads in the city.[16] The first practical problem is how to maintain continuity of green corridors across major roads. Experience from European cities show that a combination of priority crossings, permeable surfacing, wildlife tunnels, and pedestrian overpasses can enhance both ecological and human 'connectivity'.[17]

In practice progress on the green corridor network is slow, due to funding and access problems – ecology is generally low in the priority list of urban development. For existing urban areas there is a principle of added value – as planting clearly increases property values, there will be ways of forward funding and recouping such investment *(Chapter 13)*. For new development there is a simple principle – 'no net loss' in bio-mass and bio-diversity.[18] Where eco-systems, even those on derelict land, are unavoidably damaged or stressed, ample compensation should be made on or off-site. Every development proposal needs not only a landscape design, but an ecological strategy for wildlife and habitat, network connectivity, water and micro-climate, and food cultivation.

## Urban climate & ecology

The urban micro-climate effect concentrates heat, dust and traffic pollution, in the form of a 'heat bowl' several degrees higher than the sur-

15 Hough 1984

16 GM Countryside Unit 1988
17 Sukopp et al 1995
18 Green 1993

roundings.[19] The onset of climate change is now beginning to aggravate this effect: the current rate of climate change of 0.2-0.3°C per decade is several times the capacity of adaptation of most species, so many urban eco-systems will need support in adapting to new and less predictable conditions. The micro-climate functions of urban ecology will also find new roles for trees in shading, water for cooling and planting for dust filtration.[20] Some tree species can remove a tonne of $SO_2$ per year from the air, and on that basis a doubling of tree cover across the city could take up a large part of urban emissions.[21] Some reed and marshgrass species remove toxic metals from floodplains and wetlands, and should be designed into a restorative water system.[22]

Areas such as parks, roadsides and older neighbourhoods should use ecological planting and maintenance with diverse native species, at a fraction of the cost of conventional planting.[23] For suburban gardens organic fertilizer and pest control methods should be encouraged by local authorities and garden suppliers.

Inner urban areas have a tree coverage of about 2% of total area, and new planting often struggles against vandalism and neglect, while in suburban areas, tree coverage is an average of 10%.[24] Species such as the 'Manchester Poplar' were planted for their ability to thrive in polluted air, but this community is near the end of its life-cycle and needs renewal.[25] Urban tree planting on a larger scale depends on the redefinition of road and pedestrian space – if the fine-grain eco-corridor network above was fully planted it could provide for half a million trees. If, say, one fifth of vacant land and institutional grounds was also planted, the current urban tree coverage could be doubled, and some of this could be for fruit and nut cultivation.[26]

# Open space & community

For some, public parks and open space are the relics of a municipal age, and for others they are

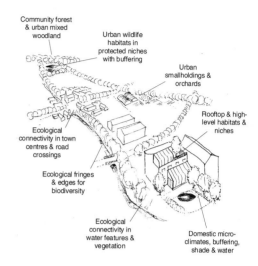

Fig 7.2                    **GREENING the CITY**

Community forest & urban mixed woodland

Urban wildlife habitats in protected niches with buffering

Urban smallholdings & orchards

Rooftop & high-level habitats & niches

Ecological connectivity in town centres & road crossings

Ecological fringes & edges for biodiversity

Ecological connectivity in water features & vegetation

Domestic micro-climates, buffering, shade & water

General themes in urban eco-morphology, including soil, water cycle, micro-climates and ecological connectivity.
Source: based on Hough 1984: Roelofs 1996

the hallmark of a civilized and creative open society. The UK national standards aim at 3.3ha of public open space per 1000 people – to meet these, the total in GM would need to be doubled to 8000ha, or 15% of the urban area.[27] In practice such standards concern quantity, rather than quality, security or accessibility, which are arguably more important. Open space and school grounds are also under pressure from development, while uses and users of open space often appear to be few, and open space and allotments are 'non-statutory' or low priority functions.[28]

The neighbourhood strategy above is the catalyst for open space – each neighbourhood unit should provide a range, from larger outer areas to inner 'pocket parks', with playing fields and institutional grounds providing public access and multiple uses. Much of the deficit could be provided simply by full-scale traffic calming – pedestrianizing half of all residential streets would generate 2000ha of publicly accessible areas in close proximity to housing.

19 Douglas 1984
20 Gilbert 1989
21 Hough 1984
22 Baylin 1979
23 Handley & Bulmer 1991
24 Est. from Salford City Council 1994 & Land Use Consultants 1993
25 'Populus nigra var.betulifolia'

26 Manchester Permaculture Group 1994; Douglas & Hart 1987
27 Greenhalgh & Worpole 1998
28 Metropolitan Planning Officers Society 1992

In practice successful open space is as much to do with community relations and social cohesion – without local involvement, vandalism, crime and neglect are much more likely. Community action can also re-use vacant or derelict sites otherwise wasted; Manchester's 'Community Initiatives' fund in the 1980s sponsored several hundred self-help landscape projects.[29] While management systems can be formal or informal, at present many projects stall as local authorities are unable to take on maintenance, and community groups are inevitably unstable and under-resourced.[30] For both residential and industrial sites, the Groundwork Trust's managed partnership approach delivers business investment, community benefits, and beneficial re-use.[31] To extend this to a city-wide programme, an eco-restoration consortium and financial package is needed. This would work with local authorities and regeneration agencies to match and coordinate potential sites, community needs and resources, neighbourhood strategies, business investment, and short or long term uses.

# GREENING THE FRINGE

The urban fringe of most large conurbations is a tangle of resources for the beginning and end of the urbanization process – economic innovation with landscape change, and opportunity alongside dereliction. Reducing pollution and re-using vacant land are valid goals, but little is achieved without looking at the wider dynamics of the urban fringe.

Of the fragmented zone of urban fringe in GM, over 90% is within 2km or direct sight and sound of urban areas. Local surveys show that farm productivity reduces with proximity to the urban areas, and nearby land shows much vacancy and fragmentation.[32] Typical fringe land-use types range from negative to positive:[33]

- disturbed landscapes: impacts from minerals, waste and dereliction;
- neglected landscapes: low intensity and marginal farming with high vacancy rates;
- industrial agriculture: high intensity monocultures with large-scale plant and buildings;
- traditional agriculture: mixed farming with variegated landscapes and eco-structure;
- amenity landscapes: woodland, country parks, large estates, open recreation;
- wilderness landscapes: unused or uneconomic upland or marshland.

Such categories overlap in a continuous flux of disturbance, reclamation, development and vacancy, and in GM most fringe areas are dominated by motorways and other infrastructure. The landscape type most obviously threatened is that of 'traditional agriculture', whose maintenance is now the aim of 'Farm Stewardship', 'Less Favoured Area' and other schemes.[34] 'Disturbance' also applies to psychological qualities – 'tranquillity' areas are defined as more than 3km from major roads or urban areas, and on that basis less than 3% of GM is undisturbed.[35]

Current land use trends are shown with 25-year projections *(Fig 7.3)*. Recreation uses could increase to 10% of open land, agricultural could reduce to 60%, and most minerals and landfill sites could be reclaimed over that period.[36] The community forest programme will also progress towards its target of 30% of rural land, while total open land could decrease on current trends by 2000 hectares or 3% of its area. This rate of urbanization would use up within 80 years the 'white' or undesignated areas, the prime source of greenfield development land.

Open land policy is dominated by the Green Belt – 47% of the GM county area is protected in principle, although there are some 'strategic deletions' for large employment sites and motor-

29 Manchester City Council 1986
30 Bradley 1986
31 Handley 1986: Brooks 1996
32 Countryside Commission 1982
33 Blair 1987

34 MAFF 1993
35 Rendel 1994
36 Data interpolated from GMR 1995 & MAFF 1994

way routes. Pressure for housing and employ-ment could impact on green belt boundaries, but much of the landscape within shows ne-glect and degradation. Green Belt policies are also restrictive of farm diversification, landscape maintenance and the rural economy in general. Other local policies such as 'landscape value' and 'river valleys' aim at similar ends, but with-out the legal status of the green belt. In practice each is hindered by the fragmentation of agri-culture, land tenure, highways and leisure ac-tivities. A national review of green belt policy would do well to consider the green belt as an 'eco-belt' – a zone of multiple use, low-impact, high value-added ecological restoration.[37]

Similar questions apply to the 29 km[2] of GM in the Peak District National Park, much of which is a reservoir catchment between bare hillsides. The national parks were reviewed recently, in an attempt to resolve conflict between 'quiet enjoyment' and economic activity. While there is a strong case that the park area in GM should be protected as 'wilderness', the landscape it-self is deteriorating from lack of maintenance. On the basis that there should be room for both, a layered approach would set areas for 'inalien-able' wilderness, for rural eco-restoration, and diversification for the local economy.

## Leisure & tourism

After agriculture, the largest rural land-use in the city-region is for leisure – golf courses cover over 7000 hectares or 10% of the area, together with diverse activities such as biking, 'horsiculture', garden centres and country parks.[38] In many ways leisure is a kind of ex-

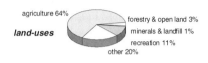

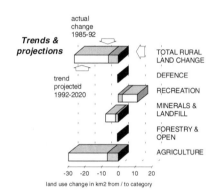

Outline of rural land-uses in GM with current trends projected to 2020.
Source: based on information supplied by GMR 1995.

tractive industry, leading to over-use, vandal-ism, traffic problems, pesticides and fertilizer run-off. Other kinds of leisure uses can meanwhile help with diversification and new opportunities for rural communities.

Outdoor leisure is likely to expand as a re-sult of early retirement, car ownership and health awareness – some activities such as biking, hang-gliding and water sports have doubled in size over the last decade. Continued growth trends, particularly for noisy activities such as scrambling, could put extreme pressure on local environments by 2020. At the same time, out-door leisure is a policy priority, as in schemes such as 'Recreation 2000', which promotes coun-tryside partnerships in the urban fringe.[39] 'Tour-ism' in GM, meaning visits with overnight stays, is mainly urban, and accounts for 1% of the city-region economy with 2 million trips and 5 mil-lion visitor nights.[40] Again this could change with a new generation of high-tech leisure de-velopments, and schemes such as the proposed 'Xanadu' in Wigan will create large gated areas with huge traffic flows.

The principle for such developments should be 'green tourism' which respects the environ-

37 Elson et al 1993
38 GM Research 1995

39 Countryside Commission 1995
40 NW Tourist Board 1995

ment and culture of its destination. But at present the tourism 'product' is usually linked to road access, fast food and packaged themes.[41] A green tourism strategy for the GM fringe should enable growth in facilities and land-use with minimal transport and other impacts. There is a ring of water parks and country parks, for instance, which is over-used and should be extended and linked in partnership schemes with local businesses. Riding, cycling and walking routes should be designed into the city-region strategic network to enable low-impact access.[42]

## Integrated fringe strategy

As with the city itself, the greening of the fringe focuses on the themes of diversity and multiple uses.[43] The driving forces in the fringe are coming from counter-urbanized and affluent life-styles, so such pressures should be steered towards more sustainable outcomes.[44] One approach is to apply the multiple-use principle:

- agriculture combined with woodlands, wild-life, small-holding;
- woodlands combined with leisure, education, wildlife, small holding and low impact housing;
- leisure combined with education, small-holding, woodlands and wildlife.

Traditional land-use policies need re-thinking for such diversified activities.[45] The former goal

of land productivity has been overtaken by farm surpluses, so organic cultivation, forest culture, horticulture and permaculture are each coming to be seen as viable job creators and maintainers of diverse and abundant landscapes. Will such moves undermine Green Belt principles and open the gates to rampant housing development? Small scale ecological settlements may be appropriate where linked to travel management, low-impact cultivation, and cooperative tenures which avoid land speculation, and the potential demand could be 5% or 50,000 households in GM. Surrounding many cities in the USA, the 'community land trust' is a means by which local people, businesses and foundations can safeguard the long term security of precious assets.[46] This should also provide for local communities: networks of rural shops, for instance, may be restructured and coordinated with employment programmes.[47]

The other side to this is the landscape itself at every scale, from the region to the neighbourhood. The NW region is the site of a unique Landscape Strategy, which provides for the first time a reference point for coordinated landscape policy and management.[48] Based on structural analysis of landscape condition and character, it sets a range of priorities: from restoring strong character areas in poor condition, to strengthening weak character areas in good condition, and creating new landscapes where both character and condition are poor.[49]

# FARMING & FOOD

Many city dwellers seem more interested in the landscape's appearance than its produce, even while buying chemically-manufactured food from multi-national chains. Is this sustainable? It is perhaps easier to say what is 'unsustainable' – soil erosion and eutrophication, species extinction, contaminated food chains and un-

healthy diets.[50] And while the conflicts between agriculture and environmental policy cause local problems, complex international subsidies and trading systems are global issues.[51]

Farmland in GM covers a full range – from upland areas in 'grade 5', medium-quality grassland , and richer areas to the south and west,

41 World Tourism Council 1994: English Tourist Board 1995
42 Roedhe & Kendle 1994
43 Countryside Agency 1999
44 Herington 1986
45 Ravetz 1991

46 Fairlie 1996
47 Tomalin 1998
48 Handley & Wood 1996 & 1998
49 Warnock & Brown 1998
50 O'Riordan & Cobb 1996
51 OECD 1989

with intensive pig and poultry, mixed cropping and horticulture. The 'self-sufficiency' ratio of food and farming in GM is about 3% in native foods, and 2% in all foods.[52] Set-aside at present takes 2% of the total area, short of the 10% target across the EU, but as most of this is marginal land, production is not greatly affected. The 'Less Favoured Area' policy aims at diversification and landscape conservation in most of the upland areas. If current trends continue, most commercial farming in GM would be livestock and horticulture on higher grade land, both of which are energy and chemical intensive. Meanwhile part-time and smaller units are growing, and tenanted farms revert to fully-owned farms, as 'hobby' farming grows alongside industrial production.[53]

Much industrial farming in GM is close to urban areas, so its effluent, waste and odour impacts are quite visible. In the longer term the 'intensification' of industrial production needs to shift towards 'extensification' or a low-impact mode of land management. The tide may now have turned for the EU set-aside and price support systems, complemented by wider shifts trends in farming practice:[54]

- 'chemical set-aside' to replace land set-aside, with 'integrated pest control' techniques;
- farm management plans within an integrated land and landscape framework;[55]
- full conversion to organic cultivation, which can take 10 years, is still a minority option.[56]

---

**Box 7.4**   *URBAN FOOD*

The 'Arid Lands' initiative has created a link between community-based agriculture in the Middle East, and a neglected council estate in Salford. Unemployed residents are now reclaiming the vacant space surrounding their flats, growing food and setting up a community enterprise with training and education facilities.

Source: Milroy 1995.

---

- alternative systems such as permaculture or bio-dynamics are growing more popular.[57]

At present less than 1% of UK farming is fully organic, compared to 10% in some EU countries – the difference in approach highlighted by the BSE disaster. The spread of higher standards throughout the EU food industry is likely to force the rate of conversion in the UK, for which support will be needed from farm subsidies, food processors, packagers, retailers and consumers. Organic conversion also encourages farm diversification, as landscape features and habitats are maintained, and employment, leisure and education are each enhanced.

## Food for the city

Does sustainable farming mean local production for local markets? At present the produce from GM joins the UK and EU processing and distribution industry, with all its impacts from chemicals and transport. Organic conversion of conventional farms reduces gross yields by a quarter, and environmental impacts by up to 90%, in contrast to more labour-intensive bio-dynamic horticulture and silviculture which can double productivity. For each alternative there is a balance of land, labour and external inputs, and the economics of the case depend on how labour and other inputs are valued and costed.

If half of GM's grassland was converted to organic horticulture, which supplies an average of two households per acre with fresh native foods, up to 10% of local seasonal food demand could be provided.[58] This would need local processing and distribution networks, similar to the Asian producer/consumer 'clubs', where a premium is paid for pedigree food.[59] It would also generate up to 20,000 land-based jobs, or six times existing farm employment. But while there is unmet consumer demand, organic growers lack access to markets and distribution. A city-region food strategy should bridge the gaps with active collaboration between retailers, land-owners, growers and consumers.

52 Estimates from data in MAFF 1994 & ONS 1998
53 MAFF 1994
54 Pretty 1999
55 Friends of the Earth 1991
56 Conford 1994

57 Mollison 1988
58 est. from Girardet 1994
59 Smith & Nasr 1992

Such potential for the fringe also applies to the urban area, where in many parts there is available land but little support or stability for its positive use. In other countries urban food is an accepted way of life, but the UK is now one of the most supermarket-dependent countries in the world.[60] For urban growers, there are the problems of air and soil pollution, drainage, vandalism and theft. An urban food strategy would provide land, suitable species, demonstrations, quality testing, equipment and technical support.[61] It would also provide distribution and storage where necessary.

The urban food potential depends very much on how land and labour are counted – with care and commitment, a household's summer vegetables can be grown in a 100m² garden, backed up by solar conservatories. By 2020 half the streets in GM could be traffic-calmed and planted with fruit trees. Assuming intensive cultivation with community involvement, an effective urban area of 15,000 hectares could support perhaps 60,000 households with seasonal native foods *(Box 7.4)*.

But why should producing food for 6% of all households be a priority? Again the principle of multiple use applies. Urban cultivation not only provides fresh food available to low-income households, it reclaims derelict and vacant sites, and helps to generate employment, training, community enterprise, social cohesion and mutual aid *(Box 7.4)*.[62] It is also another kind of special relationship between humans and other species, as valuable in its way as protected wildlife sites.

The urban area and urban fringe have great potential for combining cultivation with ecology, if an active partnership can be formed between land-owners, farmers, retailers and consumers. But food for the city-region is also a national and global issue. Consumer polls consistently show demand for better information, less industrial processing, fair trade, and less hidden chemical and genetic modification.[63] This should be the goal of a 2020 food strategy – to use every available means to enhance food quality and healthy lifestyles. Public and private organizations in education, health and social services should aim at best practice for inhouse food supplies. They should also use their purchasing power to form a core market and support system for local organic cultivation.

---

**Box 7.4**

### *LAND for URBAN FOOD*

|  | (hectares) |  |
|---|---|---|
| 15% urban vacant land | 400 |  |
| 15% other derelict land | 400 |  |
| 50% peripheral vacant land | 1200 |  |
| 50% peripheral marginal land | 2500 |  |
| 15% institutional grounds | 3000 |  |
| 25% transport-related margins | 1000 |  |
|  |  |  |
| TOTAL URBAN OPEN LAND |  | 8500 |
|  |  |  |
| 33% domestic gardens/terraces | 5000 |  |
| 50% of proposed solar conservatories | 1500 |  |
| TOTAL URBAN GROWING SPACE |  | 6500 |
| (7% of total urban area) |  |  |

Example SD scenario for land-use in urban cultivation in GM.
Source: data from GMR 1995, AGMA 1995, Garnett 1996

---

60 Noorman & Uiterkamp 1998
61 Howe & Wheeler 1999
62 Garnett 1996

63 Grove-White et al 1998

# WILDLIFE & HABITAT

The open land of GM contains a tiny fraction of the biodiversity even of the North West region, and much of that is disturbed and degraded – but it also gains by proximity to the urban population. This suggests that wildlife and eco-systems have diverse values – for economic applications in industry and property, for social roles in education or leisure, for physical functions in pest control, landscape and climate maintenance, and of course the intrinsic value of their existence. So the ecological health of a city is not only a matter of counting sites, but something deeper and more subtle – the combined set of relationships between humans and other species.

The endless diversity of possible habitats suggests that a city-region such as GM could be a garden of abundance, continuously generating new habitats and eco-systems, and compensating in part for the loss of species worldwide. In fact nature has already started – most of the 'sites of biological interest' in GM are on derelict or vacant land, and future prospects are dependent on the style of reclamation and urban development.

An underlying theme in ecological management is that of perennial flux – where traditional 'climax' communities are only one stage in a continuous cycle of succession and invasion (Fig 7.4). The balance of biodiversity and biomass, or of information content to material content, is continuously shifting and subject to intermittent catastrophes.[64] The implication is that attempts to preserve 'mature landscapes' as fixed can be unworkable and inappropriate. A similar view applies to the question of the 'value' of biodiversity – where the notion of a fixed market value is in many ways irrelevant.[65] But where does 'sustainability' fit into a picture of such continuous flux? Again, we can look at the systems perspective on the resilience and 'integrity' of human-ecological interactions:[66]

- species health and abundance in normal conditions;
- resilience and adaptability to changes in environmental pressure;
- ability to self-organize and innovate.

Wildlife conservation often seems like a losing battle – but as with heritage conservation, the opportunities can outweigh the losses. When every development and land-use in GM includes full provision for wildlife habitats and niches, then the pressure to conserve individual sites will be relieved.

## Ecological habitats

The geography of GM stretches from the Pennine uplands to the north and east, to the mosslands and rolling farmland to the south and west, with some fragments of native woodlands between. There are over 470 Sites of Biological Interest (SBIs) covering 70 km$^2$ or 5% of the total area. Every survey finds new and smaller sites, and actual trends are not easy to chart (Fig 7.5).[67] Over two thirds are in urban areas, mostly on derelict and vacant land, and very vulnerable to redevelopment and reclamation. The SBI designation appears in development plans but has no legal basis, and means little in the face of real pressure. There are also 17 Sites of Special Scientific Interest (SSSI's) taking 3% of the land area, four of which have suffered serious damage since 1990.[68] One large site in Bolton, dubbed 'Britain's ugliest SSSI', was narrowly reprieved from development for industry and waste disposal.

Again such sites do not exist in isolation, but gain ecological value and integrity through their connections – such corridors are shown on local plans, but often consist of motorway verges and other routes where conditions and continuity are difficult. The best network exists alongside the canals, themselves artificial struc-

64 Holling 1986
65 Pearce 1996
66 Kay & Schneider 1994

67 GM Ecology Unit 1995
68 English Nature 1995

Fig 7.4    ***ECOLOGICAL CYCLES***          Fig 7.5          ***WILDLIFE HABITATS***

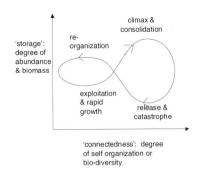

General pattern of ecological succession.
Source: Holling 1986: Kay 1994.

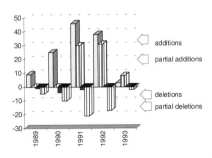

Example trends, gains & losses in numbers of 'Sites of Biological Interest' in GM.
Source: GM Ecology Unit 1996.

tures with many pressures on very narrow strips of towpath. Wildlife corridors also have to co-exist with strategic recreational routes, and land-scape management of hedgerows, woodlands and wetlands. In practice many species find their own way around – a community of foxes lives off the restaurant dustbins of south Manchester – and human intervention can raise difficult questions of management of species.

Even close to the urban areas there are some unique habitats. The western mosslands are based on a fertile layer of prehistoric peat: unfortunately peat is a marketable commodity, so the mosslands are now a tenth of their former size and on the edge of extinction, with extraction licences still standing. Some, but not all, garden supply firms have set criteria for sustainable peat supply, but to safeguard the remaining area needs a total ban on further extraction.[69]

Further afield many surrounding uplands contain bog areas with a unique community of heather and sphagnum on acidic peaty soil. Again the natural bog areas are down to 5% of their former size, the critical load for acidity has long been exceeded, and new drainage schemes are changing water tables. There is an ecological case for remedial drainage and structure planting with shelter belts and woodland exten-

sions. There is also an amenity case for doing as little as possible in areas which would be 'inalienable' wilderness. An integrated upland strategy should enable both approaches in parallel.[69a]

## Woodlands

The richest habitat type, woodlands cover only 2% of the GM area, compared to 6% across the UK and 30% in some EU countries. Native 'ancient woodlands' are only a third of this area, and would benefit from selective maintenance and better connections to other woodlands and habitats. One of the richest in GM adjoins the airport, where the second runway development is building a 300m long wildlife tunnel: another woodland in Oldham has been severed by the new orbital motorway.

Tree planting is possibly the single best way of stabilizing soil structure, enhancing biodiversity, and improving leisure and amenity in degraded fringe landscapes. The current Community Forest programme covers the western districts of GM, and aims to plant mixed woodland on 30% of the rural area over 40 years, wrapping around the built up area and penetrating along the river valleys *(Fig 7.6)*.[70]

While the Forest's aims are admirable, there are doubts on the viability of taking land out of

---

69a
70 Red Rose Forest 1994

production for several decades.[71] The Forest also needs better coordination with other policies – even while 40% of the areas to be planted are publicly owned, they have little or no status in the local UDP's. Making better progress

needs land and farm management to be integrated with 'multiple uses' as above. Leisure, tourism, education and housing providers can then each gain from the added value of planting in a connected network.

# RESOURCES

Integrated land management has traditionally been a matter of productivity – agriculture itself, the renewable resources of timber and other crops, and the non-renewable minerals and aggregates. For 'sustainable' use of resources there are several balances to be struck – local environmental impacts with economic benefit; local produce as part of urban supply chains and material eco-cycles; and conflict between physical production and competing pressures for leisure and amenity.

## Forestry

In about 50 years, a fully planted community forest, covering over a third of fringe land, could begin to meet the local demand for hardwoods of 70,000 tonnes per year. This would need a city-wide processing and distribution industry suited to furniture and garden supplies, as seen in cities such as Stockholm. 'Forest gardening' for fruit and berries is also highly productive and would be suitable for organic smallholdings or ecological settlements.[72] Permaculture methods work with the layering of many species, and combine woodland produce with ground level cultivation.[73]

Contrary to common belief, the potential for local woodlands to absorb carbon is small – the full community forest in broadleaf would take up only 30,000 tonnes or 0.03% of GM's carbon emissions, and to offset total $CO_2$ would need a forest the size of the UK *(Chapter 5)*.[74] However some species are very active in air filtration, and when complete the community forest

might help to absorb a large part of the dust and emissions of the city.

Possibly the most benign renewable energy source is bio-mass or energy crops – if a third of the city-region farmland was planted with fast-growing willow coppice, this could produce over 1% of the city's energy demand *(Chapter 9)*.[75] But using the resource to its full would need large plantations with mechanical harvesting, conflicting with amenity uses, and such crops are likely to be more for demonstration purposes.

## Minerals & aggregates

Quarrying is by nature disruptive, generating heavy lorries, dust, noise, and carving up landscapes on a massive scale. There is a good case for limiting extraction in proximity to such a dense conurbation – but on the other hand local production reduces long-distance transport, and generates other spin-offs such as voids for landfill sites, leisure activities and unusual habitats. Over 20% of local demand for aggregates is produced within GM, or two million tonnes on 600 hectares of land.[76] Surprisingly the NW region imports half of its demand: the GM 'landbanks' for sand and gravel are about seven years, and for sandstone and gritstone about 20 years, at current production levels.

Minerals are a non-renewable resource, and in principle a 'sustainable' level of consumption should be equivalent to the rate of development of substitutes, if that could be defined and measured.[77] In practice, regional reserves of sand and aggregate are huge, and the extrac-

71 Pearce 1994: Forestry Commission 1998
72 Douglas & Hart 1987
73 Mollison 1991
74 estimated from Adger & Brown 1994

75 est. fropm Energy Technology Support Unit1994
76 GM Geological Unit 1989
77 Hammersley 1996

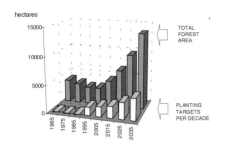

Fig 7.6 **COMMUNITY FOREST**

TOTAL FOREST AREA

PLANTING TARGETS PER DECADE

Target planting rates & total area over 40 years.
Source: Red Rose Community Forest 1995

tion rate is limited by its environmental impacts rather than the resource itself. A BAU projection of growth in minerals demand was for a doubling over 15 years. Even in a SD scenario where restructuring of urban form and fabric will take a lot of material in buildings, roads, infrastructure and so on.[78] So is there such a thing as a 'sustainable' minerals strategy?

One approach is to look at the material metabolism of the city – with a stock of 500-1000 million tonnes, and accumulation of about 25 million tonnes of material each year, the majority is from minerals and aggregates, which includes 2 million tonnes per year from local sources *(Chapter 8)*. At current rates of growth the total mass of the city would double in about 40 years, and as local sources are limited by local constraints, increasing amounts would be imported, while demolition wastes take up landfill space which is increasingly scarce.

So there is a strong case for greater efficiency in the city's material metabolism. The current UK 'landfill levy' and proposed 'quarry tax' on extracted materials are the first steps towards this, and further steps would increase the use of secondary aggregates and recycled material, an industry already established in GM. Such closed-loop material cycles could be aided by a city or regional processing system, distribution market, and standard specifications for recycled materials.

Deep coal mining in GM has now ceased, leaving a band of redundant workings across the city-region, some of which are 300 years old – an environmental jungle of contamination, instability and risk of explosion. Methane emissions from mining could be 70,000 tonnes, equivalent to 8% of total city-region climate change emissions, so stabilization of workings is a priority for that if nothing else *(Chapter 9)*. 'Areas of interest' for opencast mining cover much of northern GM; some large opencast sites have been proposed, but the huge impacts of this method are unlikely to be acceptable near urban areas. The 2020 energy-climate strategy does not encourage use of coal, the most carbon-intensive energy source, and opencasting is the least favoured option of all.

Overall, for each possible land-use there is a balance between amenity and productivity – and in the densely populated urban fringe it is likely that amenity interests will increasingly prevail. There is still a positive role for production where it supports local demand, employment or ecological diversity, as part of an integrated land-ecology and material management strategy.

# MAKING IT HAPPEN

The perennial theme of this project – integration – is a particular challenge for the land-ecology sector. Land management is a jungle of conflicting interests, from farmers, landowners, agribusiness, utilities, government agencies, NGOs and the public – and ecology is in practice 'nobody's problem'. So the 2020 land-ecology strategy is not so much about detailed planning, as building understanding and collaborative networks between very different sectors. It is also about building local capacity and resilience in the face of global pressures – the World Trade Organization trade negotiations will shape the landscape indirectly but powerfully, and a city or regional counterweight is needed.[79]

This is likely to start with a sub-regional framework, a joint initiative of the RDA, the regional Assembly and the government's Countryside Agency. This would develop a linked set of partnerships with special interests in the urban fringe, starting from an integrated landscape strategy, and extending to farming and food, urban ecology, rural development, forestry and minerals. The over-arching theme would be that of adding value through coordination and integration – so that employment, ecology, tourism, housing and so on each gain from coordination with the others.

At present local authority influence on rural issues is very limited, and the many good intentions generally lack powers and resources. So progress will depend on local authorities working closely with their partners. A menu of incentives such as development control, access to subsidy, infrastructure investment and stabilized markets, is needed to persuade developers and operators to play a sub-regional game.

In the short term, locally-led actions will focus on gathering information, demonstration projects, and collaboration with current programmes such as the Community Forest, Healthy Cities, Countryside 2000, Environmentally Sensitive Areas and others. Each of these could benefit from the contribution of community land trusts, bringing stability for investment, reconciling opposing interests, and providing incentives for localized housing, retail, transport, food and so on.

## Government

National policies quote the rhetoric of rural sustainability, but naturally find it difficult to define or set standards for such a slippery concept. Clearly more should be done, nationally and in Europe, to shift agri-business towards organic, low-impact and localized patterns of cultivation and distribution, and this might begin with changes to the finer details of land tenure and farm tenancies.[80] Localized economic development could be aided by alterations to business rating schemes, public transport investment and health or education policy. Leisure and amenity could be helped by a statutory right to roam and investment in footpath networks, and wildlife habitats could be increased by greater protection. Guiding principles should hinge on 'usufruct' – meaning that under-used assets should be turned to productive uses, whether by ramblers, farmers or smallholders.

The problem for land and ecology is that many of these goals are contradictory. The new UK Countryside Agency is charged with promoting a more integrated approach to fringe and landscape management, but it has few extra powers or resources so far, and has to try to coordinate a wide range of uncoordinated interests.[81] Neither are local authorities in the city-region well equipped to deal with rural issues, nor any other agencies or industries. The land trust concept as above may be the most effective approach for the urban fringe, in which case it would need national incentives and encouragement.[82]

---

79 Lang & Heesman 2000

80 Blair 1987
81 Countryside Agency 1998
82 Turnbull 1986

**Fig 7.7**          **LAND & ECOLOGY STRATEGY**

Outline of integrated city-region 2020 land-ecology strategy

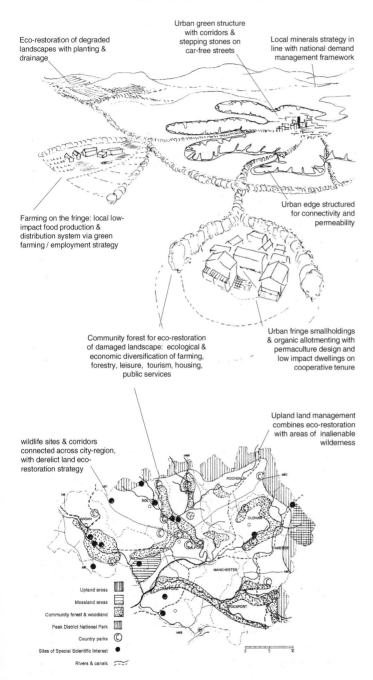

Eco-restoration of degraded landscapes with planting & drainage

Urban green structure with corridors & stepping stones on car-free streets

Local minerals strategy in line with national demand management framework

Farming on the fringe: local low-impact food production & distribution system via green farming / employment strategy

Urban edge structured for connectivity and permeability

Community forest for eco-restoration of damaged landscape: ecological & economic diversification of farming, forestry, leisure, tourism, housing, public services

Urban fringe smallholdings & organic allotmenting with permaculture design and low impact dwellings on cooperative tenure

wildlife sites & corridors connected across city-region, with derelict land eco-restoration strategy

Upland land management combines eco-restoration with areas of inalienable wilderness

Upland areas
Mossland areas
Community forest & woodland
Peak District National Park
Country parks
Sites of Special Scientific Interest
Rivers & canals

# Business & public

Farmers, landowners, developers and others are of course instrumental to any kind of joined-up multi-party strategy – and almost every community forest, organic food or eco-restoration project is such a scheme. To counter everyday commercial uncertainties, such strategies have to aim at stability and long term management, to support investments with longer returns. The 2020 food strategy, for instance, has to deliver clear added value to producers and distributors, and depends on support from farmers, retailers and public alike.

Consumer lifestyles and leisure patterns are also crucial to the future landscape, where long term eco-restoration depends on commitment from NGOs, education authorities and the public. Conflicts of interest between producers, residents, visitors and the needs of wildlife should be mediated through active consensus building and decision-making methods.

# Putting it together

Charting out the spatial implications of these strategies, the ecological and biological matrix needs to be seen as integral to the spatial dynamics of the city-region *(Fig 7.6)*. Each strand of the 2020 land-ecology strategy can then be applied to the various settlement types:

- city centres: planting in public places and semi-sheltered spaces, street planting and shelters for fauna, wildlife corridors on rivers and canals;

- development and industrial areas: eco-restoration of derelict sites, preservation of existing habitats, large scale structure planting;
- inner city areas: fine grain matrix of green spaces and corridors, allotments and planting on traffic-calmed streets, local centres and schools;
- suburban areas: connect existing garden planting across roads and along traffic-calm streets, with ecological cultivation and composting;
- urban fringe areas: eco-restoration of degraded sites, wildlife networks crossing major roads, organic conversion of farming, landscape restoration and diversification;
- upland and mossland areas: separation of inalienable wilderness areas, alongside eco-restoration of degraded landscapes with structure planting and coppice cultivation.

## Context

For a tightly bounded city-region such as GM, the focus is on the urban fringe, and we have left aside other vital issues such as coastlines and uplands, or the supply chains for timber or minerals. So the outline here aims at general lessons to be applied elsewhere at other scales – another study could push the hinterland definition to the regional scale, but even this is a partial and artificial boundary.

Urban forms are of course crucial to ecological character. Some EU cities have historic cores surrounded by large parklands and urban forests – often the legacies of former autocratic regimes, such as in Berlin or Stockholm. Other cities are more decentralized and car-dependent, with a more suburban eco-structure. Most EU populations are better equipped for food cultivation, and a retail structure better suited to local sources and farmers' markets. This shows up in very fuzzy evidence such as 'population within 15 minutes walk of green space', but urban green structures are otherwise very difficult to compare.[81]

In farmland, high nitrogen loadings are common between the UK and western EU countries, at several times the EU average, and the high UK pesticides loadings of between 3-10kg/ha are also seen in Mediterranean countries.[82] The UK has less than a tenth of the organic cultivation of Denmark and northern Germany, and the UK and Netherlands have the smallest forested areas in the EU, while total cover in the EU has increased by 10% in 30 years.

Such comparisons can only point to the complexity and diversity of land-ecology systems – few absolute targets or limits, much interdependency, and much controversy over environmental rights and territories. What stands out is the way in which the sustainability principles of integration and diversity need to be explored and interpreted at each scale from neighbourhoods to bio-regions.

---

**Box 7.5**

### *SUMMARY ~ LAND & ECOLOGY*

The 2020 landscape strategy for urban and hinterland areas focuses on integrated land management which cultivates the 'ecological metabolism' for a rich and diverse human-biological tapestry:

- networks of urban greenways and habitats, with doubling of biomass and biodiversity
- integration of urban fringe activity with rural uses, with diversified low-impact development
- organic and low-impact agriculture on the urban fringe producing food for local markets
- mixed woodlands to cover a third of the fringe area and one tenth of urban area
- eco-cycles in closed loop systems for carbon, timber, minerals and other resources.

# WASTE & POLLUTION

*The water which holds the boat is the
same as the water which sinks it'*
Tao Te Ching

It is easy to paint a picture of gloom in the city
where 'acid rain' was invented [1] – but it can be
argued that the world's most dynamic cities seem
to be naturally messy, their smoke and congestion a signal of wealth and activity. The gross
pollutants of the industrial revolution are now
being replaced by the more insidious genotoxics
and carcinogens, where even the stress of modern living is now a kind of pollutant.[2] Economic
development seems to create new pollutants and
hazards as fast as old ones are cleaned up, although it seems that the traditional $SO_x$, $NO_x$ and
VOCs are still remarkably hard to shift.[3]

Clean air, water and land are clearly essential to civilized society, but this begs the questions – how clean is clean, at what cost, and who
pays? And if pollution is defined as matter in
the wrong place and time, then the human definition of what is the right place is all-important.[4]

So here we explore the theme of 'sustainable pollution', as a dynamic balance between
material systems and human systems.

First we look at the city-region's total 'material metabolism', for the science behind the balance, and then at ways to apply the metabolic
view to goals and targets in each sector. Then
we look at each of the main environmental media
– air, water, ground and waste.

Generally, air quality management in the UK
is in an uneasy state of deadlock between policy
and practicality. Water quality and supply are
dominated by the politics of utility regulation
and deregulation. Ground remediation is tangled with hidden liabilities and avoided responsibilities. Lastly, the waste industry faces a very
uncertain future, and the ideal of integrated materials management seems a long way off.

Amidst such technical and political fragmentation and uncertainty, there is a strong case for
a city-region environmental management framework. In the space available, we have to focus
on problems directly within the city-region, leaving aside other important issues such as radiation, marine pollution and stratospheric ozone.

## Trends & tensions

Environmental quality in GM shows the poisonous legacy of several centuries of heavy industry – Manchester is labelled by the media as the
'pollution capital' of the UK, and many standards are regularly exceeded. The surrounding

1 RA Smith 1871
2 Beck 1995
3 $NO_x$ – nitrous oxides: $SO_x$ – sulphur oxides: VOC's – volatile organic
compounds: other abbreviations in appendix.
4 Douglas 1986

uplands are well over their 'critical loads' for acidity, river water quality is still the worst in the
country, and the chemicals complex on the Mersey estuary is top of the 'shame' list of corporate polluters. A quarter of all households have
water contaminated by lead, and half are seriously disturbed by noise. A tenth of urban land
is potentially contaminated and unstable, and
for the waste stream of 12 million tonnes per year,
future options are running out.

In the longer run there are trends and counter-trends, some of which could increase actual
or perceived pollution hazards. Economic growth
will tend to increase material throughput, other
things being equal, involving new and more complex substances and processes. There will also
be ever-tighter standards for health and amenity, and better evidence on environmental pathways, processes and impacts.

Such trends may be balanced by others, such
as eco-efficiency in processes and products, eco-
modernization of entire industries, and the principle of total chain management of materials and
processes. This follows from the Gaia hypothe-
sis,[5] which regards the planet as a self-regulat-
ing system, where trends such as the recent
decline in male fertility may be 'nature's way' of
containing human impacts.[6]

The result of this changing balance can be
seen in the environmental history of the city-
region.[7] A century ago, the combined hazards
of work, housing, diet and pollution resulted in
an average life expectancy of 40 years. Modern
hazards have shifted to the more insidious effects of carcinogens, trace metals and genetic
engineering, and while life expectancies have
doubled, public concerns on risks have multi-
plied.[8] The former hazards of 'production' have
shifted to those of 'consumption' – transport,
noise, waste, and food chains. And in the modern 'risk society' social divisions are as sharp as
ever. Pollution mapping shows the poor breathing the emissions of the rich, while health mapping shows a seven-year lifespan difference
between poor and affluent areas:[9] and 95% of all
industrial polluters are in poor areas.[10]

# Future prospects

With the shift of urban activity from production
to consumption, environmental management has
likewise shifted from the crude 'dilute and disperse' approach of the industrial revolution, to a
more integrated management of all environmental outputs, as with the IPC system of the UK.[11]
More recently environmental management has
been seen as a driver for business opportunity,
as in 'eco-modernization'.[12] Taking this one step
further, 'integrated chain management' coordinates all materials and processes.[13] The end-goal
is 'de-materialization', or a near-total de-linking
of economic growth from material throughput.[14]

Just as pollution control has evolved in parallel with industrialization, the future prospects
offer a similar range of alternative scenarios:

- *BAU scenario*: chemical pollution of air,
  water and land is gradually replaced by
  more insidious effects – genotoxics,
  carcinogens and genetic modifications.
  Huge waste mountains are shipped to
  developing countries.
- *technology scenario*: IT is a catalyst for
  material management, environmental
  monitoring and pollution permit trading –
  but more pollutants are released as fixed
  standards are negotiated and bypassed,
  responsibility is shifted, and production is
  further displaced from consumption.
- *SD scenario*: integrated materials management systems coordinate supply chains from
  source to disposal, and many products are
  leased on a zero-waste basis. Integrated environmental management is the principle for
  economic and urban development.
- *deep green scenario*: many shift from consumerism to low-impact lifestyles, with almost
  total recycling and re-use through neighbourhood based materials facilities. Air, water and
  land are 100% clean in the UK and overseas,
  and the world's biodiversity and renewable
  resources start to recover.

5 Lovelock 1981
6 Cadbury 1997
7 Ponting 1994
8 Beck 1995
9 NW REgional Health Authority 1997
10 Friends of the Earth (Factorywatch) 1999

11 Environment Agency 1997
12 Weale 1993
13 Wolters 1997
14 Sachs 1997

Fig 8.1  **METABOLISM of POLLUTION**

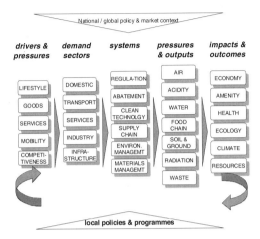

Total metabolism of waste & pollution system mapping.

Fig 8.2  **HOUSEHOLD CONSUMPTION**

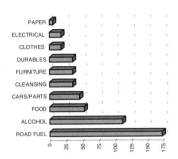

Average material consumption by UK households in kg per year per capita.
Source: based on Biffa 1997, Huttler 1997.

# Material metabolism

Steering the interactions between humans, materials and environments towards greater sustainability involves a life-cycle view of material processes from cradle to grave. It also involves a bigger picture – looking 'upstream' at the driving forces behind pollution, and 'downstream' at its eventual impacts and outcomes. A metabolic mapping of the material system shows a very simple outline of such linkages (*Fig 8.1*). Human needs and demands for shelter, mobility and comfort are the driving forces for activity in the domestic, commercial and industrial sectors. Different systems of management or regulation, in technology and industry, mediate the physical outputs of waste and pollution. Such outputs produce pressures in each of the environmental media, causing impacts and outcomes to human health, economic activity, ecological integrity, and even cultural norms.

In practice, of course, the picture is vastly more complex. Material movements are 'transboundary' with long distances from origin to destination; 'trans-media' with many processes between gases, liquids and solids; and 'transgenerational', transferring impacts and responsibilities from present to future.[15] Assessment of hazard and risk depends on how the system boundaries are drawn – even detailed life-cycle analysis (LCA) of products or processes can easily underestimate total system impacts.[16] Standards for such impacts can be set with 'thresholds' and 'critical capacities', for resource demands, industrial emissions, environmental themes such as acidification, and human or ecological health risk. However, these various kinds of standard do not often match, and there are large gaps and uncertainties between them.

One way to build up the bigger picture is by looking at the total flows of material involved, in a product, a process, an industry or a city-region. At every stage in the chain from resources, to processes, distribution, consumption, disposal and end-fate, there are 'externalities' – substances in the wrong place, time, form and ownership. Tracking these down involves a 'material flow analysis' (MFA), or balanced account of inputs, outputs, stocks and transformations, and an example MFA is shown at the end of the chapter (*Box 8.6*).[17] A good starting point is to track material flows to and from the average consumer: for a UK household, transport is the largest input, followed by alcoholic drink, food, furniture, equipment, paper and clothes (*Fig 8.2*). Different lifestyles and affluence levels have the

15 Blowers 1993a
16 Lave 1995
17 Sachs 1997

Fig 8.3

## MATERIAL INPUTS

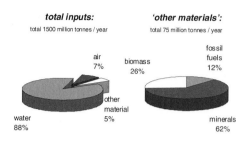

Input flows in million tonnes per year for GM system, first approximation.
Interpolated data from NW region, UK, Austria, & Germany:
Sources: DETR 1997, Biffa 1997, Baccini & Brunner 1991, Huttler 1997.

Fig 8.4

## MATERIAL BALANCE

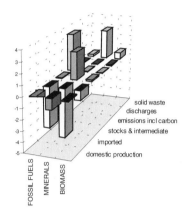

First approximation of input /output flows in tonnes per capita per year for GM
system, interpolated from data from NW region, UK, Austria, & Germany.
Sources: DETR 1997, Biffa 1997, Baccini & Brunner 1991, WRI 1997

potential to double or halve material throughput
(*Chapter 11*).

Such flows can be aggregated to the total
'direct material inputs' to an urban system, shown
here in outline for GM (*Fig 8.3*). While the majority is simply water, solid inputs amount to 30
tonnes per year per person, of which two thirds
is in mineral form. A materials balance sheet then
shows domestic production, imports, stocks,
exports and outputs, in the form of mineral, biomass and fossil fuels (*Fig 8.4*). Even this excludes indirect resource demands or 'total
material requirement' such as movement of mining spoil – the combined 'ecological rucksack',
which for GM could be about 200 million tonnes
per year, or 8kg/£GDP of economic activity.[18]

The material retained as increasing 'stocks'
is about a third of the direct material input, or
about 25 million tonnes per year in GM.[19] This
adds to an existing total mass of 500–1000 million tonnes, of which 40% is in buildings, and
the rest in infrastructure. If current material flows
continue, the entire mass of the city could double in 30 years, adding a tonne of material for
every square meter of urban area, and raising its
average ground level by over 1.5 metres per century. Such estimates are as yet very speculative,
with further research in progress.[20] Meanwhile
there are growing pressures for zero-emission

processes and supply chains, industrial ecology 'cascades' and sectoral 'sustainability strategies', each of which centres on a material flow
approach.[21]

## Towards sustainable pollution

If pollution is *de facto* wasteful and damaging,
how can it be called 'sustainable'? Such a
question hinges on the balance of environmental, economic and social values. From the scientific angle, some fundamental principles are
shown by the Natural Step 'system conditions',
although these are distant ideals more than working targets:[22]

- no net reduction in stocks of renewable resources;
- no net accumulation of artificial substances
  in the biosphere;
- no net transfer of substances from the earth's
  crust to the biosphere;
- social and economic development to enable
  the above conditions to be met.

The 'eco-indicators' approach sets thresholds
of 5% damage to eco-systems:[23] 'ecological foot-

---

18 World Resources Institute 1997
19 Baccini & Brunner 1991

20 Biffa 1998
21 Ayres & Ayres 1998
22 Hawken 1995
23 Krotscheck & Narodoslawski
24 Rees & Wackernagel 1996

print' estimates the expropriated land area of photo-synthetic product:[24] and environmental space' estimates the equal distribution of global resources and assimilation capacities (*Chapter 1*).[25] The UK Integrated Pollution Control (IPC) system is intended to provide comprehensive coverage of all environmental media; but in practice it hinges on the rather fuzzy definitions of 'best practical environmental option' (BPEO) and 'best available technology not entailing excessive cost' (BATNEEC).[26]

In practice such methods either focus on the 'product' of environmental standards, or the 'process' of management, and there are inevitable gaps in between (*Chapter 12*). Each method casts some light on the balance of environmental protection, economic cost, technical innovation and social risk. Such a balance points towards 'sustainable pollution' – in the sense of sustaining local and global ecological integrity, and sustaining society and the economy with 'acceptable' levels of safety. Defining such levels raises cultural and political questions, where the views of pressure groups and the public may be as valid as those of scientists. The precautionary principle is a guide but not the whole story, as the risks of uncertain future impacts are balanced against the risks of present-day social or economic disruption.[27] So the definition of sustainable pollution is concerned with a process of debate as much as a fixed product.[28]

The city-region itself contains only a very small slice of global eco-cycles, resources and supply chains – the average food product on the shelf in the UK has travelled 8000km. Targets for local environmental impacts and quality standards can be set, but the bulk of the agenda for 'local environmental sustainability' is only meaningful in a national and global context. So the human-environment balance above has to be interpreted for the goals, targets and management tasks which are relevant and appropriate at the local level, and again the definition of such relevance and appropriateness has to be deliberated. Such goals for the environmental balance in our city-region might include:

Box 8.1

## WASTE & POLLUTION ~ TRENDS & TARGETS

| | | 1995 | BAU 2020 | SD 2020 | Trend target index |
|---|---|---|---|---|---|
| | | | | | % |
| Material throughput/GDP factor | kg/£GDP | 3.6 | 2.8 | 1.8 | 50 |
| total waste recycled | Mt/y | 1.4 | 2.6 | 3.3 | 60 |
| Compost / digestion / spread | Mt/y | 0.1 | 0.7 | 1.5 | 40 |
| total waste arising | Mt/y | 11.4 | 7.8 | 5.3 | 60 |
| Estuary water nitrate loading | mgN/l | 14 | 23 | 10 | -100 |
| NOx total emissions | kt/y | 107 | 108 | 39 | 0 |
| CO total emissions | kt/y | 330 | 270 | 110 | 30 |
| PM total emissions | kt/y | 24 | 22 | 12 | 20 |

Summary 'core indicators' with trends & targets from ISCAM scenario accounts for GM 1995-2020.
BAU = business as usual projection from trend
SD = sustainable development scenario

Box 8.2

## WASTE & POLLUTION ~ GOALS & STRATEGIES

| | GOV | LAP | BUS | COM | PUB |
|---|---|---|---|---|---|
| **ENVIRONMENTAL STRATEGY:** | ○ | ● | ● | | |
| Integrated city-region strategy for material flows, capacities, thresholds, with fatality risk levels at 1 per million. | | | | | |
| **AIR QUALITY:** | ● | ● | ○ | | |
| Common pollutant emissions reduced by half or more to bring air quality to best practice guideline levels. | | | | | |
| **WATER QUALITY:** | ○ | ○ | ● | ○ | |
| all river quality to 'good' or 'fair' standard: sewage & effluent strategy to minimize toxics: demand management & lead-free drinking water throughout. | | | | | |
| **GROUND & SOIL:** | ○ | ● | ● | ○ | |
| Strategic programme for areas of search on contaminated & unstable land: reduce derelict / contam.land by 2/3 to 2% of urban area. | | | | | |
| **WASTE:** | ○ | ● | ● | ○ | ● |
| reduce waste arisings by 1-2% per year: BPEO for waste disposal with city-region material management system. Zero-waste economic development with consortia markets for recycling & re-use. | | | | | |

GOV ~ government & EU: LA ~ local authorities & partnerships: BUS ~ business & finance: COM ~ community & 3rd sector: PUB ~ public

25 McLaren et al 1997
26 ENDS 1994
27 O'Riordan 1996
28 RCEP 1998

- environmental management: reduce export-ed waste and pollution to levels of impact which would be acceptable as imports;
- social impact: equitable distribution of envi-ronmental hazard and risk between individu-als, communities and nations;
- economic impact: long term integrated ap-proach to cost-benefit appraisal, with envi-ronmental management as an opportunity for eco-modernization;
- risk management: define thresholds at per-haps one per million statistical fatalities per head, and apply precautionary principle to irreversible and inter-generational effects;
- integrated strategic management, including organizations and market measures to apply

these goals to the city-region environment and material metabolism.

Each of these themes should apply to the goals, targets and strategies for each environmental ef-fect from each sector. Each theme should also help to select indicators and set targets: select-ed 'core indicators' are shown overleaf with pro-jections, targets and a 'trend-target' index for the gap between (*Box 8.1*). Longer term targets can be extrapolated from the rate of change need-ed to achieve short term targets, as shown in the next section. Each theme also translates to a set of practical goals and strategies in each sector (*Box 8.2*). The practice is of course not so sim-ple, as the following cases show.

# AIR QUALITY

Manchester, the 'pollution capital of the UK', also contains some of the highest levels of res-piratory disease. There are also clusters of asth-ma, although definitive proof of a pollution link is not accepted as yet.[29] This is partly due to its location in a natural bowl, downwind of large power plants and process industries, with a shortage of green space and tree cover – a clas-sic urban heat island with seasonal peaks in air pollution verging on danger levels.

Official standards and 'exceedences' are only a starting point for air quality assessment (*Fig 8.5*). Pollution levels vary by season, time of day, location, weather temperature, second-ary reactions and synergistic effects, and their effects depend on activities and vulnerability of the recipients. Annual averages of $NO_x$ show that rural locations experience about half the levels of urban roadsides – this excludes the levels in-side vehicles, which can be several times those at the roadside.[30]

There are also countless trace elements and organic compounds in urban air and dust, many of them carcinogenics with no 'safe levels'. There

is mounting evidence, although still sketchy, of increased risk of childhood cancer of between 20% and 400% near to industrial sites.[31] Diox-ins, for instance, until recently were emitted by incinerators in GM at 60 times what is now the EU limit.[32] Many eco-systems around GM are also subject to air-borne and rain-borne acid dep-osition far in excess of their critical capacity or threshold of significant damage. The capacities of the worst affected upland and farming areas will be exceeded even after improvements such as the projected 80% reduction of $SO_x$ within a decade.[33]

Road transport is clearly the single largest polluter as the main source of $NO_x$ and CO. Man-ufacturing is responsible for most local $PM_{10}$ and $SO_x$, and process industry is the main source of VOCs (*Fig 8.6*). These data exclude upwind emissions from a large power plant 20km south-west of GM, which produces as much again as the local emissions of $SO_x$, with clouds of ammo-nia and hydrochloric acid coming from the in-dustrial cluster on the Mersey Estuary.[34] The

29 Dept of Health 1995: COMEAP 1995
30 Quality of Urban Air Review Group 1993

31 Knox & Gilman 1997
32 Greenpeace 1994: Environment Agency 1997
33 Critical Loads Advisory Group 1994
34 Lee & Longhurst 1990

Fig 8.5      **AIR QUALITY**

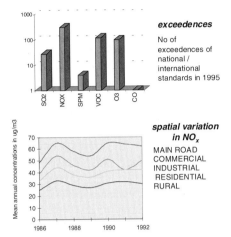

**exceedences**

No of exceedences of national / international standards in 1995

**spatial variation in NOₓ**

MAIN ROAD
COMMERCIAL
INDUSTRIAL
RESIDENTIAL
RURAL

Sample data for GM showing exceedences and spatial variation.
Source: ARIC 1994.

Fig 8.6      **AIR EMISSIONS**

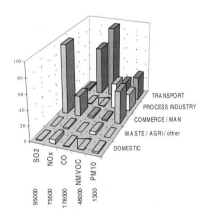

Proportions of total emissions by source, from current inventory for GM with Warrington. Figures show total emissions in tonnes per year. 'Process industry' includes metal production & processing, chemical, mineral, fuels, solvents & 'other industry'. Excludes power generation sited elsewhere.
Source: London Research Centre 1997:Lindley et al 1999

NW region also contains seven of the ten largest sources of carcinogenic emissions in the UK.

Trends and projections may be counted locally or nationally – many local emissions have risen in the last decade due to rising car ownership, while elsewhere emissions have declined with the migration of heavy industry. Emissions and quality targets for the UK are continuously revised and tightened, but many still fall short of proposed targets for the EU. Trends and targets for GM can be extrapolated to show the 'policy gap' between BAU projections and SD targets for the main air pollutants (*Fig 8.7*):[35]

- nitrogen oxides (NOₓ): many exceedences, mainly due to road traffic. While catalytic converters could halve emissions, much of their benefits will be outweighed by traffic growth. The link between emissions and air quality is complex, and reductions of up to 80% may be needed to meet local quality targets.[36]
- sulphur oxides (SOₓ): UK target of 80% reduction from 1980-2010 is on course, but there is a draft EU target being discussed which advocates a 98% reduction

- volatile organic compounds (non-methane) (VOC): a huge diversity of chemical species and sources makes controls difficult. The UK target of 30% reduction between 1988–99 contrasts with an EU target of 70%.
- tropospheric ozone (O₃): a secondary pollutant causing problems mainly for rural areas, short lived but transported long distances. Meeting ozone standards would require EU-wide reductions in its precursors, mainly NOₓ and VOCs.
- particulate matter (PM₁₀ and PM₂.₅): possibly the most difficult cases for the UK strategy, as much PM₁₀ is now thought to be long-

Box 8.3      **URBAN AIR QUALITY**

The city of Chattanooga in the USA was notorious as one of the dirtiest on that continent. In the space of 20 years, the smokestack industries have been cleaned and shifted to a number of 'eco-parks' promoting hi-tech green technology via job creation and business support. The entire business and citizen community was involved in a visioning exercise to reshape the physical and social quality of the city, and a decade later the results are bearing fruit.

Source UNCHS 1996

35 Trends & targets from QUARG 1995, AEA Technology 1997, Earth Resources Research 1992, London Research Centre 1997 and others
36 DETR 1999 (Review of the national air quality strategy)

range. Recent evidence suggests the finer particles PM$_{2.5}$ as the more damaging to health, and targets under discussion are similar to those for NO$_x$.

## Air quality management

Air quality management is a classic example of a local problem which exceeds the capability of local solutions. For road transport there are few options in the short term apart from stopping up roads, for which the local powers are as yet tenuous. The emissions source from power generation are outside the GM boundary. For minor industrial processes, Local Authority Air Pollution Control (LAAPC) has little leverage on all but the worst cases, and the majority of emissions are from small uncontrolled sources. The 27 sites in GM with 'Part A' major processes controlled by IPC produce less than 5% of total emissions for most substances.[37]

For the public, the new UK air quality banding scheme is more transparent and meaningful than before – but conflicting evidence creates fear and uncertainty, especially for people with respiratory or allergenic conditions.[38] The national report on pollution impacts suggests in a rather abstract way that up to 10% of the population may suffer 'accelerated fatality' – for those affected this is serious indeed.[39]

The economic benefits of pollution abatement appear to greatly outweigh the cost – pro rata for GM, the cost of meeting SO$_x$ targets was estimated at £50–150 million, with benefits of up to £1 billion (*Chapter 13*).[40] However, the latest exercise in the economics of air quality was exposed as vacuous and misleading, with a huge range of uncertainty.[41] An integrated approach should take into account a wide range of values and assumptions on costs, benefits and other very uncertain impacts, for a fully rounded approach to abatement policy appraisal.[42]

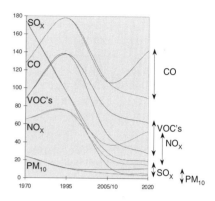

Fig 8.7 **EMISSION TRENDS & TARGETS**

'Policy gap' on selected pollutant emissions in 1000 tonnes per year: recent trends, BAU projections and SD targets for 20005/10 and 2020. Note: trends and targets are very approximate and for illustration only.
Source: interpolated data from QUARG 1993: ERM 1993: Warren Springs 1995: AEA Technology: LRC 1997: DETR 1997

While most UK cities now have air quality management (AQM) strategies, there are large gaps between policy and practice. The AQM working group in GM puts out advice and commitment to partnership, but achieving real results would need action far beyond its remit, such as the UK transport strategy, EU fuel quality standards, power generation and chemicals regulation. Local awareness campaigns are marginal, planning policies are long term, transport management awaits an integrated network, and responsibility for other pollutants is split between different agencies.[43] Meanwhile there is potential for AGM to be an integral part of transport, housing, ecology, economic development and public health strategies, as in some American and EU cities (*Box 8.3*).

37 HMIP 1996
38 DETR 1998 (air quality)
39 Dept of Health 1998
40 ECOTEC 1994
41 Dept of Health 1999
42 RCEP 1998

43 AGMA 1997

# WATER

Water forms over 90% of the total material flow through the city-region – so the water cycle in many ways is at the forefront of the theory and practice of sustainable development.[44]   The water theme hinges on an integrated view of the natural and human water system, from resource management to river quality, groundwater, sewage and effluent (*Fig 8.8*).  As with the carbon cycle, this shows the interdependency of each part of the flow on the others, and helps to see which indicators areuseful for such a system.

The onset of climate change became a public issue in the UK drought of 1995 – the worst in recent times – and raised much uncertainty over future water resources.[45]  Most of GM's supply is carried over 100 miles from the Lake District by aqueduct – one of the great enterprises of Victorian Manchester, instrumental in the growth of the city, and also stirring up one of the world's first environmental campaigns.[46]  Surprisingly,

the NorthWest with its wet climate has at 9% one of the smallest margins of supply over demand, and at the height of the drought many reservoirs were nearly empty.[47] The utility regulator's priority was to drive down consumer prices, so investment was capped, while ecological damage increased, and the next 'asset management planning' exercise showed large savings on estimated investment being returned to shareholders.[48]

Long term 'high growth' scenarios show a possible deficit of 7% in the North West by 2020, with national demand increasing by 15–45%.[49] Water leakage rates in the NW region, recently the highest in the UK, are being reduced to 'economic' levels, but within a decade UK demand may increase again, and large scale transfers from northern to southern England are a possibility. For the water industry there are clear trade-offs between shareholder returns, price reduction, forward investment, resource security and environmental protection, and the optimum balance depends on demand-side management.

Water metering is one obvious method of demand management, but raises problems of social welfare, uncertain revenue, investment and monitoring costs.  Low-flow appliances are viable but one-off replacements are costly; 'grey' water recycling is less straightforward in urban areas, while rainwater collection for gardens can be very successful.[50]  This suggests that an integrated demand management package should be carried out at every opportunity, such as in property transfers, rehabilitation and area improvements.

Drinking water quality is generally higher than ever before, but the North West has the highest levels of lead contamination in the UK, and there are possible links to genetic disorders.[51]  Most inner urban areas have occasional lead contamination over the UK 50µg/l limit, but

Fig 8.8         **WATER CYCLE**

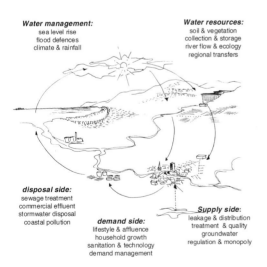

**Water management:**
sea level rise
flood defences
climate & rainfall

**Water resources:**
soil & vegetation
collection & storage
river flow & ecology
regional transfers

**disposal side:**
sewage treatment
commercial effluent
stormwater disposal
coastal pollution

**demand side:**
lifestyle & affluence
household growth
sanitation & technology
demand management

**Supply side:**
leakage & distribution
treatment  & quality
groundwater
regulation & monopoly

Outline of urban water supply-demand cycle with key system linkages

44 Newson 1992
45 Shackley & Wood 1998
46 Porter 1986
47 National Rivers Authority1994

48 ENDS Report 269:40-41
49 Dept of Environment 1996 (water resources)
50 Fewkes & Turton 1994
51 Bounds 1997: ENDS report 266:11-12
52 NW Water 1994
53 est. from data in HC Written Answers 14/10/97 Cols 816-819

the new WHO standard of 10µg/l is exceeded in perhaps a quarter of all dwellings.[52] At current rates it would take 75 years to replace all company lead piping in the NW region, at a cost of £1000 million, and private pipe replacements could be several times that.[53] At present consumers are technically responsible for pipes on their property, a task for which few households are equipped. The water utilities should be pressed as a matter of urgency to coordinate technical support with finance packages, as part of the city-region housing strategy (*Chapter 5*).

## River quality

Rivers and canals in GM have long been the worst polluted water in the UK – even with recent progress, most urban stretches are still 'poor or bad', with limited coarse fish populations. From the 5000 reported pollution incidents per year in GM, sewage, storm overflows, oil, solid wastes and process industries are the main sources. The main pollutants can be seen at the outfall to the river basin at Warrington – a purpose-designed 'Mersey index' has been developed here, and recent results can be compared against projected targets (*Fig 8.9*).[54] Ironically the water company is also the largest water polluter – its compliance rate for coastal bathing waters slipped to 50% in 1997, with 'particular dismay' expressed by the government.[55] The company has paid the third highest total pollution fines in the UK, with 35 convictions totalling £200,000 – but at 0.004% of total turnover these are symbolic gestures to a company which inherited some of the oldest infrastructure in the country.[56]

The largest river basin programme in the UK – the Mersey Basin Campaign – is halfway through its 25-year programme, having raised the proportion of its rivers in grades A-D from 40% to 60%. Its success is partly due to its partnership approach with solid core funding, and partly due to its key role in urban regeneration. Most larger schemes such as Salford Quays and the Central Manchester UDC have focused on waterfronts, and there are obvious incentives and paybacks for cleaning and greening. The Cam-

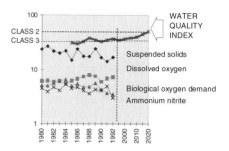

Fig 8.9            **WATER QUALITY**

Trends & targets for River Mersey at freshwater limit.
Source: DOE 1994 & Mersey Basin Campaign 1995.

paign is now complemented by a series of river catchment plans and 'river valley initiative' partnerships, where the Environment Agency aims to maximize the coordination and contributions from other players.[57]

## Groundwater

Under much of the urban area groundwater levels are rising, as abstractions for heavy industry fall, and they may cause future problems for buildings and infrastructure. The most vulnerable aquifers are under the south and west of GM, coinciding with areas of heavy industry, and leaching of toxic effluent from contaminated land in the Mersey valley is a major problem.[58] Landfill sites, chemicals and metal industries are generally the largest polluters, and up to a third of all petrol stations also cause contamination.[59] While groundwater protection is urgent, there is technical uncertainty on flows and pathways, and legal uncertainty between contaminated land and water pollution regimes.[60] Clearly the integrated catchment management framework should be extended to protect groundwater sources, pathways and receptors.

## Sewage & effluent

Sewage and effluent treatment should be an opportunity for completing the nutrient eco-cycle

54 Mersey Basin Campaign 1996
55 HC Written Answers 4/12/97 cols 289-291
56 ENDS Report No281:53

57 Environment Agency 1996 (River partnerships)
58 National Rivers Authority 1996
59 Environment Agency 1996 (Groundwater protection)
60 ENDS report 260:16-19

– so that organic wastes return safely to the land from which they came. But at present, nearly half our food is imported from overseas, processed, digested, piped, treated and then 'disposed' at large expense and consequent environmental impacts. Sewage dumping at sea has now ceased, and most plants are being converted to 'tertiary' treatment. The centrepiece of the Mersey Basin Campaign is a £2.5 billion investment in sewage treatment, including a new incinerator for GM's 64,000 tonnes (dry weight) of sewage sludge. New pipelines may also carry wet sludge to the surrounding farmland, although land spreading is now being seen as risky and controversial.

The hazards of sludge disposal would suggest that industrial and toxic effluent be separated from human waste as far as possible, but the conventional advice is still for combined treatment, and a completely new separated effluent network would be very costly. Meanwhile many household and industrial substances are being re-engineered along 'BPEO' lines, for example reducing phosphates in detergents. So a 'sustainable sewage' strategy would work at both ends – gradually improving the effluent quality, separating the most hazardous inputs, and re-engineering disposal methods for useful output. Such a city-region 'industrial ecology' in rural areas would use dry earth composting and reed-bed filtration methods. In urban areas larger scale collection and treatment is likely to continue, but following the line of an integrated eco-cycle and materials management approach.

# GROUND QUALITY

As the world's first industrial conurbation, GM contains more than its share of degraded land, and up to 60 km$^2$ – 20% of the inner urban area – is derelict, unstable or potentially contaminated. The 'areas of search' include most former sites of industry, mining, landfill, transport and utilities, and such an environmental jungle is a major obstacle to urban regeneration.[61]

Derelict land in GM has grown to cover 6% of the urban area in the last decade: half is in the public sector, a third in private, and of the rest some is in unknown ownership (*Chapter 5*).[62] Former coal workings stretch in an east-west band, with some areas of deep mining, where ground stability is suspect with regular sewer collapses, and many of the 620 'closed' landfill sites in GM are unstable, with toxic leachate and risk of explosion. One of the worst affected areas is Wigan, with many former minerals-based industries, where a pioneering survey now shows every layer from bedrock to current land-uses.[63] Local soils have high 'field capacity days' of moisture saturation, much of the urban fringe is prone to waterlogging or flooding, and in western areas soil is vulnerable to wind erosion.[64] Much of the soil contains acid levels well beyond critical capacities, contaminants such as lead and cadmium are high in some areas, and the problem of the deteriorating UK soil resource has just been recognized.[65]

## Remediation & reclamation

While dereliction is usually obvious, contamination is often invisible and concealed by owners and others – total remediation is very costly, and over half the sites are publicly owned with public liabilities. Full disclosure of all information could have severe impacts throughout the property and finance chain, and over-zealous enforcement of standards could equally hinder 'brownfield' development.[66]

The current definition of contamination – that which causes 'significant possibility' of 'significant harm' – is based on the intended use of the land, rather than as a universal standard, and this can be a very grey area.[67] There are gaps and overlaps between several legal 're-

61 Salford City Council 1994
62 National Land-Use Database 1999
63 British Geological Survey 1996

64 MAFF 1994
65 Royal Commission on Environmental Pollution 1996
66 Winter 1998
67 Graham 1995

gimes' – the Environmental Protection Act 1990, the IPC system, waste regulation, 'statutory nuisance', and the incoming EC Directive on 'integrated pollution prevention and control' (IPPC).[68] The IPPC regime is likely to require full surveys, public disclosure and remediation for a wider range of contaminants, but this would still leave out historic liabilities and 'orphan sites' with no existing owners. There is also an urgent need to define and manage 'certificates' of completed remediation, to resolve the uncertainty of liability and provide confidence for investors in remediation.[69]

In spite of this tangle there has been much progress – Wigan has reclaimed more than half of its colliery sites, and reclamation in Trafford Park and Salford Quays has led a new wave of investment. Reclamation of derelict land is about 150 hectares per year across GM, twice the rate of greenfield development and half the total of urban development. If the recent increase in dereliction turns out to be a one-off then the solution is in sight – alternatively, the easy sites may be picked off while utilities and public bodies are privatized, higher standards may increase costs, and remediation could become more difficult. If a target was set to reduce derelict land to a third of current levels, assuming that new dereliction continues at current rates, the reclamation activity would need to double (*Fig 8.10*).

## Ground strategy

How can such a minefield of technical uncertainty and legal conflict produce anything like a 'sustainable' ground strategy? Standards are rising for environmental risk assessment, and the forthcoming system of IPPC may help to coordinate ground liability with that of waste, water and industrial processes. But the higher the standard, the higher the costs of reclamation – so the more crucial it is to generate added value from development. In planning terms, the 'problem' of derelict or contaminated land is also an 'opportunity' for rapid restructuring of urban form, meaning that reclamation programmes should be part and parcel of neighbourhood strategies (*Chapter 5*).

Such strategies are not cheap – the full treatment of perhaps 5000 hectares of derelict and/or

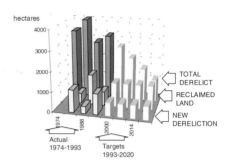

Fig 8.10                    **DERELICT LAND**

Trends and targets for derelict land: assumes target of one third of current levels, with rates of new dereliction continuing.
Source GMR 1995: AGMA 1995: DoE 1995: NLUD 1999

contaminated land in GM, assuming average costs of £250,000 per hectare, could be £50 million per year over 25 years – not impossible, but many times the national 1997 grant allowance of £16 million. The linkage between remediation and regeneration suggests the proposed 'greenfield tax' on new development, and the responsibility of certain industries for such contamination suggests a national 'superfund' levy scheme as in the USA.

But even money is not enough in itself – equally important are investor confidence, public health, community involvement, legal clarity and political accountability, and the new UK regime has yet to be tested.[70] Public registers of contamination in a city-region such as GM would be very controversial, and put at risk the values of much property in urban areas – but would it be better to grasp the nettle and set reclamation on a new level? Land 'health certificates' and technical standards should in principle be handled by a single agency – a sub-regional office of the RDA, Environment Agency, or a consortium of local authorities. Such agencies should work in a strategic programme for maximum contribution of reclamation to urban restructuring. They should also work in collaboration with community and business-based networks such as Groundwork, to fine-tune the reclamation process to local needs and opportunities.[71]

68 DETR 1997: EC Directive 96/61
69 Syms 1997

70 DETR 1999 (guidance on contaminated land)
71 Handley 1996

# WASTE & RECYCLING

Solid waste is the residue at the end of the material chains of an industrial society – a massive resource reduced to negative value by its 'entropy' or disorder. Until recently, the waste industry was mainly concerned with holes in the ground. Now, there is no such thing as a cheap and environmentally friendly method of disposal. In the longer term, the issue is not waste but materials management, where recycling, re-using and minimization are the only viable options. This involves re-organizing and re-engineering material chains throughout the city-region.[72]

The total waste arising from GM is about 12.5 million tonnes per year, of which over 1 million is 'municipal' wastes, 8 million industrial and commercial, and 3 million tonnes of 'controlled' and inert construction wastes *(Fig 8.11)*.[73] Nearly all municipal waste is taken to large landfill sites in adjacent counties, while most industrial waste is taken to the 240 private landfills. One third of the UK's imports of hazardous waste, or 15,000 tonnes also arrive every year for process-

ing in GM, which is arguably the 'waste capital' of Europe.

The growth in national waste arisings of 1– 2% per year could continue doubling every 40– 50 years in a BAU scenario – and responsibility for such a mountain is fragmented into many competing purchasers and providers. In GM, the Environment Agency regulates, the GM Waste Disposal Authority (WDA) issues contracts, GM Waste Ltd processes and transports, GM Sites Ltd operates landfills, the local authorities collect municipal waste, and 3600 private operators manage industrial / commercial wastes. At each stage there are interlocking contracts, new subsidies and taxes, new technology, new environmental standards, new legislation and commodity markets – altogether a rich mixture.

Waste disposal in GM, as in other cities, cannot continue as it is, and viable alternatives are few. At present landfill space is scarce, with less than five years of 'void' left, technical standards are rising, costs could double in the near future, and the UK landfill tax is expected to rise. Current thinking on BPEO for landfill is divided between mixing and segregation of wastes, and between dry or wet landfills, and there are few long term test results. The alternative of incineration or 'waste to energy' is commercially viable but controversial – a proposed network of incinerators won approval for the UK renewable energy subsidy ('NFFO'), but naturally aroused strong public opposition.[74] Composting, digestion and other methods are promising but untested on a large scale. Several strategic options were investigated by the GMWDA, with a highly charged public consultation process. Alternative combinations were assessed for economic and environmental impact relative to the 'base case' of continuing with landfill *(Fig 8.12)*.[75]

The first principle of waste policy is the now familiar 'waste hierarchy' – waste minimization, material recycling, recovery of energy or bio-mass, and landfill as the last option. Howev-

Fig 8.11   **WASTE ARISING & DISPOSAL**

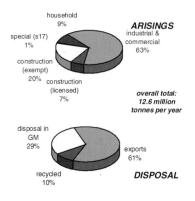

Summary of waste arisings & disposal in GM as of 1995-96.
Source: GMWRA 1996.

72 Biffa 1997
73 Current data estimated from various sources with large margin of uncertainty: GM Waste Regulation Authority 1996: Environment Agency NW 1998: Biffa 1997

74 ENDS report 266:13-14
75 GM Waste Disposal Authority 1997: ERM 1997

er there is conflicting evidence on the total life-cycle impacts of each option, and conflict between the UK policy and the rather uncertain draft EU Waste Directive, which will require pre-treatment of all landfill waste and a shift to other methods.[76] The emerging UK waste strategy is also aiming at a regional management framework, but in practice the BPEO appears to vary locally, making national standards difficult. Even the current modest targets of recycling 25% of household waste, and recovering 40% of municipal waste, are unlikely to be achieved.[77]

Waste disposal has also been the subject of the UK's first fully fledged eco-tax, with a landfill levy now standing at £10 per tonne for 'active' and £2 for inert wastes. The tax revenues offset 0.2% of employers' insurance contributions, and up to 20% of the duty can be offset against tax for environmental projects (*Chapter 13*).[78] The results so far are mixed, with increased illegal disposal and shortages of engineering material, but the main benefit is in the strong signal to waste producers and operators. An improved tax in future could be the central plank of an integrated waste system, extended to other disposal methods, other parts of the material chain, other tax differentials, and incentives for eco-efficient collection (*Box 8.4*).

## Recycling & minimization

Recycling is the traditional response to waste problems – but in the industry view, the environmental benefits are not always clear, the economics depend on unstable markets, and success depends on the unstable commitment of consumers. In GM about 10% of industrial wastes

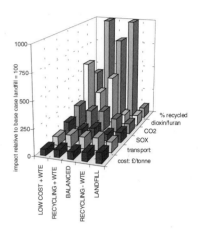

Fig 8.12    **WASTE DISPOSAL OPTIONS:**

Environmental impact & cost per tonne for selected indicators in each of 5 main options, for municipal waste in GM: shown relative to 'base case' of continuing landfill, including for offsetting of emissions via energy recovery. Source: GMWDA, Coopers & Lybrand & ERM 1997.

and 15% of construction wastes are recycled commercially, but of municipal wastes only a tiny 3.5%, about half the national average.[79]

Meanwhile there are cities in EU and North America with up to 75% recycling rates, lower municipal costs and large-scale job creation programmes. The London Waste Strategy draws on such experiences, and sets a new standard for large cities.[80] Recycling rates of 60-80% can be achieved not just as ends in themselves, but as part of an overall market transformation with environmental, economic and social benefits.

The environmental benefits of recycling compared to landfill can be summed up by the reductions in $CO_2$ emissions of up to 5 $tCO_2$ per ton of waste, many times that of incineration.[81] Up to 2500 recycling jobs could be created pro rata in GM, and up to 5000 in related materials management industries. There are huge savings in the eventual costs of full kerb-side recycling systems which can be a fraction of landfill or incineration methods. However, there is a 'hump' of increased capital and start-up costs to be overcome, which might be overcome by diverting other revenues, or local levies on waste streams. Funding could also involve private finance initiatives (PFI) with potential materials operators and

---

**Box 8.4    *INNOVATIVE RECYCLING***

New ways of collecting waste for recycling have to be invented. In a rural area in Finland, the postal service also collects waste paper  – a very neat way to close a loop in the paper cycle. This is one programme in a LA21 partnership which recycles or recovers 70% of municipal waste.

Source Euronet 1998

---

76 DETR 1998: (Less waste more value)
77 Dept of Environment 1995
78 Entrust 1998

79 Audit Commission 1997
80 Murray et al 1998
81 US EPA 1997

markets – newsprint, metals, plastics and so on – and in each case the public sector will need to expand its remit from waste to materials management.

The recycling strategy also has interesting implications for a successful post-industrial 'green collar' business – customer focused, ICT responsive, supply-demand integration, just-in-time logistics, and a networked rather than monolithic structure.[82]

Such a business also has to coordinate with schemes such as packaging recycling – the first sector to trial an internal trading system based on the producer responsibility principle, with 'packaging recovery notes' (PRNs) required for all medium and larger businesses.[83] So far there are rival collection schemes, dispute on who 'owns' the waste, a windfall for incinerator companies, and much PRN trading rather than a true BPEO. An active material management sector would transform the PRN system by collaboration between packaging producers, consumers and operators.

In the longer term we have to rethink the concept of waste itself with a further set of 'Rs' – re-design, re-use, repair and re-conditioning.[84] Forward looking companies such as Rank Xerox are now leasing services rather than selling products, and aiming at zero waste processes. 'Project Catalyst' in GM showed how 14 companies could avoid 12,000 tonnes of waste with a saving of several million pounds, about half of which required no new investment (*Chapter 10*).[85] But while larger process companies are keen to sign up to such schemes, it is still difficult to engage the majority of SMEs, and for these a more comprehensive kind of support network may be needed.[86] Trafford Park in GM may shortly be the site of an innovative industrial ecology scheme, turning wastes into resources for a network of collaborating firms.[87]

## Integrated material strategy

Overall the prospects for waste management in GM show pressing problems and uncertainties – but on the horizon, a new kind of material metabolism in production and consumption. Non-essential throughput would be minimized, all products would be designed for re-use and recycling, and remaining waste would be sorted on collection. Organic and nutrient-rich materials from households, agriculture, and industry would be linked through local and regional ecocycles. The total system of material flows and processes would be managed for efficiency and effectiveness by the 'City-Region plc'. The first step towards this is improving the information base – monitoring and accounting systems for total material flow as per the example below (*Box 8.5*).

Box 8f

### MATERIAL ACCOUNTS

| MATERIAL METABOLISM | 1995 Output | 2020 BAU output | 2020 SD output | 2020 SD to stock | 2020 SD inputs | 2020 SD input/ GDP | Change 95/SD |
|---|---|---|---|---|---|---|---|
| RESOURCE INPUTS / OUTPUTS | Mt/y | Mt/y | Mt/y | Mt/y | Mt/y | t/£1000 | |
| bulk mineral/aggregates | 0.3 | 0.4 | 0.3 | 9.8 | 10.1 | 0.31 | |
| organic: food/timber/paper | 0.4 | 0.5 | 0.3 | 1.3 | 1.7 | 0.05 | |
| manufactured & other | 2.5 | 3.2 | 2.1 | 10.1 | 12.2 | 0.37 | |
| fossil fuel excl.power | 0.0 | 0.0 | 0.0 | 9.7 | 9.7 | 0.29 | |
| solid waste | 11.3 | 14.6 | 9.5 | -9.4 | 0.1 | 0.00 | |
| water borne | 1.2 | 1.6 | 1.0 | -1.0 | 0.0 | 0.00 | |
| air-borne incl carbon | 42.0 | 54.3 | 35.3 | -9.2 | 26.0 | 0.79 | |
| TOTAL material input/output | 57.7 | 75 | 48.5 | 11.3 | 59.7 | 1.8 | -16% |

| WASTE & RECYCLING | disp. | Disp. | disp. | Recyc | %recyc | Arising | Change 95/SD |
|---|---|---|---|---|---|---|---|
| Municipal | 1.2 | 1.4 | 0.7 | 0.3 | 30% | 1.0 | |
| industrial / commercial | 7.1 | 8.7 | 4.6 | 2.0 | 30% | 6.6 | |
| special (section 17) | 0.2 | 0.2 | 0.1 | 0.1 | 30% | 0.2 | |
| construction (licensed) | 0.7 | 0.9 | 0.5 | 0.2 | 30% | 0.7 | |
| construction/mineral (unlic.) | 2.2 | 2.7 | 1.5 | 0.6 | 30% | 2.1 | |
| agricultural (unlicensed) | 0.1 | 0.1 | 0.0 | 0.1 | 80% | 0.2 | |
| sewage sludge | 0.1 | 0.1 | 0.1 | 0.0 | | 0.1 | |
| TOTAL to conversion/disposal | 11.5 | 14.1 | 7.6 | | | 10.9 | -34% |
| TOTAL WASTE RECYCLED | | | | 3.3 | | | 131% |

| CONVERSION & DISPOSAL | disp. | disp. | disp. | Energy | % WTE disp | | Change 95/SD |
|---|---|---|---|---|---|---|---|
| | Mt | mt | mt | PJ/y | | shares | |
| Landfill incl compaction | 11.3 | 4.9 | 3.0 | 0.0 | 50% | 40% | |
| Compost / digest / spread | 0.1 | 0.7 | 1.5 | 0.8 | 50% | 20% | |
| Incineration (WTE) | 0.1 | 8.5 | 3.0 | 16.4 | 80% | 40% | |
| Reduction incineration(75%) | -0.1 | -6.3 | -2.3 | | | | |
| TOTAL WASTE to disposal | 11.4 | 7.8 | 5.3 | | | | -54% |
| TOTAL energy recovery | | | | 17.2 | | | |

Summary of ISCAM scenario accounts for material & waste sector in GM.
Output only for 1995 account & BAU = business as usual projection.
Full breakdown for SD = sustainable development scenario at 2020.

82 Murray 1998
83 DETR 1997 (producer responsibility)
84 Biffa 1997
85 Aspects International 1994
86 Groundwork Foundation 1997
87 National Centre for Business & Ecology 1997

To achieve this vision, the institutions of the city-region would have to deliver functions which are appropriate and achievable, and this is not a simple task. Public intervention in commercial materials markets would be one option for stabilizing prices and commodity banks, but this starts along the road towards a very different kind of public sector. Again the logic for environmental solutions needs to come from social and economic programmes – with a 'solu-

tions-multiplier' approach, the city-region environmental management strategy would look for added value by combining job creation, competitiveness, new business, cost savings, environmental benefit and quality of life factors. In this sector, like few others, there are now enough practical examples from around the world to enable new ways of thinking between waste operators, businesses, development agencies, local authorities and voluntary sectors.

# MAKING IT HAPPEN

Coordination of problems and opportunities in pollution and material flow needs a pro-active city-region framework or 'environmental management strategy'. This has many roles – setting standards for local and regional limits and thresholds, strategic management of air, water, land and waste, active coordination with sectors such as transport and energy, and possibly intervention in markets for materials and pollution trading. As an integral part of the GM 'sustainable development framework', the environment strategy would be implemented by a consortium of the local authorities, RDA, Environment Agency, utilities, major industries, professional and NGO groups.

As with similar environmental programmes, success will come not so much from regulating

environmental 'problems', as from enabling social and economic 'opportunities'.[88] So it is essential that the city-region environment strategy is linked closely with others in health, housing, transport and economic development.

Meanwhile local authorities have to make headway while the legal and financial basis is often unclear – a breakdown of responsibilities shows a fragmented situation, even after the establishment of the UK Environment Agency *(Box 8.6)*. Environmental action for local authorities may start with the standard menu:

- inhouse environmental management
- environmental surveys and audits
- best practice demonstrations
- regulation and policy incentives
- coordination of grants, subsidies, levies and trading networks.

Beyond that, there are opportunities on the technical side, where the city-region level is the key to added value and critical mass in expertise, purchasing power and new partnership structures. There are also opportunities with 'hearts and minds' issues, where LA21 and similar activities are essential for raising political and public commitment.

## Government

The principles of integrated environmental management have been grasped at a national level,

---

**Box 8.6**

### ENVIRONMENTAL MANAGEMENT

| | |
|---|---|
| Air quality: | Districts technically responsible but lacking powers & resources: |
| Air emissions: | EA for larger IPC processes: Districts for smaller LAAPC processes |
| Water quality: | EA , water utilities: river catchment partnerships |
| Land quality: | Districts, EA, utilities, minerals, property, insurance |
| Waste | EA, Districts, packaging chain, waste operators |
| Noise, nuisance, environmental health: | Districts & civil law |
| Occupational risks, civil defence: | HSE & Districts |
| Ecology & bio-diversity: | EN, CA, Districts, GMEU |
| Soil & land | MAFF, CA, agricultural operators. |

Key responsible bodies for environmental management and regulation in GM.

88 Gouldson & Murphy 1998
89 HMGUK 1999

Fig 8.13

## WASTE & POLLUTION STRATEGY

Outline of integrated city-region 2020 environmental management strategy.

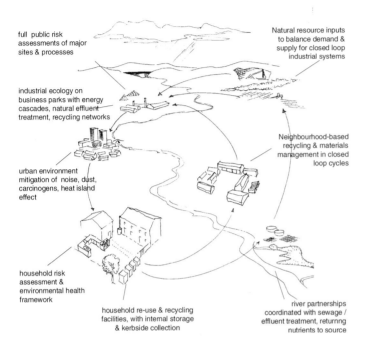

full public risk assessments of major sites & processes

industrial ecology on business parks with energy cascades, natural effluent treatment, recycling networks

urban environment mitigation of noise, dust, carcinogens, heat island effect

household risk assessment & environmental health framework

household re-use & recycling facilities, with internal storage & kerbside collection

Natural resource inputs to balance demand & supply for closed loop industrial systems

Neighbourhood-based recycling & materials management in closed loop cycles

river partnerships coordinated with sewage / effluent treatment, returnng nutrients to source

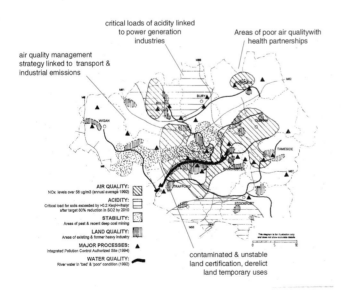

critical loads of acidity linked to power generation industries

Areas of poor air qualitywith health partnerships

air quality management strategy linked to transport & industrial emissions

**AIR QUALITY:**
NOx levels over 56 ug/m3 (annual average 1992)

**ACIDITY:**
Critical load for soils exceeded by >0.2 Keq/H+/ha/yr after target 60% reduction in SO2 by 2010

**STABILITY:**
Areas of past & recent deep coal mining

**LAND QUALITY:**
Areas of existing & former heavy industry

**MAJOR PROCESSES:**
Integrated Pollution Control Authorized Site (1994)

**WATER QUALITY:**
River water in 'bad' & 'poor' condition (1992)

contaminated & unstable land certification, derelict land temporary uses

and the UK Strategy for sustainable development sets out the principle of a far-sighted agenda.[89] But the issue here is the gap between rhetoric and reality, and the practical implications for local and regional players. Clearly government has to provide the frameworks to help 'internalize' environmental costs and benefits in all markets and policy areas. Legal clarity is needed for pollution standards and liabilities, and such standards should be raised progressively over time. The regulation of utilities, and other large scale infrastructure, should incorporate BPEO alongside economic and social objectives. The recent introduction of eco-taxation is welcome, and this should be extended to all activities with environmental impacts, in a structured, gradual and progressive market transformation for both producers and consumers.

To achieve this needs both national and local actions, and it needs powers and resources to be devolved to regional or local levels. This would enable and encourage much greater levels of integrated environmental management for cities, city-regions and regions as appropriate. In particular, investment and equity sharing mechanisms may be the key to enable the new structures of regional governance to be fully effective in the transformation to a de-materialized economy.

## Business & public

Most businesses need to accelerate their environmental management practice, for short term cost savings and long term growth. In many sectors, international competitors from the EU, USA and Asia have been setting higher environmental standards for some time, and local and regional businesses need to move fast to ensure their future competitiveness.

For the environmental industries themselves there is a need for coordination, and complex activities such as waste management and land remediation need common standards, best practices and greater accountability.

As the public are both causes and recipients of local pollution, changing attitudes and lifestyles is perhaps the first step. In practice environmental control can easily conflict with individual freedoms – so positive social norms should be reinforced at every point in education, health, retail, transport and other sectors. Individuals can run cleaner cars, use bio-degradable household chemicals, and sort their waste for recycling, given the right kind of encouragement. This can be accelerated via positive guidance and examples from local authorities, employers, retailers and other service providers.

## Putting it together

A total picture of environmental conditions can be seen by putting together environmental pressures and qualities into an overall 'pollution index'.[90] What this often shows is the perennial division of rich and poor. The mapping here shows a summary of key themes across the city-region *(Fig 8.13)*, and for each area type there is a typical menu of problems and opportunities:

- city and town centres: air and traffic management, water quality, commercial waste
- industrial and development areas: process emissions, water quality, land remediation, industrial ecology
- inner city areas: air quality and traffic management, reclamation of dereliction
- suburban areas: air and traffic management, organic wastes
- urban fringe: water quality, pesticides, soil erosion, organic wastes
- countryside: ozone & acidification, pesticides, soil erosion, farm wastes.

## Context

In international comparison the city-region of GM contains some extreme conditions, but its spread of problems is broadly typical of older industrial cities:[91]

- air quality: worse acidification in eastern EU and CIS cities, worse summer smog in Mediterranean areas, and worse ozone in southern rural areas;
- water: many EU cities are on multi-state river systems with severe problems of toxics, BOD/ COD and eutrophication, with shortages in arid regions of Spain, Italy, Greece;
- ground and soil: contamination affects all cities with older industry: erosion severe in some southern states;
- waste management: much greater arisings in countries such as Norway, and much less in equally affluent Alpine region cities: recycling most advanced in northern EU and Scandinavia;

In general the northern and western EU cities – Stockholm, Amsterdam, Copenhagen – have much better developed environmental management systems, but also suffer from the problems of affluence. Eastern and CIS cities tend to have industrial air and ground problems, and peripheral cities have water and transport problems. While there are no ready-made solutions, the general theme applies throughout – an integrated technical, economic and political framework.

---

**Box 8.79**

### *SUMMARY ~ WASTE & POLLUTION*

The 2020 environment strategy aims to upgrade eco-efficiency in the material metabolism. Waste itself will be a potential resource in a closed loop cycle of production and consumption:

- environmental standards for maximum risk and exported substances in pollution 'bubble'
- transport air emissions contained by demand management and cleaner technology
- water demand management for climate risk, total supply quality with lead replacement
- waste and materials consortium to develop materials handling, re-use and re-design for a zero-emission and zero-waste economy

---

90 Wood & Lee 1974
91 European Environment Agency 1996

# ENERGY & CLIMATE

*'The energy that moves mountains, moves the people'*
Mullah Nasruddin

Energy is fundamental to the life of cities and regions – but the energy which powers them is now disrupting the basis of life itself, the global ecological balance. Climate change, possibly the greatest single threat to the global environment, is a problem for which every nation has to accept responsibility and work together – a new kind of global order. In turn, every city and region bears some kind of responsibility to play its part and move towards best practice. The question is then what kind of responsibility – and the answer has to be found in opportunities for economic growth, environmental improvement and social welfare.

A sustainable energy path is clear in principle and technically quite viable – but the technology is only the starting point for a huge economic and political transformation. And while such a transformation is debated at the global and national level, only a few cities or regions have any kind of coordinated response in the shape of an energy-climate strategy.

So our aim here is to sketch the outline of a fully integrated energy-climate strategy for the city-region – including 'supply-side' actions on fuels and markets, 'demand-side' actions for housing, transport, industry and others, and adaptation and defensive actions for climate change itself. Renewables and CHP are then the long term energy sources and networks of choice, in the transformation of the total energy metabolism. And, as always, success depends on integrating such an energy-climate strategy with parallel actions, in sectors such as housing, property, regeneration, transport and economic development.

## Trends & tensions

The total system of supply, conversion and demand of the city-region – the energy metabolism – has transformed in three decades, from a time when the air was thick with soot and acid gases from coal burning. Overall energy use per person in GM may be up to 5% higher than the UK average, due to an older and less fit housing stock, higher road transport distances, a rapid expansion in services, and clusters of older industry.[1] Current energy data for fuels and sec-

1  All GM energy data from McEvoy 1997: March 1986: DTI 1995: DTI 1996

tors shows that housing, transport and industry each take about 30%: and that gas and oil between them account for 75% of 'final energy' delivered to consumers *(Fig 9.1).*[2]

The majority fuel for all sectors except transport is now gas, but electricity is the fastest growing energy source. Current BAU ('business as usual') projections show that total UK 'final demand' could rise at between 11-20% per decade – but these depend on many assumptions on utility regulation, international fuel prices, technological change and economic growth. Transport energy is by far the fastest growing at 32% per decade, followed by services, industry and domestic demand at 6% per decade.[3]

At present the international energy industry is in a period of hectic change and restructuring, and GM is now the home base of a combined energy-water utility company, a leading player in the new deregulated energy market in the UK and abroad.[4] However few of the utilities show much concern on the total picture of demand, distribution, supply and external impacts, and the main agenda for the industry and regulators alike is competitiveness and prices.[5]

The single largest impact of energy use is through carbon dioxide ($CO_2$) emissions from burning of fossil fuels, the main cause of climate change *(next section).* National $CO_2$ emissions under BAU projections could rise between 8-25% by 2020 – in direct conflict with the scientific advice for a worldwide reduction of 60%.[6] Alongside climate change there are many related impacts from the energy industry, with the fossil fuel and nuclear plant life-cycles. For consumers in the city-region, the GM housing stock is one of the least efficient in Europe, and even with falling energy prices a third of all households suffer from some form of energy poverty.[7] Climate change also has other human causes including methane, nitrous oxide, other chemicals and deforestation.

## Future prospects

Energy-climate systems are the focus of much scenario modelling on a national and global

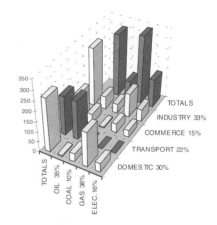

**Fig 9.1**          **ENERGY CONSUMPTION**

TOTALS
INDUSTRY 33%
COMMERCE 15%
TRANSPORT 22%
DOMESTIC 30%

TOTALS
OIL 35%
COAL 10%
GAS 38%
ELEC. 16%

Final energy demand in GM in GWh/yr, by fuel and end-use sector;
Source: est. from DTI 1995, March 1988, McEvoy 1997, ISCAM accounts

scale. On a city or regional level, the uncertainties of climate impacts and the opportunities in responses show that computer modelling needs to be combined with a more deliberative kind of scenario approach, which may use citizen panels or futures workshops.[8] Here is one possible way to structure a set of scenarios:

- *BAU scenario:* energy demand continues to rise, and supply draws on the cheapest 'brown' fossil fuels. Climate disruption sets in with massive storms, floods and droughts. By 2020, total emissions increase by 20%.
- *technology scenario:* smart IT systems and micro manufacturing stabilizes the demand for energy, and $CO_2$ emissions stay level. Renewable sources are developed, but smart metering divides the rich from the poor.
- *SD scenario:* integrated demand management at local and city-region level stabilizes energy demand. Integration of supply technologies helps rapid spread of renewables: city-region $CO_2$ emissions reduce by 35%
- *deep ecology scenario:* downshifting lifestyles reduces consumption, mobility and energy demand heavily. With large

2 Final energy or 'final demand' refers to energy consumed at point of use: 'Primary energy' is the energy content of the raw fuel before conversion or distribution
3 DTI 1995
4 United Utilities plc 1998
5 DTI 1998

6 IPCC 1995
7 DETR 1997 (Energy report): Leather & Morrison 1997
8 Ravetz 1998a

## ENERGY METABOLISM

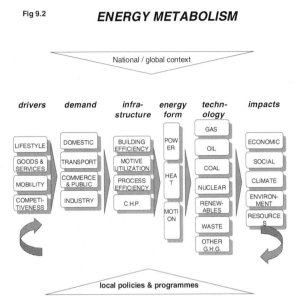

Fig 9.2

Integrated assessment system mapping of total energy metabolism

### Energy metabolism

Energy supply and demand are calculated in enormous detail by engineers and economists, but the wider role of energy in human society includes many other factors. One approach is to look at energy as an ecological dynamic, which dissipates from high intensity sources, through natural and human systems, towards entropy and disorder.[9] Another approach is to put together physical and human factors with an 'integrated assessment' mapping of the total energy metabolism *(Fig 9.2)*.

This shows how the 'drivers' on the left – the human needs of shelter, comfort and mobility – translate to demand sectors in housing, transport and industry. On the other side of the balance are the many energy technologies and their possible impacts on the economy, society and environment.

Such a mapping shows that single issues such as climate change are linked to almost every activity in the city-region. Most energy model-

investment in renewables and CHP this cuts $CO_2$ emissions in 2020 by 50%, and the most severe climate effects are avoided.

ling assumes for instance, supply-demand equations or 'elasticities', but these may be very dependent on management, political and lifestyle factors.[10] The UK's climate change targets could be met now if all consumers wore thermal clothing at all times – but this is unlikely within current social norms. So any change in the overall balance of the metabolism and its impacts is likely to be a combination of cultural, economic, political, infrastructure, technology, scientific and ethical actions – a rich mixture.

### Towards sustainable energy

The goals and scope of a 'sustainable' energy strategy are clear in principle – to manage equitable levels of demand and efficient means of supply within local and global environmental limits.[11] But when we look for such clear limits, we find many layers of risk and uncertainty across space and time, and balancing these with economic and social demands is complex and controversial. For instance in GM, the fastest growing energy demand sector is air travel, and the airport is also the economic powerhouse of the region. Energy taxes to reduce consumption can be seen either as a brake on the economy, or as an incentive for modernization. In practice most businesses and consumers have little real commitment to energy efficiency – progress depends on linking energy-climate strategies with problems and opportunities in housing, transport, economic development and so on, in a diverse and responsive approach.

In terms of the physics and technology there are several strands to an integrated energy-climate strategy:

- climate change adaptation or defence
- mitigation of emissions through demand efficiency measures
- cleaner fuels and supply technologies
- renewable and low-impact energy sources
- co-generation (CHP) and direct heat distribution networks.

9 Odum 1983
10 Ekins 1995

11 Krause et al 1995

The technical strategy aims at the optimum balance of these options, which also meets the many social, economic and environmental goals.

There is also a social agenda for increasing efficiency and equity, especially for those in energy poverty, and for countries and people more at risk from climate impacts. There is an economic agenda for internalizing the true costs of energy use, and using the efficiency factor to drive innovation and eco-modernization. There is also a political and cultural agenda in creating the institutions for planning and investment in a deregulated market.

Overall targets can be drawn from the global emissions reductions needed to maintain the maximum rate of ecological adapation.[12] With an environmental space calculation of the quota for UK and GM, using a range of assumptions on world population and climate sensitivity, the central estimate for the UK is for reduction in climate emissions of 88% from 1990-2050, which equates to 65% reduction at 2020.[13] This equates to the 'deep green' scenario above, and such a target is a reference point for comparison with opportunities on the ground in housing, transport and industry, and particularly the economic and political constraints. The targets for energy markets, renewables and CHP are based on 'best practice' scenarios within anticipated policies and market conditions, and each of these has been modelled for the city-region using the ISCAM scenario method *(Chapter 1)*. The indicators and targets shown here are the most critical and sensitive 'core indicators' drawn from the scenario accounts *(Fig 9.1)*.[14] Following these is a summary of goals and strategies, which outline the general direction and main targets for an integrated energy-climate strategy *(Fig 9.2)*.

---

**Box 9.1**

### ENERGY & CLIMATE ~ TRENDS & TARGETS

| | | 1995 | BAU 2020 | SD 2020 | Trend target index |
|---|---|---|---|---|---|
| | | | | | % |
| total final energy demand | PJ/y | 333 | 474 | 284 | -100 |
| total renewable supply | PJ/y | 2 | 7 | 25 | 20 |
| CHP heat output | PJ/y | 5 | 14 | 26 | 40 |
| total primary energy | PJ/y | 406 | 561 | 355 | -100 |
| total CO2 emissions | mt | 31 | 37 | 22 | -70 |
| total CO2 / total GDP | kg/£GDP | 1.58 | 1.14 | 0.66 | 50 |
| total CH4 emissions | kt | 220 | 55 | 22 | 80 |
| total HFC / PFC emission | kt | 2.60 | 4.20 | 0.25 | -70 |

Summary 'core indicators' with trends & targets from ISCAM scenario accounts for GM 1995-2020.
BAU = business as usual projection from trend
SD = sustainable development scenario

---

**Box 9.2**

### ENERGY & CLIMATE ~ GOALS & STRATEGIES

| | GOV | LAP | BUS | COM | PUB |
|---|---|---|---|---|---|
| **CLIMATE CHANGE STRATEGY:** | ○ | ● | ● | | |
| Planning for 1° temp rise, 40cm sea-level rise, ecological stress, floods, storms, droughts. Integrated environment-economic planning for total final energy reductions 20-25%: CO$_2$ reduction 35-40% (1995/2020) | | | | | |
| **ENERGY SUPPLY & DEMAND:** | ● | ● | ● | | |
| National strategy for power & utilities: market incentives for efficiency: city-region partnership energy agency | | | | | |
| **RENEWABLE SOURCES:** | ○ | ○ | ● | | ○ |
| 5-10% of energy demand from localized solar, wind, bio-mass, waste | | | | | |
| **COMBINED HEAT & POWER:** | ○ | ● | ● | | ○ |
| 30% of housing & businesses to have access to CHP network | | | | | |

GOV ~ government & EU: LA ~ local authorities & partnerships: BUS ~ business & finance: COM ~ community & 3rd sector: PUB ~ public

---

12 McLaren et al 1997
13 World Energy Council & IIASA 1995
14 Ravetz 2000

# ENERGY–CLIMATE STRATEGY

Almost every year sees a new record for world temperatures – affluent tourists and peasant farmers alike are now subject to increasing levels of floods, droughts, storms and heatwaves.

The global climate is a hugely complex system, and its disruption could have catastrophic effects far beyond the calculations of the models. On the other hand, humans have always lived and adapted to climate hazards, and change may bring benefits as well as costs, a feature which emerged in the NW regional impacts studies.[15] Some argue that the pace of social and economic change is far beyond that of the climate, and that climate mitgation or adaptation is a relatively minor item on the world agenda.[16] Much hinges on how scientific uncertainty is interpreted by different worldviews and cultures, and the implications for political commitment and management styles in climate strategy.[17]

Climate change is caused mainly by the emissions of carbon dioxide ($CO_2$) from burning fossil fuels *(Fig 9.2)*.[18] The emissions from GM, including those from power stations, air travel and heavy industry which supply the city, are about 32 million tonnes of $CO_2$ per year – about 1/7th of 1% of the world total.[19] The largest single source of $CO_2$ is from coal-fired power generation, and the fastest growing sources of $CO_2$ are from road transport and air travel.

The current scientific best estimate is that average temperatures are rising by 1 degree every 40–50 years, or 0.2–0.25° per decade. For most eco-systems this is a greater rate of change than any in recorded history, at several times the maximum rate of natural adaptation, and the result is likely to be ecological damage, loss of land, extreme weather conditions, and increased risk of more catastrophic effects. Worldwide, about half a billion people could be directly affected, and many more could suffer from increased morbidity and economic instability. The effects of climate change for GM and the NW region are modest in comparison, but ecological stress is likely and low-lying areas such as the Lancashire coast could be below sea-level within a hundred years *(Box 9.3)*.[20]

## Climate targets & policies

World $CO_2$ emissions could rise by 50% over the next 25 years, with the bulk of the increase in developing nations. For the UK, the BAU emissions could rise by 8-25% by 2020, but the current uncertainty in markets and technologies makes such projections quite speculative. Meanwhile the scientific community recommends cuts of at least 60% world-wide, as soon as possible, on the basis that temperature rise should be contained at 0.1° per decade. The international agreement of Kyoto in 1997 is a legally binding commitment by most developed countries to stabilizing the growth of $CO_2$ emissions, but this is only the first step on a very long road *(Box 9.4)*.

The UK government is now putting together a post-Kyoto climate emissions reduction strategy, which focuses on the target of 12.5% reduction (1990–2002/2012) for a basket of climate emissions, together with a domestic target for

Fig 9.3    **CLIMATE CHANGE**

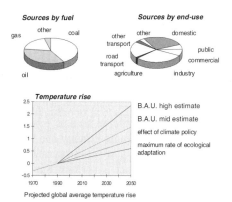

Causes & effects for the UK of global climate change.
Source: IPCC 1996: DETR 1998.

15 Shackley & Wood 1998
16 Ausubel 1993
17 Rotmans & de Vries 1997
18 Houghton 1997

19 $CO_2$ estimates include a pro rata allocation of the UK power system, and a full allocation for air travel direct emissions, as in Chapter 7
20 DETR 1998: Hulme 1998

**Box 9.3**
## CLIMATE IMPACTS: NW–UK

- temperature increase between 0.5 - 1.4° from 1970-2020: average 0.2° per decade
- winter rainfall increases 6-14%: summer rainfall reduces 1-10%: more variability and risk of storms & floods
- climate in GM similar to the present climate of London in 2020
- sea level increase 15cm by 2050: problems on Lancashire coast
- ecological habitats shift northward by 50-80km per decade:
- increase in soil erosion & drought
- increase in some infectious diseases & morbidity
- 10% reduction in heating, larger increase in cooling energy
- productivity increase for some crops & timber
- possible benefits for outdoor recreation & tourism but much uncertainty on local cloud cover

Source: Climate Impacts Programme 1998: Shackley & Wood 1998:

**Box 9.4**
## KYOTO PROTOCOL

The 1997 Kyoto Agreement negotiated a multilateral global agreement for an aggregate 5.2% reduction of $CO_2$ emission equivalents (including a basket of 3 gases) from all developed nations from 1990-2010 (averaged 2008-2012). The EU collectively agreed to a reduction of 8% apportioned internally, from a 27% increase in Portugal to a 21% reduction in Germany. The UK's international commitment is to a reduction of 12.5% in the basket of gases, alongside a 'domestic' target of 20% reduction in carbon emissions alone.

In practice the Kyoto agreement is only the start of a very long process which will eventually include all nations. Due to the large stock of atmospheric $CO_2$, by 2100 Kyoto as it stands will produce only marginal effects on climate change processes already in motion. A similar commitment from developing countries after 2020 could reduce temperature rise in 2100 by a quarter, while the 60% emissions reduction recommended by the IPCC could reduce temperature rise in 2100 by over half, to 0.1° per decade or the maximum rate of ecological adaptation.

Source: DETR 1998: Grubb et al 1998

**Fig 9.4** **DE-CARBONIZATION**

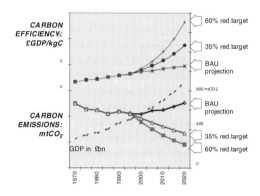

Ratio of economic activity to carbon production from all sources of primary energy. Projections & targets for 35% and 60% $CO_2$ emission reductions for UK to 2020. Assumes GDP growth at 2.25% p.a.
Source: based on DTI 1995: Krause 1995

20% reduction in carbon emissions alone.[21] While the previous UK strategy was very modest, the 'dash for gas' in power generation, the extended life-cycle of nuclear plants, and the effect of climate change itself, have helped to meet the targets easily – national $CO_2$ emissions have in fact reduced by 8% since 1990.[22] However another such windfall is unlikely in future decades, and even to stabilize emissions, let alone reduce them by 12.5% or 20%, will need much stronger actions. Even these targets hardly register on the longer term agenda.

Energy–climate policy generally starts with a 'no-regrets' approach, in other words that the costs of emissions reduction should be less than the 'benefits' of avoided damage and improved efficiency.[23] In practice such a balance is based on many assumptions, such as the value of human life and the long term discount rate, and the costs of efficiency can also be seen as a benefit for the eco-modernization of industry and infrastructure.[24] This process of eco-modernization can be tracked with what is perhaps the most fundamental indicator of any in sustainable development – 'carbon restructuring'. This shows the rate of change in 'carbon efficiency' or the economic output per unit of carbon emissions

21 DETR 1998 (Climate change consultation paper)
22 HC Written Answers 13/04/98 Col 121-2
23 Chesshire 1992
24 Pezzey 1994

*(Fig 9.4)*.[25]  Current carbon efficiencies can be estimated:

- for GM, about £2.80/kgC[26]
- for the UK, £3.20/kgC, rising at 2% per year
- for the world about £0.80/kgC, with little change.[27]

The rate of increase in carbon efficiency in the UK is about 2.25% – similar to that of long term economic growth – and so long term emissions trends are relatively static. In practice much of this efficiency gain has come from the migration of heavy industry, which substitutes direct emissions with indirect, via imported goods and materials.  But to achieve stringent energy–climate targets while maintaining economic growth, the rate of carbon restructuring would have to accelerate sharply.  The chart shows alternative targets of 35% and 60% reduction by 2020, which require a rate of carbon restructuring of several times current levels.

## City-region climate strategy

Local energy–climate strategies in the UK until recently have been restricted to a few dedicated cities and counties.[28]  With the growing awareness of climate change, many local and regional authorities are now looking at energy strategies in a broader context:

- the Home Energy Conservation Act 1995 requires plans (not necessarily actions) for the improvement of housing efficiency by up to 30% by 2010. This may be combined by an Energy Efficiency Bill which requires home energy audits at purchase.[29]
- the Heidelberg Declaration of EU Mayors aims at 20% CO$_2$ reduction 1987–2005.[30]
- the FoE Climate Resolution for local authorities proposes 30% reduction from 1990–2005.[31]

While ambitious targets are proposed, most have little research to back them up. In contrast to many in Europe, local authorities in the UK have little influence or even information on the fast-moving, deregulated and commercially sensitive energy market *(Box 9.5)*. For a city-region such as GM, its older housing stock, obsolete industry and fragmented transport networks are problems and also opportunities. The technology to achieve CO$_2$ reductions of 30–40% is available and proven, but up to now, improved efficiency has been outweighed by rising demand for space, mobility and goods – an economic and lifestyle issue. A parallel challenge is to create institutions which can enable and coordinate long term planning and investment – a political issue.

In the context of national and global markets and policies, a localized energy–climate strategy, raises the question – what is the effective territory and remit of city-region actions and agencies? The evidence from sectors such as housing, transport and so on, shows that energy-climate issues are embedded in technology, infrastructure, regulation, markets, institutions, and not least the physical nature of the city or region. And as energy is rarely a top priority for individuals or organizations, success depends on linkages with housing, transport, economic development and so on. For example the first priority for emissions reduction is the housing stock, where every dwelling in the city-region should be upgraded to best practice standards, but there is no way of achieving this in the present system. So a city-region energy agency

---

**Box 9.5**

### URBAN CLIMATE STRATEGY

Amidst its rapid restructuring, the city of Berlin has placed a strong emphasis on energy–climate policies. In line with its commitments to the European Climate Alliance, the city government aims to reduce CO$_2$ emissions by 50% per head between 1990 and 2010. A plan of action with funding of DM 430 million has been committed, and the reduction in CO$_2$ emissions is estimated at 10% in the first 2 years.

Source UNCHS 1997

---

25 Ravetz 1999d
26 shown in kg carbon: 1 kg carbon = 3.7 kgCO$_2$
27 World Resources Institute 1997
28 Chell & Hutchinson1993: Newcastle City Council 1997: Leicester City 1995: Bristol Energy-Environment Programme 1992
29 Association for the Conservation of Energy 1996
30 EU Expert Group 1997
31 Friends of the Earth 1995

would aim to capture the potential added value by coordinating efficiency programmes with re-habilitation and regeneration at every opportunity.

The goals and targets of a city-region strategy can be drawn from the energy–climate scenario below. This is based on the ISCAM scenario accounting system, using a combination of 'top-down' and 'bottom-up' government projections, industry models, renewables studies and assessment of local conditions. Several possible emissions targets were investigated:

- 20% 'pale green' reductions, based on local authority estimates, with commercially viable actions under modest levels of eco-taxation.[32]
- 35% 'sustainable development' reductions: best practice in every sector including power generation with stronger eco-tax package.
- 65% 'deep green' reductions as per the environmental space case: a total re-engineering of all buildings, transport, production and consumption in GM.

The focus here is on the middle 'SD' scenario – a full scale application of 'best practice', within reasonable assumptions on technological, economic and political constraints. The charts show sectoral scenarios for final energy and emissions *(Figs 9.5 and 9.6)*:[33] and the table shows a breakdown and rate of change from 1995 to 2020 *(Box 9.6)*. Such broad energy–climate targets then form the backdrop to more detailed strategies, policies and programmes in each sector.

## Sectoral strategies

The starting point for an integrated strategy is energy efficiency in housing, where application of best practice over 25 years could reduce $CO_2$ emissions by 40% *(Chapter 5)*. This assumes that new and renovated housing is built to the highest practical standards, that all other housing is upgraded, that household numbers and appliances continue to increase, and that climate change has significant effects on heating and cooling.

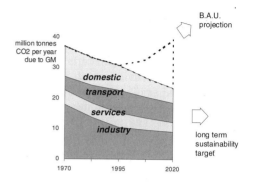

Fig 9.5     **CARBON SCENARIO**

Emissions source targets for CO2 reductions in GM by 2020, from UK & NW data, incl. air travel apportioned per capita.
Source: ICAM scenario accounts, based on DTI 1995:
Cambridge Econometrics 1998, IPPR 1996

The 2020 transport strategy aims to stabilize growth in overall travel levels, while shifting private to public transport, and together with improved efficiencies and power sources, this could achieve a $CO_2$ reduction of 15-20% *(Chapter 6)*.[34] Even this fairly moderate target implies major changes to travel, leisure and work patterns, with other benefits such as air quality, public health and urban regeneration.

Energy–climate targets for public and commercial sectors follow a similar approach as for housing, but due to the many obstacles in the commercial sector, the pace of growth and the backlog of older buildings, the $CO_2$ targets are lower at 25-30%. For manufacturing industry a similar case is based on projected GDP shares and sectoral 'best practice' efficiencies, in the context of economic growth and energy-intensive automation *(Chapter 10)*.[35]

## Other climate effects

The effects of other emissions including methane, nitrous oxide and HFCs, account for between 20% and 40% of the total climate effect, depending on the allocation method for emissions

32 Cambridge Econometrics 1994
33 Energy calculations use many units including: joules, mtoe, barrels, kWh, therms. Units for the city-region total energy use are converted here to Petajoules (PJ, or 10^15 joules): 1 PJ = 277 million kWh (kilowatt hours) = 22000 tonnes of oil equivalent.

34 Hughes 1994
35 HM Treasury 1998 (Marshall Report)

**Fig 9.6** ***ENERGY DEMAND SCENARIO***

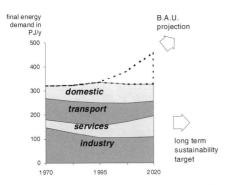

Scenario targets for final energy consumption by sector including power in GM by 2020, from UK & NW data, incl. air travel.
Source: ISCAM scenario accounts, based on DTI 1995: Cambridge Econometrics 1998, IPPR 1996

**Box 9.6**

### ENERGY-CARBON SCENARIO ACCOUNTS

| FINAL ENERGY: PJ/y | 1995 | BAU 2020 | SD 2020 total | SD 2020 DOM | SD 2020 TRAN | SD 2020 SERV | SD 2020 IND | SD 2020 share |
|---|---|---|---|---|---|---|---|---|
| Gas | 122.4 | 161.8 | 91.3 | 44.3 | 8.8 | 13.8 | 24.3 | 32% |
| Oil | 123.6 | 181.5 | 68.7 | 1.8 | 47.9 | 6.9 | 12.2 | 24% |
| Coal | 30.2 | 23.5 | 9.9 | 0.9 | 0.0 | 0.9 | 8.1 | 3% |
| Renewables | 0.0 | 3.0 | 16.7 | 10.6 | 0.0 | 3.7 | 2.4 | 6% |
| Direct heat (CHP) | 4.7 | 14.0 | 26.0 | 13.3 | 0.0 | 4.6 | 8.1 | 9% |
| Power | 52.0 | 89.8 | 71.0 | 17.7 | 11.2 | 16.1 | 26.0 | 25% |
| TOTAL FINAL DEMAND | 332.9 | 473.5 | 283.7 | 88.6 | 67.9 | 46.1 | 81.1 | |
| Shares of total | | | 0% | 31% | 24% | 16% | 29% | |
| Sectoral change 1995/2020 | | | -15% | -8% | -18% | -4% | -24% | |

| CARBON EMISSIONS MtCO2 | | | 2020 SD total | 2020 SD DOM | 2020 SD TRAN | 2020 SD SERV | 2020 SD IND | 2020 SD POW |
|---|---|---|---|---|---|---|---|---|
| Gas | 7.3 | 12.3 | 7.2 | 2.4 | 0.5 | 0.8 | 1.3 | 2.1 |
| Oil | 10.8 | 16.9 | 6.8 | 0.1 | 4.0 | 0.5 | 0.9 | 1.1 |
| Coal | 11.3 | 4.9 | 2.6 | 0.1 | 0.0 | 0.1 | 0.8 | 1.6 |
| Waste | 0.9 | 2.4 | 4.9 | 0.0 | 0.0 | 0.0 | 1.2 | 3.6 |
| Nuclear | 0.4 | 0.6 | 0.2 | 0.0 | 0.0 | 0.0 | 0.0 | 0.2 |
| Total $CO_2$ ex.power | | | 21.7 | 2.7 | 4.6 | 1.4 | 4.4 | 8.7 |
| Power share | | | 100% | 25% | 16% | 23% | 37% | |
| Power allocation | | | - | 2.2 | 1.4 | 2.0 | 3.2 | |
| TOTAL $CO_2$ Incl power | 30.6 | 37.1 | 21.7 | 4.8 | 5.9 | 3.4 | 7.5 | |
| Share incl.power | | | 99% | 22% | 27% | 15% | 34% | |
| Sectoral change 1995/2020 | | | -29% | -41% | -16% | -29% | -28% | |

Summary of ISCAM scenario accounts for final energy demand & carbon emissions in GM. This shows:
total output only for 1995 account & BAU (business as usual projection):
breakdown for SD (sustainable development): change from 1995-2020.
DOM – domestic: TRAN – transport: SERV – commercial & public: IND – industry: POW—power generation.
Sources: based on DTI 1995, DETR 1998, March 1988, McEvoy 1997.

sources and end-users.[36] The inventory for GM, as compared to the NW and UK, shows a high proportion of $CO_2$ from transport and industry, and a high proportion of methane from many landfill sites *(Box 9.7)*.

Methane ($CH_4$) from agriculture, waste disposal, gas distribution and mining accounts for 12-17% of climate change effects. The many closed landfills and mineworkings in GM make this a priority issue, and some mines are at risk of explosion. Methane collection from new landfill sites is now a viable renewable energy source which could meet 1–2% of total energy demand.

Nitrous oxide ($N_2O$) accounts for 8% of the UK climate emissions, mainly from nylon manufacture and use of agricultural fertilizers. The GM sources are mainly from catalytic converters in road transport – an example of how solving one environmental problem tends to create others. If the GM proportion is allocated by end-users, $N_2O$ is a major issue for the farming and food industries, pointing to the organic conversion of the food chain *(Chapter 7)*.

HFCs (hydro-fluorocarbons) are used as substitutes for the 'ozone depletors' CFC's and HCFC's in refrigeration, foams and fluids. CFC's

**Box 9.7**

### CLIMATE EMISSIONS

| | GM | NW | UK |
|---|---|---|---|
| CO2 | 80.0 | 59.0 | 76.9 |
| Methane | 17.0 | 17.3 | 12.7 |
| Nitrous Oxide | 2.0 | 4.6 | 8.1 |
| HFC | 0 | 18.6 | 2.1 |
| PFC / SF6 | 0 | 0 | 0.2 |
| TOTAL % | 100 | 100 | 100 |
| TOTAL global warming potential in MtCO2 equiv. by emission source | 17.1 | 80.7 | 720.9 |
| TOTAL MtCO2 by end-user | 22.6 | 61.1 | 543.2 |

Percentage proportions of climate change effect from 6 gases, weighted by global warming potential at 100-year time horizon, allocated by emissions source.
Source: London Research Centre 1997: Manders et al 1999

---

36 Allocation of these emissions by 'source' or by 'end-user' shows different results. The GM, regional and national proportions each differ. Emissions can be totalled by their GWP (global warming potential) expressed as carbon equivalents for either a 25 or 100 time horizon. Details in Mander, Buchdahl & Shackley 1999.

are now being phased out due to their effects on the ozone layer, but most of them are long-lived and will stay in the atmosphere for many years. Nearly all HFCs in the UK are now from a plant on Merseyside which is being replaced. International agreements cover the phasing out of CFC production by 1996, and HCFCs by 2015, but emissions will continue for some time due to the stock of older plant and equipment.

Overseas deforestation and land-use change accounts for an additional third on the total world climate effect – a complex tangle of development politics and international trade. Within GM itself, forestry and other forms of carbon storage could at most absorb 1% of carbon emissions *(Chapter 7)*. Local strategies are more effective by targeting the supply chains for minerals, timber and food.

## From strategy to action

An integrated climate strategy combines three kinds of response – mitigation, defence and adaptation – of which mitigation is the first and main agenda for the city-region. Climate defences concern sea-levels, rising groundwater, flood risks, soil erosion and other effects. Climate adaptation is a new agenda, with timescales beyond the horizons of most organizations.[37] The NorthWest UK has started with some pioneering impacts studies, which combine technical evidence with stakeholder surveys – the next step is to develop integrated responses.[38]

In practice an energy–climate strategy, whether at national or local level, cannot operate as if managed by objectives by a single agency – it is more a case of diverse actions in many sectors, coordinated for added synergy – a kind of 'zen and the art of climate maintenance'.[39]

There are also several proposed national and global mechanisms which could complicate the issue, with potential for local applications, but also the possibility that action will be substituted for paper targets. 'Joint implementation' is an arrangement where emissions targets may be substituted from one country to another, through forestry planting or others. The Clean Development Mechanism encourages development of carbon offsets as part of overseas development activity. 'Carbon trading' is a national or international market in emissions permits to be traded, and large energy companies are already piloting internal trading schemes .[40]

The dialogue now starting between the UK government and industrial sectors will have to work within this more complex picture of diffused responsibility. For cities and regions, there will be questions raised on the appropriate responsibility and territory for climate strategy, and it is likely that area-based programmes could run in parallel to sector-based activity.

# ENERGY SUPPLY & DEMAND

The technical case for improving supply efficiencies and reducing impacts hinges on power generation, and its effect on the ratio between 'primary' and 'final' energy.[41] At present power in the UK comes from gas, coal, oil and nuclear, together with small amounts of hydropower and other renewables, and the generation industry is the largest single source of $CO_2$ emissions. The total system efficiency and impacts depends on:

- the proportion of electricity in the energy mix: electricity being the most versatile but inefficient of fuels. Substitution by gas has benefits and is viable in refrigeration and large-scale motive power;

- the primary fuels used for power generation – gas produces half the carbon for the same heat output as coal, but UK resources are limited. Nuclear produces little carbon but has many other risks;

---

37 Cline 1992
38 Sustainability NW 1998: Shackley, Wood et al 1998
39 Rayner & Malone 1997
40 Collier & Lofstedt 1997

41 For power generation the difference between 'final' and 'primary' energy is mainly due to generation and distribution losses which total about 60-70%.

Fig 9.7   **POWER SCENARIO (UK)**

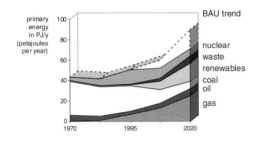

'Sustainable Development' power generation scenario for UK by primary
fuel source in PJ/year, pro-rata for consumption in GM, excluding local
variations from embedded generation.
Sources: based on ISCAM scenario accounts, data from DTI 1995,
National Grid 1994.

- the proportion of power from renewables
  and CHP, and proportion of direct heat,
  which displace power and other fuels.

Each of these – substitution, fuel switching, and
displacement – is an objective for energy–climate strategy. In practice power is distributed
through the national grid, mostly outside local
influence, although there is a large 'own-use'
industrial generation capacity in GM. So a local
energy-climate strategy has to make assumptions
on a future 'green power' scenario, based on
climate targets, national projections and scenario
modelling.[42] The SD scenario shown here shows
UK power demand increasing by 30%, mainly
due to increased use in transport – while its $CO_2$
emissions reduce by 15%, due to a further shift
from coal to gas, and a major contribution from
renewables *(Fig 9.7)*.

In practice the UK power industry is in great
flux, rapidly liberalizing with pressures from the
remaining coal industry, limited gas resources,
unstable oil markets, uncertainty on the nuclear
option, fierce global competition, and new climate change commitments.[43] With a context of
falling world prices and a deregulated market,
such technical and political uncertainties make

prediction very difficult, and the most sophisticated computer tools depend on assumptions
which are up in the air.[44] Both nationally and
locally, any strategy is likely to be more oppor-
tunistic as planned.

## Energy markets

The transformation of the UK energy industry
over the last decade is now being completed,
with the final stages of deregulation in generation, distribution and consumer choice – with
the regulators in the sensitive role of mediating
between economic, social and environmental interests, in roughly that order. As a result, market
structures have shifted from a former monolithic
'supply-led' industry, to a much more diverse
interaction of contracts, subsidies, subsidiaries,
environmental constraints, and 'consumer interests' as defined by the regulators.[45] In this commercial jungle the main attention is on the big
money, either in mergers and acquisitions, in
overseas markets, or in horizontal integration
between services. The utility company of the
near future may be selling anything from mort-
gages to groceries alongside its core business.

In GM, the first integrated energy–water
company in the UK, United Utilities plc, was
formed in 1996 as a major force in the regional
economy and the global market. The bulk of its
profits come from regional distribution and supply, but these are closely regulated. Growth opportunities lie in other areas such as generation
and parallel utilities, and such diversification may
well be suited to renewable sources and energy
services.[46] In practice the potential is constrained
by falling energy prices in the UK and world markets – even while the total environmental costs
of energy use are several times its direct price,
and the UK is alone in Europe in taxing efficiency
measures more than fuel use. A UK business
energy tax is now forthcoming, although the tax
rates and exemption details are still highly controversial. The UK is aiming at a negotiated dialogue with major energy-using sectors, although
the evidence so far is that the rates envisaged
will make little difference to climate targets. The

42 Patterson 1998
43 DTI 1998 (review of energy sources)

44 Ravetz 1998a
45 Guy & Marvin 1996
46 NORWEB & ETSU 1993

best approach would be a gradual, comprehensive and progressive taxation package, to reduce costs for basic needs, increase costs for surplus demand, incentives for innovation and modernization, and recycle public funds into forward investment.[47] At the national level this could be coordinated by a UK energy agency.[48]

Such progressive energy taxation would work mainly at the national level – but the deregulated market also enables new patterns of local purchasing and distribution. Manchester, for instance, is aiming at bulk purchasing for its 80000 properties, which could enable not only price reductions, but a progressive recycling of funds for further investment.[49] A 10% levy on all public energy bills in GM could generate £40 million per year for the upgrading of all public housing, in a 25-year programme, which would show direct annual profit after 10 years *(Chapter 5)*. The combined GM public sector energy spend also offers substantial bargaining power and leverage which could encourage 'green energy' markets from renewable sources.[50]

## Integrated energy agency

Such market transformation points the way towards a more responsive and 'post-Fordist' energy industry. This would use ICT to target 'cold spots' of under-used capacity, and 'hot spots' where demand exceeds supply.[51] Demand side management aims to coordinate demand with supply capacity, and is now a common technique – and trading of 'negawatts' in efficiency via integrated least-cost planning is now an active

part of the USA energy market.[52] At present DSM is aimed at commercial ends, but it also has potential for direct benefits to consumers and the environment.

In practice, consumers' actual needs are for warmth and light rather than heat or power – energy 'services' rather than energy as such. 'Energy services companies' (ESCOs) could be the future one-stop providers – coordinating efficiency investment, DSM, local generation and CHP distribution.[53] At present market uncertainty undermines long term planning and investment, with technical and legal issues in defining 'savings', and progress with ESCOs is slow.

All this strengthens the case for a coordinating body to implement the local energy–climate strategy in a deregulated and diversified market – a city-region or regional 'energy agency' *(Box 9.8)*.[54] This would coordinate the climate mitigation, adaptation and defence themes. Building on EU examples, it would provide an interface between financiers, generators, suppliers, consumers, developers and the public sector, for both domestic and commercial applications:[55]

- broker for third-party and lease contracts for energy plant and conservation measures;
- finance packages for housing upgrading and brokering for mortgage companies;
- coordination of consortium purchasing and progressive pricing policy in public housing;
- technical coordination and investment vehicle for city-wide CHP networks;
- agency and purchasing consortium for installers and suppliers for consumers and small businesses;
- promotion and technical support for low-energy demonstration projects;
- comprehensive energy audits and advice to householders and small businesses.

The scope of such a city-region energy agency would go far beyond the current 'local energy

---

Box 9.8

### *URBAN ENERGY AGENCY*

The city of Amsterdam has set up a partnership consortium to coordinate all energy demand and supply in the city. The national 2% energy levy is being raised locally, to fund a comprehensive programme of efficiency upgrading and supply innovation.

**Source OECD 1996**

---

47 Local Government Association 1998
48 Green Alliance 1999
49 Manchester City Council 1996
50 Elliott 1996
51 Guy & Marvin 1996

52 von Weizsacker & Lovins 1997
53 NORWEB 1995
54 Local Government Association 1999
55 March Consulting 1995

advice centres' which cover only the last function above. In a deregulated market it could form a city-region consortium for supply and distribution, with the local utility or any other in the market. Its purchasing power would enable a progressive tariff structure, to encourage efficiency investment, nega-watt trading and others, while tackling energy poverty and management issues at source. It would also coordinate the climate response side of the strategy with a wider set of stakeholders as above.

# RENEWABLES

Renewable energy taps resources from the sun or from the earth's gravity. Such sources are generally more diverse, decentralized, and variable than fossil fuel or nuclear sources, and well suited to the deregulated market.[56] Detailed assessments of national and regional potential have been made, from which estimates for GM are drawn.[57] Current UK policy is to achieve 5000MW of renewable capacity, or 10% of power demand by 2010 – but this would require rapid acceleration in the rate of development, and while renewable output prices are falling, fossil-fuel energy prices are falling faster. The recent Non-Fossil Fuel Obligation (NFFO) round of subsidies for pilot projects allocated 40% of funding to windpower, and other sources such as landfill gas and waste incineration are also achieving near-commercial prices.[58]

For the NW region, up to 30% of current power demand could be met in theory from renewables.[59] The proven technologies of hydro-electric and landfill gas have been operated by United Utilities, but each is a limited resource with major planning constraints.[60] The largest regional resource is tidal power, but wind, waste and bio-mass are also viable if environmentally acceptable with stable fuel supplies.

The regional and national resource is an indirect component of the GM targets, and a 25% renewables contribution by 2020 is assumed here for the national 'green power' scenario. Within GM itself the resources are fairly marginal, but may also serve other objectives such as urban regeneration, rural diversification or housing im-provement. 'Best practice' estimates show that renewables within GM could provide a 'maximum practical resource' of perhaps 5% of current demand if fully developed *(Fig 9.8)*.[61]

## Wind & solar power

GM is adjacent to some of the largest windfarms in the north, and windspeeds on many Pennine uplands are technically adequate. Outline 'areas of search' might show a potential resource for 200 turbines covering 20 km², and with current technology this might provide 50 MWe 'declared net capacity', or 1.5% of average power demand in GM. However the effect of large turbines on the landscape arouses intense opposition, even where the same landscapes are in fact degraded by acid rain from power generation.[62] There may be novel solutions, such as the substitution of new turbines for existing pylons by putting grid cables underground – this might also address the perceived or potential risks from overhead power lines.[63]

'Photo-voltaic' (PV) panels convert sunlight directly to power, and are possibly the cleanest and simplest power source. Prices are high, but reducing at a rate which suggests that by 2010–20 they will be approaching commercial levels – in the meantime the most viable approach is to install PV panels as replacement cladding on the south-facing sides and roofs of larger buildings. If installed on all commercial buildings the potential resource could be 200 MW, or 6% of the GM peak power demand. If installed wherever feasible on domestic roofs during life-

56 Johansson et al1994
57 Energy Technology Support Unit 1994
58 DTI 1999 (New & renewable energy sources)
59 NORWEB & ETSU 1989

60 NORWEB & ETSU 1993
61 McEvoy, Gibbs & Longhurst 1997
62 Nuclear Free Local Authorities 1991
63 Talbot 1997

cycle renewal, by 2020 the resource could be over 700 MW or 20% of GM peak demand, continuing the pace of the European '500,000 solar homes' scheme.[64]

Even in dense urban areas there is scope for passive solar energy, with valuable spin-offs in domestic amenity and living space. It is also the most diffused and decentralized energy source, and has little interest for commercial utilities. Solar spaces fitted on the south side of houses or flats, operated correctly, can provide up to 20% of annual consumption in new houses at the beginning and end of the heating season.[65] Assuming that half of new dwellings and a quarter of existing dwellings were covered in a rolling programme, this low-temperature heat source would amount to 1–2% of total GM energy demand, increasing with climate change.

Passive solar design for larger commercial buildings is especially suitable for public buildings and shopping areas. Active solar water heating operates 40,000 systems in the UK, and could make further contributions, especially in multi-purpose buildings and industrial processes.

## Biomass & waste

Short-rotation coppice planting or 'biomass' for wood burning has great potential for farm diversification *(Chapter 7)*. Half the future GM community forest, together with a third of the remaining agricultural land, would produce over 1% of the total GM energy demand. Biomass fuel is in principle 'carbon neutral' as emissions are re-absorbed in further growth. In practice, industry studies have found difficulty in securing stable supplies from large land areas, and the overall eco-efficiency is very dependent on transport distances.[66] Other biomass crops, such as rape-seed for transport fuels, may also become more viable as world oil prices rise in future.

Power generation via methane gas from organic wastes in landfills is now common in many cities, and the latest NFFO round included three landfill gas schemes in GM. The total landfill gas resource could be 1% of total power demand, however there are technical uncertainties on long

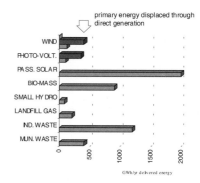

Fig 9.8

### RENEWABLE ENERGY

Outline potential renewable energy resources within GM: in GWh/yr delivered energy.
Source: outline estimates based on ETSU 1994: NORWEB 1989 & 1993

term outputs, and landfill itself is becoming the option of last resort. Although the energy production is not great, prices are close to commercial, and there is also a climate change objective in capturing the methane. Biogas schemes using methane from sewage are also common in GM, but further expansion is limited.

Industrial and special waste incineration in GM could provide about 1.5% of total energy demand, and municipal wastes about 0.5%. Their viability increases if integrated with CHP generation and local heat distribution. However the energy gained from incineration is generally less than the energy saved by recycling of the same material:[67] and the potential risks from emissions such as dioxins and aromatic hydrocarbons are controversial. A proposed network of urban CHP incinerators taking the bulk of GM's municipal waste stalled, due both to public opposition and to uncertainty on waste supplies.[68]

## Renewables strategy

Within the densely populated GM, the main contribution of renewable sources will be where they serve other objectives with minimal external impacts. Interestingly, the largest local resource is that of passive solar, and this intermittent low-

64 European Solar Taskforce 1997
65 Energy Conscious Design 1980
66 NORWEB & ETSU 1993

67 Taylor 1995
68 March Consulting 1995

grade resource is more significant to building design and consumer lifestyles, than the energy industry as such. Photovoltaics will become a growing urban resource as their costs become competitive. Most of the remaining resources are either small, such as hydropower, or constrained by social or environmental impacts, such as waste incineration and wind power. This sug-gests that renewables development has to link with other sectors such as housing or waste management, in order to tap diverse energy resources as part of the total urban metabolism. In the face of a rather uncertain national policy on regulation and innovation, there is an urgent need for city-region level incentives for renewable energy.[69]

# CO-GENERATION

Co-generation or CHP (combined heat and power) re-uses the waste heat from power generation, as hot water or steam supplied to buildings or industrial processes. This can increase the total efficiency of power generation from an average of 33% up to 75–85%, and is a commercially viable technology for larger buildings and process industries.[70] District heating (DH) then distributes the heat directly across local or urban areas – combined CHP-DH networks operate in UK cities such as Sheffield and Nottingham, and one of the first was built in 1911 in Manchester.[71]

The national target is to increase CHP use from 5% to 8% of power generation or 5000 MWe capacity by 2000, and double this by 2010, while the CHP Association points to the potential to provide 25% of UK generation by 2020.[72] In comparison, the current EU average is 10% of total power, with some cities and countries at 30%. In general, CHP schemes are most viable when serving mixed uses with stable heating baseloads, while selling excess power to the grid. In spite of government policy the current spread of CHP has slowed, as a result of market deregulation, technical unreliability, and particularly falling energy prices. CHP-DH in particular requires large fixed investments which are difficult where land-uses, buildings and energy technologies change rapidly – even climate change affects heat load projections over the life of an installation – so any CHP strategy needs to be as responsive and diversified as possible.

## CHP development

Despite a large process industry sector in GM, local industrial CHP is under-developed; there are only 34 plants producing 43 MWe or 1.5% of industrial power demand. The most likely growth area is in small-medium scale packaged schemes for multi-purpose buildings and process industries, as at the airport and various leisure centres; however many of these have experienced technical problems.[73] If we assume improvements in market conditions, reliability and ease of grid connections, the industry estimate of 15% of all power from CHP could be achieved by 2020.

---

**Box 9.9**          *CITY-WIDE CHP*

The Swedish city of Goteborg has linked two thirds of its housing to a CHP-DH network, together with most of the city centre. Energy is supplied from municipal waste and the large chemical works and refineries downriver, an excellent example of industrial ecology.

Source EURONET 1997

---

69 DTI 1999 (Renewable energy sources)
70 Energy Technology Support Unit 1997
71 Babus Haq & Probert 1994
72 Combined Heat & Power Association 1997

73 McEvoy, Gibbs & Longhurst 1998

As for the fuel source, gas is the first choice, as it is efficient, clean and easily supplied to urban areas, but gas-powered CHP could be vulnerable to the expected price rises.[74] Some process industries produce surplus heat, and in some cities nearby power stations are a potential source of heat for distribution.[75] Industrial or municipal waste is an alternative, with the attraction of reducing the waste volume going to landfill, but large waste flows and emissions cause problems *(Chapter 8)*. The 2020 energy–climate scenario assumes a likely fuel mix for CHP of gas, waste and other renewable sources.

## District & city heating

There are a number of smaller CHP-DH schemes in public housing, but for greater coverage and efficiency a wider network across the city is needed. For this the density of housing and heatloads is crucial – net densities of 100 pph or 15–20 dwellings per acre (gross) appear to be about the minimum viable.[76] About a quarter of the population live at such densities in the inner urban areas, but this proportion could increase rapidly as a result of the 'clustering' of the 2020 neighbourhood strategy *(Chapter 5)*. Mixed areas of housing, services and industrial uses contain diverse daily variations and stable heatloads suited to CHP, of which there are many in GM.

Such 'areas of search' were covered in a major proposal for the regional centre with the health and education quarter, using municipal waste as the energy source – this failed due to uncertain waste supply and public controversy.[77] The Trafford Park industrial estate was also the site of a multi-company proposal, which again was stalled by commercial uncertainty.[78]

While such CHP-DH schemes are ideal in principle, they rely on favourable fuel prices, stable building uses and heatloads, institutional commitment and long term contracts – a combination which is difficult to achieve in the current market, especially as increasing demand efficiency tends to reduce the viability of CHP supply. So there is a strong case for the city-region energy agency to map out 'areas of search' as part of integrated local energy strategies, to assess all larger developments for CHP potential, and coordinate investment for supply and demand with strategies for housing, regeneration and economic development. The result would be the forward-funding of pilot schemes, which would be the building blocks of a wider network to take shape over several decades.

# MAKING IT HAPPEN

Energy production is organized at the global and national level, distribution is regional, energy consumption is mostly localized, and climate policies apply at every level – so there is a clear need for 'vertical' integration. And in practical terms an energy-climate strategy will be most effective in full coordination with other strategies for housing, planning, transport, infrastructure, land-use, economic development and regeneration – this implies a fully 'horizontal integration'. Such coordination then depends on partnership between public, private and civic sectors, or 'institutional integration'.

The city-region is possibly the most effective arena for such an integrated energy–climate strategy, a key component of its over-arching sustainable development framework *(Chapter 14)*. Such a strategy should be implemented by a city-region energy agency, acting on behalf of the city-region association and the RDA, and bringing together partnerships for integrated planning and investment:

- partnership consortium for energy distribution, with terms and tariffs to favour demand

74 DTI 1998 (Review of energy sources)
75 Newcastle City Council 1992 & 1997
76 Owens & Cope 1992: Hutchinson 1991

77 Manchester City Council 1994
78 March Consulting 1995

management DSM, nega-watt or carbon budgeting, and energy poverty strategy;

- investment coordination – least-cost planning and long term finance packages for efficiency and demand management;
- economic coordination – combined purchasing to enable market leverage on suppliers and new technologies;
- infrastructure coordination of local energy balances including supply, distribution and demand;
- political coordination of regeneration, housing, land-use and economic development programmes.

For local authorities, the 1996 Home Energy Conservation Act set an agenda which has yet to be pursued by most cities – home energy and efficiency audits should be put into practice by local consortiums which maximize the leverage on lenders, developers, utilities and materials suppliers. Local regeneration programmes should include energy efficiency priorities, while planning consents and public property leaseholds should encourage best practice by every means possible. Investment consortiums should integrate sources, distribution and demand management, again with a typical local authority menu:

- inhouse actions for efficiency;
- surveys and audits on local energy balances;
- demonstration schemes and services;
- regulation and incentives via planning policy;
- coordination of grants, subsidies and levies;
- vertical, horizontal and institutional collaboration.

## Government actions

Energy has always been a national concern, and even the current deregulated market is highly sensitive to the politics of monopoly and utility regulation. The results so far are an interesting experiment, but show fragmentation and diversity, rather than the integration and stability needed for longer term investment.[79] As a return to state ownership is not on the agenda, and all the trends point to technical and economic glo-

balization, national strategy should focus on what is viable and achievable, locally and regionally, in a deregulated and diversified market. Utility regulation and electricity trading systems should raise environmental priorities, enable local or regional equity and purchasing schemes, enable the ESCO concept to take off, and provide incentives for market transformation for renewables and CHP. Housing finance should promote comprehensive 'nega-watt' investment packages between lenders, borrowers and utilities, and taxation should shift incentives from consumption to efficiency.

This all comes to a focus on the price of fuel, as in the political controversy on VAT and energy poverty – so it is essential that basic consumption at affordable rates is subsidized by progressive taxation applied above a certain threshold, with revenues put back into integrated supply and DSM programmes.[80]

## Business & households

The energy expenditure of most businesses is below 4% of turnover, with few incentives and many barriers to increasing efficiency. The newly deregulated market offers many opportunities for business chains, consortiums, trade associations or property owners to negotiate for supply packages and for ESCOs offering integrated energy services. Larger businesses, utilities, financiers and other stakeholders should be in partnership with the city-region energy agency.

Energy efficiency should in principle lower the costs of energy to consumers, and particularly the third of all households who are in some form of energy poverty. Over 10% of energy demand can be reduced simply by daily practice, and such savings should be encouraged through 'energy feedback' schemes and a network of local energy advice centres.[81] Meanwhile the success of CHP depends on consumer take-up, and renewables such as windpower and biomass also depend on public acceptance. Urban energy sources such as passive solar will gain by providing other benefits such as increased living space, to be encouraged by regeneration and rehabilitation programmes.

---

79 Patterson 1999: Ravetz 1996b

80 Chesshire 1993
81 Energy Efficiency Office 1995

# Putting it together

Within the city-region, integrated energy strategies for sub-regions and their settlement types will contain different menus for demand management, fuel switching, renewables and CHP. Together with the transport managment theme, these provide a menu for detailed neighbourhood and industrial estate programmes *(Fig 9.9)*:

- City and town centres would focus on commercial building efficiency, CHP networks, PV cladding, and passive solar atriums and micro-climates.
- Industrial and development areas would focus on process efficiency, CHP, landfill and waste incineration, together with other forms of industrial ecology and energy cascades.
- Inner city areas will focus on domestic efficiency in social flats and terrace housing, with passive solar conservatories running along terraces, PV on roof conversions and CHP networks.
- Suburban areas will focus on domestic efficiency programmes for owner-occupied tenures, and domestic-scale renewables.
- Urban fringe areas bring greater opportunities for localized renewable sources such as solar, landfill and biomass.
- Countryside areas may provide larger-scale renewable sources such as windpower or biomass, where these are compatible with other countryside uses.

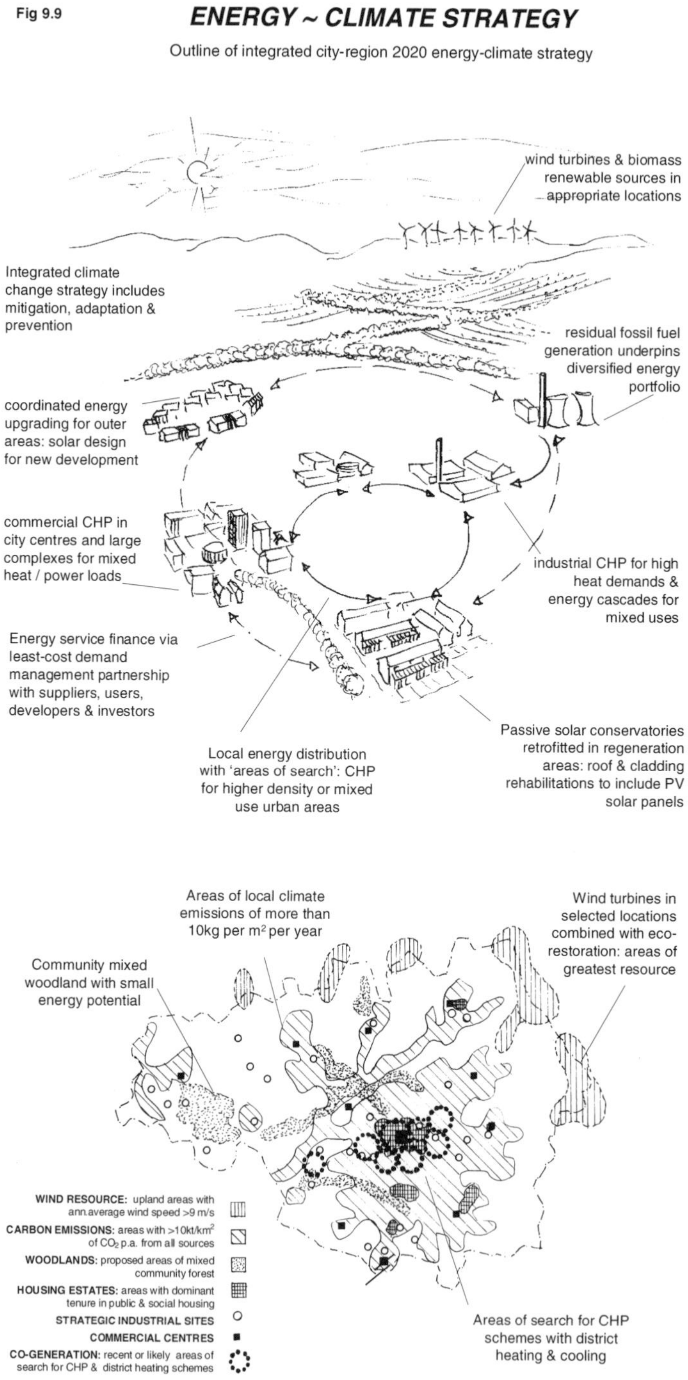

Fig 9.9

## ENERGY ~ CLIMATE STRATEGY

Outline of integrated city-region 2020 energy-climate strategy

wind turbines & biomass renewable sources in appropriate locations

Integrated climate change strategy includes mitigation, adaptation & prevention

residual fossil fuel generation underpins diversified energy portfolio

coordinated energy upgrading for outer areas: solar design for new development

commercial CHP in city centres and large complexes for mixed heat / power loads

industrial CHP for high heat demands & energy cascades for mixed uses

Energy service finance via least-cost demand management partnership with suppliers, users, developers & investors

Passive solar conservatories retrofitted in regeneration areas: roof & cladding rehabilitations to include PV solar panels

Local energy distribution with 'areas of search': CHP for higher density or mixed use urban areas

Areas of local climate emissions of more than 10kg per m² per year

Wind turbines in selected locations combined with eco-restoration: areas of greatest resource

Community mixed woodland with small energy potential

WIND RESOURCE: upland areas with ann. average wind speed >9 m/s
CARBON EMISSIONS: areas with >10kt/km² of CO₂ p.a. from all sources
WOODLANDS: proposed areas of mixed community forest
HOUSING ESTATES: areas with dominant tenure in public & social housing
STRATEGIC INDUSTRIAL SITES
COMMERCIAL CENTRES
CO-GENERATION: recent or likely areas of search for CHP & district heating schemes

Areas of search for CHP schemes with district heating & cooling

The combined result will help to transform the former energy metabolism – a monopoly supply industry with inefficient end-uses – towards a more integrated and diversified pattern of localized energy supply and demand, within an integrated energy–climate strategy.

## Context

The total system of energy supply and demand operates at every scale from global to local, of which the city-region is one, and energy was perhaps the first fully globalized industry. So in the limited space here we have focused on what is directly relevant to the city-region – leaving aside other questions such as oil resources, the nuclear industry and global climate policy. The aim is to show what is possible, and indeed essential and inevitable, for a typical post-industrial European city-region.

In its international context, GM lies between the effects of affluence and the problems of poverty, as shown by some basic indicators of the energy metabolism:[82]

- energy intensity, or consumption per person, in the UK is midway between affluent and land-rich countries such as USA or Sweden, and poorer EU countries such as Portugal;
- energy intensity per unit GDP shows less variation, but some CIS countries with much obsolete industry, such as Poland, have much higher ratios;

- renewable sources in the EU account for 9% of production, mainly through hydro-power, several times greater than the UK, while nuclear sources are 35% or twice the UK ratio;
- CHP is much more advanced in northern EU countries, with cities such as Berlin producing 16% of power through CHP;
- in Japan there are detailed plans for a zero-energy city, and also a floating city with fully integrated environmental services.[83]

While any detailed energy–climate strategy is of course unique to each city or region, the general theme is common to all – the integration of technological, environmental, economic and political strategy.

---

**Box 9.10**

### SUMMARY ~ ENERGY & CLIMATE

The 2020 energy-climate strategy aims to transform and de-carbonize the total energy metabolism. Integration of demand, supply, conversion and distribution, can reduce climate emissions by 35% by 2020 and 60% by 2050:

- climate response and mitigation programme to monitor risks and opportunities
- energy services firms and partnership energy agency to accelerate efficiency in all sectors
- local renewable energy sources where appropriate, for up to 10% of peak demand
- combined heat and power programme for all inner urban and industrial areas, for a quarter of total energy demand.

---

82 International Energy Agency 1996: Nijkamp & Perrels 1994
83 International Environment Reporter 1998

# 10

# ECONOMY & WORK

*'All progress is based on the universal desire of
every organism to live beyond its income'*
Samuel Butler, 1872

The simple question – what is a sustainable local or regional economy? – has many answers.[1] A local or regional economy constantly innovates, competes, adapts and evolves, with countless layers from local to global. It is embedded in the culture and lifestyles of its people and its institutions, and for every trade in money there is another in social or environmental resources. But even the most complex of economies can have simple outcomes – as in the case of GM, where rising affluence is accompanied by social exclusion, environmental degradation, and economic dependency. It is perhaps easier to say what is unsustainable, as the evidence is there to see.

Manchester, arguably the world's first industrial city, is a topical place to explore. There is every possibility that its post-industrial economy could soon be based on locally-owned zero-emission ethical trade. But many trends in the short term point the other way, and there is an equal possibility of increasing dependency, polarization and decline.

So here we bring current thinking to the question of a sustainable regional economy, with each of its environmental, social and financial dimensions. Then we take several cross-sections.

First is the urban development agenda of sites, premises, location and access. This is parallel to the 'greening of business' agenda of environmental management and eco-efficiency in firms and sectors. 'Greening the economy' is about driving the process of ecological modernization through public policy and programmes. This links to 'sustainable employment' and the prospects for work, workers and workplaces. Finally 'sustainable livelihoods' goes beyond the mainstream money-based economy to look at other kinds of activities and trading systems.

The focus here is more on the environmental and social aspects of the regional economy, as mainstream economic questions are covered by many others. Related questions of public sector economics are in Chapter 11; economic regeneration in Chapter 12; and environmental cost-benefit and investment in Chapter 14.

## Trends & tensions

As in many northern conurbations, manufacturing in GM has been declining for decades, while its service sector struggles to compete with other more favoured regions. The result is that many indicators of the city-region economy are 5–10%

1 Here we use the term 'regional' as shorthand for the 'city-region'

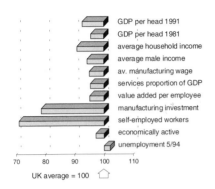

**Fig 10.1**    *ECONOMIC INDICATORS*

GDP per head 1991
GDP per head 1981
average household income
average male income
av. manufacturing wage
services proportion of GDP
value added per employee
manufacturing investment
self-employed workers
economically active
unemployment 5/94

70    80    90    100    110

UK average = 100

Data for Greater Manchester relative to UK average.
Source: ONS 1998.

below the national average – some communities have double shares of unemployment, and self-employment, training, added value and investment ratios are all way down. It is also a divided city-region – the GDP per head in the central and southern half is nearly 50% more than that in the northern half.[2] For a city-region which aims to build a knowledge-based value-added economy on the remains of its former manufacturing base, the results so far are mixed. The NW regional strategy put forward a series of 5- and 10-year goals, but the indicators show that few of these are being achieved.[3]

The general shift towards the service sector continues, but GM is behind the national shift by about 15 years, with a 62% share compared to 66%. Manufacturing jobs may lose 2% per year, and for the medium term to 2020 the prospect is for another 5% shift towards services *(Fig 10.1)*.[4] Certain producer sectors such as chemicals, paper and electronics industries could see GDP expand at up to 5% jobless growth while most others contract. Other traditional sectors such as defence and textiles, the basis of GM's historic wealth, appear to be in long term contraction.

Meanwhile there are immense assets – universities and research centres, financial services and media, an international airport, and world-class sports and arts. These resources are crucial to inward investment and skills development, and there is an army of agencies trying to promote them. But the rate of change in economic activity seems faster than ever – former patterns of production and consumption, or of ownership and control, are shifting towards a more volatile and flexibilized structure, locally and globally.

## Future prospects

While economic projections are notoriously uncertain, there are trends and counter trends running in parallel *(Chapter 3)*. One is globalization, driven by international trade and capital flows, trans-national corporations and accelerated innovation.[5] A counter-trend is 'localization', down-sizing, and a new generation of service industries based on human-scale interactions. ICT facilitates both trends and is transforming the 'nervous systems' of all organizations and networks large and small.[6] One result is in new patterns of division and exclusion, where whole occupations and communities become redundant to global capital.

Another new factor is the environmental agenda, and the process of 'ecological modernization' or structural transition with technical, economic, political and cultural dimensions.[7] This brings opportunities for environmental goods and services, market profile and credibility, and a culture of quality management.[8] Its logical conclusion is the 'de-materialization' of economic growth from physical throughputs, and such a 'factor four' or even 'factor ten' is now mainstream thinking.[9] In parallel with this are immense structural changes in the organization of businesses and markets:[10]

- markets: rapid shifts where success and stability depends on corporate integrity;

2 ONS 1998
3 Government Office NW & Merseyside 1998
4 Cambridge Econometrics 1996

5 Dicken 1998
6 Gates 1999
7 Hajer 1995
8 Roberts 1995
9 Business Council for Sustainable Development 1993
10 Elkington 1997

- values: greater emphasis on the trust of consumers, employees and stakeholders;
- transparency: increasing stakeholder and and consumer awareness through media and ICT;
- life-cycle technology and chain management for cradle-to-grave responsibility;
- partnerships: between competitors, suppliers and many other stakeholders;
- space extension: from global supply chains to new priorities for local amenity and cachet;
- time extension: from just-in-time logistics to inter-generational responsibility;
- corporate governance: from shareholding to stakeholding in equity and accountability.

A further transition is in the nature of work – from a former nine-to-five model, to more fluid combinations of production and consumption, carried out be a flexible-time sub-contracted workforce with portfolios of transferable skills.[11] And as jobs in the globalized economy become ever more competitive and insecure, there is increasing need and opportunity for useful activity which is localized, inclusive and ethically sound. The narrow shareholding model of globalized capital is perhaps the most efficient system yet devised for allocation of resources, but its internal contradictions could shift it rapidly towards 'stake-holding', 'stake-owning' and other forms of shared responsibility.[12]

Such trends and counter-trends can be picked out in alternative scenarios for the future economy:

- **BAU scenario:** current trends continue with 'jobless growth' and growing resource consumption via automation. Work-rich and poor are increasingly polarized as knowledge-based tasks become dominant.
- **technology scenario:** ICT transforms retail markets, supply chains, technological diffusion, labour markets and capital flows; global capital is increasingly volatile as corporations appear and disappear.
- **SD scenario:** a balance is struck between global and local economies; much service trading takes place in various layers of local

Fig 10.2          **GREEN ECONOMY**

sustainable livelihoods: human workplace: social economy

environmental management: clean technology: resource efficiency

ECONOMY

SOCIAL & POLITICAL          ENVIRON-MENT

Green consumption: ethical investment : environmental regulation

currencies. Total environmental management is the guiding theme for all firms and products.
- **deep green scenario:** most people downshift to de-materialized ethical lifestyles, consuming and travelling less. Economic activity shifts from planned obsolescence to 'quaternary' public services, and third sector quality-of-life activity.

## Total economic metabolism

Defining a 'sustainable regional economy' could be an endless quest – but without some kind of map there is little to go on. To tackle this we bring the 'integrated assessment' methods to throw light on the many layers of the regional economy *(Chapter 1)*.

A good starting point is to look at real problems – for instance 15,000 tonnes per year of hazardous waste are imported to GM, more than any other European city: this creates jobs, makes waste harmless, and keeps industry in the region. It can also be argued that there is no safe disposal method, that firms should deal with their own waste, and we should move to cleaner processes anyway. Is such an industry 'sustainable'? If not, what can be done, and who should decide?

Such questions contain three strands – environmental, economic and social *(Fig 10.2)*. A similar logic is the basis for a practical business tool, the 'triple bottom line', which extends

Fig 10.3     ***ECONOMIC METABOLISM***

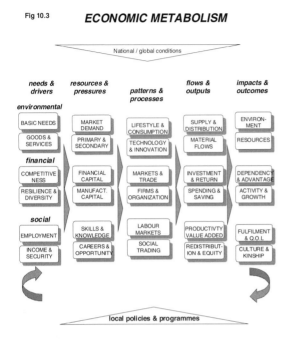

Very simplified 'integrated assessment' system mapping of physical environment.
financial & social dimensions of an economic total metabolism

For the social dimension, the question is how far economic activity meets human needs for goods and services, employment and incomes, equity and fulfilment.[17] These might be measured as 'stocks' of human welfare, and the 'limits' of acceptability or risk. The 'dynamics' which turn problems into opportunities might be consumer responsibility on the demand side, and business responsibility on the supply side.[18] The 'third sector', or non-monetary social economy, can also address some of the failures and shortcomings of the mainstream economy.

The economic or financial dimension focuses on the internal viability of the regional economy, as an open sub-system within national and global economies. Economic 'stocks' can be measured with balance sheets for financial and other assets, and their 'flows' as profit and loss accounts in GDP and similar measures. The 'limits' can be seen as the viable and sustainable levels of liquidity, investment, saving and gearing ratios. The 'dynamics' which turn problems into opportunities are in competitiveness, innovation, shareholder value, entrepreneurship, learning culture, labour skills, management integrity and other more intangible factors.

Each of these themes – environmental, social and economic – shows a complex and self-organizing system, a long way from the machine-like equilibrium models of neo-classical economics.[19] The overall balance of needs and outcomes, as delivered and mediated through the regional economy, can be seen with a 'metabolic mapping' of the total system *(Fig 10.3)*. Shifting the balance towards greater fulfilment with less impact involves actions and changes at every link in the chain. This kind of mapping also shows how 'sustainability' in a regional economy is not so much a fixed menu as an evolution of a complex system, inextricably tangled with national and global economies through trading linkages, technological diffusion, dependency and advantage.

But does a sustainable and successful economy for GM mean that other city-regions are out of business? As with natural eco-sys-

financial accountanting to environmental and social issues.[13] The overlap between the circles shows how economic activity needs to be 'de-materialized' from its environmental impact, so that one can grow while the other reduces. It also shows how economic activity needs to be 're-socialized', so that greater human welfare is delivered for the same amount of economic activity.[14] Following the logic through, we can look at the 'stocks', 'flows', 'limits' and 'dynamics' for each circle *(Chapter 1)*.[15]

The environmental theme can be seen in terms of eco-cycles and ecological capacities, in layers of space and time *(Chapter 1)*. Environmental 'stocks' should be conserved and their 'flows' managed at local and global levels. Environmental 'limits' are the ultimate containers for economic activity – showing that de-materialization is essential for long term economic growth. The 'dynamics' are the factors which turn problems into opportunities – innovation on the supply side, or green consumers on the demand side.[16]

14 Robinson & Tinker 1997
15 Ravetz 1999d
16 Howes Whelan & Skea 1997

17 Max-Neef 1992
18 Hutton 1995
19 Ormerod 1999

tems, activity levels in each city or region generally emerge through competition, and competition inevitably produces winners and losers. But the ecological concepts of resilience, integrity and corridors of stability can also apply to economic competition.[19] Rather than the current system where 'winner takes all', this aims to temper competition with social justice and environmental responsibility, maintaining and sustaining both the game and its players.

So finally, coming back to the hazardous waste example, we can bypass the question of total 'Sustainability' which is practically unworkable. Instead we can look at the effectiveness and resilience of the industry's eco-cycles, social welfare, economic viability, and role in the wider process of eco-modernization.

## Sustainable growth and jobs?

All this points to the million dollar question – how to get sustainable economic growth?

What is often meant by this is conventional growth which does not fall prey to the next business cycle or wobble on the capital markets. A simple response would be that where economic growth helps to reduce environmental damage, then it is 'less unsustainable', at least environmentally. But this shifts conventional notions of economic growth as 'quantity' of consumption, or the 'tonnage ideology', towards development as 'quality' of human welfare.[20] The United Nations saw five kinds of unsustainable growth – destroying either jobs, democracy, cultures, social equality, or environmental resources.[21] The economic metabolism mapping above throws some light on the nature of the balancing act in generating sustainable economic growth.

The other crucial question is – how to create sustainable jobs for all? There is consensus that strong environmental policies combined with 'revenue neutral' eco-taxation, all other things being equal, could increase total employment by 2–3%.[22] Further added value comes through the 'double dividend', combining jobs, environmental improvements and social regeneration.[23]

More uncertain are the effects of multipliers, displacements, innovation and competitiveness in a globalized market. Some very rough estimates for GM are outlined at the end of the chapter, with further research in progress. The evidence suggests that structural changes to employment will come not through marginal changes, but through

---

**Box 10.1**

### ECONOMY & WORK ~ TRENDS & TARGETS

| | | 1995 | BAU 2020 | SD 2020 | Trend target index % |
|---|---|---|---|---|---|
| Serv.floorspace / GDP | m2/£GDP | 0.86 | 0.78 | 0.60 | 30 |
| Serv.new blg.intensity | GJ/m2/y | 2.9 | 2.6 | 2.0 | 30 |
| Serv.final energy demand | PJ/y | 47.9 | 67.8 | 46.1 | -100 |
| Serv.CO$_2$ emissions. incl power | MtCO2/y | 4.7 | 5.4 | 46.1 | 0 |
| Ind.energy intensity /GDP | MJ/yr/£GDP | 16.4 | 14.8 | 8.2 | 20 |
| Ind. final energy demand | PJ/y | 106.2 | 136.2 | 81.1 | -100 |
| Ind. CO$_2$ emissions incl power | MtCO2/y | 10.5 | 11.2 | 7.5 | -20 |
| Business EMAS/BS7750 reg | % | 1% | 6% | 50% | 10 |
| Total GDP relative to UK av. | % | 96% | 92% | 100% | -100 |
| Ind.added value/job /UK av. | % | 95% | 92% | 100% | -60 |
| Ind. Investment/job/UKav | % | 78% | 73% | 100% | -20 |
| Total unemployment / UK av. | % | 105% | 108% | 100% | -60 |

Summary 'core indicators' with trends & targets from ISCAM scenario accounts for GM 1995-2020.
BAU = business as usual projection from trend
SD = sustainable development scenario

---

**Box 10.2**

### ECONOMY & WORK ~ GOALS & STRATEGIES

| | GOV | LAP | BUS | COM | PUB |
|---|---|---|---|---|---|
| **SITES, PREMISES, DISTRIBUTION:** | ○ | ● | ● | ○ | ○ |
| mixed uses & local services: stabilize freight, shift 20% to rail: local distribution networks, employers commuting schemes & car clubs | | | | | |
| **GREENING OF BUSINESS:** | ○ | ○ | ● | ○ | ○ |
| 15% final energy, 25% carbon reduction: full env. management, accounting, labelling: all material industries in env.strategy | | | | | |
| **GREENING ECONOMIC DEVELOPMENT:** | ○ | ● | ● | ○ | |
| env.-business networks, technology transfer & finance: env./ethical investment policies: green growth pole & development fund: | | | | | |
| **SUSTAINABLE EMPLOYMENT:** | ● | ○ | ● | ○ | ● |
| Environmental / employment joint strategy; re-skill labour for eco-modernization: promote stakeholding & stakeowning | | | | | |
| **SUSTAINABLE LIVELIHOODS:** | ○ | ○ | ● | ● | ● |
| cooperatives, voluntary sector, local trading, cultural industries & third sector: community audits & social trading partnerships | | | | | |

GOV ~ government & EU: LA ~ local authorities & partnerships:
BUS ~ business & finance: COM ~ community & 3rd sector: PUB ~ public

---

19 Beckenbauer 1994
20 Ayres & Simonis 1996
21 UNDP 1996
22 Forum for the Future 1998
23 Jackson & Roberts 1997

market transformation which changes the balance between producers and consumers, or monetary and social economies, and such changes cannot be calculated by models *(Chapter 13)*.

With so many themes in so many layers, how is it possible to select indicators and set targets? Global environmental limits provide some guidance; energy–climate targets can be used as proxies for other more complex problems, and contrasted with 'best practice frontiers' for what is technically achievable.[24] Local environmental targets can be defined to some degree by the city-region environment strategy for air, water, land, waste and urbanization.

For social issues the goals are naturally more fuzzy, but general goals and working targets can be set for unemployment, poverty, and third sector activity. These might draw on the regional policy objective to attain UK and EU averages across a spread of economic indicators.[25] A selection of actual trends and selected targets, based on the ISCAM model, is shown by the 'core indicators' overleaf, each with its 'trend-target' index *(Box 10.1)*. These then apply to the 20–25 year policy goals and strategies in each theme *(Box 10.2)*.

# SITES & PREMISES

So much for the grand theory – the practical questions start with the physical call of industry and commerce on sites and premises, the traditional theme of economic development. Surprisingly, while economic activity is de-materialized through ICT and the shift to services, its footprint on the ground still seems to increase. This raises the long term question – where will we work?[26]

For this, the traditional factors of production – 'land, labour and capital' – may need some re-thinking. Capital is now internationally mobile, and so is increasingly knowledge-based labour – leaving land as the local resource which is the most finite and vulnerable. As with housing, there is scope to build multi-storey or even underground, but in practice industry and distribution thrive on space-intensive automated handling.[27] Most service businesses demand rising standards for parking and amenity, and while IT enables telework and 'hot-desking', the complexity of information-based activity still tends to increase floorspace per job. Trafford Park in GM, the world's first industrial estate, now contains 35,000 jobs or less than half its

former workforce. Industrial and commercial floorspace appears to be linked with economic growth, at about 2% long term growth per year, and in GM this growth would fill the total stock of vacant land area in 30 years *(Chapter 5)*. As with transport, 'delinking' is inevitable sooner or later, for continuing economic growth on a finite amount of land.[28]

The geography of employment suggests that industrial conurbations such as GM are losing jobs at 10% per decade, while rural growth areas attract both jobs and housing.[29] For male full-time industrial jobs the losses are several times as great, with female part-time jobs the winners. ICT is crucial to future developments – current trends suggest that by 2020 up to half of all information-based activity, or a quarter of all employment, could be done at a distance *(Chapter 3)*.[30] This could transform the property markets, and related patterns of commuting, retailing, distribution, and business services. Meanwhile, as a knowledge-based economy revolves around 'exchange', leading-edge producers may cluster in high-amenity science parks, while distributors cluster in retail parks.[31]

24 Tyteca 1996
25 NW Development Agency 1999
26 Breheny 1999
27 Whelan 1997: Grimley 1997

28 Fothergill, Monk & Perry 1987
29 Turok & Edge 1999
30 Graham 1996
31 Castells & Hall 1994

At the other end of the scale, telematics also has great potential for local economic and social development, and each neighbourhood may need a range of multi-purpose ICT centres for itinerant hot-deskers, not only for the hardware as for the social benefits.[32]

A perennial problem is the tendency for property development to cluster in growth areas and withdraw from declining areas – polarizing local economies and increasing commuting distances. Much current advice aims to bring the jobs closer to the people, but in reality modern labour markets are increasingly specialized and stratified, with long distance commuting and dual career households working in different locations. Such a situation is unlikely to be restricted by planning or any other kind of policy, and a more effective approach might be to encourage 'what works', both for business and wider interests:

- generating added value through business clusters and cultural amenities, higher density and mixed use business development on public transport nodes, with integrated travel management strategies;
- using ICT to enable networking and distribution of employment locations, space provision, and commuting pressures;
- greater incentives for renewal and reclamation of existing employment areas, through the rating system, contract and purchasing policies, infrastructure works and others.

## Business travel demand

Transport is on the frontline of the battle of economic vs environmental goals, and at present hardly covered in environmental management. The projected growth in freight and business travel is double that of domestic traffic, and most major route capacities in the city-region are already at or over capacity.[33] One approach is via accessibility planning with the 'ABC' system, but in a city-region such as GM there are few sites which meet the requisite standards for integrated public transport *(Chapter 6).*[34]

As the rate of change in business practices generally outstrips the inertia of development planning, the onus for travel management is more on the business travel demand side. Future business development will be more closely monitored for its freight and business travel demand, coordinated with city-region transport and environment strategy. The current 'sequential test' for retail sites, for instance, is likely to spread to other uses, and policies for 'reducing the need to travel' will gradually alter the trends of the property markets, especially for large travel generators such as retail and leisure.[35] Economic development and business strategy will work in parallel with integrated transport measures, such as area licensing, lorry route management, local distribution networks and trans-shipment depots *(Chapter 6).* Transport demand will be an integral part of environmental management systems, not only for manufacturing but for service businesses.

# GREENING OF BUSINESS

The 'greening of business' is one step in a long evolution. From the 'smokestack' approach of the industrial revolution, to integrated pollution control (IPC) and eco-modernization, the de-materialize ideal of a post-industrial era has yet to be defined *(Chapter 8).* The new-born business-environment agenda contains several layers – management of the local impacts of production: extended supply chains and product life-cycles: and wider indirect trading and investment linkages. In each case there are physical questions on materials and processes, and wider questions on management techniques and market structures. It also leads to the questioning of goals and values, inside and outside the firm, for the firm's reason for being.[36]

32 Manchester Telematics Partnership 1996
33 DETR 1997 (National Road Traffic Forecasts)
34 Amundsen 1995: DETR 1998 (Sustainable Urban Development)
35 CB Hillier Parker 1998: Guy 1998

36 Welford 1995

## Energy & business

The primary resource for all economic activity is energy; nearly half of total consumption is in public services, commerce and industry, and half of this is in buildings and equipment. In modern shops and offices, lighting and equipment often use 30%, and air-conditioning can take 40% of total energy.[37] Many 'best practice' programmes show that 10% savings come simply from good management, and a further 20% savings are generally viable with a payback of less than three years.[38] For new buildings such as supermarkets, low-energy design can save 60% on current standards by integrating equipment with building systems, and there is technical potential for 90% reduction – the longer term factor-of-ten goal.[39]

In contrast, city-regions such as GM contain many older and inefficient commercial buildings, and with a 2% growth rate in demand for floorspace, and many low intensity uses to fill low-value space, many will stand for a long time to come. For such property, low asset values, split responsibility, multiple leaseholds and falling energy prices make forward investment much more difficult, and such property also tends to house the SMEs which are most vulnerable and short of capital. To bridge the gap, as with housing, a city-region energy agency should coordinate an energy efficiency investment package in partnership with energy services companies, providing incentives for landlords, and trading in nega-watts (Chapter 5).

Industrial processes and motive power account for a third of business energy use. Applying the best cost-effective technology can deliver between 5–30% savings, and applying the 'theoretical best' shows 15–40% savings. There are different cost-efficiency profiles for intensive industries with energy costs of 20% of turnover, such as cement; medium-impact industries such as food and light manufacturing; and low-impact industries with average energy costs of 2% of

turnover.[40] The larger the plant, the longer the investment times, so efficiency upgrading has to coordinate plant life-cycles with new processes and best-available technology (Chapter 9). However, long investment cycles, complex contract conditions, falling energy prices and market deregulation each undermine the theoretical efficiency potential. Each industrial sector is now negotiating possible

**Box 10.3**

### ECONOMY-ENVIRONMENT SCENARIO ACCOUNT

| | unit | 1995 Total | BAU 2020 Total | SD 2020 Total | SD shares / rates | Cha-nge 95/SD |
|---|---|---|---|---|---|---|
| **POPULATION** | million | 2.57 | 2.70 | 2.70 | | 5% |
| GDP | £ bn | 19.60 | 32.93 | 32.93 | | 68% |
| GDP per head | £1000/cap | 7.62 | 12.19 | 12.19 | | 60% |
| Industry/primary | £bn | 6.47 | 9.22 | 9.88 | 30% | 53% |
| Commerce & public | £bn | 13.13 | 23.71 | 23.05 | 70% | 76% |
| **SERVICE SPACE** | | | | | | |
| Floorspace/GDP | m2/£1000 | 0.9 | 0.8 | 0.6 | | -30% |
| Current stock | M.m2 | 16.8 | 14.3 | 11.8 | | -30% |
| New development | M.m2 | 0.0 | 11.4 | 8.0 | | # |
| TOTAL FLOORSPACE | | 16.8 | 25.7 | 19.8 | | 18% |
| Total energy/serviceGDP | MJ/y/£GDP | 3.6 | 2.9 | 2.0 | | -45% |
| Exg.blg.intensity | GJ/m2/yr | 2.85 | 2.71 | 2.57 | | -10% |
| New blg.intensity | GJ/m2/yr | 2.85 | 2.57 | 2.00 | | -30% |
| Exg.blg.final demand | PJ/y | 47.9 | 38.7 | 30.2 | | -37% |
| New blg.final demand | PJ/y | # | 29.2 | 16.0 | | # |
| TOTAL DEMAND | PJ/y | 47.9 | 67.8 | 46.1 | | -4% |
| **SERVICES USES** | | | | | | |
| Space heat | PJ/y | 12.4 | 14.2 | 11.5 | 25% | -7% |
| Water / cooking | | 3.8 | 4.7 | 4.2 | 9% | 8% |
| Lighting | | 13.4 | 17.0 | 11.5 | 25% | -14% |
| Refridge | | 7.7 | 17.0 | 7.4 | 16% | -4% |
| Other power | | 10.5 | 14.9 | 11.5 | 25% | 9% |
| TOTAL FINAL DEMAND | | 47.9 | 67.8 | 46.1 | 100% | -4% |
| **SERVICES ENERGY** | | | | | | |
| Electric | PJ/y | 11.9 | 27.1 | 16.1 | 35% | 36% |
| Gas | | 15.8 | 20.4 | 13.8 | 30% | -13% |
| Oil | | 18.0 | 14.9 | 6.9 | 15% | -62% |
| Coal | | 1.4 | 1.4 | 0.9 | 2% | -36% |
| Direct renewable | | 0.0 | 0.7 | 3.7 | 8% | # |
| Heat | | 0.7 | 2.7 | 4.6 | 10% | 541% |
| TOTAL DEL.ENERGY | | 47.9 | 67.2 | 46.1 | 100% | -4% |
| **INDUSTRIAL** | | | | | | |
| Energy intensity | MJ/yr/£GDP | 16.4 | 14.8 | 8.2 | | -50% |
| Electric | PJ/y | 22.7 | 34.1 | 26.0 | 32% | 14% |
| Gas | | 43.2 | 57.2 | 24.3 | 30% | -44% |
| Oil | | 22.3 | 23.2 | 12.2 | 15% | -45% |
| Coal | | 14.4 | 16.3 | 8.1 | 10% | -44% |
| Direct renewable | | 0.0 | 0.0 | 2.4 | 3% | # |
| Heat | | 3.6 | 5.4 | 8.1 | 10% | 125% |
| TOTAL INDUSTRIAL | PJ/y | 106.2 | 136.2 | 81.1 | | -24% |
| **$CO_2$ EMISSIONS** | | | | | | |
| Commercial | | 4.7 | 5.4 | 3.4 | | -29% |
| Industry | | 10.5 | 11.2 | 7.5 | | -28% |

Summary of sustainable development scenario for 2020 commercial / industrial energy strategy in GM.

'BAU' = business as usual projection: 'SD' = sustainable development scenario

'SHARES' shows percentage proportions of SD total: 'RATE' shows annual growth rate for SD total: 'CHANGE' shows growth from 1995 – SD 2020 scenario.

37 Energy Efficiency Office 1988
38 BRECSU 1995
39 von Weizsacker & Lovins 1997
40 International Energy Agency 1991: March Consulting 1989

voluntary agreements with the government, and city or regional partnerships should provide the added value and incentive on the ground.[41]

The business use of energy may shortly be the target of the UK's first major energy tax. While there is intense negotiation on exemptions, reliefs and internal trading systems, the tax is widely seen as a tax on the industrial north of England to subsidize the service-based south. For all the pain, the tax is expected to reduce business $CO_2$ emissions by only 2%, and increased energy costs could well be absorbed in falling prices. Nevertheless the tax sends a signal to industry which should be followed up by progressive increases in the coming years.[42]

The business-energy SD scenario overleaf below assumes that institutional moves can overcome such barriers, to promote 'best practice' efficiency levels *(Box 10.3)*. For services, the rate of increase in floorspaces is slowed, and the efficiency levels of new space are doubled from those of the BAU trends. Integrated building design keeps air-conditioning demand to a minimum, and electricity is switched to gas, solar and direct heat supply wherever possible – this would stabilize final energy demand and reduce $CO_2$ emissions by 30%. For industry, an aggregated scenario assumes that physical throughput is stabilized, unit efficiency raised by 25%, and fuels switched to low-impact sources wherever possible – the effect is to reduce final demand by 25% and $CO_2$ again by 30% *(Box 10.3)*.

## Integrated Pollution Control

The Integrated Pollution Control (IPC) system was a milestone, one of the first systems in the world to coordinate site-based environmental regulation, based on the far-reaching and fuzzy concepts of 'best practical environmental option' (BPEO) and the 'best available technology not entailing excessive cost' (BATNEEC). In GM there are 29 IPC sites with major 'Part A' processes, regulated by the Environment Agency, and over 3000 'Part B' processes which are monitored by local authorities. The IPC system for sites and processes should run in

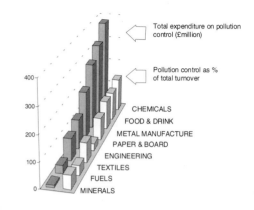

Fig 10.4   **ENVIRONMENTAL MANAGEMENT**

Total expenditure on pollution control (£million)

Pollution control as % of total turnover

400
300
200
100
0

CHEMICALS
FOOD & DRINK
METAL MANUFACTURE
PAPER & BOARD
ENGINEERING
TEXTILES
FUELS
MINERALS

Industries vulnerable to environmental regulation: UK data.
Source: data based on ECOTEC 1996: DTI 1996: OECD 1997

parallel to life-cycle analysis (LCA) of products and materials, as a fully comprehensive, transparent and accountable system, but since its inception in 1991 there has been controversy on the sensitive negotiation of standards versus costs.[43] In any case the system will change with the draft EU Directive and UK Bill on 'integrated pollution prevention and control' (IPPC), and environmental assessment may extend to wider issues:[44]

- freight, business travel and commuting;
- energy use and climate emissions;
- integrated supply chain and life-cycle analysis;
- human and ecological risk assessment;
- ethical criteria for suppliers, contractors, distributors and investors.

The IPPC framework also raises the possibility of integrated management within a local or regional environmental strategy. This highlights a missing link – between individual sites or processes, and area-based environmental management. At present the IPC 'environmental quality standards' and 'relative assessment levels' are calculated on national averages.[45] In future, with growing pressure from industry and

41 Jackson 1991
42 HM Treasury 1998 (Marshall report)

43 ENDS 1994
44 DETR 1997 (Implementation of EU Directive 96/61)
45 Environment Agency 1997

Fig 10.5     **THE 'SUSTAINABLE' FIRM**

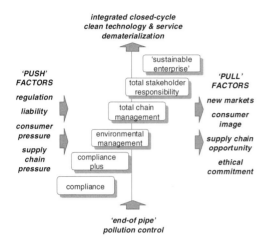

integrated closed-cycle
clean technology & service
dematerialization

'sustainable
enterprise'

'PUSH'                           'PULL'
FACTORS     total stakeholder    FACTORS
            responsibility
regulation                       new markets
            total chain
liability   management           consumer
                                 image
consumer    environmental
pressure    management           supply chain
                                 opportunity
supply      compliance
chain       plus                 ethical
pressure                         commitment

            compliance

'end-of pipe'
pollution control

Push and pull motivation for shift from end-of-pipe to 'sustainable firm'.
Source: adapted from Wood 1995: Gouldson & Murphy 1998

rising sensitivities in the local environment, targets should be based on pollution 'bubbles' – thresholds for resource flow and assimilative capacities, managed through an integrated city-region environment strategy.[46]

Such a strategy will also look at questions of location and distribution – recent surveys have found, not surprisingly, that clusters of polluting industry are in areas of poverty and unemployment, with statistical links to clusters of ill-health.[47] It would also consider the links between environmental management, industrial sector profiles, competitiveness, innovation and regeneration policy.

## Environmental management

A pioneering demonstration, 'Project Catalyst', showed how 14 major companies in the NW region could reduce both costs and impacts by pro-active environmental management.[48] The total saving was over £600,000 per company, in some cases up to 5% of turnover: a third of this was at zero capital cost, and a further third had payback periods of less than three years. As similar programmes penetrate through the regional economy, reductions of 10–20% in waste, effluent and emissions to air are quite feasible

and cost-effective. If combined with an integrated package of taxation, market incentives and institutional moves, the proportions could double.

Environmental management techniques have been a growth industry in the last decade. EMAS ('Environmental Management and Audit System') was promoted by the EU, and British Standard 7750 was a UK system used internationally: both were overtaken by ISO 14001, which is now used on over 700 sites in the UK, with numbers doubling every two years. In practice, most environmental reviews and audits take place internally with less bureaucracy and management time input. One of the first firms in Europe to register with EMAS was the Manchester-based Ciba-Clayton.

However, while environmental management systems are the first step in controlling environmental impacts, many registered firms are among the largest polluters in the UK. And while the spread of such systems may be reaching critical mass in some industry supply chains, there is a general lack of interest and take-up by SMEs. This huge number of firms cause the bulk of environmental impacts, but often lack expertise, time or commitment to achieving better practice.[49]

Formal management systems are also seen as a 'licence to pollute' – meeting short term paper targets by end-of-pipe fixes, rather than the real challenge of cleaner technology, process substitution and product innovation.[50] A sectoral breakdown of environmental expenditure shows a measure of the problem rather than the solution – substitution and innovation would often show smaller expenditure with greater effect *(Fig 10.4)*. Green labelling is also problematic – uncontrolled labels are often misused on products which are far from green, and many firms who equate 'green' with inefficiency avoid such labels in any case.[51]

In the longer term, environmental management systems are one tool among many. Environmental accounting systems, supply-chain management, risk assessment, best practice frontiers, eco-efficiency standards, eco-balance LCA, sectoral benchmarking, product eco-labelling,

46 Welford & Gouldson 1993
47 Friends of the Earth 1999
48 Aspects International & DTI 1994

49 Groundwork Foundation 1996
50 Gouldson & Murphy 1999
51 Design Innovation Group 1996

life-cycle leasing and others, each show a slice
of the total picture and need to combine in a
wider framework.[52]   Forward looking firms will
seek to climb the steps towards the goal of a
'sustainable firm', where corporate values are the
dynamic behind technical change *(Fig 10.5)*.[53]

## Industrial ecology

While most environmental management systems
focus on firms, sites and processes, a wider view
looks at the combined impact of whole industries
and sectors.  Large variations can be seen in the
climate and acidification burden of different
sectors in GM;  for example the chemicals sector
has the highest overall impact, while non-metallic
industries have the highest impact per added
value *(Fig 10.6)*.[54]   Such sectoral profiles are
the basis for the UK industry and trade
association voluntary agreements now being
discussed with government.[55]  The prospects for
high impact sectors in GM, such as chemicals,
textiles and light manufacture, should be a key
part of the city-region environment strategy, as
in the examples below.

Sectoral profiles are also the basis for
developing 'industrial ecology' systems which
cascade energy, resource and waste flows from
a variety of industries *(Box 10.4)*.[56]  Such
coordinated networks of material flows are suited
to areas of heavy industry, and integrated design
is most common in large chemicals complexes.
A prototype industrial ecology network is now
setting up in the Trafford Park industrial park,

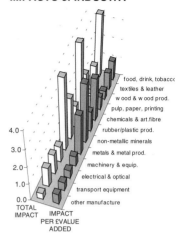

Fig 10.6    **IMPACTS of INDUSTRY**

food, drink, tobacco
textiles & leather
wood & wood prod.
pulp, paper, printing
chemicals & art.fibre
rubber/plastic prod.
non-metallic minerals
metals & metal prod.
machinery & equip.
electrical & optical
transport equipment
other manufacture

TOTAL    IMPACT
IMPACT   PER £VALUE
         ADDED

Aggregated climate change / acid rain impacts per economic value of sector.
(1) shows total environmental impact: (2) shows ratio of impacts to added value.
Source ECOTEC 1996:  DTI 1996: OECD 1997

possibly the best location in GM. At the regional
level established materials industries could
develop markets and trading networks, anchored
on a cluster of materials reclamation and
disassembly plants. Such a 'green growth pole'
could stimulate development in the same way
that chemicals or car plants did in previous
decades.[57]

A prime example would be the chemical sector, and adjacent to GM on the Mersey estuary
is one of the largest complexes in Europe – this
has a long history of accidents, and even now
produces two thirds of the UK's large scale carcinogenic emissions. The Chemical Industries
Association (CIA) set up a 'responsible care'
programme, even though 40% of its member firms
lacked EMAS or ISO 14001 registration.[58]  Certain economies of information came to light – for
instance half of BP's reported improvements were
due to plant sales and accounting changes,
rather than actual achievements.[59]  In contrast,
market leaders such as Dow Chemicals have pioneered 'eco-efficiency', setting standards for
others to follow.[60]

Another example would be textiles, the origi-
nal motivator of growth in  GM, and the first

---

**Box 10.4**

### INDUSTRIAL ECOLOGY

One of the most integrated energy-materials cascades in a modern economy is in Kalundborg in
Denmark.  A coal-fired power plant sends waste
heat to housing, greenhouses and other industries, and sends its ash for conversion to building
materials.  It also exchanges fuel, heat and water
with an oil refinery, chemicals and pharmaceuticals works.

**Source: Ayres & Simonis 1996**

---

52 Bennett & James 1999
53 RSA Inquiry 1995:  Wood 1996
54 Based on UK data from ONS 1998: adjusted for sectoral multipliers

55  DETR 1998 (Sustainable Business)
56 Ayres & Simonis 1997
57 Roberts 1995
58 Chemical Industries Association 1994
59 ENDS Report 259
60 Business Council on Sustainable Development 1993

global industry. Textiles has suffered more than most from overseas migration, and most remaining plants in GM are in value-added operations such as printing and design. The EU textile sector is finally moving towards agreement on an eco-label scheme, but this covers only a small part of the LCA 'tree' of effluent, emissions, packaging and synthetic fibres. Much of the GM fashion trade now deals in sweat-shop imports where sources are confidential and standards are difficult to enforce, using materials such as cotton with large indirect impacts. On the other hand most textile products are highly sensitive to consumer pressure, and forward looking firms should capitalize on the opportunity of the 'Benetton factor' – rising standards in both demand and supply sides, plus the marketing to link them.

# GREENING THE ECONOMY

The next stage is to extend the greening of business to the entire  city-region economy – . the wider spread of environment–business activity, the effect of environmental policy on the regional economy, and its opportunities and risks. This leads to the crucial question of how to steer economic development towards combined environment-economic-social benefit.

There is a unique opportunity as each of the English Regional Development Agencies (RDAs) prepares and implements its first full Regional Economic Strategy ('RES'. That of the NW region aims to be as 'sustainable' as any. But in practice it is difficult to break out of conventional thinking on supply-side 'sites and skills', and the powers and resources for more far reaching actions are still fuzzy and distant.

## Business–environment links

For all the talk it is early days yet, and out of many schemes there are fewer successes *(Box 10.5)*. Following the 'Project Catalyst' above, the 'Manchester Energy - Environment Agency' had difficulties with a subsidized consultancy scheme for subscriber firms. Meanwhile the larger business community, with greater expertise and investment power, established an internal forum for environment-business opportunities, and this is now running *Evolve*, a green benchmarking scheme.[61] The Manchester-based Coop Bank has taken a profitable lead with its green and ethical policies, and preferential lending for environmental investment.[62] The bank also sponsored the National Centre for Business and Ecology in partnership with the four universities, and is instrumental in the regional partnership and its pioneering agency, 'Sustainability North West'.

At ground level the slow response of SMEs to environmental regulation and opportunities causes concern, as shown by a local survey which confirmed national findings:[63]

- 10% of SMEs think they have significant environmental impact
- 20% have some form of environmental review or written policy
- 30% claim interest in a green business club, but only 1% attend meetings
- 65% have no knowledge of environmental issues.

Generally, there are mixed signals on the spread of business-environment schemes:  the management time required is often seen as not cost-effective, and many environmental reviews lack accreditation or credibility. Regional surveys show a jungle of competing agencies, often reaching the already converted, or only those on the run from the regulators.[64]

Meanwhile, of the 60,000 businesses in GM, about 10% are registered for some environmental facility, including 4000 sites with IPC Part A or B, 2000 producers of trade effluent, and 3500 licensed waste producers or carriers.[65] Perhaps

61 Sustainability NW 1999
62 Co-operative Bank 1998

63 Hooper & Gibbs 1995: Groundwork Foundation 1996
64 Douglas & Lawson 1997
65 data from HMIP 1995: GMWRA 1996: NW Water 1996

**Box 10.5**

**ENVIRONMENT-BUSINESS ACTIVITY**

- Sustainability North West: umbrella partnership agency
- Coop Bank environmental marketing & lending schemes
- 'Evolve' environmental benchmarking for large firms
- National Centre for Business & Ecology 'Green Competitive Edge' programme & network
- Groundwork: business-environment consultancy network
- Manchester Energy & Environment Agency
- Manchester Chamber of Commerce programme
- Bolton Institute Technology / Environment programme
- Mersey Basin Campaign & Business Foundation
- NW Business Team, Environmental Action Group:
- Ethical Investment Research & Information Service
- Trafford Park Energy Strategy & Quality Initiative
- 'Enviro-Net 2000': promotions for 80 firms
- Research R&D at HEI's
- DTI 'Envirotech' assisted consultancy scheme
- DTI 'Project Catalyst' demonstration: 14 firms
- DTI national programmes SCEEMAS & EDAS

Data for GM 1990-1997: Ravetz 1999d & NW Partnership 1997

**Box 10.6**

**ENVIRONMENT-BUSINESS PENETRATION**

< 0.1% of businesses registered ISO 14001, BS 7750, EMAS
< 0.5% of GDP in 'environmental' industries (excl. water)
< 1% have inhouse / informal EM systems
< 10% have active environmental reviews / policies
< 10% are registered polluters or waste producers
> 20% show interest in EM
> 50% of businesses have significant material throughput

Approximate estimates for GM as of 1997:
Source Ravetz 1999d

another 40% of businesses in manufacturing, construction, distribution, catering or retail have significant material throughput, while the service-based remainder still consume office supplies, premises, energy and transport. Such broad estimates show that formal management systems are used in about one in a thousand businesses in GM, and in-house or informal reviews and audits have spread to perhaps one in a hundred, although these proportions are weighted towards larger firms *(Box 10.6)*.

If recent trends can be interpreted as a doubling of environment-business activity every 5-10 years, and registrations every 2–3 years, then we might anticipate full environmental management coverage of businesses with significant material throughput in 20–30 years. If systems for monitoring and target-setting are only the first steps towards the bigger picture – fully integrated chain management, stakeholder responsibility and the 'sustainable firm' in corporate culture – then 50-100 years would not be unrealistic for such a transition.[66]

# Economy–environment links

Environmental policy may have positive or negative impacts on economic activity, and for each policy or strategy, local and regional economic impacts can be identified, if not calculated, as shorter term adjustment or longer term adaptation.[67] For GM, with its many older and heavier industries, areas of employment growth would include:

- 'environmental' industries and internal activity in other regulated industries;
- other sectors with increased competitiveness through price increases in regulated sectors;
- sectors dependent on environmental quality such as leisure and tourism;
- public sector environmental infrastructure.

In contrast to this, sectors at risk of economic or employment decline would include:

- producers of 'defensive' products and end-of pipe technology;

---

66 World Wildlife Fund 1996
67 Jacobs 1994

- sectors which are economically 'vulnerable', and more sensitive to increased costs, market shifts, redundancy of plant, and willing to migrate to less regulated locations.

For these vulnerable industries the style and flexibility of regulation are crucial, as seen in the sensitive negotiations of the 'BATNEEC' approach.[68] The 'vulnerability' of any industry sector can be seen by its exposure to energy or transport costs, length of the investment cycle, and the proportion of SMEs who are less able to adapt and invest *(Fig 10.7)*. Extrapolating from other surveys might suggest that up to 30,000 jobs in GM could be at risk in certain vulnerable sectors such as paper, textiles, food, chemicals and distribution.[69]

There is also case for 'counter vulnerability' – in the sense that slow or weak environmental regulation can inhibit incentives and undermine competitiveness in world markets, where higher standards are already enforced elsewhere, where responsible firms risk being undercut by irresponsible firms, and where 'first-mover' status is a crucial advantage.[70] European experience suggests that the overall impacts of environmental regulation so far tend to be neutral or positive, although there may be 'accelerated obsolescence' in some older and more vulnerable industries.[71]

In the longer term, there are wider effects of environmental policy on the regional and national economy, few of which have been worked out in detail.[72] One is the share of manufacturing to services – in a low-impact de-materialized closed-loop economy, service shares may increase, as products are leased and re-used within the service sector. There is also a changing balance of investment to consumption, or internal/financial costs to external/societal costs, where internalization requires longer term investment. There are effects on the balance of capital and labour, where social goals may favour low-skill job creation, while economic goals favour high-skill and capital-intensive jobs *(next section)*.

Finally, there are effects on the balance of the private, public and third sectors – and in this picture, market transformation may see new kinds of institutions take the place of conventional share-equity firms *(Chapter 13)*. Many environmental industries such as recycling are naturally labour intensive, and will achieve greater economic efficiency if tasks are 'embedded' in cultures and lifestyles – where for instance householders are happy to pre-sort their waste. In other words, less formal jobs may achieve greater eco-efficiency with added social benefits.

## Green economic strategy

Urban and regional policy documents now exude green ideals, and the first question is the gap between rhetoric and reality.[73] The previous NW 'sustainable' RES aimed for a 'green and pleasant region', but counted this in purely local anecdotal terms with little reference to global impacts.[74] Likewise the previous Regional Planning Guidance (RPG) aimed to reduce traffic while developing motorway sites for business parks.[75] The GM Operational Programme for EU funding carried out 'tick-list' environmental appraisals, but no assessment of impacts against current trends or targets in transport, energy or waste.[76] One of its five programmes was 'regeneration and the environment', with 17% of the funds, of which 'promoting environmental practice' was a small component.[77]

So with the rhetoric now in place, there is an even greater challenge in the green conversion of the mainstream economic development agenda – sites, premises, infrastructure and regeneration.[78] Such thinking in progress can be seen in the recent NW region RES, together with related transport and environment components, where each heading could form the basis of an expanded 'green' agenda:[79]

- *knowledge base*: environmental expertise, R&D and technology diffusion should be linked to resources in further and higher education.

68 ENDS 1994
69 ECOTEC 1991
70 DTI / DoE 1994
71 Hitchen 1997
72 Ravetz 1999d

73 Gibbs 1996
74 NWRA 1993
75 Dept of Environment 1996 (RPG 13)
76 GONW 1994 (Single Programme Document)
77 Gibbs, Longhurst & Braithwaite 1995
78 Centre for Local Economic Strategies 1994: LGMB 1994
79 North West Partnership 1996

- *workforce skills:* environmental skill and awareness should be an essential component in human resources development.
- *restructuring and redeployment:* vulnerable sectors need assistance in adaptation and promoting environmental market opportunities.
- *small firms support:* the SME sector is more vulnerable to regulation, and needs support, incentives and access to markets.
- *inward investment:* should focus on low-impact high added-value clean technologies
- *strategic sites:* should be based on low-impact development and transport modes.
- *telematics:* to enable clean technology diffusion, skills development and low-impact consumerism.
- *arts, leisure, culture and image:* promote quality of life investment and the spread of low-impact lifestyles.

The regional partnership remit now extends far beyond that of local government, with a key role in the new landscape of RDAs, regional chambers and assemblies, City Challenge and SRB Boards, Chambers of Commerce, TECs and Business Links, and many other professional and industry bodies. There is no simple formula to bringing the green economic agenda to such a mixed community – it may be carried out within such organizations, as a free-standing initiative, or a mixture of both. In the NW a partnership non-profit company was set up, 'Sustainability North West', to catalyse new initiatives, advice, assistance and stimulation of its parent bodies. For this kind of venture the crucial factor may be not only technical resources, but again the corporate culture and commitment.

To promote such 'vision factor', each area and territory has to evolve its own approach. In many free-standing cities there are active and self-supporting business–environment forums.[80] In the NW the Groundwork Trust links a network of specialist offices in smaller cities. While the need and potential are as great in GM, the size and complexity of the conurbation means that one central organization or network may not be

Fig 10.7  **INDUSTRIAL VULNERABILITY**

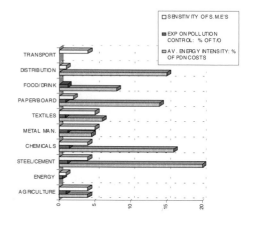

Indicators for the vulnerability of industrial sectors to environmental regulation. Proportion of SME's in the sector shows short planning cycles. Energy expenditure as proportion of t/o shows sensitivity to energy prices. Data for UK: with industries by SIC code.
Source: based on ECOTEC 1994

appropriate, and different models may be suited to each business type and size band:

- larger companies: policy and development role for city-region environmental management framework, technology R&D, infrastructure;
- medium-sized manufacturing: access to specialist consultancy and finance: networks for collaboration on transport, energy, waste;
- local SMEs: general promotions, access to technology, information, financial packages;
- local micro and start-up businesses: basic guidance and access to support and services;
- commercial and retail services: green-ethical supply chains, purchasing and marketing;
- financial and producer services: green-ethical investment policies and projects;
- public or quasi-public services, particularly health and education: purchasing and contracting, social trading networks.

More than ethics and ideals, the practical motivation for green economic strategy is to maximize opportunity and minimize risk. For the first, the 'environmental industries' market is about £300 million pro rata for GM – including pollution control, land remediation, water and waste management. European and world markets are growing at perhaps 50% per decade in the near future.[81] Further business opportunities will follow from environmental policy in each key sector – construction, energy, transport, countryside management, producer services such as packaging and printing, consumer products, and the 'Urban Mines' theme of creating jobs by converting waste to resources.[82]

At the same time GM contains many vulnerable industries as above – while the RES has something of a bullish 'invest in success' attitude, there is a strong case for targetted support to almost all materials-based industries and sectors. Initial approaches to the 10,000 plus SME's involved might come from the regulators, but would be more effective from the all-important banking and accountancy system.

## Green development fund

The financial sector itself could do more to promote new green products and markets, bridging the gap between dwindling public resources, narrow business programmes, and short-termist bank finance *(Chapter 13)*. In Germany for instance, banks, R&D organizations and businesses agencies establish partnerships and networks for long term investment and equity holding.[83] Similarly in the UK there is a strong case for a urban or regional investment fund targeted on green business opportunities. Such a fund might be run by a partnership of commercial banks and venture capital funds, public sector authorities and TECs, with a direct relationship to the resources of the RDA and regional government office. The main objective of such a fund would be in bridging market barriers to enable viable long term investment:

- clean technology 'growth pole' with technology transfer network, linking R&D, HEIs and industrial bodies;
- market development programme, linking green investment and purchasing policies to venture capital and potential suppliers;

- central database of green and ethical goods, services, recyclable materials, and business opportunities;
- preferential finance for environmentally accredited businesses, as piloted by the Coop and NatWest banks;
- other business services, such as insurance and accountancy focused on environmental best practice;
- infrastructure development: long term equity or underwriting to environmentally-led schemes such as CHP and public transport;
- partnership agencies: preferential capital, equity investment and underwriting to the city-region energy agency and similar consortium bodies;
- employment development programme: tackling unemployment and local business development, supporting the New Deal with energy efficiency and similar programmes.

Such a green investment fund would have much in common with a general local or regional banking system, along the lines of the USA Community Banks, or the regional development banks of Europe which are successful by virtue of their social and financial stake in the region.[84]

## Local resilience

The potential for such development funds raises the question of how far an open economy could or should be localized or regionalized, and how far city-region public intervention should seek to influence the free market flow of global capital.

This, of course, is an intensely political question. On one hand the 'small is beautiful' approach aims at local employment, reducing transport impacts, and environmental costs.[85] On the other is a tide of globalization and integration, supported not only by market pressure but the technical case for cleaner production in larger plants. GM's position as a provincial capital in a peripheral location might suggest an economic philosophy of strengthening local diversity and resilience by import substitution.[86] A profile of GM's critical

81 OECD 1997: Environmental Industries Commission
82 Roberts & Pike 1998
83 Gudgin 1996

84 Mayo 1997: Laulageinan 1998
85 Schumacher 1973
86 Jacobs 1985

factors shows a strong need and opportunity for steering away from branch-plant investment, towards a more self-sustaining and self-reliant regional economy:[87]

- local equity: about half all businesses in GM are locally owned, 80% of large businesses are external, but 60% of new jobs come through SMEs;
- local diversity: the size of GM enables a full spread of sectors, although the manufacturing–services share shift is still behind the UK;
- local 'added value': current GM added value is 5% below the UK average, and manufacturing added value is 20% below;
- local resources: GM has critical mass in business services, media, HEI's, sports and arts, and the airport;
- skills, entrepreneurship and learning culture: qualifications are below UK averages, self-employment is down, business start-ups and failures are above average, while Manchester has a strong self-image as an innovator;
- internal markets and supply chains: the GM public sector market is about £7–8 billion, with great scope for policy-led initiatives;
- access to finance, entrepreneurs and investors: GM has the largest financial and professional centre outside London.

But in spite of this financial concentration, much apparent regional autonomy is undermined by London-based investment funds, with the result that economic strategy tends to reinforce branch-plant dependency by default.[88] Even the very concepts of local economic development focus on 'basic' industries which by nature are those which globalize, rather than the indigenous loops which in reality generate the bulk of local activity.[89] Clearly, for the success of the 2020 green economy strategy above, city-region autonomy and self-reliance need to increase. One approach is the long uphill march of rebuilding entrepreneurial capacity in a post-industrial city. Another is the potential for structural change from within – through stakeholding or stakeowning for employees and customers, as in the next section.

## Investment & purchasing

The bulk of industrial production is now in external and overseas operations, where environmental and social impacts are indirect and invisible. Ethical investment is the main means by which policy can affect the production cycle at source, and the evidence so far is that its profit levels, if anything, can out-perform the market average.[90] GM is a national centre for ethical investment research, and the Manchester-based Co-operative Bank is the first high street bank to promote publicly and profit from its ethical policies. All public bodies should adopt out of principle active ethical investment policies for their capital and pension funds, and link these with city-regional development funding as above.[91]

Greening the economy is also linked to the other end of the chain – the 'checkout revolution' – and again GM is a national centre for green consumer research.[92] Pressure for change may come from firms, supply chains, scientific evidence, the media or from public opinion, and frequently from a confusing and controversial mixture of these. For organic food for instance, there is a compounding of consumer demand, retail supply chains, and producer innovation, but the result so far is unmet demand. In Japan, by contrast, vertically integrated producer–consumer food cooperatives have grown into major businesses, showing the way for similar ventures in the UK. Again, market failure is due to many factors, but the lead role falls to public bodies to coordinate in-house purchasing with distribution networks for green and ethical products.

87 data from ONS 1998
88 Martin & Minns 1995
89 Williams 1997

90 Holden Meehan 1994
91 Simpson 1994
92 ICLEI database 1999

# SUSTAINABLE EMPLOYMENT

What is 'sustainable employment'? It concerns the labour component of the process of eco-modernization. It also concerns perennial goals for social justice and human fulfilment. Leaving aside the time-worn debates on labour and capital, we explore the prospects for 'green jobs' – the employment opportunities of environmental strategy. We also touch on local actions for quality of work and workplaces. For the question – how many jobs? – purely for illustration we show some ball-park estimates, subject to many assumptions and further research.

The GM labour market of about 1 million workers contains more craftsmen and operatives, and less professional and self-employed than the national average. The regional centre draws two thirds of its workforce from within GM, but only 15% from the more deprived areas within a 3-mile radius. There are now more women than men in work, albeit more part time and insecure, and this has profound implications for family structure and male self-identity. Jobs are migrating from the conurbations to rural and 'retirement' areas, while GM itself is a complex mix between older industrial centres and newer service economies of its outer satellites.[93]

Unemployment for GM is marginally worse than the UK average, and its mixed economy has survived recent recessions better than some other regions. However there are still wards with 20–30% structural unemployment, and areas of over 10% cover most inner city and peripheral estates. Recent projections are for an overall loss of jobs at about 0.3-5% per year, partly compensated by higher education and early retirement.[94] There is local evidence for an adapted '30-30-30' model, where 30% are unemployed or low waged, 30% are in part-time or insecure employment, 30% in secure employment, and 10% are outside of any simple category.[95]

## Work & society

A wider view looks at future trends in work, the relationship of employees to enterprises, and the structural shift from primary and secondary activity, to tertiary and quaternary activity *(Chapter 1).*[96] The previous 'Fordist' mode of male breadwinners doing 'undesirable' work is now shifting to a more post-Fordist aspiration of 'desirable', fulfilling and high earning jobs which enable high-spending leisure, and in some cases downshifting with reduced earning or spending *(Fig 10.8)*. In practice, few attain the aspirations of both value and quality, and many occupations experience stress, insecurity and 'time poverty'.[97] While economic policy tends to assume a universal aspiration for high-achieving high-spending lifestyles, in GM itself there are high levels of depression, suicide, divorce and stress, due in some part to workplace conditions *(Chapter 11)*. Employers can ease these pressures and improve their human resource capacity, by enabling sabbaticals, flexible hours, parental leave, childcare and others.

The shifting boundaries between work and leisure are also crucial for environmental policy. In transport strategy, for instance, drivers' time is counted as a cost as if they were at work, while there is much counter evidence that driving is a leisure activity, and so on the other side of the balance sheet.[98] Some cultures are happy to grow food for leisure, while for others it would be counted as work and therefore uneconomic. On principle, damaging activities ought to be miminized as 'work', and restorative activities ought to be maximized as 'leisure', but of course things are rarely so simple.

The relationship of workers to enterprises is also shifting. Downsizing, networking and out-sourcing are everyday trends in a knowledge-based, value-added, human-resource economy. Such an economy also involves new kinds of relationship between labour to capital, and

93 Wong, Baker & Gallent 1999
94 Peck & Emmerich 1992
95 Hutton 1995

96 Rifkin 1994
97 Burchell 1999
98 Stradling & Simpson 1998

Fig 10.8        **WORK & LEISURE**

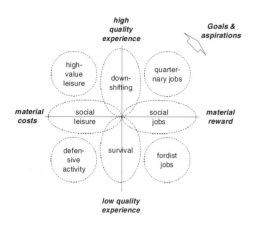

Changing balance of quantity of material reward and quality experience
in work and leisure in post-industrial societies.
Source: adapted from Handy 1995; Rifkin 1994

Fig 10.9        **IMPACTS of EMPLOYMENT**

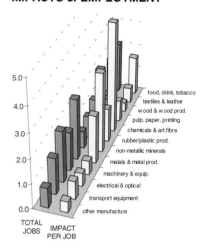

Aggregated climate change / acid rain impacts per job by manufacturing sector.
(1) shows total jobs in UK sector (2) shows ratio of impacts to employees.
Source ECOTEC 1996: DTI 1996: OECD 1997

producers to consumers, in various combinations of 'stake-holding':[99]

- entrepreneurial ownership, where more start-up companies are employee owned;
- equity pay schemes, enabling employees to be paid in part with shares and options;
- employee ownership in the SME sector, to spread equity through firm life-cycles;
- employee ownership in the corporate sector as incentive and enabler for team management and participatory governance;
- 'stake-owning' and other extended corporate responsibility, to and from a wider circle of suppliers, clients, employees, financiers, regulators and others.[100]

Finally, the traditional divisions between public and private sectors are shifting, particularly in the voluntary and education sectors. An 'intermediate labour market' is forming around the problem of youth unemployment, both by accident and by design.[101] The UK government proposal to enlist the unemployed as school assistants is the tip of an iceberg, which will see the merging of many voluntary and education activities as the solution to pressing problems.

While this opens up the prospect of new thinking in public services, it also risks the casualization and exclusion of lower-income groups.

## Jobs in a green economy

Such transitions are crucial for environmentally-based employment, and the pattern of work and leisure in a de-materialized economy. Future eco-taxation may shift the burden from labour to resources, enabling increased employment with lower resource use *(Chapter 13)*. This would change the 'employment intensity' for many sectors – for instance, substituting public for private transport could increase transport sector jobs by 10%.[102] Shifting waste disposal towards waste recycling increases employment by up to five times. The shift towards service-based leasing and re-use, rather than manufacture, also changes the mix of occupations and activities.[103]

Eco-modernization for more vulnerable industries may also result in accelerated investment and ICT-led rationalization, with resulting job losses. An estimate of the 'jobs at risk' in vulnerable industries in GM would be 20–40000, if environmental controls were applied too rigidly and rapidly.[104] The chart shows for

99 Leadbeater 1997
100 Gates 1998
101 Sanderson Walton & Campbell 1997

102 Friends of the Earth 1997
103 Murray 1998
104 estimated from ECOTEC 1994

key sectors the overall environmental impact per job, highlighting the most vulnerable industries where support should be targeted *(Fig 10.9)*.

The challenge is to balance environmental goals with the development of human resources, labour skills and business competitiveness. Taking the environmental agenda as a learning curve benefits individuals, firms and the city-region, where 'learning' culture and 'networking' capacity are now seen as crucial for competitiveness.[105] This suggests different approaches to green employment policy.

One is to re-skill the labour market for environmentally-led growth industries, where knowledge-based skills and human resources are needed to maximize future opportunities.[106] Another is to prioritize environmental actions for their linkage with employment. Full-scale energy upgrading across GM, for instance, could create 10–15,000 jobs, mostly local and manual.

A third approach is to promote environmental strategy as a catalyst which encourages new forms of service sectors, social economy and human resource development. Developing public transport-based neighbourhood centres, for instance, would increase demand for retail, maintenance and security employment. Some of this could be full time employment, some intermediate, and some third sector activity, which is of course less easy to estimate.

## Green jobs

Estimates of environmentally-based jobs can be drawn from OECD or national studies, adjusted for the economic structure of GM, and allowing for rapid change in labour markets and occupations. Current employment in 'environmental industries' in GM, including public administration, environmental managers, export production and landscape-related activity, would be in the region of 10–15,000.[107] A 70% growth is estimated in Europe over the last decade, with world projections for 3-4% per year growth beyond that. The result could be a total of 40,000 jobs by 2020 in all environmentally-linked sectors in GM, with a range of manual, semi-skilled and specialist occupations. Many of these would be adjustments to existing occupations, and not necessarily all labelled as 'new jobs' in the environment.

In each key sector the investment and development programme could also generate a similar order of jobs, in the region of 30–40,000. These would include energy efficiency, public transport, waste re-use and recycling, CHP and others. The proposed EU and UK eco-taxation packages would also generate an estimated 30,000 jobs in GM, not only via the environmental activities counted above, but through the lowering of labour

---

| Box 10.7 | |
|---|---|
| **GREEN EMPLOYMENT** | |

| **ENVIRONMENTAL INDUSTRIES** | |
|---|---|
| Environmental management in industry | |
| Environmental control goods & services | |
| Environmental export production | |
| Environmental public administration | |
| water & effluent | |
| Landscape & amenity | |
| waste recycling & re-use | |
| | 40 |

| **ECO-TAXATION** | 30 |
|---|---|
| general stimulus of falling labour costs | |

| **ENVIRONMENTAL KEY SECTORS** | |
|---|---|
| Construction & energy efficiency upgrading | 15 |
| public transport, ICT & re-engineering | 15 |
| organic agriculture & forestry | 5 |
| CHP, renewable energy, smart systems | 5 |
| | 40 |
| jobs at risk in vulnerable industries | (10) |
| **Total direct employment** | **100** |

| **THIRD SECTOR** | |
|---|---|
| Voluntary sector – fte equivalent | 10 |
| cultural industries - fte equivalent | 10 |
| Community & cooperative - fte equivalent | 10 |
| LETS social trading - fte equivalent | 10 |
| Public service trading - fte equivalent | 10 |
| TOTAL THIRD SECTOR JOBS | 50 |

| **Combined job equivalents** | **150** |
|---|---|
| (existing unemployment total, 6/96) | 136 |

Aggregated estimates for illustration only, of potential 'green employment' growth. Estimates pro-rata for GM in gross 1000's of jobs 1995-2020, excluding multipliers and displacements, with very large margin of error.

Sources: based on ECOTEC 1994, FOE 1995 & 1998, Jacobs 1994, ESI 1994, IPPR 1997, Cambridge Econometrics 1998

---

105 Morgan 1997
106 Gallie & White 1997
107 est. from OECD 1997: Environmental Industries Commision 1998

108 Cambridge Econometrics 1998: Jenkins 1997

costs via employers' National Insurance contributions *(Chapter 13)*.[108]

Allowing for possible losses in vulnerable industries, and not including multipliers or displacements, total increased employment in the SD scenario is in the region of 100,000, which is the same region as the average unemployment in GM *(Box 10.7)*. Adding in notional figures for the job equivalents in 'third sector' activity could add 50% to this total, depending on how such activity is estimated. In practice unemployment may not be reduced directly by new jobs created, as the labour market is highly segmented with many mismatches between occupations and skills.

Again we should stress that these estimates are purely for illustration only at this stage.

# Tackling unemployment

Can sustainable development solve the greatest threat to global capitalism and the social order – unemployment? The above case seems to be saying yes and no – that there will be jobs, but not necessarily for the unemployed. There is an argument that 'inflation-stable' levels of unemployment are here to stay, as long as ICT replaces jobs faster than new markets create them.[109] But for multi-national corporations, the dominant institutions of the 20th century, labour is a commodity to be expended for profit.[110] In the UK, average unemployment is at a historically low level, but within the average there are many clusters where unemployment is the largest common factor in mortality, crime and drug abuse. Meanwhile many unemployed and 'economically inactive' invent roles in the informal or black economy – such talent and energy should in principle be harnessed.[111]

The UK government's New Deal 'supply side' approach promotes employment skills and aptitudes with a range of welfare-to-work 'gateway' options – subsidized employment, voluntary sector placements, full-time education or training, or an environmental task-force. Each type of scheme has had mixed success in the past, and it may be that after drop-outs, free-rider substitutes, artificial 'workfare' and demand side limits, the number of real permanent jobs created will be small and quite costly.[112] In Manchester the 'gateway' package is managed by the TEC for the City Pride partnership, as part of an intermediate labour market framework – but the 5000 'gateway' places in GM would have to multiply many times to make serious inroads on unemployment.[113]

Beyond welfare to work, there are other approaches to be explored in future years. An institutional approach would look again at the new UK 'working families tax credit', and the potential for universal negative income taxes for loosening the boundaries between formal work, leisure, voluntary activity, training and unemployment.[114] A human resources approach looks at the possibility of a 'social contract' basic income in exchange for community contributions and personal training.[115] This points to a third sector 'social trading' approach for supplying public services through an intermediate labour market, contributing to social security, health, education, crime prevention, housing, landscape, leisure and others.

Many argue that the key to success is not only the economics but the culture of employment, the all-important networks of contacts and opportunities, and the changing balance of work and leisure.[116] Meanwhile the numbers of economically active but not seeking work are growing – many people apparently have other things to do with their lives. Marginalized, criminalized or alternative sub-cultures with total distrust of 'officials' and 'schemes' may have little time for well-intentioned work placements, and lateral thinking may be more effective for mixed activity in work-public-leisure-training .[117]

Overall, a sustainable city-region employment strategy would aim to extend conventional thinking on job creation and skills training. It would look at problems and opportunities from the viewpoints of alternative cultures, third sector economy and environmental strategy, to capitalize on the opportunities and added value of coordination.

109 Rifkin 1995
110 Korten 1999
111 Douthwaite 1996
112 Institute of Public Policy REsearch 1999
113 Manchester Training and Enterprise Council 1998

114 Offe & Heinz 1994
115 Lipietz 1995
116 Kruger 1997
117 Sanderson Walton & Campbell 1997

# SUSTAINABLE LIVELIHOODS

While the global economy booms, half the world's population is getting poorer, and even those who are richer are not necessarily better off.[118] Purely economic indicators of turnover and employment can mislead as to true wealth and human resources – hence the growing awareness of the informal, social or 'third sector' economy, an umbrella concept for almost any common enterprise and exchange of goods or services outside the monetary system.[119] Of course there is no firm line between the informal, grey, and black economies, and the fuzziness of the concept is a problem when dealing with the public and private sectors. But GM has long been a centre for social movements, and there is huge scope for the future.

## Cultural industries

In the transition to a post-industrial economy, cultural industries can bridge the gap between voluntary sectors, community identity, and the cultural cachet favoured by investors and professionals.[120] Manchester itself is a regional capital with world class music, sport and fashion – the Northern Quarter of the city centre is the 'cultural quarter', Castlefield is an 'urban heritage park', the Manchester Host uses ICT for cultural networks, and many developments and regeneration schemes are anchored on sports, arts or leisure.[121]

However, the actual size of the cultural industries is small, new activities are rare in poorer areas, and the majority are still passive consumers of global media. While the image of cultural industries is glitzy and 'happening', the reality is often on the edges of the black economy and drug culture. Are the cultural industries the plaything of an educated minority, a marketing ploy by developers, cultural colonization by the knowledge-based classes, or are they the catalysts for transformation of civic society?

Each of these views is valid. Together they show how cultural industries are a vital strand in the re-invention and 're-imagineering' of post-modern urban life in all its contradictions.[122]

## Cooperation & mutuality

Cooperatives are a form of enterprise through common ownership, an alternative to the system of shareholding for externalized risk and profit. The 'mutual' institutions were founded with a similar ethos, for responsibility and self-help for members through preferential terms and dividends. GM is the headquarters of the UK and world cooperative movement: the large financial, retail and producer cooperatives are market leaders, and the Co-op Bank in particular has taken a profitable lead with its green and ethical policies.[123] Now the principle of mutuality itself is under attack from capital buying in, and from members selling out, and the near success of a take-over bid for the Cooperative Wholesale Society group showed the need for innovation in the cooperative sector.

Worldwide the majority of co-ops are now in the east Asian 'tiger' economies. Smaller co-ops in the UK tend to draw on particular sub-cultures and lifestyle niches, and in GM there are over 90 local co-ops with 700 jobs.[124] Manchester City has in the past spent £500,000 per year on cooperative development, creating jobs at a fraction of the cost of high-tech enterprise support.[125] Although most of these jobs are low-paid, this shows the scope for the cooperative sector as a vital interface between formal and informal economies, as training grounds for social entrepreneurs and a vital strand for intermediate labour markets.

Alternative employment is often generated by communities with few alternatives – in parts of East Manchester, for instance, half the people may be living on 'unofficial' activity.[126] Of the local or community-based enterprises which do

---

118 Daly & Cobb 1989
119 other terms: Third Force Organization (TFO): Citizen-Based Organization (CBO): Voluntary Sector Organization (VSO): Non-Governmental Organization (NGO): Not-for-profit (NFP)
120 Bianchini & Parkinson 1994
121 O'Connor & Hill 1996:

122 Soja 1995
123 Co-operative Bank 1999
124 data from GM Council for Voluntary Service as of 1995
125 Manchester City Council 1995 (Economic development statement)
126 Jones & Partridge 1989

spring up despite the odds, many are stymied by
lack of finance – one in five households in GM,
and in some parts half the population, have no
access to any financial services. Credit unions
offer facilities to households and start-up
businesses with no other access to finance. In
Ireland one in four people are credit union
members; a network in GM has started over 20
schemes in the last five years, with excellent
repayment rates.[127]   Many urban areas such as
GM need to reinvent what still goes on in some
rural areas – local collective investment in
facilities such as open space, public shelters, and
opportunties for youth and elderly.

## Local & social trading

Meanwhile it is curious that 100,000 people are
unemployed in GM, and yet there is work to do
everywhere, from cleaning up pollution, to caring
for the elderly. The missing link is money. And
yet money is little more than a system of social
exchange and indirect trust – if two neighbours
swap or share, anything from childcare to DIY
equipment, no money changes hands, but both
are better off.[128]

Local Exchange Trading Systems (LETS) are
based on this principle. A local currency is based
on time value, with computerized accounts,
automatic overdrafts, and zero interest rates –
members pay for goods and services by cheque,
and a growing number of businesses take part
payment in LETS units. The Manchester LETS
scheme was one of the largest in the UK, and its
rapid growth suggested that it might cover large
parts of the local service economy. In the event
it has split into different networks for different
areas, and it is still early days – the services on
offer are limited to discretionary services, not
always relevant to lower income groups. But
LETS offers one of the best prospects around,
for fostering a degree of resilience and self-
reliance from the volatile winds of global capital.

On a wider scale, there is also scope for
extending LETS networks to public services for
'social trading'. In the Brazilian city of Curitiba,
for instance, recycled materials collected locally
are exchanged by the authorities for free public

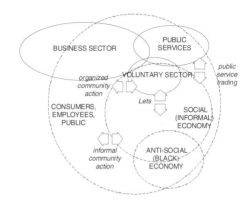

Fig 10.10          **LOCAL ECONOMIES**

Summary of alternative trading systems.
Source: adapted from Friedman 1994:  Offe & Heinz 1995

transport passes – increasing the viability of
both recycling and public transport, and
benefiting low-income people.[129]  This principle
can apply to any services which are locally
value-added and suitable for non-specialist
labour – street cleaning, security services,
caretaking and wardening, gardening and food,
re-use and recycling, youth provision and
supplementary education are all potential
candidates for a community contribution. The
services provided in exchange could be anything
with small marginal costs – spare seats in public
transport or leisure facilities, re-used furniture
and equipment, short-life housing and business
premises.

Such trading networks are a democratic
extension of the more elite 'favours' of political
and business circles, where senior figures
contribute to the community for a return of
intangible influence. The mounting pressures
on public services, as in the next chapter, show
that such 'social trading' may be not only
desirable but an essential strand of an
intermediate labour market – providing job
creation, expanded services and environmental
improvements.[130] Many North American cities
are experimenting with variations on the theme.
At one end of the scale are self-organized
networks such as 'time dollars', enabling one-

---

127 Joseph Rowntree Foundation 1994
128 Lang 1994: Croall 1999

129 Rabinovitch & Lietman 1996: Gilbert 1996
130 Friedman 1995

off trades between individuals or organizations. At the other end are comprehensive local currencies, where the majority of local businesses trade in combinations of national and local dollars.[131] In principle there is every possibility that GM could set up a local currency for specific local added-value service exchange – it would certainly have critical mass. The degree of self-containment would be a question, and any serious revenue diverted away from government would be controversial. While this sounds radical, the City Pride partnership in GM is even now looking in the same direction, and the long term scope of such a concept is huge.

## Voluntary & third sector

Traditional social trading has been through the voluntary sector, whose diversity and 'fuzziness' is both a problem and an asset. The UK has one of the largest voluntary sectors of any nation, and GM has one of the largest clusters in the UK. There are about 10,000 organizations, of which 7–8000 are charitable status, and about 20,000 including all those which are neither strictly public or private – a third of the number of commercial firms in GM.[132] The income of registered charities is in the region of £800 million, or 3% of total GDP, employing about 20,000 part- and full-time workers, with about 1 million adults in some form of voluntary activity. About 40% of organizations are in the health and social services sector, and another 30% in youth and recreation.[133] While the economic output of the sector is twice that of further and higher education, and the social output could be estimated at anything up to half of total GDP, there are problems in short termism, displacement of paid jobs, and potential for fraud or abuse.[134]

Some voluntary sector social services bodies are developing 'service agreements' with local authorities, and such schemes could be extended to many other organizations, particularly in disadvantaged neighbourhoods. Regeneration schemes have shifted towards community participation and partnership, but in practice the voluntary sector is often under-funded, under-managed and sidelined by bigger players. This suggests that each district or neighbourhood should set up a 'compact' as a basis for public–voluntary sector coordination.[135] Local authorities are unlikely to find much funding, but they can assist in kind with the marginal value goods above such as premises, facilities and other exchanges.

The voluntary sector itself is one component in the overall concept of a 'third sector' economy. This emerged in the EU in the 1980s as a response to structural unemployment, early retirement, cultural industries, and the crisis in the public services.[136] One practical outcome was the 'staircase policy', where the unemployed could contribute quasi-voluntary services by caretaking in and around buildings and estates.

The third sector theme is also linked with that of the 'stakeholder economy', where cooperation and cohesion is as important as competition for sustainable wealth creation.[137] The third sector theme is also parallel to the emerging philosophy of the 'third way' *(Chapter 15)*. This applies to both bottom-up activities such as community and voluntary sector, activity. It also ap-

| Box 10.8 | |
|---|---|
| **THIRD SECTOR ACTIVITY** | |
| Outline of activities in the third, mutual, voluntary, community and not-for-profit sectors. | |
| *LAND* | Community land trusts: Development Trusts: community woodlands: Managed workspace: city farms: community gardens |
| *HOUSING* | Community self-build: green homes: housing cooperatives |
| *TRANSPORT* | Car & lift sharing: community transport: railway opening: bus security: |
| *FOOD:* | Organic box schemes: subscription farming: food co-ops: permaculture: eco-villages |
| *ECOLOGY* | Wildlife conservation: landscape maintenance: urban greening: |
| *ENERGY:* | Community renewable schemes: domestic energy services: eco-feedback: |
| *WASTE* | Community composting: community recycling & re-use: |
| *TRADE* | Community enterprise: Fair Trade: telecottages: community shops & pubs: ethical shops |
| *FINANCE* | LETS:Community trusts: Credit Unions: time dollars: ethical investment |
| *PUBLIC SERVICES* | social care, community services, neighbourhood education, health & crime prevention |
| Source: adapted from New Economics Foundation 1997 | |

131 Boyle 1998: Pacione 1999
132 est.by GM Council for Voluntary Service & NCVO 1993
133 Kendall & Knapp 1996

134 Lang 1994
135 Home Office 1998: Craig et al 1999
136 Lipietz 1995
137 Mulgan 1995

plies to larger quasi-public and quasi-private organizations, in housing, education, health and many others *(Chapter 13)*.

For the majority of the population who are not the winners of global economic competition, the third sector is a viable way forward – not necessarily a replacement for incomes and jobs, but a complement in several ways:[138]

- allows unemployed and 'economically inactive' more satisfying and productive lives;
- contributes to social cohesion through constructive activity and mutal interaction;
- contributes to general welfare by unlocking local resources and providing public services.

A holistic picture shows how different approaches to the third sector, informal economy and local trading intersect and overlap *(Fig 10.10)*.[139]  This kind of thinking opens up a new dimension for public services – few local authorities are fully informed on the problems and needs of their areas, on the outcomes of service delivery, or even what people do with their time. A continuous social, economic and environmental auditing process should highlight needs and opportunities, in the areas where local authorities or major employers can best work in partnership with the third sector. But such an audit cannot work if it is 'top-down' and externally imposed – a more effective process will be user-driven, client-focused and 'bottom-up'. This leads towards a paradox for local authorities, who try to encourage bottom-up approaches from a top-down position.[140]  So there is a strong case for an arm's-length agency to mediate between public sector 'purchasers' and voluntary sector 'providers' – an active coordinator for needs and resources across the city-region.

# MAKING IT HAPPEN

As local, regional, national and global economic systems are all entangled, there is no simple answer to the question 'who does what?' to generate a sustainable economy.  At present the UK has perhaps the best opportunity in recent times to combine social, environmental and economic priorities, but the hard questions still stand – the balances of market and state, and of 'carrots' and 'sticks', have still to be worked out at every level.

The regional development 'coalition' is now a powerful force, combining the RDA and regional assembly, EU funding, mainstream government spending and a host of business agencies – any city-region green economic strategy will have to find its role within this context *(Chapter 14)*. On the other hand, for many purposes the city-region is more of a functional territory than the NW region, with scope for particular added value in conurbation-wide functions and networks:

- economic infrastructure development such as freight transport, CHP and business energy, industrial ecology and materials networks;
- economic development activity including green business forums, specialist resources, and investment / development fund;
- green and ethical investment policies through purchasing, contracting, pension funds;
- employment programmes based on environmental task force, intermediate labour markets and social trading schemes;
- partnership 'compacts' with the third sector, community regeneration and intermediate labour markets;
- coordination of economic strategy with other key sector strategies, including: urban development, neighbourhoods, property, construction, transport, ICT, environment, energy-climate, regeneration and investment.

138 Dauncey 1988: Douthwaite 1996
139 Offe & Heinze 1994
140 Young 1996

While local economies are increasingly global, local authorities still have significant influence, through planning, infrastructure, and not least their roles as landlords and purchasers.[141] Local authorities are also learning a more pro-active role as developers and entrepreneurs in new forms of partnership, for regeneration, training and business development. And while there is much inertia, each of these activities can be steered towards a green and ethical agenda, both in long term strategy and short term actions. Actions 'now' with low cost and high benefit would include the common menu:

- inhouse measures, in public services, policy development, purchasing and contracting;
- information: audits of environmental and human resources;
- regulation: standards to support pollution control and clean technology;
- market measures: local authority funds are scarce, but small seed-funding can be found for demonstrations, networks, promotions;
- partnership with other agencies: for business clubs, clean technology networks, investment funds, and social economy initiatives.

## Government

As the UK government attempts to balance economic, social and environmental goals with global pressures, the intention and the rhetoric are encouraging. But while the concept of eco-modernization is moving up to the main agenda, dematerialization is still off the horizon. Much of the green business agenda is being approached through voluntary negotiation, although the experience so far is not all positive; utility regulation is a case in point, where market frameworks should enable least-cost long-term investment partnerships which coordinate supply and demand between many parties. There is an array of initiatives for cleaner production, sustainable technology, sustainable consumption, and market transformation in key sectors.[142] In reality the infighting and horse-trading typical of any

sector or industry suggests caution in assessing future prospects.

Generally to enable and support the wholesale and rapid green conversion of the city-region economy, government needs to go much further in putting ideas into actions:

- in-house: green-ethical policies for all contracting, purchasing and investment; as yet the 'greening of Whitehall' is failing;[144]
- fiscal measures: full and comprehensive eco-taxation or progressive internalizing of environmental impacts, with incentives for cleaner production and consumption;
- regulation: long term strategic development of standards for emissions and resource use
- markets: clean technology promotion in industry and supply chains, material flow trading systems;
- common standards for consumer information and advice, mandatory eco-labelling for all products and services;
- local powers and resources, for infrastructure and local investment: enabling of non-monetary social economies via flexible controls on local authorities.

## Producers & consumers

For most businesses environmental 'best practice' is a key to competitiveness and export growth – the challenge is to coordinate re-engineering with emerging markets, changing standards and supply chain pressure. For material-intensive industries, environmental strategy is causing a re-think of product life-cycles and services. For less intensive service sectors, environmental management focuses more on indirect effects, supply chains and investments. Business in general needs clear signals from government on markets and regulation, to enable forward investment on long cycles.

Much pressure for greening comes from consumers and public concern – and there are mixed signs on whether this is rising or falling. Forward looking enterprises such as the Co-operative Bank have capitalized on green and

141 Centre for Local Economic Strategies 1994
142 DETR 1998 (Sustainable Business)
144 ENDS Report: April 1998

ethical opportunities. In principle all goods sold in GM should have comprehensive eco-labelling, and every means possible should be used to persuade and motivate suppliers to provide this.

## Putting it together

On the ground, green economic strategy has to be fitted to the local balance of problems and opportunities:

- city centres, dominated by service sectors: green investment, supply-chain and consumer campaigns;
- inner cities with high unemployment and disadvantage, with environmental strategy and social economy as a generator of jobs and public services;
- regeneration areas with industrial decline and restructuring: support for vulnerable SME's: low-impact transport and energy infrastructure: materials and waste networks;
- suburbs with few jobs and services: teleworking and social economy as generator of local employment and services;
- urban fringe, generally an area of innovation and investment: clean technology and R&D networks and growth poles.

**Fig 10.12**     *ECONOMY & WORK STRATEGY*

Outline of integrated city-region 2020 economic development strategy

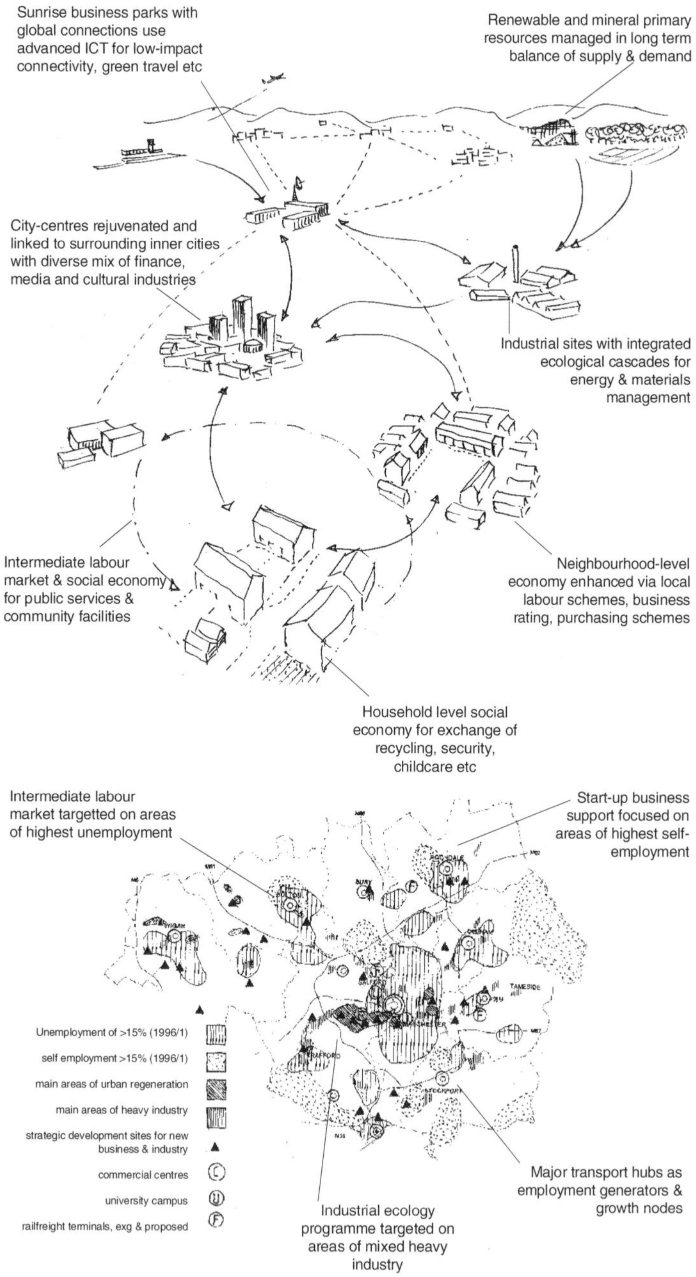

Sunrise business parks with global connections use advanced ICT for low-impact connectivity, green travel etc

Renewable and mineral primary resources managed in long term balance of supply & demand

City-centres rejuvenated and linked to surrounding inner cities with diverse mix of finance, media and cultural industries

Industrial sites with integrated ecological cascades for energy & materials management

Intermediate labour market & social economy for public services & community facilities

Neighbourhood-level economy enhanced via local labour schemes, business rating, purchasing schemes

Household level social economy for exchange of recycling, security, childcare etc

Intermediate labour market targeted on areas of highest unemployment

Start-up business support focused on areas of highest self-employment

Unemployment of >15% (1996/1)

self employment >15% (1996/1)

main areas of urban regeneration

main areas of heavy industry

strategic development sites for new business & industry

commercial centres

university campus

railfreight terminals, exg & proposed

Major transport hubs as employment generators & growth nodes

Industrial ecology programme targeted on areas of mixed heavy industry

*Putting together the key sectors throws the spotlight on the social and economic questions which make or break any environmental strategy. 'Lifestyles' investigates the health, security and education services and their constant struggle for funds. 'Regeneration' applies sustainability thinking to the age-old urban question – the seemingly inevitable polarization of wealth and poverty. 'Funding' takes the questions of cost and value as the keys to market transformation and financing urban restructuring. 'Running the city-region' tackles the question 'who decides': with a new agenda for local and regional authorities, a collaborative 'sustainable development framework' aims to generate synergy and added value.*

# LIFESTYLE & COMMUNITY

*'..café-bar society integrating lifestyle...*
*.......shape innovative aspirational catering...*
*.........vibrant design trend city sound evolving venue...'*
Frogmore Investments (marketing copy) 1998

Only a century ago, most people lived in deprivation and squalor which is almost unimaginable today – but even now, under the surface of the consumer society, there is widespread stress, insecurity and conflict. And while individuals, communities or societies are at war with themselves or others, there can be little progress on environmental sustainability, or any other kind.

But the perennial themes of peace, justice, quality of life and meaning of life are an endless quest in themselves. It is easier to focus on providing material affluence, but this meets only a fraction of human needs – a 'sustainable' community or society, if such a thing were possible, might aim to meet most if not all human needs. But who is to say which are the needs, and which are extraneous desires or demands?

In exploring such questions, this chapter is the most free-ranging so far in our journey. Here is not the place to tackle all human problems, but we can apply the sustainability thinking outlined so far to urgent problems in social strategy and public services. And while many social issues hinge on national policy or individual choice, local actions can and do have significant influence. So our main focus is on the problems and opportunities which are relevant at the city-re-

gion level. Then for each sector within the city-region, we explore its links to lifestyle issues, environmental issues, community issues, and overall strategy.

This begins with the question of lifestyle, culture, place and space – where social norms and choices may win or lose environmental strategy. This leads to the questions of poverty and exclusion, which underpin the whole agenda in one of the richest nations in the world.

For public services such as health, education and crime prevention, the themes of joined-up policy and the input of the third sector, appear to be the best prospect for the future. Each of these points to the theme of 'sustainable communities', as the guiding principle for social strategy at every level.

## Trends & tensions

On the face of it, the people of GM have never had it so good – in less than a century the goalposts of poverty and deprivation have clearly shifted a long way. But many now suffer from the problems of affluence – traffic pollution, allergic conditions, fear of crime, job insecurity and family stress. And under the surface of the consumer society, both relative and absolute poverty is on the increase – while water, power and television are almost universal, many still go short of healthy food, decent housing, useful education and a place in society. Economic restructuring has thrown whole communities on the scrapheap, and even in the affluent suburbs breakdown is rife – one in ten people are clinically depressed in Manchester, which is also the 'suicide blackspot' of the UK. The indicators below hardly scratch the surface – but GM's downbeat position relative to the national average is clear *(Fig 11.1)*:

- more single parents, drug abuse, dependency;
- poor health and mortality rates for young and old;
- poor education and over-crowded schools;
- more crime and fear of crime, with less detection;
- more unemployed and excluded from society.

What such indicators cannot show is the positive side. GM has long been a power-house of social innovation and self-help, its communities are diverse and active, and its sports and arts are second to none. It might not be the world's most beautiful city, but it could possibly be one of the friendliest. It is the most cosmopolitan city in northern England, in its global connections, cultural diversity and the 'structure of feeling' of people in the street.[1]

Meanwhile these people have come and gone – the city has lost half a million in the last 30 years, and many inner areas were cleared to a fraction of their former populations, while suburban areas mushroomed. The map of 'health and wealth', at the end of the chapter, shows the polarization of inner and outer areas – while the successful got up and out, the remainder became trapped in dysfunctional communities and environments *(Fig 11.14)*. Former class divides have shifted towards new social patterns, along the lines of an adapted '30-30-30' model: the insiders, the insecure, the outsiders, and the unclassifiable *(Chapter 10)*.[2]

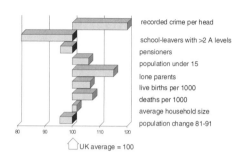

Fig 11.1

## SOCIAL INDICATORS

recorded crime per head
school-leavers with >2 A levels
pensioners
population under 15
lone parents
live births per 1000
deaths per 1000
average household size
population change 81-91

UK average = 100

Key indicators of social conditions for GM, shown relative to UK as at 1995.
Source: CSO 1996:

## Future prospects

As for which way the evidence points from here, some key trends over the last generation, both positive and negative, can be drawn and projected *(Fig 11.2)*:[3]

- average household size reduced from 3 to 2.2;
- average number of children reduced from 2.5 to 1.7 per family;
- inequality between top and bottom 10% of incomes increased to 14:1;
- school-leavers in further and higher education doubled;
- reported crime doubled, and 'fear of crime' tripled;
- homelessness doubled and 20–25% more new dwellings needed by 2020;
- average life expectancy rising by two years per decade, but reducing for the unemployed.

Such accelerating trends, both positive and negative, show the structural dynamics of 'fragmentation' and 'individuation' – the shifting of previously stable social structures and norms towards more complex and fluid patterns.[4] Divergent lifestyles in a post-industrial city are encouraged by economic globalization, rising affluence, mobility and ICT, and polarization of

1 Taylor, Evans & Fraser 1996
2 Hutton 1995

3 Policy Studies Institute 1993
4 Lash & Urry 1994: Harvey 1989

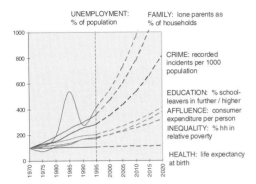

Fig 11.2 **SOCIAL TRENDS**

UNEMPLOYMENT: % of population

FAMILY: lone parents as % of households

CRIME: recorded incidents per 1000 population

EDUCATION: % school-leavers in further / higher

AFFLUENCE: consumer expenditure per person

INEQUALITY: % hh in relative poverty

HEALTH: life expectancy at birth

Key social trends extrapolated from 1970-1995 average over 25 years, to 1995-2020, for GM and UK, relative to 1970 base.
Source: CSO 1996.

rich and poor. GM is not quite at the point of the 'ecology of fear' of Los Angeles, but many of its trends point strongly in that direction.[5]

Fragmentation lies behind the practical problems of health, crime or education – where cultural differences and compounded exclusion undermine well-intentioned public services. Meanwhile the dynamic of individuation enables many groups and sub-cultures to gain empowerment through diversity – women, youth, ethnic groups, sexual subcultures and others. Global media and ICT generate a common culture, connexivity and a kind of cohesion, even while accelerating the diversity of cultures and identities.[6] This dual theme – cohesion and diversity – underlies the concept of 'sustainable communities' which we revisit at the end of the chapter.

And what lies over the horizon? The prospects over the next generation for lifestyles and communitie already stretch the imagination, even in the 'business as usual scenario':

- average lifespan in the developed world may be over 100, and there will be more people over 50 than under;

- bio-technology may provide artificial brain implants, genetic surveillance, nano-robotic surgery, full ICT-based medicine;
- ICT is the organizing medium and nervous system for almost all work, education, leisure, sub-cultures and kinship groups;
- surveillance of all individuals and organizations is routine and automated;
- paid work, voluntary work, training, cultural activity and leisure all overlap in different combinations;
- stress, neurosis, paranoia, drug abuse and cyber-addiction increase in parallel with aspirations, affluence, opportunity and choice.

Such a tangle of contradictory trends and dynamics can play out with infinite variations – but following the logic of the previous chapters generates several alternative scenarios:

- *Technology scenario:* accelerated innovation and diffusion in the three current scientific revolutions – bio-technology, digital technology, quantum science, changing life itself as we know it.[7]
- *Sustainable development scenario*: a balanced evolution of state, market, community, technology and infrastructure results in greater equality, diversity and cohesion.
- *Deep green scenario*: fundamental shifts in lifestyles, cultures, communities and organizations, rapidly reduces environmental impact and social inequality.

## Social metabolism

Social structures – families, organizations, communities, societies and cultures – appear to be complex balances of opposing forces. At every level there are the dynamics of dependency and exploitation, cooperation and conflict, altruism and competition, security or risk, or love and hate. Individuals reproduce their patterns in organizations and societies, and vice versa. Human nature seems to hinge on a fundamental duality of ideals and reality – we can imagine

5 Davis 1998
6 Mulgan 1997

7 Kaku 1999

utopias where every person and community is
fulfilled, empowered and totally 'sustainable', but
there are few examples to follow. We have to
apply such perennial ideals to the endless
evolution of social systems – at each step on the
way, a little more fulfilment, empowerment,
equality, and so on.

For this kind of journey, the logic of the
'integrated assessment' system mapping can be
very useful. Charting the chains of cause and
effect in the metabolism of social institutions and
public services, helps to highlight the bigger
picture – linkages and conflicts between one
sector and another *(Fig 11.3).*

Again this shows, in a very general way, a
set of balances between 'what we need' – the
drivers of social process and patterns – and 'what
we get', in terms of outcomes. The 'needs' on
the left of the chart are drawn from organizational
psychology, and the 'outcomes' on the right
show common functions and dysfunctions.[8]
Everywhere there are conflicts, tensions and
imbalances – people and communities need
security and identity, but often they get insecurity
and alienation.[9] A 'sustainable' community or
society aims at a better balance, by changes at
each stage in the process – in values, activities,
institutions, outputs or outcomes.

The map shows that multiple needs drive
multiple activities with multiple outcomes. The
perennial debate between right and left can be
disaggregated into alternative sets of inputs,
outputs, value-systems and 'discourses' of
social patterns and processes.[10] Neo-liberalism
sees free markets as the organizing dynamic of
structured cultural patterns: while social
democracy sees state institutions as the
organizing dynamic of structured economic
patterns. Each approach reproduces and fulfils
its own discourse and produces a mixed bag of
benefits and impacts. The 'third way' approach
sees that the trends of globalization,
individuation, democratization and ecological
issues have moved beyond both right and left
agendas, but still holds certain values as self-
evident *(Chapter 15).*[11]

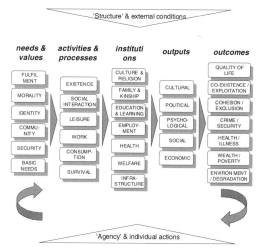

**Fig 11.3      SOCIAL METABOLISM**

A very approximate 'integrated assessment' mapping of the social metabolism.
Source: adapted from Maslow 1970, Max-Neef 1994

In practical terms it is clear that tackling social
problems with public services, for instance in
crime or health, has to distinguish between
service 'outputs' and downstream 'outcomes'.
Such public services also have to look upstream
to tackle the causes behind the problems – a
much wider agenda. This is not the place for a
history of social theory, but we should note some
of the alternative approaches to such an agenda:

- economic structural patterns and processes,
  as in the Marxist analysis of class conflict
  and capital accumulation.[12]
- social patterns and processes: as in social
  'norms' and a 'human ecology' view of
  communities.[13]
- cultural patterns and processes, as in
  anthropology and the new study of social
  economies, movements and subcultures.[14]
- in-depth research now uses techniques such
  as focus groups to explore the 'structure of
  feeling' – the patterns of experience in
  everyday life. A major study of Manchester
  and Sheffield contains much evidence for the
  discussion here.[15]

8 Maslow 1970
9 Max-Neef 1994
10 Giddens 1994 & 1998
11 Powell 1999

12 Harvey 1976
13 Gans 1972
14 Castells 1989
15 Taylor, Evans & Fraser 1996

On the trail of 'sustainable communities', we might take each of these approaches as useful in its own terms. We might apply the systems thinking of Chapter 1, to identify the viability, integrity and sustainability qualities of any social system – adaptability, resilience, self-organization, co-existence and so on.[16] Taking these at each level – individuals, families, organizations, communities, cultures, societies – we can build up a multi-dimensional picture of social patterns and processes. Bringing this rounded picture back to the practical problems of public services, helps to highlight some very practical goals:

- coordination and integration between sectors such as housing, crime, health and education;
- environmental best practice in lifestyles and public services, to deliver 'more for less';
- long term balance of supply and demand for public goods and services;
- lateral thinking on social cohesion and cultural diversity, as the key to this balance.

Such goals apply, for instance, to the health service – to move on from its present role as a 'sickness service', it needs far greater integration with lifestyles and cultural patterns, with other public services, with environmental strategy, and with the 'third sector' social economy.

Finally this kind of analysis is not only about political economy, but about a deeper agenda of values and ethics. While state religion in the UK is now a fraction of its former size, there are many other faiths and broader moralities not far below the public surface. As summed up by the 'Real World' programme, the ethical agenda includes ecological responsibility, community cohesion, cultural diversity and political participation.[17] Of course such ideals are much abused – most individuals and communities survive day-to-day amidst competition and materialism. So again the 'sustainable' social strategy needs to balance idealism and practicality. For this, a guiding theme might be 'lateral thinking for enlightened self-

interest' – the win-win actions which benefit both individuals, communities and society at large.

## Social strategy

It remains to be seen how local and global political processes can balance ideals with practice – the 'third way', or whatever title comes next, is an endless quest, and the future shape of the education or health sectors can hardly be guessed. So in this chapter we focus on longer range strategy, several steps ahead of the swings and roundabouts of the political process.

One very practical theme stands out – in almost every public service there is conflict between needs and resources, or demand and supply. Economic resources limit health and education. Physical resources limit housing and transport provision. For market goods such as housing, market inequalities are acceptable within limits, while for 'public' goods such as health, different values apply. In each case the problem can be tackled on the supply side, with greater efficiency and effectiveness – or on the demand side, via lifestyle shifts and community

---

**Box 11a**

### LIFESTYLE & COMMUNITY ~ GOALS & STRATEGIES

| | GOV | LA | BUS | COM | PUB |
|---|:---:|:---:|:---:|:---:|:---:|
| **LIFESTYLES & ENVIRONMENT:** promote low-impact lifestyles: explore multi-cultural values, attitudes, place & locality | ○ | ● | ● | ● | ● |
| **POVERTY:** preventative support networks: basic needs met at marginal cost: self-help advocacy | ● | ● | ○ | ● | ● |
| **HEALTH:** preventative & lifestyle support networks: environmental monitoring: integrate paramedic & complementary medicine | ● | ○ | ○ | ● | ● |
| **CRIME & SECURITY:** design for public security: upgrading service for households: local presences for public safety: support networks for prevention | ● | ● | ○ | ● | ● |
| **EDUCATION:** environment core curriculum: schools eco-centres: city design for children & youth: project-based self-directed learning: | ● | ● | ○ | ○ | ● |
| **SUSTAINABLE COMMUNITIES:** social cohesion & cultural diversity: integrated public services with 3rd sector | ○ | ● | ○ | ● | ● |

GOV ~ government: LA ~ local authorities: BUS ~ business: COM ~ community: PUB ~ public

---

16 Clayton & Radcliffe 1996
17 Jacobs 1996

action. There is huge potential in the 'third sector' social economy for unlocking human resources, not only as an economic input, but as a catalyst for social cohesion and cultural empowerment.[18]

How can such goals translate to practical targets? For each sector we can look at long term trends and pressures, assess opportunities for change and restructuring, and translate these into practical targets and strategies. Of course the prospects for each sector are highly uncertain and controversial. For social issues, such targets are often 'aspirational' – if we aim to halve crime rates, for instance, this does not necessarily

follow from doubling the police force, but from many other factors beyond our control. And in practice each sector, and each level from local to national, is intimately linked – health depends on housing and education, education depends on security and social cohesion, and so on. The whole is clearly greater than the sum of the parts.

In practice, general targets might be based on the attainment of UK or EU averages, stabilizing negative trends, or halving negative outcomes *(Box 11.1)*. General strategies include the building of new institutions and networks in public services to enable lifestyle changes.

# LIFESTYLE & ENVIRONMENT

Lifestyle changes are a key to environmental strategy in each and every sector of the city-region – for instance, if everybody in GM wore several layers of thermal clothing, $CO_2$ emissions could be reduced by 20%. This might achieve more than any other single action, and yet such a move seems very unlikely. The cultural norms and values behind lifestyle choices need to be explored in order to target policies and strategies for greater effect.

The theme of 'risk' is central to environmental strategy, and there is a new awareness of social divides in terms of exposure or fear of technological risk.[19] The 'precautionary principle' aims to link risk assessment with rational choices, but often fails to recognize that most individuals and organizations survive amidst many kinds of short and long term risk.[20] The 'cultural theory' matrix in Chapter 1 shows different levels of risk aversion for different social types, and this is also a very useful management technique in areas such as energy policy.[21] A city-region such as GM in aggregate is possibly more risk-tolerant than others – containing, for instance, more unhealthy lifestyles and criminal activity than the national average.

Such a 'portfolio' of risk shows in public attitudes to the environment: opinion polls tend to show an inverse relationship between environmental concern and unemployment, with green issues peaking in the late 1980s – if people are worried about their jobs today, the environment of the future is a lesser priority *(Fig 11.4)*. Going beyond statistical surveys, a new generation of in-depth focus groups and visioning exercises shows how environmental and social concern can be overshadowed by a deep distrust of government, experts and 'the system' in general.[22] Such alienation is the real-world context for sustainable development. This is shown by recent responses to well meaning initiatives such as the 2020 project:[23]

> *'nice idea but it will never happen'*
> *'why should we believe the experts?'*

Every community contains alternative 'discourses', ways of seeing the world and reproducing power and self-identity.[24] In GM the 'growth coalition' expresses a culture very different from that of youth, ethnic, or other marginalized groups.[25] Even if the growth

18 Friedman 1994
19 Beck 1995
20 O'Riordan 1995: Adams 1996
21 Rotmans & van Asselt 1996: Energy Efficiency Office 1995

22 MacNaghten & Urry 1997
23 Darier 1998
24 Hajer 1995: Rydin 1991
25 Logan & Molotch 1987: Cochrane et al 1996

Fig 11.4    **SOCIAL ATTITUDES**

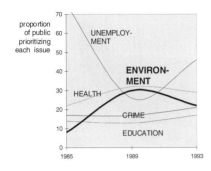

Issues needing government action of greatest concern to public sample:
Source: DOE 1994.

Fig 11.5    **LIFESTYLE IMPACTS**

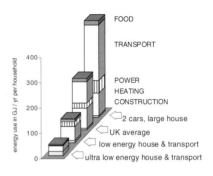

Environmental impact estimated via energy use in GJ / yr per household
for various lifestyle options.
Source: Christensen 1998.

coalition was suddenly converted to a full-blown environmental strategy based on expert advice, there would still be problems in crossing deep-rooted cultural barriers. And on close inspection, such expert advice is often uncertain and dependent on social values and priorities – so the wide and fuzzy theme of sustainability can be interpreted in almost any way to suit the discourse of the elite.[26] The upshot is that sustainability is not so much a blueprint but a moving agenda for continuous debate at every level of society.

## Affluence & environment

Most would agree that the gap between rich and poor must be narrowed – but if the poor in GM levelled up to the standards of the rich, the environmental impacts would be serious, and a world-wide levelling up would need the resources of several planets.[27] In each sector, the 'drivers' of environmental pressure can be seen as the material desire for space, mobility and affluence. This is shown by various lifestyle options and their global impacts *(Fig 11.5)*: the average person in GM is reponsible for nearly 6 tonnes of $CO_2$ per year from housing and transport. A large house and high mileage will double this, while an effi-

cient house and local lifestyle can halve it.[28] To raise awareness of lifestyle impacts, 'eco-feedback' schemes are now on trial with equipment and software for personal assessments.[29] But experience of energy feedback shows that the catalyst for change is not so much technology, but norms and expectations from friends, neighbours, media and advertising. Countering such messages often fails to bridge cultural gaps – a poster campaign for 'sustainability' in Manchester, for instance, was a joke for the converted and incomprehensible to others. A lateral approach would aim to show low-impact lifestyles as stylish and 'happening', rather than moral and 'folksy', and Manchester's cultural industries of fashion, music and sport could be a major asset in this.[30]

Of course material consumption is the sacred cow of global capitalism, and challenging it goes against the grain. Another approach is to redirect lifestyle goals and expectations, as in the American 'downshifting' movement – doing more with less, buying quality rather than quantity, and sharing resources rather than private ownership.[31] While downshifting is an individual choice, far-sighted employers should enable such moves through part-time working,

26 Rydin 1997
27 Rees & Wackernagel 1996

28 Christensen 1995: Noorman & Uiterkamp 1998
29 BT Environment City 1995
30 Chapman 1997
31 Dauncey 1991

flexible and sabbatical leave *(Chapter 10)*. Finally, consumption is a spiritual matter – people who are more fulfilled may simply have less need for material wealth. The 'eco-psychology' of environmental awareness is a key to changing hearts and minds.[32]

## Place & locality

Many lifestyle questions revolve around the 'locality' principle – the simple case that people who are happy in their neighbourhoods will need to travel less and consume less. This tends to ignore wider trends, where local 'places' are turned into commodities, and where global communications create 'virtual space' disconnected from any physical location.[33] But there is also a counter trend towards new patterns of 'localization':

- competition between cities and regions for 'place advantage' and amenity to attract investment;
- telecommunications which enable localized lifestyles within globalized networks;
- rising affluence which encourages awareness of quality of life and 'sense of place';
- a resurgence of informal economies and subcultures based on urban territories.[34]

Some evidence from GM shows that most people value their own neighbourhood in comparison to others *(Fig 11.6)*.[35] But the public 'structure

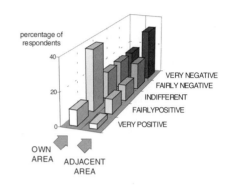

Fig 11.6    **LOCAL PERCEPTIONS**

Perceptions of general quality of life in local & adjacent neighbourhoods: from sample survey of inner areas in GM, Merseyside & Tyneside. Source:  Robson et al 1994.

of feeling' often shows places of fear and insecurity as manifestations of social conflict and division.[36] People continuously adjust their routes and boundaries to excluding the urban 'others' and the 'dangerous places', while desirable and safe places are 'consumed' as commodities. Bringing together diverse communities in public places may enable social cohesion, but also creates tension and insecurity. 'Localized' strategies for housing, transport, regeneration, open space and others, need to be based on in-depth exploration of local perceptions, local networks and local resources.[37]

# POVERTY & EXCLUSION

The gap between rich and poor has widened in recent years –  but it is clear that large-scale redistribution of resources is not on the current agenda.  And yet the effects of poverty are endemic in both city and country, fragmenting the social fabric, hindering economic

development, and creating insecurity even for the affluent.[38] The theme of deprivation itself is shifting from lack of money to lack of expectations, aspirations and networks. There are several kinds of response:[39]

32 Roszak 1991
33 Lash & Urry 1993
34 Borja & Castells 1996
35 Robson et al 1994

36 Campbell 1993
37 Taylor 1998
38 Pacione 1997

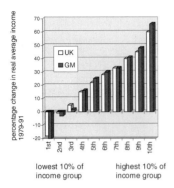

Fig 11.7    **TRENDS in INEQUALITY**

percentage change in real average income 1979-91

lowest 10% of income group

highest 10% of income group

Income inequality showing change from 1979-91 in distribution by deciles in average per capita income after housing costs:
Source: JRF 1995: NOMIS 1996.

- reducing inequality of provision, as in traditional 'welfare' socialism;
- reducing inequality of opportunity, as in the new Labour 'stakeholder' theme;
- lateral approaches to poverty through prevention, adaptation and self-help, as in the community development theme – this is the particular focus here.

Whichever way poverty is measured, whether relative or absolute, nearly 40% of households in GM – a million people – live with a household income of less than half the national average.[40] The growth of inequality over the last 20 years is a national issue, but the picture for GM is even more extreme.[41] *(Fig 11.7).* While the top 10% of households have enjoyed a 60% growth in real incomes, and average households a 32% increase, the bottom 10% have suffered an 18% decline, and a third of the population is no better off now than 20 years ago. Such material poverty tends to cluster in areas with over 50% dependency, and up to 80% in 'official' poverty.[42] The modern low-wage casualized economy is rarely a viable alternative to dependency or street

life – local surveys show that half the jobs on offer would pay less than £100 per week.[43]

Alongside the official count is 'hidden' unemployment, at a third or half higher, as found in local area studies.[44] Homelessness in GM is officially estimated at 10–15,000 households, but there is evidence of three times that level – similar in fact to the number of vacant dwellings.[45] While about 1000 people live on the street in the city centre, it is ironic that the *Big Issue* magazine won a national award for sustainable development.[46] The size of the hidden class can be guessed through Census under-enumeration – the UK's 'missing million' – and the doubling of unregistered voters with the poll tax.[47] A tenth of the central area population may be unregistered, or a quarter of men aged 20–30, a total hidden population of over 50,000 which is vulnerable to poverty, crime and drug abuse.[48]

## Poverty & environment

Environmental pollution, poor housing, derelict land and declining services all serve to compound income poverty with social 'disadvantagement'. In housing, the poor are more likely to suffer energy poverty, damp and condensation, health problems and building decay *(Fig 11.8).* Public estates are more likely to be overcrowded and lacking security, and the replacement of neighbourhood shopping by out-of-town sites excludes lower income groups.[49] Older deprived areas are often devoid of vegetation, newer estates contain useless grassed areas and derelict sites, while healthy diets are out of reach *(Chapter 7).*[50] Much of the public transport network is becoming a 'place of fear' and used as a last resort, while the Metrolink tram, the icon of modernizing Manchester, is handy for suburban commuters but unaffordable by the poor.[51]

Such poverty-environment linkages suggest that for basic urban services, such as energy or transport, there is a strong case for progressive pricing and subsidy to support access for lower

39 Kruger 1997
40 CSO 1996
41 Joseph Rowntree Foundation 1995
42 Policy Studies Institute 1994

43 Low Pay Unit 1994
44 Jones & Knight 1993
45 Shelter 1995
46 Homeless International 1996
47 Simpson, March & Sandhu 1993
48 Dorling 1995
49 Sennet 1992
50 Low Income Project Team 1994
51 Taylor 1991

income groups. Public transport policy already aims at such goals, but is hindered by funding shortages and deregulation – so 'social trading' systems should be used to exchange transport credits for other public services *(Chapter 10)*. Affordable energy would be a priority for the pricing policy of the city-region energy agency *(Chapter 9)*. One of the simplest barriers to self-help and employability is the lack of a telephone – so a city-region telecoms consortium should provide a basic service to every low-income household at marginal cost.

## Poverty & exclusion

Beyond material factors, a wider view looks at the social processes which are cause and effect of poverty. The arrival of the street-dwellers confirmed Manchester as a 'beggars capital', a world city where 'these things happen'. Mental maps of the city are structured by no-go areas, based on psychology as much as fact, and for vulnerable women, elderly, children, and ethnic groups, these landscapes divide the city.[52]

Social exclusion is an intractable problem for the EU and developed world.[53] The transition from a male-dominated Fordist manufacturing economy is devastating the social structures and norms of industrial cities; many men cannot provide role-models to their children, and struggle with a new gender balance – over half the GM labour force is now female, albeit more casual and part-time.[54] With general loss and insecurity, greater rewards are found in the street-level 'anti-social economy' or 'wild zones'.[55]

Policies for social exclusion tend to come with a 'managerial' culture which is part of the problem. The community development approach struggles to reach the 'non-joiners', while the economic development approach tends to bring jobs for outsiders. The cultural industries approach can be more inclusive, on the interface between drug culture and the anti-social economy.[56] Social exclusion strategies have to recognize the realities of marginalized communities and cultures, and target resources more effectively:

Fig 11.8  **ENERGY POVERTY**

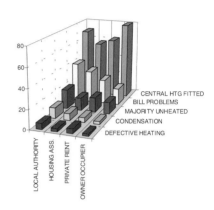

Proportion of energy problems in housing by tenure in NW region.
Source: DOE 1995: Engish Housing Condition Survey.

- reduce the cultural barriers into 'the system' via media, music, sports and new social movements;
- encourage self-help in enterprise development and training, through education and youth work;
- provide personal challenges and routes to status and identity, in business training and work schemes.

## Poverty & social strategy

Manchester and surrounding districts have several faces – to business they show a dynamic optimism for investment; to the government they show cautious trust that money can solve their problems; while around them is a swathe of inner and outer cities on the brink of decline. In response each has developed variations on a social strategy, such as Manchester's headings – local services, crime and anti-social behaviour, the voluntary sector, children and youth, special housing, participation, and research.[57] Backing this up are brave words as in the City Pride and similar documents.[58] In reality, local authorities are almost powerless against the compound spiral of decline into poverty. A holistic anti-poverty strategy should look at the roots more

52 Taylor Evans & Fraser 1996
53 CEC 1995
54 Peck & Emmerich 1992
55 Lash & Urry 1995
56 Bianchini & Parkinson 1993

57 Manchester City Council, Chief Executives Dept 1996

than the symptoms, with perhaps three perennial themes – prevention, adaptation and 'empowerment'.

For prevention, the threshold factors in poverty are crucial – unemployment, debt, housing stress or drug abuse. Social services often come in after the damage is done – so there is a case for a wider network of 'social support' for emerging problems. This would work in partnership with housing, health, education, police and others, providing personal advocates for households and communities. Basic support for the most vulnerable of the one million in some kind of poverty might take a doubling of voluntary sector activity through an expanded 'social trading' system *(Chapter 10)*.

Adaptation to poverty sounds like an apology for 'no new money', but there are parallels in the downshifting movement and

similar sub-cultures. The third sector approach bypasses some of the need for money, by matching useful activity to social needs and resources. All these revolve around the theme of 'empowerment' – many are unwilling to join any 'scheme' until it offers a similar status or reward as the street. So the challenge for social strategy and public services is to bridge cultural gaps, 'get real' about marginalized communities, and look what works at street level.

The UK government's anti-poverty strategy aims at some redistribution, incentives to work through the Working Families Tax Credit scheme, with experimental projects in health, education and housing, and a targetted budget for the worst affected areas.[59] Where it could go much further is in helping those unsuited to any kind of paid work to be active in intermediate, social or self-help economies.

# HEALTH & WELL-BEING

Public health was at the roots of local government a century ago, and much of GM was built as a model of Victorian sanitation. The 'healthy city' movement is now world-wide, looking at physical, economic and social environments, and a linking theme for almost every part of this project.[60] One starting point is the WHO 'health fields' framework, of which we focus on the first two themes:[61]

- lifestyle: work, leisure, risk, food, culture;
- environment: housing, pollution, accessibility, employment, security;
- health care: resources, access and participation to community, primary and specialist services:
- biology: genetics, nutrition, demographics

GM is a very topical place for this theme – Manchester is notorious as possibly the least healthy and most dangerous place in the

country.[62] Nearby, Liverpool has pioneered the WHO 'healthy cities' project in the UK.[63] Now that the large scale epidemics of the former industrial city are contained, there is a backlog in the 'diseases of affluence' – cancers, cardiac conditions, allergies, drug and food abuse – many of them linked to stress, insecurity and depression. For each of these, the NW regional figures are 5–10% above the national average, and for some areas such as Manchester, the death rate excess are twice that. One in ten people in Manchester are clinically depressed, and 100 people take their own lives every year.[64] Recent trends can be seen in key indicators such as perinatal mortality: while these have improved threefold in the last 20 years, the NW is still about 10% or 10 years behind the UK average.

There is growing awareness of health as a positive quality, more than the absence of disease – a holistic fulfilment of human needs at every level. Linkages can be traced between income,

58 Manchester / Salford / Trafford Partnership 1997
59 Dept of Social Security 1999
60 Ashton 1997: Davies & Kelly 1993
61 WHO 1992

62 OPCS 1998
63 The 'Liverpool Declaration', in Ashton & Knight 1988
64 ONS 1998 (Population trends 93): Raleigh & Kiri 1998

housing and health conditions with an integrated system mapping *(Fig 11.9)*.[65] This shows that definitions of health and illness vary with expectations, family, religion, employment, leisure and lifestyle; and that a wide range of services and institutions surrounds the statistics for waiting lists and 'finished consultant episodes'.

## Health & lifestyle

Images in the media and popular culture often promote unhealthy diet and risk-taking activity, and as large-scale epidemics and industrial injuries have reduced, the culture of risk has become integral and endemic to a modern society.[66] Young males are driven towards new forms of risk, through physical activity, drug experience or crime, in a culture of 'aggressive masculinity', and the effect of poverty is to focus lifestyle choices on the present rather than the future.[67]

Smoking, for instance, is a key indicator of personal health risk; the proportion of smokers in GM is 13% higher than the national average, with rising trends among teenagers and young people.[68] The rational health case has to overcome cultural alienation, media images, and personal survival strategies. Some organizations have a special role to play – football, for instance, demands ultimate fitness, but is packaged for a male-dominated culture of drinking and smoking. If Manchester United, the sporting flagship of the city, shifted its image and facilities towards promotion of personal fitness, large improvements in its supporters' health might result.

Spending on alcohol and tobacco is 13% higher than nationally, and consumption of fruit and vegetables is 10% lower.[69] National standards for food advertising and labelling are essential, but local actions can also combat the cultural barriers and commercial interests which promote unhealthy diets, with school dinners being the first priority. There are many community-based activities such as food co-ops, community cafes and home delivery networks, and these should be linked to the 2020 food strategy *(Chapter 7)*.[70]

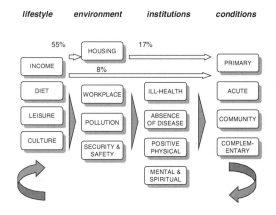

**Fig 11.9**          **HEALTH METABOLISM**

General linkages in WHO 'health fields', arranged in social metabolism framework. Percentages show example causal factors from NE Region.
Source: adapted from Byrne 1986: Lalonde 1976.

## Environment & health

The environmental health agenda is linked to poverty and lifestyle risk – but a risk which is involuntary, long term, and uncertain. For environmental pollution a common standard might be set at one statistical fatality per million for any one substance, where this can be identified – in practice, causal links for many pollutants are difficult to prove.[71] Meanwhile a blanket application of the 'precautionary principle' could be impractical for the 100,000 substances in common use – a more in-depth social risk assessment process is needed for topical issues, including citizens' juries and science forums *(Chapter 12)*.[72] One method is 'prospective health impact assessment', which investigates causes-effect linkages as 'calculable', 'estimable', 'definite not measurable', and 'speculative' types; this is a useful basis for assessment of any programme or project [73].

Housing is the first priority for environmental health, and yet current monitoring or control goes little beyond the building regulations.[74] In a city-region such as GM, 40% of housing is unfit or in need of repair, and the health costs of

65 Byrne et al 1986
66 Beck 1995
67 Measham, Newcombe & Parker 1994
68 Manchester Health Authority 1996
69 CSO 1994
70 Low Income Project Team 1994: National Food Alliance 1999

71 DoH & DoE, 1996
72 Crosby 1997
73 Ardern 1996
74 Byrne et al 1986

Fig 11.10    **HEALTH INEQUALITY**

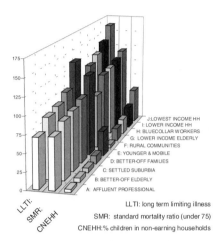

Age standardized ratios for 'social areas' in GM, Lancashire & West Pennine.
Source:  NW Regional Health Authority 1998.

## Health & wealth

There is at long last a recognition of the linkages between social class, employment and health, which surfaced controversially in the 1980s.[77] Analysis of 'social area' health in GM shows that long-term limiting illness and standard mortality ratios (SMR) for the lowest income groups is twice that of affluent professionals *(Fig 11.10)*.[78] The proportion of children in non-earning households, a key indicator of childhood and adult health, shows a tenfold difference between the highest and lowest income groups. The social mapping at the end of the chapter shows ill-health and mortality closely linked to poverty, unemployment, and poor housing.

The linkage of 'health and wealth' is now a key to public health policy, but again there are cultural and class barriers, where many people are disadvantaged by lack of cars, telephones, literacy and negotiation skills. Public health programmes recognize the linkages with poverty and unemployment, but can do little on their own – and the wider approach conflicts with medical structures and practices, with all the pressures for increasing 'throughput' rather than personal engagement with patients. So there is a case for new directions in public health, such as the community-based multi-cultural service, integrated with education, crime prevention and anti-poverty strategies as below.

energy poverty alone have been estimated at £80 million per year.[74] Upgrading and energy efficiency in housing can aggravate other problems in ventilation, and energy programmes need to take account of the whole-building context. There is also a case for standardized health monitoring of all housing, either five-yearly or at point of sale, in parallel with the energy programme *(Chapter 5)*. A similar approach applies to workplaces, particularly in the less regulated service industries – employee health is a key to any business and yet often neglected. Business agencies should go beyond conventional 'health and safety' advice towards positive environmental health for employees and customers.

Healthcare premises are of course the first item on this agenda.[75] For the urban environment in general, many standards are based on risk assessment with uncertain information, and monitoring is generally scarce; 'integrated environmental zoning' can be used to build compound maps of environmental risks.[76] These should be combined with self-help household or community-based monitoring for common health hazards. For localized traffic pollution and its controversial asthma linkage, for instance, the public is beset by ignorance and uncertainty, and information and support are needed.

## Healthy city strategy

In the face of rapid change, the UK National Health Service maintains one constant – continuously increasing pressure on resources. The internal responses of 'rationing', 'streamlining' or 'marketization' are unlikely to resolve the basic problem of the generational and sectoral investment gap. Health education is perhaps the most cost-effective measure of all, and yet takes less than 0.5% of total health spending. The public health costs of traffic pollution in GM are about £500–1000 million per year, which could be largely avoided by a more modest investment in transport *(Chapter 13)*.[79]

74 Boardman 1992
75 Hosking & Haggard 1999.
76 Kozlowski & Hill 1993: deRoo 1993

77 Townsend, Davidson & Whitehead 1988: Dept of Health 1998b
78 NW Regional Health Authority 1994
79 Maddison & Pearce et al 1996

This suggests firstly that health costs should be assessed alongside those of transport, housing, education and others, to see where financial and human resources can be best be targetted. The overlap in GM of ten districts, six health authorities and many other agencies suggests that the city-region is perhaps the most effective level for integration of costs and benefits, within the NHS and between other sectors.

For compound problems in health, poverty and unemployment, the social economy might provide 'barefoot' community paramedics as personal health advisors and advocates in every neighbourhood or organization. Longer term community care and support for chronic patients, the vulnerable elderly and other disadvantaged, should be carried out by neighbourhood-based carers.[80] The human resources needed for this would need an expanded voluntary sector with various 'social trading' systems, as now operating in the USA *(Chapter 10)*.[81]

For the health service itself, a new direction is needed for primary and appropriate care, overcoming the 'throughput' syndrome, and using the potential of ICT for self-help diagnostics and back-up to medicinal treatment. The health service should also coordinate with alternative and complementary medicine, so that the resources of non-western techniques can be brought to bear on positive health, both physical, mental and spiritual.

One of the first 'Health Action Zones' is now setting up in Manchester, Salford and Trafford, building on the work of 'Healthy Manchester 2000' and similar programmes, and starting with the most urgent priorities of coronaries, dental health, accidents, drug abuse and sexual issues. Beyond that is a golden opportunity to develop a new model of positive health services, coordinating with regional development and regeneration agencies, to begin to tackle the compound cycle of health, poverty, unemployment, housing, education, crime and others.

# CRIME & SECURITY

Crime is perhaps the first indicator of a dysfunctional society, and perhaps the greatest challenge for the future of 'social cities' as civic entities. Here we focus on local problems and opportunities with three themes:

- linkages of crime to unemployment and poverty;
- security through physical planning and design;
- security in social cohesion and community action.

Since 1950 average recorded crime rates have risen by over 10 times to one incident per 10 people – while the steepest rises were in the early 1990s, rates have fallen for some incident types in recent years. There is also new recognition of 'hidden' crime at several times the official figures, unreported through lack of confidence in the police, or acceptance of minor crime as a fact of life.[82] GM, and Manchester in particular, is seen as a 'crime capital' – areas such as Moss Side are notorious for gun-related crime, with one result being a raised profile and status for such activity. Recorded crimes are 30% higher in GM than the national average, with burglaries at 50% higher, and while the number of active officers per head of population is also 30% higher, the rate of detection is a third lower than average *(Fig 11.11)*.[83] Although the great majority of incidents are in 'property crime', the most trau-

80 Illich 1975
81 Boyle 1999: Williams & Windebank 1997

82 Mayhew et al 1993
83 GM Police Authority 1997: Taylor 1997

Fig 11.11      **CRIME & SECURITY**

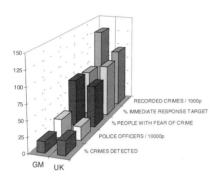

Comparison of key statistics for GM & UK, 1994:
Source: Audit Commission 1996.

matic crimes of violence, robbery and sexual offences have increased by 70% in a decade. 'Perceived' crime problems in inner cities have
worsened recently, and the 'security gap' between inner areas and suburbs is still widening.[84]

## Crime & social trends

Crime has wider social effects of insecurity and
stress for the affluent and poor alike – for instance in the NW region in 1993–95, 'fear of
crime' increased while actual rates dropped.[85]
The city-scape is divided into zones of security
and danger, with rising tension between genders,
classes, age-groups, ethnic groups and subcultures.[86] Crime may be perhaps the largest single
factor in migration to the suburbs, and policies
for re-urbanization may achieve little until public
security is increased.[87] Meanwhile the total cost
of the criminal justice system has doubled in a
decade, at over £500 million in the GM public
sector, and £200 million in property insurance
and security measures.

Crime is a rich hunting ground for social scientists, and there are several ways to trace the
wider picture of cause and effect:

- 'social disorganization' focuses on the loss
  of social 'norms' in rapid social and
  economic change;[88]
- a 'subculture' approach looks at pressures
  on individuals and groups in defining their
  identity;
- an 'environmental' approach looks more
  closely at the physical design of neighbourhoods and housing, and the urban
  geography of crimes and offenders;[89]
- the 'new criminology' looks at crime in its
  total social and economic context.[90]

For 'rational' crime such as burglary, there are
clear linkages to poverty, unemployment and
drug abuse.[91] For 'impulsive' crime such as vandalism, there are linkages to urban environments,
education, housing and cultural exclusion. Less
visible is 'white-collar' crime such as workplace
fraud, and traffic offences (a topical point for
any transport strategy). A wider trend is anti-
social behaviour or 'disorder', the conflict of different lifestyles and cultures in public places. A
general picture emerges – that the justice system and the wider social norms are failing to contain social tensions and conflicts – and that
longer term and more integrated solutions are
needed for both physical and social structures
in the city-region.

## Security & environment

The links between urban design and security can
be controversial – one approach tends towards
secure private enclaves, while another aims at
natural surveillance in public streets and spaces.
'Defensible space' was coined to describe the
layering of territory and public security, and 'community of interest' aims at clustering of homoge-
neous populations where social norms can be
reinforced.[92] The 'communitarian' philosophy
goes further towards the 'gated city', with community enclaves to deter or contain crime and
disorder.[93] The practical result is found in current advice on 'crime-free housing', avoiding dark
corners, undefined spaces and multiple escape
routes.[94]

84 Robson et al 1994
85 NW REgional Association 1996
86 Campbell 1993
87 Shostak 1997
88 Shaw & McKay 1942

89 Herbert 1982
90 Taylor Walton & Young 1973
91 Field 1990
92 Newman 1981
93 Etzioni 1996

This is a challenge for the physical city – large areas in GM lack any kind of definition between major roads and declining industry, many new estates lack even fencing, and older housing contains back lanes with easy access to insecure housing. In the neighbourhood strategy, pedestrian routes need to be designed for intrinsic security, with public overlooking, clear routes, and good lighting. At present the property market tends towards target hardening, at the expense of the public realm, and civic design input is needed at the planning stage. The UK has more video surveillance than anywhere in Europe – there are successes in many town centres, but also doubts on its effectiveness and wider implications, which should be debated at every level.[95] Video may be especially useful for transport nodes and interchanges, which in any case should be designed around retail and public services. Parking arrangements are also crucial – estates in Stockport were successfully redesigned around cul-de-sacs and car spaces adjacent to dwellings.[96]

Physical security in housing needs to extend the 'locks and bolts' approach to a wider household management; children's movements require a careful layering of social territory, and rising temperatures need new techniques for windows and ventilation. In many areas there are simple actions waiting to happen – on one estate in Rochdale, burglaries were halved by removing domestic slot meters.[97] This suggests a household security programme which covers every vulnerable house in the city, in parallel with the energy and environment strategies *(Chapter 5)*. The investment cost should be offset by lower insurance and policing costs, with a finance package coordinated by a city-region consortium.

## Security & community

'Zero tolerance', as famous in New York, is seen by many as the solution to rising public disorder, but also opens the door to police brutality and oppression of minorities. Other USA cities have seen similar or greater crime reductions with an opposite approach – neighbourhood-based preventative schemes, based on a rebuilding of social cohesion.[98]

This quality of cohesion – the capacity for mutual aid and social norms – is crucial to the security of any city, and perhaps the least understood. Indicators of 'disorganization' can be used to trace the linkages between crime and cohesion – ethnically mixed areas may be more prone to burglaries for the same degree of disadvantagement.[99] 'Homewatch' schemes in the UK include about 130 000 projects covering 5 million people;[100] but while there are benefits in affluent areas, they may achieve little in disadvantaged areas.[101] A more integrated approach to social cohesion is through local presences for natural surveillance, such as in corner shops, small businesses, and housing concierges; incentives such as preferential business rating should be used to encourage this.

Large organizations employ their own security staff, but such costs are not viable for most communities. In many EU countries, civilian 'guardians' or 'watchers' are used to maintain street presences and create jobs for the unemployed, and trials in Manchester and Liverpool are in progress.[102] The next step is with community businesses, as in Scotland, which employ estate residents to police their own areas, possibly more effectively than external services, with savings to housing and insurance costs.

High levels of social cohesion may help to rebuild social norms – but many communities are under such pressure that crime is the norm, an inevitable way of life. A longer term integrated approach is the aim of community safety partnerships, which aim to coordinate police, probation, education and other services – but many such schemes show signs of 'partnership fatigue' and an emphasis on short-term defensive measures.[103] As with health, preventative programmes take less than 0.5% of the total criminal justice budget, and there is a strong case for increasing this – such investment can be recouped many

94 Poyner & Webb 1991
95 Graham 1996: Brooks & Heery 1996
96 Safe Neighbourhoods Unit 1993
97 Forrester et al 1988
98 Shapiro 1997

99 Hirschfield & Bowers 1997
100 Home Office 1998
101 Viz the criminology data problem: perceived, recorded and actual crime statistics may each show different trends
102 Lipietz 1996
103 Osborne & Shaftoe 1995

times by savings in social services, psychiatric care and the justice system itself.[104] Integrated youth programmes including sports, music, skills training, advice and advocacy, also show that recidivism is reduced.[105] Other programmes work with pre-school children and parents, targeting vulnerable households with job or marital stress.[106] This kind of security programme coordinates with education, health or anti-poverty programmes, and unlocks human resources through neighbourhood self-help and 'social trading' systems *(Chapter 10).*

# EDUCATION & HUMAN RESOURCES

Education is perhaps the key to human resources in sustainable development. For economic innovation, social cohesion, environmental responsibility, the schoolchildren of today will be the decision-makers of 2020. But in practice few children actively enjoy schooling, and for many it is irrelevant and alienating. So here we look at three themes:

- schools, colleges and the environmental agenda;
- a city for children and young people;
- education for social cohesion and cultural diversity.

Educational attainment levels in GM are 10% lower than the UK average, with many pockets of severe deprivation. Across the city, the quest for educational choice and quality is a key factor in house values, migration patterns and polarization of communities. For the 'growth coalition', from the region to the districts, education is the key to competitiveness and prosperity, and increasing amounts of regeneration funds are targeted on training and business skills. The profile shows the city-region relative to national and regional averages *(Fig 11.12):*

- a third more children under five in education;
- primary pupil/teacher ratios 25% greater;

- 20% more pupils leave with no qualifications;
- 5% more pupils gain five GCSE passes at grade A-C;
- 20% fewer pupils leave with two or more A levels.

While pre-school provision is more widespread, primary schools are overcrowded, and delinquency is rife in many areas. The result is a less skilled and more alienated generation of young people – with results such as the rate of teenage pregnancies of three times the national average.[107] This contrasts with the highlights – two Manchester schools with 'university' catchments are among the national top ten A-level achievers. GM contains at present four universities or Higher Education Institutions (HEIs), and numerous colleges.[108] The full-time student population of 56,000 is the largest outside London, with as many again in related activity, building on a long history of workers' education and public libraries. This floating 10% of the inner urban population has much to do with the cultural industries which have put Manchester on the map in recent decades. The HEI sector accounts for over 3% of total GDP, but even here there is evidence of widening gaps between needs and provision for business and the professions.[109]

---

104 Cavadino 1997
105 Allen 1997

106 Safe Neighbourhoods Unit 1994
107 Manchester Health Authority 1996
108 HEIs (higher education institutions) include: Victoria University of Manchester: UMIST: Manchester Metropolitan University: University of Salford. (The University of Bolton is anticipated in 1999-2000).
109 Robson et al 1994

# Environment & education

The quarter million children in school buildings in GM are a major part of the urban metabolism – the energy used in education is nearly half of public sector consumption, and with outdated design and poor maintenance, wastage in schools and colleges is higher than average.[110] Surrounding unfit and unhealthy buildings are acres of bare asphalt, while many 'surplus' grounds have been sold for development. Transport to school encourages car dependency, while school dinners encourage unhealthy diets. There is huge scope for environmental management, purchasing and contracting, but this is undermined by financial constraints and political restructuring.

The national 'Eco-schools' project involved 500 schools in a programme of classroom education and practical action, but has yet to translate the environmental agenda into the requirements of the national curriculum.[111] The more informed higher education community should coordinate building management, teaching and student projects, critical mass is lacking;[112] in Manchester, for instance, a transport management project for 3000 university staff has run into the sand.[113] Meanwhile the 'sustainable communities' projects as at Middlesex and Central Lancs universities aim to raise commitment for low-impact lifestyles and positive futures.

Environmental education is often slotted into 'science' or 'geography' – but urban studies, current affairs, business and personal/social education each link to the environmental agenda. The education system also contains a hidden agenda of competition, exploitation and pessimism, and this demands to be countered with pro-active education for peace, equality, sustainable development and positive visions, using 'circle sessions', discussion groups, practical projects, and self-learning programmes.[114] Arts and media projects are perhaps the best way to overcome inbuilt cultural and generation gaps – in Manchester over 1000 pupils built their own environmental sculptures in the 'Art in Schools' project, achieving a rare vision.[115]

Fig 11.12                  **EDUCATION**

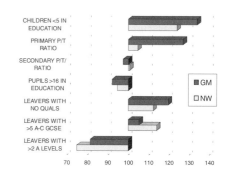

Comparison of key statistics for GM & NW, base 1995: relative to UK = 100.
Source: CSO 1996.

These show the 'hands-on' value of 'sustainable education' –improved school buildings and grounds, food gardens and wildlife habitats, internal trading systems and arts/media projects. Such projects should be geared to pupil's lifestyles and self-directed learning, and coordinated with intermediate labour markets and integrated public services.

# A city for young people

The modern city is a dangerous place for children, and for all the policies on education, there is little room for street parties, skinny dipping or tree-houses.[116] The city is structured by hostility and danger, for both young people and for those threatened by them, and the results show in crime and drug abuse.[117] Manchester's own town hall prints youth policy reports, while banning skateboarders from the town hall square.

Bridging the generation gap needs a new focus on young people's space and activities, in the design and management of housing, neighbourhoods and city centres. This starts with reclaiming the streets – the 'Home Zone' traffic calming of all residential areas, pedestrian routes, wildlife corridors and water habitats, to enable

110 Energy Efficiency Office 1990
111 Renton 1993
112 Toyne 1994
113 Banister 1996
114 Hutchinson

115 Art in Schools Project 1994: Martin 1996
116 Ward 1978
117 Bartlett et al 1999

freedom for play and exploration.[118] Economic restructuring for more flexible and localized activity will enable greater contact between children, parents and workers, for work experience and attitude.

Yet while the generation gap grows in education, crime and health, most youth and pre-school services have been cut to the bone. Pre-school provision is the key to fostering a culture of education – with locally based personal advisors who facilitate parent–child contact and shared learning.[119] For youth work, active out-of-school and work experience projects are needed in collaboration with employers, voluntary organizations, sports and media. Such programmes must start from young people's daily experience – drug use, for instance, is regarded as a danger to society, and so the majority of young people are criminalized at an early age. In the absence of intelligent discrimination, many fall into the spiral of hard drug addiction. A holistic drugs programme starts from realistic experience of positive use and negative abuse, to bridge the 'trust gap' between the generations.[120] Opening the political system is one approach, and in Wigan for instance a 'young people's council' is being set up, hopefully to take on some real responsibilities.[121]

## Education & community

While education is a key to social and economic vitality, it is also instrumental in the reproduction of social exclusion and a technocratic elite.[122] For many the values and methods of the 'system' fail at an early age, and the majority of under-11s experience boredom, alienation and resentment.[123] There is a growing gap between education and the experience of most young males – as shown in media images, computer games, globalized marketing, and anti-academic peer pressure. The result is that children with supportive backgrounds conform enough to pass exams and 'join the system', while others are pushed towards a future of exclusion and disadvantagement.

The human and financial wastage involved is huge and unnecessary. Experience shows that confidence and enthusiasm for learning are enhanced by multi-cultural project-based activity, within and outside of schools and colleges.[124] Practical skills can be acquired for a fraction of the time and cost of the school system, once the commitment to learning is there. So a more efficient and holistic education system would focus on commitment and confidence, with personal self-help projects in lifestyle areas such as technology, music, fashion, design, IT and business – with the added time input coming from employers, parents and the voluntary sector.

The pilot Education Action Zone now setting up in Salford and Trafford is a huge opportunity for such creative innovation – but there are signs that the focus will be the traditional 'paper-chase' of grades and certificates. In the education system overall there is a growing resource gap, and with little 'new money' a rethink of priorities and methods is needed:

- fostering confidence and commitment in pre-school, inter-school, post-16 and lifelong learning;
- encouraging parental and employer involvement, with voluntary input to bridge the resource gap;
- coordination between education, youth provision, public health, crime prevention and social services;
- targeting of curricula and methods for greater relevance, with practical self-help community-based projects where possible;
- ICT as a relatively 'free' resource – not only a computer in each class, but a terminal for every pupil.[125]

This restructuring of a massive system, with internal stresses on every side, will not be simple or quick – teachers and administrators need educating and inspiring as much as pupils and students, and much depends on parents and other influences. The UK government has made

118 Stine 1997
119 Safe Neighbourhoods Unit 1994
120 Leeds Environment City 1996: Measham Newcombe & Parker 1994
121 Wigan MBC 1997
122 Illich 1971
123 National Commission on Education 1993: Bentley 1999

124 Connell 1993: Ravetz 1973
125 McKinsey 1997: Taylor Powell & Speake 1996

a heroic effort to re-establish standards of excellence – but current trends appear to be leading towards excellence for a few, a marginal level of semi-transferable skills for most, and exclusion for the remainder. A city-region 2020 education strategy needs a more positive vision for the problems and opportunities of a fluid and fragmented post-industrial society.

# PUTTING IT TOGETHER

The ultimate goal of social strategy – the 'sustainable community' – is perhaps a paradox of the future, always out of reach.[125] But for cities such as Manchester, many social problems are so pressing that such a concept is being re-invented, for practical guidance in running the city.[126] Here we look at the implications for social strategy and public services, firstly in area-based 'local communities', and then for social 'communities of interest'.

Individuals, groups and communities each contain an ever-changing set of cultural, social, economic, political and environmental needs – if these are unfulfilled, conflict and tension result in a community which is 'unsustainable' for its people and for itself. Any community or society maintains its resilience and integrity with two complementary qualities:

- cohesion: self-organizing linkages, networks, and capacity for self-help and mutual support, within and between communities;
- diversity: a healthy mix of cultures and interactions based on mutual co-existence, essential to the innovation and adaptability of the system.

Of course, cohesive communities can be exclusive and intolerant: and diverse communities can suffer from lack of cohesion – charting the combinations shows positive and negative possibilities *(Fig 11.13)*. The globalization and restructuring of post-industrial cities can work both ways, accelerating global 'mono-culture' alongside empowerment of diverse sub-cultures.[127] In practice things rarely stay still – as with ecological communities, any social community shifts from one dominant mode or pattern to another.[128]

The practical question is whether it is possible to influence the level of cohesion and diversity, and if so how to do it. But such qualitities are complex and subtle, and there is no ultimate standard by which streetlife, for instance, is better or worse than middle-class affluence. For practical purposes there are several kinds of definitions and indicators:

- An economic view starts with dependency, or lack of diverse incomes – in Manchester the threshold is defined as one third of households on benefit, which makes half the city 'unsustainable'. Adequate money is clearly essential, but informal activities in the social economy can be as important.[129]
- A social perspective on diversity looks at indicators of class, age or ethnic mixing, with linkages to social cohesion through crime and other forms of disorganization.[130] Again formal indicators can easily overlook informal qualities for which more in-depth exploration is needed.
- An environmental approach looks for physical signs of anti-social activity such as the 'broken window' threshold, where unattended problems can lead to a spiral of decline. Poverty and crime are clearly linked with poor environments, but while affluence can solve many problems, it can also undermine social cohesion.

---

125 Handy 1994
126 Manchester Housing 1996
127 Townroe 1996

128 Thompson 1997:
129 Williams & Windebank 1997

## Fig 11.13 **SUSTAINABLE COMMUNITIES**

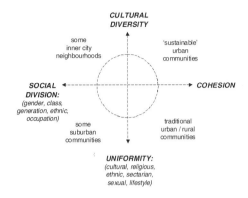

Sample communities showing dual themes of diversity & cohesion.

Most urban communities are in continuous flux and transience. Inner city neighbourhoods, for instance, can be vibrant and diverse, with cheap housing and workspace, but with high levels of dependency and migration. Social policy often sees them as 'problems' to be solved, while an alternative view sees opportunities for lower-income groups to pass through while finding a niche in society.[131] While individuals come and go into wealth or poverty, the neighbourhood as a whole can be 'sustainable' by playing an essential role in the city-region.

On the ground, such neighbourhoods are in a constant flux, polarizing into rich or poor, black or white, and skilled or unskilled. Such polarization appears to be cause and effect of added value – as in 'quality education', 'desirable suburbs', and 'secure' out-of-town shopping. Such added value might be enhanced by a 'community of interest' or the 'communitarian' approach – aiming for internal cohesion through neighbourhood enclaves and the 'gated city'.[132] Such internal cohesion has to balance with a wider cultural diversity, encouraged by a strong civic realm in urban places and facilities – the 'richness of cities'.[133] Such multiple overlapping communities can be seen in alternative spatial patterns for neighbourhood units, and in policies for housing, health, education and others *(Chapter 5)*.[134]

## A city for all

In a post-industrial city-region, many 'communities' based on neighbourhoods or local industries are being replaced by 'subcultures' based on social and economic networks. Recent decades have seen much progress in the empowerment of women, ethnic groups, disadvantaged groups and other sub-cultures, but there is still a never-ending task in balancing cohesion with diversity to create a 'city for all'.[135]

Women outnumber men in GM, for instance, but at present their experience of the city is often that of fear, insecurity and exclusion: many women cannot travel at night, have less control over housing, and less access to public space and facilities.[136] The majority live in suburbs based on an outmoded model of working men serviced by dependent housewives. Meanwhile, as women attain better education, social skills and life expectancy, former patterns of male dominance are shifting.[137] In each area of public services there are positive responses to the changing gender balance:

- for crime prevention, there are community safety and awareness programmes, domestic violence and support networks;[138]
- for health, there are well-women's centres, womens' support groups and networks;
- for transport, there are women-only taxi services, accessible design in vehicles and

---

**Box 11.2**

### *MULTI-CULTURAL SOCIAL ECONOMY*

The Ashram Acres project in Birmingham has worked with local ethnic groups for 15 years to create an Asian allotment project, growing specialist foods and herbs for the local community. The project has trained several hundred people in gardening and business skills, and reclaimed five acres of derelict land for productive social and economic activity.

**Source: Homeless International 1996**

---

130 Blau 1977
131 Jacobs 1965
132 Newman 1982: Etzioni 1996
133 Worpole & Greenhalgh 1997

134 Carley 1995
135 Black Environment Network 1991
136 Darke 1996
137 Peck & Emmerich 1994
138 Morrell 1996

buildings, car sharing clubs and lift networks.[139]

- for employment, there are childcare and after-school projects, positive employment policies, training and business development, support networks, and anti-poverty programmes.

Similar approaches work for ethnic, disadvantaged, disabled, cultural and other disadvantaged minorities – in general, the majority of the population who are not white, male, able-bodied, heterosexual, middle-class and economically-active *(Box 11.2)*.

## Social strategy

While public services were created alongside local government itself, many other actors are now involved – churches, health, education, unions, business, regeneration agencies and the voluntary sector. This broad spread is the basis of partnerships such as City Pride, aiming to bring together many groups for a common vision.[140]  In practice this and similar ventures are seen by many as public relations stunts of the 'growth coalition' with the 'same old faces'.[141]

To overcome the barriers between the majority 'nonjoiners' and the active civic elite, new patterns of public involvement are needed – 'one good community entrepreneur is worth a dozen civil servants'.[142]  This contains a political agenda for participation and the spreading of power and in-

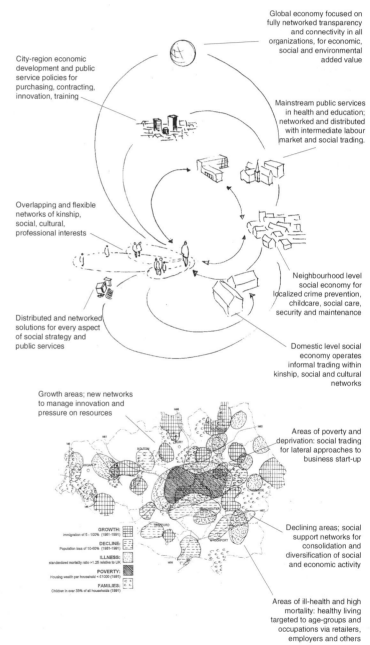

**Fig 11.14**          ***LIFESTYLE & COMMUNITY ~ THEMES***

General themes in lifestyle and community issues which underlie an integrated city-region strategy for public services and social economy.

Global economy focused on fully networked transparency and connectivity in all organizations, for economic, social and environmental added value

City-region economic development and public service policies for purchasing, contracting, innovation, training

Mainstream public services in health and education; networked and distributed with intermediate labour market and social trading.

Overlapping and flexible networks of kinship, social, cultural, professional interests

Neighbourhood level social economy for localized crime prevention, childcare, social care, security and maintenance

Distributed and networked solutions for every aspect of social strategy and public services

Domestic level social economy operates informal trading within kinship, social and cultural networks

Growth areas; new networks to manage innovation and pressure on resources

Areas of poverty and deprivation: social trading for lateral approaches to business start-up

GROWTH:
Immigration of 5 - 100% (1981-1991)
DECLINE:
Population loss of 10-60% (1981-1991)
ILLNESS:
standardized mortality ratio >1.25 relative to UK
POVERTY:
Housing wealth per household < £1000 (1991)
FAMILIES:
Children in over 33% of all households (1991)

Declining areas; social support networks for consolidation and diversification of social and economic activity

Areas of ill-health and high mortality: healthy living targeted to age-groups and occupations via retailers, employers and others

139 Hill 1996
140 Manchester Salford Trafford Partnership 1997
141 Cochrane et al 1996
142 Henderson 1978

fluence to all levels of society *(Chapter 14)*. There is a parallel economic agenda for the third sector and the promise of free resources for public services *(Chapter 10)*. One practical result is an environmental agenda, where local services and facilities are more viable and effective with community input *(Chapter 5)*. A cultural agenda underlies each of these, generating new social movements and local-global networks and alliances.[143] And yet there are many obstacles – political, economic and cultural – and as 'communities' are replaced by 'sub-cultures', alienation and passive consumerism are as widespread as ever.

There is an equal set of barriers between each of the public services – social services, health, crime prevention and education each tackle a small slice of the symptoms rather than the causes. The result is that people and communities with compound problems fall through the gaps, with massive waste of resources and human suffering. The growing problems of civic fragmentation and social exclusion raise crucial questions on the future of cities as we know them.[144]

From such themes we can sketch the components of a more integrated social strategy for public services:

- multi-sectoral coordination: bringing together strategy and action in public services such as housing, unemployment, anti-poverty, health, crime prevention, and education;
- multi-agency coordination: bringing together voluntary sectors, churches, unions, employers, business agencies, neighbourhood bodies and others;
- in-depth social audits and assessment, using both technical data and street-level exploration of perceptions, problems and quality of life factors;
- unlocking human resources through the third sector, social economy and social trading systems to enhance public services and social cohesion;

- multi-cultural approach: extending beyond the 'technocratic' paradigm to engage with other generations, sub-cultures and ethnic groups on their own terms.

While these themes include the remit of local authorities they go far beyond, and in practice public services are delivered by a complex web of organizations at neighbourhood, district, regional and national level. There is not necessarily a single point of responsibility for 'making it happen', rather an extended framework for cooperation and coordination.

For the city-region level there may be particular opportunities for added value – for coordination between areas and between sectors, for specialist resources, for purchasing power and political leverage. A city-region 'social strategy' partnership should work in parallel with environmental and economic strategies, within an umbrella 'sustainable development framework' *(Chapter 15)*. Such a partnership can then evolve its roles and functions within the emerging regional development structures.

---

**Box 11.3**

### *SUMMARY: LIFESTYLE & COMMUNITY*

The 2020 social strategy tackles the fragmentation and underfunding of public services by applying sustainability principles for social cohesion and cultural diversity. The result are in three key themes: responsive services, third sector inputs, and civic regeneration:

- changing attitudes and lifestyles to reduce the impacts of consumption
- anti-poverty strategy for diverse cultures with integrated preventative and adaptive measures
- health strategy, with holistic community and complementary medicine for positive health
- crime prevention strategy coordinated with environmental, social and economic measures
- education for human development potential and lifelong learning, for knowledge-based eco-modernizing society
- integrated public services and social strategy to promote social economy, voluntary sector, social cohesion and cultural diversity .

---

143 Borja & Castells 1996: Grove-White 1997
144 Parkinson 1998

# 12 REGENERATION

*'The axis of the earth sticks out visibly from the
centre of each and every town or city'*
Oliver Wendell Holmes 1857

From the top floors of the city-centre office
blocks, beyond the commercial glitz, there is a
long view on endless miles of urban sprawl. Unemployment, derelict land, crumbling housing
and obsolete workspace combine to suck the life
out of local economies, property markets and
communities. The urban question hinges on the
ominous sounding 'restructuring' – the inexorable tide of economic development which seems
to create losers alongside winners, globally and
locally. 'Regeneration area' is a polite heading
for the urban dumps and 'human landfills' of the
city-region,[1] where the cyclical process of adaptation and renewal has failed, demanding public
intervention with 'schemes' and 'programmes'.

Managing urban change is a challenge in
both rising and declining areas. While several
decades of urban regeneration efforts have
turned around areas with waterfront or other
special cachets, many larger surrounding areas
are in worse condition than a generation ago.
This suggests that such deep-seated and compound problems cannot be 'fixed' in isolation.
One approach is to look at the city-region as a
composite unit, where inner city problems are
likely to be part and parcel with suburban oppor-

tunities. Another looks at the whole spectrum –
jobs, skills, property, services, security and environments – as a total package.

The 'sustainability' agenda adds further layers to the mix. From the angle of our investigation, regeneration and managing change should
be catalysts for environmental sustainability, not
only for problem areas, but for the city-region as
a whole. Added to this is a new agenda for social and economic sustainability, aiming at participation, empowerment, skills, competitiveness,
diversity, local services and informal economies.

So this chapter does not aim to be a blueprint or manual – more an exploration of the 'city
as process' – in this case, the process of reaching the goals set out in previous chapters. We
aim to bridge the gaps between the urban agenda
and the sustainability agenda – firstly with a review of the dynamics of urban change, and the
meaning of 'sustainable regeneration'. Then we
look at the reality of regeneration as a physical,
social and economic process. This leads to the
wider theme of managing urban change through
integrated planning – the holy grail of integrating spatial, environmental, economic and social
development.

---

1 Davis 1998

Fig 12.1 **URBAN DEPRIVATION**

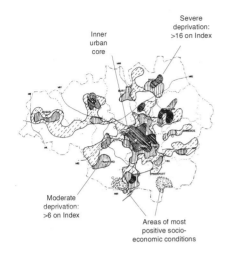

Pattern of urban deprivation as shown by 'Carstairs' index, with ward boundaries adjusted for urban area: composite indicators including unemployment, dependency, lack of car and housing stress.
Source:  based on DoE 1991: DETR 1998: data from 1991 Census

## Trends & tensions

The physical problems above are highly visible, their causes in economic failure are clear, but the resulting social stress then clusters in pockets which are largely hidden from view.  While the statistics can be debated endlessly, the practical perception is that a large crescent around the urban core of GM, plus many outer estates, is on the brink of a downward spiral.[2]  The mapping above shows by ward areas the worst and best 98th percentile, or the 2% most extreme conditions, for a basket of indicators from the Index of Local Deprivation *(Fig 12.1)*:[3]

- unemployment: 16–52% (NW average 9%);
- dependency ratio: 0.7–1.1 (NW average 0.63)[4]
- dwellings lacking indoor w.c, bath, shower or central heating: 22–70%  (average 20%).

The overlaps are clear between unemployment, dependency and poor housing, and many other indicators could be added.  For each of these the worst quartile is about 50% higher than the regional average, and 60% higher than the national average.  Such concentrations are common in the inner areas of Manchester, Salford and some other districts, but there are also large peripheral estates with similar problems.  The areas of non-overlap are also revealing – for instance, high dependency ratios in the affluent suburbs of Bury, or high unemployment in the transient but aspiring middle-classes in south Manchester.

The trends over time are also mixed. Derelict land has returned to its 1970s level, while housing conditions have improved in line with national trends.[5]  Public health and education standards have improved relatively slowly; households without work and single parents have increased in some areas faster than the national average.  In contrast, the proportion of 'higher' social classes has risen, due to some inward middle class migration.  This suggests that in a diverse city-region such as GM, each area type contains a different profile of regeneration problems and opportunities:

- central areas: many parts of the regional centre show success with fast-rising values based on leisure, retail and cultural industries. However the centre is still an island surrounded by a ring of decline and disorganization.
- inner city areas: older or public housing stock with falling values, transient populations and fragmented urban form; some market potential via proximity to city centres.  Mixed fortunes in GM so far, with some success in flagship estates such as Hulme, but less so with others.
- peripheral areas: generally public estates, lacking local employment and services, with potential for diversifying tenures and household types. A very mixed picture in GM, where larger estates such as Langley or Wythenshawe are still in decline.
- former industrial, mining, railway or shipping areas:  shattered communities and acute dereliction. Some success in GM with the river valleys, Ship Canal corridor and sports developments; more difficult without waterfronts or other catalysts of added value.

2 Manchester City 1996, pers.comm.
3 DOE 1991 & DETR 1998
4 defined as ratio of persons under 5 or over 70, to persons 5-70

5 Policy Studies Institute 1994

- suburban areas: apparently moderate problems but many vulnerable areas alongside affluent areas
- urban fringe towns: in spite of intense activity around the motorway ring, many smaller industrial towns struggle with declining local economies and ageing populations.

## Future prospects

With this kind of area profile, far wider than the conventional agenda for inner urban areas, we can draw from the trends in motion some alternative 25-year regeneration scenarios:

- *BAU scenario:* regeneration continues to move the symptoms of structural problems around the city. More communities and occupations are redundant to the global economy, while investment withdrawal and physical decline is endemic.
- *technology scenario:* urban property-led re-urbanization is aided by ICT which encourages 'gated communities', on-street surveillance, privatized service delivery and other forms of social engineering.
- *SD scenario:* structural trends are stabilized, as many urban areas become more attractive, with greater social mixing, re-investment and rebuilding of values, coordination of public services, and incentives for local businesses.
- *deep green scenario:* neighbourhood renewal leads to a rapid re-urbanization of inner areas, while co-ops and social trading schemes spread in housing estates, promoting low-impact community-based businesses.

---

**Box 12.1**
### HULME REGENERATION

Hulme Regeneration was a 5-year City Challenge programme, just south of central Manchester, on a former local authority estate. It includes a locally-based Economic Forum of small businesses and investors, partnership with 4 major developers and social housing providers, and a development masterplan with an urban design framework. The local construction labour scheme has resulted in 300 local jobs, with over 3500 new dwellings.

Source: Hulme Regeneration Ltd: Harding 1998

---

Fig 12.2 **TRENDS IN LOCAL DEPRIVATION**

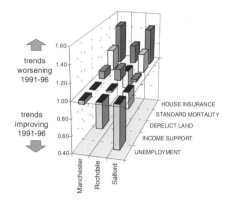

Trends from 1991-1996 in selected indicators from 'Index of Local Deprivation' for 3 worst Districts in GM: scale shows ratio of 1996 / 1991 values.
Source: data from DoE 1991 & DETR 1998 (Index of Local Conditions).

## The state of the art

All this is a very well-trodden path – it seems that each generation comes up with a solution, and by the time it has had some effect, evaluation is rare and difficult, and the agenda moves on.[6] GM has been a test-bed for regeneration schemes, starting in the 1960s with the Community Development approach.[7] The 1980s saw the Inner City Partnership, Task Forces, City Action Teams, Enterprise Zones, Urban Programme and others. Then in the 1990s another generation took over:

- Urban Development Corporations: Central Manchester and Trafford Park DCs were wound up 1995-97.
- City Pride partnership: Manchester, Salford, Trafford.
- City Challenge flagship schemes: Manchester, Bolton, Wigan.
- Single Regeneration Budget (SRB): about 20 areas active at any one time.
- Urban Regeneration Agency: was English Partnerships, now subsumed in the Regional Development Agency.
- European Regional Development Fund: Objective 2 area covering most of GM is at the

---

6 Robson et al 1994
7 Community Projects Foundation 1976

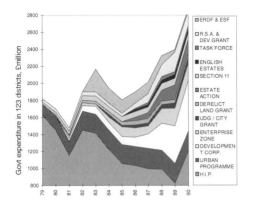

Fig 12.3  **REGENERATION FUNDING**

Total housing, urban regeneration & regional development funding, 1979/80 - 1990/91, excluding Rate Support Grant, in 123 most deprived authorities in England.
Source:  Bradford & Robson 1995.

time of writing awaiting new a programme and criteria.

• recently a national 'New Commitment to Regeneration' and a New Deal for Communities, one of the pilot areas being in East Manchester.

In spite of the glossy front of such schemes, they account for a small part of total local authority funding in urban areas, which itself has declined by a third in 20 years.[8]  The 1980s saw property and economic development as the catalyst for a 'trickle-down' effect, and the Development Corporations of that era have just wound up – but the property-led supply-side approach ran into problems in the 1990s recession, and often failed to re-skill and re-vitalize local communities.[9]  The current Single Regeneration Budget and New Deal programmes have at least the intention of partnership with small businesses and local communities, and represent more or less the state of the art.[10]  The European structural funds are intended to complement local initiatives, but there is still conflict on allocation and 'additionality' of funding.[11]  The chart

shows the complexity of the many schemes over the last 20 years *(Fig 12.3)*.

All this experience raises questions on short termism, accountability, environmental appraisal and community participation. The competitive bidding process is a problem – half the districts in GM have lost City Challenge competitions, wasting much investment and energy for partnership.[13]  The problems of short-term funding, rigid targets, and onerous matching finance can be seen in failed projects such as the Ancoats Development Trust just north of the city centre.[14]  Regeneration expertise in GM is equal to that of anywhere, but a recent survey found the same general picture of fragmentation, outputs rather than outcomes, and lack of long term vision.[15]  The flagship City Challenge and follow-on partnership in Hulme and Moss Side has promoted a property market, local businesses and a pioneering urban design guide, but its very rapid rate of physical change is not easily transferable *(Box 12.1).*[16]

## Urban metabolism

Much regeneration activity tends by default to address the symptoms rather than the causes – but such causes are deeply embedded in the complex and interlocking dynamics of urban and global systems. There is not yet or ever likely to be a single and final 'theory of the city'. But we can link some of the key themes to new thinking coming from the sustainability agenda.

Perhaps the most fundamental dynamic is global 'capital accumulation' – or in plain words, making money. There is also a dynamic of 'centre-periphery' competition between cities and territories, where cities are simultaneously the organizers, exploiters and residuals of their hinterlands.[17]  Another is the dynamic of polarization, where certain social and economic problems cluster and accelerate themselves to the point of civic breakdown.[18]  The combined results can be seen as various levels of 'uneven development':[19]

8 Bradford & Robson 1995
9 Roberts & Whitney 1993
10 Parkinson 1996
11 Lloyd & Meegan 1996

13 Healey & Davoudi 1995
14 Robson 1995
15 Carley 1998
16 Hulme Regeneration 1996: Harding 1998
17 Morgan 1978
18 Robson 1988
19 Savage & Ward 1993

- cities in competition through international restructuring – global uneven development;
- spatial concentrations of deprivation within the city-region – local uneven development;
- barriers in the cyclical renewal of industries and infrastructure – technological uneven development;
- stratification of labour and social class – social uneven development..

Each of these symptoms is glaringly visible in a city-region such as GM. As to the causes and dynamics behind such uneven development, there are endless debates on the system of land, labour, capital, advantage, Fordist and post-Fordist modes of production, and its implications for urban forms and activities:

- urban evolutionary theory looks at new kinds of urban form as responses to new modes of production;[20]
- the 'new international division of labour' looks at the competition between cities in a global hierarchy;[21]
- 'internal contradictions of capital' sees investment in property as a second circuit or alternative to investment in markets;[22]
- 'regulation theory': looks at the role of the state apparatus and its interest groups in managing the transition from fordist to post-fordist modes of production.[23]

Each of these economic dynamics may be valid in its own terms, but on the ground they are compounded by social and environmental problems, into a vicious spiral of material 'deprivation' and cultural 'exclusion'.[24] Magnified by poor education, security, housing, health, drug abuse and alienation, such compound effects can spiral into the 'wild zones' – the 'dangerous places' of the darker side of the city. Even the possibility of such a spiral affects a much larger population who are vulnerable to any one of the symptoms above, and for whom it can appear that the entire apparatus of the state is hostile.[25]

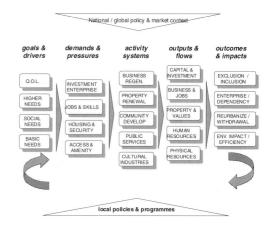

Fig 12.4   **REGENERATION METABOLISM**

Urban regeneration seen as a metabolism translating needs into outcomes.

The obvious goal is to turn such vicious spirals into virtuous circles, to set up frameworks for holistic thinking and joined-up action, for 'win-win' circles whereever possible. In principle, re-urbanization should bring investment to the city, promoting local economies, in turn to enable further re-urbanization. Improved local services encourage housing markets, normalizing deprived areas, and increasing the viability of the same local services. In reality such approaches often fail where they are piecemeal, uncoordinated, and tackling the symptoms rather than the causes.[26] But who is to say which is cause and effect in the urban system?

For a wider picture we can use again a 'system mapping' of the urban metabolism – here focused on the theme of regeneration and balancing of uneven development *(Fig 12.4)*. Again this shows multiple goals, multiple outcomes and many possible complex feedback effects. It does not pretend to explain the whole system, but gives a holistic view of the balance between needs and outcomes.

Within this balance are many layers of activity, from global to local, and from formal to informal. Where such layers are fragmented or disconnected, within cities or between cities, the

20 Hall & Hay 1980
21 Frobel Heinrichs & Krege 1977
22 Harvey 1974
23 Harvey 1989
24 Pacione 1996
25 Lash & Urry 1993: Campbell 1993

26 Perri 6

**Fig 12.5** **REGENERATION STRATEGIES**

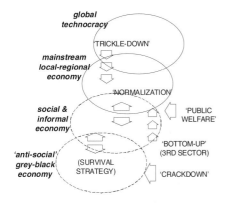

Different levels of local economies with alternative regeneration responses.
Source: adapted from Friedman 1994.

resulting system effects are likely to be dysfunctional, with the outcomes of uneven development, unemployment and social stress. This suggests a family tree of different layers of regeneration activity, each of which aims to re-connect different layers of the economic fabric, from the 'global technocracy' of mobile capital to the street-level 'anti-social' or black economy *(Fig 12.5)*:

- the 'welfare' approach of the 1960s aimed at redistribution of collective goods such as housing, targeted to disadvantaged groups;
- a 'bottom-up' or 'third sector' approach which emerged in the 1970s aims to tap local human resources in the social economy to enhance the mainstream economy;[27]
- the 'trickle-down' approach of the 1980s invests in property and infrastructure, and risks the displacement of local communities in order to attract the colonizing middle classes and global entrepreneurs;
- a 'normalization' approach of the 1990s aims to spread concentrations of deprivation, not necessarily to 'solve' the problems directly but to re-integrate them into mainstream society;[28]

- a perennial 'survival strategy' is also shown, not as a policy, but as real activity on the boundaries of the informal, grey and black economies.[29]

Such economic fabric itself is not a single agenda, but a combination of business competitiveness, property markets, inward investment, skills and learning, cultural assets, institutional 'thickness' and so on – each of which is crucial to the prospects of each of the layers.

## Towards sustainable regeneration

Just as the urban system has many dimensions, regeneration has many strands, and so does the fuzzy label 'sustainable regeneration' – coming back to the question 'sustaining whom or what?'[30] The role of regeneration in relation to our main agenda has two themes in particular:

- public intervention to solve the most acute and urgent problems;
- strategic management as the catalyst for steering the whole urban system towards a more sustainable path.

For the environmental agenda, 'environmentally sustainable' regeneration would include the re-engineering and restructuring of the city-region to meet its strategic targets for energy, transport, waste and others. This would start with the worst concentrations of pollution and deprivation, and extends to the entire city-region. The result might be seen as local greening side by side with city-region networks.

Achieving this depends on 'financially sustainable' regeneration – technically, the continuation of private investment after public funding exits. This agenda also now extends to the rebuilding of local economies and social cohesion through community banking and trading schemes. The result might be a global investment partnership in partnership with a community credit union.

It also involves 'socially sustainable' regeneration, which promotes inclusion and empow-

27 Gibson 1996
28 Carley 1995b & 1999

29 Friedman 1994
30 Mitlin & Satterthwaite 1996

erment through community participation, mutual aid and self-help. This might see a business park side by side with local childcare schemes and community gardens.

The post-Fordist agenda focuses on 'culturally sustainable' regeneration, where global inward investment may be attracted by cultural industries and a 're-imaging' of industrial areas, and also where local human resources are enhanced by cultural activities. This could result in an opera house side by side with a community arts project.

Each of these strands combines for a 'structurally sustainable' regeneration process – the successful re-starting of indigenous cyclic renewal, and re-connecting the fragmented layers of a dysfunctional urban system, without future backsliding into decline and dependency.

One useful view likens the city to a human body, and regeneration to a healing process *(Chapter 1)*. Many parts of the city are clearly 'sick' by any measure, but local sores may be symptoms of underlying conditions – the 'quick fix' of medical surgery may be one step in a longer term programme, which follows acute treatment

with positive therapy for holistic health. Likewise, regeneration is as much a 'process' as a 'product', which may need to continue over decades in certain areas. Such a long term programme might be seen as a drain on public funds, or as continuous re-investment, if not redistribution, to heal the gaps in a vulnerable urban system. The UK 'Urban Renaissance' programme is heading in the same direction, although with a more narrow remit for the physical problems of inner urban areas.[31]

Such a holistic and process-oriented view is more complex and less certain than many would like to believe – just as with human health – but it does point towards goals for 'sustainable' regeneration and management of urban change:

- environmental best practice within a city-region strategy;
- economic eco-modernization and human resource development;
- social and cultural development for cohesion, diversity and empowerment;
- regeneration programmes which are holistic, self-sustaining and entrepreneurial;
- planning mechanisms which are integrated between sectors, themes and agencies.

## Indicators & targets

From such goals, different kinds of targets can be drawn for each layer of regeneration and intervention, and different layers of criteria will suit different targets.[32] Programmes such as SRB focus on hard 'outputs' such as jobs created, training places and employment floorspace, and there are problems when the output targets take over the process to the detriment of outcomes. The 'normalization' targets might look for the statistical profile of clusters of uneven development. A welfare approach might set absolute thresholds or limits for each indicator of poverty, housing condition and so on. A property-led approach would select market-based targets such as housing mix and property values. An environmental approach looks at access and equity in energy, transport and so on, within strategic targets for the city-region as a whole.

---

**Box 12.2**

### REGENERATION ~ GOALS & STRATEGIES

| | GOV | LAP | BUS | COM | PUB |
|---|---|---|---|---|---|
| **PHYSICAL REGENERATION:** Promote environmental best practice & eco-modernization via city-region environmental strategy | ○ | ● | ● | ○ | |
| **ECONOMIC REGENERATION:** Support inward investment, local business capacity, vulnerable industries, local services, human resources | ○ | ● | ● | ○ | ○ |
| **SOCIAL REGENERATION:** Enhance local capacity & diversity through training, participation, self-help, community networks, social & intermediate economies, small businesses & cultural industries | ○ | ● | ○ | ● | ○ |
| **PLANNING & MANAGEMENT:** Integrate development planning with economic/ social: integrated environmental planning for all physical activities | ○ | ● | ○ | ○ | ○ |

GOV ~ government & EU: LA ~ local authorities & partnerships: BUS ~ business & finance: COM ~ community & 3rd sector: PUB ~ public

---

31 Urban Task Force 1999
32 CAG Consultants 1997

Clearly a holistic regeneration programme should include different kinds of targets and monitoring measures for each theme. The summary below shows the range of goals and strategies for regeneration and planning in a city-region context.

Finally, it is clear that 're'-generation is in many ways a misnomer – the old conditions are now long gone, and life in an industrial city was pretty grim anyway. The agenda is much more about simply 'generation' – the invention of new ways of living and working in a post-industrial urban order.

# PHYSICAL REGENERATION

Most industrial cities are hollowing out – Manchester itself has lost 20% of its population and 30% of its jobs in three decades, partly a result of planned 'deconcentration', partly from massive industrial shake-out and restructuring.[33] The results are gaping holes in the urban fabric, where property values and expectations have fallen through the floor.[34] Demolition of physically sound properties is almost the only option for public and social landlords, but this is incredibly wasteful, and even the possibility is enough to damage values and expectations. A large crescent from the west to the south-east of inner urban GM is vulnerable to what is seen as a spreading contagion, as estate managers watch anxiously for signs of 'broken windows' and other threshold indicators. Only intensive and costly life-support inputs of physical renewal and economic schemes are managing to hold the line.

As to the remedies, the conventional departmental approach of 'schemes' with hard targets is clearly prone to failure. The physical and design-based approach to recycling land and buildings of the 'urban renaissance' is also not very appropriate where jobs are scarce and values are non-existent.[35] This crucial task – rebuilding values – includes actual markets in traded property; the security of income to support the property; and the expectations and aspirations of its users, landlords and lenders.[36] The 'colonization' approach aims to create enclaves for middle-class incomers, less risky in property terms, but

more divisive of existing communities. In contrast, the 'inclusion' approach aims at joined-up coordination between the housing market, benefit system, intermediate labour markets and social trading networks – less certain in property terms, unless public funding can be used to underwrite it.[37] This is perhaps the largest challenge for any regeneration agency.

At the conurbation level, derelict land still stands at about 7% of the urban area, and new dereliction has kept pace with reclaimed land for two decades. Vacant land has reduced by a third over the last decade, but much is still concentrated in industrial areas, with complex ownerships, obsolete infrastructure, contamination and negative image. Alongside such problems are opportunities for innovation in urban form – larger regeneration areas, such as Trafford Park, Salford Quays or East Manchester are the catalysts for new urban villages of housing, leisure and workspace.[38] Over several decades some of these areas have been turned around, mainly where there is added value from waterfronts, location or cultural assets. The greater challenge will be spreading the process to surrounding areas which lack these assets, and this could take much more money and power than any public agency is likely to have.

At the neighbourhood and street level, there is a huge agenda for new kinds of workspace and social space, restructuring of neighbourhoods, converting streets to public spaces, en-

33 Turok & Edge 1999
34 Power & Mumford 1999
35 Urban Task Force 1999
36 George Mills, pers.comm.

37 Forrest & Kearns 1999
38 Urban Villages Forum 1995

ergy efficiency and renewable energy, ecological design, healthy and adaptable building
*(Chapter 5)*. Each of these requires investment
which is more cost-effective when combined with
the others – energy upgrading is costly on its
own, but very cheap when combined with life-
cycle maintenance. So the regeneration process
is a one-off opportunity to combine social and
economic goals with an integrated programme
for a sustainable built environment *(Fig 12.6)*.
This depends on coordination, and the perennial joined-up action, between developers, financiers, owners, landlords, utilities, transport and
other services.

## Housing improvement

Over half a million slum dwellings were cleared
in GM, and half as many again were upgraded to
basic health standards. Overcrowding, as defined by more than one person per habitable
room, has also reduced by half in the urban core,
but the dwellings 'unfit or in need of major repair', have increased by a third in the last decade, and now stands at nearly 40% of the total
stock in GM.[39] The city's 128,000 dwellings 'in
need of replacement' might stand for a century if
planned renewal went ahead, but current rates
of activity are about a tenth of this – a major
problem for the future.

Housing fitness problems are spread between older private housing and the newer public estates. Much private housing was built with
now obsolete materials and standards, with a
natural life-cycle which can be extended through
indigenous renewal. In contrast the untimely
decline of much public housing is a compound
failure in design, construction, allocation, and
maintenance. The capital and maintenance programme for Manchester's housing has halved in
a decade, the right-to-buy with capital receipts
controls has produced sinks of deteriorating
housing, and there are signs that voluntary housing estates are going the same way.[40]

The problems of housing investment seem
to dwarf the funds available – at the national
level, the housing benefit system is an example
of waste and inefficiency, and there is a strong

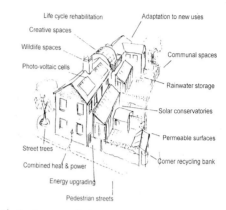

Fig 12.6   **PHYSICAL REGENERATION**

Life cycle rehabilitation
Creative spaces
Wildlife spaces
Photo-voltaic cells
Street trees
Combined heat & power
Energy upgrading
Pedestrian streets
Adaptation to new uses
Communal spaces
Rainwater storage
Solar conservatories
Permeable surfaces
Corner recycling bank

Integration of many types of policy and programmes into the
physical fabric of regeneration areas.

case for redistribution of benefit towards social
housing investment, with a new framework for
partnership Housing Companies.[41] At the local
level, there is great potential in combining housing maintenance and renewal with community
cohesion, local business development and training.[42] The self-build movement shows how new
houses can be built on marginal sites at a fraction of the normal cost.[43]

## Ecological regeneration

In the re-engineering of the city-region towards
environmental sustainability, regeneration programmes are *de facto* catalysts for rapid change
and new urban forms. Designated regeneration
areas in GM cover at present about 3000 hectares, or about 6% of the urban area, in programmes of 3–10 years duration. But to meet the
ambitious targets of previous chapters, for land-
use, neighbourhood structure, housing fitness,
energy efficiency and healthy building, the process of restructuring or 'regeneration' will need
to extend to much larger areas.

Assuming that area regeneration programmes aimed to upgrade every building in the
city-region over 25 years, as required by the energy–climate strategy, they would need to take
on about 2000 hectares per year. This would be
several times the current rate of activity, with a

39 NWRA 1994
40 Power & Mumford 1999

41 Priority Estates Project 1997
42 Groves et al
43 Broome 1993

50–100% increase in total output of the construction industry. Such a comprehensive process could only be self-financing, with an array of subsidies and levies, recycling of utility savings, land assembly and re-investment of rising values, as at the end of this chapter. [44]

Physical regeneration is material- and energy-intensive, with heavy demands on local and global environments. For each regeneration programme there is a wider environmental or eco-balance, whose scope is far beyond the current 'environmental appraisal' of policies and programmes.[45] One problem is that regeneration areas do not exist in isolation – investment and jobs are often transferred from adjacent areas, and likewise many environmental impacts are indirect and displaced. Re-using vacant land may consolidate urban form at the cost of local wildlife, or transport infrastructure may unlock investment while increasing total traffic.[46] Environmental assessment of regeneration needs a city-wide baseline and scenario to show the wider effects.[47]

Such a city-wide context is also the basis for a strategic approach to environmental best practice. Regeneration investment should be targeted on locations with good public transport and transport management plans, and the biodiversity of derelict sites should be channelled into wildlife habitats in new developments.

A typical SRB programme, such as in Salford, estimates 3600 jobs, 1500 houses and 75,000m$^2$ of workspace, at a direct cost of £37 million public and £19 million private funding.[48] The $CO_2$ emissions embodied might be about 75000 tonnes, or 1/400th of the GM annual total – design of buildings to NHER 10 or equivalent, would produce annual $CO_2$ emissions at a third or quarter of this level. This would still add to the emissions of the city, but at reduced levels within the context of the city-region energy–climate strategy. Again, environmental actions are much more effective where combined with social and economic, as in estate regeneration in Glasgow *(Box 12.3)*.

---

**Box 12.3**   *ECO-REGENERATION*

The WISE partnership agency in Glasgow has successfully linked environmental and social regeneration. WISE has pursued energy efficiency with employment training, public health, education, housing and crime prevention. Over three years 5000 dwellings were brought up to NHER 8 efficiency, and generating 300 training jobs for local people.

Source: Brooke 1994

---

# ECONOMY & COMMUNITY

The impact on the city of globalization and restructuring can be seen as different kinds of economic gaps, barriers or other market failures; these need to be bridged with public resources before private investment can begin to circulate.[49] Such gaps might be in property values, labour skills, entrepreneurial resources, infrastructure, or simply image and confidence. Economic regeneration, in many ways, is simply the intervention needed to fill the gaps, overcome the barriers and re-connect activity at each layer, from global technocracy to local informal economy. To do this action on all fronts is needed:

- infrastructure to encourage new investment, support market values, image and confidence;
- promote local economic activity, start-up enterprises and business networks;
- assist the flexibilization and re-skilling of the labour force;
- develop human resources through the social economy.

---

44 TCPA 1997: (Finding the land for 4.4 million homes)
45 Seamark 1996
46 Pauli 1998

47 Ravetz 2000
48 Salford Partnership 1995
49 Jensen-Butler 1995

## Investment gaps

While this is now common knowledge, the arguments then start around the hard choices for
scarce public funds. A successful Urban Development Corporation (UDC), such as in Central
Manchester, could achieve a direct gearing ratio
of public to private expenditure of five times, with
an indirect ratio double that. Property-led regeneration in GM, as elsewhere, focuses on flagship
areas, where rising values can be generated from
the added value of waterfronts or commercial location – Salford Quays, Trafford Park, and various quarters of the regional centre.[50] In such
areas of loft living and small business unit mills,
there is visible success in changing image and
functions from material-based to information-
based modes of production and consumption.
But while many sites and buildings were reclaimed, the effect of a fast rising property market was to disrupt many local businesses with
insecure tenures and vulnerable clientele.

Surrounding them are larger areas where the
winning formula of funding, infrastructure and
confidence has yet to emerge. As a post-industrial city in perpetual state of restructuring and
re-imaging is likely to continuously produce a
surplus of floorspace with low values, this suggests we have to look for ways to turn such problems into opportunities. Where vacant or
low-value property can be released for low-cost
or temporary workspace, new micro-businesses
and cultural networks can begin to rebuild the
local economy, with property values following
on.[51] Where such value appreciation can be retained and recycled through local development
trusts or partnerships, then the 'virtuous circle'
of re-investment can begin to work.[52] The new
generation of urban regeneration agencies just
springing up will take this as their guiding theme.

## Employment gaps

The effects of concentrated economic regeneration can be seen for a sample Task Force area,
where recession of the 1990s raised unemployment only slightly, at a lower rate than the national average, while long term unemployment
stayed level *(Fig 12.7)*. But in the surrounding

Fig 12.7          ***UNEMPLOYMENT TRENDS***

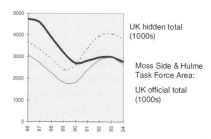

UK hidden total
(1000s)

Moss Side & Hulme
Task Force Area:

UK official total
(1000s)

Sample: unemployed in Moss Side & Hulme Task Force Area.
Source: NOMIS 1995 & Unemployment Unit 1997.

city, unemployment increased by 25% over the
previous decade – youth unemployment declined in most areas, but in Manchester increased
by 15%, so that a quarter of all 16–19 year olds
are now unemployed.[53] The city also saw the
largest rise in households with no working member, at twice the national increase *(Chapter 10)*.

Such evidence suggests some improvement
in the regeneration target areas – but across the
inner city as a whole, there is widespread structural unemployment, even while training achievements improve.[54] This is not a simple issue – it
can be argued that the post-industrial flexibilized
and deregulated service economy depends on
reservoirs of low-skill casual labour, and attempts
to 'solve' such problems locally are undermined
by national and global trends and pressures.[55]
In practice there are different kinds of unemployment gaps or mismatches, some needing an approach beyond that of mainstream programmes:

- skills mismatch due to industrial restructuring, or lack of basic skills from mis-directed
  education;
- cultural mismatch or attitude gap, particularly
  in the shift from former skilled occupations
  to new low-status service sector;
- incentive mismatch or poverty trap, especially for tenants with dependants: this may
  be partly solved by the new UK Working
  Families Tax Credit scheme;

50 Law 1994
51 Jacobs 1982
52 Monaghan 1997

53 GMR 1996
54 Bradford & Robson 1995
55 Hayton 1998

- demand-side business failures, from short-term finance policies, restrictive legislation, management shortcomings, multi-national competition;
- youth unemployment, a total combination of education, poverty, family stress, crime and general alienation.

This range of mismatches suggests that several kinds of policy approach may be needed, and that to lump them all together in a single development agency or programme may not be effective. Likewise, area-based schemes such as the new 'Employment Zones' may be less appropriate than sectoral schemes which can be coordinated with area-based actions. Youth exclusion is possibly the most intractable problem of all, and demands a new approach to integrated cultural action, education and training *(Chapter 11)*. And it is possible that in a post-industrial globalized economy, full employment may be unachievable anyway – suggesting a re-think of the boundaries between formal, intermediate and informal economies *(Chapter 10)*.

## Community gaps

In the healing of a fragmented and dysfunctional city, the 'process' – of social cohesion and empowerment – may be as important as the 'product' of jobs and houses.[56] Even the accelerated change of regeneration can bring insecurity and displacement – in the 1950s, wholesale clearances, and in the 1980s, wholesale gentrification. A city-region such as GM contains large transient and marginal populations, and there is evidence of regeneration 'moving the poverty' around the city – as soon as one area is improved, others nearby are nearer the threshold of decline. Middle class colonization of newly gentrified areas is countered by the colonization of vulnerable and 'dangerous places' by drug dealers and others below the radar.[57] The solution must be to generate and retain rising incomes and upward mobility within the area – but this invites conflicts where the newly affluent may reject their former neighbours on the wrong side of the tracks. There is no ready solution to this, but for

responsive neighbourhood-based regeneration programmes to work closely with local people, businesses and landlords, retaining not only material success but confidence and aspirations in the area – more like gardening than development as we know it.[58]

The conditions of the inner city are the 'zones of transition' and by-products of an post-industrial society, and the 'wild zones' where anti-social behaviour can flourish.[59] They are also seedbeds for new lifestyles, social movements and cultural industries, and even run-down housing is a social asset – the squatting movement showed how regeneration and rising values could follow spontaneously from 'anti-social' activity.[60] A holistic approach aims to turn such problems into opportunities, by encouraging diversity of lifestyles and activities in the social economy. At the moment any community group or enterprise faces huge hurdles in getting established – financial, legal, organizational, premises – and public agencies should aim for the opposite.

Neighbourhood-based regeneration cannot solve wider structural problems, but provides a visible focus for positive action and capacity building. Parallel actions for economic, social and political development can then be set in motion, generating the 'institutional thickness' which empowers local businesses and communities.[61] To encourage this there is a case for 'community zones', where regeneration planning and investment are devolved to the most local level, with capacity building for decision-making and business development *(Box 12.4)*.[62]

---

**Box 12.4** **COMMUNITY ZONES**

In Detroit, USA, a large scale regeneration programme has been run since 1984 by a community-based non-profit organization. Within the city's 'empowerment zone', the 'City Centre Neighbourhoods' agency is managed and staffed by local people, and has combined large scale urban village development with continuous neighbourhood improvements.

Source McCarthy 1997

---

56 Williams & Windebank 1999: MacArthur 1999
57 Campbell 1993

58 Forrest & Kearns 1999: Benn 1998
59 Lash & Urry 1993
60 Wates 1980
61 Amin & Thrift 1995
62 Urban Task Force 1999

# INTEGRATED PLANNING

The theme of holistic regeneration for sustainable development demands new ways of planning and managing urban activity. And the concept of 'planning' itself needs rethinking – the traditional model of 'strategic decisions taken by enlightened decision-makers in the public interest' is becoming outmoded in an era of post-fordist uncertainty and multiple discourses.[63] Here we look at the implications for the sustainability agenda – for physical 'development planning', for 'environmental planning', and in 'integrated urban management'.

These various layers are shown, for instance, with the energy-climate strategy – where success depends on how far 'planning' can engage with the levers of the urban system *(Fig 12.8)*. In this case, 'development planning' might achieve 15% reduction in climate emissions at the most, through policy to reduce the need to travel. 'Environmental planning' might achieve 25% reduction with infrastructure development, and 'environmental management' could reach 35% by including alternative modes. 'Integrated urban management' might achieve 50% reduction by putting together cultural and lifestyle factors on the demand side, with advanced technology and comprehensive regulation on the supply side *(Chapter 9)*.[64]

## Development planning

Land-use and development planning is a key point of reference in sustainable development – land is effectively the ultimate 'finite' resource on which all else depends. While much store is placed on development planning to 'achieve' or 'deliver' sustainability, as if this was a fixed product, there are obvious constraints:[65]

- planning has little power to counter wider trends – 'reducing the need to travel', for instance, might increase the desire to travel;

- planning is a political medium for vested interests, and tends by default to marginalize others – even the current 'urban renaissance' can be seen as a conspiracy by the rural affluent against the urban masses;[66]

- planning, as a non-spending function whose main power is that of veto, depends on the resources of others beyond its control;

- planning only controls direct physical change, with little influence on subliminal trends or pressures – for all its policies on reducing travel, traffic continues to grow.

In the 1980s planning became more concerned with 'regeneration' than 'redevelopment'. Various approaches emerged in the changing balance of public and private sectors – a 'responsive' mode with a broadening of technical inputs, and a 'partnership' style with a broadening of investment sources.[67] Each of these types and modes can be seen in GM, and the spatial dynamics in each settlement type is some guidance to the appropriate mode of planning *(Chapter 3)*.

There has always been tension between spatial planning and economic development – the emerging EU agenda aims to bridge the gap, and the future case may be that of 'no plan – no funding'.[68] Both EU and UK funding regimes are likely to be more regionally based than national or local, which requires a greater coordination between unitary authorities than seen so far. There are great expectations of the new framework for 'regional planning guidance' (RPG), but the reality is already falling short.[69]

Development planning also faces hard decisions for scarce resources, which are not often covered by official 'guidance'.[70] The pressures on both housing and transport, for instance, are extending the role of planning from the supply side to the demand side. And the concepts of housing and transport are being shifted from market goods which can be freely traded, to wel-

63 Healey 1995
64 CO$_2$ emissions reductions est. from BAU scenario 1990 / 2020. Based on ECOTEC 1993, Owens & Cope 1994
65 Owens & Cope 1992

66 Lock 1999
67 Brindley, Rydin & Stoker 1996
68 Morphet 1997
69 DETR 1998 (PPG 12)
70 DETR 1998: 'Sustainable Urban Development'

Fig 12.8 **PLANNING for SUSTAINABLE DEVELOPMENT**

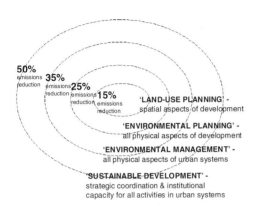

**50%**
emissions
reduction
**35%**
emissions
reduction
**25%**
emissions
reduction
**15%**
emissions
reduction

'LAND-USE PLANNING' - spatial aspects of development

'ENVIRONMENTAL PLANNING' - all physical aspects of development

'ENVIRONMENTAL MANAGEMENT' - all physical aspects of urban systems

'SUSTAINABLE DEVELOPMENT' - strategic coordination & institutional capacity for all activities in urban systems

Shows alternative paradigms for integrated planning: with estimates for possible transport emissions reduction from BAU scenario to 2020. Sources: Owens 1994, Hughes 1994, ECOTEC 1993.

fare goods to be 'managed and monitored' if not rationed. The results are often contradictory – one practical dilemma is that of highways and parking, where conventional good practice is being turned upside down by policies to reduce the need to travel. Another is that of density, where the pressure for brownfield development conflicts with enshrined wisdom on space between dwellings.[71] For these and many others there are policy gaps which can only be resolved in the wider context of integrated urban management.

## Environmental planning & management

'Environmental planning' is the logical extension of the planning system to the spatial aspects of environmental systems. 'Environmental management' at the city-region level then takes on the coordination of the entire physical and environmental metabolism of the urban system.[72] Current techniques link causes and effects at various levels, from the 'project' to the 'city-region' and its global context *(Chapters 1 and 8)*. Alternative assessment methods can operate 'outwards' from projects to their context, or 'inwards' from

local or global capacity limits to the project *(Fig 12.9)*.[73]

A city-region level of environmental management aims to use each of these techniques and link them to strategic management of the urban system – in other words, a pro-active environment strategy. A 'weak' version might be seen in current policy appraisals, EMAS and similar auditing schemes. A 'strong' version would seek positive links between individual policies and programmes, and integrated development scenarios for the city-region and all its components. In practice again there are many gaps in methods and techniques:

- gaps between 'specifics' (products, firms or impacts), and 'systems' (spatial or functional);
- gaps between the environmental 'goals' and the 'means' in business and policy performance;
- gaps between end-of-pipe abatement and complete redesign with clean technology.

In each case there is an information problem, where huge amounts of data are needed – and an uncertainty problem, where for many urban and ecological systems no amount of data would ever be enough for accurate prediction of ends and means. There is also a 'values' problem, where different communities have perceptions, goals and worldviews which are different and often incommensurable, so that the goal of the 'greatest good' is unattainable by definition.[74] Such problems suggest that environmental planning works more effectively as an 'adaptive' process with many stages of technical and social understanding.[75]

## Integrated urban management

Such problems can be approached via the concept of 'integrated assessment', which aims to combine environmental, economic, social and cultural dimensions with spatial development.[76] Integrated assessment is a newly emerging field, where established systems modelling has dis-

71 Breheny 1997:
72 Lusser 1994: Buckingham-Hatfield 1996

73 Ravetz 2000
74 Arrow 1956
75 Holling 1986
a76 Bailey 1997

covered that different cultural perspectives per-
ceive and manage reality in very different ways.[77]
One method uses 'sustainable development
records' which track the ratios between social,
economic and environmental 'efficiency', 'efficacy' and 'effectiveness'.[78] The ISCAM method
in this report is another approach which aims to
link simple and complex forms of knowledge
through generates system mapping and scenario
accounts *(Chapter 1).*[79] The Best Value management framework for local authorities in the
UK aims at an integrated assessment of the links
between inputs, outputs and outcomes, although
there will be problems fitting any bureaucratic
scheme with the over-arching goals of
sustainability *(Chapter 15).*[80] In general the
wider the field of view, the more value-judge-
ments are built into the assessment.[81]

On the technical side, ICT is a key to understanding complex systems, and a new generation of computer models attempt to simulate the
more subtle aspects of urban systems.[82] The
value context of such models can then be explored by a holistic planning process with civic
'deliberation' and discourse.[83] Local Agenda 21
is one kind of forum, and there are many other
new techniques such as vision building, scenario
workshops, focus group explorations and others *(Chapter 14).*[84] Such deliberative findings
can then be linked back to technical models,
plans and policy debates, in a two-way learning
and consensus-building process of 'collaborative planning'.[85] For problems with high uncertainty, high risk and high controversy,
'environmental planners' will be ethically aware
and reflexive agents rather than supposedly neutral advisors –the post-modern or 'post-normal'
scientist.[86]

Such planners will not only produce plans
and policies, but they will be enablers and
facilitators of new forms of economic and community development, networking and awareness-
raising *(Box 12.5).* In GM, an innovative

**Fig 12.9**   *ENVIRONMENTAL PLANNING*

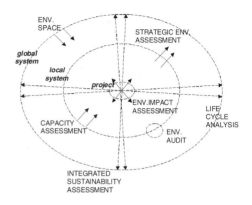

General scope and method of alternative techniques in environmental
assessment, management and life-cycle analysis.

'Sustainability Atlas' project and website combines an interactive 'Sim-Region' model for generating future scenarios, a GIS visualization
module which allows real-time animation of current conditions and trends, and a multi-media
databank of images, people and other links.[87]

All this adds up to a challenging agenda for
integrated planning, for which this report aims
to show an example. Integrated planning for sustainable development applies exactly that principle – integration – in each dimension of the
city-region system:

- horizontal or sectoral integration: coordinate
  land-use and spatial development with sectors such as housing, education or transport;
- environmental integration: coordinate policies and programmes within an integrated
  city-region environment framework;
- vertical integration: coordinate EU, national,
  regional, local and neighbourhood level policies and programmes;

77 Ravetz 1998a
78 Nilsson & Bergstrom 1995
79 Ravetz 2000
80 CAG Consultants 1998
81 Tillman 1997
82 Batty 1995: Ravetz 1998a
83 Hajer 1995
84 Street 1997
85 Healey 1996
86 Funtowicz O'Connor & Ravetz 1994

87 Ravetz 2000b

- policy integration: coordinate policies and programmes with environmental, economic, social and technology impact assessment;
- supply-demand integration: coordinate supply-side and demand-side policies and programmes in each sector;
- time integration: consider long term dynamic trends, pressures, goals and targets, with a strategic horizon of at least 25 years.

Such a tangle of linkages is the natural result of applying sustainability principles, which tend to extend areas of responsibility in all directions.[87] And operating such a process involves much more than the conventional 'survey-analysis-plan' approach – it is likely to need further layers of integration in human resources, technical expertise and institutional capacity:

- technical integration: using ICT with GIS, systems modelling, and interactive decision support tools to support the above;
- political integration, for participation from many interests and communities, with democratic and collaborative mediation;

- resource integration: coordinate with funding resources, programmes and projects to fulfil planning objectives;
- institutional integration: establish partnerships and agencies with capacity for implementation;
- communications and network integration: action-centred networks with learning management style, rather than monolithic organizations.[88]

---

**Box 12.5**  **COMMUNITY I.T. PLANNING**

In the Edinburgh area of Craigmillar a community 'intranet' information service has been set up to link local businesses, the local authority, community groups and residents. With internet facilities, training and support, it provides bulletin boards, local trading schemes, support for local education and health, targetted training, and access to jobs, opportunities and available resources in the city.

Source: Carley & Kirk 1999

---

# REGENERATION STRATEGY

All this takes place in the context of seemingly intractable problems – cities are structured by competition and conflict, their regeneration is a messy and uncertain process, vulnerable to the swings of the global economy, and the result will be a future urban order which has yet to be imagined. It is no wonder that regeneration activity can be failed on many counts.[89] And now that the focus of regeneration and planning is shifting from 'hard' outputs such as property and land, to 'soft' factors such as image and creativity, questions of accountability, legitimacy and value for money are even harder to answer.

Regeneration activity, as most public services, contains two kinds of parallel goals – 'effi-ciency' or competitiveness, and 'equity' or social welfare. Each is a counterpart to the other, but each leads towards different styles and outcomes:[90]

- invest in success – or targeting failure;
- focus on opportunities – or on problems;
- investment in places – or in people;
- market mechanisms – or policy and regulation.

Such multiple agendas can be seen in several layers of parallel policy approaches, and this is a useful mapping for the different roles to be played by different agencies at different levels (*Fig*

87 TCPA (Reinventing Planning)
88 Carley & Christie 1996
89 Healey & Davoudi 1995

90 Solesbury 1990

*12.10*).[91] Technology growth poles, for instance, are likely to require regional partnerships: housing improvements might be led by district-based public agencies; and youth training schemes may run better with locally-managed neighbourhood agencies.

At the same time there is a pressing need for coordination and integration – the aim of the newly formed Regional Development Agencies (RDAs), the regeneration 'one-stop-shops'.[92] The North West RDA (NWDA) is a powerful body, spending about £90 million per year in GM, about 1% of the total public sector expenditure and 10% of capital investment; but for the next few years the great majority of this is locked up in existing commitments. And as yet there are many unresolved questions – the relation of the RDAs to local and regional government, their linkage to the planning process, their environmental and social responsibilities, and their relation to other spending departments of government *(Chapter 14)*. One of the biggest opportunities missed is an integrated regional strategy or vision framework – as yet there is continuing fragmentation between the RDA's Regional Economic Strategy, the RPG for spatial development, the Environment Strategy, the Action for Sustainability reports and others.[93]

The multiplicity of themes in 'sustainable regeneration' highlights some key points for the scope and structure of the RDA's. Their first remit is that of sites and premises, an important function in itself. Beyond that, the RDA's have the potential, and the responsibility, to be a vital catalyst for the city-region sustainable development framework, through a set of coordinating functions which echo the 'integrated planning' principles above:[94]

- political coordination with existing institutions, partnerships and networks;
- physical coordination with local regeneration of housing, land, services and infrastructure;
- economic coordination of investment with business development and labour skills;
- policy coordination, from regional and district to local and neighbourhood level.

**Fig 12.10   REGENERATION STRATEGIES**

Outline of dual strategy approach at several levels of regeneration activity
Source: based on Breheny & Hall 1988.

- all regeneration activities managed within the city-region sustainable development framework *(Chapter 14)*.

## Regeneration funding

The million-dollar question is, of course, the money – the source and management of regeneration funding – and as direct public investment is unlikely to increase greatly, other means have to be found. The context for this is the city-region sustainable development framework itself, which includes for new patterns of economic flows and linkages *(Chapter 13)*. The economics of regeneration have up to now centred on private sector leverage, but this has proved over-vulnerable to national fluctuations and regional hierarchies in the property market. In the wider picture there are several kinds of fiscally-neutral 'redistribution' of financial flows, some of which are on the current agenda:

- public-private redistribution;
- national-local redistribution;
- 'defensive' to 'forward' redistribution;
- risk redistribution via public-private partnerships and equity schemes.

91 Breheny & Hall 1988
92 DETR 1997 ('RDA's: Partnerships for Prosperity')
93 TCPA 1997: (Regional Development Agencies)
94 Gibbs 1997: Sustainability NW 1999

Fig 12.11     **GREEN ACTION ZONES**

**Institutional framework**
development partnership to
coordinate public equity,
collateral, planning consents,
remediation and infrastructure

**Financial framework:**
for coordination of equity, capital,
loan finance, leasing, subsidies,
pre-lets, rental structure, revenue
costs from all parties

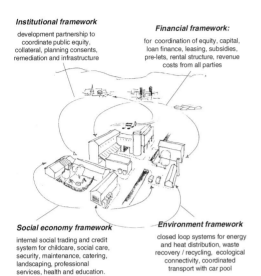

**Social economy framework**
internal social trading and credit
system for childcare, social care,
security, maintenance, catering,
landscaping, professional
services, health and education.

**Environment framework**
closed loop systems for energy
and heat distribution, waste
recovery / recycling, ecological
connectivity, coordinated
transport with car pool

Outline of integrated neighbourhood framework for environmental and socially
sustainable regeneration.

The menu of immediate possibilities for funding physical inner city regeneration in the UK was considered in depth by the Urban Task Force, and it is worth reviewing their conclusions:[95]

- Urban Priority Areas which encourage partnership investment companies to assemble land, attract investment and coordinate development, as well as the actions below:[96]
- harmonization of VAT between new-build and conversion work – the most obvious and urgent item;
- new institutional vehicles for attracting investment into the private rented sector;
- impact fee system for new development, to rationalize the fuzzy and uncertain system of planning gain;
- local authority measures include cancellation of housing debt to encourage stock transfers, retention of business rates and council tax, and further encouragement of PFI schemes;
- private tax incentives and exemptions including stamp duty, council tax banding, business rating, with grants, loans, equity stakes

and tax relief to encourage home improvements – in effect, paying the middle classes to re-colonize the inner city;
- possibilities which are difficult and contentious, for further research and debate: tax on possession of vacant brownfield sites, and tax on greenfield development.

However, the Task Force was set tight boundaries and a physical inner city focus. For the city-region agenda we should look beyond the inner city, beyond the physical side of regeneration, beyond current political constraints, and beyond the margins of the urban regeneration game. The result is a more far-reaching menu of possibilities for consideration:

- redistribution of mainstream fiscal flows such as housing benefit should aim at pump-priming or guarantee funding, with a restructuring of national rent control and benefit systems.[97]
- restructuring of mortgage finance systems might see more portability and flexibility of house lending, geared to the mobile professionals suited to inner city colonization;
- redistribution of local government finance allocations would see greater redistribution between wealthy shire counties and poor urban districts;
- regulation of the finance and banking sector would aim at positive criteria for community re-investment, so that savings accruing in urban areas not only were retained but were enhanced with flows from elsewhere, underwritten by long term public securities.[98]

Shifting from defensive to forward expenditure is a general theme for utilities and public services – for instance, a city-wide energy efficiency programme could be self-financing where coordinated by an energy agency with partnership finance packages (*Chapter 9*). Employment, health and crime prevention each have a similar agenda, where preventative measures and interdepartmental coordination are the keys to more effective spending. This also points towards the role of the social economy in catalysing indig-

enous human resources, which can match financial input both on paper and in practice *(Chapter 10)*.

# Green action zones

There is a perennial debate for and against the
'area' focus of regeneration – the current UK
'action zone' approach in health, education and
employment aims partly to tackle the worst conditions, partly to try out new solutions. What if
the same concept was applied to urban
sustainability? A 'Green Zone' would define an
area where normal controls and financial flows
are deliberately adjusted to encourage integrated
sustainable development.[99] While the Greenwich
'Millennium Village' and similar schemes are aiming in this direction, a Green Zone regeneration
programme would aim at wider application to existing neighbourhoods. Their particular objective would be to set up mechanisms for
environmental best practice which were transferable to other areas *(Fig 12.12)*.[100]

The starting point for a Green Zone is its
engineering services, the utilities of energy, water, waste, transport and communications – each
of which can gain added value from integrated
neighbourhood-level infrastructure. Zero emission buildings would complement CHP distribution, with similar networks for water filtering and
recycling, waste collection and sorting, transport and ICT services. Normal building regulations and planning controls would be adjusted
to encourage integrated environmental design;
special housing tenures would encourage co-
ownership and collective management; ecological goods and services would integrate the
domestic with the local economy.

The key would be the finance and regulatory framework – special incentives for utilities
to offer 'negawatts', water efficiency and others
would be set up, and the total financial package
would be geared to life-cycle cost/benefit rather
than normal short-term returns. The marginal
extra cost of zero-emission and zero-waste performance would be funded through the added
value from site assembly and appreciation – another form of financial recirculation.

The Green Zone concept is in many ways a
model version of the case for the city-region, so
it is worth reviewing its key 'frameworks':

- 'environmental framework': this coordinates
  and integrates utilities and material flows on
  both supply and demand sides, for added
  value and efficiency;
- 'services framework': coordinates supply and
  demand between residents and businesses
  of on-site services such as childcare, cleaning, landscape, maintenance or security, with
  an internal trading system;
- 'financial framework': this generates upfront
  funds from several sources to re-invest in
  long term added value and efficiency in use,
  with the end result being enhanced profit-
  ability.
- 'development framework': coordinates the
  institutional partnerships between investors,
  owners, policy-makers, developers, users and
  others, in order to promote a viable, effective
  and transferable development process.

Finally, the process of development is as important as the product – so rather than a fixed blueprint for an entire neighbourhood, a more organic
approach would aim to harness the resources of
local businesses, residents and owners in a continuing programme. With the current generation
of pilot 'zones' in the UK, it is clear that the time
has come for an urban Green Zone programme.

---

**Box 12.6**

### SUMMARY ~ REGENERATION

The 2020 regeneration strategy aims at a continuous healing of the 'urban metabolism' itself, rather
than a short term fix. It puts together the physical,
economic and social restructuring, re-engineering
and re-invention of the city-region:

- physical restructuring, continuous and city-
  wide, for strategic environmental targets
- economic and employment diversification to
  balance the risks of globalization
- social empowerment through community action and the third sector economy
- urban and environmental integrated planning
  and assessment with new communication
  methods, via the city-region 'sustainable development framework'.

---

99 Ravetz 1991
100 Rudlin & Dodds 1998

# FUNDING the CITY-REGION

*'If you can actually count your money you are not really a rich man'*
Jean Paul Getty

Our modern economy contains many paradoxes. We know that our energy use is disrupting the global climate irreversibly and unpredictably – yet energy is too 'cheap' to be worth saving. We saw in the last chapter how the life is being sucked out of large parts of the city – yet the UK, one of the richest countries in the world, cannot 'afford' to do more than tinker at the edges. The economic order which allocates resources is full of such gaps and failures.

For sustainable development to tackle the physical city it also has to tackle its economic metabolism. The necessary re-engineering and restructuring will depend on large investments, and will produce large returns. Such returns are direct and financial, in avoided costs and lost oppportunities, and in quality of life. Calculating the balance is complex and uncertain, but it starts with two very practical questions:

- what are the costs and the benefits?
- who puts up the money, and who gets the return?

Answers to such simple questions could fill many libraries, and here we can only provide some pointers. So far in this book, the Introduction sketches some outlines for a sustainable economy: 'Economy and Work' looks at the greening of production and consumption *(Chapter 10):* and 'Regeneration' looks at redistribution to balance uneven development *(Chapter 12)*. Now we need a wider picture of 'values', with a practical picture of funding and investment.

So this chapter is a non-specialist review of the 'total economy' of the city-region, and a practical investment case for its sustainable development. We review the scope of environmental economics and market measures, and how they might apply at the city-region level. Then we look at the outline cost-benefit balances and possible market actions for each key sector. Finally we point towards the general prospects for market transformation, to achieve social and environmental goals.

In general we aim at possibilities beyond the 'good idea' stage of environmental policy. We flag up for further research some viable investment opportunities and economic mechanisms to encourage sustainable development at the city-region scale.[1]

# Economy & ecology

Almost all economic activity generates 'market failures' or 'externalities' – financial and other costs born by other sectors and the public, local or global environments, or future generations. Such externalities include both social costs, such as the costs of traffic accidents, and ecological costs, such as destruction of wildlife. Sustainable development in a market economy needs to 'internalize' these externalities, to bring such costs into mainstream market activity as far as possible. In principle this internalization should bring economic, social and environmental benefits – the so-called double dividend – but in practice there are many questions.

Every investment appraisal, for instance, has to assume a discount or interest rate – but higher rates devalue costs and benefits to future generations, while lower rates reduce the present benefits. This is one of many dilemmas underlying 'valuation' methods, which try to define money equivalents for environmental assets through hypothetical 'shadow' markets. Such shadow values often seem to depend on the way the question is put, whether pricing 'free goods' through surveys of 'willingness-to-pay' for an asset, 'willingness-to-accept' its loss, dose-response linkages, or other economic multipliers.[2]

There is also a fundamental question on 'growth' versus 'development'. Current economic methods tend to assume material consumption as equivalent to increasing human welfare – but continuous material growth will sooner or later conflict with environmental limits. In contrast ecological or 'new' economics aims at an alternative view based on non-material welfare within ecological limits which cannot necessarily be traded or substituted. The entire global environment has now been 'valued' at about £30 trillion – while this sounds impressive, it is equivalent to only two years' GNP or 1 month's international capital flows, and in reality the global environment cannot be traded for any amount of money or human activity.[3]

The many types and layers of costs, from internal to external, can be seen in a range – at one end are direct, present-day, tangible costs,

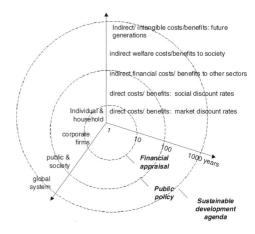

Fig 13.1 **EXTERNAL COSTS & SUSTAINABLE DEVELOPMENT**

Scope of external costs, cost-benefit appraisal, investment & returns.
Source: adapted from Lichfield & Lichfield 1998

calculated at market discount rates, such as the cost of energy to consumers. At the other end are those which are indirect, long term, uncertain, irreversible and often intangible, such as the impacts of climate change on lost species for future generations. Such cost levels are linked to different time horizons, from the individual or firm with perhaps a 1–10 year horizon, to a global society with a much longer view *(Fig 13.1)*.

Such external or indirect costs then affect human activity and economic systems through the effects of damage, adaptation or prevention. Each of these generates a particular approach:

- damage costs, or direct financial impacts on producers or consumers: for example damage to buildings by pollution or climate change;
- adaptation or defensive costs: such as the cost of air filters or sea defences;
- investment or prevention costs: investment in infrastructure or technology to minimize future damage, such as renewable energy or public transport.

In practice it is often unclear whether a particular action is a defence or an investment. A process or an industry may require a mixed package of

2 Bowers 1995
3 Constanza et al1997

**Fig 13.2** *ECONOMIC VALUE METABOLISM*

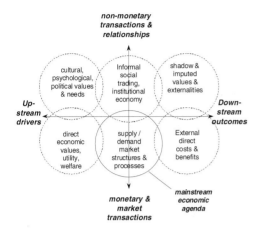

Integrated assessment system mapping of total metabolism of ecological-social-economic 'values'. Dotted lines show where quantified economic relationships may be appropriate to a degree.
Source: Ravetz 2000b.

end-of-pipe abatement and clean technology, where one is a cost and the other an investment – accounting systems, whether standard and green, have problems in placing these on the balance sheet.[4] Such ambiguity is integral to complex ecological-economic systems.

## Value metabolism

For a wider picture we can draw again on the 'total metabolism' theme and the systems mapping approach *(Chapter 1)*. This helps to chart out a 'value metabolism', which underlies and links many more visible kinds of economic activity *(Fig 13.2)*. Conventional economics is focused on resources and activities traded in markets, through a universal medium of exchange, or money. Upstream of the supply-demand balance is the fuzzy area of human 'needs' and how these can be manifest in economic 'welfare' or 'utility'. Downstream of this are the environmental or social externalities which can be directly costed or otherwise brought to market interactions.

On the other side of the equation are those values, assets, resources which are non-monetary, and for which market conditions apply very

tenuously, if at all. Cultural, political, psychological 'needs' have their own internal logic: informal, social or institutional trading are embedded likewise in cultures and politics: and downstream there are other kinds of externalities which are far removed from any kind of market – such as the imputed value of the global environment as above.

Why do we bring this up? Because the very concept of sustainability points beyond the assumptions of market-based economics – human needs, ecological values, social cohesion and so on. The implication is that cost-benefit evaluation of sustainability policy is very sensitive to the assumptions made, in other words on the institutional, cultural or social context. For example, the GM energy-climate strategy aims to upgrade every building to best practice standards, but a conventional financial appraisal would show a 10–15 year payback, making it hardly viable *(Chapter 9*. But if we could assume coordination with building maintenance, incentive systems, nega-watt tariff structures, long term equity finance packages, and a culture where people want to save energy, the economic case suddenly looks very positive. This suggests that there are 'competing rationalities' at work, in other words different ways to frame the economic equations; and that markets and institutions can and should be designed around social and environmental goals, as below.[5]

A further point on the ecological economics axis is that markets are more akin to biological eco-systems than generally thought.[6] Conventional economic theory makes a whole raft of assumptions, such as perfect information, rational consumers, 'sovereign' or autonomous firms, market equilibrium – in other words a society which is selfish and lonely. As a result much of the theory has difficulty even with core economic questions such as inflation or the business cycle. If, on the other hand, a market or an economy is seen as a self-organizing 'system' of firms and consumers who interact and learn from each other, it can be understood in quite a different way, and apparently chaotic patterns start to make sense. Such a systems perspective has so far been applied to the macro level, but the 'total

4 Schaltegger 1996

5 Ravetz 1999c
6 Ormerod 1998: Clark, Allen & Perez 1997

value metabolism' picture above suggests strongly that every level of an economy, both monetary and non-monetary, can be looked at in this way.[7] Local trading systems, for instance, are not simply material exchanges to maximize utility, but an institutional pattern which depends on certain kinds of social and cultural cohesion.[8]

## Markets & eco-taxation

As many environmental problems seem to be a result of market failure, their solutions might also lie in market adjustment. The economics of pollution tends to assume simple cause-effect linkages, but in practice the causal chains between processes, products, sources, emissions, impacts, damage and economic costs are usually complex and uncertain. Assuming that the external costs of market failures or 'inefficiencies' can be defined, the economic goal is then the 'efficient' or optimal level of subsidies or levies.[9] In theory this can be estimated by the costs of damage and restitution, by the 'shadow' costs above, or by least-cost planning to meet targets defined by other means.[10] In practice very little is simple, and common problems such as the valuation of climate change show that the answer is totally dependent on the highly debatable assumptions made.[11]

That being said, while valuation-based market mechanisms are very imperfect, other options are also. Again, the many alternative types of market measures can be seen in context with another version of the total metabolism systems mapping. This shows different kinds of external costs in the causal chain from demand to supply, different points of application for charges and levies, and different points of application for the recycling of revenues *(Fig 13.3)*. Practical market measures include:[12]

- emissions or volume charges: used in many countries, in the UK with landfill tax and shortly with business energy;
- tradeable permits: extensive use in USA for sulphur and organic air emissions, now discussed for carbon emissions;

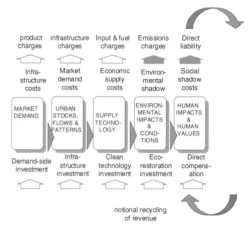

**Fig 13.3  EXTERNAL COSTS & MARKET MEASURES**

Market instruments for internalization of external costs, through revenue recycling: integrated assessment mapping.

- infrastructure charges, such as roads or open space – such resources are often 'indivisible' and 'non-excludable', and charging can be difficult;
- product charges: direct impact on industrial competitiveness and consumer prices;
- deposit-refund schemes: application to packaging, with possible extension to others;
- legal liability and compensation: application to land contamination and other specific effects, but complex and costly to negotiate.

Each of these alternative options has pros and cons, to which the general criteria for taxation design would apply – clear benefits to the environment, minimal administration costs, signals and incentives for improvement, gradually tapered effects, least disruption to business, and 'fairness' in distribution.[13] But the quality of 'fairness' is not a simple question – the division between public services and market goods is a social and political issue. Any policy generally has secondary effects – road pricing, for instance, can easily displace traffic into adjacent areas, or benefit affluent drivers to the detriment of lower-income people.[14] Such

7 Strathern 1992
8 Offe & Heinze 1994
9 Pigou 1926
10 Turner & Pearce 1991
11 Global Commons Institute 1997

12 DoE 1993 (Making markets work)
13 OECD 1989
14 Webster Bly & Paulley 1989

questions show how ecological and welfare economics are each inter-linked with social or ethical judgements.

Ecological tax reform (ETR) aims to combine various one-off market measures into coordinated fiscal packages serving multiple goals.[15] In general these aim to shift the burden of taxation from the 'goods' of labour to the 'bads' of pollution and resource depletion. Many ETR packages are based on 'revenue neutrality', where total public income is unaffected – such as taking environmental revenues to reduce employers' national insurance rates. Environmental benefits or 'dividends' may then be combined with employment dividends, to correct inefficiencies and distortions in the wider economy.[16]

Hypothecation or 'earmarking' of tax revenues for specific expenditure is a thorny question – where the traditional view is against hypothecation on financial and political grounds.[17] But there is also a case for hypothecation or 'presentation' in order to gain public acceptance with at least the impression that the money is returned.[18] In practice there is a large grey area between general 'taxes', one-off 'levies', and specific 'charges' for services: and many of the economic measures discussed below are in this grey area. A range of ETR systems have been established in most northern EU countries, some of them combining emissions charges with product charges *(Box 13.1)*.

Following the 1999 budget, the UK at present has a basic ETR package which includes:

- Road fuel duty, escalating at 6% per year;
- Differentials on vehicle licensing duty;
- Business energy tax (forthcoming);
- Landfill waste disposal tax;
- Possible primary minerals tax (proposed);

Several 'revenue neutral' models of the UK economy reach similar conclusions: that half a million jobs could be generated in 10 years, either by a road fuel duty escalator of 10% per year, or a general carbon tax of £12 per barrel of oil equivalent, with the revenues used to offset employers' National Insurance contributions.[19]

For GM this would equate to about 25,000 jobs, mostly in full-time male occupations *(Chapter 10)*. However, the estimated job potential – about 2–3% of the economy – is at a similar level to the uncertainties in the economic model, and the swings of the business cycle.

## Local & regional markets

Most market measures are designed and applied at the national level, with increasing influence from Europe – the few fiscal powers of local government are tightly limited, at least in the UK, and regional agencies as yet have none. Some of the most powerful city-region bodies are the social or monopoly providers of health, housing, or utilities, and each of these exists in a complex balance of regulation and market autonomy. But the application of national eco-tax market measures is often most practical at the local level – parking charges, road pricing or business rates.[20] A spectrum from national to local shows the range of economic measures which could be relevant at the city-region level:

- national economic measures or taxes with clear local effects, such as the ETR package above;
- national measures which are administered locally, such as business rates;
- local taxes, precepts, or levies, applied around the UK, such as car parking fines;
- local taxes, levies, charges or differentials, which can be controlled and managed locally, with revenues recycled locally.

---

**Box 13.1**

### *ECO-TAXATION in EUROPE*

Sweden has been developing an advanced ETR package for the last decade. Fiscal levies or permit trading systems include fossil fuels, new cars, aviation fuels, fertilizers and pesticides, batteries, and direct emissions of NO and SO . While there is a long way to go, such taxes have encouraged take-up of cleaner technologies, and the revenues have been used to reduce income taxes.

Source Gee 1997

---

15 O'Riordan 1997
16 Ekins 1997
17 Spackman 1997
18 Mulgan 1997

19 Barker 1997: IPPR 1996: ESI 1994
20 Templett & Glenn 1992

There is also a scale of possibilities for intervention – direct tax or subsidy; indirect differentials or trading schemes; and indirect influence through market regulation and adjustment. A coordinated package would include several levels. An integrated energy efficiency programme, for instance, might combine national direct energy taxes, regional differential rating bands, regional consumption tariffs, regional infrastructure investment, local improvement subsidies, and local supply-chain schemes for accredited businesses. Such a package should aim towards a strategic 'market transformation' as below, rather than simply raising funds at one point in the chain.

The question of which measure works at which level, and who gets the money, is naturally controversial. Many sustainable development strategies imply that local authorities should extend their fiscal powers to more pro-active tax-raising, subsidies, and forward investment. In practice this on a wider scale would impact on many industries, as well as the national public debt and trade balance. There is also a fine line between local levies under existing powers, and 'artificial' trade barriers, which could conflict with European harmonization and the worldwide trend towards deregulation and liberalization. It is not easy to talk about local eco-tax without questioning global capitalism.

The principle of subsidiarity suggests that that as much freedom as possible is devolved to regional or local authorities, within certain defined limits. Such limits might be defined as a 'sustainability allowance' – another component in the complex calculation of the UK local government settlement. Beyond the local level, this theme could be pursued by the English regional assemblies, which in due course may demand increased tax and spend powers. The NWDA is now discussing with the UK Government the possibility of varying taxation rules and labour charges in order to encourage regional job creation. This and similar ideas would begin steer the entire public sector economy towards a more federated structure, with far-reaching implications.[21]

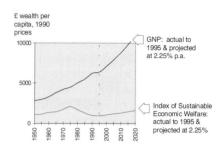

Fig 13.4    ***INDEX OF SUSTAINABLE ECONOMIC WELFARE***

Chart of 'sustainable economic welfare' with projection to 2020, data for UK as at 1990:
Source: Jackson & Marks 1994, New Economics Foundation 1996; Hanley & Moffat 1999.

## Total economic welfare

Part of the success of market capitalism comes from its efficiency in providing signals to producers and consumers, through the medium of money. But clearly for many kinds of private needs and public goods, such signals can be incomplete or misleading.

An alternative approach starts with human needs, and how they may or may not be satisfied by economic goods.[22] Many public assets, for instance, are 'indivisible' and only work as wholes, such as an airport runway, while others are 'non-excludable', such as public space – and for these the distribution of costs and benefits is a political question. Economic systems can be seen not only as trading activity between producers and consumers, but as patterns of social and institutional power and dependency.[23] Moving beyond a narrow economic appraisal needs a wider view – taking account of the multiple linkages between markets and society at every level, and explored through a process of open and deliberative debate.[24]

Meanwhile it is clear that conventional traditional economic indicators, such as GDP, fail to measure the true wealth of environmental resources, social welfare and quality of life – traffic accidents increase GDP, while road safety

21 Gudgin 1996

22 Max-Neef 1994
23 Daly & Goodland 1994
24 Jacobs 1994

Fig 13.5    **TOTAL ECONOMIC WELFARE**

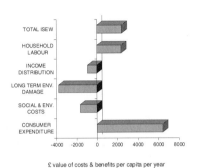

£ value of costs & benefits per capita per year

Analysis of 'sustainable economic welfare calculation: data for UK as at 1990: Source Jackson & Marks 1994, New Economics Foundation 1996.

decreases it. Taking account of such plusses and minuses produces something like an 'index of sustainable economic welfare' (ISEW).[25] The widening gap between GDP and ISEW over the recent decades is a result of rising affluence bought at the cost of environmental damage and social inequality *(Fig 13.4)*. The breakdown of the ISEW is also revealing – net economic welfare after pollution, defensive measures and social inequality, is roughly equal to the value of unpaid domestic labour *(Fig13.5)*.

Other accounting methods look directly at the ecological resources, capacities, energy throughput, or expropriations, each with pros and cons. A recent survey compared the progress over time of six variations on the ISEW indicators for Scotland, and found little agreement between them.[26] But such methods can be useful where suited to the purpose. For a firm or organization, such integrated accounting can be shown with a 'triple bottom line' – a balance and profit / loss account for financial, social and environmental stocks and flows.[27] Every project or programme should contain some form of integrated assessment, both in money values and with ecological accounting. Alternative methods such as 'environmental capital' look at natural assets in terms of functions and possible substitutions, which bypasses the problems of adding

or monetizing environmental, social and economic values.[28]

The 2020 project looked for ISEW-type methods which were relevant to a city-region – a highly open system with many possible boundaries in time, space and functionality. In such a system, flows are much greater than stocks, and most environmental impacts are indirect; the complexity of economic interactions needs many indicators; and social conditions are relative to the region and nation. One response to this challenge is the above total-economy / value-metabolism approach above, a small slice of which can be expressed in the ISCAM scenario accounts and trend-target indices. This approach shifts the focus from a static single 'index' of ISEW to a dynamic picture where change is compared between alternative scenarios.[29]

# Market transformation

Each of these themes – eco-taxation, economic subsidiarity, and total economy accounting – adds up to a wider view of how markets can serve society, rather than the other way round. The investment case for energy efficiency, as above, depends on the assumptions on market gaps, cultural commitment or political opportunities. To achieve best practice in every building which is called for by the energy-climate strategy, would need all market gaps to be closed, and all market signals and incentives to work in synchrony – adding up to a total 'market transformation'.[30]

The logic of such market transformation comes via the total economy / value metabolism approach, so that the systems qualities of 'integrity' and 'co-existence' are the result of feedback and self-organization in economic flows and patterns *(Chapter 1)*.[31] In practical terms such transformation will only happen where it is commercially and politically viable – and this is likely to depend on several kinds of integration. The proposed city-region energy agency consortium is a good example:

- institutional integration, with consortiums for stakeholding and 'stake-owning', so that

25 Jackson & Marks 1991: NEF 1996
26 Hanley et al 1999
27 Elkington 1997

28 CAG & Land-Use Consultants 1997
29 Ravetz 2000
30 Hawken 1995
31 Ormerod 1998

market gaps and split responsibilities can be integrated between investors, providers, developers, purchasers and consumers;[32]

- supply-demand integration: so that total least-cost planning and investment can coordinate supply and DSM with developer and consumer practice;
- fiscal integration, so that utility regulation, tariff structures, levies and subsidies are coordinated with positive incentives for environmental best practice and equitable distribution;
- political integration, so that energy market regulation and capital flow control is geared to social objectives, nationally and locally.

The example of energy efficiency is one of the simpler cases, where there are clear linkages to technology, infrastructure, innovation and the financial regime. Other sectors such as transport are more complex to begin with. In general, market transformation is not a quick fix – it will be as complex and messy as the markets from which it starts, the industries which it influences, and the social goals to which it aims. And as markets are continually changing in any case, it will be a continuous process rather than a final solution.

---

**Box 13.2**

### FUNDING & MARKETS ~ GOALS & STRATEGIES

| | GOV | LAP | BUS | COM | PUB |
|---|---|---|---|---|---|
| **MARKET MEASURES:** Eco-taxation package for all production and consumption with environmental impact, with revenues recycled to re-investment. | ● | ● | ○ | | |
| **LOCALIZED INVESTMENT:** promote new linkages & partnerships for investment & return between public, private, community & consumer sectors. | ● | ○ | ● | ○ | ○ |
| **TOTAL ECONOMIC ACCOUNTING:** integrated financial social & environmental accounting & reporting for private & public sector | ● | ○ | ● | ○ | |
| **MARKET TRANSFORMATION:** market regulation with incentives for new market-based activities with least-cost planning, integrated supply-demand management & environmental best practice | ● | ○ | ● | ○ | ○ |

GOV ~ government & EU: LA ~ local authorities & partnerships: BUS ~ business & finance: COM ~ community/3rd sector: PUB ~ public

---

# MARKET PROFILES

Integrated economic appraisal of sustainable development may be complex and uncertain, and dependent on many questions and assumptions. To provide a grounding it would be useful to have a very rough and simple idea of the relative scale of costs, benefits and returns, implied by the city-region SD framework.

So here we review the prospects for market measures and a wider market transformation in each key sector.

Following the 'value metabolism' logic, external costs are shown for demand-side, infrastructure, supply-side and non-monetary impacts. For the building and transport sectors, monetary estimates combine financial flows with shadow costs, for present day, 'business as usual' (BAU) trends, and a 'sustainable development' (SD) scenario.

We should stress that such costings are for discussion and illustration only, and exclude discounting, displacement, multipliers and re-spending. More detail could be got with input-output or dynamic modelling, but each of these makes many dubious assumptions. External shadow costs are even more questionable, both in their amount and in their significance.[33]

---

32 Leadbeater 1997: Jacobs 1997

33 Bowers 1995

Current estimates for the shadow costs of sulphur emissions, for instance, vary by a factor of ten, and the shadow costs of energy supply vary by a factor of 10,000 – so all the figures here contain huge margins of ambiguity and uncertainty.[34] Likewise the possible market measures are shown strictly for discussion and further research.

## Buildings & energy

Buildings are responsible for over half of the total energy demand and climate emissions in GM, with a direct monetary cost – or energy bill – of over £1 billion per year. For the whole building life-cycle, including construction and maintenance, the table shows many other effects, from external costs of mineral extraction, to the public health costs of toxic materials *(Box13.3)*.

For building energy and construction together, current external costs of energy in buildings could be several times the direct costs *(Box 13.4)*. Total direct/indirect costs remain similar with the BAU scenario, where a rise in demand could be offset by gradual improvement of supply technology, while the SD scenario is based on investment in efficiency, infrastructure and clean technology. In practical terms, an investment programme of about 10% of the energy bill, or about £100 million per year, could over 25 years reduce running costs by over a third, and the external costs by over half; it would also generate up to 15,000 jobs, mostly in areas of high unemployment *(Fig13.6)*.[35]

This very simplified case depends on how far energy upgrading is combined with maintenance and renewal, how far building tenures encourage investment, and whether such a programme would take labour which is otherwise unemployed.[36] At present the market is fragmented by deregulation, complex ownerships and short-term financial horizons. One approach is for life-cycle costing in public finances and commercial accounting – ecological low-energy construction can be over 15% cheaper for landlords than its standard equivalent over a 60-year building life, and its external impact less than a quarter of the average.[37]

Where would such investment come from? As far as possible by market measures which rearrange the huge flows of finance around the property, construction and energy industries. National level revenues could be raised by direct taxation, trading of carbon permits, levies on producers, or tax breaks for energy investment. At the local level there is scope for differential rating by efficiency, planning obligations linked to energy footprint; or direct infrastructure

---

**Box 13.3**

### EXTERNAL COSTS ~ BUILDING

|  | DEMAND SIDE | INFRA-STRUC-TURE | SUPPLY SIDE | ENVIRON-MENT | SOCIAL COSTS |
|---|---|---|---|---|---|
| DAMAGE COSTS | en.costs | Fabric damage waste dereliction | energy minerals toxics | climate acid rain ecology | en.poverty health |
| ADAPT ATION | climate | climate | climate acid | eco-system | Lifestyles |
| INVEST MENT | energy eff. eco-blg healthy blg | CHP | clean tech renewable energy | restoration | |

---

**Box 13.4**

### COSTS & BENEFITS ~ BUILDING

|  | 1995 | BAU 2020 | SD 2020 | notes |
|---|---|---|---|---|
| EXPENDITURE | | | | |
| Domestic energy | 500 | 500 | 300 | excl transport |
| Comm/ind.energy | 600 | 750 | 450 | |
| Const./ maintain | 1300 | 1300 | 1300 | total GDP in const. |
|  | 2400 | 2550 | 2300 | |
| EXTERNAL COSTS | | | | |
| Climate | 900 | 1150 | 400 | see energy notes |
| Air | 1500 | 1200 | 750 | based on energy factor |
| Resource 'rent' | 500 | ?600 | 250 | fossil fuel depletion |
| Ecology | ?500 | ?600 | ?250 | equiv.to rent |
| Materials | ?650 | ?650 | ?325 | equiv.to 50% of GDP |
| Health | 100 | 100 | 25 | energy poverty cost |
|  | ?4250 | ?4300 | ?2025 | |
| INVESTMENT: | | | | |
| Energy eff. | | | 150 | see notes |
| eco-construction | | | 50 | est. on LCA study |
| CHP | | | 50 | notional est. |
| **TOTAL COSTS: direct, external & investment** | **?6650** | **?6850** | **?4400** | |

- from CSERGE 1994,1996, Boardman 1992, March 1987, ONS 1996
- all figures 1995 value, excluding discount, displacement, respending
- italics show national external cost estimates pro-rata for gm.
- ? shows very speculative estimates where little data exists.
- financial data not validated: general error margin of +/- 50%.
- external cost estimates with uncertainty margin of at least x 2

---

34 Stirling 1995
35 Taylor 1993
36 Boardman 1993
37 Whitelegg, Smith & Williams 1998

charges. For building materials, minerals taxation is likely in the near future, and the principle could then be extended to toxic materials and components.

Such revenues could be recycled into direct investment in CHP networks and energy upgrading; into tax breaks for efficiency investment; underwriting of energy services companies; technology and R&D support; or financial guarantees for energy infrastructure. Otherwise the revenues could simply offset employment costs as in the ETR models.

As ever, the distributional effects are highly political – for instance the lowering of VAT on domestic energy brought marginal social benefits, but sends the wrong signals for environmental improvements. More progressive would be a graduated tax, based on property bands or energy audits, which allowed for each household or business a basic energy quota at marginal cost, with increasing tariffs for excess consumption.[38]  This would be coupled with a large scale investment programme for housing and commercial buildings.

## Urban development

For land and development, the relationship between internal activities and external costs is much more complex, and even ball-park estimates are not easily generated.  Generally, counter-urbanization and the road infrastructure generate

Fig 13.7

### COSTS & BENEFITS

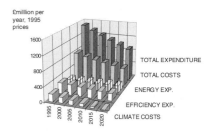

£million per year, 1995 prices

TOTAL EXPENDITURE
TOTAL COSTS
ENERGY EXP.
EFFICIENCY EXP.
CLIMATE COSTS

Expenditure & social / environmental costs of 25 year programme for energy efficiency in buildings in GM, with assumptions and uncertainties as sources.
Source:  adapted from RCEP 1994, Pearce 1996, Boardman 1992.

added value on the urban fringe, while the economic vitality of urban areas declines, leaving derelict sites and infrastructure, and increasing transport demand *(Box 13.5)*.

The policy goals of neighbourhood clustering and re-use of buildings tends to go against the grain of the property market – as renovation, mixed use and brownfield reclamation are perceived to have lower capital values, with higher risks and management costs.[39] Restructuring the property industry is no easy matter, but an integrated package of levies and subsidies is essential to an urban development strategy.  Some of these are now on the agenda of the 'urban renaisssance', and some could be based on the spatial boundaries of the proposed 'urban priority areas' *(Chapter 12)*.[40]

For the development process itself, there is scope for national fiscal measures through every possible route – capital gains tax, stamp duty and VAT on new build versus restoration. At a local or regional level, the possibility of levies on green field development is being discussed, although there are problems of definition.[41]  Other charges could be levied on density standards, with differential rating according to density and mixed use.  For infrastructure charges, possibilities are a standard planning gain levy or differential rating based on commercial parking, site plot ratio, or ecological disturbance.[42]

---

Box13.5

### EXTERNAL COSTS ~ DEVELOPMENT

|  | DEMAND SIDE | INFRAST-RUCTURE | SUPPLY SIDE | ENVIRON-MENTAL | SOCIAL |
|---|---|---|---|---|---|
| **DAM-AGE COSTS** | property values | transport demand vacancy | loss of land local services | transport demand ecology dereliction | amenity community accessibility |
| **ADAPT ATION** | | Restruct-uring | | transport demand ecology | travel demand |
| **INVES TMENT** | public services | Neighbour-hood dev. Public transport | blg renovate | land reclaim | |

---

38 Local Government Association 1998

39 Rydin 1994
40 Urban Task Force 1999
41 KPMG 1999
42 TCPA 1997 'finding the land for 4.4. million homes'

Perhaps as significant as any fiscal measures is the ability of a public agency to assemble land – the RDA, local authorities, the new urban agencies, and others will be falling over themselves to unlock stagnant property markets. Few of the other options are straightforward, in the sense of being equitable, transparent, enforceable and easy to collect, and the previous failures of the 'betterment tax' should be borne in mind.[43]   Possibly the first priority would be reform of the council tax and business rating system, with a return to local control of banding and recyling of revenue.[44]   Following that, transparent and progressive charges could be absorbed over a period, which would include levies on vacancy, parking, road infrastructure, mixed use and density criteria.

As always, the distributional effects are complex and contentious.  Counter-urbanization is justified by the industry as market demand – 'nobody wants to live in the rust-belts'.[45]  But if the externalities of such market activity are seen to be greater than the marginal private benefits, there is a strong case for market intervention – in effect, paying people to move back to the city. At present many financial incentives point the other way – affluent suburbs are often 'free-riders' in terms of urban facilities and welfare provision – so redistribution at a regional level, through rating or infrastructure levies, may be the logical solution.

## Transport

Transport imposes severe costs on local and global environments and human health – at the same time the 'benefits' of transport are clear to consumers and businesses, and totally embedded in lifestyles and economic activity *(Box 13.6)*:

Estimates of the external costs of transport are as always very uncertain, and the UK figures which are supposed to be state of the art have doubled in five years.[46]  The general result is that road users in the UK pay in taxes only a fraction of their total external costs – even while they are angry at receiving in investment only a

fraction of what is paid in taxes.  Such figures are translated to a breakdown for GM, which includes notional estimates for items usually excluded such as the production life-cycle of vehicles and infrastructure, the social costs of community severance, and damage to eco-systems *(Box 13.7)*.  Some rough and ready totals include, pro rata for GM:

- total direct spend:              £2500m
- fuel and excise duty paid:       £800m
- maintenance / investment:        £330m
- total external costs             £5700m
- unpaid / 'free-ride' costs:      £4500m
- unpaid costs per vehicle:        £4300

The effect of very simple investment scenarios can be seen on direct and external costs.  The BAU projection sees some clean technology, while car travel increases by 60% and air travel by 300%, increasing external costs to £12 billion. The SD scenario anticipates shifting a third of car travel to public transport, while air travel growth is halved, with environmental investment at a notional 10% of revenue – direct costs are stable, and total costs reduce by 25%.

The internalization of current external costs could double the aggregate cost of travel – as fuel accounts for about a quarter of the running cost of a private car, its price would need to increase by over eight times, other factors being equal.  Obviously many journeys would not be undertaken if this were the case; such a feedback effect can be estimated with an 'optimal pricing'

Box 13.6

### EXTERNAL COSTS ~ TRANSPORT

|  | DEMAND SIDE | INFRAST-RUCTURE | SUPPLY SIDE | ENVIRON-MENTAL | SOCIAL |
|---|---|---|---|---|---|
| **DAM-AGE COSTS** | travel demand | displacemt. Severance blight, land | operating costs | climate air, water, land,ecology oil industry | Accidents Health Congestion Noise |
| **ADAPT-ATION** | lifestyles congestion | parking minerals | congestion | congestion roadspace | Congestion Disturbance Severance |
| **INVES-TMENT** | car sharing teleworking cycleways greenways | accessibility planning | clean tech. Public transport railfreight | clean tech. public transport | lifestyle & business change |

43 Reade 1987
44 Institute of Public Policy Research 1995
45 House Builders Federation, quoted in Guardian 29/5/97
46 Pearce 1996

approach, where the marginal external cost is set as equivalent to the total tax revenue. Drawing from national estimates, the result could be a reduction in travel demand of perhaps a third, and a tax revenue in the region of £3500 million, as in the SD scenario. This excludes displacement and multiplier effects in the transport industry and national economy.[47]

Direct levies on fuel are at present over 40% of the final cost, and the UK fuel duty 'escalator' increases the rate by 6% per year. However, with falling world oil prices and rising income, the real costs of fuel are static or falling, and a much higher escalator rate may be needed to seriously influence travel demand.[48] Excise duties are now adjusted by size of vehicle, but at present the amounts are small, and differentiated taxes on new vehicles would be more effective. A common standard of vehicle 'eco-labelling' would enable differentiation in many other transactions, such as company cars, travel tax allowances, employer's mileage rates, road lane occupancy and parking charges.

Infrastructure charges on roads or parking are more 'efficient' in the sense of reducing congestion at source, and experiments are underway in some UK cities, including one in Manchester. The 'stick' of road pricing is more likely to work in combination with the 'carrot' of park-and-ride and multi-modal public transport, in cities with well-defined commercial centres. But for a complex conurbation such as GM, charging for urban roads or parking could easily accelerate the drift to peripheral sites, undermining the urban development policies above. Such effects might also be tackled by adjusting the incentives for car ownership, through employers' schemes, car sharing and neighbourhood mobility schemes.

As always, there are distributive questions – while the local costs of transport are large, so are the local benefits, but the two often fall to different groups. Levies on private cars tend to exclude lower-income drivers, and localized actions will tend to displace both problems and opportunities to surrounding areas. The 'win-win' SD scenario assumes that surrounding areas have similar policies, and that public transport can be a viable alternative. However, the city-region transport strategy recognizes that transport *per se* is linked with social inequality and environmental damage, and that any market measures are only partial solutions *(Chapter 6)*.

## Land & ecology

In an urban fringe of marginal agriculture, urban infrastructure, leisure uses and protected habitats, there are few clear patterns on which to base external costs or investment returns *(Chapter 7)*. Likewise in the urban area, most green space and wildlife have little direct function in the marketplace. One approach is to look for indirect shadow costs and benefits through linkages with amenity and property values, as per the breakdown in the table below *(Fig 13.8)*.

Some very approximate sample costs can be shown, not as 'real' prices, but to illustrate an economic approach which might support the land-ecology strategy. For urban green space a property value approach has found that a 10% increase in street trees correlates with a £400 in-

---

**Box 13.7**

### COSTS & BENEFITS ~ TRANSPORT

| | 1995 | BAU | SD | Notes |
|---|---|---|---|---|
| **EXPENDITURE** | | | | |
| cars/lorries | 2000 | 3200 | 1300 | incl fuel & other road transport |
| bus/rail | 250 | 250 | 750 | Incl. Water |
| Air | 300 | 1000 | 500 | incl. total journeys allocated |
| | 2550 | 4450 | 2550 | |
| **EXTERNAL COSTS** | | | | |
| Climate | 500 | 800 | 400 | RCEP: incl. air @ 2 x CO2 effect |
| Air | 1200 | 1200 | 600 | incl. Nox, SOx, PM, VOC & Pb |
| Noise | 200 | 250 | 100 | based on WTP studies |
| Congestion | 1000 | 1600 | 600 | (debatable category) |
| Accidents | 500 | 500 | 250 | based on £2million value of life |
| road damage | 100 | 150 | 50 | Pro rata est. |
| Ecology | ?500 | ?600 | ?400 | equiv. to climate change |
| Community | ?500 | ?700 | ?300 | equiv. 50% congestion cost |
| Production LCA | ?1200 | ?1800 | ?800 | total life-cycle: equiv. to air |
| | ?5700 | ?7600 | ?3500 | |
| **INVESTMENT:** | | | | |
| LRT& rail: | | | 100 | excl domestic/ business |
| buses: | | | 50 | expansion to 10% of urban travel |
| street works | | | 50 | expansion to 30% of urban travel |
| | | | | pedestrianization 8000km streets |
| **TOTAL: direct / external & investment costs** | ?8250 | ?12050 | ?6050 | |

- Estimates mainly based on CSERGE 1996: RCEP 1994
- All figures at 1995 values: excl. discounts, displacement, responding
- *Italic figures show national external cost estimates pro-rata for GM.*
- ? shows very speculative estimates where little data exists.
- Financial data not validated: general error margin of +/- 50%.
- External cost estimates contain margin of uncertainty of at least x2

---

47 Tindale & Holtman 1996
48 HMG 1997 (Indicators of sustainable development)
49 Willis & Garrod 1994: Adams 1996

crease in average house prices. On that basis a doubling of trees in the city might produce a 5% increase in relative house prices, amounting to £3000 million across the city, or about ten times the investment cost.[49] Extrapolating from trees to other amenities, various kinds of 'ecological added value' can be sketched:

- land reclamation; 1% avoided cost: £600 million
- public space: 1% added value: £600m
- traffic calming: 2% added value: £1200m
- urban greening: 5% added value: £3000m
- community forest: 1% added value: £600m
- total package: 10% added value: £6000m (25% of annual GDP)

Further to this would be public health benefits, outdoor leisure, bio-diversity and quality of life, with the latter almost impossible to estimate. The total added value would of course be indirect, intangible, diffused and long term, hence not easy to recoup and recycle into investment, and long term property movements would be absorbed into the regional pattern of house prices.

Direct charging methods would include a development or disturbance levy, based on area of habitat or tree loss, or an ecological levy, based on costs of eco-restoration or compensation. Such revenues might be directly earmarked for investment in acquisition and planting of open space. In practice, landscape investment costs are very dependent on relations with owners and

communities – the cultural and institutional context as above – and a partnership approach to eco-restoration generally delivers results for a fraction of the commercial costs.[50]

## Air quality

For pollution in general, the typical 'polluter pays' and precautionary principles are not enough when jobs or lifestyle changes are at stake. A general cost breakdown shows the areas of application for pollution control *(Box 13.9)*. The nature of pollution as often uncertain and irreversible would suggest an extended '4P' – 'polluter pays precautionary principle'. This would operate a system of advance-paid bonds or 'escrow' accounts, where the onus is on polluters to prove that their activities are not environmentally damaging.[51]

The economics of air emissions and air quality has focused on the common pollutants, many of which are from fossil fuels in energy or transport. One example is a shadow estimate for $SO_2$, historically the worst common pollutant, of damage, adaptation and investment in the international 'Sulphur Protocol', shown here pro rata for GM, with a relatively modest range of uncertainty *(Fig 13.8)*:[52]

- total costs of Protocol: £50–150 million
- total benefits of Protocol: £150–1000 million.

For this and many others, the benefits of pollution control are valued at many times the external costs of continuing pollution. Investment in air quality is often also on a short internal payback, and the majority of firms authorized by LAAPC experience no extra cost from the new regulatory system.[53] If all emissions to air were charged, or permits traded, clean technology incentives would increase and could outweigh 'end-of-pipe' abatement. In practice there are market barriers to such apparently rational investment, particularly among SMEs, and other approaches through producer networks or supply-chain pressure may be more effective.[54]

---

Box 13.8

### EXTERNAL COSTS ~ LAND & ECOLOGY

| | DEMAND SIDE | INFRAST-RUCTURE | SUPPLY SIDE | ENVIRON-MENTAL | SOCIAL |
|---|---|---|---|---|---|
| **DAM-AGE COSTS** | consumer costs | vacancy dereliction opportunity costs | production costs | soil quality soil erosion water poll. pesticides. eutrophicatn | health amenity leisure |
| **ADAPT-ATION** | leisure | urban form | new tech. | Climate ch. Eco-system | travel demand |
| **INVES-TMENT** | food markets | Conservatn | organic farm sust.forestry | woodlands eco-restoration | social capacity |

50 Handley & Bulmer 1997

51 Costanza & Cornwell 1992
52 ECOTEC 1994
53 OECD 1997
54 Gouldson & Murphy 1998

## Water & waste

The economics of the water industry highlight the relationship between costs and benefits, both in quantity, quality and the effects on freshwaters and coastal areas. The privatization of the industry and then the recent drought also exposed many previously hidden costs, and controversy hinged on the costs and benefits to shareholders or consumers. Recent UK data shows:[55]

- the rise in investment at privatization recently fell to £2.5bn per year;
- doubling of dividends to £1.5bn;
- reduction in tax paid to £170 million.

North West Water consulted on its investment options, including bathing water, river pollution, sewer problems, drinking water taste and lead piping.[56] The most popular option with consumers was river improvement, and this was also the most expensive at £12 per household. Generally, the economics of water supply highlight the question of how to charge for what is still in many ways a 'public good'. Depending on the effects of climate change, much of the UK could be under-supplied by 2020; while most domestic consumers still pay flat rate charges unrelated to volume, direct charging with water meters is a controversial issue. Meanwhile, valuation methods for river quality were shown in sharp relief by a recent case, where the calculation was

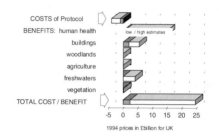

Fig 13.8        **ENVIRONMENTAL COSTS & BENEFITS**

Example costs & benefits of implementing UNECE Sulphur Protocol for UK.
Source:  ECOTEC 1994.

found to have boundary assumptions which were completely artificial.[57]

For solid waste, external cost estimates have to rely on risk analysis more than direct dose-responses – however, waste is the first industry in the UK with the beginnings of an active ETR system, in the form of the landfill levy, the recycling credit scheme, and the packaging recovery system.   The landfill levy is currently set at £11 for mixed waste and £2 per tonne for inert waste, based on shadow values for the external costs of waste disposal:  these rates in the UK are a fraction of those in other EU countries.   Recycling credits to reflect avoided costs of waste disposal are set at £11.29 per tonne in GM, but have not yet greatly increased recycling. On this basis, municipal waste costs in GM would be:[58]

- public costs of disposal & regulation:  £36m;
- avoided costs via recycling credits:  £144m;
- external costs reflected in landfill levy:  £73m.

As with water, current household charges are flat rate, with no relationship to the type and volume of waste, and no economic incentive to re-use or recycle.  Commercial and industrial charges, in contrast, are finely tuned but still exclude the full external costs.  The complex 'packaging recovery note' system aims to transmit external costs right through the distribution chain, but in practice encourages speculative dealing in notes. A full economic

Box 13.9

### EXTERNAL COSTS ~ WASTE & POLLUTION

|  | DEMAND SIDE | INFRAST- RUCTURE | SUPPLY SIDE | ENVIRON- MENTAL | SOCIAL |
|---|---|---|---|---|---|
| DAM- AGE COSTS | consumer costs | dis- investment | lost production, material waste | air quality water quality soil & land | health amenity |
| ADAPT ATION | green consumer | sewers, landfills | end of pipe | adaption | filters noise ins. |
| INVES TMENT | green products re-use | clean disposal | clean technology Recycling | remediation |  |

55 Environment Agency, quoted in Guardian 27/5/97
56 NWWater 1993

57 Hills et al 1999
58 GMWRA & GMWDA 1995

package would seek to go beyond the limited measures so far, towards restructuring the total material metabolism of key industries. On the demand side, product taxes on toxic goods such as batteries are already in use in Europe. On the disposal side, graduated waste collection systems to reflect types and toxicities of waste would include for charges escalating over a period to allow adaptation and investment.

## Energy & climate

The external costs of energy production and use underly each of the estimates for buildings and transport above. And yet climate change effects are spread between many nations and generations, and cost estimates have to make many questionable assumptions on uncertainty, 'statistical value of life', discount rates, risk aversion, and equity between gainers and losers, or between present and future generations.[59] The current 'standard' shadow value of £12/tonne carbon ($20/tC) shows a total cost of the emissions from GM of £100 million per year – a figure which seems totally unrelated to the scale of the risk involved.[60] On close inspection this excludes most factors where an economic cost is not easily identified, and a broader estimate shows the longer term cost of doubling atmospheric $CO_2$ as 6% of world GDP. Pro-rata for GM, this would amount to an external cost of £150 per tonne or a total of £1.2bn.[61] Even this excludes impacts such as morbidity, human migration and ecological stress; including a notional value for these could bring the total shadow cost for energy in GM to £1.5bn, which is on a par with total energy expenditure. But if different assumptions are made on human and ecological values, then the 'cost' estimate increases more than tenfold.[62]

The reality is that such estimates stretch the shadow costing approach beyond its sensible limits. The risks of severe disruption to the global climate are uncertain, irreversible, and continuously increasing. In the worst case such disruption could damage the world economy beyond recognition, while in the best case, such gradual disruption might hardly be noticed in the context of global development.[63] Hence the solutions to the economic problem lies beyond calculation, in a realm of politics and ethics, and the logic of the CBA is not only uncertain but possibly misleading.[64]

# MARKET TRANSFORMATION

These sketches of sectoral market profiles each point to an agenda far beyond simple ETR levies and subsidies – nothing less than a full market transformation of each sector in the context of the wider economy. Of course such transformations are in continuous process in any case, with new patterns emerging, and in particular new economic linkages between public, private and community sectors. This is nothing new – the reality behind the textbook 'perfect market' of firms and consumers has always been a rich mixture of cooperation, exploitation and dependency between interlocking parties and their interests.[65] Such economic alliances and linkages include three basic combinations – public–private, private–community and public–community *(Fig 13.9)*.[66] Each sector has certain strengths, weaknesses, institutional logic, and an agenda to pursue. This three-way picture goes a little way towards mapping the complex mutual interactions which may occur at every level of an advanced economy, and provides an essential context to the two-way axis of ETR.

Public–private linkages include the recent UK 'private finance initiatives' (PFI), various brands of partnerships and consortiums, ethical investment and purchasing, supply chain initiatives, and most forms of economic development

59 Pearce 1995
60 Fankhauser 1996
61 Cline 1992
62 Meyer & Cooper 1995

63 Ausabel 1993
64 Adams 1996
65 Ormerod 1996
66 The 'community' sector includes local informal or social economies, 'civic' or non-profit institutions, associations, unions, churches and so on.

activity. Public intervention has generally aimed to close 'market gaps' – in contrast private finance is now seeking to close a 'public gap' in access to capital, and many public services could be operated or financed by business as the boundaries between the sectors merge. It is essential for such businesses to be run with some local control or equity to counter 'branch-plant' dependency, and any PFI schemes should be based on such principles. However, the PFI framework is attracting more criticism, as to maximize commercial reward, it has to introduce economic logic and differentiation within the public sector – in the health service, PFI is accused of favouring wealthy over poor areas and masking a decline in real assets.[67] The public sector pension funds, likewise, are generally managed from the City with little responsibility to their constituencies, and an obvious move would be to redirect their policies towards local re-investment.[68]

Activities on the private–community axis include local business or regeneration partnerships, social investment funds, what remains of the 'mutual' financial institutions, corporate trusts and guarantee companies, producer or consumer clubs and networks, cooperatives and community development trusts. In some ways the consumer market for any product or service can be a form of alliance or 'community of interest'. Such potential synergy and influence can be mobilized either for commercial gain, as with advertising, or for social benefit through consumer lobbies, NGOs and other networks. The genetic foods episode of 1999 was perhaps a turning point, when the fate of a large transnational firm was seriously affected by public opinion. Nearer home, voluntary and charitable activity is already a large sector with about 4% of GDP, and is likely to expand rapidly to take on a new generation of devolved public services.

For the third linkage, on the community–public axis, the mandate of local government itself depends on alliances or 'social contracts', such as between representatives and electorate. Linkages and alliances include the emerging Best

Fig 13.9  **NEW ECONOMIC LINKAGES**

franchising
public/private partnerships
deregulation
marketization

*private*          *public*

trade associations                            public services
responsive markets                          best value & NPM
consumer clubs          *community &*      city contracts
community enterprise        *civic*         social trading

General linkages and potential alliances between public, private and civic / nonprofit / third / community sectors.

Value regime, voluntary sector compacts, neighbourhood forums and partnerships, resident or customer charters, social trading schemes and many others. Newly emerging groups and networks in local and wider communities demand new responses from local government – and while local government is perennially strapped for cash, it may yet gain enough financial autonomy to enable some new and creative economic moves. These in turn will enable new forms of investment alliance between local authorities, local communities, NGOs and other interest groups.

## City-region strategy

All this analysis should help in the practical question of city-region strategy for economic incentives, long term investment and market transformation. Again, the city-region level is caught between the districts and emerging regional agencies, but it may yet be the most effective level for many policies and strategies *(Chapter 14)*. Each strategy and sub-strategy of the SD framework will have different and unique economic implications and political constraints. However, a common pattern of fiscal measures and investment packages will help to build added value, synergy and bargaining power.

---

67 British Medical Association 1999 ##
68 Martin & Minns 1996

Fig 13.10          **TOTAL ECONOMY ~**
                   **CYCLIC METABOLISM**

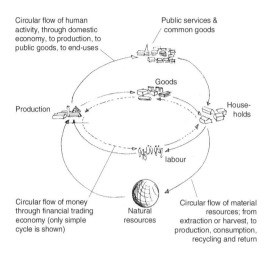

Circular flow of human
activity, through domestic
economy, to production, to
public goods, to end-uses

Public services &
common goods

Goods

Production

House-
holds

labour

Circular flow of money
through financial trading
economy (only simple
cycle is shown)

Natural
resources

Circular flow of material
resources; from
extraction or harvest, to
production, consumption,
recycling and return

Outline of financial, physical and human resource flows to be mobilized in the
city-region 2020 funding and investment strategy

The financial sector is a key in all this, following on from the Co-operative Bank's lead in 'green' lending.[69] Ethical funds outperform the long term average, and cover a tenth of all funds on the New York stockmarket. Managed funds targeted at community development, regeneration and a local equity base, are operating in many developing countries and North America.[70] Insurance companies are taking a keen interest in the risks of climate change and the liability of contamination, and venture capital firms are hunting for growth prospects through environmental regulation. While much of the world economy looks distinctly shaky, in many areas of financial services the market transformations already in progress are focusing on the 'shareholder value' factor and its 'triple bottom line'.[71] It is not unrealistic to imagine a city-region managed fund, venture capital and equity scheme targetted at urban regeneration and infrastructure, combining public backing and social responsibility with financial sector expertise.

For the public sector, the Best Value regime is an opportunity to re-examine all activities against objectives, performance standards and cost-effectiveness *(Chapter 14)*. If some services are marketized and franchised as a result, this may spend public money more efficiently, but would it lead towards market transformation? A future concept might be something like 'Better Value', which would look more creatively at the scope for fiscal and institutional integration. The public sector role in the city-region energy agency, for instance, could be a minimal deal for public tenants, or a more pro-active lead in a multisectoral partnership covering all dwellings.

The community, voluntary or third sector is unlikely to be a channel for large funding flows, but is in another way a catalyst for the vital factors of shareholder value, consumer approval and customer loyalty. At present only a fraction of the money saved in inner city areas is re-invested locally – the poor are unwittingly subsidizing the affluent. The third sector's role is likely to be in mobilizing local support and stakeholding and stakeowning alliances, alongside the social economy and social trading networks.

Each of these will combine in the city-region sustainable development framework as in the next chapter. For this, an integrated package of market measures, long term investment and market transformation is integral to success.

---

Box 13.10

**SUMMARY ~ INVESTMENT**

The 2020 'investment strategy' funds restructuring and re-engineering in many sectors. With changing boundaries between public, private and non-profit organizations, new financial mechanisms aim at a better balance of costs and benefits:

- eco-taxation package for all environmental consumption, with revenues re-invested
- long term investment partnerships to bridge market barriers and split responsibilities
- integrated financial social and environmental accounting for policies, programmes and organizations
- market transformation for least-cost planning and integration of supply and demand.

---

69 Co-operative Bank 1998
70 Tennant 1997
71 Schmidheiny 1996: Elkington 1997

# 14 RUNNING the CITY-REGION

*'I have come to the conclusion that politics is too serious a matter to be left to the politicians'*
Charles de Gaulle

In the crowded islands of the UK, cities, and those who would run them, seem to have little control over their destinies – their existence is at the mercy of national government, and their economies dangle on the strings of the global marketplace. In many ways a city or region is simply another place where the national sustainable development process may or may not happen.

Alternatively, a city, a region, or a city-region can take a positive lead as a coherent unit – it can define its vision, assume global responsibilities, coordinate its services, empower its citizens, and strive for best practice. There is a strong case that the metropolitan area or city-region is the best level to motivate and organize sustainable development – large enough for critical mass, and small enough to be manageable.[1] To achieve this, effective and appropriate 'governance' is crucial. Meanwhile, former political structures of representation and decisionmaking are shifting to new and more complex patterns, and there are now many more players, with wider set of objectives than ever before.

In particular, the challenge of sustainable development – where the whole is greater than the sum of the parts – demands a high level of coordination and integration, for synergy and added value. Such integration is needed between sectors, between agencies, between national and local levels, and between needs and outcomes. To encourage and enable such integration we propose a city-region 'sustainable development framework' – an over-arching vision and strategy, embedded in collaborative structures and networks.

So here we look at the context and future prospects for such a framework, and for integrated governance at regional, local and city-region levels. First we review political structures and processes, applying the sustainability agenda to perennial questions of governance. Then we apply the findings to the practical issues of decision-making and public services in cities and regions. We put a special focus on 'local agendas', participation and subsidiarity. All this provides foundations for the city-region sustainable development framework, which must find its place in a changing political landscape.

1 Cohen 1993: Roberts 1999

## Trends & tensions

As each nation searches for its version of a 'sustainable' social and economic development path, the search revolves around time-honoured questions – social welfare versus free markets, centralization versus devolution, and the changing balance of economic, social and environmental priorities. Apparently sovereign governments are caught in forces beyond their control, of globalization and liberalization – and they also struggle with problems beyond their control, of polarization and exclusion.

Such national and global questions are mirrored in the politics of the city-region. The ten districts which make up GM are freestanding 'unitary' authorities, major local employers now struggling under huge financial pressure, and with many public services now devolved to the market or quasi-public bodies. Most local regimes have shifted from their traditional power-bases towards corporate public-private alliances – all but one of the districts are under Labour control, and the current parliamentary seats are 26 Labour, two Conservative and one Liberal-Democrat. GM has a voluntary association for coordination of joint functions, the Association of Greater Manchester Authorities (AGMA). However for many purposes, if not most, GM is now a 'sub-region' of the northwest of England. Here a very active partnership has established a regional development agency (NWDA), alongside a local authority regional Chamber, which is well on the way to being an elected Assembly.[2]

Whatever their political colour, city administrations are in a transition to a new and uncertain world. Local government was established on a 'Fordist' model of centralized public services, planning, regulation, and clear channels for representation and decision-making.[3] From the 1980s onwards, 'post-Fordist' local government shows a much more diverse pattern. There are many new kinds of institutions shifting and merging the boundaries between market, state and community, and inventing new alliances between sectors and agencies:[4]

- shift from universal 'provider' to selective 'enabler' through diverse alliances and partnerships;
- new agenda for economic development, with many agencies and alliances from business and others;
- new agenda for social welfare, with increasingly the private sector and third sector as service providers;
- new approaches to management by objectives, performance monitoring and dedicated agencies, as now seen with 'Best Value' and similar schemes;
- international competition of cities and regions for EU subsidy and/or global investment.

Each district in GM has its version of an environment or sustainability 'charter', and most now have Local Agenda 21 'statements'. In reality such visions are fairly marginal to most mainstream activity – the districts have diminishing control, influence, or even information, on the essential services and levers of the urban system. At the same time they remain the natural or residual 'stewards' of their territory and the city-region, even while the people and the economy of the city-region are globalized and distributed in cyberspace. This territorial role should not be underestimated, and any future mode of governance should aim to enhance it.

## Future prospects

While political structures and processes are changing and evolving at a hectic pace, some perennial themes keep recurring. Many future scenarios show clearly the tension between globalization and localization of power and influence.[5] How this tension plays out, between traditional public sector structures, and corporate representation of diverse interest groups, can be seen in a range of possible scenarios:

- ***BAU scenario:*** political fragmentation continues the decline of the public sector and the rise of the corporate sectors. There is mounting conflict and in-fighting

---

2 Williams 1998
3 Painter 1991
4 Mayer 1995

5 Science Policy Research Unit 1999

between regions vs districts, EU vs UK, public vs corporate, and urban vs rural.[6]

- **technology scenario**: rapid spread of ICT enables new forms of direct democracy and integrated management. However it also accelerates the polarization of centre and periphery, or the info-rich and poor, and the dissolution of locally-based communities and networks towards global cultures.
- **SD scenario**: a combined city-region vision and strategy brings together all sectors for consensus, if not total agreement, on integrated management of the city-region. Meanwhile new forms of local democracy and direct decision-making are developed.
- **deep green scenario**: this sees a rapid shift towards devolved neighbourhood-based decision processes, where important local questions are decided by focus groups and deliberative poll. Regional and national issues are informed by advanced ICT tools with consensus-based citizen conferences.

## Metabolism of governance

Political theory is of course a labyrinth in itself, and linkages to the sustainability agenda are many and diverse.[7] Looking beyond the formal structures of 'government through representative democracy in the public sector', to the wider picture of decision-making in the common interest, there are many layers to the theme of 'sustainable governance':

- a process of collective negotiation which translates 'needs' into 'outcomes';
- new modes of communication and decision-making;
- new patterns of institutions, networks and representation;
- engagement of groups and communities on the periphery;
- alliances and integration of public, private and civic sectors;
- the wider political debate – if sustainable development means what it says about 'equity', does this mean social redistribution, and if so on what terms?

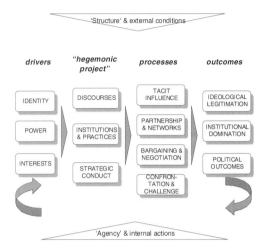

Fig 14.1     **POLITICAL METABOLISM**

Political process seen as a metabolism translating drivers to outcomes.
Source: adapted from Hajer 1993: Giddens 1984

The first and last points revolve around the 'balance' concept of sustainability. If we adapt our 'needs-outcomes' metabolism model and the systems approach to the political process, it helps to untangle some of the links in a causal chain *(Fig 14.1)*. 'Upstream', the needs for power and identity are manifest in the 'projects' of the dominant elite; these are expressed through negotiation or confrontation, with outcomes 'downstream' which may be tangible or intangible.[8] This kind of analysis is useful in highlighting political networks and alliances, both inside and outside formal structures, as explored through 'regime' theory.[9] It also shows political processes and power structures at any level, as expressing the 'discourse' or implicit values of the dominant elite, which are then reproduced by political institutions.[10]

Such a political model also highlights the shift towards a mode of governance which is enabling and entrepreneurial – as much to do with selling images as with policies. Such images revolve around the communications functions of cities, now being transformed via ICT – reinforcing the hierarchy of central hubs, while diffusing power and influence across 'electronic

6 Travers 1999, in the Guardian 21/4/99
7 Baker & Kousis 1997

8 Ravetz 1999b
9 Stoker 1995
10 Hajer 1995

Fig 14.2          **AGENCY & POWER**

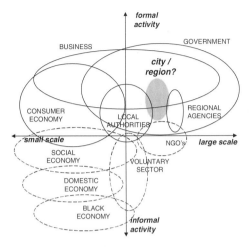

Showing very approximate role and size of activity sectors.
Source: adapted from Friedmann 1995

space' rather than 'urban place' *(Chapter 3).*[11] Such new modes of communication are integral to governance as a decision-making system, which like any system needs internal feedback in order to adapt and innovate.[12] In practice many ICT-based networks are rapidly moving far beyond the control or even the knowledge of governments, in a jungle of private and privatized lobbies and sub-cultures.[13] Meanwhile cities are also re-inventing their role as hubs for informal networks and social movements, and the resulting distribution of power might be more elitist and exclusive, or more pluralist and open.[14]

A common theme on the post-Fordist agenda is the restructuring of local institutions and networks – a simple mapping shows the range of both formal and informal institutions, from transnational businesses to the black economy *(Fig 14.2).* Such institutions and networks are now seen as key factors in global competitiveness, whether for learning, innovation, technology diffusion and so on.[15] The cities and regions most admired for economic vitality – Silicon Valley, or Baden-Wurtemberg – each contain a great 'thick-

ness' of institutions and networks, which are simultaneously competitive and cohesive.[16]

An institutional view also focuses on small-scale informal groups and networks – the 'power to the people' agenda. While community participation is often seen as an end in itself, in practice it can be as elitist and self-interested as any other political process. Among the UK public there is widespread distrust of the political system – turnouts are falling towards zero at many local elections, and the ratio of representatives to electorate in the UK is about 1:4000, the lowest in Europe.[17] But while the public sector diminishes, countless groups and networks deliver increasing power and influence to individuals and communities – most are marginal to the political system, many are formed in opposition, and others are more concerned with cultural than political 'space'.[18] Their common feature is that of life on the physical or cultural periphery, in a do-it-yourself mode far removed from the power games of the centre.[19] Effective governance should seek to engage and build consensus with such informal and transient groups and networks.[20]

This emergence of the community sector is mirrored by a restructuring and merging of other sectors – as with 'market transformation', there are new linkages emerging between private, public and community sectors *(chapter 13) (Fig 14.3).* While the traditional lines of political debate were on the balance of market and state, the franchising and deregulation of public services is blurring such boundaries, and the 'third sector' now has increasing influence, from LA21 forums to consumer lobbies *(chapter 11).* One result is the spread of new neighbourhood alliances, creating services and activities which would not otherwise exist.[21] Another result is seen with urban services such as energy, water or transport, where the deregulated utilities are shifting their engagement towards profitable clients and away from low-income consumers.[22] Another is seen with the 'mutual' mode of or-

11 Castells 1993
12 Portugali 1996
13 Marvin & Graham 1996
14 Stoker 1991
15 Morgan 1997

16 Amin & Thrift 1995
17 MacNaghten 1995
18 Grove-White 1996
19 Worpole 1999
20 Gibson 1996
21 Greenhalgh & Worpole
22 Marvin & Graham 1995

ganization, whose traditional savings base is now being sold out and replaced by other forms of stakeholder involvement.[23] Effective governance in theory should combine the best features of each sector, in a framework of responsive and responsible partnerships and consortiums. This is, of course, easier said than done.

Finally, coming back to the great debate on equity and redistribution, it turns out that UK society, one of the most liberal, is one of the most unequal in the world.[24] There are also signs that the exclusion at the bottom of the social ladder is now being matched by voluntary opting out at the top.[25] The greater part of this question appears to lie outside the scope of the city-region – except that in a world of inter-dependency, every level is relevant. In practical terms, the fundamental theme of social justice and equity has to be the foundation for a host of practical decisions on public services and environmental management, in the city-region as elsewhere *(Chapter 11)*.

## Towards sustainable governance

A sustainable development path implies a political transformation, as with the economic, social and physical transformations in previous chapters. And as with the others, the political agenda is not a fixed blueprint, but a dynamic process, at every level of society. Such an agenda applies the common principles of sustainability or responsibility – themselves an extension of the time-honoured principles of human rights and social justice:

- equity, or responsibility to present generations;
- futurity, or responsibility to future generations;
- ecology, or responsibility to other species;
- 'empowerment', or responsibility to communities and society.

Such principles can be held up as self-evident fundamental human rights, and the moral justifi-

Fig 14.3          **NEW LINKAGES**

business agencies
monopoly regulation
corporate partnerships
quango boards

*private*          *public*

stakeholder mutuals                    area & user forums
consumer/interest groups               Best Value & NPM
industryassociations      *community &*   third sector services
media & advertizing          *civic*      direct democracy

General types of alliances now emerging between public, private and civic/community sectors.

cation for environmental policies.[26] They are also pre-conditions for practical progress towards environmental sustainability. Citizen empowerment is essential for effective action in planning, transport and others; and equity between communities is essential to enable both rich and poor to choose ecologically responsible lifestyles.

The crunch comes with the contradictions. 'Equity' is an admirable goal, but how many of the rich would hand over real power and money to the poor? Empowerment of communities sounds ideal, but how can local self-interest fit with strategic planning? Should public money be invested in successful or declining areas, and who gets to decide? In principle, wealthy communities should take responsibility for the social order via redistribution, and local communities should take responsibility for wider issues via strategic planning. In practice society and its collective decision processes is an ever-more complex pattern of interlocking self-interests.

The quest for the 'third way' or the 'stakeholder society' – a social and economic order beyond market capitalism or welfare socialism – attempts to bridge such gaps.[27] Each person, community and institution should embody a balance of rights and responsibilities, to themselves and to others, in an open society

23 Mulgan & Landry 1995
24 UNDP 1996
25 Giddens 1998

26 Boyle & Anderson 1996
27 Hutton 1995: Giddens 1998

based on public accountability.[28]  Naturally, the third way struggles with definitions of principle and practice, and its central debate on redistribution is far from resolved.[29]  It finds application in the agenda for 'joined-up government', which addresses perennial problems with new modes of operation for public services *(Chapter 11)*:[30]

- forward investment and prevention, rather than curative action after the problem;
- integration between sectors, with a focus on 'outcomes' rather than 'outputs';
- unlocking the potential of the third sector, community and social economy;
- soft approaches to shifting values and perceptions as much as hard incentives and enforcements.

The practical agenda for the city-region brings together these diverse themes. Many programmes for 'sustainable governance', for instance from the Global Forum 94 in Manchester, have focused on the 'people's agenda' as the ultimate mandate, and local authorities as the ultimate providers – forming by default a 'public and populist' agenda *(Box 14.1)*.  Most programmes for urban development and regeneration tend to assume that local authorities can and must take the lead.[31]  But much practical experience, particularly from the corporate sector, shows that most of UK society is non-joining, materialistic and individualistic – forming by default a more private, privatized, individualist and pluralist agenda.[32]  Democratic institutions, with their cumbersome committees and wide-ranging and fuzzy objectives, can hardly compete with the sophisticated and single-minded marketing of multi-national firms. So how can such different worlds be combined?  No agenda for sustainable governance can ignore such a challenge.

One result is that many sustainable development strategies demand that citizens or businesses 'own' their responsibility for taking action, as an alternative to having it enforced upon them. Therein lies the choice, as hard for politicians as it is for consumers.

We cannot prejudge the outcome of such a choice. What we can say in general terms, is that the agenda for sustainable city-region governance will cover a vertical dimension, a horizontal dimension, a management dimension, and the added value of an over-arching framework *(Box 14.2)*.

---

**Box 14.1**     *CITY GOVERNANCE*

- Define & protect citizen's rights in an urbanizing world
- Community action for participation & accountability
- Responsibilities of national governments for local action
- International action for sustainable development in cities
- Education to change attitudes to development and environment
- Decentralize decision-making to neighbourhood level
- Checks and balances for accountability and proper use of public funds

Manifesto for sustainable city governance, agreed at Global Forum 94 international key sectors forum.
Source:  Manchester City Council 1994

---

**Box 14.2**

| *GOVERNANCE ~ GOALS & STRATEGIES* | G O V | L A P | B U S | C O M | P U B |
|---|---|---|---|---|---|
| **LOCALIZING GOVERNANCE:** Township, neighbourhood & street forums with open, flatter & more responsive structures | ○ | ● | ○ | ○ | ○ |
| **ACTIVE DEMOCRACY:** Education, ICT, market research, conflict mediation & vision building for active citizenship & institutional capacity | ○ | ● | ● | ● | ○ |
| **PARTNERSHIPS:** Partnerships, consortiums, joint forums to combine investment & return for public, private & community sectors | ○ | ● | ● | ○ | |
| **CITY-REGION S.D. FRAMEWORK:** Strategic partnership for coordination of city-wide environmental management, economic development & social policy: representing regional & local government. | ○ | ● | ● | ○ | |

GOV ~ government & EU: LA ~ local authorities & partnerships: BUS ~ business & finance: COM ~ community & 3rd sector: PUB ~ public

---

28 Soros 1996
29 Powell 1999
30 Perri 6 1999
31 Urban Task Force 1999
32 McNaghten & Urry 1997

For levels of governance which are appropriate and effective, there is a strong case for including townships, neighbourhoods and streets. This will enable and catalyse active participation, integrated public services, and the resources of the social economy.

Within this framework there is scope for new kinds of partnerships and alliances, between public, private and community sectors, to integrate and coordinate investment, power and responsibility from each sector.

It also suggests the management style of sustainable local governance as multicultural, transparent, pluralist and responsive – using new techniques in direct democracy, ICT access, management by objectives, consensus and vision building.

Finally, to achieve the synergy and integration needed for sustainable development, there is a strong case for the extension of local and regional governance to the city-region level – a 'sustainable development framework'. This will aim to coordinate and integrate environmental management, economic development and social strategy.

# CITY & REGIONAL GOVERNANCE

## Territory & function

One principle of effective governance is to match appropriate territories to their functions and institutions.[33] The 'city-region' is a very appropriate kind of territory for many functions. But at present it is excluded from the UK political landscape, which only recognizes local authorities, counties and regions. The traditional concept of a city-region was based on a hinterland providing resources for a city to manufacture and export – but in a globalized economy such material flows may be less relevant than other social or cultural factors.[34] There is a campaign for city-region government, as the natural unit for economic and political functions, which builds on a long history of local government reform.[35] This has now fulfilled its first objective with the re-establishment of  metropolitan government in London.[36]

Where there is similarity between economic and environmental territories in areas such as GM, the city-region is perhaps the most appropriate level for the integrating theme of sustainable development.[37] At this level, environmental objectives can be matched to economic incentives, and gain from critical mass in political and social institutions.  In contrast to the localized version of eco-efficiency, operations and regulatory systems for recycling, energy efficiency or public transport tend to be more efficient and effective at the city or regional scale.[38] The proposed Metropolitan Planning Guidance, for instance, would coordinate all physical development in an over-arching strategy, aiming at a high degree of political integration.[39]

In reality, the 'eco-eco' scale of sustainable development is contested and controversial – different levels will serve different interests with different outcomes, and different winners and losers.  The reality, in the UK at least, is that 'regions' will be the main focus of political activity in the near future – while city-region metropolitan areas clearly need strategic management, they will have to work with the trends in motion. The emerging regional agencies and assemblies are complemented by the regionalizing of government agencies, EU funding, public utilities, major providers, and even the logistics of major businesses.

33 Friedman & Weaver 1988
34 Dickinson 1964
35 Warren-Evans 1996
36 Graham & Hebbert 1999
37 Roberts 1994

38 Gouldson & Murphy 1998
39 Roberts, Thomas & Williams 1999

In this project we have taken existing political boundaries for simplicity, but there are other possible patterns of function and territory surrounding the conurbation – as seen both in geographical space and an 'equal population' cartogram *(Fig 14.4):* [40]

- city-region as a political unit: includes the AGMA districts in the former GM County;
- city-region travel to work area: a wider functional zone used for economic and infrastructure planning;
- 'bio-region': river catchments and/or landscape types, as contained in the Mersey Basin;
- 'planning' region: the official North West now includes Cheshire, Lancashire, Merseyside, and Cumbria;
- a northern 'super-city' based on the M62 corridor is in many ways a functional unit equal in size to London;[41]
- urban catchment: another level of gravity boundary between Strathclyde, West Midlands, and West/South Yorkshire;
- European city-region on the periphery: in this case GM is the largest single conurbation on the edges of the 'Atlantic Arc' and 'North Sea' mega-regions.

Each of these 'regions' represents a different matching of layers of function and territory, and even for the region defined as the North West, the actual boundaries differ for planning, health, water, telecoms and so on. Different activities and functions in supply or demand are served by various institutions and activities which may overlap or compete. For the record, we show below a breakdown of responsibilities in each territory and sector *(Box 14.3).*

## Subsidiarity & residuarity

GM itself, in contrast to other more free-standing cities, is a kind of paradox – both a distinct functional unit, and a collection of fragmented parts. The name Greater Manchester is itself a bureacratic invention, and the division of GM into 10 unitary 'districts', with eight metropoli-

**Fig 14.4**

### CITY-REGION TERRITORIES

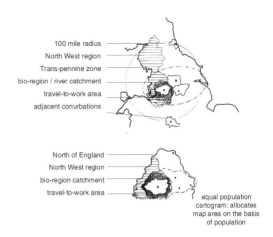

100 mile radius
North West region
Trans-pennine zone
bio-region / river catchment
travel-to-work area
adjacent conurbations

North of England
North West region
bio-region catchment
travel-to-work area

equal population cartogram: allocates map area on the basis of population

Alternative definition of city-region territories: (1) in geogaphical space, and (2) in equal population cartogram format.
Source: based on Dickinson 1964: Dorling 1996

**Box 14.3**

### TERRITORY & FUNCTION

| | North Eng-land | NW reg-ion | M62 sup-er city | Bio-reg-ion | Tra-vel work area | GM | Dist-rict | neigh bour-hood |
|---|---|---|---|---|---|---|---|---|
| land & development | ○ | ○ | | ○ | | ● | ● | ○ |
| housing | | ○ | | | | ○ | ● | ○ |
| retail & property | ○ | ○ | | ○ | | ● | ○ | ○ |
| public transport | ○ | ● | | ○ | | ● | ○ | ○ |
| highways | ● | ○ | | ○ | | ○ | ○ | ● |
| airport & TEN's | | ○ | | ○ | | ● | | |
| ecology & landscape | | ○ | ● | | | ○ | ○ | ● |
| agriculture & food | | ○ | ○ | ● | | ○ | ○ | ○ |
| air quality | | ○ | ○ | ○ | | ● | ● | |
| water & minerals | ○ | ● | ○ | ● | | ○ | ● | |
| ground & soil | | ○ | | ● | | ○ | ● | |
| waste & recycling | | ○ | | | | ● | ○ | ● |
| energy supply | ○ | ● | ○ | | | ○ | | |
| energy demand | | ○ | | | | ● | ○ | ○ |
| economic dev. | | ● | ○ | | | ● | ● | |
| urban regeneration | ○ | ○ | | | | ● | ● | ○ |
| health | ● | | | | | ○ | ○ | ○ |
| higher education | ○ | ○ | | ○ | ○ | ○ | | |
| finance & media | ○ | ● | | ○ | ○ | | | |
| SD framework | ● | ○ | ○ | ○ | ○ | ● | ● | ○ |

Analysis of effective territories for each key sector
● shows formal political or economic linkage
○ shows other function-territory linkage

---

tan boroughs and two cities, is artificial in many ways. Manchester City in particular contains regional services and world-city aspirations, alongside extreme poverty and deprivation, and there is mounting pressure to alter its boundaries and balance its economic base.[42]

Within such a city-region are many layers of activity, and there is often no one 'right' layer for governance and management. The spatial hierarchy for GM includes 10 unitary districts, 363 local authority wards: perhaps 1000 neighbourhoods, about 35,000 roads and streets, and over 1 million households. Each of these is more or less of a spatial unit or territory with various functional patterns.[43] Such a hierarchy can be seen with energy efficiency, which is normally thought a matter for householders *(Box 14.4)*.

Such examples demonstrate the dual principles of 'subsidiarity' and 'residuarity'. Subsidiarity aims to push or devolve responsibility to the lowest level consistent with effective decision-making.[44] Behind the principle is conflict and competition, for instance where the problems of traffic reduction are handed to local authorities, but without adequate powers and resources to deal with them. In reverse, the theme of residuarity legitimates the 'pull' or the claiming of responsibility by lower levels, where higher levels fail to carry out necessary functions. Much activity under the banner of local sustainability assumes residual responsibilities which are sidelined in mainstream institutions. A typical

result is that marginal agendas, for example green space, are either pushed out by the centre or pulled in by the 'community', leaving more mainstream agendas such as economic development under central control.[45]

The upshot for the city-region agenda is that any future political powers and resources will come from one of three directions, as a result of pushing, pulling, or redistribution of new roles and functions:

- powers and resources devolved down from the regional or higher level;
- powers and resources devolved up from the local authority level;
- new functions on the interface of public, private and third sectors.

## The European city-region

The context for sustainable development in GM is its place in larger spatial structures – and whether the pace of integration is faster or slower, the enlarging European Union of over 400 million people is becoming a primary political and economic framework. The EU dimension has many far-reaching implications for city-region strategies:[46]

- economic integration, competitiveness and the single currency;
- policy integration, as seen with the Environmental Action Programme and others;
- structural funding for economic and social development, infrastructure and regeneration;
- spatial implications of a peripheral location, access and communications.

EU economic integration centres on the dual theme of regional cohesion and competition. GM is a typical industrial conurbation receiving 'Objective 2' funding for areas of declining industry, providing physical, economic and social infrastructure. In the UK these programmes have been managed autonomously from the regional government offices, and their delivery has not

---

**Box 14.4**

### SPATIAL HIERARCHY in ENERGY EFFICIENCY

- typically a matter for individual buildings & owners
- street or block level: organization of upgrading contracts
- neighbourhood level: area based packages for infrastructure
- district level: technical management, finance and admin
- city-region level: for regeneration, utilities, finance packages
- regional level: coordination of utilities, government and development agencies
- national level: policies, investment, market regulation

---

42 Leese R, in Manchester Evening News 21/07/97
43 Friedmann & Weaver 1986
44 Pateman 1970

45 Rydin 1997
46 Roberts, Hart & Thomas 1993

always coordinated with the many other sources of regeneration and development funding.

EU environmental policy is coordinated through the Fifth Environmental Action Programme from 1993–2000 – unlike previous programmes, this is a more strategic framework to be negotiated in the detail.[47] Countries such as Sweden, Netherlands and Denmark stand as role models for environmental policy, even while struggling with the impacts of economic growth and urbanization. The theme of sustainability now permeates EU policy at every level, but the interpretation is often stuck on the 'tonnage ideology' of material consumption.[48]

The evolving EU 'social model' is also a powerful theme, even as the problems of ethnic minorities, unemployment and exclusion threaten to undermine the economic model of competiveness and cohesion.[49] Such models are also a means of integrating economic, social and environmental issues at appropriate levels including regions and city-regions.

The EU planning framework of 'Europe 2000+' and the 'European Spatial Development Perspective' is an outline of the problems and prospects in a community of 400 million people, as a guide for planning and investment.[50] The GM city-region straddles two EU 'mega-regions' – the 'Atlantic Arc' of coastal areas reaching from Scotland to Portugal, and the 'North Sea' region of the UK, Netherlands, Denmark and northern Germany, characterized by older industrial cities. While the 2000+ documents have an advisory role to national planning systems, they provide an overview for national policies and for EU-wide activity on transport, energy, agriculture, regeneration and environmental protection.

## Regional governance

Many public services and economic activities are organized at the level of the North West region, of which the GM city-region contains 40% of the population on 9% of the land area.[51] The North West is one of the most advanced of the English regions, in bringing together a public-private partnership, and a very active regional level of governance is now taking shape:[52]

- Regional Development Agencies (RDAs) are integrated 'one-stop shop' regeneration and development outfits with a long list of objectives, including that of 'promoting sustainable development'. One of their first tasks is to prepare a Regional Economic Strategy, although much of this agenda consists of bringing together the work of others.

- a Regional Chamber is now operating with an interim format, paving the way for a future Regional Assembly with statutory powers, and possibly spending functions. One of their first tasks is to prepare a review of Regional Planning Guidance (RPG) and a linked transport strategy.

- other strategies such as environment, health and competitiveness are run via the Government Offices of the Regions, related quango's or other public agencies.

Until recently in the UK little real progress was made on the regional level of planning and development, and in some areas there has been conflict and 'contested governance' between the EU, UK, local authorities and the regional quangos.[53] In recent years the 'single programming documents' for EU funding have become less partial and opaque, while RPG has been extended to included greater detail and stronger strategic vision. The regional Government Offices have achieved some inter-departmental coordination, but still have a long way to go in bringing together central departments, deregulated providers and marketized public services.[54]

The RDAs aim to provide such coordination, bringing together budgets of around £100 million per year in GM alone. Their objectives include economic development and regeneration, business support, skills, employment, and 'sustainable development' – with the latter generally interpreted as environmental protection which directly promotes economic growth.[55] A NW regional forum examined the RDA remit for sus-

47 European Environment Agency 1996
48 Simonis 1994
49 CEC 1994 (Social model)
50 CEC 1997 (EU 2000+)
51 This includes Cumbria which is in the DETR 'planning' region but excluded from the 'standard' region

52 Roberts & Lloyd 1998
53 Lloyd & Meegan 1995
54 European Institute for Urban Affairs 1996
55 Gibbs 1998

tainable development, amidst uncertainty and concern on the RDAs' powers and resources, its linkage with land-use planning, and general mismatch between economic and environmental goals.[56]    Whichever way the boundaries are drawn, the RDAs will have a key role in economic, social and environmental strategies, so it is essential that their operation is suited to the potential synergy of sustainable development at the regional level:[57]

- physical development planning on rolling programmes which integrate land-use, economic, social and environmental objectives, for longer time horizons;
- devolving of specific functions to sub-regional forums, local partnerships, or to executive agencies;
- open democratic structure, accountable to local authorities and voluntary sectors, and as soon as possible to the regional chamber;
- coordination to avoid overlap in bidding, partnership forming, and implementing EU funding and other major investments;
- transparent monitoring and targetting which shows as far as possible both 'outputs' and 'outcomes'.

It is also essential that sub-regional and sectoral working is encouraged to enable greater detail and closer links between planning and implementation.[58]  While the RDAs were set up with the aim of coordination and integration, the result so far is still fragmented – with many diverging controls and agendas on economic development, EU funding, RPG, environmental strategies and so on.  There is a strong case for putting these together in an over-arching regional vision and strategy, combining the democratic accountability of the Assembly with the clout of the RDA.[59]  However, in the short term this is not on the cards, and it is possible that forcing through such an integration at the regional scale would be an unnecessary and complex diversion.  Instead, the sub-region or metropolitan level offers a different kind of opportunity for integration, which by fitting a natural economic-environmental ter-

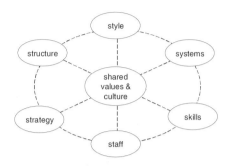

**Fig 14.5    CORPORATE MANAGEMENT**

Organizational systems showing McKinsey "7-S" management model.
Source: adapted from Peters & Waterman 1982

ritory may well be more viable and effective.  This is the theme of the SD Framework below.

## Local government

Many sustainable development functions can and should be delivered by local authorities – but most local authorities in the UK are in a state of flux, balancing the finances, pressurized to 'modernize or die', competing for influence and struggling for public interest at the polls.[60]  Internally, the 'new public management' of compulsory tendering and the private finance initiative has reached a new phase with the Local Government Review.[61]  The result is likely to include many actions which increase the performance and accountability, but definitely not the funding demands, of local government.  At the same time such change can be disruptive and open to abuse – the perennial 'empire-building' which tends to occupy the best attentions of management.[62]

One of the most significant moves is the 'Best Value' programme, a framework for fundamental reviews and  operational audits, using management objectives, monitoring targets and performance indicators.[63]  The guidance headings of Best Value are the '4Cs – 'challenge, compare, consult and compete' – and their 'SMART'

56 Sustainability North West 1998
57 Gibbs 1998: Hitchens 1997
58 Roberts & Lloyd 1998
59 TCPA 1997 (RDAs)

60 Stoker & Young 1994
61 Leach & Barrett 1998
62 Stoker 1998
63 Local Government Chronicle 1998

Fig 14.6     **CORPORATE MANAGEMENT**

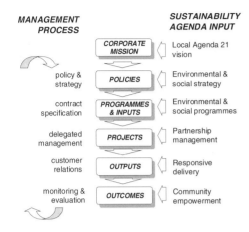

| MANAGEMENT PROCESS | | SUSTAINABILITY AGENDA INPUT |
|---|---|---|
| | CORPORATE MISSION | Local Agenda 21 vision |
| policy & strategy | POLICIES | Environmental & social strategy |
| contract specification | PROGRAMMES & INPUTS | Environmental & social programmes |
| delegated management | PROJECTS | Partnership management |
| customer relations | OUTPUTS | Responsive delivery |
| monitoring & evaluation | OUTCOMES | Community empowerment |

General inputs of environmental & social priorities to public sector management process.
Source: adapted from Hambleton 1992

management objectives – 'specific, measurable, achievable, relevant and time-bound'. At present 23 local authorities and public bodies are piloting the Best Value evaluation scheme, those in GM including Manchester, Oldham and the GM Police Force.

The Best Value framework could be an essential catalyst for more efficient and effective services. It could also see another step away from universal service provision, with 'needs' targetting, separation of purchasing and providing, and reinforcing the traditional 'policy silos' where the real problems are pushed around between departments.[64] For the sustainability agenda, Best Value could force the pace of structured thinking on goals and targets, and lead towards integrated audits and management plans.[65] There is also a risk that the sustainability agenda is reduced to a management paper-chase where easily measured 'outputs' take priority over more complex 'outcomes'. Some environmental indicators, such as greenspace per person, are easily defined. More subtle questions, such as whether that greenspace is secure and cared for, will be endlessly debated, and the quality and accountability of such debate is crucial.

But how can local authorities deliver more sustainable services, when they struggle to deliver any services? Their autonomy has dwindled, their financial policy is all about how to make the largest cuts with the least pain, they are lumbered with a legacy of restrictive practices, and the new UK government turned out to have an even more rigorous approach than their predecessors. Even so, the input of sustainability principles can take place in every dimension of activity:

- in-house measures and management;
- structured targetting and monitoring;
- longer term policies, plans and programmes;
- ethical contracting, purchasing, investment;
- active governance and decision-making

As important as any policies or programmes is the management ethos and internal operating structures which encourage awareness and commitment to the sustainability agenda. Typical organization models show how each aspect of internal structure links to others, as a guide to management change *(Fig 14.5)*.

For public policies, plans and programmes, each stage on the management chain from strategy to outcome is a potential input for the 'sustainability' agenda, either in substance or in style *(Fig 14.6)*. Local authorities are also large employers, purchasers and investors – environmental and ethical policies should be built into

---

Box 14.5     **ENVIRONMENT CITY**

The UK's first Environment City was Leicester, which has over eight years fostered a wide range of actions for sustainable development:

- Environ – an independent agency providing environmental & community development services, employing 50 people
- Eco-house – a demonstration refurb with state of the art ecological construction & services
- Vision 2020 - an outline for longer term programmes, including energy, transport, waste, ecology and education

Source: BT Environment City 1995 (www.sustainablecity.org.uk)

---

64 Hambleton 1992
65 CAG Consultants 1998

all economic transactions, and individual authorities should form city-region consortiums to enhance their expertise and bargaining power *(Chapter 10)*.

Finally, there is an agenda for new forms of representation, legitimation and decision-making, as with the current move towards directly elected mayors and executive cabinet-style management.[66] But voter interest may still stagnate while local authorities are seen as obsolete relics of party politics with little real power – in GM the average turnout for local elections is falling below 30%, and some wards are down to a 5% turnout. It may be that new kinds of social economy, sub-cultures, ICT networks and environmental lobbies will be the catalysts for revived local democracy.[67] The implications for local authorities contain many possibilities: they could extend horizontally to other sectors; vertically to township and neighbourhood levels; and laterally by reclaiming former commercial and social activities. Each of these options may bring new life to old institutions, but may also put at risk the performance indicators carefully constructed by their paymasters.

Each district in GM contains such pressures and opportunities with different responses – Manchester has set up inter-agency partnerships with health, police and other agencies; Rochdale has decentralized many functions to township forums and area committees. Salford is running a 'community safety' anti-crime partnership, and using performance indicators as the basis for all management processes.

The problem for a large and fragmented city-region such as GM is that most districts lack specialized functions, bargaining power, and city-wide coordination for strategic issues, while financial pressures leave little room for ideals and innovation. The current proposals for 'corporate plans' and 'community plans' may work well for individual districts; models for similar frameworks exist in free-standing cities such as Leicester or Leeds, where multi-sector partnerships have taken an active role *(Box 14.5)*. For a larger and more complex city-region such as GM this points towards an over-arching linking device, a 'SD Framework' as below.

# LOCAL AGENDAS

Almost every practical action on the sustainable development agenda is more effective and efficient with local involvement and cooperation – land reclamation, recycling, traffic calming, car-sharing, childcare and many others. The principle of subsidiarity aims to take decision-making to the level which is most viable – enhancing both effectiveness in the 'product', and empowerment through the 'process'.

Neighbourhood level action also enhances community 'capacity' where this is lacking, and this depends on a common interest, access to resources and legitimate authority.[68] But local democracy cannot expect everyone to 'join' – many informal networks are already operating in

pubs, clubs and elsewhere, and only come together in the face of problems or threats.[69]

One natural focus for neighbourhood groups is the local built environment – including reclamation, housing, ecology, transport and community services. Town or neighbourhood forums with delegated powers can set out strategies, carry out appraisals and surveys, and carry out small scale works *(Chapter 5)*. Such activity can then extend to the social economy, including LETS schemes, shared facilities, neighbourhood services and others. An effective town or neighbourhood forum will also be a meeting point, trading post, training facility and information hub. Where such a hub is also a

66 DETR 1998 'Modernizing Local Government'           69 Young 1996
67 Grove-White 1996
68 Twelvetrees 1988

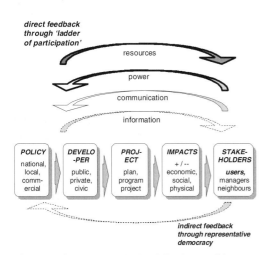

Fig 14.7    **PARTICIPATION PROCESSES**

direct feedback
through 'ladder
of participation'

resources

power

communication

information

| POLICY | DEVELO-PER | PROJ-ECT | IMPACTS | STAKE-HOLDERS |
|---|---|---|---|---|
| national, local, commercial | public, private, civic | plan, program project | +/-- economic, social, physical | users, managers neighbours |

indirect feedback
through representative
democracy

General model for constructive participation on built environment policies,
programmes and projects.
Source: based on Arnstein 1969: Ravetz 1995:

channel for public services and intermediate labour markets, it can move towards operating larger scale development trusts and community businesses *(Chapter 10)*.

While such activities are highly localized, there is a strong case for a coordinated package of powers and responsibilities, a menu which can be drawn down from local authorities in a phased programme. This would include:

- ready access to information, land, premises, equipment;
- training in management and financial skills and resources;
- coordination of public services with local needs;
- devolving of public functions such as security and maintenance to the third sector.

## Participation

While community participation is generally held to be a 'good thing', it is cursed by fuzzy thinking. The 'law of oligarchy' shows that in any group, large or small, an inner elite will emerge to manipulate the majority.[70] While relationships between centre and periphery are mediated by the checks and balances of democratic structures, direct participation aims to extend or to challenge these structures, and is often seen as dangerous by those in the centre. The 'ladder of participation' shows different levels in this centre-periphery relationship, from 'placation' to 'citizen power' *(Fig 14.7)*.[71] Such models tend to assume that 'the community' has a single voice and single agenda – but in practice most communities are diffused and divided. In a globalizing post-industrial city based on consumption and ICT, the nature of community itself is changing rapidly, from one of collective identity through circumstance, to a search for self-identity through lifestyle choice.[72] One result is that the members of environmental groups now exceed the members of trade unions, and such trends are likely to continue.[73]

In principle, participation is a guiding theme for almost every aspect of urban decision-making, from strategic planning to neighbourhood regeneration *(Box 14.6)*. In practice there are many problems – strategic issues are complex and dominated by corporate interests, while at the neighbourhood level most structural decisions have already been taken. Defining the 'community' is a perennial problem, and the need for speed, commercial confidentiality and institutional inertia all serve to distance the community from the real decision point. Participation processes themselves tend to create a community elite – the 'usual suspects' who learn to work the system to their own advantage.[74] While each local authority has to evolve its own approach, there is again a case for a city-region framework of best practice for participation:

- common standards for decentralized decision-making in public services, using citizens juries and focus groups;[75]
- specialist resources such as internet hosts and community technical aid as channels from communities to authorities;
- participation framework for other city-region functions such as transport or health;

---

70 Michel 1968

71 Arnstein 1976
72 Henley Centre 1999
73 Grove-White 1997
74 Jeffrey 1997
75 Stewart 1994: Barbour & Kitzinger 1996.

- forward budgets such as 'per-cent for participation' for audits and feasibility studies'. This aims at a 1% slice of any major budget to be targetted on participative decisionmaking.[75]

## Local Agenda 21

The 1992 Rio Summit advised all local authorities to consult with their citizens to produce a statement on local issues and actions for sustainable development – a Local Agenda 21 (LA21).[76] The UK is seen as a leader in LA21, and a recent survey shows interesting results:[77]

- half of all UK local authorities showed 'tentative support' with a LA21 forum or similar;
- over half of authorities were committed to a LA21 statement by 1996 or later;
- over a third of authorities are working on indicators for sustainable development;
- less than 10% of authorities had formal environmental management registrations.

Fig 14.8                    **LOCAL AGENDA 21**

Overview of alternative themes and directions for Local Agenda 21.
Source: adapted from UNED-UK 1995

---

Box 14.8

### COMMUNITY PARTICIPATION
### in the BUILT ENVIRONMENT

| DEVELOPMENT STAGE | SPATIAL SCALE | METHODS & ORGANIZATION |
|---|---|---|
| Strategic or regional planning guidance | Conurbations, counties | Sustainability indicators & forums |
| local authority UDP | Cities, towns, districts | focus groups, alternative plans |
| Neighbourhood /area strategy/programme | Neighbourhoods | area partnerships, community planning |
| site allocations & development briefs | Development sites | Planning for real, urban design events |
| Building design & mix of uses | Larger buildings & sites | Design participation, local audits |
| Detailed design, facilities, externals | Buildings & surroundings | Models, workshops, simulations, visits |
| Construction, access, local employment | Larger buildings & surroundings | Business / community partnerships |
| Medium-long term use, management & access | Buildings, sites, community facilities | Community development, trusts & associations |

Summary of community participation in time, space and organization.
Source: Ravetz & Community Architecture Group 1995

---

The attitude of most authorities in GM towards such an idealistic programme is generally receptive but sceptical. In Manchester the LA21 Forum was seen as a vehicle for radical factions, and its core budget was withdrawn after the 'statement' came out; while the Environment Forum in Oldham continues open discussion on many topical issues. For most, the reality of running a problematic conurbation tends to take priority over the visionary but fuzzy theme of LA21.

The unique asset of LA21 is at the same time its problem – a broad focus not only on every aspect of the local environment, but also complex and challenging social and economic issues. The 'agenda' of LA21 can extend from global to local, and from present to distant future *(Fig 14.8)*. It also includes several kinds of 'discourse' – from welfare reform to a political programme, and from community services to cultural space *(Fig 14.9)*.[78]

From the LA21 programmes and statements now piling up around the UK, there are several themes which stand out:

- For 'quality of life', public discussion of 'QOL' is valuable and can influence political action. But the QOL agenda can also tend

---

75 Ravetz & Community Architecture Group 1996
76 HMG 1998: 'Local Agenda 21'
77 Tuxworth 1996

78 Freeman, Littlewood & Whitney 1996

Fig 14.9 **AGENDAS for LOCAL ACTION**

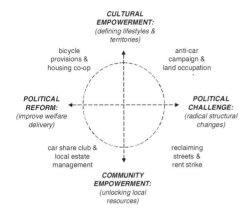

**CULTURAL EMPOWERMENT:**
*(defining lifestyles & territories)*

bicycle provisions & housing co-op

anti-car campaign & land occupation

**POLITICAL REFORM:**
*(improve welfare delivery)*

**POLITICAL CHALLENGE:**
*(radical structural changes)*

car share club & local estate management

reclaiming streets & rent strike

**COMMUNITY EMPOWERMENT:**
*(unlocking local resources)*

Outline of political & cultural discourses, with generalized examples from transport & housing.
Source: adapted from Castells 1987

towards 'motherhood', glossing over harder conflicts and contradictions.

- For the vision factor, envisioning of future goals and scenarios is an essential step for any community, but often the participants are self-selected, with wish-lists disconnected from the real world.
- For direct democracy, LA21 is a potentially valuable feedback channel for the electorate, and brings groups and networks together in new ways. LA21 forums can also be unfocused and marginal, with little formal legitimacy and accountability.
- For the environmental agenda, LA21 is valuable for networking and open discussion, but information and expertise are lacking on complex environmental issues, and key players such as utilities and government agencies show only token interest.

A sceptical view of LA21 might see local authorities as 'playing along' with a public relations exercise, until it challenges the political order as in Manchester.[79] A more positive view sees local democracy in the UK in a great state of flux, and LA21 as a catalyst for new networks with social and environmental agendas.[80] LA21 appears to be supported by the UK government,

but at the same time the new 'community planning' framework may sideline or replace it altogether. From either viewpoint, LA21 is taking the first steps along a very long road – so what might be its long term role in the sustainable development of the city-region?

LA21 should build on its assets, in the vision factor, consensus building, new cultural and social networks, and catalysing of practical projects. It would address its weaknesses, in accountability, in technical resources, and in its limited constituency. The future possible scenarios for local government point to similar options for LA21:

- a topic-based approach, such as for transport or health, developing technical resources and expertise for more effective input to sectoral decision-making;
- an interest-based approach, representing for instance employers, churches or unions, building on existing partnerships, and seeking consensus on social and environmental goals;
- an area-based approach, for townships, neighbourhoods, or parishes, bringing together local authorities, local communities and other stakeholders;
- an action project approach, focused on practical and visible projects which change hearts and minds;
- a multi-sectoral communications approach which sets goals and targets, monitors indicators, distributes information and access, facilitates and coordinates actions by others. Such a model at the regional level now exists with Sustainability North West, a unique catalyst agency set up by the NW partnership.[81]

Such possibilities are equally relevant to the city-region SD Framework as below. For this the unique LA21 contribution would be essential – a vision-based, ethical, direct democracy input, – to what could otherwise be a very complex if not tangled agenda.

---

79 Kitchen 1997
80 Church 1995

81 Sustainability NW 1999

# SUSTAINABLE DEVELOPMENT FRAMEWORK

The final challenge is that the 'whole is greater than the sum of the parts' – that the problems and solutions in sustainable development are each linked, between sectors, activities, agencies and individuals. Even for existing functions there is much overlap, competition and fragmentation, and for the wider agenda of sustainable development there is an even greater need for integration.

How can we put it all together?

For a city-region sustainable development strategy it would be simple to propose an over-arching authority which controls, plans, invests, regulates and takes hard decisions on behalf of its constituency. But at present this is not a viable proposition, either politically or technically.

The reality, in the UK at least, is intense activity at the regional level, with the North West being one of the most advanced of any region. There is also intense activity for local authorities, in the transition from providers and regulators, to enablers and entrepreneurs, and shifting many functions to the market or the local level. The result is that the integrated city-region or metropolitan area is not at present a top priority on the political agenda. But the practical and operational needs for coordination and integration still remain, as do the many functions which are still managed now at the city-region level.

This situation is not a one-off case to be fixed with a new formula for a new institution – it appears to be endemic to the way that a complex post-industrial society and economy works, or fails to work. At every level, power and responsibility are diffused and fragmented, and there is rarely a single body with the powers and resources and mandate to take final decisions. National governments themselves are in a similar transition in the European and global arenas – compromised and co-dependent on every side.

This suggests a more subtle, variegated and post-Fordist approach to integrated management. Rather than 'command and control', this aims to 'communicate and coordinate'. It would gain added value from many activities between many agencies in many sectors, forming the 'neural networks' of a learning economy and innovation society. As a demonstration of the current buzz for 'joined-up government', it would aim at preventative action, long term investment, integration for policy outcomes, the contribution of the third sector, and the soft agenda of changing attitudes and perceptions.[82] In practical terms this emerges as a diverse menu of 'partnerships', 'joint strategies', 'co-decision processes', and 'action-centred networks' – self-organizing chains of collaborative bodies as a model for inter-sectoral working at any level.[83] At the city-region level such partnerships or networks can be organized in various ways:

- strategic partnerships as over-arching fora, as in the public-private North-West Partnership;
- sectoral partnerships, bringing together relevant agencies around themes such as transport or health;
- client-based partnerships targeting specific problems, as for the young unemployed;
- area-based partnerships, as in the current generation of consortia of regeneration programmes;
- project-based partnerships or consortia, for specific actions such as reclamation or waste minimization.

In practice there may be no single 'right' approach – each of the above is valid in its own terms, in dealing with problems beyond the capacity of any one agency. But is there a danger that such partnerships may become talking shops or paper-chases, bogged down by detail, tangled with

82 Perri 6 1998: Christensen 1999
83 Carley & Christie 1996

Fig 14.10 ***S.D. FRAMEWORK ~ STRUCTURE***

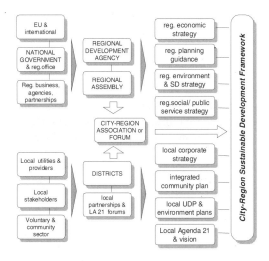

tion between strategic direction and service provision, and this remains to be worked out for each theme and activity. The framework shown here focuses on physical development and environmental management, and this includes specific goals and targets for each of the key sectors. Surrounding this are the many social and economic activities which link to environmental themes. The diagrams below show one possible solution for the scope and structure of such a framework *(Figs 14.10–14.12)*:

The 'Structure' diagram shows the general pattern of relationships between the many stakeholders involved;

- above, the regional assembly and RDA represent national government and regional bodies. Between them they produce and implement the regional strategies for economy, development, environment and public services;
- below, the local authorities and other local partnerships and forums represent the district and other levels and sectors within it. They produce and implement together the corporate strategy, community plan, development plan, LA21 programme and others;
- the city-region Association, in this case AGMA, is strengthened and constituted to act on behalf of the region and the local authorities for appropriate functions. The Association is responsible for operating the SD Framework;
- The SD Framework acts as a coordinating mechanism for the sub-regional components of the regional strategies; and an integrating mechanism for local strategies from the public, private and third sectors.

The 'Scope' diagram outlines the divisions of the SD Framework into key sectors, and the direct and indirect linkages to each programme within them:

- the SD Framework acts as overall coordinating device, with indicators, targets, auditing, management systems, technical coordination and communications;

institutional inertia, and failing to grasp the bigger picture? This possibility strengthens the case for an over-arching SD Framework.

## Integrating vision & strategy

Some kind of integrating mechanism is needed to bring together all the sectors and agencies involved in sustainable development – in other words, the totality of the city-region. But such a mechanism cannot work along the lines of a fixed blueprint, as if carried out by a single organization under known conditions. It will inevitably be more of a 'framework', an indicative outline for strategic goals and targets, within the uncertainties of shorter and longer time horizons. It will also be an 'enabling' mechanism which catalyses and coordinates actions by others; and a 'learning' mechanism which continuously innovates, adapts and communicates.

Such a 'SD Framework' can take shape at regional, city-region, local or neighbourhood level, each with a different set of opportunities and responsibilities. The framework proposed here for GM is a demonstration for discussion purposes of how it might work.

The key to providing slim-line coordination without top-heavy bureaucracy, is in the distinc-

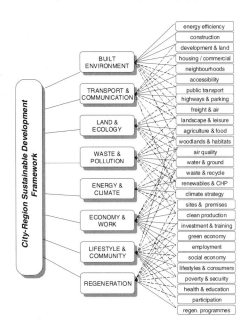

Fig 14.11    **S.D. FRAMEWORK ~ SCOPE**         Fig 14.12    **S.D. FRAMEWORK ~ OPERATION**

- over 30 programmes and action strategies are directly linked or indirectly coordinated with the 8 key sector strategies;
- each programme involves the actions of many other bodies, such as utilities, education or health, and provides a common format for collaborative management, planning and investment.

Finally the 'Operations' chart shows some of the essential functions needed to make the SD Framework efficient and effective, in coordinating the actions of many diverse bodies:

- a 'management' theme with a common framework for semi-autonomous partnership 'agencies', for multi-lateral functions such as energy or housing, where none exist already;
- a 'finance' theme which coordinates the finances of such agencies for investment, borrowing and underwriting from public-private consortia;
- a 'planning' theme which coordinates physical development, environmental manage-

ment, infrastructure and the spatial dimensions of all activities;
- a 'communications' theme, which provides common information formats, indicators and targets, monitoring and audits, together with public access, awareness-raising, education and training.

Such an SD Framework contains and links many specific strategies, but is not itself a strategy to be carried out by a single body. The number and complexity of the issues and actors involved implies that any meaningful 'strategy' either cannot be agreed, or makes unfounded assumptions, or is out of date before it can be printed. So the SD Framework aims to be a more flexible and enabling device which continuously coordinates, adjusts and negotiates the more detailed strategies contained within it. But this begs the questions – what kind of 'clout' would it have, and to what kind of organization or democratic mandate is it accountable?

# Integrating the city-region

The UK is alone in Europe in having no strategic authorities for its major conurbations – many functions of the urban system are dispersed or privatized, making planning and strategic investment more difficult and complex.[84] The functions which relate to the city-region as a natural unit are many, and suggest that city-region coordination, if not government, is essential. However, the experience of the metropolitan county councils, including that of GM from 1974–86, was not wholly positive, and few would propose to revive another two-tier system. At present coordination through the GM association of AGMA works for a limited range of functions:[85]

- public transport, through the PTE and PTA, and transport investment via the joint local transport plan system;
- police, emergency services and civil defense;
- waste disposal and landfill operations;
- joint units for ecology, minerals, transport, heritage, tourism, records and research;
- spatial development through a planning forum, coordinating the UDPs and producing 'strategic planning frameworks' and similar.[86]

In practice, inter-authority coordination through AGMA is voluntary and sometimes fragile – real-time issues such as parking and out-of-town development generate conflict, and coordination of the many public and private agencies is often ad-hoc. A perennial problem is the core-periphery linkage, where Manchester City provides most of the regional facilities, but has the highest poverty levels in the conurbation, and hence there are periodic calls for a GM 'Assembly'.[87]

To operate an effective city-region 'SD Framework', the current voluntary association needs to be extended and strengthened – in the form of a constituted 'Association', or possibly an 'assembly', 'forum' or similar body. Its functions would be designed to fit political constraints and opportunities – with some functions devolved from the regional level, others devolved from the districts, and others created on the public-private-community interface. In each case ultimate authority and accountability would rest above with the region, and below with the districts, while the city-region Association would take delegated operational control on specific issues. It would also act as the sub-regional forum for all RDA strategy and activity relevant and appropriate to that level. Its operation and constituency could be based on that of AGMA, and could evolve in several stages over the next decade, following on from the establishment of the RDA and regional assembly.

What would the city-region Association do? Its aim would be to manage the sustainable development framework, for all activities which are most effective at a scale larger than the districts and smaller than the region. Firstly it would extend the scope of coordination for existing activities:

- a more integrated provision for existing 'joint' public services such as transport and waste;
- coordination of marketized services such as health, training, social housing, tourism;
- enhanced coordination with regional providers and utilities such as energy, water, telecoms and railways.

Following on from there it might develop a range of new services and activities, based on the primary objective of the SD Framework:

---

**Box 14.7**

## *INTEGRATED CITY MANAGEMENT*

A cost-benefit analysis was applied to the government structure of Tilburg in the Netherlands, as it was realized the city was not being run efficiently or effectively. The Tilburg model redesigned the structure into divisions where achievements are measured by quality of outcome, and level of transparency and accountability. Performance indicators were developed and applied to many areas such as housing, safety, transport and environment. Citizens are consulted on a neighbourhood basis and common priorities established by consensus and vision-building.

Source UNCHS 1995

---

84 Roberts & Thomas 1995
85 Williams 1998
86 AGMA 1997
87 R.Leese, in Manchester Evening News 21/07/97

- agencies and investment partnerships for services and infrastructure: such as housing, public transport, vehicle fleets, local food markets, CHP networks, energy efficiency, woodlands;
- regulation and coordination at the city-region level: public purchasing / contracting, environmental management, energy/climate strategy, green corridors, land reclamation;
- coordination and management role for investment by the RDA, EU funding programmes, major infrastructure and others;
- enabling role for strategic resources: inward investment, arts and sports, higher education, technology development, ICT, strategic sites and large scale regeneration.

Achieving such an Association will be a balancing act between a top-heavy bureaucracy and a lightweight entrepreneurial agency – democracy and accountability generally carries a price. Each city-region around the world evolves its own model, and the nearest examples can be seen in Europe, where the Copenhagen, Frankfurt and Paris city-regions have each evolved streamlined agencies for strategic functions.[88] In the UK, the special case of London is now the test-bed for a new generation of metropolitan governance. For a provincial capital such as GM, the role of its Association and SD Framework will emerge, as the surrounding regional structures and the new local authorities take shape *(Box 14.7)*.[89]

It might be argued that such an Association would add further layers to an already over-complex cake. On the other hand, it is clear that the sustainable development agenda demands a much higher level of integration, in whichever functional units are appropriate and effective –

and city-regions are such units, with a unique set of problems and opportunities.

One example of an urgent policy imperative is the issue of climate change – where in one of the world's richest nations, we are unable to put even basic insulation into each house in the city. So the SD framework would enable the city-region energy-climate strategy to bring together the political, economic, technical and social means to do this, and coordinate the result with other sectors for social welfare and economic opportunity.

Every chapter in this book contains similar examples. At the end of the day, the issue here is not the detail of political structures – it is the principle of coordination and integration for sustainable development. There is much to gain from doing this, and little time to lose.

---

**Box 14.8**

### *SUMMARY ~ S.D. FRAMEWORK*

The 2020 governance strategy will see new structures and processes of decision-making, to manage a 'sustainable development framework', integrated between all sectors:

- decision-making with responsive, ICT-enabled, multi-cultural, consensus techniques
- strengthen powers, legitimacy and efficiency of districts, towns and neighbourhoods
- extend Local Agenda 21 to community planning with technical grounding
- set up a city-region 'sustainable development framework' as a coordinating and enabling platform in the context of regional governance
- set up city-region 'agencies' where needed to carry out city-region 'strategies' and 'programmes'.

---

88 Hall 1988
89 Roberts, Thomas & Williams 1998

# SUMMARY & CONCLUSIONS

The principles of sustainability are now accepted by governments, businesses and others. But there are huge gaps between principle and practice, which need to be tackled at every level from the local to the global. The city-region is a vital link in this chain.

Greater Manchester, the world's first industrial city, is a very topical case-study for this inquiry into 'integrated planning for long term sustainable development'.

In *City-Region 2020* we take a strategic view of the dynamics of this industrial and post-industrial conurbation over 25 years. In each sector we look at the principles and practice of sustainable development, from each of many angles:

- environment – tuning up the material metabolism;
- time – the dynamics of restructuring of city and regional systems;
- space – the dynamics of where it happens on the ground;
- economics – patterns of production, work, trade, competition;
- politics – roles and institutions for management and decision-making;
- technology – risks and opportunities
- society – enhancing lifestyles, communities, public services and social economy;
- culture – globalization, affluence, exclusion, diversity, media and networks.

We also look at how each sector – housing, transport and so on – fits with the others, for a wider picture of the conflicts and synergies between them.

To bring together such a wide range of knowledge we have introduced some new tools. A 'system mapping' of the environmental, economic and social metabolism of each sector helps to untangle the linkages. It also helps to form strategies to coordinate actions, identify the agencies to carry out the actions, and operate accounts to help manage the system.

The research itself has three main outcomes:

- a detailed scenario which explores the dynamics and opportunities in the case-study;
- general policy implications for cities and regions in the developed world;
- general methods and tools for wider use around the UK and the developed world.

# The city-region

Greater Manchester is a dynamic, complex and problematic conurbation. It is a world city and thriving centre for finance, education, sport and culture – it also has a million people living in poverty, amidst obsolete industry and crumbling buildings. The city contributes 1/700th of the world climate change effect, air pollution is high, life expectancies are short, and the city casts a huge 'footprint' on the world.

Possible futures for the city-region are shaped by the trends of globalization, liberalization, ICT and social exclusion. Such trends could lead to alternative scenarios, from 'business as usual' to 'deep ecology'. *City-Region 2020* looks in detail at a middle way or 'sustainable development' scenario. This draws from a composite 25 -year vision for each area type:

- urban centres can be vibrant, diverse, vibrant, green and safe;
- development areas can evolve new kinds of environment for working and living;
- the inner cities can regenerate themselves using the potential of the third sector;
- the suburbs can reinvent their neighbourhood centres, local economies and services;
- the urban fringe and rural areas can be a rich and diverse landscape.

Such a scenario can be encouraged by short term 'baseline' actions from local authorities:

- environmental and social audits, accounts and management systems;
- green and ethical purchasing, contracting and investment policies;
- strategic planning and partnership building for long term investment;
- consensus and vision building through an expanded Local Agenda 21 or similar.

## The built environment

The city-region *2020 development strategy* aims to restructure and consolidate the physical and spatial form of the city-region, to encourage strong local economies, cohesive communities, and diverse lifestyle patterns:

- urban form: restructuring for diversity and balance of housing, services, access, ecology;
- neighbourhood strategy which clusters and revitalizes local centres, jobs and services;
- housing development to provide over 20% new dwellings in all sizes and tenures;
- property development to promote local centres, mixed uses, travel management;
- vacant and derelict land re-used as short or long term resource in urban restructuring;

The *2020 buildings strategy* aims to reduce the environmental impact of the building stock metabolism. This will provide for rising standards of comfort and health, while reducing $CO_2$ emissions by 40%:

- every new building built and operated to energy-environment best practice standard;
- every existing building to be upgraded to best practice via city-wide regeneration;
- all buildings to be monitored regularly and environmental health hazards minimized.

## Travel & transport

The *2020 transport strategy* aims to balance mobility, efficiency and equity in the transport 'metabolism'. There are three themes – integration of modes, diversification of technologies, and coordination with other sectors:

- demand management via accessibility planning, integrated travel management, and re-engineering for walking and cycling;
- promote clean vehicles, smart systems, and clubs for car access without ownership;
- stabilize traffic growth, with large shift to other modes and low-impact vehicles;
- fully integrated and responsive ICT-based public transport to rival car performance;
- freight and distribution coordinated with multi-mode interchanges and local networks;
- air travel growth within environmental limits; the airport as an integrated transport hub.

# Land & ecology

The *2020 landscape strategy* for urban and hinterland areas follows the theme of integrated land management, cultivating the 'ecological metabolism' for a rich and diverse human-biological tapestry:

- networks of urban greenways and habitats, with doubling of biomass and biodiversity;
- organic and low-impact agriculture on the urban fringe producing food for local markets;
- mixed woodlands to cover a third of the fringe area and one tenth of urban area;
- closed loop eco-cycles for carbon, timber, minerals and other resources.

# Waste & pollution

The *2020 environment strategy* aims to upgrade eco-efficiency in the material metabolism. Waste itself will be a potential resource in a closed loop cycle of production and consumption:

- environmental standards for maximum risk and exported substances in the city-region pollution 'bubble';
- transport air emissions contained by demand management and cleaner technology;
- water demand management for climate risk, total supply quality with lead replacement;
- waste agency to develop materials handling, re-use and re-design for a zero-emission and zero-waste economy.

# Energy & climate

The *2020 energy-climate strategy* aims to transform and de-carbonize the total energy metabolism. Integration of demand, supply, conversion and distribution, can reduce climate emissions by 35% by 2020 and 60% by 2050:

- climate response and mitigation programme to monitor risks and opportunities;
- energy services firms and partnership energy agency to accelerate efficiency in all sectors;
- local renewable energy sources where appropriate, for up to 10% of peak demand;

- combined heat and power programme for all inner urban and industrial areas, for a quarter of total energy demand.

# Economy & work

In the face of globalization and restructuring, the *2020 green economy strategy* aims at local resilience and capacity, via long term ecological modernization, diversifying employment and skills, intermediate labour markets, social credits and the third sector:

- integrated environmental management for sites, premises, transport, energy, resources;
- cleaner production and waste minimization as drivers for innovation and competitiveness;
- green economic development with clean technology nodes, specialist networks, supply chain management and green investment fund;
- stakeholding and stakeowning approach for diversification of employment and skills, with potential 10% increase in jobs;
- realizing the potential of the third sector, through intermediate labour markets, cultural industries, mutuals and social credit networks.

# Lifestyle & community

The *2020 social strategy* tackles the fragmentation and underfunding of public services by applying sustainability principles, in the context of social cohesion and cultural diversity. The result will be responsive services, third sector inputs, and civic regeneration:

- changing attitudes and lifestyles to reduce the impacts of consumption;
- anti-poverty strategy for diverse cultures with integrated preventative and adaptive measures;
- health strategy, with holistic community and complementary medicine for positive health;
- crime and security strategy coordinated with preventative environmental and social action;

- education for human development potential and lifelong learning, for knowledge-based eco-modernizing society;
- integrated public services and social strategy, for individual empowerment, social cohesion and cultural diversity.

## Regeneration

The *2020 regeneration strategy* is a continuous healing of the 'urban metabolism' itself, rather than a short term fix. It puts together the physical, economic and social restructuring, re-engineering and re-invention of the city-region:

- physical restructuring, continuous and city-wide, for strategic environmental targets;
- economic and employment diversification to balance the risks of globalization;
- social empowerment through community action and the third sector economy;
- urban and environmental planning for the city-region 'sustainable development framework'.

## Funding the city-region

The *2020 investment strategy* funds restructuring and re-engineering in many sectors. With changing boundaries between public, private and non-profit organizations, new financial mechanisms aim at a better balance of costs and benefits:

- eco-taxation package for all environmental consumption, with revenues re-invested;
- long term investment partnerships to bridge market barriers and split responsibilities;
- integrated financial social and environmental accounting for programmes and organizations;
- market transformation for least-cost planning and integration of supply and demand.

## Running the city-region

The *2020 management strategy* will see new structures and processes of decision-making, to form a city-region 'sustainable development framework' which coordinates all sectors:

- decision-making with responsive, ICT-enabled, multi-cultural, consensus techniques
- strengthen powers, legitimacy and efficiency of districts, towns and neighbourhoods
- extend Local Agenda 21 to community planning with technical grounding
- a city-region 'sustainable development framework' as a coordinating and enabling platform in the context of regional governance
- city-region 'agencies' where needed to carry out city-region 'strategies' and 'programmes'.

## Outcomes

The result is a detailed sustainable development scenario and policy framework, as a demonstration for other cities and regions in the developed world. It also has lessons for the UK Sustainable Development Strategy, for urban and regional policy, and the 'third way' in general.

Since its start in 1994, the Sustainable City-Region programme has run in parallel to many regional and sub-regional policy initiatives:

- The GM Strategic Planning Framework has endorsed the principles of the 2020 development strategy.
- The NW Economic Strategy is focused on the greening of business.
- The GM Local Transport Plans aim at an integrated transport system.
- The NW Landscape Strategy integrates policy for the fragmented urban fringe

The Sustainable City-Region programme continues its theme with related projects, including management tools, economic evaluation, resource flow audits, scenario visioning workshops and an ICT-based interactive 'Sustainability Atlas'.[1]

---

1 Sustainable City-Region Programme 1999: details on http//:www.art.man.ac.uk/planning/cure

# SIGNPOSTS & NEXT STEPS

Looking back and taking stock, we can distill some key themes on city-region strategy and agency. We can look beyond the 25-year horizon, beyond the current paradigm of the 'third way', and beyond the case-study of GM, towards other city-regions around the world. Then we can take stock of 'where we are at' at the present time, as a guide to the next steps on the journey.

First we should recap on what is not in this report. The 2020 project is about a city-region system, so we have focused on issues most relevant to that level, and said less about others such as radiation, ozone or world trade. The project is also about a longer time-horizon, so we have said less about now or next year. The scenario we draw is strongly integrated – assuming that environmental, economic and social changes can and should mesh together – so we have said less about contingencies, and what to do in 'win-lose' situations. Finally we have assumed that strong support comes from national government, Europe and the world in turn – essential to significant progress in the city-region. In turn, sustainable cities and regions are instrumental to peace and justice at the world level.

## Strategy & agency

Can such a wealth of problems and opportunities be boiled down to a simple menu – 'sustainable development in ten lessons'?

Sustainable development in principle is simply a way of achieving the perennial 'greatest good for the greatest number'. In practice, such a theme is as complex and contradictory as the world which it seeks to influence. *City-Region 2020* highlights some key principles for strategic management, each centred on the theme of 'integration':

- horizontal integration, between sectors or 'policy silos' such as housing, education, transport and ecology;

- vertical integration: between national, regional, local and neighbourhood levels;
- environmental integration: between pressures, media and impacts;
- spatial integration: between land-uses, activity patterns and spatial dynamics;
- time integration: between trends, targets and strategies for short, medium and long terms;
- resource integration: between supply- and demand-side in each sector and industry;
- economic integration: between short term cost and long term return to different groups;
- political integration: between many interests, agencies, cultures and communities.

Such a list could go on and on. The point is that the city-region is in many ways an integrated functional territory. To realize its potential and added value, it should aim at a high level of coordination and synergy, across each of the dimensions above – an integrated 'strategy'. Then to put the strategy into practice requires new mechanisms for institutions to work together – an integrated 'agency'. For instance this applies to the energy-climate sector *(Chapter 9)*:

- 'energy-climate strategy': many actions coordinated between many bodies;
- 'energy-climate agency': an institution or partnership which coordinates, catalyses and achieves such actions.

Finally, we have the central challenge of sustainable development, of delivering more for less – better housing in less space, better access with less traffic, and so on. Each of these cases shows an irreducible problem of quantities – to support the global population at western levels would take not one but at least three planets.[2] The key is to focus on the quality, not the quantity, and of course this takes a paradigm shift and a transformation in politics, if not in human nature itself. There may be little alternative, but as the political battles over transport or energy taxation show, it is not an easy road to travel.

## Beyond 2020

A generation is not such a long timespan – a child born today might finish school in 2020, and live to see the 22$^{nd}$ century. But for *City-Region 2020* we took a generation as the practical maximum for current trends and projections, and a practical minimum which could show the restructuring of the city-region. The unknowable question is – what might lie beyond?

One way into this would be to look at the structural transitions in human activity over the last few centuries – starting with the shift from primary to secondary and tertiary 'Fordist' activity *(Chapter 1)*. The post-modern and 'post-Fordist' city is in the transition from tertiary to quaternary services – complex cultural and knowledge-based activities, which challenge the Fordist paradigms of economy, society and urban form.[3]

Following that, we might just dimly imagine an outline of so-called 'quintenary' activity. As ICT replaces the bulk of tertiary service activities, bio-technology and quantum technology are likely to open up the possibilities of artificial life and intelligence.[4] Genetically-designed chemical and cyber-drugs are likely to greatly extend the range of alternative states of consciousness, and the connectivity and diversity of different groups and networks. The quintenary mode of activity which results might be centred on what we can only understand now as poetry or psychic activity – far beyond current concepts of production, consumption, work or leisure.

What could this mean for the future of the city-region? From past observation we would expect such transitions to be compounded, so that many manual and service activities continue, even while quintenary activity becomes a dominant mode – while most restaurants use cyber-waiters, for the most select venues only human waiters will do.

Physical urban form might be less relevant in a functional sense, in that nearly all activity is networked, but more relevant in a human sense,

in that people will be more desirous of places and experiences with psychic or aesthetic qualities – if the city is not beautiful it may cease to exist. Many aspects of the city-region will be universal, and ordering a pizza may involve a global chain of ICT – while other aspects will be very local, and the same pizza may be delivered by the neighbourhood trading system. But the physical dimension is perhaps the one which cannot ultimately be networked – the optimum combination of territory and location may always be the prize of the rich, while the poor make do with virtual equivalents. A city-region such as GM was formed in the full spate of the industrial revolution, and new reasons and cultural norms for several million people to live in post-industrial proximity are just now being invented.

As in the eco-fable of Chapter 3, it is possible to imagine a sustainable city which is the victim of its own success. Following the instructions in this report, for instance, could help to raise quality of life to such levels that local property markets escalate, the inner cities are re-colonized by wealthy enclaves, others are pressed into compact 'sustainable neighbourhoods', and the excluded and marginalized practice their own colonization, in a new geography of wild zones.[5]

As always, such transitions offer both opportunities and risks, and the scenarios outlined through this report can be projected forward into a garden of forking paths which are simultaneously utopias and nightmares. But we would suggest that many of the most interesting problems are those which are here to stay – the polarization of rich and poor, centre and periphery, enterprise and social justice. A series of 50-year 'Futures Workshops' in GM found that in each sector, the debate was not so much about growth rates or technology as such, but these very human perennial questions.[6]

## Beyond the third way

How does this local case-study relate to the wider debate on cities, economic growth and the social model?

At the national level the UK Sustainable Development Strategy is an umbrella which links

---

3 Handy 1995
4 Kaku 1999
5 Davis 1998

6 Gough, Ravetz & Shackley 2000

many components.[7]  Most of these are under review and consultation, and in sectors such as utility regulation, transport strategy and eco-labelling, it is clear that economic, social and environmental goals are pulling in opposite directions. The UK Strategy as a whole follows an 'eco-modernization' discourse, anticipating that the enlightened self-interest of car-driving middle England will be enough to achieve its goals without too much pain.

Here we cover similar ground with several added points.  The first is that the city and regional dimension is the key to success – that national strategy has to work in terms of action on the ground, and coordination on the ground will gain in effectiveness and added value. Another is that the diversity of sub-cultures and new kinds of network are also keys – that the theme of local people acting through local democracy in the common interest is in many ways overtaken in a networked age. A further point is that this double-edged sword of empowerment sees social exclusion and polarization rising in parallel, and that issues of ecology and risk could become the fulcrum for political conflict far beyond what is envisaged in the UK Strategy.[8]

Such themes are also relevant to the urbanist or 'urban renaissance' theme – in the UK, focused on the physical revitalization of declining urban areas, with less to say about urban economies, communities or regional linkages.[9]  The 2020 project hopefully addresses these gaps, with a rounded view on a globalizing economy, a networked society, the regional dimension, and a long-term view on the metabolisms of materials, energy, spatial development and so on.

Finally, the 'third way' as a political philosophy appears to be an inevitable step forward from neo-liberalism on the right, and social democracy on the left.[10]  The third way incorporates the dynamics of globalization, individuation, democratization and ecological modernization – and it also re-asserts the values of 'one-nation' citizenship, an open society, and a delicate balance of rights and responsibilities.[11]

Our multi-dimensional view of sustainable development overlaps a long way with this programme, but again it raises further points. One is the barely imaginable impact of global ICT on cultural divergence, where an open society will be stretched to its limit to accommodate growing social differences. Another is the growing divide between rich and poor, or insiders and excluded, with perhaps wider conflict than envisaged so far – even while the excluded also create their own forms of inclusion, to which the centre has to adapt. These questions are put into sharp focus by the long term prospects for ecological modernization, which behind its green rhetoric is also a device for maintaining social differentials.[12] As local and global limits become tighter by 2020 and beyond, transforming the environmental metabolism is likely to create new social conflict alongside new opportunities.

## Other city-regions

This study has been done as a demonstration project, with the aim of learning both local and general lessons.  Most of the principles, and many of the strategies and actions, are equally relevant to other cities of a similar size, in the UK and elsewhere in the developed world.

Looking at other city-regions across Europe and beyond highlights the inter-dependency of scales between urban, regional and national levels. Each city-region has a unique development path, a unique mix of problems, assets, and position in the regional and national context.  While there may be some common and fundamental goals, such as climate emission targets, the means of achieving them is not a fixed blueprint, more a process of investigation, building consensus and assembling the tools – technical, economic, political and so on.  With this in mind we can review the prospects for different types of European cities.[13]

Urban development shows many variations on the pattern seen in GM, arguably the world's first industrial city-region.  Many European cities have retained more of a historic core with active local economies, but the problems of

7 HMG 1999
8 Beck & Giddens 1991
9 Urban Task Force 1999
10 Giddens 1998
11 Powell 1999

12 Hajer 1995
13 Scheicher-Tappeser & Strati 1999

suburbanization and counter-urbanization are widespread. Cities in peripheral areas, such as Lisbon or Athens, are generally still at the urbanization stage of rapid growth and assimilation of rural communities. Cities in the CIS or former Soviet bloc, such as Warsaw or Budapest, are in the throes of large-scale modernization. Cities in older industrial areas, such as Hamburg or Lyon, display many problems similar to GM, of polarization and exclusion alongside rising affluence, suburbanization and counter-urbanization. Between each city and region there is intense competition for position in the urban hierarchy, which translates to the imperative for economic growth.[14]

Environmental conditions vary greatly, and a pan-European survey shows the complexity of trends and pressures.[15] Environmental management is more advanced in northern and Scandivanian countries, and cities such as Stockholm, Amsterdam and Zurich lead the way for others. In eastern Europe the demise of heavy industry has improved local conditions, while road traffic growth is set to replace $SO_x$ with $NO_x$. Southern European cities show the impacts of rapid growth, mass tourism and lack of infrastructure, with many air and water problems. Most city-regions include both high and low quality environments as part of a functional whole, just as with rich and poor people. Urban environmental metabolism or material flow is generally related to income levels, geography and cultural factors, and few cities take active account of their external impacts.

Urban economic and social problems are recognized at the EU level through regional policy and the 'social model', even while the process of restructuring for competitiveness might exacerbate the situation. Unemployment, exclusion, migration, poor housing, poor health and simple poverty are compounded into a huge and intractable problem. Cities in southern countries tend to have more active kinship networks and informal economies, and may fare better even while their official indicators show worsening problems. Some cities in northern countries also contain high institutional capacity, such as

Baden-Wurtemberg, where the regional economy has prospered from a cohesive model of investment and innovation.

On a wider scale, a general 'European model' of urban development can be contrasted with others around the world, and global urban strategies can be drawn from these.[16] The 'American' model of unrestricted expansion appears to lead to intense polarization and exclusion of class and ethnic groups. The 'less developed' or postcolonialist model in Africa and Asia is also a result of unrestricted growth, in this case with huge unofficial populations of rural migrants on the margins of existence, coming into cities built around the remnants of former administrations. A modernizing Asian model, as in Singapore or Kuala Lumpur, shows levels of physical density and local economic activity almost unknown in the West, managed by corporatist regulation, extended kinship and corporate networks, with intensive use of ICT.

If there is a lesson to be drawn from such an overview, it is perhaps on the linkage of urban development, economic growth and environmental sustainability. Certain levels of affluence and technical sophistication appear to be necessary to meet human needs while reducing environmental impacts. The risk is that increasing economic growth and worldwide affluence to western levels will overload global environmental resources, while undermining the social capacity to deal with such problems. The 'safe window' of opportunity is to manage all three themes in a viable balance, and this will be a perennial theme for the next century.

## Where we are at

For each theme in sustainable development, there is a ferment of policies, literature, research and publicity. Is this leading towards a sustainable future, or simply re-arranging the deckchairs on a sinking ship? Much corporate publicity would say the former – while most scientific evidence would say the latter. Taking a step back, we can make out an overall assessment of 'where we are at':

14 Hall & Hay 1982
15 European Environment Agency 1996                    16 UNCHS 1996

**Fig 15.1**        **SHIFTS & TRANSITIONS**

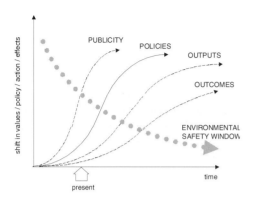

General patterns of change in social systems, with diminishing margin
of safety in environmental systems.
Source: adapted from Elkington 1994; Meadows 1991

protection and social justice. At the same time
the great majority in a city-region such as GM
perhaps 'don't give a toss' – inbuilt values have
hardly changed.[17] Corporate publicity glows with
'sustainability', while many environmental trends
steadily worsen. Public and private policies and
investment plans are all caught up in the inertia
and complexity of the system, and few are in a
position to take a lead. The actions and effects
of policies generally lag behind, until something
comes up which changes the whole agenda – for
instance a century ago a major urban problem
was horse manure, for which the motor car became the solution. But now that human activity
affects world systems, for many problems there
is a diminishing 'window' of opportunity between increasing risks and reducing safety margins.

## Next steps

Most of the scenarios and actions throughout
the report are focused on the year 2020. But the
first question for practical action is – where to
start?

   As in the 'key sector' chapters, each of the
targets and measures can be addressed in the
short, medium and longer term. A typical target,
such as for $CO_2$ reductions, will contain both
'demand side' and 'supply side' components,
both 'physical' actions and 'human' actions, and
will need both technical and economic resources.
The 'next steps' are the actions which cost little,
use available technology, gain political viability
and generate social benefits – the ideal win-win
situation. In general these will include:

- vision: generate scenarios, projections and
  visions in combination with all stakeholders;
- resources: build institutional 'capacity' for
  cohesion, cooperation and longer term thinking;
- action: strategic business planning for short,
  medium and longer terms.

For local authorities, the primary stewards and
guardians of the city, there are some practical
'horizontal' actions in the short term which pre-

- local environment: improvement for some
  problems, deterioration for others, and a long
  way to go;
- global environment: international trade, global agreements and new technology solve
  some problems while creating new ones;
- local economy: some improvement, but need
  to accelerate progress to stay level and reverse trends of inequality, exclusion, and insecurity;
- lifestyles and communities: empowerment for
  some groups, alienation and exclusion for
  others.

In each of these themes there is a transition or
restructuring process, and different trend curves
can be drawn for each kind of transition *(Fig
15.1).* At any one time we may be at several
points on several curves, as the changes perco-
late through the system:

- shift in stated values and publicity;
- shift in policies and strategies;
- shift in investment and actions;
- shift in outcomes and effects;

At present our conscious values have shifted
some way – most now agree on the principle of
balancing economic growth with environment

pare the ground for longer term strategy *(Chapter 3)*:

- corporate policy and mission: promote LA21 & other vision building exercises;
- information and management: full state of the environment & social audits;
- in-house measures: green purchasing policies, environmental management systems;

- prepare for integrated city-region sustainable development framework.

Some of these next steps are already in hand, while others are waiting to happen. If this project has succeeded at all, it will show that more sustainable, and enjoyable, futures are there to be invented.

## 10th June 2024

*What will a sustainable GM be like for our children? Some changes will be very obvious, others will be more subtle. Hopefully the biggest change will be in quality of life – almost impossible to measure, but we know its lack by the stress and alienation of the city today. A sustainable city should be first and foremost an enjoyable and beautiful city.*

*By coincidence, on the 125th anniversary of the Town & Country Planning Association, we come into the city, where silent trams whisk down tree-lined avenues. In residential areas children are playing in the streets amidst wildlife and greenery. While cars are kept firmly in their place, there is a new generation of electric city-bugs, charged from renewable sources across the region.*

*Inside our house we feel immediately comfortable as the low-energy 'breathing' design spreads warmth and relaxation. Even though the house is in a converted terrace,*

*the full length solar conservatory is abundant with exotic and edible plants. On the 'smart panel' we press a few buttons, and within minutes a responsive minibus arrives with a day's journeys ready planned.*

*A trip to the centre shows how GM will equal any of the great world cities in style and quality – fantastic galleries and gracious tree-lined squares. Flexible and creative work patterns mean that workers can enjoy the city with family or friends, any time of day or night. For others, unemployment and homelessness are almost in the past, as local trading networks now include and provide for those outside the global money system.*

*Out in the countryside the landscape seems somehow more green and full. Many people now work the land in organic cultivation, growing fresh produce for local markets. The rivers are clean and the air is pure. Is this utopia, or just sustainable development?*

# ABBREVIATIONS & ACRONYMS

| | | | |
|---|---|---|---|
| ABC | Dutch system of matching land-uses to their accessibility profile | DTI | UK Department of Trade & Industry |
| AGMA | Association of Greater Manchester Authorities: umbrella body for 10 unitary Districts | dw/acre | dwellings per acre: 10 dw/acre = 25 dw/hectare |
| ALARA | 'as low as reasonable achievable': principle for environmental management | EA | Environment Agency: new govt. body as from April 1996 absorbed NRA, HMIP and WRA's |
| AQS | air quality standards for forthcoming pollution control regime | EAL | Environmental Assessment level: measure of average safe background level |
| BAU | 'business as usual': effect of continuing trends with current policies & commitments | EEA | European Environment Agency |
| BANANA | 'build absolutely nothing anywhere near anyone' | EEO | Energy Efficiency Office: Government agency for energy advice and information |
| BATNEEC | 'best available technology not entailing excessive cost': the application of IPC | EHCS | English House Condition Survey |
| BOD | biochemical oxygen demand: overall indicator of water quality | EIA | Environmental Impact Assessment: applies to projects |
| BPEO | 'best practical environmental option': the main principle behind IPC | EMAS | Environmental management & audit system: for management & monitoring |
| BREEAM | Building Research Establishment Environmental Assessment Method for buildings | ENDS | ENDS Report: environmental journal |
| BS 7750 | British Standard on Environmental Management | EPA | Environmental Protection Act 1990: formalized the IPC system |
| CAA | Civil Aviation Authority of the UK | EPAQS | Expert Panel on Air Quality Standards: government review committe |
| CAP | Common Agricultural Policy of the EU: sets subsidies and levies for all food markets | EQS | Environmental quality standards: statutory pollution limit |
| CBA | cost-benefit analysis for both direct & indirect costs | ESI | electricity supply industry |
| CBO | citizen-based organization (voluntary sector) | EST | Energy Saving Trust: government-backed fund for subsidy of energy efficiency |
| CEA | cost-effectiveness assessment | ETR | ecological tax reform: taxing activities with environmental impacts, not social benefits |
| CEC | Commission of the European Community | EU | European Union |
| CEST | Centre for the Exploitation of Science & Technology | FGD | flue gas desulphurisation: removal of $SO_2$ emissions from fossil fuel combustion |
| CFCs | Chloro-fluorocarbons: the main cause of damage to the ozone layer | GDP | Gross domestic product: annual value of goods & services in the national economy |
| $CH_4$ | methane: the 2nd most potent greenhouse gas, mainly from landfills & agriculture | GIS | graphical information system: computer-based mapping and geographical analysis |
| CHP | Combined heat & power: local power generation with use of waste heat | GJ | (energy unit): 1 gigajoule = 9.5 therms = 278 kWh |
| CIA | Chemical Industries Association: UK trade body | GM | Greater Manchester (comprising 10 unitary local authority Districts) |
| CLAG | Critical loads advisory group: govt. expert panel | GMC | Greater Manchester County: (abolished in 1986) |
| CO | carbon monoxide: toxic gas emitted mainly by diesel engines | GMEU | Greater Manchester Ecology Unit |
| $CO_2$ | carbon dioxide: from fossil fuels: responsible for 2/3 of the global warming effect | GMR | Greater Manchester Research, Information & Planning Unit |
| ONS | Office of National Statistics | GONW | Government Office for the North West |
| DIPSIR | 'driving forces, pressure, state, impact, response': EU indicators system | GQA | General Quality Assessment: standard method for freshwater quality |
| DfEE | UK Department of Education & Employment | GWG | global warming gas: generic term for any atmospheric cause of climate change |
| DETR | UK Department of Environment, Transport and the Regions | GWP | global warming potential: weighted factor of propensity for climate impact for each gas |
| DoE | former UK Department of the Environment | GWh | (energy unit): 1gigawatt-hours = 1 million kilowatt-hours (Kwh) = |
| DoH | UK Department of Health | | |

| | |
|---|---|
| H⁺ | Hydrogen ion (measure of acidity) |

$H^+$ — Hydrogen ion (measure of acidity)

ha — hectare: 1 hectare area = 10000 $m^2$ = 2.4 acres = 1/100 of 1 $km^2$

HAG — Housing Association Grant

HFC's — hydro-fluorocarbons: developed as a substitute for CFC's: significant GWG's

HEES — Home Energy Efficiency Scheme: govt fund for basic efficiency improvements

HEI — Higher Education Institution i.e. universities (4 in GM, shortly 5)

hh — household:

HMG — Her Majesty's Government of the UK

HMIP — Her Majesty's Inspectorate of Pollution: former body now subsumed in Environment Agency

HSE — Health & Safety Executive: govt agency

IA — integrated assessment of environmental, social & economic impacts

ICT — information and communication technologies, or 'telematics'

IDA — Improvement and Development Agency: training and development agency for local authorities

IPC — 'Integrated Pollution Control': the UK system of regulation for air, water & waste pollution

IPPC — 'Integrated Pollution Prevention & Control': draft EU directive for environmental framework

IPCC — Intergovernmental Panel for the Scientific Assessment of Climate Change

ISCAM — 'Integrated Sustainable Cities Assessment Method': systems analysis / scenario accounts

ISEW — 'Index of sustainable economic welfare': a measure of total benefit to society

ISO 14001: — International Standards Organization: standard on environmental management

$km^2$ — 1 square kilometre = 100 hectares = 0.38 square miles

kT — Kilo-tonne = 1000 metric tonnes

kWh — Kilo-watt hour: unit of energy: 1kWh = 3600 joules

LA — local authority: in GM there are 10 LAs (8 Districts and 2 Cities)

LA21 — Local Agenda 21: the production of sustainability plans by community consensus

LAAPC — Local Authority Air Pollution Control: licensing of less polluting processes by LA's

LCA — life-cycle analysis: total assessment of impacts for goods and processes

LCP — 'least cost planning': method of allocating resources between multiple objectives

LETS — Local exchange & trading systems: network for non-monetary exchange

LGA — Local Government Association: newly merged organization for all local govt.

LGMB — Local Government Management Board: former information & training agency, now the IDA

LOTS — Living Over the Shop scheme: promotes re-use of vacant space

LRT — Light rapid transit: in GM, the Manchester MetroLink

$m^2$ — square meter: 1 $m^2$ = 10.76 $ft^2$

M6, M62 — principal north-south and east-west motorways with GM at the intersection

MAFF — UK Ministry of Agriculture, Food & Fisheries

MBC — Metropolitan Borough Council

mg m⁻³ — milligrams per cubic metre

MIPS — 'material input per unit service': measure of physical impacts of material production

mg m⁻³ — micro gram per cubic metre: = $10^{-6}$ g / $m^3$

mT — mega-tonne = 1 million metric tonnes

mtC — million tonnes of carbon: 1mtC equivalent to 3.67 million tonnes of $CO_2$.

mtoe — (energy unit): 1 million tonnes of oil equivalent: = 12700 GWh primary energy

MW — power unit: 1 mega-watt = 1000 kW (kilowatt) = 1000 kWh per hour

NCBE — National Centre for Business & Ecology: partnership agency with Coop Bank & HEI's

NFFO — 'Non-fossil fuel obligation': levy charged on energy companies

NFLA — Nuclear Free Local Authorities: UK association coordinated from Manchester

ng m⁻³ — nanogram per cubic metre = $10^{-9}$ g / $m^3$

NGO — non-governmental organization

NHER — National Home Energy Rating: a measure from 1-10 of domestic energy efficiency

NHS — National Health Service of the UK

NIMBY — 'not in my back yard'

$N_2O$ — nitrous oxide, a significant GWG

$NO_2$ — nitrogen dioxide, the most common oxide of nitrogen

$NO_x$ — nitrogen oxides incl. nitrogen dioxide and nitrous oxide, the largest pollutant from transport

NRA — National Rivers Authority: former govt. body with responsibility for freshwaters: now EA

NW — North West region of the UK: including GM, Merseyside, Cheshire, Lancashire, Cumbria

NWBLT — North West Business Leadership Team: private sector consortium of large employers

NWDA — North West Development Agency for regeneration & economic development

NWP — North West Partnership: umbrella consortium of NWBLT and NWRA

NWRA — North West Regional Assembly of local authorities (formerly Association)

NWRHA — North West REgional Health Authority of the NHS executive

$O_3$ — tropospheric or low-level ozone: formed from VOC's and acid gases in sunlight

OECD — Organization for Economic Cooperation and Development:

ONS — Office of National Statistics: govt.agency

OPCS — Office of Population & Census Surveys: government statistical body

p.a. — per annum or per year

| | | | |
|---|---|---|---|
| p.c. | per capita or person | SMR | Standardized Mortality Rate: statistical death rate allowing for age distribution |
| PAC & PAH | polycyclic aromatic compounds: polycyclic aromatic hydrocarbons | SNW | 'Sustainability North West' partnership agency |
| Pb | Lead: contamination in air, water or land | $SO_2$ | sulphur dioxide, the main component of acid rain: mainly from power generation |
| PFI | Private Finance Initiative: capital investment by the private sector for public sector assets | SPD | Single Programming Document: programme for EU regional funding |
| pH | chemical measure of acidity: values below 7 indicate acid: above 7, alkaline | SRB | Single Regeneration Budget: combination of government funds for regeneration |
| PJ | Peta-joule: unit of energy: 1 PJ = 277 million kWh or 22000 tonnes of oil equivalent | SSSI | 'Site of Special Scientific Interest': a statutory designation of natural habitat |
| $PM_{10}$ & $PM_{2.5}$ | Particulate matter less than 10ug or 2.5ug diameter | SWQO | Statutory Water Quality Objectives: official standards for river quality |
| ppb | parts per billion, by volume: pollution measure | TCPA | Town and Country Planning Association |
| PPG | Planning Policy Guidance: series of DETR papers on interpretation of planning law | TEC | Training and Enterprise Council: DTI sponsored agency for business development |
| pph | persons per hectare: planning measure for urban density | therm | (energy unit for gas): 1 therm = 29.3 kWh = 0.105 GJ = 100 000 BTU |
| PTA & PTE | Passenger Transport Authority & Passenger Transport Executive | LTP | Local Transport Plan: system of bidding for local integrated transport strategy |
| PV | photo-voltaics: synthetic panels which generate power directly from sunlight | TTWA | 'Travel to Work Area': area with >70% containment in local labour & employment |
| QUARG | Quality of Urban Air Review Group: govt. expert panel | UDP | Unitary Development Plan: statutory land-use plan by local authorities |
| R&D | research & development: of new technologies | UTC | Urban Traffic Control: electronic regulation of traffic lights and vehicle flows |
| RCEP | Royal Commission on Environmental Pollution: publishes series of major reports | VOCs | volatile organic compounds: large class of hydrocarbons: mainly from industry / transport |
| RDA | regional development agency | vpd | transport unit: vehicles per day in both directions |
| RES | regional economic strategy: RDA framework for economic development & regeneration | ward | smallest unit of metropolitan government: 263 in GM, average 10000 population |
| RIBA | Royal Institute of British Architects | WCED | World Commission on Environment & Development: produced Bruntland Report |
| RPG | Regional Planning Guidance: framework for planning set by government | WDA | Waste Disposal Authority |
| SBI | Site of biological interest: a non-statutory designation used in GM | WRA | Waste Regulation Authority: now within EA |
| SD | sustainable development scenario | WHO | World Health Organization: agency of United Nations |
| SEA | Strategic environmental assessment: EIA applied to policies & programmes | WTE | Waste-to-energy: incineration with energy recovery |
| SME | small and medium enterprise: firm with up to 500 employees | | |

# CORE INDICATORS

This table brings together the 'indicators and targets' boxes from each Key Sector *(chapters 5-10)* with further information. It summarizes a linked set of 'core indicators' from the ISCAM (Integrated Sustainable Cities Assessment Method) scenario accounts *(Chapter 1)*. The core indicators are those selected as being the most sensitive to both the environmental performance of the total city-region system, and to economic and social policy opportunities. This simple accounting system is designed as a counterpart to the more qualitative 'systems mapping' technique of the ISCAM. Each indicator is shown with a value and an annual rate of change (average linear growth over 25 years):

- Historic value for 1970 where possible, although much of this data is scarce and unreliable.

- Current value, with a 1995 baseline. This is taken from 'bottom up' data for GM wherever possible, otherwise estimated from regional or national data.

- BAU (business as usual) projection from current trends, assuming current policies and market conditions, drawn from government or industry data where possible.

- SD (sustainable development) scenario, designed to meet the scientific consensus on targets where possible, in combination with other plausible social and economic goals

- A 'trend-target' index shows the 'policy gap' between the BAU and SD rates of change, as the ratio of (trend – current) / (target – current). Large negative values are shown as a maximum of –100%, indicating a trend which is equal and opposite to the direction of the desired target. Trend-target indices in the shaded areas show average index values for that sector.

- 's' identifies 'satellite' indicators which are not linked directly to the main accounting system.

The ISCAM scenario accounting system is designed to help with strategic environmental management, environmental reporting, scenario work, sustainability appraisal and comparitive accounting between cities and regions. Further details and prototype software are available on www.art.man.ac.uk/planning/cure.

| CORE INDICATORS (1) | | 1970 | 1995 | 2020 BAU | | 2020 SD | | trend/ target | |
|---|---|---|---|---|---|---|---|---|---|
| | UNIT | | (C) | Rate p.a | TOTAL (P) | Rate p.a. | TOTAL (T) | (C-P) (C-T) | NOTES |
| **GENERAL** | | | | | | | | | |
| POPULATION | million | 3.3 | 2.6 | 0.2% | 2.7 | 0.2% | 2.7 | | Based on DETR projections |
| GDP | £ bn | 7.0 | 19.6 | 2.9% | 33.9 | 2.9% | 33.9 | | |
| GDP per head | £1000/cap | 2.1 | 7.6 | 2.4% | 12.2 | 2.4% | 12.2 | | |
| industry/primary | £bn | 4.3 | 6.5 | 1.7% | 9.2 | 2.1% | 9.9 | | Assumed effect of SD policy |
| commerce & public | £bn | 5.6 | 13.1 | 3.2% | 23.7 | 3.0% | 23.1 | | |
| **BUILT ENVIRONMENT** | | | | | | | | *8%* | |
| total urban land | km2 | 435 | 550 | 0.2% | 578 | 0.1% | 564 | 50% | Est.from Best 1981: GMC 1986 |
| new hsg gross pop.density | pp/ha | | 82 | | 88 | | 120 | 73% | |
| industrial land/GDP | m2/£1000 | | 4.25 | -0.7% | 3.55 | -0.9% | 3.34 | 77% | |
| transport land/pass.travel | m2/1000km | | 3.82 | -1.2% | 2.67 | -1.1% | 2.75 | 93% | Incl.dedicated routes, excl streets |
| total derelict land | km2 | 37.0 | 32 | -0.3% | 30 | -2.6% | 11 | 10% | |
| s hh within 400m of local centres | % | | 18% | -1% | 14% | 3% | 30% | -38% | Est.from map surveys |
| s retail space % out of town | % | | 19% | 5% | 42% | -1% | 15% | -100% | Based on 86-93 trend |
| s % households exposed >1000 vpd | % | 10.0% | 20% | 4.0% | 40% | -3.0% | 5% | -100% | Est.from historic traffic data |
| **HOUSEHOLDS** | | | | | | | | *-14%* | |
| energy intensity new stock | GJ/m2/y | | 1.25 | -0.8% | 1.00 | -1.6% | 0.75 | 50% | Est. From ETSU 1996 |
| total final energy demand | PJ/y | 102.0 | 96.1 | 0.8% | 115.8 | -0.3% | 88.6 | -100% | |
| % energy via direct renewables | | | 0.01% | 1064% | 2.0% | 6404% | 12.0% | 17% | |
| % energy via CHP heat | | 2.0% | 0.4% | 49.4% | 5.0% | 156.2% | 15.0% | 32% | |
| domestic $CO_2$ emissions incl power | mtCO2/y | 10.1 | 8.2 | -0.3% | 7.5 | -1.6% | 4.8 | 21% | |
| unfit hsg in need of replacement | 1000's | 220 | 129 | 2.0% | 193 | -1.6% | 78 | -100% | Data NWRA 1994 |
| s % hh in energy poverty | | | 28% | 1.0% | 35% | -4.0% | 0% | -25% | Est.EHCS 1996 |
| s % homeless / hsg stress/ neg.equity | | | 20% | 1.0% | 25% | -4.0% | 0% | -25% | |
| s % new hsg with BREEAM or similar | | | 3% | 8.0% | 9% | 129.3% | 100% | 6% | Digest data for construction 1996 |

| CORE INDICATORS (2) | UNIT | 1970 | 1995 (C) | 2020 BAU Rate p.a | 2020 BAU TOTAL (P) | 2020 SD Rate p.a | 2020 SD TOTAL (T) | trend/target (C-P) (C-T) | NOTES |
|---|---|---|---|---|---|---|---|---|---|
| **TRANSPORT** | | | | | | | | *-21%* | |
| pass.travel economic intensity | km/y/£GDP | 1617.1 | 2460 | -0.4% | 2214 | -1.2% | 1722 | 33% | Shows linkage of travel with economy |
| freight economic intensity | t.km/y/£GDP | 0.5 | 0.42 | 0.4% | 0.46 | -1.3% | 0.28 | -30% | |
| cycle/walk>1km | Mkm/y | | 695 | 2.5% | 1133 | 8.7% | 2204 | 29% | Depends on definition of walking |
| total surface pass.travel | Mkm/y | 11320 | 18739 | 2.0% | 28334 | 0.7% | 22037 | 34% | Excl walking |
| total air pass.travel | Mkm/y | 3000 | 10549 | 8.0% | 31648 | 4.0% | 21099 | 50% | Manchester airport figures |
| total freight traffic | Mt.km/y | 3600 | 8210 | 3.4% | 15172 | 0.5% | 9241 | 15% | |
| total final energy demand | PJ/y | 51.5 | 82.7 | 3.5% | 154.3 | -0.7% | 67.9 | -100% | Excl.LCA of vehicles / roads / fuels |
| total $CO_2$ from transport incl power | MtCO2/y | 4.4 | 7.1 | 3.3% | 13.0 | -0.7% | 5.9 | -100% | Excl.LCA of vehicles / roads / fuels |
| s av.pers.travel car / noncar owners | ratio | 1.3 | 3.0 | 2.7% | 5.0 | -1.3% | 2.0 | -100% | |
| s % children emissions-related asthma | % | | 15% | 4.0% | 30% | -3.2% | 3% | -100% | Link with trans.emissions not yet confirmed |
| s total transport fatalities | no | | 146 | -1.5% | 91 | -3.6% | 15 | 42% | Incl accidents only |
| **OPEN LAND & ECOLOGY** | | | | | | | | *-8%* | |
| urban open/green space | km2 | | 55 | -0.9% | 43 | 1.1% | 70 | -100% | Est.from Best 1981: GMC 1986 |
| total rural land | km2 | 848 | 733 | -0.1% | 709 | -0.1% | 723 | 42% | |
| total woodland area | km2 | 16 | 23 | 4.3% | 48 | 11.7% | 90 | 37% | Est.GMC 1986 |
| other designated habitat | km2 | | 15 | 4.0% | 30 | 6.4% | 39 | 63% | Est.trend 1989-94: GMEU |
| s % food supply organically grown | % | | 0.5% | 16.0% | 2.5% | 156.0% | 20.0% | 10% | Est. Soil Association 1996 |
| s % soil with >7% organic matter | % | | 10% | -2% | 5% | 4% | 20% | -100% | Est RCEP 1997 |
| **WASTE & POLLUTION** | | | | | | | | *2%* | |
| material throughput/GDP factor | kg/£GDP | | 3.6 | -0.9% | 2.8 | -2.0% | 1.8 | 46% | Est Biffa plc |
| total material output | Mt/y | 42.5 | 57.7 | 1.2% | 74.6 | -0.6% | 48.5 | -100% | |
| total waste recycled | Mt/y | | 1.4 | 3.4% | 2.6 | 5.2% | 3.3 | 64% | Est GMWDA 1996 |
| compost / digestion / spreading | Mt/y | | 0.1 | 20.5% | 0.7 | 48.5% | 1.5 | 42% | |
| total to final disposal | Mt/y | | 11.4 | -1.3% | 7.8 | -2.1% | 5.3 | 60% | |
| s estuary water nitrate loading | mgN/l | | 14 | 2.6% | 23 | -1.1% | 10 | -100% | Trend 1988-96: Mersey Basin 1994 |
| NOx total emissions | kt/y | 82.0 | 107 | 0.1% | 108 | -2.5% | 39 | -3% | incl utilization/efficiency per final demand |
| S CO total emissions | kt/y | | 330 | -0.7% | 270 | -2.7% | 110 | | |
| S PM total emissions | kt/y | | 24 | -0.3% | 22 | -2.0% | 12 | 17% | Incl $PM_{10}$ ($PM_{2.5}$ data n/a) |
| **ENERGY & CLIMATE** | | | | | | | | *-18%* | |
| total final demand | PJ/y | | 333 | 1.7% | 474 | -0.6% | 284 | -100% | Final demand calc.bottom up from sectoral totals |
| total renewable supply | PJ/y | | 2 | 12.4% | 7 | 60.3% | 25 | 21% | Incl.direct localized sources of heat & power |
| CHP heat output | PJ/y | | 5 | 7.9% | 14 | 18.2% | 26 | 43% | Heat refers to distributed heat or CHP |
| total primary energy | PJ/y | | 406 | 1.5% | 561 | -0.5% | 355 | -100% | primary energy: raw fuel before processing |
| total $CO_2$ emissions | mt | 37.2 | 31 | 0.8% | 37 | -1.2% | 22 | -72% | |
| total $CO_2$ / total GDP 'intensity' | kg/£GDP | | 1.58 | -1.1% | 1.14 | -2.3% | 0.66 | 48% | 'carbon intensity': fundamental SD indicator |
| S total $CH_4$ emissions | kt | | 220 | -3.0% | 55 | -3.6% | 22 | 83% | excl.agricultural emissions |
| S total CFC / HCFC emissions | kt | | 2.60 | 2.5% | 4.20 | -3.6% | 0.25 | -68% | based on 19995 trend |
| **SERVICES & INDUSTRY** | | | | | | | | *-31%* | |
| serv.floorspace / total GDP | m2/£GDP | 11.0 | 0.86 | -0.4% | 0.78 | -1.2% | 0.60 | 30% | |
| serv.new blg.intensity | GJ/m2/y | | 2.9 | -0.4% | 2.6 | -1.2% | 2.0 | 33% | |
| serv.final energy demand | PJ/y | 33.5 | 47.9 | 1.7% | 67.8 | -0.1% | 46.1 | -100% | |
| serv.$CO_2$ emissions incl power | MtCO2/y | 4.7 | 4.7 | 0.6% | 5.4 | 35.1% | 46.1 | 2% | |
| ind.energy intensity / ind.GDP | MJ/yr/£G | 34.6 | 16.4 | -0.4% | 14.8 | -2.0% | 8.2 | 20% | |
| ind. final energy demand | PJ/y | 148.7 | 106.2 | 1.1% | 136.2 | -0.9% | 81.1 | -100% | |
| ind. $CO_2$ emissions incl power | MtCO2/y | 17.9 | 10.5 | 0.3% | 11.2 | -1.1% | 7.5 | -23% | |
| s Business with EMAS/BS7750 | % | | 1% | 20.0% | 6% | 196.0% | 50% | 10% | |
| s total GDP relative to UK av. | % | | 96% | -0.2% | 92% | 0.2% | 100% | -100% | |
| s ind.added value/job /UK av. | % | | 95% | -0.1% | 92% | 0.2% | 100% | -60% | |
| s ind. Investment/job/UKav. | % | | 78% | -0.3% | 73% | 1.1% | 100% | -23% | |
| s total unemployment / UK av. | % | | 105% | 0.1% | 108% | -0.2% | 100% | -60% | |

# RIO PRINCIPLES & AGENDA 21

- People are entitled to a healthy & productive life in harmony with nature
- Development today must not undermine the development and environment needs of future generations
- Nations have the sovereign right to exploit their own resources, but without causing environmental damage beyond their borders
- Nations shall develop international laws to provide compensation for damage that activities under their control cause to areas beyond their borders
- Nations shall use the precautionary approach to protect the environment. Where there are threats of serious or irreversible damage, scientific uncertainty shall not be used to postpone cost-effective measures to prevent environmental degradation.
- In order to achieve sustainable development, environmental protection shall constitute an integral part of the development process, and cannot be considered in isolation from it.
- Eradicating poverty and reducing disparities in living standards in different parts of the world are essential to achieve sustainable development and meet the needs of the majority of people
- Nations shall cooperate to conserve, protect and restore the health and integrity of the earth's eco-systems. The developed countries acknowledge the responsibility that they bear in the international pursuit of sustainable development in view of the pressures their societies place on the global environment and of the technologies and financial resources they command.
- Nations should reduce and eliminate unsustainable patterns of production and consumption, and promote appropriate demographic policies
- Environmental issues are best handled with the participation of all concerned citizens. Nations shall facilitate and encourage public awareness and participation by making environmental information widely available.
- Nations shall enact effective environmental laws, and develop national law regarding liability for the victims of pollution & other environmental damage. Where they have authority, nations shall assess the environmental impact of proposed activities that are likely to have a significant adverse impact.
- Nations should cooperate to promote an open international economic system that will lead to economic growth and sustainable development in all countries. Environmental policies should not be used as an unjustifiable means of restricting international trade.
- The polluter should, in principle, bear the cost of pollution.
- Nations shall warn one another of natural disasters or activities that may have harmful transboundary effects.
- Sustainable development requires better scientific understanding of the problems. Nations should share knowledge and innovative technologies to achieve the goal of sustainability.
- The full participation of women is essential to achieve sustainable development. The creativity, ideals and courage of youth and the knowledge of indigenous people are needed too. Nations should recognize and support the identity and interests of indigenous people.

- Warfare is inherently destructive of sustainable development, and nations shall respect international laws protecting the environment in times of armed conflict, and shall cooperate in their further establishment.
- Peace, development and environmental protection are inter-dependent and indivisible.

1.      Preamble to Agenda 21

## SOCIAL & ECONOMIC DIMENSIONS

2.      International cooperation
3.      Combating poverty
4.      Changing consumption patterns
5.      Population & sustainability
6.      Protecting & promoting human health
7.      Sustainable human settlements
8.      Making decisions for sustainable development

## CONSERVATION & MANAGEMENT OF RESOURCES

9.      Protecting the atmosphere
10.     Managing land sustainably
11.     Combating deforestation
12.     Combating desertification & drought
13.     Sustainable mountain development
14.     Sustainable agriculture & rural development
15.     Conservation of biological diversity
16.     Management of bio-technology
17.     Protecting & managing the oceans
18.     Protecting & managing fresh water
19.     Safer use of toxic chemicals
20.     Managing hazardous wastes
21.     Managing solid wastes & sewage
22.     Managing radio-active wastes

## STRENGTHENING THE ROLE OF MAJOR GROUPS

23.     Preamble to strengthening the role of major groups
24.     Women in sustainable development
25.     Children & youth in sustainable development
26.     Strengthening the role of indigeneous people
27.     Partnerships with NGO's
28.     Local authorities
29.     Workers & trade unions
30.     Business & industry
31.     Scientists & technologists
32.     Strengthening the role of farmers

## MEANS OF IMPLEMENTATION

33.     Financing sustainable development
34.     Technology transfer
35.     Science for sustainable development
36.     Education, training & public awareness
37.     Creating capacity for sustainable development
38.     Organizing for sustainable development
39.     International law
40.     Information for decision-making

# REFERENCES

Abbott, J (1996) *Sharing the City: Community Participation in Urban Management,* London, Earthscan

Ache, Bremm and Kunzmann, K, with University of Dortmund (1990) *Spatial impacts of the Single European Market,* FGR, University of Dortmund

Adams, J (1989) *London's Green Spaces: what are they worth?,* London Wildlife Trust and Friends of the Earth

Adams, J (1996) *Risk,* London, University College Press

Adger, W. and Brown, K (1994) *Land use and the Causes of Global Warming,* Chichester, Wiley

AEA Technology (1997) *Review of Nitrogen Oxide Pollution in the UK,* Warren Springs

AGMA (1989) *Issues for Strategic Guidance,* Wigan, AGMA

AGMA (1992) *Strategic Sites for Industry and Business in Greater Manchester* Wigan, AGMA

AGMA (1994) *Strategic Guidance Monitoring Report,* Wigan, AGMA

AGMA (1997) *Clearing the Air: the Greater Manchester Air Quality Management Strategy,* Wigan, AGMA

AGMA and GMPTA (1994) *Greater Manchester Package Bid 1995/6,* Wigan, AGMA

Alberti M (1996) Measuring Urban Sustainability *Environmental Impact Assessment Review* Vol 16/4-6:381-423

Alexander, C (1986) *A Pattern Language,* Oxford University Press

Allen, R (1997) *Crime Prevention: A Fighting Chance,* National Association for the Care and Resettlement of Offenders

Amin, A and Thrift, N (1995) *Globalization, Institutional Thickness and the Local Economy,* In: Healey, P et al (Eds) *Managing Cities: the New Urban Context,* Chichester, Wiley

Amundsen, C (1995) *Right business, right place - simple as ABC,* In: Town and Country Planning, Vol 63/1

Ardern, K (1996) *Guidance Notes for Prospective Health Impact Assessment for Single Regeneration Budget Proposals,* Public Health Dept, Liverpool Health Authority

Arnstein S.R (1969), *A Ladder of Public Participation* In: Journal of American Institute of Planners, 7/69 Vol 35:216-224

Arrow, K J (1986), *Social choice and multicriterion decision-making,* Cambridge, Mass, MIT Press

Ashby, W.R (1956) *Principles of Cybernetics,* London, Methuen

Ashton, J and Knight, L (1988), *Proceedings of the first UK Healthy Cities Conference,* Dept of Public Health, University of Liverpool

Ashton, T.S (1934) *Economic and Social Investigations in Manchester, 1833-1933,* London, King Publishing

Aspects International and Dept of Trade and Industry (1994) Best Practice Programme, *"Project Catalyst: Report to the DEMOS Project Event,* March Consulting, W.S.Atkins, and Aspects International, London, DTI

Audit Commission (1995) *Local Authority Performance Indicators, Vol 3, Police and Fire Services,* London, HMSO

Audit Commission (1995) *Safer Streets: More Effective Police Patrols,* London, Audit Commission

Audit Commission (1997) *It's a Small World: local government's role as a steward of the environment,* London, Audit Commission Publications

Ausubel J (1993) *Costs, Impacts and Benefits of $CO_2$ Mitigation,* International Institute of Applied Systems Analysis, Austria

Averley, J (1997) *Remaking Manchester,* In: Town and Country Planning Vol66/1

Ayres, R and Simonis, U, (Eds) (1997) *Industrial Metabolism: restructuring for sustainable development,* New York, United Nations University Press

Babus'Haq R and Probert, S.D (1994) *Combined Heat and Power Market Penetration in the UK: Problems and Opportunities,* Applied Energy Vol 48:315-334

Baccini, P and Brunner, P H (1993) *The Metabolism of the Anthroposphere,* Berlin and New York, Springer Verlag

Bain, R, Pettit, T, and Community Transport Association (1993) *Social Car Schemes: a guide to organized car-sharing,* Hyde, Cheshire, Community Transport Association

Baker, S, Kousis, M, Richardson, D, Young, S.C (1997) *Introduction: the Theory and Practice of Sustainable Development in the EU Perspective,* In: Baker et al (Eds), *The Politics of Sustainable Development,* London, Routledge

Barbour R.S and Kitzinger J (Eds.) *Developing Focus Group Research: Politics, Theory and Practice,* London, Sage Publications

Bartlett School (1999) *Landscape of change: the built environment of the digital age,* London, Ballast Wiltshier

Bartlett, S, Hart, R, Satterthwaite, D, de la Barra, X and Missair, A (1999), *Cities for Children: Children's Rights, Poverty and Urban Management,* London, Earthscan

Barton, H and Bruder, N (1995) *A Guide to Local Environmental Auditing,* London, Earthscan

Barton, H, Davis, G, Guise, R (1995) *Sustainable Settlements: a guide for planners, designers and developers,* Luton, Local Government Managerment Board and University of the West of England.

Batty, M (1995) *Cities and Complexity: implications for modelling sustainability,* In: Brotchie, M, Batty, M, Blakely, E, Hall, P and Newton, P, (Eds), *Cities in Competition: productive and sustainable cities for the 21st century,* Melbourne, Longman Australia

Baylin, F (1979), *Solar Sewage Treatment,* In: Popular Science Journal, New York, Vol26/3

BDOR et al (1995) *Community Involvement in Planning and Development,* HMSO, London

Beck, U (1995) *Ecological politics in an age of risk,* Cambridge, Polity Press

Beckenbach F and Pasche M (1996) Non-Linear Ecological Models and Economic Perturbation: sustainability as a concept of stability corridors, In: Faucheux S, Pearce D, Proops J (Eds) *Models of Sustainable Development,* Cheltenham, Edward Elgar

Bell M and Morse S (1998) *Sustainability Indicators: measuring the immeasurable,* London, Earthscan

Benn, M (1998) *Livelihood: work in the new urban economy: Richness of Cities paper 6,* London, Demos Foundation

Bennett M and James P (Eds) (1999), *Sustainable Measures: Evaluation and Reporting of Environmental and Social Performance,* Sheffield, Greenleaf Publishing

Bentley, T ((1999)) *Learning Beyond the Classroom: Education for a changing world,* London, DEMOS Foundation

Best, R (1981) *Land-use and Living Space,* London, Methuen.

Bhatti, M, Brooke, J and Gibson, M, (Eds) (1994) *Housing and the Environment: a new agenda,* London, Chartered Institute of Housing

Bianchini, R and Parkinson, M (1994) *Cultural Policy and Urban Regeneration,* London, Routledge

Biffa plc (1997) *Great Britain plc: the Environmental Balance Sheet,* High Wycombe, Biffa

Binde J (1997) Habitat II and the art of city management, *Futures* Vol 29

Black Environment Network (1991) *The Black Environment Network Report: working for ethnic participation in the environment,* London, BEN

Blair, A.M (1987), *Future Landscapes of the Rural-Urban Fringe,* In: Lockhart D.G. and Ilbery, B (1987), *The Future of the British Rural Landscape,* Norwich, Geo Abstracts

Blau, P.M (1977) *Inequality and Heterogeneity: a Primitive Theory of Social Structure,* New York, Free Press

Blowers, A (1993), Pollution and Waste, In Blowers, A (Ed), *Planning for a Sustainable Environment,* London, Earthscan

Blowers, A and Smith, D (1992) *Waste Location: Spatial Aspects of Waste Management, Hazards and Disposal,* London, Routledge

Blowers, A, (Ed) (1993) *Planning for a Sustainable Environment,* London, Earthscan

Boardman, B (1992) Social Aspects of Energy Efficiency, In: Christie I (Ed) *Energy Efficiency: the Policy Agenda for the 1990's,* London, Policy Studies Institute

Borja, J and Castells, M (1997) *The Local and the Global: Management of Cities in the Information Age,* London, Earthscan

Bossel, H (1996) *20/20 Vision: Explorations of Sustainable Futures,* Centre for Environmental Systems Research, University of Kassel, Germany

Bound, J.P (1997) *Archives of Disease in Childhood,* 76:107-112

Bowers, J (1997), *Sustainability and environmental economics: an alternative text,* Harlow, Longman

Boyle D (1999) *Funny Money: in search of alternative cash,* London, Harper Collins

Boyle, A and Anderson, M (1996) *Human Rights Approaches to Environmental Protection,* Oxford, Clarendon Press

Bradley, C (1986) *Community Involvement in Greening,* Birmingham, Groundwork Foundation

Bramley, G (1995) *Too high a price: homeless households, housing benefit and the private rent,* London, Shelter

Bramley, G and Watkins, C (1996) *Circular Projections: housing need and housing supply in context,* London, Campaign for the Protection of Rural England

Brand., S (1994) *How Buildings Learn: what happens after they're built,* New York, Viking

BRE (Building Research Establishment) (1998) *The Green Guide to Specification,* London, CRC Ltd

BRECSU (Building Research Energy Conservation Support Unit) (1995) *Energy Management Guide, organizational aspects of energy management,* General Information Report No 12, Watford, Building Research Establishment

Breheny, M (1991) *The Contradictions of the Compact City:* a review, In Breheny, M (Ed.) (1992) *Sustainable Development and Urban Form,* London, Pion.

Breheny, M (Ed) (1999), *The People: Where Will They Work? The TCPA project on household growth and the changing geography of jobs.* London, TCPA

Breheny, M and Hall, P (1996), *The People – Where Will They Go? (National report of the TCPA regional inquiry into housing need and provision in England)* London, TCPA

Breheny, M and Rookwood, R (1993) Planning the Sustainable City Region, In: Blowers, A (Ed) *Planning for a Sustainable Environment,* London, Earthscan

Breheny, M J, Hall, P (1988) *Northern Lights: a Development Agenda for the North in the 1990's,* Preston, Derrick Wade and Waters

Breheny, M, and Ross, A (1998) *Urban Housing Capacity: What Can Be Done?,* Final Report of the TCPA Urban Housing Capacity and the Sustainable City Project, London, TCPA

Breheny, M, Gent, T, Lock, D (1994) *Alternative Development Patterns: New Settlements,* London, DOE Planning Research Programme.

Breheny, M.J (1995) *Counter-urbanization and sustainable urban form,* In: Brotchie, M, Batty, M, Blakely, E, Hall, P and Newton, P, (Eds): *Cities in Competition: productive and sustainable cities for the 21st century,* Melbourne, Longman

Brindley, T, Rydin, Y, Stoker, G (1996) *Remaking Planning: the politics of urban change,* London, Routledge

Bristol Energy and Environment Programme (1992) *Bristol Energy and Environment Plan'*

British Airways (1994) *Environment Report,* London, BA

British Geological Survey (1995) *A Geological Background for Planning and Development in Wigan,* Technical Report WN/95/3, British Geological Survey, Nottingham

British Medical Journal, Editorial, July (1999)

Brooke, J (1994) *Towards an Ecological City: poverty and urban regeneration in Glasgow,* In: Bhatti, M, Brooke, J and Gibson, M, (Eds) (1994) *Housing and the Environment: a new agenda,* London, Chartered Institute of Housing

Brooks, A (1996) *Re-establishing Contact between People and Nature: the creation of nature areas by Groundwork in Greater Manchester,* In: Urban Nature Magazine, Vol 2/4

Brotchie J, Hall P and Newton D, (Eds) (1987) *The Spatial impact of technological change,* London, Croom Helm

Brown, K and Adger, N (1993) *Forests for International Offsets,* CSERGE Working Paper GEC 93-16, University of East Anglia and University College London

BT Environment City (1994) *The Big Picture: all eight topics under one roof,* Lincoln, The Wildlife Trusts and British Telecom plc

Buchanan, A and Honey, B (1994) *Energy and Carbon Dioxide Implications of Building Construction,* In: Energy and Buildings International Journal, Vol 20, p 205.

Burchell, B et al (1999), *Job Insecurity and Work Intensification: flexibility and the changing boundaries of work,* York, York Publishing Services

Byrne, D.S, Harrisson, S, Keithley, J and McCarthy, P (1986) *Housing and Health,* Aldershot, Gower

Cadbury, D (1997) *The Feminization of Nature: Our Future at Risk,* London, Hamish Hamilton

CAG and Land Use Consultants (1997) *What matters and why: a new approach to environmental* capital, Report to Countryside Commission

CAG Consultants (1998), *Best Value: integrating sustainable development into Best Value (Draft Report),* Luton, Local Government Improvement and Development Agency

Cahill, A (1999), *More Than Just a Job,* National Housing Federation

Calthorpe, P (1993) *The Next American Metropolis: ecology, community, and the American dream,* New York, Princeton Architectural Press

Camagni, R, Capello,R and Nijkamp,P (1998) *Towards sustainable city policy: an economy-environment-technology nexus,* In: Ecological Economics Vol 24:103-118

Cambridge Econometrics (1994) *Prospects for Reducing CO2 Emissions to the Year 2020: Report submitted to the Nuclear Free Local Authorities,* Manchester, NFLA

Cambridge Econometrics (1996), *Cambridge Regional Economic Review,* University of Cambridge

Cambridge Econometrics (1998), *Industrial Benefits from Environmental Tax Reform in the UK: Technical Report 1,* London, Forum for the Future and Friends of the Earth

Campbell, B (1993) *Goliath: Britain's Dangerous Places,* London, Methuen

Carley M and Kirk K (1999) *Sustainable by 2020: a strategic approach to urban regeneration for British Cities,* Bristol, Policy Press

Carley, M (1995b) *Community Participation in Urban Regeneration: case studies in Edinburgh and Manchester,* Edinburgh, Scottish Homes

Carley, M and Christie, I (1992) *Managing Sustainable Development,* London, Earthscan

Carley, M and Spapens, P (1997) *Sharing the world: sustainable living and global equity in the 21st century,* London, Earthscan

Castells M (1998) *End of millennium, (The information age: economy society and culture: Vol 3)* Oxford, Blackwell

Castells, M and Hall, P (1994) *Technopoles of the world: the making of 21st century industrial complexes,* London, Routledge

Cavadino, P (1997) *Families and Crime,* London, National Association for Care and Resettlement of Offenders

Caves, R (1992) Aviation Policy, In: Roberts, J et al (Eds), *Travel Sickness: the need for a sustainable transport policy for Britain,* London, Lawrence and Wishart

CB Hillier Parker and Savill Bird Axon (1998), *The Impact of Large Foodstores on Market Towns and District Centres,* (Report to the DETR) London, TSO

CEC (Commission of the European Communities) (1990) *Green Paper on the Urban Environment,* CEC, Brussels

CEC (Commission of the European Communities) (1990) *Green Paper on the Urban Environment,* Brussels, CEC

CEC (Commission of the European Communities) (1990) *Green Paper on the Urban Environment,* Brussels, CEC

CEC (Commission of the European Communities) (1992) *Towards Sustainability: (5th Environmental Actioni Programme),* Brussels, CEC

CEC (Commission of the European Communities) (1994) *Europe 2000+: Cooperation for European Territorial Development,* Brussels, EC

CEC (Commission of the European Communities) (1995) *Medium Term Social Action Programme 1995-97,* Brussels, CEC

CEC (Commission of the European Communities) (1995) *Potential Benefits of Integration of Environmental and Economic Policies - an incentive based approach to policy integration,* Brussels, EC

Centre for Local Economic Strategies (1992) *Social Regeneration - Directions for Urban Policy in the 1990's,* Manchester, CLES

Centre for Local Economic Strategies (Gibbs, D C) (1994) *"The Green Local Economy: Integrating Economic and Environmental Development at the Local Level",* Manchester, CLES

Champion, T, Atkins, D, Coombes, M and Fotheringham, S (1998), *Urban Exodus: a report for CPRE,* London, Campaign for the Protection of Rural England

Chapman, G (1997), *Environmentalism and the Mass Media: the north-south divide,* London, Routledge

Checkland, P and Scholes, J (1990) *Soft Systems Methodology in Practice,* Chichester, Wiley

Chell, M and Hutchinson, D (1993) *London Energy Study,* London Research Centre

Chesshire, J (1992) *Economic Aspects of Energy Efficiency,* In: Christie, I and Ritchie, (Eds), *Energy Efficiency; the Policy Agenda for the 1990's,* London, Policy Studies Institute

Christensen, K S (1999) *Cities and Complexity: Making Inter-Governmental Decisions,* London, Sage

Christensen, P (1995) *Impact of Different Lifestyles on the Environment,* ERP International Sustainable Development Research Conference Proceedings 1995

Christie I and Levett R (1999) *Towards the Ecopolis: sustainable development and urban governance; Report no 12 of the Richness of Cities project,* Leicester, ECOS Distribution

Civil Aviation Authority (1997) *Air Traffic Forecasts for the United Kingdom,* London, DETR

Clark N, Perez-Trejo F and Allen P (1997), *Evolutionary Dynamics and Sustainable Development,* Cheltenham, Edward Elgar

Clark, M, Gibbs, D, Brime, E and Law, C.M (1992) *The North West,* In: Townroe, P and Martin, R, (Eds) *Regional Development in the 1990's,* London, Jessica Kingsley Publishing

Clarke, P (1997) *Urban Capacity Methodologies,* In: Town and Country Planning Vol 66/9

Clarke, P (1997), Urban Capacity Methodologies, *Town and Country Planning* **66**/9:237-241

Clayton, A, Radcliffe, N (1996) *Sustainability: a systems approach,* London, Earthscan

Cline, W (1992) *The Economics of Global Warming,* Cambridge University Press

Cochrane, A, Peck, J, Tickell, A (1996) Manchester Plays Games: Exploring the Local Politics of Globalization, *Urban Studies* **33**/8:1319-1336

Cohen M (1993) Mega-Cities and the Environment, *Finance and Development* **30** (2): 44-47

Cohen, M.J (1996) *Risk Society and Ecological Modernization: alternative visions for post-industrial nations,* In: Futures Vol 29/2,105-119

Collier,U and Lofstedt, R (1997) *Cases in Climate Change Policy: Political Reality in the European Union,* London, Earthscan

Combined Heat and Power Association (1997) *Response to the Government's CHP Strategy,* London, CHPA

COMEAP (Committee on the Medical Effects of Air Pollutants (1995) *Asthma and Outdoor Air Pollution,* London, HMSO)

Comedia and Demos (1999) *The richness of cities: urban policy in a new landscape,* Leicester, ECO Distribution

Community Development Foundation (1999) *An Environment for Everyone: social exclusion and environmental action,* London, CDF Publications

Community Projects Foundation (1986), *Community work in the U.K. 1982-6: a review and digest of abstracts by Marilyn Taylor,* London, Library Association Publishing and Community Projects Foundation

Confederation of British Industry (1994) *Missing Links: the Problem with British Transport Policy':* London, CBI

Conford, P (Ed), *A Future for the Land: Organic Practice from a Global Perspective,* Bideford, Green Books

Connell, R.W (1993) *Schools and Social Justice,* London, Pluto Press

Coop Bank (1999) *Partnerships Report,* Manchester, Coop Bank

Cooperative Bank plc (1995) *Ethical Policy,* Manchester, Coop Bank

Cooperative Retail Society (1995) *The Right to Know,* Manchester, CRS

Costanza R, d'Arge R, deGroot R et al (1997) The value of the world's ecosystem services and natural capital, *Nature* 387:253-260

Costanza, R, Cornwell, L (1992) *The 4P Approach to Dealing with Scientific Uncertainty,* In: Environment Vol 34/12:20-42

Countryside Agency (1999) *Vision 2020: Englands, Green and Pleasant Countryside,* Cheltenham, CA

Countryside Commission (1986) *Farming in the Fringe,* London, HMSO

Countryside Commission, 1976, *The Bollin Valley: a study of land management in the urban fringe,* Cheltenham, CC

Craig, G, Taylor, M, Szabo, C, Wilkinson, M (1999) *Developing Local Compacts: relationships between local public sector bodies and the voluntary and community sectors,* York, York Publishing Services

Critical Loads Advisory Group, for the DOE (1993) *Critical Loads of Acidity in the United Kingdom,* London, HMSO

Croall, J (1999), Local, Mutual, Voluntary and Simple: the power of local exchange trading schemes, In: Worpole, K (Ed), *Richer Futures: Fashioning a New Politics,* London, Earthscan

Crosby, N (1997) *"The Citizens Jury Process and Environmental Decisions",* In: Sexton K and Burkhardt, T, (eds.) *Better Environmental Decisions: Strategies for Governments, Businesses and Communities,* (forthcoming)

CSO (Central Statistical Office) (1997) *Regional Trends 32,* London, HMSO

Curwell, S, March C, Venables R (Eds) (1990) *Buildings and Health: the Rosehaugh Guide,* London, RIBA Publications

Daly, H and Cobb, J.B (1990) *For the Common Good: Redirecting the economy towards community, environment and a sustainable future,* London, Green Print

Daly, H and Goodland, R (1994) *An Ecological - Economic Assessment of Deregulation of International Commerce under GATT,* In: Ecological Economics, Vol 9/1, Elsevier

Darke, J (1996) *The Man-Shaped City,* In: Booth, C, Darke, J and Yeandle, S (Eds), *Changing Places: Womens Lives in the City,* London, Paul Chapman Publishing

Davies, J K and Kelly, M P (1993) *Healthy Cities: Research and Practice,* London, Routledge

Davis M (1998) *The Ecology of Fear: Los Angeles and the imagination of disaster,* New York, Metropolitan Press

Davis, J and Kelly, M (1993) *Healthy Cities: research and practice,* London, Routledge

de Roo, G (1993) *Environmental Zoning, the Dutch struggle towards integration,* European Planning Studies, 1:3, 367-377).

Deakin, N and Edwards, J (1993) *The Enterprise Culture and the Inner City,* London, Routledge

Dept for Education and Employment (1997) *Superhighway for Training,* Sheffield, DfEE

Dept for Education and Employment (1998) The Learning Age: a renaissance for a new Britain, Cm 3790, London TSO

Dept for Education and Employment (1999) *Excellence in Cities,* DfEE Publications. URL: http://www.standards.dfee.gov.uk/library/publications/excellence [cited: 1st December, 1999]

Dept of Energy (1989) (Martin and Shock), *Energy Use and Energy Efficiency in UK Transport up to the year 2010,* London, HMSO, ETSU

Dept of Energy, Energy Efficiency Office (1990) *Energy Use and Energy Efficiency in the UK Domestic Sector up to the year 2010,* London, HMSO

Dept of Environment (1989) Planning Policy Guidance Note: *Strategic Planning Guidance for Greater Manchester,* London, DoE

Dept of Environment (1993) *Making Markets Work for the Environment,* London, HMSO

Dept of Environment (1993c), *Crime Prevention on Council Estates,* London, HMSO

Dept of Environment (1994) *Housing and Construction Statistics,* London, HMSO

Dept of Environment (1994) *Sustainable Development: the UK strategy,* London, HMSO

Dept of Environment (1994), *MPG 6: Guidelines for Aggregate Provision in England and Wales,* London, TSO

Dept of Environment (1995) *Digest of Data for the Construction Industry,* London, HMSO

Dept of Environment (1995) *Draft Guidance on Determination of Whether Land is Contaminated Land: under the provisions of Part IIA of the Environmental Protection Act 1990,* Consultation Paper, DOE

Dept of Environment (1995) *PPG13: a Guide to Better Practice,* London HMSO

Dept of Environment (1995) *Projections of Households in England to 2016,* HMSO

Dept of Environment (1995) *Rural England - a Nation Committed to a Living Countryside,* (CM 3016: the Rural White Paper), London, HMSO

Dept of Environment (1996) *Water Resources and Supply: an agenda for action,* London, TSO

Dept of Environment (1996) *Digest of Environmental Protection and Water Statistics No 18,* London, HMSO

Dept of Environment (1996) *Indicators of Sustainable Development for the UK,* London, HMSO

Dept of Environment (1996) *Review of the Potential Effects of Climate Change in the UK,* London, HMSO

Dept of Environment (1996) with Dept of Transport, *Planning Policy Guidance Note 13: Transport,* London, HMSO

Dept of Health (1995) *Asthma: an Epidemiological Overview,* Central Health Monitoring Unit, HMSO

Dept of Health (1997) *Health Inequalities,* London, TSO

Dept of Health (1998) New ambitions for our country: a new contract for welfare, Cm 3805, London TSO

Dept of Health (1998) Our Healthier Nation: a contract for health, Cm 3854, London TSO

Dept of Health (1998) *The Acheson Report: an independent enquiry into inequalities in health,* London TSO

Dept of Health (1998) *The Quantification of the Effects of Air Pollution on Health in the UK,* London, TSO

Dept of Health (1999), *Economic Appraisal of the Health Effects of Air Pollution: report of the Economic Appraisal of the Health Effects of Air Pollution Group,* London, TSO

Dept of Health (1999) *Economic Appraisal of the Health Effects of air pollution,* London, DoH (www.doh.gov.uk/hef/airpol/airpolh)

Dept of Health and Dept of Environment (1996) *The UK National Environmental Health Action Plan,* (Cmd 3323) London HMSO

Dept of Social Security (1999), *Poverty: Opportunity for All,* London, TSO

Dept of Trade and Industry (1993) *"A Guide to the Eco-management and Audit Scheme for UK Local Government",* London, HMSO

Dept of Trade and Industry (1994) *The UK Environmental Industry: Succeeding in the Changing Global Market,* London, HMSO

Dept of Trade and Industry (1995) *Energy projections for the UK,* Energy Paper No 65, London, HMSO

Dept of Trade and Industry (1997) *Digest of UK Energy Statistics 1997,* London, TSO

Dept of Trade and Industry (1998) *Energy Sources for Power Generation,* London TSO

Dept of Trade and Industry (1998) *Our Competitive Future: building a knowledge-based economy,* CM4176, London TSO

Dept of Trade and Industry (1999) *New and Renewable Energy: prospects for the 21st century,* London TSO

Dept of Trade and Industry (1999), *New and Renewable Energy: Prospects for the 21st Century,* London, DTI Publications

Dept of Trade and Industry (1998) *Review of Energy Sources for Power Generation,* London, DTI

Design Innovation Group (1996) *The Commercial Impacts of Green Product Development,* DIG, Open University, Milton Keynes

DETR (1996), *Energy Report 1996, supplement to the English House Condition Survey 1991,* London, HMSO

DETR (1997) *UK Implementation of EC Directive 96/61 on integrated pollution prevention and control,* London, DETR

DETR (1997), *Draft Producer Responsibility Obligations (Packaging Waste) Regulations 1997,* London, TSO

DETR (1998) *1998 Index of Local Deprivation: a summary of results,* London, DETR

DETR (1998) *A New Deal for Transport: Better for Everyone,* CM3950, London TSO

DETR (1998) *Improving Local Services Through Best Value,* DETR

DETR (1998) *Making biodiversity happen,* DETR Free literature

DETR (1998) *Planning for the Communities of the Future,* London DETR

DETR (1998) *Review of the UK National Air Quality Strategy,* London DETR

DETR (1998) *Sustainability Counts,* DETR Free literature

DETR (1998) *Sustainable Business,* DETR Free literature

DETR (1998) *Sustainable Construction,* DETR Free literature

DETR (1998) *Sustainable Regeneration: a Good Practice Guide,* London DETR

DETR (1998) *The UK Climate Change Consultation Paper,* DETR free literature

DETR (1998) *UK Climate Change Programme Consultation Paper,* London, DETR

DETR (1998), *Less Waste, More Value: consultation paper on the waste strategy for England and Wales,* DETR Free Literature

DETR (1998) *Sustainable Urban Development: towards better practice,* London, TSO

DETR (1998), *Sustainability Appraisal for Regional Planning Guidance,* Interim Report, London, DETR

DETR (1999) *A better quality of life: a strategy for sustainable development for the UK,* Cm4345 London TSO

DETR (1999) *From Workhorse to Thoroughbred: a better role for bus travel,* (daughter document to CM3950) DETR Free Literature

DETR (1999) *New Projections of Households to 2021,* London, DETR News Release 311

DETR (1999) *Regional Development Agencies' Strategies,* DETR URL: http://www.local-regions.detr.gov.uk/rda/strategy/index.htm [cited: 1st December, 1999]

DETR (1999) *Revision of Planning Policy Guidance Note 3: Housing,* DETR Free Literature

DETR (1999) *Sustainability Counts: consultation paper on a set of headline indicators of sustainable development,* London, DETR Free literature (also: www.la21-uk.org)

DETR (1999) *Sustainable Distribution: a Strategy,* DETR Free Literature

DETR (1999), *Contaminated Land: Implementation of Part IIA of the Environmental Protection Act 1990,* London, DETR

DETR (1999), *National Road Traffic Forecasts.* on www.transport.detr.gov.uk

DETR (1999) *Proposals for a Good Practice Guide on Sustainability Appraisal of Regional Planning Guidance,* London DETR

DETR LGA and LGMB (1998) *Sustainable local communities for the 21st century: how and where to prepare an effective Local Agenda 21 strategy,* London TSO

Dicken, P (1998) *Global shift: transforming the world economy,* (3rd ed), London, Paul Chapman

Dickinson, R (1964) *City and Region: a geographical interpretation,* London, Routledge and Kegan Paul

Dodds N, and Rudlin, D (1999), The Autonomous Neighbourhood: a European funded project, *Sustainable Urban Neighbourhoods Newsletter,* **6**:2-4

Dodds, F and Biggs, T (1997) *The UN Comission on Sustainable Development,* In: Dodds, F. (Ed), *The Way Forward – Beyond Agenda 21,* London, Earthscan

Dorling, D (1995) *A New Social Atlas of Britain,* London, Wiley

Douglas M (1984) *Purity and danger: an analysis of the concepts of pollution and taboo,* London, Ark

Douglas, Sholto J and Hart, R A. (1987) *Forest Farming,* London, Watkins

Douthwaite, R (1995) *Short Circuit,* Hartland, Green Books

Dreborg, K.H (1996) Essence of Backcasting, *Futures* 28/9:813-828

Duffell, R (1995), *Taking responsibility: engineering and manufacturing industry,* London, Pluto in association with WWF

Earth Resources Research (1989) *Atmospheric Emissions from the use of Transport in the UK, Vol 2, the Effect of Alternative Policies,* London, WWF and ERR

Eco-Logica Ltd (1995) *Life-Cycle Analysis of Housing: Report for Scottish Homes,* White Cross, Lancaster, Ecologica

ECOTEC (1991) *The Implications of Environmental Pressures: (report to Warwickshire County Council, Coventry City Council and the BOC Foundation),* Birmingham, ECOTEC

ECOTEC (1993) *Reducing Transport Emissions through Planning,* London, DOE .

ECOTEC (1994) *Sustainability, Employment and Growth: the employment impact of environmental policies,* (Working Paper No 1), Birmingham, ECOTEC

ECOTEC (1995) *Costs and Benefits of Sulphur Abatement in the UK,* (unpublished Report to the DOE)

ECOTEC (1996) *Environmental Protection Expenditure by Industry,* (Report to the DoE) London, HMSO

EEA (European Environment Agency) (1995) *Environment in the European Union 1995: Report for the Review of the Fifth Environmental Action Programme,* EEA, Copenhagen / London, HMSO

EEA (European Environment Agency) (1995) *Europe's Environment: The Dobris Assessment,* (Eds) Stanners, D and Bourdeau, P, EEA, Copenhagen / London, Earthscan

Ekins P (1994) *A Four Capital Mode of Wealth Creation,* In: Ekins P and Max-Neef (Eds) *Real Life Economics: Understanding Wealth Creation,* London, Routledge

Ekins, P (1995) *Revisiting the Costs of CO2 Abatement,* In: Barker, T, Ekins, P and Johnstone, N, (Eds) *Global Warming and Energy Demand,* London, Routledge

Ekins, P (1997), The Kuznets Curve for the environment and economic growth: examining the evidence, *Environment and Planning A* **29**:805-803

Ekins, P (1998) *Ecological Tax Reform, Environmental Policy and the Competitiveness of British Industry,* London, Forum for the Future and Friends of the Earth

Elkington, J (1997) *Cannibals with Forks: the triple bottom line of 21st century business,* Oxford, Capstone Publishing

Elkington, J and Hailes, J (1998) *The Green Consumer Guide,* London, Victor Gollancz

Elliott, D (1997) *Energy, Society and Environment: Technology for a Sustainable Future,* London, Routledge

Elson, M, Walker, S, MacDonald R, Edge, J (1993) *The Effectiveness of Green Belts,* London, DOE, HMSO

Employment Studies Institute (1994) *Taxing pollution instead of jobs,* Economic Reports Vol 8 No 9, London, ESI

ENDS (1996-8) *BS7750 Reaches Century Mark,* ENDS Report No 258:7, *Major Companies Sign Up for ISO 14001 and EMAS,* No 275:6-7, *BP Opts for EMAS at all European Sites,* No 278:5

ENDS (Environmental News Data Services) (1994) *Integrated Pollution Control: the First 3 Years,* London, ENDS

Energy Technology Support Unit (1993) *Managing and Motivating Staff to Save Energy,* Guide No 84, Energy Effiiciency Office, Watford, BRECSU

Energy Technology Support Unit (1994) *Renewable Energy in the UK,* Harwell, ETSU and Dept of Energy.

Energy Technology Support Unit (1997), *Assessment of Combined Heat and Power: Final Report,* Harwell, ETSU

Energy Technology Support Unit and NORWEB (1989) *Prospects for Renewable Energy in the NORWEB Area,* Manchester, NORWEB.

Engels, F (1845) *The Condition of the Working Class in England,* Oxford, Blackwell, 1958 edition

English Tourist Board (1994) *Tourism and the Environment: maintaining the balance,* London, ETB

ENTEC UK for the DETR (1997) *The Application of Environmental Capacity to Land-Use Planning,* London, TSO

Environment Agency (1996) *Evaluation of the Extent and Character of Groundwater Pollution from Point Sources in England and Wales,* Bristol, Environment Agency

Environment Agency (1997) *A Review of Dioxin Releases to Land and Water in the UK,* Bristol, EA

Environment Agency (1997) *Best practicable environmental option assessments for integrated pollution control,* (Technical guidance note. Environmental, E1), London, Stationery Office

Environment Agency (1997), *River Valley Inititatives in the North West Region,* Warrington, EA

Environment Agency NW Region, *Greater Manchester, Lancashire and Cheshire Single Programming Document: Environment Section,* Warrington, EA

Environment Industries Commission (1998), *The EIC Guide to the UK Environmental Industry,* Croydon, Faversham House Group Ltd for the EIC

Environment Resource and Information Centre (1996) *Public Attitudes to Transport Policy and the Environment,* London, ERIC, University of Westminster

Environmental Resources Management (1997) *Development of an Integrated Waste Management Strategy for Greater Manchester: Environmental Analysis,* Oxford, ERM

Ernst and Young (1996) *Business Competitiveness and Transport Policy,* (Report to Dept of Transport), London, DoT

Etzioni, A (1996) *Spirit of Community: Rights, Responsibilities and the Communitarian Agenda,* New York, Harper and Row

EU Expert Group on the Urban Environment (1994) *European Sustainable Cities,* 1st Annual Report to European Conference on Sustainable Cities and Towns, Lisbon.

EURONET, *Sustainable Cities Project,* (internet database from University of West of England and International Council for Local Environmental Initiatives), http://cities21.com/europractice

European Commission (1999) *European Spatial Development Perspective,* Luxembourg, EC

European Institute for Urban Affairs (1996) *Regional Government in Britain: an Economic Solution,* Bristol, Policy Press

European Solar Taskforce (1997) *Statement to Ministers,* Brussels, EC DG5

Fairlie, S (1996) *Low Impact Development: planning and people in a sustainable countryside,* Yeovil, Jon Carpenter Publishing

Fankhauser, S (1995) *Valuing climate change: the economics of the greenhouse,* London, Earthscan

Fewkes, A and Turton, A (1994) *Recovering rainwater for w.c. flushing,* In: Environmental Health 94/2:42-46

Field, S (1990) *Trends in Crime and their Interpretation,* (Home Office Research and Planning Unit Report), London, HMSO

Forrest R and Kearns A (1999) *Joined up Places? Social cohesion and urban inclusion for disadvantaged neighbourhoods,* Joseph Rowntree Foundation, York, The Policy Press

Forrester, D, Chatterton, M, Pease, K (1988) *The Kirkholt Burglary Prevention Project,* Paper No 13, Home Office Crime Prevention Unit

Fothergill, S, Monk, S and Perry, M (1987) *Property and Industrial Development,* London, Hutchinson

Freeman, C, Littlewood, S and Whitney, D (1996) *Local Government and Emerging Models of Participation in the Local Agenda 21 process,* In: Journal of Environmental Planning and Management, Vol 39 (1)

Freund, P and Martin, G (1993) *The Ecology of the Automobile,* New York, Black Rose Books

Friedmann J. and Weaver C (1979), *Territory and Function,* Edward Arnold, London

Friedmann, J (1992) *Empowerment: the Politics of Alternative Development,* Oxford, Blackwell

Friend, J. K and Hickling, A (1987) *Planning under pressure: the strategic choice approach,* Oxford, Pergamon

Friends of the Earth (1992) *Less Traffic, Better Towns,* London, FoE

Friends of the Earth (1994) *A Working Future? Jobs and the Environment,* London, FoE

Friends of the Earth (1995), *A climate resolution for local authorities,* Luton, FoE

Friends of the Earth (1999), *Factorywatch: a Top Ten List of Corporate Polluters,* FoE, URL: http://www.foe.co.uk/factorywatch/ [cited 1st December 1999]

Friends of the Earth, *Less Traffic More Jobs: direct employment implications of a sustainable transport strategy for the UK,* London, FoE

Frobel, F, Heinrichs, J and Kreye, K (1980) *The New International Division of Labour,* Cambridge University Press

Funtowicz, S, O'Connor, M, Ravetz, J (1994) *Emergent Complexity and Ecological Economics,* In: van der Straaten and van den Bergh (Eds), *Economy and Eco-systems in Change,* NY, Island Press

Galbraith, J K (1977) *The affluent society,* London, Deutsch

Gallie, D and White, M (1997) *Employee Commitment and the Skills Revolution,* London, Policy Studies Institute

Gandy, M (1994) *The Politics of Urban Waste,* London, Earthscan

Gans, H J (1972), *People and Plans: essays on urban problems and solutions,* (abridged edition), Harmondsworth, Penguin Books

Garnett, T (1996) *Growing Food in Cities: a report to highlight the benefits of urban agriculture in the UK,* London, SAFE and National Food Alliance

Garreau, J (1991) *Edge city: life on the new frontier,* New York, Doubleday

Gates, J (1996) *Revolutionising share ownership: the stakeowner economy,* London, Demos Foundation

Gates, W (1999) *Business @ the speed of thought,* New York, Harper and Row

Geddes, P (1915) (New Ed.1968) *Cities in evolution: an introduction to the town planning movement,* London, Benn

Gee, D (1996) Economic Tax Reform in Europe: opportunities and obstacles, In: O'Riordan, T (Ed) *Eco-Taxation,* London, Earthscan

Gibbs, D (1998), Regional Development Agencies and Sustainable Development, *Regional Studies* 32/4:365-369

Gibbs, D.C ,(1995) *European Environmental Policy: the Implications for Local Economic Development,* In: Regional Studies, Vol 30 No1, p93

Gibbs, D.C, Longhurst, J, and Braithwaite, C (1996) *Moving Towards Sustainable Development: integrating economic development and environmental management in local authorities,* J. Environmental Planning and Management Vol 39/3:317-332

Gibson, T (1996) *The Power in Our Hands: neighbourhood based world shaking,* London, Jon Carpenter Publishing

Gibson, W (1984) *Neuromancer,* New York, Viking

Giddens, A (1994) *Beyond Left and Right: the Future of Radical Politics,* Cambridge, Polity Press

Giddens, A (1998) *The third way: the renewal of social democracy,* Cambridge, Polity Press

Gilbert, O (1989) *The Ecology of Urban Habitats,* London, Chapman and Hall

Gilbert, R, Stevenson, D, Girardet, H and Stren R (1996) *Making Cities Work; the role of local authorities in the urban environment,* London, Earthscan

Gillespie, A and Giannopoulo, G (Eds) (1993) *Transport and communications innovation in Europe,* London, Belhaven Press

Girardet, H (1993) *Cities: The Gaia Atlas,* London, Gaia Books

GM Countryside Unit (1986), *A Nature Conservation Strategy for Greater Manchester,* GM County Council

GM Countryside Unit (1988) *A Strategic Network of Recreation Routes in Greater Manchester,* GMCU (now GM Ecological Unit)

GM Countryside Unit (1989) *The Mosslands Strategy,* GMCU (now GM Ecological Unit)

GM County (1977) *Alternative Strategies Report,* Dept of Planning, GMC

GM County (1979) *Greater Manchester County Structure Plan,* Manchester, GMC

GM Geological Unit (1989) *Greater Manchester Minerals Local Plan'*

GM Passenger Transport Executive (1993) *Strategic Development Plan for Public Transport,* Manchester, GMPTE

GM Police Authority (1995) *How Your Police Perform,* Salford, GMPA

GM PTE (1994) *Trends and Statistics 1984 - 1993,* Manchester, GMPTE

GM PTE (Passenger Transport Executive) (1999) *Green Transport Plans: A Greater Manchester Guide,* Manchester, GMPTE, AGMA and Manchester Airport

GM Transportation Unit (1996) *Transport Statistics Greater Manchester 1995,* GMTU Report no 308

GM Waste Disposal Authority (1997) *Waste Management Strategy for Greater Manchester: consultation document,* Manchester, GMWDA

GM Waste Regulation Authority (1996) *Waste Disposal Management Plan,* Manchester, GMWRA (now Environment Agency)

GMR (GM Research, Information and Planning Unit) (1996) *Greater Manchester: Facts and Trends,* Oldham, AGMA.

Gordon, P and Richardson, H.W (1995) *Sustainable Congestion,* In: Brotchie, M, Batty, M, Blakely, E, Hall, P and Newton, P, (Eds), *Cities in Competition: productive and sustainable cities for the 21st century,* Melbourne, Longman Australia

Gough, C, Ravetz, J, Shackley, S (1999) *Visions for the North West: Interim Report:* Manchester School of Management, UMIST

Gouldson A and Murphy J (1999) *Regulatory Realities: the implementation and impact of industrial environmental regulation,* London, Earthscan

Government Office for the North West (1994) *Single Programming Document for Greater Manchester, Lancashire and Cheshire,* GONW, Manchester

Government Office for the North West and Merseyside (1997) *Action for Competitiveness,* Manchester and Liverpool, GONW and GOM

Government Office for the North West and Merseyside (1999) *Action for Sustainability,* Manchester and Liverpool, GONW and GOM

Graham, S and Marvin, S (1996), *Tele-communications and the City: electronic spaces, urban places,* London, Routledge

Graham, S, Brooks, J and Heery, D (1996), Towns on the Television: closed circuit TV in British Towns and Cities, *Local Government Studies* **22**(3):1-27

Graham, D & Hebbert, M (1999) Greater London, In: Roberts, P, Thomas, K & Williams, G (Eds) *Metropolitan Planning in Britain: a comparitive study,* London, Jessica Kingsley

Graham, T (1995) *Contaminated Land,* Bristol, Jordan Publishing

Green Alliance (1999) *The Case for a Sustainable Energy Agency,* London, Green Alliance

Green, R and Holliday, J (1993), Countryside Planning, In: Blowers, A (Ed) *Planning for a Sustainable Environment,* London, Earthscan

Greenhalgh L and Worpole K (1997) *Park life: urban parks and social renewal,* London, Demos Foundation

Greenhalgh L and Worpole, K (1998), *Urban Policy in New Landscape: Richness of Cities Final Report,* Leicester, Ecos Distribution

Greenpeace (1994) *Achieving Zero Dioxin: an Emergency Strategy for Dioxin Elimination,* London, Greenpeace

Greenwood, W (1932) *Love on the Dole,* London, Penguin

Grimley JR Eve (1997), *Strategic and Operational Property Needs of the Manufacturing Sector,* London, Royal Institute of Chartered Surveyors

Groundwork Foundation (1996) *Small Firms and the Environment - a Groundwork Status Report,* Birmingham, Groundwork Foundation

Groves, R, Morris, J, Murie, A, Paddock, B (1999), *Local Maintenance Initiatives for Home Owners; good practice for local authorities,* York, York Publishing Services

Grove-White, R (1997) Currents of Cultural Change, *Town and Country Planning,* **66**/6:169-173

Grove-White, R, MacNaghten, P, Mayer, S, Wynne, B (1997) *Uncertain World: Genetically Modified Organisms, Food and Public Attitudes in Britain,* Centre for Study of Environmental Change, 1997

Grubb, M, Brack, D and Vrolijk, C (1999), *The Kyoto Protocol: A Guide and Assessment,* London, Earthscan with the Royal Institute of International Affairs

Gudgin, G (1996) *Prosperity and Growth in UK Regions,* In: Local Economy May 1996 p7

Guy S and Marvin, S (1996) *Disconnected Policy: the Shaping of Local Energy Management,* Environment and Planning C: Government and Policy Vol 14:145-158

Guy, S (1998), Developing Alternatives: Energy, Offices and the Environment, *Int. Journal of Urban and Regional Research* **22**/2:264-282

Guy, S and Marvin, S (1996) Infrastructure Networks and the Emergence of Demand Side Management, *Town and Country Planning* **65**/1

Gwilliam M, Bourne C, Swain C and Prat A (1999) *Sustainable Renewal of Suburban Areas,* York, York Publishing Services

Hajer, M.A (1995) *The Politics of Environmental Discourse: ecological modernization and the policy process,* Oxford, Clarendon Press

Hall, P (1988) *London 2001,* London, Unwin Hyman

Hall, P and Hay (1980) *Growth Centres in European Urban Systems,* Berkeley, University of California Press

Hall, P and Ward, C (1998) *Sociable Cities; the legacy of Ebenezer Howard,* Chichester, Wiley

Hall, P, and Breheny, M (Eds), *The People - Where Will They Go? (National Report of the TCPA Inquiry into Housing Need and Provision in England),* London, TCPA

Hambleton R (1999) *Local Government and Political Management Arrangements: an International Perspective,* London TSO

Hammersley, R (1995) An Inquiry into Prospects for Sustainability in Minerals Planning, *Sustainable Development,* Vol 3/ 2, ERP Environment, Chichester, Wiley

Handley J and Wood R (1996) *Greening the North West: a Regional Landscape Strategy,* Manchester, Sustainability North West

Handley J and Wood R (1998) Defining Coherence for Landscape Planning and Management: a regional landscape strategy for North West England, *Landscape Research* **23**/2:133-158

Handley, J (1996) *The Post Industrial Landscape: a resource for the community, a resource for the nation,* Birmingham, Groundwork Foundation

Handley, J and Bulmer, P (1991) *Making the most of Greenspace: the Design and Management of Cost Effective Landscapes,* St Helens, Groundwork Trust

Handy, C (1994) *The Empty Raincoat: Making Sense of the Future,* London, Hutchinson

Hanley N Moffat I Faichney R and Wilson M (1999) Measuring Sustainability: a time series of alternative indicators for Scotland, *Ecological Economics* **28**:55-73

Hannigan, J (1998), *Fantasy Cities: pleasure and profit in the post-modern metropolis,* London, Routledge

Harding, A (1998), *Hulme City Challenge - did it work?* Manchester City Council

Harding, A (Ed) (1994), *European cities towards 2000: profiles, policies and prospects,* Manchester University Press

Hardy, D (1991) *From Garden Cities to New Towns: campaigning for town and country planning 1899-1946,* London, EandF Spon

Harvey, D (1973), *Social Justice and the City,* London, Edward Arnold

Harvey, D (1989) *The Condition of Post-Modernity,* Oxford, Blackwell

Hass-Klau, C (1992) *Civilised streets: a guide to traffic calming,* Brighton, Environmental and Transport Planning

Haughton, G and Hunter, C (1994) *Sustainable Cities,* London, Jessica Kingsley

Hawken, P (1993) *The Ecology of Commerce: A Declaration of Sustainability,* Harper Business, New York, 1993

Hayton, K (1998) *A Big Issue Approach,* Town and Country Planning Vol 67/ 3:104-106

Healey, P (1997) *Collaborative Planning: Shaping Places in a Fragmented Society,* London, Macmillan

Healey, P and Davoudi, S (1995) *City Challenge – sustainable mechanism or temporary gesture,* In: Hambleton, R and Thomas, H (Eds): *Urban Policy Evaluation: Challenge and Change,* London, Paul Chapman Publishing

Henley Centre for Economic Forecasting (1998), *2020 Vision,* London, Henley Centre

Henley Centre for Forecasting (1994) *Local Futures 94,* Oxford, Henley Centre

Hens, L and Honari, M (1997), *Health Ecology,* London, Routledge

Herbert, D (1982) *The Geography of Urban Crime,* London, Longman

Herington, J (1990), *Beyond green belts: managing urban growth in the 21st century,* London, Jessica Kingsley and the Regional Studies Association

Hill, D and O'Connor, J (1996) *Cottonopolis and Culture: Contemporary Culture and Stuctural Change in Manchester,* In: City Vol 5/6 p109

Hills R, Huby M and Kenway P (1999) *Fair and Sustainable: paying for water,* London, New Policy Institute

Hirschfield, A and Bowers, K.J (1997) *The Effect of Social Cohesion on Levels of Recorded Crime in Disadvantaged Areas,* In: Urban Studies Vol 34/ 8:1275-1295

Hitchens, D (1997) *Environmental Policy and Implications for Competitiveness in the Regions of the EU,* In Regional Studies Vol 31/8:813-819

HM Government (1994) *"Sustainable Development: The UK Strategy"* London, HMSO

HM Government (1997) SI 1997 No 648 *Producer Responsibility Obligations (Packaging Waste) Regulations (1997)* London TSO

HM Treasury (1998) *Economic Instruments and the Business Use of Energy (Marshall Report),* London, HM Treasury, TSO

HMG, *Energy White Paper: conclusions of the review of energy sources for power generation, (CM 4071)* London TSO

HMG, *Modern Local Government: in touch with the people,* CM4014, London TSO

HMIP (Her Majesty's Inspectorate of Pollution) (1995) *Chemical Release Inventory,* (Search for authorizations in Greater Manchester) London, HMIP

Hoggett, P et al (1994) *The Politics of Decentralisation,* Macmillan, Basingstoke

Holden Meehan (1994) *An independent guide to ethical and green investment funds,* London, Holden Meehan

Holden R (1995) *Aesthetics and the post-industrial landscape,* Bradford, ERP International Conference on Sustainable Development Proceedings

Holdsworth, W (1993) *Healthy Buildings,* London, Longman

Holling, C.S (1986) The Resilience of Terrestrial Eco-systems: Local Surprise and Global Change, In: Clark, W.M, and Munn, R.E (1986) *Sustainable Development in the Biosphere,* Cambridge University Press

Holling, C.S, (Ed) for IIASA (1980) *Adaptive Environmental Assessment and Management,* Chichester, Wiley

Home Office (1998) Getting it right together: the compact on relations between government and the voluntary and community sectors in England, CM4100, Home Office

Home Office (1998) The 1998 British Crime Survey'; Home Office

Homeless International (1996) *Living in the Future: 24 Sustainable Development Ideas from the UK,* Coventry, Homeless International

Hooper, P and Gibbs, D.C (1995) *Profiting from Environmental Protection: a Manchester Business Survey,* (Report to the Cooperative Bank), Dept of Environmental Sciences, Manchester Metropolitan University

Hosking, L and Haggard, S (1999), *Healing the Hospital Environment: design, management and maintenance of healthcare premises,* London, EandFN Spon

Hough, M (1984) *City Form and Natural Processes,* London, Routledge

Houghton, J T (1997), *Global Warming: the complete briefing,* Cambridge University Press

Housebuilders Federation (1996) *Families Matter,* London HBF

Howard Humphreys and Partners (1994) *Managing Demolition and Construction Wastes,* London, DOE, HMSO

Howard, Ebenezer (1898) (reprinted 1985), *Garden cities of to-morrow: a peaceful path to real reform,* Eastbourne, Attic

Howe J and Wheeler P (1999) Urban Food Growing: the experience of two UK cities, In: *Sustainable Development* 7:13-24

Howes, R, Skea J and Whelan B (1998) *Clean and Competitive: Motivating Environmental Performance in Industry,* London, Earthscan

Hughes, P (1993) *Personal Transport and the Greenhouse Effect,* London, Earthscan

Hulme City Challenge (1994) *Rebuilding the City: A Guide to Development in Hulme,* Manchester City Council and Hulme Regeneration Ltd

Hulme, M and Parry, M (1998) *Adapt or Mitigate? Responding to Climate Change,* Town and Country Planning Vol 67/2:50-51

Hutchinson, D (1992) *Towards Sustainability: the combined production of heat and power,* In: Breheny, M (Ed) (1992) *Sustainable Development and Urban Form,* London, Pion.

Hutchinson, F (1996) *Educating Beyond Violent Futures,* London, Routledge

Huttler, W, Payer H and Schandl H (1996) *Material Flow Analysis Austria,* Vienna, IFF

Hutton, W (1995) *The State We're In,* London, Vintage

ICLEI (1999) Municipal Green Purchasers Network, ICLEI. URL: http://www.iclei.org/europe/ecoprocura/ [cited: 1st December, 1999]

Illich, I (1975) *Medical Nemesis,* London, Calder and Boyars

Institute of Development Policy & Management (1999) *Sustainability Appraisal of Proposed WTO New Round of Multilateral Trade Negotiations,* Phase 2 report, Manchester, IDPM

Institute of Environmental Health (1996) *Indoor Air Quality in the Home,* University of Leicester, IEH

International Energy Agency (1991) *Energy Efficiency and the Environment,* Paris, IAE and OECD

International Environment Reporter (1996) *Ebara announces plans for zero-emissions city,* International Environment Reporter, June 1996

INWARD, quoted in *Region Fails to Punch its Weight,* In: The Guardian, 21/8/96

IPCC (International Panel for the Scientific Assessment of Climate Change) (1996) *Climate Change: the Second Assessment,* Cambridge University Press

Jackson, T and Marks, N (1994) *Measuring Sustainable Economic Welfare - a Pilot Index 1950 - 1990,* York, Stockholm Environment Institute

Jackson, T and Roberts, P (1997) *Greening the Fife Economy: Ecological Modernization as a Pathway for Local Economic Development,* J.Environmental Planning and Management Vol 40/5:615-630

Jacobs M and Dutton C (1999) , In: Roberts P and Sykes H (Eds) Urban Regeneration, London, Sage.

Jacobs, J (1965) *The death and life of great American cities,* Harmondsworth, Penguin

Jacobs, J (1982), *Cities and the Wealth of Nations: principles of economic life,* London, Viking

Jacobs, M (1994) *Green Jobs? The Employment Implications of Environmental Policy,* Report to the World Wildlife Fund, Godalming, WWF

Jacobs, M (1994) *The Limits to Neo-classicism: Towards an Institutional Environmental Economics,* In: Redclift, M and Benton, E (Eds), *Social Theory and the Global Environment,* London, Routledge

Jacobs, M (1997) Environmental Valuation, Deliberative Democracy and Public Decision-Making Institutions, In: Foster, J (Ed) *Valuing Nature: Economics, Ethics and Environment,* London, Routledge

Jacobs, M (1997) *Making Sense of Environmental Capacity,* London, CPRE

Jacobs, M, for the Real World Coalition (1996), *The Politics of the Real World: meeting the new century,* London Earthscan

Jeffrey, B (1997) *Creating Participatory Structures in Local Government,* In: Local Government Policy Making Vol23/4 p25

Jenks, M, Burton, E, Williams, K, (Eds) (1996) *The Compact City: a Sustainable Urban Form?,* London, E and FN Spon

Jensen-Butler, C (1995) *A Theoretical Framework for Analysis of Urban Economic Policy,* In: Lever, W and Bailly, A (Eds), *The Spatial Impact of Economic Changes in Europe,* London, Avebury

Johansson, T, Kelly, H, Ruddy, A; and Williams, R, (Eds) (1993) *Renewable Energy,* London, Earthscan and San Francisco, Island Press.

Jones P (1996) *Mass Balance and the UK Economy,* In: Environmental Excellence 7/96

Jones, B and Partridge, J (1989) *West Gorton: an Economic Survey,* Manchester City Council

Joseph Rowntree Foundation (1995) *An Inquiry into Income and Wealth,* York, York Publishing Services

Joseph Rowntree Foundation (1999) *Food Projects and how they work,* York, York Publishing Services

Kaku, M (1998) *Visions: how science will revolutionize the 21st century,* Oxford University Press

Kay, J.J, and Schneider, E.D (1994) Complexity and Thermodynamics: Towards a New Ecology, In: *Futures,* Vol26/6

Keating, M (1993), *The Earth Summit's Agenda for Change,* Geneva, Centre for Our Common Future

Kendall, J and Knapp, M (1996) *The Voluntary Sector in the UK,* Manchester University Press

Khakee, K and Stromberg, K (1993) *Applying Future Studies and Strategic Choice Approach in Urban Planning,* Journal of the Operational Research Society, Vol 4/3: 213

Kitchen, T (1995) *Towards a More Sustainable Manchester,* In: Whittaker, S (Ed), *First Steps: Local Agenda 21 in Practice,* London, HMSO

Kitchen, T (1996), The Heart of the North? *Town and Country Planning* **65**/1:7-12

Kitchen, T (1997) *People, Politics, Policies and Plans: the city planning process in contemporary Britain,* London, Paul Chapman Publishing

Knoflacher, H (1994) *On the Harmony of People and Traffic,* (unpublished English translation), *Zur Harmonie von Stadt und Werherh'*

Knox, G and Gilman, E (1997) Incidence of Childhood Cancer in proximity to Industrial Sites, *Journal of Epidemiology and Community Health,* Vol 51/151-159

Korten D (1999) *When Corporations Rule the World,* London, Earthscan

Kozlowski, J and Hill, G (1993) *Towards Planning for Sustainable Development: a Guide for the Ultimate Environmental Threshold Method,* Aldershot, Avebury

KPMG Peat Marwick (1999), *Fiscal Incentives for Urban Housing: Exploring the Options: a report to the Urban Task Force,* London, DETR Free Literature

Krause, F et al (1993) *Energy Policy in the Greenhouse: the International Project for Sustainable Energy Paths,* Report to the Netherlands Ministry of Housing, Planning and Environment

Krotscheck, C and Narodoslawski,M (1996) *The sustainable process index: a new dimension in ecological evaluation,* In: Ecological Engineering Vol 6:241-258

Kruger, D (1997) *Access Denied? Preventing information exclusion,* London, Demos Foundation

Kuznets S (1955), Economic Growth and Income Inequality, *American Economic Review* 45:1-28

Lancashire County Council (1951), *Draft County Development Plan,* Preston, LCC

Land Use Consultants (1993) *Trees in Towns: a survey of trees in 66 towns and villages in England and Wales,* Dept of Environment, HMSO

Land Use Consultants (1995) *Sustainable Development for Archaeology and the Historic Environment,* Consultation paper for English Heritage

Landry C and Bianchini F (1997) *The creative city,* London Demos Foundation

Lang, P (1994) *Rebuilding the Local Economy,* London, New Economics Foundation

Lang, T and Heasman, M (2000), *Food, Health and Globalization,* London, Earthscan

Lansley, S (1994), *After the gold rush: the trouble with affluence, consumer capitalism, and economic growth,* London, Century Books and the Henley Centre for Economic Forecasting

Lash, J and Urry, J (1993) *Economies of Signs and Space,* London, Sage

Lave, L, Cobas-Flores, E, Hendrickson, C, McMichael, F (1995) *Using Input-Output Analysis to Estimate Economy-Wide Discharges,* Environmental Science and Technology, 29/9: 421-426

Law, C (1992) *Property-led Urban Regeneration in Inner Manchester,* In: Healey et al (Eds), *Rebuilding the City: Property-led Urban Regeneration,* London, E and FN Spon

Leach, R and Barnett, K (1998) *New Public Management and the Local Government Review,* , Local Government Studies, Vol 23/1: 37-54

Leadbeater C (1998) Welcome to the knowledge economy, In: Hargreaves A and Christie I, (Eds), *Politics of the Future: the third way and beyond,* London, Demos

Leadbeater, C (1997) *A piece of the action: employee ownership, equity pay and the rise of the knowledge economy,* London, Demos Foundation

Leather, P and Morrison, T (1997), *The State of UK Housing,* Bristol, The Policy Press

Lee, D.S, and Longhurst, J (1990) *Estimates of Emissions of SO2, NOx, HCl and NH3 from Greater Manchester and the North West of England,* Manchester Metropolitan University, Atmospheric Research and Information Centre

Leeds Environment Business Forum (1995) *Good Environmental Business Practice Handbook,* Leeds, LEBF Ltd

Leeds Environment City (1996) *Children, Young People and the Environmnet,* Leeds City Council

Leicester City Council, *Leicester Energy Strategy,* Environment Unit, Leicester City Council

Levett, R (1996) *Linking the Indicators,* In: Town and Country Planning Journal, Vol 65/12

Lichfield, N (1987) *The Economics of Urban Conservation,* Cambridge University Press

Lichfield, N & Lichfield, D, (1997) *Community Impact Evaluation in the Development Process* In: Kirkpatrick, C & Lee, N (Eds): *Sustainable Development in a Developing World,* Aldershot, Edward Elgar

Lipietz, A (1995) *Green Hopes: the Future of Political Ecology,* Cambridge, Polity Press

Llewellyn-Davies (1997), *Sustainable Residential Quality; a report to LPAC, Government Office for London and DETR,* London, LPAC

Lloyd, P, Meegan, R, *Contested Governance: European Exposure in the English Regions,* In: Alden, J and Boland, P (Eds), *Regional Development Strategies: a European Perspective,* London, Jessica Kingsley

Lloyd, P.E (1980) *Manchester: a Study in Industrial Decline and Economic Restructuring,* In: White, P, (Ed), *The Continuing Conurbation: Change and Development in Greater Manchester,* Aldershot, Gower

Local Government Association (1998) *Energy Services for sustainable communities: the local government position,* LGA (www.gov.uk/policy/energyservices)

Local Government Management Board (1994) *Greening the Local Economy,* Luton, LGMB

Local Government Management Board (1995) *Environmental Management and Auditing Systems: a Guide for Local Authorities,* Luton, LGMB

Local Government Management Board (1996) *Sustainability reporting: a practical guide for UK local authorities,* Luton, LGMB

Local Government Management Board / Touche Ross (1994) *Sustainability Indicators Research Project – Report on phase 1,* Local Agenda 21 Steering Group, Luton, LGMB

Logan, M (1992) *Environmental Capacity of Airports: a method of assessment,* In: Roberts, J et al (Eds), *Travel Sickness: the need for a sustainable transport policy for Britain,* London, Lawrence and Wishart

Logan, R and Molotch, L (1987), *Urban Fortunes: the Political Economy of Place,* Berkeley, University of California Press

London Research Centre (1997) *Inventory of Atmospheric Emissions from Greater Manchester,* London, LRC

Longhurst, J, et al (1995) *Air Quality in Historical Perspective: a case study of the Greater Manchester Conurbation,* In: Power, H, (Ed), *Urban Air Pollution Vol.2,* Southampton, CMP

Lovelock, J (1995) *The ages of Gaia: a biography of our living earth,* Oxford University Press

Low Income Project Team (1996) *Low Income, Food, Nutrition and Health: Strategies for Improvement,* Nutrition Task Force, Dept of Health

Low Pay Unit (1994) *Survey of the Labour Market in Manchester,* Dept of Education and Employment

Lowe R and Bell M (1999) *Towards Sustainable Housing: Building Regulation for the 21st Century,* JRF, York Publishing Services

Lowe, S and Petherick, A (1989) *Living Above the Shop,* In: Housing Review Vol 38 No2, 1989.

Lusser, H (1997) *ZEUS Takes the Green Car to Market,* In: Town and Country Planning Vol 66/1

MacArthur A (1999) Making the Link: childcare, employment and area regeneration, *Local Economy* 2/99:327-338

MacFarlane, R (1998), What – or Who – is Rural Britain? *Town and Country Planning* 67/6:184-189

Macnaghten, P and Urry, J (1998), *Contested natures,* London, SAGE

Macnaghten, P., Grove-White, R., Jacobs, M. and Wynne, B (1995), *Public Perceptions and Sustainability in Lancashire - Indicators, Institutions, Participation,* (Lancashire County Council and Lancaster University / CSEC).

MAFF (1993) *At the farmer's service,* (compendium of official publications and grant schemes), London, MAFF

MAFF (1994) (Ministry of Agriculture, Fisheries and Food), *Census Data for Greater Manchester 1983-1993.,* Crewe, MAFF

MAFF (1995), *Farming in Britain,* London, TSO

Manchester /Salford /Trafford City Pride Partnership, *"A focus for the future", 1994.*

Manchester Airport (1993) *Development Strategy to 2005,* MIA

Manchester Airport (1994) *Environment Plan: consultation draft,* MA

Manchester City Council (1945), *City of Manchester Development Plan,* MCC

Manchester City Council (1986) *Community Landscapes,* (Information Pack), MCC

Manchester City Council (1991) *Taking Involvement Seriously: a guide to involving the public in your work,* MCC

Manchester City Council (1994) *Economic Facts'*

Manchester City Council (1994) *The Manchester Report: Outputs of Global Forum 1994,* MCC

Manchester City Council (1995) *City Development Guide,* Manchester

Manchester City Council (1995), *Economic Development Statement,* MCC

Manchester City Council (1996) *Manchester: 50 Years of Change,* London, HMSO

Manchester City Council, Chief Executives Dept (1995) *The Best Way to Save is to Share: development of a Manchester Energy Agency,* (internal paper), Manchester City Council

Manchester Health Authority (1996) *Public Health Annual Report 1996,* MHA

Manchester Housing (1996) *Sustainable Communities: Policy Implications,* (Unpublished) report to neighbourhood strategy sub-committee, Manchester City Council

Manchester Permaculture Group (1994), *Urban Tree Cultivation in Manchester: a proposal,* Manchester, MPG

Manchester Telematics Partnership (1997), *Manchester, the Information City: promoting economic regeneration through use of telematics,* Manchester City Council, Economic Initiatives

Manchester Training and Enterprise Council (1998), *A New Deal for 18-24 Year-olds,* MANTEC

March Consulting (1995) *Multi-Client CHP Scheme for Trafford Park, Manchester,* In: Energy Management Journal, July 1995

March Consulting and City of Manchester (1994) *Integrated Energy Saving and Production Strategy for the City of Manchester,* (unpublished) Manchester City Council

March Consulting Group (1987) *Energy Study of the North West Region of the UK,* Report to DG5 of the Commission of the European Communities, DG11

Martin, R and Minns, R (1995) Undermining the Financial Basis of Regions: the spatial structure and implications of the UK pension fund system, *Regional Studies Vol 29 No2, p125*

Maslow A (1970) *Motivation and Personality,* New York, Harper and Row

Max-Neef, M (1992) *Development and Human Needs,* In: Ekins, P and Max-Neef, M, (Eds) *Real-life Economics, understanding wealth creation,* London, Routledge

Mayer, M (1995) *Urban Governance in the Post-Fordist City,* In: Healey, P, et al (Eds), *Managing Cities: the New Urban Context,* London, Wiley

Mayhew, P, Maung, N and Mirlees-Black, C (1993) *The 1992 British Crime Survey, ,* Home Office Research Study 132, London, HMSO

Mayo E (1997) *Community Banking: a review of the international policy and practice in social lending,* London, New Economics Foundation

McCarthy, J (1997), Empowerment Zones: the story so far, *Town and Country Planning* **66**/10:309-311

McEvoy, D, Gibbs, D.C, Longhurst, J (1997) *Assessing Carbon Flow at the Local Scale – Greater Manchester, a UK case study,* Energy and Environment Vol 8/4:297-313

McKinsey and Co (1997) *The Future of IT in British Schools,* London, McKinsey and Co

McLaren, D, Bullock, S, Yousuf, N (1997) *Tomorrow's World: Britain's Share in a Sustainable Future,* London, Earthscan

McLoughlin, J.B (1969) *Urban and Regional Planning: a systems approach,* London, Faber

Meadows, D, Meadows, D and Randers, J (1992) *Beyond the Limits: Confronting Global Collapse and Envisioning a Sustainable Future,* Chelsea Green, Post Mills, Vt, USA

Measham, F, Newcombe, R and Parker, H (1994) The Normalization of Recreational Drug Use among Young People in the North West, *British Journal of Sociology,* July 1994

Mersey Basin Campaign (1995) *Changing for the Better: First Periodic Report,* Mersey Basin Campaign Unit, Manchester, Government Office for the North West

Meyer A and Cooper T (1995) *A recalculation of the social costs of climate change: GCI critique of IPCC WG3,* Cambridge, Global Commons Institute

Michels, R (1968) *Political parties: a sociological study of the oligarchical tendencies,* London, Collier-Macmillan

Miles, I (1995), I.T. Makes Itself At Home, *Town and Country Planning,* **64**/1: 13-16

Milroy,A (1995) *Urban Oases - Greening the Urban Desert,* In: Town and Country Planning Journal, Vol 64 No 10.

Ministry of Housing and Local Government (1970) *Living in a Slum: a study of St Mary's, Oldham,* MHLG, London, HMSO

Mitchell, W J (1999) *City of Bits: Space, Place and the Info-bahn,* Boston, MIT Press

Mitlin, D and Satterthwaite, D (1996) *Sustainable Development and Cities,* In: Pugh, C, (Ed), *Sustainability, the Environment and Urbanization,* London, Earthscan

Mollison, W (1988) *Permaculture: a designer's manual',* NSW Australia, Tagari Institute

Monaghan, A (1997) *Here to Stay: a Public Policy Framework for Community-based Regeneration,* London, Development Trusts Association

Morgan, E (1978) *Falling Apart; the rise and decline of urban civilization,* London, Abacus

Morgan, K (1997) *The Learning Region: Institutions, Innovation and Regional Renewal,* In: Regional Studies Vol 31/5:491-504

Morphet, J (1997) *There'll be planning, but not as we know it,* In: Town and Country Planning, Vol 66/4: 122

Morrell, H (1996) *Women's Safety,* In: Booth, C, Darke, J, and Yeandle, S, (Eds), *Changing Places: Women's Lives in the City,* London, Paul Chapman Publishing

Mulgan G and Landry C (1995) *The other invisible hand: remaking charity for the 21st century,* London, Demos

Mulgan, G (1995) *The other invisible hand: remaking charity for the 21st century,* London, Demos Foundation

Mulgan, G (1996), Functional Hypothecation as a potential solution, In: O'Riordan, T (Ed) *Eco-Taxation,* London, Earthscan

Mulgan, G (1997) *Connexity,* London, Calder and Boyars

Munasinghe, M and Shearer, W (1995), An Introduction to the Definition and Measurement of Bio-geo-physical Sustainability, In: Munasinghe, M and Shearer, W (Eds), *Defining and Measuring Sustainability,* Washington, World Bank and International Bank for Reconstruction and Development

Murray R et al (1999) *Re-inventing Waste: towards a London Waste Strategy,* London, Ekologica

Murray, R (1999), *Creating Wealth From Waste,* London, DEMOS

National Centre for Business and Ecology (1997) *A Green Competitive Edge for the North West,* University of Salford, NCBE

National Centre for Economic Alternatives (1994) *Index of Environmental Trends,* Washington USA, NCEA

National Commission on Education (1993) *Learning to Succeed: Report of the Paul Hamlyn National Commission on Education,* London, Heinemann

National Food Alliance (1998), *Food Poverty: what are the policy options?* London, National Food Alliance

National Rivers Authority (1994) *Irwell Basin Catchment Management Plan,* Warrington, NRA (now Environment Agency)

National Rivers Authority (1994) *Policy and Practice for the Protection of Groundwater: (with NW Regional Appendix),* Bristol, NRA

National Rivers Authority (1994) *Water: Nature's Precious Resource. An Environmentally Sustainable Water Resources Development Strategy,* Bristol, NRA

National Rivers Authority (1995) *The Drought of 1995,* Bristol, NRA

NCVO (National Council for Voluntary Organizations) (1993) *Facts and Figures on the Voluntary Sector,* (Information Briefing) London, Community Matters

Neighbourhood Initiatives Foundation (1994) *Planning for Real.* (training package), Telford, NIF

New Economics Foundation (1997) *Community Works: a guide to community economic action,* London, NEF

Newby, H (1996) *Social Change in Rural England,* In: Town and Country Planning Journal Vol 65 No 2

Newcastle City Council (1992) *Energy and the Urban Environment: Strategy for a major urban centre,* Newcastle City Council

Newman, O (1981) *Community of Interest,* New York, Anchor / Doubleday

Newman, P and Kenworthy, J (1989) *Cities and Automobile Dependence,* Aldershot, Gower

Newman, P, Kenworthy, J and Vintila, P (1992) *Housing, Transport and Urban Form,* Institute for Science and Technology Policy, Murdoch University, Australia

Newson, M (1992) *Water and Sustainable Development: the turn-around decade,* J. Environmental Planning and Management 35/2:175-184

Nicholas, R and McWilliam, G A (1962), Planning the City of the Future, In: Carter C F, (Ed) *Manchester and its Region: a survey prepared for the British Association,* Manchester University Press

Nicholson-Lord, D (1987) *The Greening of the Cities,* London, Routledge

Nijkamp, P, and Perrels, A (1994), *Sustainable Cities in Europe,* Earthscan, London

Nijkamp, P, Lasschuit, P, Soeteman, F (1992) *Sustainable development in a regional system,* In: Breheny, M. (Ed) (1992) *Sustainable Development and Urban Form,* Pion, London

Nilsson, J and Bergstrom, S (1995) *Indicators for the assessment of ecological and economic consequences of municipal policies for resource use,* Ecological Economics, Vol 14: 175-184

NLUD (National Land-Use Database) (1998) *Survey of vacant and derelict land in England and Wales* (DETR) URL: http://www.nlud.org.uk/ [cited: 1st December, 1999]

Noorman, K J and Uiterkamp, T S, (Eds) (1998), *Green Households? Domestic consumers, environment and sustainability,* London, Earthscan

North West Economic Research Consortium (1994) *The Greater Manchester Economy,* (unpublished), Salford University Business Services

North West Partnership (1997) *Greening the North West,* Wigan, NWP

North West Regional Association (1994) *Greener Growth: Advice to Regional Planning Guidance for NW England,* Wigan, NWRA.

North West Regional Association (1994) *Regional Transport Strategy for North West England,* Wigan, NWRA

North West Regional Association (1994), *Environmental Action for North West England,* Wigan, NWRA

North West Regional Association (1996) *The First NW Quality of life and Sustainability Audit,* Wigan, NWRA

North West Regional Association, PIEDA plc with Hall Aitken Associates (1993) *Regional Economic Strategy for North West England,* Wigan, NWRA and North West Business Leadership Team

North West Regional Health Authority (1997) *Patterns of Health in the North West,* Warrington, NWRHA

North West Tourist Board (1994), *Annual Report,* Bolton, NWTB

North West Water (1993) *A time to decide: Future Investment Proposal,* Warrington, NWW

North West Water (1994), *Partnerships in Action: Conservation, Access and Recreation Report,* Warrington, NWW plc

North West Water (1995) Mersey Valley Sludge Disposal, Phase 2, (consultants report)

North West Water (1997) *Improving the Quality of Life: Environment and Performance Report 1996-7,* Warrington, NW Water

NorthWest Development Agency (1999), *Draft Strategy for North West England,* Warrington, NWDA

NORWEB (1995) *Annual Report 1994-5 on the Standard of Performance in Energy Efficiency,* Manchester, NORWEB

NORWEB and Energy Technology Support Unit (1989) *Prospects for Renewable Energy in the NORWEB area,* Harwell, ETSU with NORWEB.

NORWEB and ETSU (1993) *Deploying Renewables: the NORWEB Perspective,* London, Dept of Trade and Industry

Nuclear Free Local Authorities (1991) *Developing Wind Energy: The Planning Issues,* Manchester City Council, Nuclear Policy and Information Unit

NW Green Party (1996) *If Pigs Could Fly: a critique of the case for the Manchester Airport second runway,* Manchester, NW Green Party

NW Tourist Board (1995) *Annual Report,* Chorley, NWTB

NWRA (1997), *Urban Capacity: the North West Study,* Wigan, NWRA

O'Connor, J and Hill, D (1996) *Cottonopolis and Culture: contemporary culture and structural change in Manchester,* In: City, Vol5-6, London

O'Regan, B and Moles, R (1997) *Applying a Systems Perspective to Environmental Management,* In: Journal of Environmental Planning and Management, Vol 40/4:539-543

O'Riordan, T (1995) The Politics of Sustainable Development, In: Turner, K and Bateman, I, (Eds) *Sustainable Development and Environmental Resource Management,* Aldershot, Edward Elgar

O'Riordan, T (1996) *Eco-taxation and the Sustainability Transition,* In: O'Riordan (Ed), *'Ecotaxation,* London, Earthscan

O'Riordan, T, (Ed) (1995) *The Precautionary Principle,* London, Earthscan

O'Riordan, T, and Cobb, R (1996) *That Elusive Definition of Sustainable Agriculture,* In: Town and Country Planning Journal, Vol 65 / 2.

O'Connor, M. (Ed.). (1994). *Is Capitalism Sustainable? Political Economy and the Politics of Ecology,* New York, Guildford Press

Odum, H.T (1983) *Systems Ecology,* NY, Wiley

OECD (1991) *Energy Efficiency and the Environment,* Paris, OECD

OECD (1991) *Environmental Indicators: a preliminary set,* Paris, OECD

OECD (1992) *The OECD Environment Industry: Situation, Prospects and Government Policies,* Paris, OECD

OECD (1995) *Urban Energy Handbook: Good Local Practice,* Paris, OECD

OECD (1997), *Environmental Policies and Employment,* London, TSO

OECD (1997), *Sustainable Development: OECD Policy Approaches for the 21st Century,* Paris, OECD

OECD (1997), *The World in 2020: towards a new global age,* Paris, OECD

Offe, C and Heinze, R.G (1992) *Beyond Employment: Time, Work and the Informal Economy,* (Trans. Braley, A) Cambridge, Polity Press

Office of National Statistics (1998) *The UK Environmental Accounts,* London TSO

OFWAT (1997), *The Proposed Framework and Approach to the 1999 Periodic Review,* London, OFWAT

Oldham MBC (1996), *Sustainability Indicators for Oldham,* Dept of Technical Services, Oldham MBC

Ormerod, P (1994) *The Death of Economics,* London, Faber

Ormerod, P (1998), *Butterfly Economics: a new general theory of social and economic behaviour,* London, Faber and Faber

Orr, D.W. (1992) *Ecological Literacy: Education and the Transition to a Post Modern World,* Albany, NY, State of New York Press

Osborne, S and Shaftoe, H (1995) *Safer Neighbourhoods? Successes and Failures in Crime Prevention,* London, Safe Neighbourhoods Unit

Owens S (1999) Better for Everyone?, *Town and Country Planning* **67**/10:329-331

Owens, S and Cope, D (1992) *Land Use Planning Policy and Climate Change,* Planning Research Programme, DOE, HMSO

Pacione, M (1997), Urban Restructuring and reproduction of inequality of Britain's cities, In: Pacione, M (Ed) *Britain's Cities: Geographies of Division in Urban Britain,* London, Routledge

Pacione, M (1999), The Other Side of the Coin: Local Currency as response to the globalization of capital, *Regional Studies,* **33**/1:63-72

Pahl, R (1984) *Divisions of Labour,* Oxford, Blackwell

Panayotou, T (1998), *Instruments of Change: motivating and financing sustainable development,* London, Earthscan

Pateman, C (1970) *Participation and Democratic Theory,* Cambridge University Press

Patterson W (1999) *Transforming Electricity: the coming generation of change,* London, Earthscan

Pauli, S (1998), Beyond Standard Assessment Tests, *Town and Country Planning* **67**/2:77-79

Pearce, D (1995) *Blueprint 4: Capturing Global Value,* London, Earthscan

Pearce, D (1996) *The True costs of Road Transport (Blueprint 5)*, London, Earthscan

Pearce, F (1994), *Community Forests in the Balance,* New Scientist 20th July 1994

Peck, J and Emmerich, M (1992) *Recession, Restructuring and Recession Again: the Transformation of the Greater Manchester Labour Market,* School of Geography Working Paper 17, University of Manchester

Percy, M (1996), The Best Laid Plans: Institute of Contemporary History Witness Seminar on the Making of Milton Keynes, *Town and Country Planning* **65**/3:75-83

Perri 6 (1997) *Escaping poverty: from safety nets to networks of opportunity,* London, Demos Foundation

Perri 6, Problem-Solving Government, In: (Ed) Hargreaves I, and Christie, I (1998) *Politics of the Future; the third way and beyond,* London, DEMOS

Perry, J (1997) *Sustainable home ownership: new policies for a new government,* Coventry, Chartered Institute of Housing

Peters, T and Waterman, R (1982) *In Search of Excellence,* New York, Harper and Row

Pezzey, J (1993) *The Impact of CO2 Control Strategies on Industrial Competitiveness*, (Report to the Dept of Trade and Industry) London, HMSO

Pieda plc with Allott and Lomax (1995) *Sustainable and Accessible Urban Areas for the 21st Century,* Report to GMPTA

Pigou, A.C (1952) *The Economics of Welfare*,

Plowden, S (1993) *Taming the Truck: Freight Policy and the Environment,* (Transport Retort Vol 16/1), London, Transport 2000

Policy Studies Institute (Ed P.Wilmott) (1994) *Urban Trends 2: a decade in Britain's deprived urban areas,* London, PSI

Policy Studies Institute and Northcott, J, *Britain in 2010: The PSI Report,* London, PSI

Ponting, C (1992) *A green history of the world,* Harmondsworth, Penguin

Porter, E (1978) *Water Management in England and Wales,* Cambridge University Press

Porter, M.E (1990) *Competitive Advantage of Nations,* London, Macmillan

Portugali, M (1997) *Self-Organizing Cities,* In: Futures Vol 29/4-5:353-380

Powell M (1999) (Ed), *New Labour, New Welfare State?,* Bristol, Policy Press

Power A and Mumford K (1999) *The slow death of great cities? Urban abandonment or urban renaissance,* Joseph Rowntree Foundation, York Publishing Services

Power, A (1995), *Swimming against the tide: polarisation or progress on 20 unpopular council estates,* York, Joseph Rowntree Foundation

Poyner, B and Webb, B (1991) *Crime Free Housing,* Oxford, Butterworth Heinemann

Pre' Consultants (1995) *The Eco-Indicator 1995,* Pre' Consultants, Bergstraat 6, 3811 Amersfoort, Netherlands

Pretty, J (1999), *The Living Land: agriculture, food and community regeneration in the 21st century,* London, Earthscan

Priority Estates Project (1997) *Residents Service Organizations: a new tool for regeneration,* Stretford, PEP

Quality of Urban Air Review Group (1993) *Urban Air Quality in the UK: 1st Report,* London, DOE

Rabinovitch, J and Lietman, J (1996), Urban Planning in Curitiba, *Scientific American* **274**/3:46-53

Rabl, A (1996) *Discounting of long-term costs: what would future generations prefer us to do?,* In: Ecological Economics Vol 17/3, Elsevier

Raleigh, V S, and Kiri, V (1997) *Journal of Epidemiology and Community Health* 12/97

Rapaport, A (1977) *Human Aspects of Urban Form: towards a man-environment approach to urban form and design,* Oxford, Pergamon

Ravetz, J (1973), Practical Deschooling, In: Buckman, P (Ed) *Education without Schools,* London, Souvenir Press

Ravetz, J (1991), St Aidan's on the Aire, (2ⁿᵈ prizewinner in Tomorrow's New Communities, competition) In: Lock, D, Hall, P and Darley, G (Eds) *Tomorrow's New Communities,* York, Joseph Rowntree Foundation

Ravetz, J (1996a) *Towards the Sustainable City Region*, In: Town and Country Planning, Vol 65 No5

Ravetz, J (1996b), How long to the sustainable city, *Eco-Design Journal,* Stroud, Vol 5/4: 13-17

Ravetz, J (1997) Strategic planning for sustainable development of an urban system, In: Christie, I, (Ed) *Planning for Local Change,* London, Henley Centre for Economic Forecasting

Ravetz, J (1997a), *Place and Space in the Sustainable City,* In: Streetwise 31, Vol 8/3:5-8, Brighton, Places for People

Ravetz, J (1998), Capacity Problems – Sustainability Solutions, *Town and Country Planning Journal* **67/5**: 173-175

Ravetz, J (1998a), Integrated Assessment Models: from global to local, *Impact Assessment and Project Appraisal*, **16/2**:147-154

Ravetz, J (1999) Urban neighbourhoods: sustaining whom or what?, In: *Sustainable Urban Neighbourhood Newsletter* Vol 8:4-5, Manchester, URBED

Ravetz, J (1999b), Citizen Participation for Integrated Assessment: new pathways in complex systems, *Int. Journal of Environment and Pollution* **11**/3:331-350; special issue on citizen participation

Ravetz, J (1999c), Urban Form and the Sustainability of Urban Systems: theory and practice in a northern conurbation, In: Jenks M, Burton E and Williams K (Eds), *Achieving Sustainable Urban Form,* London, E and F Spon

Ravetz, J (1999d), Economy, Environment and the Sustainable City: Notes from Greater Manchester, In: Roberts P and Gouldson A (Eds), *Integrating Environment and Economy: Local and Regional Strategies,* London, Routledge

Ravetz, J (2000), Integrated Assessment for Sustainability Appraisal in Cities and Regions, *Environmental Impact Assessment Review*, **19/6**

Ravetz, J (2000a), *Integrated sustainable cities assessment method, (ISCAM),* Dept Working Paper, Dept of Planning and Landscape, Manchester University

Ravetz, J (2000b), *Regional Interactive Sustainability Atlas: Workshop Summary,* Dept of Planning Occasional Paper, University of Manchester

Ravetz, J (2000c), *Integrated Assessment and Economic Evaluation for Sustainable Development in the City-Region: final report to the Global Environmental Change Programme,* Swindon, Economic and Social Research Council

Ravetz, J with Carter, C (1996) *Manchester 2020 - Sustainable Development in the City Region: Overview,* Centre for Employment Research, Manchester Metropolitan University

Ravetz, J with the Community Architecture Group (1995), *Feasibility Studies: a Guide to Good Practice,* London, RIBA Publications

Ravetz, J with the SCR Working Group (1996), *Manchester 2020 Working Paper 5: Built Environment,* Centre for Employment Research, Manchester Metropolitan University

Ravetz, J with the SCR Working Group (1996b), *Manchester 2020 Working Paper 6: Travel and Transport,* Centre for Employment Research, Manchester Metropolitan University

Ravetz, J with the SCR Working Group (1996c), *Manchester 2020 Working Paper 7: Land and Ecology,* Centre for Employment Research, Manchester Metropolitan University

Ravetz, J with the SCR Working Group (1996d), *Manchester 2020 Working Paper 8: Waste and Pollution,* Centre for Employment Research, Manchester Metropolitan University

Rayner, S and Malone, E (1997) *Zen and the Art of Climate Maintenance,* In: Nature Vol 390, 27/11/97: 332-335

RCEP (Royal Commission on Environmental Pollution) (1994) *18th Report, Transport and the Environment,* London HMSO

RCEP (Royal Commission on Environmental Pollution) (1996) 19ᵗʰ Report, *Soil Quality in the UK,* London, HMSO

RCEP (Royal Commission on Environmental Pollution) (1998) *21 st Report: Setting Environmental Standards, (Cm 4053)* London TSO

Reade, E (1987), *British town and country planning,* Milton Keynes, Open University Press

Red Rose Forest (1994) *The Forest Plan,* (consultation draft) Manchester, Red Rose Forest

Rees, W, and Wackernagel, M (1995) *Our Ecological Footprint: Reducing Human Impact on the Earth,* British Columbia, Gabriola Island , New Society Publishers

Rendel, S (1994) *Tranquillity - an Essential Commodity,* Town and Country Planning Journal, Vol 63 No 11

Renton, L (1993) *The school is us: a practical guide to successful whole school change,* World Wide Fund for Nature

Rifkin, J (1995) *The end of work: the decline of the global labor force,* New York, G.P.Putnam's Sons

Roberts P and Jackson T (1999) Incorporating the Environment into European regional programes – evolution, progress and prospects, *Town and Country Planning* Vol 67:85-88

Roberts P and Lloyd S (1998) *Developing Regional Potential: monitoring the development of the RDA's,* London, British Urban Regeneration Association

Roberts P and Pike J (1998) Mining the Urban Waste Stream, *Town and Country Planning* **67**/10:324-326

Roberts, P (1995) *Environmentally Sustainable Business: a Local and Regional Perspective,* London, Paul Chapman Publishing

Roberts, P (1997) Strategies for the Stateless Nation: Sustainable Policies for the Regions in Europe, *Regional Studies* 31/9:875-822

Roberts, P (1998), Retrospect and Prospect, In: Roberts, P, Thomas, K, Williams, G (Eds), *Metropolitan Planning in Britain: a comparitive study,* London, Jessica Kingsley

Roberts, P and Hart, T (1996) *Regional Strategy and Partnership in European Programmes: experience in four UK regions,* Joseph Rowntree Foundation, York Publishing Services

Roberts, P and Thomas, K (1995) *Strategic Planning without Strategic Plans: an analysis of the metropolitan areas of England,* In: Regional Studies, Vol 29, No..

Robinson, J (1990) Backcasting;.... *Futures...*

Robinson, J and Tinker, J (1995), *Reconciling Ecological, Economic and Social Imperatives: towards an analytical framework,* British Columbia, Sustainable Development Research Institute

Robson, B (1988) *Those Inner Cities: Reconciling the Social and Economic Aims of Urban Policy,* Oxford, Clarendon Press

Robson, B (1998) *The impact of urban development corporations in Leeds, Bristol and Central Manchester,* London, DETR

Robson, B and G (1994) *Forward with Faith: experience from the Miles Platting and Ancoats Development Trust,* Town and Country Planning Journal, Vol 63 /3

Robson, B, Bradford, M.G, Deas, I, Hall, E, Harrison, E, Parkinson, M, Evans, R, Garside, P, Harding, A (1994) *Assessing the Impact of Urban Policy,* Inner Cities Research Programme, DOE, HMSO

Robson, B. T (1988), *Those inner cities: reconciling the economic and social aims of urban policy,* Oxford, Clarendon

Rodgers, B (1986) *Manchester: metropolitan planning by collaboration and consent* In: Gordon, G, (Ed), *Regional Cities in the UK 1890-1980,* London, Paul Chapman Publishing

Roelofs, J (1996) *Greening Cities: Building Just and Sustainable Communities,* New York, Bootstrap Press

Rose, C (1990) *The Dirty Man of Europe: the Great British Pollution Scandal,* London, Simon and Schuster

Roszak, T (1993) *Eco-psychology,* British Columbia, Island Press

Rotmans, J and de Vries B (Eds) (1997) *Perspectives on Global Change: the Targets Approach,* Cambridge University Press

Rotmans, J and de Vries, B (1997), *Perspectives on Global Change: The TARGETS approach,* Cambridge University Press

Rotmans,J and van Assaelt,M (1996) *Integrated Assessment: a growing child on its way to maturity,* Climatic Change 34:327-336

RSA Inquiry (1995) *Tomorrow's Company: the role of business in a changing world,* London, Royal Society of Arts

Rudlin D and Falk N (1999) *Building the 21ˢᵗ Century Home: the sustainable urban neighbourhood,* Oxford, Architectural Press

Rudlin D for Friends of the Earth (1998) *Tomorrow: a peaceful path to urban reform,* Luton, Friends of the Earth

Rydin, Y (1995) *The Greening of the Housing Market,* In: Bhatti, M et al (Eds) *Housing and the Environment; a new agenda,* London, Chartered Institute of Housing

Rydin, Y (1997) *Policy networks, local discourses and the implementation of sustainable development,* In: Baker, S, Kousis, M, Richardson, D, Young, S.C (Eds), *The Politics of Sustainable Development,* London, Routledge

Sachs W (1998) *Greening the North: a post-industrial blueprint for ecology and equity,* London, Zed Books and Wuppertal Institute, GDR

Safe Neighbourhoods Unit (1993) *Crime Prevention on Council Estates,* (Report to DoE), London, HMSO

Sale, K (1985) *Dwellers in the Land: the Bioregional Vision,* San Francisco, Sierra Club

Salford Partnership, Salford's Bid to the SRB 1995/96; *Supporting the City Pride Initiative,* Salford City Council

Salford, City of (1991) *Internal Environmental Audit,* Salford City Council

Sanderson, I, Walton, F and Campbell, M (1997), *Back to Work: local action on unemployment,* York, York Publishing Services

Sardar, Z and Ravetz, J (1996) Reaping the Technological Whirlwind In: Sardar, Z and Ravetz, J (Ed) *Cyberfutures: Culture and Politics on the Information Super-highway,* London, Pluto Press

Satterthwaite, D (1996) (Ed), *An Urbanizing World: The Second Global Report on Human Settlements,* Oxford University Press

Savage, M and Ward, A (1993) *Cities and Uneven Development,* London, Macmillan

Schaltegger, S, with Muller, K and Hindrichsen, H (1996) *Corporate Environmental Accounting,* Chichester, Wiley

Scheicher-Tappeser R, and Strati P (1999) *Progress Towards Regional Sustainable Development: results from the EU research programme on human dimensions of environmental change.,* (Working Paper) Brussels, EC DG12-D5

Schlesinger, A (1999), New Deal for Communities – One Year On, *Town and Country Planning* **68**/11:345-348

Schmidheiny, S (1992) *Changing course: a global business perspective on development and the environment,* Cambridge, Mass, MIT Press

Schumacher, E (1973), *Small is Beautiful: a study of economics as if people mattered,* London, Blond and Briggs

Schumann, M (1995) *Impact of NOₓ Emissions from Aircraft at 8-15km,* In: Schumann, M, (Ed), *Overview of Aeronox,* London, EC-DLR Publications

Schumpeter, J.A (1939) *Business Cycles: a theoretical, historical and statistical analysis of the capitalist process,* NY, McGraw-Hill

Schwartz P (1996) *The Art of the Long View,* New York, Black Rose

Science Policy Research Unit et al (1999), *Non-Climate Futures Study: Report to UK Climate Impacts Programme,* Oxford, UK Climate Impacts Programme

Scottish Homes (1994) *Environmental Issues in Housing,* Edinburgh, Scottish Homes

Seamark, D (1996), European Funding and Environmental Appraisal, *Town and Country Planning* **65**/12:340-342

Sennet, R (1991) *The Conscience of the Eye: the Design and Social Life of Cities,* London, Faber and Faber

Shackley S and Wood R (1998) *Everybody has an Impact: Climate Change Impacts in the North West of England,* Wigan, NW Regional Association

Shapiro, B (1997) *One Violent Crime,* New York, Harper Collins

Shelter (1998), *Behind closed doors: the real extent of homelessness and housing need,* London, Shelter

Sherlock, H (1990) *Cities are Good for Us,* Transport 2000, London

Shirley, P (1996) *Urban Wildlife,* London, Whittet Books, British Natural History Series

Shoard, M (1983) *This Land is Our Land,* London, Paladin

Shostak, L (1997) *A Choice-Driven Approach,* In: Town and Country Planning, Vol 66/4:106

Simpson, A (1994) *Local Authority Investment and the Environment,* In: Agyeman, J and Evans, B, (Eds)*'Local Environmental Policies and Strategies,* Harlow, Longman

Simpson, S, March, C, Sandhu, A (1993) *Validation of Census Coverage by Other Means,* Manchester Census Group Occasional Paper, University of Manchester

Smit J and Nasr, P (1992) *Urban Agriculture for Sustainable Cities';* In: Environment and Urbanization, Vol 4 No 2, London, International Institute for Environment and Development

Smith, R.A (1872), *Air and Rain: the beginnings of a chemical climatology,* London, Longmans, Green and Co

Soja, E.W (1999), *Postmetropolis,* Oxford, Blackwell

Solesbury W (1999) Get Connected, *Town and Country Planning* 99/2:52-53

Solesbury, W (1990) *Property Development and Urban Regeneration,* In: Healey, P and Nabarro, R (Eds), *Land and Property Development in a Changing Context,* Aldershot, Gower

Solow, R.M (1970), *Growth theory: an exposition,* Oxford , Clarendon

Spackman, M (1996), Hypothecation: a view from the Treasury, In: O'Riordan, T (Ed) *Eco-Taxation,* London, Earthscan

Stead D, Titheridge H, Williams J (1999) Land-use Change and the People: identifying the connections, In Jenks M, Burton E and Williams K (Eds), *Achieving Sustainable Urban Form,* London, E and F Spon

Stewart, J, et al (1994) *Citizens, Juries,* Institute of Public Policy Research, London,

Stine, S (1997) *Landscapes for Learning: Creating Outdoor Environments for Children and Youth,* Chichester, Wiley

Stirling, A (1997) *Multi-Criteria Mapping: mitigating the problems of environmental valuation,* In: Foster, J (Ed), *Valuing Nature: Economics, Ethics and Environment,* London, Routledge

Stockport MBC and Taylor Young Partnership (1994) *The Green Development Guide: New Housing,* Stockport MBC

Stoker, G (1995) *Regime Theory and Urban Politics,* In: Judge, D, Stoker, G, Wolman, H (Eds) *Theories of Urban Politics,* London, Sage Publications

Stradling, S, Meadows, M and Beatty, S (1998), *Psychological Benefits and Disbenefits of Driving,* Wokingham, Transport Research Laboratory

Strathern M (1992) Qualified Value: the perspective of gift exchange, In: Humphrey C and Hugh-Jones S (Eds) *Barter, Exchange and Value: an Anthropological Approach,* Cambridge University Press

Street, P (1997), Scenario Workshops: a participatory approach to sustainable urban living? *Futures* **29**/2:139-158

Stren, R, White, R and Whitney, J (1992) *Sustainable Cities: Urbanization and the Environment in International Perspective,* Oxford, Westview Press.

Sukopp, H, Numata, M, Huber, A (1995) *Urban Ecology as the Basis of Urban Planning,* Amsterdam, SPB Academic Publishing

Sustainability North West (1998) *Sustainable Development and the North West Regional Development Agency,* SNW, Manchester University

Symes M and Pauwels S (1999) The Diffusions of Innovation in Urban Design: the case of sustainability in the Hulme Development Guide, *Journal of Urban Design* **4**/1:97-117

Syms, P (1997) *The Redevelopment of Contaminated Land for Housing Use,* London, ISVA, also in Findings 225, York, Joseph Rowntree Foundation

Talbot, J (1997) *Cables of Concern,* In: Town and Country Planning, Vol 66/2

Taylor, I (1991) *Not Spaces in which you'd linger: Public Transport and Public Well-Being in Manchester,* Survey and report to the GMPTE, Manchester

Taylor, I (1997), New York / Manchester, Zero Tolerance or Reclaim the Streets? *City* Vol 8:139-149

Taylor, I Evans, K and Fraser, P (1996) *A Tale of Two Cities: Global Change, Local Feeling and Everyday Life in the North of England,* London, Routledge

Taylor, I, Walton, P and Young, J (1973) *The New Criminology':* London, Routledge and Kegan Paul

Taylor, L.P (1992) *Employment Aspects of Energy Efficiency,* In: *Energy Efficiency,* London, Policy Studies Institute

Taylor, P, Powell, J, Speake, T (Eds) (1996) *The potential of the information superhighway to deliver appropriate interactive training,* Gemisis 2000 Report, University of Salford

TCPA (1997), *Finding the Land for 4.4 Million Households,* London, TCPA

TCPA (1999), *Your Place and Mine: Reinventing Planning. The report of the TCPA inquiry into the future of planning,* London, TCPA

Templet, P.H, Glenn, J and Farber, S (1991) *Louisiana ties environmental performance to tax rates,* New York, Environment Finance, Autumn (1991) pp271-277.

Thompson, M, Ellis, R, and Wildavsky, A (1990) *Cultural Theory,* Boulder USA, Westview Press

Tindale, S and Holtman, G (1996), *Green Tax Reform: pollution payments and labour tax cuts,* London, Institute of Public Policy Research

Town and Country Planning Association (1987) *The North-South Divide - a New Deal for Britain's Regions,* London, TCPA

Town and Country Planning Association (1993) *Strategic Planning for Regional Development,* London, TCPA

Townroe, P (1996) *Urban Sustainability and Social Cohesion,* In: Pugh, C, (Ed), *Sustainability, the Environment and Urbanization,* London, Earthscan

Toyne, P (Ed) (1993), *Environmental Responsibility in Further and Higher Education: The Toyne Report,* London, Dept of Education

Travers A (1999) Restructuring Government, In: *The Guardian* 27/01/99

Turnbull, S (1986) Cooperative Land-Banks, In: Ekins, P (Ed), *The Living Economy: a New Economics in the Making,* London, Routledge and Kegan Paul

Turok, I and Edge, N (1999) *The jobs gap in Britain's cities: Employment loss and labour market consequences,* York, Joseph Rowntree Foundation, Policy Press

Tuxworth, B (1996) *From Environment to Sustainability; surveys and analysis of LA21 process development in UK local authorities,* In: Local Environment Vol 1/3, Wiley

Tyteca, D (1996) *On the Measurement of the Environmental Performance of Firms - a literature review and a productive efficiency perspective,* In: Journal of Environmental Management Vol 46, p281, Academic Press

UNDP (United Nations Development Programme) (1996) *Human Development Report,* Oxford University Press

United Nations Centre for Human Settlements (1996) *Best Practices for Human Settlements: Database,* Nairobi, UNCHS, URL: http://www.bestpractices.org [cited: 1ˢᵗ December, 1999]

United Utilities plc (1998) *Environment Report 1998,* Warrington, United Utilities plc

Urban Research and Policy Evaluation Regional Research Laboratory (1994) *The North West of England 1991 Census Atlas,* University of Liverpool, URPERRL

Urban Task Force (1999) *Towards an Urban Renaissance: the final report of the Urban Task Force,* London, E and FN Spon

Urban Villages Group (1992) *Urban Villages: A Concept for Creating Mixed-Use Urban Developments on a Sustainable Scale,* London, Urban Villages Group

URBED and Hillier Parker (1995) *Vital and viable town centres,* London, HMSO

URBED and Newbury King (1998) *Valuing the Value-added: the role of housing plus in creating sustainable communities,* (Working Paper 3) London, Housing Corporation

URBED, MORI and School for Policy Studies (1999) *But would you like to live there? Shaping attitudes to urban living,* London, DETR

Urry, J (1995), *Consuming places,* London, Routledge

Vale, R (1995) *Selecting Materials for Construction,* In: *European Directory of Sustainable and Energy Efficient Building,* London, James and James

Vale, R and B (1991) *Green Architecture: Design for a Sustainable Future,* London, Thames and Hudson

Vickerman, R, Spiekerman, k, Wegener, M (1999) Accessibility and Economic Development in Europe, *Regional Studies,* **33**/1:1-16

von Weizsacker, E, Lovins, A and Lovins, L.H (1997) *Factor Four: Doubling Wealth, Halving Resource Use,* London, Earthscan

Wall, D (1999) *Earth First! and the Anti-Roads Movement: radical environmentalism and comparitive social movements,* London, Routledge

Ward, C (1978) *The Child in the City,* New York, Pantheon

Ward, C (1989) *Welcome, thinner city: urban survival in the 1990s,* London, Bedford Square

Warnock S and Brown N (1998) A Vision for the Countryside, *Landscape Design* April 1998

Warren-Evans, R (1996) *Building a New Britain: an alternative democratic vision for the UK,* London, City-Region Campaign

Wates, N and Knevitt, C (1979) *Community Architecture,* Harmondsworth, Penguin

WCED (World Commission on Environment and Development) (1987) *"Our Common Future",* Oxford University Press

Weale, A (1993) *The New Politics of Pollution,* Manchester University Press

Webster, F.V, Bly, P.H, Paulley, N.J, (Eds), and ISGLUTI (1988) *Urban Land-Use and Transport Interaction: Report on the International Study Group on Land-Use / Transport Interactions,* Aldershot, Avebury

Welford, R (1995) *Environmental Strategy and Sustainable Development,* London, Routledge

Wennberg S et al (1998) Science Vol 279:534-542

Whelan, J (1997) A Brake on Manufacturing Productivity, *Town and Country Planning* **66**/11:311-313

White, R and Whitney, J (1992) *Cities and the Environment: an Overview,* In: Stren, R, White, R, Whitney, J, (Eds), *Sustainable Cities - Urbanization and the Environment in International Perspective,* Colorado, Westview Press

Whitelegg, J (1993) *Transport for a Sustainable Future,* London, Belhaven Press

Whitelegg, J (1995) *Freight Transport, Logistics and Sustainable Development,* (Report to the World Wildlife Fund), Godalming, WWF

Whitelegg, J, Smith, M and Williams, N (1998) *The Greening of the Built Environment,* London, Earthscan

Wilbert, C (1996) *Wilderness and Working Landscapes,* In: Town and Country Planning Journal, Vol 65 No 2

Wilkinson, S (1986) *Manchester's Warehouses: their History and Architecture,* Salford, Neil Richardson

Williams, C (1997) *Consumer Services and Economic Development,* London, Routledge

Williams, C and Windebank, J (1999), *A Helping Hand: harnessing self-help to combat social exclusion,* York, York Publishing Services

Williams, G (1998), Greater Manchester, In: Roberts, P, Thomas, K, Williams, G (Eds), *Metropolitan Planning in Britain: a comparitive study,* London, Jessica Kingsley

Williams, R (1965), *The Long Revolution,* London, Penguin

Willis, K and Garrod, G.D (1993) Valuing Landscape: a contingent valuation approach, *Journal of Environmental Management,* **37**/1 p1-22

Winter, P (1998), Urban Housing Capacity 3: Where There's Muck, There's Liability, *Town and Country Planning* **67**/3: 116-121

Wolman, H (1995) *Local Government Institutions and Democratic Governance,* In: Judge, D, Stoker, G, Wolman, H (Eds) *Theories of Urban Politics,* London, Sage

Wong, C Baker, M and Gallent, N (1999), *The People: Where Will They Work: the geography opf employment in the North West,* London, TCPA

Wood, C (1996) *Trading in Futures: the role of business in sustainability,* Lincoln, Wildlife Trusts

Wood, C.M, Lee, N, Luker, J.A, Saunders, P (1974) *The Geography of Pollution: a study of Greater Manchester,* Manchester University Press

World Business Council for Sustainable Development (WBCSD) (1998), *Making it into the 21st Century,* Geneva, WBCSD

World Business Council on Sustainable Development (1993) *Changing Course,* Geneva, BCSD

World Health Organization (1992) *Twenty Steps to Developing a Healthy Cities Project,* New York, WHO

World Resources Institute et al (1997) *Resource Flows: the material basis of industrial economies,* Washington DC, WRI

World Resources Institute with UNEP and UNDP (1997), *World Resources 1997-8,* Oxford University Press

Worpole, K and Greenhalgh, L (1999) *Urban Policy in a New Landscape: final report on the richness of cities programme,* Leicester, ECOS Distribution

Young, S.C (1993) *The Politics of the Environment,* Manchester, Baseline Books

Young. S.C (1996) *Promoting Partnerships and Community-based Participation in the context of Local Agenda 21,* European Policy Research Unit, University of Manchester

Zimmerman, J.F (1986) *Participatory Democracy: Populism Revived,* New York, Praeger

# INDEX